Legal Aspects of
Managing Technology

Legal Aspects of Managing Technology

Lee B. Burgunder

Professor of Business Law and Public Policy
California Polytechnic State University
San Luis Obispo

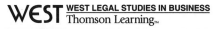

WEST LEGAL STUDIES IN BUSINESS
Thomson Learning™

Australia • Canada • Denmark • Japan • Mexico • New Zealand • Philippines
Puerto Rico • Singapore • South Africa • Spain • United Kingdom • United States

Legal Aspects of Managing Technology, 2nd edition by Lee B. Burgunder
Vice President and Publisher: Jack Calhoun
Senior Acquisitions Editor: Rob Dewey
Developmental Editors: Bob Sandman/Alana O'Koon
Marketing Manager: Mike Worls
Production Editor: Peggy Buskey
Manufacturing Coordinator: Charlene Taylor
Cover Design: Envoi Design
Production and Composition: Trejo Production
Printer: Webcom

Printed in Canada
2 3 4 5 03 02 01 00

For more information contact West Legal Studies in Business, South-Western College
Publishing, 5101 Madison Road, Cincinnati, Ohio, 45227 or find us on the Internet at
http://www.westbuslaw.com

For permission to use material from this text or product, contact us by
• **telephone: 1-800-730-2214**
• **fax: 1-800-730-2215**
• **web: http://www.thomsonrights.com**

Library of Congress Cataloging-in-Publication Data

Burgunder, Lee B., 1955–
    Legal aspects of managing technology / Lee B. Burgunder.—2nd ed.
        p. cm.
    Includes index.
    ISBN 0-324-02720-6 (alk. paper)
    1. High technology industries—Law and legislation—United States. 2. Intellectual
property—United States. 3. Computer contracts—United States. I. Title.
KF1890.H53 B87 2001
346.7304'8—dc21
                                                                    00-025869

Preface

As we enter the new millennium, no topic generates more excitement and interest than technology. Investment dollars are pouring into technology companies that are breaking new ground with innovations in computers, biotechnology, electronic commerce, and the Internet. The media now blankets audiences with technology stories, reflecting both its importance and the public's fascination with the issues. For managers, the rapid-paced world of technology offers both unlimited opportunities and difficult challenges. It is no wonder that business executives have insatiable appetites for educational programs addressing the very latest developments in technology management.

This book is designed to address the legal issues that must be understood by any manager involved with technological innovations. Technology has caused nothing short of a revolution in strategic business thinking. Managers appreciate that their most prized possessions are ideas, and that ideas may be quickly and easily lost if they are not handled in the appropriate fashion. This has led to staggering interest in the ways that the law protects intellectual assets so that firms may maintain strategic advantages. Companies involved with the Internet, for instance, have an endless set of concerns and questions. Can Internet business methods be patented? How extensively do copyrights prevent others from posting or downloading materials on the Web? Who has rights to domain names? What kinds of contracts can customers be required to accept, and how might agreement be arranged? The questions from other fields, such as biotechnology, are no less daunting. In fact, legal systems now have to address whether businesses may own rights to life, itself.

Since intellectual property clearly is the new mantra for technology concerns, this book focuses substantial attention on it. However, new technologies raise numerous other legal, social and regulatory issues that this book addresses as well. For example, the book focuses considerable attention on privacy, especially in the context of the Internet and electronic communications. It also deals with emerging controversial issues in electronic commerce, such as with click-wrap licenses. In addition, the book considers how antitrust issues may affect strategic decisions, a topic that obviously has been given renewed life since the Microsoft litigation.

INTENDED AUDIENCE

This book is designed specifically for students and businesspersons who need exposure to the legal aspects of managing technology, but who do not have the immediate intention of becoming lawyers. Those interested in managing technologies come from a wide spectrum of disciplines, including management, engineering, architecture, industrial technology, biology, and computer science. The overriding goal of the book is to stimulate and inform such individuals without regard to their background or training.

The explosive growth in the importance of technology has motivated universities to offer a variety of courses that address the legal concerns of technology enterprises. Many of these take a general law and technology approach, while others are more narrowly focused on Internet or e-commerce issues. This book has been painstakingly conceived to be an exceptional instructional tool in all of these types of courses. This book rests on the philosophy that all aspects of technology law are rooted on a common core of principles. As we shall see, most of the legal policies regarding the Internet have been developed though analogies to more traditional technological contexts. Thus, the approach of this book is not to treat the Internet as something distinct and separate. Rather, the book builds a complete understanding of Internet-based legal principles by dealing first with general notions of technology law in tangible contexts, and then by applying those considerations to the often more nebulous realm of cyberspace. In this way, students not only will come away with a thorough understanding of the legal policies applicable to Internet commerce, but they also will appreciate the rationales for those laws. Such a solid grounding in fundamental principals also will help students predict how the laws likely will adapt to the inevitable future changes in Internet technologies.

This book also would be an excellent selection for a general education course dealing with law, technology and society. One of the purposes of this book, as described in the next section, is to stimulate students to address the many social, political, religious, economic, and ethical issues raised by technology and addressed by the law.

PURPOSES OF THE BOOK

Focus Attention on Integral Technology Topics

The objective of this book is to focus on those topics that are important and interesting to every person involved with managing technology. The goal is not to be the definitive treatise on every conceivable topic that might be pertinent to managers of technology. For example, the book does not deal with telecommunications law. Although the field may be very important to certain businesses, the issues nonetheless are relatively specialized and do not pertain to most technology concerns. Having said this, the book does concentrate substantially on computers and the Internet. Although this may seem at odds with the core-topics approach, these fields have become so ubiquitous that virtually all businesses are involved with them. In addition, the book spends some considerable time with biotechnology issues, particularly the debates arising in the patent arena. This choice was made due to the widespread concern and interest that the public currently has with this particular area of technology.

The book tries to avoid the trap of becoming mired in every nuance of the law. That aspect is an attribute of so many law-related texts, which makes them unappetizing to readers. The guiding philosophy here is to simulate the reader by presenting the most pressing and interesting issues without necessarily covering every legal angle than might come into play. The book is not intended to enable its readers to become legal experts. Instead, the goal is to allow managers to understand the fundamental legal issues pertinent to technology management so that they can competently create strategic plans in consultation with their attorneys.

Analyze the Most Current and Interesting Issues

As with the first edition, every effort has been made to make the text as current as possible while at the same time predicting the changes that may be forthcoming in the near future. Obviously, a lot has changed since the first edition was published in 1994. The Internet was hardly a blip on the radar at that time, but it now has become one of the fundamental forces in modern society. Perhaps the greatest achievement of this text is that it fully integrates discussions of the major issues raised by the Internet and other important new technologies. As you will see, discussions of the Internet were not just added on to the existing text. Rather the book was completely rewritten so that it addresses the most pressing issues in a coherent and logical fashion.

As a sneak preview, the following list provides a small sample of the recent issues that have been fully assimilated into the book:

- Copyright infringement and piracy issues on the Internet
- The legality of framing and linking on the Web
- Music and video issues on the Internet, including the debates over MP3 portable audio players and the Secure Digital Music Initiative
- The responsibilities of Internet service providers for defamation
- Domain names, cybersquatting and trademark rights
- Other trademark issues on the Web, such as with metatags and "suck" sites
- Privacy debates on the Internet, including such issues as data mining, cookies, encryption, and industry initiatives to protect privacy
- Employer monitoring of employee e-mail communications and Internet usage
- The regulation of indecent materials on the Web
- Proposed model laws to govern e-commerce issues, such as UCITA and UCC Article 2B
- Y2K Issues
- The antitrust case against Microsoft
- The laws that apply to interstate and international Internet activities, and the jurisdictions in which suits may be brought
- Patents for computer programs and Internet business methods
- New developments in copyright protection for computer programs and user interfaces

- New developments in biotechnology, such as cloning and the controversy over labeling genetically engineered ingredients in food products
- Recent piracy and international trade issues, including a comprehensively revised discussion of the World Trade Organization
- New patent laws in the United States
- New developments with trade secrets, such as passage of the federal Economic Espionage Act

Engage Readers in Controversial and Important Social Issues

The legal issues of managing technology are so fascinating because they raise numerous controversial issues having social, ethical, religious, political, and economic dimensions. This book involves readers in the following important debates:

- *Biotechnology Issues.* Protection of biotechnological inventions through patents raises fundamental and controversial notions regarding the ownership of life. Students are forced to inquire whether there should be any limits on the abilities of human beings to play God. Is it ethical to create an incentive system that rewards the creation of animals having deformities? Should humans be entitled to own human genes? This is an excellent opportunity to probe the reactions of the public policy process when human fears are raised and religious convictions are challenged.
- *Freedom of Speech and the First Amendment of the U.S. Constitution.* The Internet has raised free speech concerns in several contexts. The Communications Decency Act, encryption export regulations, unauthorized uses of trademarks, and laws protecting copyright management systems are a few examples discussed in the text. Digital sampling and spamming, among several other technology law topics, also involve first amendment issues.
- *International sovereignty.* Through the Internet, foreign firms can transact business in a local community just as if the were located there. Should local laws apply to their conduct even when their operations take place overseas? The book raises this issue in several contexts, such as with domain names and trademark infringement. It also addresses international sovereignty in other realms, such as with antitrust.
- *Responsibility for the unlawful conduct of others.* One consequence of many new technologies is that they have decentralized the opportunities for individuals to infringe rights. The VCR, for instance, makes it easy for individuals to copy movies or TV shows. The Internet enables individuals to engage in many troubling actions, such as copyright violations and defamation. Under circumstances such as these, enforcement is an enormous problem for those who suffer losses. Thus, they often attempt to locate major businesses that they can morally and legally blame for their grief. The book examines numerous examples, such as accusations against VCR and MP3 portable audio player manufacturers, and the potential liabilities of Internet service providers for the unlawful conduct of their users.

- *Business rights versus personal rights, including privacy.* Firms are entitled to take steps to protect their assets and property rights. What happens, though, when those steps intrude on personal rights enjoyed by employees or other individuals? Drug testing is a classic historical example. More recent examples include e-mail and Internet usage monitoring, genetic testing, invention assignment requirements, and the collection of personal information. Business and personal rights clash in other contexts, as well, such as when high technology companies with trade secrets take steps to prevent employees from working with competitors.

- *Government responsibilities versus individual rights.* Governments often are expected to take steps that are reasonably necessary to protect citizens from harm. Sometimes these measures intrude on individual rights, raising questions about their propriety. One example followed in the book involves government regulation of encryption products, which pits the interests of law enforcement against the desires of individuals and businesses to protect the privacy of their communications.

- *Personal responsibility for harmful conduct.* The book examines negligence and strict products liability, which both raise questions about when consumers can blame manufacturers for injuries. The latter is more controversial since it involves blame without fault.

- *Protection of Children.* The Internet allows merchants and information providers to open direct channels of communications with children. Family values are at the heart of controversies regarding such matters as the display of indecent materials, the use of manipulative selling devices, and unwarranted intrusions on privacy.

- *Economic Development and Intellectual Property Rights.* Sometimes, the economic needs and cultural traditions of less-developed countries lead to very different views about the appropriate role of intellectual property protection. The book examines how these differences may frustrate the economic goals of developed nations, and considers the suitability of potential responses. The advantages of multilateral agreements, such as the World Trade Organization, are highlighted in these discussions.

Demonstrate the Public Policy Process

This book immerses its readers in the public policy process. Rapid changes in technologies raise complex debates within the realms of ethics, religion, sociology, philosophy, and economics. From the myriad of viewpoints, the public policy process, based on the workings of governments, legal systems and politics, must devise solutions. This book provides an excellent means to discuss not only the "should," but also the "how" and the "why" of the public policy process. It also is a vehicle to contrast differences between the United States and other countries, such as the European Union and Japan.

Readers will learn how courts behave when forced to make policies about novel issues. For example, resolution of issues within the intangible world of the Internet has required judges to seek solutions through analogies to the physical world. The debates over copyright infringement, defamation, framing and linking over the Internet, for instance, all are being argued with reference to preexisting methods of commerce. This form of analysis lends itself well to critical thinking. In addition, it demonstrates how public policies tend to move incrementally from what is known into the realm of the unknown.

Use of Cases

One of the fascinating challenges in developing this book was determining the correct balance between theory and practice. On one level, the book articulates the current state of the law and suggests practical strategic decisions that logically follow. However, strategic decisions also must account for how the law might change in the future. Such an exercise requires a somewhat sophisticated appreciation of the concepts and reasoning that shape legal policies. To this end, the book presents a blend of key historical landmark cases and recent important judicial decisions. Regarding the latter, this book adds the following new cases to those that were included in the first edition:

- *Reno v. American Civil Liberties Union*—Internet indecency laws
- *Recording Industry Association of America v. Diamond Multimedia Systems*—MP3 portable audio players and copyright infringement
- *Sidney Blumenthal v. Matt Drudge and America Online, Inc.*—ISP responsibility for defamation
- *Religious Technology Center v. Netcom On-line Communication Services, Inc.*—ISP liability for copyright infringement
- *Panavision International v. Dennis Toeppen*—Domain names and cybersquatting
- *ProCD v. Zeidenberg*—Shrink-wrap and click-wrap licenses
- *State Street Bank & Trust Co. v. Signature Financial Group*—patents for business methods
- *Lotus Development Corp. v. Borland International, Inc.*—Copyright protection for user interfaces
- *Michael A. Smyth v. The Pillsbury Company*—Monitoring of employee e-mail communications
- *Hasbro, Inc. v. Clue Computing, Inc.*—Internet jurisdiction

All of the cases have been carefully edited so that the reader may focus on the major facts and issues involved in the dispute without being distracted by nuances of the legal system. In addition, the court's original language has been preserved as much as possible. And, unlike many legal texts, the cases are preceded by explanations of what the reader should expect and are followed typically by summaries of their major principles.

The Audio Enhancement System (AES) Example

In chapter 2, the text introduces a hypothetical example about the development and sale of an invention called the Audio Enhancement System or AES. This example is used throughout the text to illustrate how diverse legal solutions often may apply to typical technology-based innovations. Each time that the book addresses the AES, an icon appears in the margin to alert the reader. By focusing attention on the AES, the book clearly demonstrates that technological problems often require managers to decide among a variety of potential legal solutions that offer different degrees of benefits and deficiencies depending on the context.

Other Important Features

EXPANDED INTERNATIONAL COVERAGE   International affairs have become substantially more important to technology managers since the first edition was published. The book strives to address international strategic matters in a much more comprehensive fashion. For instance, the international policy perspective presented in Chapter 1 is greatly enhanced, and includes thorough discussions of the World Trade Organization and the reach of international laws. Throughout the book, major international issues are addressed, especially when differences may have important strategic consequences.

SUBSTANTIAL REFERENCES TO ADDITIONAL SOURCES OF INFORMATION   This book contains a substantial number of footnotes. There are times when the footnotes provide additional important details or insights that might prove confusing if they appeared in the text. However, more often, they steer the reader to sources of information that provide interesting additional details and examples of topics discussed in the text. Often these references are to articles in the popular press or legal magazines. Every effort has been made to select references that are appropriate for the managers and students who are within the intended audience of this book. For the most part, the footnotes stay clear of scholarly law review articles that likely would only interest lawyers and law students. The references also help the reader find original sources of information by providing citations for cases, statutes and regulations.

SAMPLE SOFTWARE DEVELOPMENT CONTRACT   The book provides a simplified software development contract at the end of Chapter 9 to illustrate how many problems raised in the book might be handled through contracts. The sample contract can be easily located by flipping to the pages with the shaded margins.

Brief Contents

Contents

6   **Copyright Policy: Specific Technology Applications 297**

Table of Cases

I

An Overview of Intellectual Property Protection: A Policy Perspective

INTRODUCTION

You are about to embark on an important journey. This book will guide you through the maze of legal policies that affect the strategic decisions of those managing new technologies. What you will find may surprise you. The pace of inventions is advancing at an ever-increasing rate, constantly challenging the legitimacy of legal frameworks that govern how new technologies should be developed, controlled, and used. You will see how the law struggles to keep up as new realities test traditional legal norms. The chaos in the realm of computer programs, including the notion of "look and feel" protection, provides one stunning example. The Internet, though, is clearly the new frontier, and its challenges are even more pervasive and difficult. The fact that it symbolically resides in a completely separate world—cyberspace—demonstrates that it may require new ways of thinking about governing doctrines. This journey will take you to these new worlds, and in the process you will learn numerous principles that will be crucial for your future in high-technology enterprises.

As you might expect, this book provides a current snapshot of the most important legal policies affecting the technological environment. Having knowledge of these key concepts will allow you to make the most informed strategic business decisions possible. However, you will also become painfully aware that the knowledge you acquire from reading this book may no longer be valid when it comes time to implement decisions in the future. Thus, you will come to understand that managers never can rest content with what they have learned. Rather, they must continually find ways to become aware of new developments so that they can appropriately adjust their business strategies. You will find that the best answer is never obvious. Instead, you will see that in the world of high technology, managers are offered a large array of different legal opportunities offering distinct advantages and disadvantages. This book, by explaining what is possible, provides only the necessary foundation for developing business strategies. It will be up to you, using your business acumen, to determine what choices may be most appropriate for any particular venture.

Finally, you will come to grips with how the complexity of legal issues is compounded when one must deal in the international environment. The wide array of legal systems that have been developed around the globe often are based on far different principles from those in the United States. Managers who focus their attention solely on the laws of the United States often find that their strategic decisions are inappropriate, even devastating, when they decide to broaden operations internationally. Thus, from reading this book, you also will recognize that one needs to consider international options in the early stages of the strategic decision process.

This book will take you into the most rapidly developing and exciting forum that currently exists in the legal environment of business. Those involved in developing new multimedia technologies, for instance, have found that the legal issues are as important and complex as the technologies themselves. Genetic engineering has opened a host of questions about the morality and legality of creating and owning new life forms. Computer programs are written works, in a sense, but they also serve critical functions in machines. This combination has strained the traditional legal doctrines that were designed to treat these subjects differently. The Internet seems to raise new questions every day. What domain name may one use? Is it legal to link to other sites, or frame them within a home site? May users download materials off the Web or copy them to a bulletin board? What responsibilities do service providers have when their customers act unlawfully? The range of Internet questions appears to be boundless. Also, the advent of new technologies, including the Internet, has magnified certain business and societal problems, such as piracy and intrusions on privacy. Issues such as these make this area of the law so interesting and important.

It is no longer possible to open a newspaper without reading accounts of disputes between the world's most powerful companies over legal rights to technological innovations. For example, Polaroid's patent infringement suit against Kodak garnered a lot of attention in the press in the 1980s, not only because the result effectively drove Kodak out of the instant camera market but also because Polaroid asked the court to award it $12 billion in damages. Making headlines today are controversies between leading computer companies, involving such names as Apple, Hewlett-Packard, Microsoft, Digital Equipment, Intel, and IBM. Genetic engineering has drawn tremendous publicity, with firms such as Genentech, Amgen, and Genetics Institute battling over rights to erythropoietin ("EPO"), tissue plasminogen activator ("TPA"), and other innovative drugs. The international intrigue of industrial espionage has made headlines, as when Hitachi and Mitsubishi stole technological secrets from IBM. And the Internet, of course, has opened a new floodgate of legal disputes. Substantial media attention focused on the browser wars between Microsoft and Netscape, culminating in the U.S. government's antitrust action against the software giant. But clearly, this is just the tip of the iceberg, with accusations stemming from a wide range of issues such as privacy, domain names, and handheld devices that can store and play music from the Web.

This first chapter sets the foundation for the specific issues, cases, inquiries, and strategic recommendations that follow. Here, we will consider why there are public policies in the United States allowing firms to obtain legal rights to technological innovations. We will also explore how such legal policies are developed in the United States by the various state and federal government institutions. Finally, we will broaden our perspective to the international policy arena, the increasingly important frontier affecting high-technology practices today.

THE INTELLECTUAL PROPERTY SYSTEM

Many things can make a firm profitable. The innate abilities of the managers and employees, coupled with hard work, are almost always critical to the success of an organization. The business also may have unique situational advantages, such as its proximity to buyers or distributors. In addition, the firm may have access to relatively cheap sources of raw materials and power. All of the above—labor, land, and natural resources—are tangible ingredients for success.

Profitability depends on much more than such tangible aspects, however. Novel production techniques may reduce costs through increasing the efficiency of the physical plants. New managerial methods may lead to better quality control and more industrious employees. Development of unique product features and characteristics may result in greater customer satisfaction and sales. A stylish brand image may create consumer interest. Unlike tangible assets, however, these qualities are more elusive in that their value is derived from the novel implementation of ideas. For this reason, such resources are called intangible or intellectual assets.

In a competitive economy, such as that of the United States, the mere possession of assets, whether they be tangible or intangible, may not be sufficient to generate profits. Implicit in the foregoing was the assumption that the firm's assets were as good as, or better than, those held by competitors. Thus, for example, a piece of land may not be profitable unless that parcel is comparatively well situated for its uses. The land may be relatively close to the firm's customers, for instance, thereby yielding lower transportation costs than those enjoyed by competitors.

The importance of comparative advantages to profitability leads to problems in a free market economy. First, if one possesses a lucrative asset, then competitors will attempt to take it for their own uses. Just consider what might happen if you were the first to discover a gorgeous lake within 50 miles of Los Angeles. As long as you are the only one to know about it, your life will be improved through enhanced recreational freedoms. But when others learn of your advantageous lifestyle, they too will want to share your asset. Soon will come a free-for-all, with numerous individuals using acts of aggression to lay claim to their particular portions of the lake. In order for you to maintain your advantage, you will need to control the asset, backed up by the authority of the government. This is one of the reasons that property rights are created and protected by law.

Legal protection of property, even with its private exclusivity, results in social benefits. Reflect again on your newly discovered pristine lake. Certain improvements, such as tastefully conceived lakefront houses, roads, and boating facilities, may be socially desirable. But would you be willing to invest time and money in these construction projects if visitors could freely take them when they were completed? With this prospect in mind, you likely would abandon the concept and refrain from any labor or investments in the region. Only with property rights enforced by law would you be willing to undertake such efforts. This social justification for property conforms to the philosophical teachings of John Locke. Put simply, the premise is that people must be motivated to perform labor, and the best way to encourage and reward it is through property protection.[1]

Property protection is no less vital for intellectual assets than for tangible ones. For example, assume that you believe that you can create a handheld radio capable of clear FM reception from a distance of up to 500 miles. Your theory is based on adjusting such factors as transistor numbers, their placement, circuitry, and materials. After three years of expensive research and development (R&D), your theory is confirmed, and an affordable working prototype is completed. You then embark on production, distribution, and marketing.

After the new radio is publicly distributed, various events may take place in the competitive market. Persons interested in the radio business will take the radio apart to determine how its extended range was achieved. This exercise likely will be much easier than the effort you expended during the initial R&D. Once this knowledge is cheaply in the hands of competitors, they may choose to produce similar radios. However, these firms will be more profitable than yours since they have fewer start-up costs to cover.[2] Also, once firms are in possession of your novel radio ideas, they may come up with associated concepts that yield a greater range, or they may make other beneficial improvements. Competitors may now have an even better radio than yours, and without incurring your initial R&D outlay. Finally, firms that have expertise in mass production may find ways to manufacture your radio more cheaply than you do, again without the initial risks and expenses of development.

These competitive effects are advantageous to the consumer and society, at least on first glance. After all, the result may be a better product produced possibly with fewer resources and sold at a lower price. This is why free competition is cherished in the U.S. economy and why it serves as the fundamental tenet of most social policies. However, under these circumstances, you might be reluctant to risk putting the time and capital into the development of this radio in the first place. Why go through the expense when everyone else can just take a free ride on your efforts when you are done? In this environment, you might logically conclude that you would be better off if you simply waited for some other foolish individual to develop the radio, thereby allowing you to learn from that person with minimal costs. In the end, rational market participants, such as yourself, likely will forgo useful and creative investments based on ideas. Therefore, if firms are allowed to compete freely without regard to property rights, the net result may be that creativity is stifled to the detriment of social welfare.

Patents

Components of the intellectual property system are designed to maintain the incentives for inventors to create new products in a free market environment. Patents in the United States, for instance, provide property rights to creators of innovations that are useful, novel, and nonobvious. They also bestow similar benefits on originators of novel and nonobvious ornamental designs. Patents, though, last for only limited periods of time. For inventions that are useful, the patent term begins when the patent application is filed and lasts for 20 years. Patents for ornamental designs last for 14 years, but this period begins only when the patent becomes effective. Inventors have the right to control their new developments and designs while the patents are in force, and have the legal authority to prevent anyone from making or selling in the United States any products that incorporate them. Assuming the improvements are good ones, the periods of exclusive control potentially may be very profitable. The duration of the patent is intended to achieve a delicate balance, providing inventors sufficient incentives to undertake the risks of development while returning the inventions as early as possible to the public domain, where free competition can begin. Also, during the lives of patents, the details of the inventions are fully disclosed to the public for scrutiny, thereby increasing the likelihood that competitive improvements will hit the market either immediately on the expiration of protection or sooner if the inventors approve.

Copyrights

Copyright protection serves similar public goals for certain creative expressions. Imagine that you have a writer's gift and an intriguing story to tell. Unfortunately, the novel probably will take two years to develop. Although you look for some assurance that you will be adequately compensated, faith in yourself is all that you gather. Nonetheless, you decide to take the risk and create the piece. When the book is finally completed, you know you have a winner. You therefore contact a publisher with an established distribution network, and, based on sales projections, you jointly decide to price the book at $29.95. This figure is intended to compensate you adequately for your years of effort and to reward you for the risks of undertaking a project that could have totally failed. It also should be sufficient to compensate the publisher for the expenses and risks it incurs in marketing and distributing the book.

One week after your novel hits the shelves, however, another author introduces a book exactly like yours, but selling for $7.95. How did this happen? This author simply bought one copy of your novel, scanned the pages into a computer printing system, and created his own copies to sell. His price, albeit much lower than yours, is sufficient to comfortably cover his costs of operation. In addition, this business enterprise has relatively few risks, given that the novel was already completed and so obviously desirable. In the end, you do not make nearly enough money to justify the time and risk you dedicated to the project, but the subsequent author makes a tidy profit. Under these circumstances, it is doubtful that you will ever create another novel. To the world's dismay, your artistic genius never again will be publicly enjoyed.

The U.S. copyright system is designed to prevent others from copying creative expressions that are fixed in tangible media, so that artists will have sufficient incentives to share their talents. Items such as books, sculptures, movies, and paintings clearly may be protected with copyrights. Debate begins, however, when considering artistic creations that also are useful, such as computer programs or handsomely sculpted industrial products. Such issues become important because the period of copyright protection is much longer than with a patent, sometimes lasting well over 100 years. Also, copyright protection is much easier to obtain. From an economic perspective, these differences normally are easy to explain. A patent provides protection to a product idea or design, effectively allotting a limited form of monopoly power to the owner. A copyright, on the other hand, merely protects one expression of an idea and does not extend to the idea itself. Therefore, in theory, the copyright should be less intrusive on competitive markets. We will discover, though, that products such as computer programs sometimes blur the distinctions between ideas and expressions, leading to potential misapplications of copyright protection.

As noted, copyright protection in the United States primarily is designed to provide sufficient economic incentives to reward creative investments. This again follows the philosophy of John Locke, who believed that individuals are not willing to undertake labor unless there are reasonable prospects for compensation. Copyrights, by providing property rights over expressions, offer the requisite opportunities for economic rewards. Copyrights, therefore, are merely tools for their owners to achieve economic ends and may be exploited in the market as their owners wish. This means that the owners can completely sell or otherwise transfer all their copyright privileges to others, if that best suits their economic objectives.

Copyrights, though, may also be justified in somewhat different philosophical terms.[3] According to philosophers such as Georg Hegel, artists self-actualize by extending their personas on to external physical objects.[4] A painting, for instance, may be beautiful, but it also reflects the very being of the artist. It becomes, in a sense, a mirror to the artist's soul. Accordingly, there is an intimate bond between the artistic work and the painter's unique personality. Under this conception, copyrights provide property-like protection to creative expressions to prevent others from interfering with the self-actualizing process. This, in turn, permits artists to continue their personal growth. Artists always may sell their paintings, thereby allowing purchasers to satisfy their own personal needs through ownership of the creative pieces. However, the painters cannot give up all claims to the works, since to do so would be to totally alienate their own personalities. Thus, an artist always will have some personal or moral rights to a creation even after disposing of it to others. As we shall see, this view has been adopted by many other countries, notably in Europe, and recently it also has been followed to a limited degree in the United States.

Trade Secrets

Another important component of the intellectual property system is trade secret protection. Trade secret laws protect valuable information that is not publicly known and that is subject to measures to preserve its secrecy. Again, the rationale for protection is to stimulate the development of new inventions, techniques, and other creations, as well as to preserve high moral standards of corporate conduct.

For example, suppose you start a beverage company. You are sure that a combination of prunes, apples, and apricots will make a fabulous new drink, but you do not have the skills to create it. Thus, you hire a product development staff of experts to create a formula based on these fruits. Finally, the staff finds the proper proportions in conjunction with other ingredients needed for coloring, additional flavor, and preservation. If one of these experts could freely take the formula and either start his own company or sell it to a competitor, the potential profitability of your R&D efforts might quickly diminish. Indeed, without some means to prevent such occurrences, one would be reluctant to share ideas or information with others, even employees, in order to commercially improve and develop those ideas. Trade secret laws allow one to control such secret information by preventing those entrusted with the information, or those who otherwise steal it, from using or disclosing it.

Trademarks

The final major arm of the intellectual property scheme is trademark protection.[5] Trademarks serve somewhat different public goals from the goals served by patents, copyrights, and trade secrets. The role of trademarks is not to provide creative incentives; rather, trademarks function to increase distributional efficiency by making products easy for consumers to locate without confusion.

For a simple but illustrative demonstration of the importance of trademarks, imagine that you are in a managerial position at a hypothetical detergent company. Your company invests significant capital in the production of its detergent to ensure that its product is among the best laundry agents on the market. In addition, great pains are taken to guarantee that the quality of the product is consistently maintained so that the purchasing public will be continually satisfied. You package the detergent in a white box, which bears the name "Denton's" on it.

Soon after introduction of the product, you become aware of a menacing competitive response. Another company freely copied the characteristics of your packaging and began selling its detergent in a white box with the name "Denton's" on it. Inside is a cheap and ineffective substance closely akin to sawdust. The effect on your customers was both swift and detrimental.

Many buyers who previously enjoyed your product and who wanted it again purchased that of the competitor by mistake. Of course, when they used the product this time, their clothes were not adequately cleaned. The customers became confused. What is going on here? Maybe this company, which makes "Denton's," doesn't perform enough quality control? Clearly, the negative repercussions on the goodwill of your company may be substantial. Some sophisticated customers may question whether the recently purchased box came from the same manufacturer that made the previous ones. How many Denton's are out there? Committed individuals even may take steps to try to find the right "Denton's." Perhaps your detergent has a different smell. Customers with adequate time may sniff the boxes before purchase. Of course, the competitor may foil these efforts by copying your product's odor also. Other steps might include discussions with the retailer, ripping open boxes, and/or buying substantial quantities when the right cleaner is located.

The ability of the competitor to compete freely by copying your packaging has resulted in a number of socially undesirable consequences. First, your incentive to maintain consistent quality is diminished, since many customers, after being fooled, will attribute their annoyance to spotty production techniques. Also, why should you continue to make a premier product at great expense when competitors can so easily pass off sawdust for the same retail price? Indeed, the competitor's business is the more lucrative, so maybe it is time to move into sawdust sales yourself. In addition, many purchasers are wasting a lot of time and money to search for and obtain your product.[6]

Providing legal exclusivity through property protection of identification symbols and characteristics can solve these problems. If your company had exclusive rights to use the name "Denton's" on the packaging, then the competitor's attempts to fool customers would be foiled, for whenever that name appeared on a box, buyers could be sure that it came from you. No longer would customers have to engage in time-consuming search efforts to find your detergent. All they need do is locate a box marked with "Denton's." Your investments in quality and consistency now would pay off because your customers would be constantly satisfied with their purchases. Also, these benefits could be enjoyed in most situations without any countervailing social harms. Those competitors who try to legitimately compete will not be disadvantaged simply because they cannot use the name "Denton's." Certainly there is nothing special about that word that might give your company an unfair advantage in the marketplace. There are hundreds of other words competitors can use to equally identify their products. In fact, the only persons who will be harmed are those who wish to compete unfairly by misleading your customers.

At one time, technology managers may not have had to give special attention to trademark issues. However, this is no longer the case. For instance, trademarks are raising major headaches on the Web, such as when they are used in domain names or to designate links. Also, the law with regard to trademarks has broadened rapidly in recent years, allowing many new product characteristics to be protected. The "look and feel" of computer software interfaces, for instance, now may possibly serve as trademarks. Further, international issues such as the gray market and counterfeiting are increasingly important to those persons involved with managing technology.

In sum, the intellectual property system confers varying degrees of protection on intangible assets. The most important rationale is to stimulate creativity without unduly displacing the benefits that normally flow from free competition. Patents, copyrights, and trade secrets all are grounded substantially on this principle. Patents and copyrights also encourage public disclosure of ideas and expressions so that the public can learn and enjoy. The intellectual property system also may foster the development of self-identity through the protection of moral and personal attributes. Copyright protection serves as one vehicle for this overseas, while in the United States, such concerns are just starting to arise. Finally, intellectual property, notably by way of trademarks, promotes distributional efficiency and the maintenance of high-quality standards. Exhibit 1.1 on the following page outlines the respective roles played by these fundamental forms of intellectual property protection in the United States.

THE PUBLIC POLICY PROCESS IN THE UNITED STATES

The Power Struggle: Federal vs. State

Public policies in the United States emanate from an interrelated structure consisting of federal and state domains. When separate spheres of influence attempt to expand their respective realms of control, tension usually results. The public policy process that establishes the ground rules for managing technology provides a classic example.

The founding of the United States was a difficult feat requiring the union of separate and distinct state governments, which theretofore had controlled the policies within their respective borders. As you can imagine, state participants were extremely wary of relinquishing power and control to a federal government. After all, a state is only one of many voices within a national entity, whereas in its own state policy structure, it is the sole determinant. The U.S. Constitution provided the great compromise that brought the states together by defining and limiting the authority that the federal government could exert over the various state governments.

Article I, Section 8, of the U.S. Constitution specifically lists those activities in which the federal government may engage if its policy makers so choose. The list is actually fairly short, including such things as the power to tax, spend, regulate foreign affairs, and provide military forces. Of most importance for this book, also included are the rights (1) to promote the progress of science and useful arts by securing for limited times to authors and inventors exclusive rights to their writings and discoveries and (2) to regulate commerce among the several states. Clearly the federal government has the authority to regulate patents and copyrights, as it has done. However, by virtue of its power over interstate commerce, the federal government also may make policies regarding trademarks and trade secrets, as long as a business is involved in some interstate activity. As we shall see, the federal government has been substantially involved in trademark policy for some time but only recently has entered the trade secret arena. In addition, the federal

Exhibit 1.1
Important Forms of Intellectual Property Protection in the United States

FORM OF PROTECTION	WHAT IT PROTECTS	STANDARDS FOR PROTECTION	WHAT IT PROTECTS AGAINST	LENGTH OF PROTECTION	REGISTRATION REQUIREMENTS?
Patent Utility	Inventions	Useful, novel, nonobvious	Independent creation, copying, use, sale	20 years after filing the patent application	Yes
Design	Designs	Ornamental, novel, nonobvious	Independent creation, copying, use, sale	14 years after the patent issues	Yes
Trade Secret	Information	Secret, subject to reasonable security measures	Misappropriation	Potentially unlimited	No
Copyright	Expressions in tangible media	Original	Copying, display, distribution, performance, transmission†	Life of Author plus 70 years*	No, but recommended Simple procedure
Trademark	Identification symbols and features	Distinctive	Similar use causing a likelihood of confusion or dilution	Potentially unlimited	No, but recommended

†Protection against transmissions is somewhat limited.
*For certain works, the length of copyright protection is 95 to 120 years.

government has the authority to regulate other aspects of interstate commercial activity, such as contractual relationships and liabilities for product defects, but here again, it has remained somewhat on the sidelines.[7]

A few additional points are worth noting here. First, Article I of the U.S. Constitution, with few exceptions, delineates the entire permissible sphere of federal influence. If an activity is not on the list, or is not at least somehow necessary and proper to accomplish a power on that list, it is subject to state control only. Second, state governments generally have simultaneous authority to regulate in those areas that are listed. This is why we see state governments making laws affecting trademarks and trade secrets, as well as contracts and products liabilities. However, this state power is qualified by the Supremacy Clause, which provides that federal policies are the supreme laws of the land. Thus, if the federal government passes a law, then the states cannot do anything that undermines the intent of the federal policy.

Supremacy issues sometimes are simple to resolve, but more often they are complicated and contentious. The easy situations are when the federal law explicitly articulates that the federal policy is to be exclusive and that the states are forbidden from exercising any authority. In such a situation, there is no question that any state law regulating the same activity would undermine the very clear intent of the federal law. The federal copyright law provides a good example. Section 301 of the federal copyright law provides that no person may receive equivalent protections under state law. Thus, the states are restricted from passing laws that protect expressions written on tangible media. However, as we shall see later, the federal copyright laws do not extend to oral expressions or ideas. Thus, the explicit federal supremacy related by the copyright law does not apply to state influence over these matters.

The more difficult situations result when the federal law does not explicitly preempt state regulation. In that case, the intent of federal lawmakers must be indirectly discerned. Usually, supremacy will be established when a state law stands as an obstacle to the accomplishment of the purposes and objectives of federal lawmakers. When a state law serves to strengthen or otherwise further the federal policy, the two may coexist. The mutual existence of federal and state trademark policies serves as an example. However, when a state law detracts from federal policy, then that state law, including its requirements, prohibitions, and penalties, must fall.

In 1989, the Supreme Court addressed Supremacy issues in *Bonito Boats, Inc. v. Thunder Craft Boats, Inc.*[8] In this case, the Court reviewed a Florida state law that prevented boat manufacturers from using the "direct molding process," a technique that is very effective for copying boat hull designs. Thunder Craft used the direct molding process in Florida to copy an unpatented boat hull sold by Bonito Boats and was sued for violating the Florida statute. Thunder Craft asked the Supreme Court to invalidate the Florida statute, arguing that it unduly interfered with the objectives of the federal patent laws.

The Court agreed with Thunder Craft and ruled that the state statute violated the Supremacy Clause. According to the Court, the federal patent laws embrace a limited exception to the overriding principles of free competition, based on carefully crafted criteria designed to provide incentives for creative acts and to stimulate public disclosure of ideas. In a somewhat sweeping statement, the Court declared that "the federal patent laws must determine not only what is protected but also what is free for all to use." The Florida statute, by preventing companies from using an efficient method for duplicating unpatented designs, interfered with the federal policy that makes such designs free for all to copy and use.

In reaching its decision, the Supreme Court had to address why the patent laws should preempt the state boat hull statute, but not state trademark and trade secret laws, which also serve to protect unpatented designs and inventions from duplication. The difference, the Court said, is based on the fundamental purposes of the state protection schemes and the reduced degree to which each interferes with the policy objectives of the patent laws. State trademark laws, for instance, may protect product designs from copying, but they do so only to prevent consumer confusion and not to provide incentives for creative activities. Thus, as a general rule, trademark laws do not conflict with patent policies. However, we shall see in Chapter 7 that companies sometimes want trademark laws to do more for them than merely to protect identification symbols, such as by making it difficult for other companies to compete with alternative products. In these situations, state trademark laws become problematic and their application may offend patent policies.

The Supreme Court also confirmed in *Bonito Boats* that state trade secret laws are compatible with the federal patent laws, despite the fact that they operate to prevent the disclosure of ideas. Since disclosure is a primary objective of the patent laws, trade secret laws raise perhaps more substantial concerns than do trademark laws. Nonetheless, the Court concluded that they still pass muster. One reason is because their objectives are to preserve trust and deter espionage, goals that are outside the interests of the patent laws. However, of more importance, the Court believed that trade secret laws are so much weaker than patent policies that companies usually rely on them only when they believe that their inventions are not patentable. Thus, trade secret laws tend to preserve the secrecy of information only when such information would not be disclosed through the patent process anyway. In reaching this conclusion, the Court referred to its previous analysis in *Kewanee Oil Co. v. Bicron Corp.*, a case that is presented in Chapter 4. The Court also noted that state trade secret laws, as well as trademark laws, have coexisted with the federal patent laws for almost 200 years, and Congress had not yet indicated any disapproval. That Congress had tolerated any potential tension raised by the state laws for so long further diminished any argument that they conflict with federal objectives.

Bonito Boats typifies the struggle between the federal and state domains over control of intellectual property. Members of the Florida legislature resolved to protect the research and development efforts of Florida boat manufacturers from those competitors using the direct molding technique. Why the Florida legislature was motivated to pass such a law is open to debate, an exercise that will not be entertained here. However, you can easily imagine a scenario wherein all 50 states pass a multitude of such laws in a variety of contexts. If allowed, the resulting patchwork of intellectual property laws would severely restrain commercial activity on any but a local scale. Similarly, the effectiveness of federal patent policy, which is designed to provide uniformity in this context, would be extremely hampered. That is why the Supreme Court repeatedly has struck down such forays by state governments to control intellectual property.[9] However, as *Bonito Boats* indicates, protection of trade secrets by state governments does not conflict with federal patent policy, nor with any other federal policy to date. Likewise, state trademark or unfair competition laws do not run afoul of federal policies as long as they are carefully tailored only to protect consumers from confusion.

The net result can be summarized as follows. The federal patent laws serve as the national umbrella policy to provide the proper level of incentives for inventive activity in useful products. Although most state laws that insulate useful inventions from competition are not tolerated, state trade secret protection survives. The relatively limited context of trade secret protection, along with the needs to preserve business ethics, bring it outside the purview of patent policy. In addition, Congress made it clear when passing a relatively new federal trade secret law that the measure was designed to supplement and strengthen state trade secret laws, rather than to supplant them. Federal copyright laws explicitly direct that all similar state protection schemes are void. Thus, there are no state laws that protect creative works of authorship expressed in tangible media. Federal trademark laws, as we shall see, were developed for the most part to rectify certain procedural deficiencies in existing state trademark policies and were intended to work hand in hand with the various state laws. Therefore, one finds policies to combat customer confusion simultaneously at both the federal and state levels. Exhibit 1.2 on the following page illustrates how these principles have been applied to allocate power between the federal and state systems of regulation.

How Intellectual Property Policies Are Made in the United States

Intellectual property policies are made in similar fashions at both the federal and state levels. We will review the basic concepts here to provide a framework for understanding the more specific elements presented in the chapters that follow. The discussion focuses on the federal policy process, but the principles can be applied readily to the various state methods.

The Federal Process

The dynamic nature of the policy process can best be understood by first taking a quick look at patents. When Congress passes a statute, it usually will speak in broad terms. The representational nature of Congress often makes agreement on specifics impossible. Also, details may best be left to experts acting within the general directives from Congress. The Patent Act, for example, provides that one is entitled to a patent upon inventing a novel and nonobvious process, machine, manufacture, or composition of matter. Which governmental body should decide whether these criteria have been met in particular cases? In 1997, there were over 235,000 requests in the United States for patents.[10] Clearly, neither Congress nor the president has the time to focus on such minutiae. Therefore, as it has done for

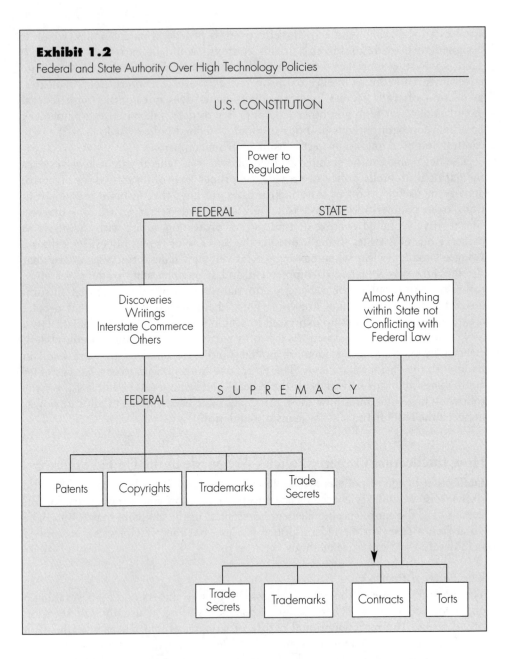

Exhibit 1.2
Federal and State Authority Over High Technology Policies

U.S. CONSTITUTION

Power to Regulate

FEDERAL   STATE

Discoveries
Writings
Interstate Commerce
Others

Almost Anything
within State not
Conflicting with
Federal Law

FEDERAL ——— S U P R E M A C Y

| Patents | Copyrights | Trademarks | Trade Secrets |

| Trade Secrets | Trademarks | Contracts | Torts |

most statutes requiring administration, Congress formed an administrative agency to make these determinations. For patents (as well as trademarks) Congress created and funded the Patent and Trademark Office (PTO) to review such applications. The PTO is within the Department of Commerce and is headed by a commissioner, who serves at the pleasure of the president.

Let's assume that the PTO receives a request to patent a genetically engineered living bacterium that is useful for dispersing oil floating on water. If you were the expert at the PTO in charge of examining this file, would you grant the patent? Did Congress intend that living things be patentable? This is certainly a far cry from the more typical situations involving machines or chemicals. Obviously, your job would be easier if Congress had specified in the statute the fact that bioengineered microorganisms may be patented, but unfortunately nothing so explicit was drafted. Ultimately you interpret the vague terms of the Patent Act so as to prohibit patents on living things, and therefore you reject the application. Such an action by agency personnel thereby establishes the policy that living things are not patentable.

The inventor here likely will feel wronged and become bitter, wondering how a single bureaucrat can make such an improper decision, which may ruin an otherwise bright future. Fortunately for the inventor, Congress subjects all administrative agencies, including the PTO, to procedural safeguards, which allows others to review the examiner's decision. In the PTO, the inventor may appeal to a board, which has the power to correct the examiner's interpretation. If the agency appeal board agrees with the examiner's interpretation, then the inventor may appeal that ruling to the federal court system. As we shall study in the next chapter, such a case actually occurred, and the federal courts ultimately interpreted the statute differently, thereby concluding that living things were patentable. This then became the new policy, and the inventor was granted a patent under it.

To summarize, Congress makes policies, in conjunction with the president, through the passing of statutes. Administrative agencies administer the details of those policies. In carrying out their responsibilities, the agencies may have to interpret vague terms and conditions in the statutes, thereby establishing new policies. Likewise, courts make policies by interpreting statutes when deciding cases. This may happen in appeals from administrative actions, as described, or may arise in other contexts, such as disputes between private parties. *Bonito Boats* actually was an example of the power of courts to make policies by interpreting statutes. There, the U.S. Supreme Court interpreted the terms of the Patent Act and concluded that reverse-molding statutes conflicted with the wishes of Congress.

Two other elements of the dynamic are worth noting here. First, if Congress were opposed to the determination by the courts that living things are patentable, it could (subject to presidential action) amend the statute to explicitly state that living things may not be patented. After such a clarification, the door would be closed on those in the PTO or the courts who felt the policy should be otherwise. Thus, in these matters, Congress has the ultimate say. However, Congress moves very slowly, and such clarification amendments often come relatively late, especially in technological fields where rapid change is common. We will see this dynamic often in this book, such as when we study the course of copyright protection for computer software.

Congress also has given the PTO the power to make regulations about patent procedures. A regulation is simply a law passed by an administrative agency, which conforms to the benchmarks articulated by Congress. A host of such regulations passed by the PTO can be found in the Code of Federal Regulations. The PTO also can make guidelines offering its views up front about certain issues. For instance, the PTO has developed guidelines for use by its patent examiners about the patentability of computer programs.

Federal trademark and copyright policies arise through similar dynamics. Trademark policy is controlled by the Lanham Act, with administration conducted, again, by the PTO. Copyright law is derived from the Copyright Act, which is administered by the Copyright Office, a branch of the Library of Congress. As with patents, the administrative agencies in these instances make registration decisions, which are subject to appeal in the federal courts. They also issue regulations. Exhibit 1.3 provides a summary of the federal government policy-making institutions and indicates how each may affect the development of intellectual property policies in the United States.

State Policies

Policies made at the state level are controlled by analogous principles. Legislatures make laws that are subject to interpretations by courts and administered, if necessary, by administrative agencies. State policies, however, raise a new issue. You can imagine how potentially burdensome it might be for a national or international company to deal with state laws if those laws varied greatly from state to state. For instance, if you had valuable information that was protected by trade secret laws in some states but not all, your advantage could be lost if you do not exercise special care within certain borders. Fortunately, in a variety of contexts, the states have taken steps to unify their individual policies. For example, trade secret policy has been brought into substantial conformity in many states through adoption of the Uniform Trade Secrets Act, a document that was developed by experts to serve as a model for legislative action. Also, in the contracts arena, all states except Louisiana have adopted Article 2 of the Uniform Commercial Code (UCC), thereby unifying policies dealing with the sale of goods. However, Article 2 of the UCC started to show its age in the face of technological changes, such as with computers and the Internet. For this reason, the National Conference of Commissioners on Uniform State Laws and the American Law Institute began work in the mid-1990s to modernize Article 2, and in particular to add a new Article 2B, dealing specifically with software contracts and licenses of information. This effort to revise the UCC stalled in 1999, perhaps because it was too ambitious. Nevertheless, other model laws, such as the Uniform Computer Information Transactions Act, quickly appeared to take its place. Therefore, despite the seeming failure to finalize Article 2B, there is little question that the nation soon will enjoy the benefits of uniformity in these modern technological contexts.

Another area of law controlled primarily by state law is torts, which includes negligence and strict products liability, among other things. In this area, state laws vary more widely, although the American Law Institute has published the so-called Restatement of Torts, which serves as an authoritative guide to prevailing legal principles. Although the Restatement is not a law, it promotes uniformity because state court judges tend to rely on it to guide their decisions in tort cases. In 1997, the Institute published its third revision of the Restatement, including a hotly

Exhibit 1.3
Powers of U.S. Government Policy Makers

BRANCH	FORMAL METHODS OF POLICY MAKING
Congress	1. Pass legislation articulating policy
	a. The Patent Act
	b. The Copyright Act
	c. The Lanham Act (Trademarks)
	d. The Economic Espionage Act
	(Trade secrets)
	2. Pass legislation affecting administrative
	agencies
	a. Authorize powers of agencies
	b. Designate budgets for agencies
	3. Approve president's nominees for
	administrative agencies and courts
President	1. Nominate administrative agency heads*
	2. Nominate court justices
	3. Approve or veto legislation
	4. Manage administrative agencies
Courts	1. Interpret statutes and constitutions
Administrative agencies	
— Department of Commerce	1. Administer legislative directives
— Patent and Trademark Office	2. Interpret statutes
— Library of Congress	3. Promulgate regulations
— Copyright Office	4. Establish guidelines
— Others	

*Exception: The register of copyrights, who heads the Copyright Office, is selected by the librarian of Congress.

debated new provision on strict products liability. We will take a look at how the new Restatement handles this controversial body of law in Chapter 8.

The Expanding Scope of Intellectual Property Protection

Before moving on to the international arena, one should be aware that there has been a substantial trend toward increasing intellectual property protection within the United States. Since 1982, Congress has passed numerous new laws and amendments that have served to strengthen intellectual property rights. Many of these policy steps will be discussed in detail later in this book. However, here is just a small sample of the relatively recent changes made by Congress on the domestic front:

1. Congress passed the American Inventors Protection Act, which provides for earlier publication of certain patent applications, allows patent term

extensions when there are lengthy administrative delays, and permits greater public involvement in the patent reexamination process.

2. Congress gave trademark owners enhanced remedies against individuals and companies that register Internet domain names in bad faith.
3. The Copyright Act was amended simplifying the procedures to receive protection and expanding the range of coverage.
4. Congress passed the Digital Millennium Copyright Act, which, among other things, protects Internet service providers from copyright infringement claims, and strengthens digital copyright management systems and technological safeguards.
5. Owners of copyrights in sound recordings received new rights in the Copyright Act, giving them added controls over digital transmissions of their works.
6. Congress lengthened the term of copyright protection.
7. The federal trademark statute—the Lanham Act—was revised, allowing one to register a trademark earlier and extending the breadth of protection under federal law.
8. Criminal penalties for counterfeiting were increased under the Lanham Act.
9. Congress added new federal criminal laws dealing with trade secret misappropriation.
10. Criminal penalties under the Copyright Act were expanded and now cover situations that are not necessarily motivated by personal financial gain.

The other players in the U.S. policy process reinforced the expansion and solidification of intellectual property rights. Presidents Reagan, Bush, and Clinton were committed to strengthening intellectual property protection both at home and abroad. This was demonstrated not only in their speeches and legislative proposals but in their various governmental appointments as well. Those appointed to head the relevant administrative agencies worked diligently to modernize and improve their departments. For example, the PTO embarked on a program to computerize its operations and otherwise utilize new technologies in order to handle the rapidly increasing number of patent and trademark applications. The PTO made other administrative adjustments as well so as to respond to the burgeoning number of patent filings in the new technology fields such as biotechnology and data processing. Those in the intellectual property agencies also liberalized their interpretations as to protectible assets. One striking example was the decision of the PTO in 1988 to issue a patent on a genetically engineered mouse. Seemingly, patent protection is now available for any form of nonhuman life.[11] In addition, the enforcement agencies contributed to the power of those companies holding intellectual property rights. For instance, the Justice Department's Antitrust Division, which polices the markets for anticompetitive actions, clearly indicated in its enforcement guidelines that businesses could exercise more control over the uses of their intellectual property.[12]

The U.S. presidents also affected the opinions from the federal judiciary by nominating judges when vacancies on the bench arose. The nominees ultimately appointed under the Reagan and Bush administrations consistently held conservative judicial philosophies, while those appointed under President Clinton were more moderate. Whatever differences these judges may have had in general philosophical sentiments, however, did not translate into any recognizable changes of approach regarding the protection of intellectual property rights. The somewhat consistent trend in the federal judiciary during this period was to cast an increasingly sympathetic ear to the needs of intellectual property owners. The clearest explanation for this may be that all three presidents were vocal advocates of a strong system of intellectual property protection. One is hard pressed to find a predictable relationship between judicial philosophies and support for intellectual property laws. Perhaps one might expect conservatives in general to show greater support—which may partially explain the trend—but the strength of this relationship, if it exists, is not very compelling. Therefore, the judges simply may have been moved more by the expectations of the presidents, members of Congress and the public. Whatever explanation one accepts, the federal judiciary had a clear role in elevating the status of intellectual property in the United States. It is interesting to note, for instance, that patent rights are upheld in 80% of cases now, whereas before 1982, the likelihood was closer to 30%.[13] In addition, the courts, through their interpretations, expanded the range of intellectual property protection to new varieties of technology, such as computers and biotechnology. The only perceivable exception to this trend may have emerged in the copyright area.[14] Nonetheless, the judiciary was highly criticized from many corners for years regarding the generous degree of copyright protection it afforded to computer programs. Now the criticism has moved to other arenas, such as patents for computer-related inventions and licensing practices, among many others. In any event, U.S. companies obviously have noticed the sympathy of the courts toward their intellectual assets. For instance, the number of patent-related lawsuits filed in federal courts grew from around 700 in 1982 to 1,500 in 1992 to over 2,100 in 1997.[15] Undoubtedly, the heat has been turned up within the domestic technology policy arena. It should come as no surprise that developments are occurring rapidly within the international domain as well.

AN INTERNATIONAL POLICY PERSPECTIVE

The U.S. policy process clearly has recognized the importance of protecting intellectual property. To that end, numerous laws have been constructed to allow firms operating in the United States to profit from their investments in creativity and to enjoy the fruits of their valued names. Laws on the books, however, would not be enough without enforcement. Predictably, U.S. policy makers have provided for effective enforcement of these laws as well. The various statutes generally articulate that wrongdoers must cease their activities and are responsible to compensate their victims. And the courts have carried out their role in ordering these remedies by using the various tools of authority at their disposal.

If the United States were an insular economy, then one probably could rest comfortably with the aforesaid state of affairs. However, markets now are unquestionably global, within which the United States is only one, albeit important, piece of the puzzle. Most high-technology firms now compete and trade on an international scale. If laws are not developed and enforced within other borders as in the United States, protection may be lost. The United States does not have the authority to dictate policy within other sovereign countries or to enforce its own laws within those other jurisdictions. Thus, U.S. companies managing high technologies are dependent on foreign governments to establish strong intellectual property protection policies, such as those that have been established in the United States. If those policies are not developed, then the ground rules may be completely different when firms engage in commercial activities in international zones. Even if intellectual property protection is established by law overseas, it may be useless if the enforcement mechanisms are insufficient. It is one thing to state that something is wrong; it is quite another to do something about it.

The problems have become especially acute as technology has advanced. It is becoming increasingly easy and inexpensive to transmit, store, copy, and print huge volumes of data in very short periods of time. The time has passed when effective enforcement could be aimed at a few major business users, distributors, or manufacturers. Now, substantial violations may occur in even the smallest of homes. Under these circumstances, therefore, enforcement may be problematic even in the United States. In countries with less developed intellectual property protection mechanisms, the magnitude of the issue is extreme. And withdrawing operations from those countries does not necessarily avoid the problems. Access to the valued information anywhere in the world allows pirates to make duplicates within the hospitable environments and then channel their copies into the international distribution network. Exports of intellectual property assets from the United States more than doubled in the 1980s, and by 1990 accounted for more than 25% of total U.S. exports.[16] Some estimates in the early 1990s suggested that inadequate international protection of U.S. patents, trademarks, and copyrights cost the U.S. economy $80 billion in sales and 250,000 jobs every year.[17] A more recent study in 1997 put the sales losses for the U.S. software industry alone at over $11 billion, suggesting that software piracy was the norm in a host of countries, including China, Indonesia, Italy, Argentina, Paraguay, Turkey, Bulgaria, Vietnam, and Taiwan.[18] It is no wonder that international protection of intellectual property ranks high on the U.S. foreign policy agenda.

Raising the level of intellectual property protection across the globe to that level currently enjoyed in the United States and other industrialized countries is a formidable task. After all, there is no world government with the power to establish international intellectual property laws and the authority to enforce their provisions without regard to sovereign boundaries. Therefore, other avenues must be used to reach such uniformity.

Of course, it would be convenient if all governments developed economic policies based on the philosophical principles of the United States. Then one might expect at least some continual movement toward continuity among world governments. However, the wide diversity of cultural, economic, political, and social backgrounds that defines the various policies of the independent nations precludes the occurrence of a natural transformation. For example, many developing countries, especially in Latin America and Asia, consider intangible ideas, forms, symbols, and processes as belonging to the common heritage of mankind.[19] Treating such public goods as private property is inconsistent with those countries' cultural orientations, especially when the intangible items are controlled by foreign entities. National pride is an imposing force in such domains. In addition, these countries believe that it is in their economic self-interest to deny protection. Inexpensive access to the developed world's technology is seen as the quickest way to move along the modernization curve. Indeed, piracy-based business ventures continue to thrive in Asia, Eastern Europe, and South America.[20] Clamping down with intellectual property protection may have serious short-term consequences to the current economic bases of nations in these and other regions. The least developed nations logically fear that stronger intellectual property laws would raise their prices for consumption goods and for key components of their manufactured items while simply transferring additional profits outside their countries. Thus, if one can find intellectual property policies at all within those borders, they are usually weakly drawn and even more casually enforced. Expecting those nations to reform these fundamental notions on an independent basis would be a naive hope.

Deterrence of international pirating can be accomplished through unilateral, bilateral, and/or multilateral means. Unilateral options usually are the easiest to implement but tend to be the least effective, especially for companies with widespread international marketing activities. Bilateral agreements are an improvement, but they lead to a patchwork of varying international standards. Multilateral methods should provide the most extensive protection but can be frustrating to achieve. We will review some important considerations and developments on all of these fronts.

Unilateral Steps

A unilateral action can be defined as an independent step by a country, such as the United States, to protect its citizens from foreign pirating activities. It is a law or measure designed to protect businesses within the national borders. Given that it has only national extent, such a law is most useful for firms that concentrate their marketing activities within those borders. Organizations with more multinational visions will find that other efforts are needed to combat the global effects of piracy on their operations.

Actions Against Imports Into the United States

The U.S. patent, copyright, and trademark laws all provide remedies for the importation of pirated copies into the United States. Thus, if Microsoft Excel were pervasively copied in Thailand, for instance, then Microsoft would be entitled to legal recourse if these copies were imported into the United States. So, if Microsoft discovers a distributor in Seattle, Washington, reselling the pirated software, Microsoft could bring suit against that distributor in a federal trial court located in that area. If it persuades the court that the distributor indeed did sell illegal copies, then the court could order the distributor to compensate Microsoft for lost profits from forgone sales, and it could forbid the distributor from selling any more pirated Microsoft items in the state.

Although these laws provide some measure of protection for Microsoft, their overall effectiveness, even within the United States, can be somewhat limited. First of all, litigation in the United States often takes three to five years, a long period in any context, but especially burdensome in the fast-paced technology climate. Second, and more important, the suit by Microsoft is against an individual distributor. If the overseas pirating activity is widespread, then the illegal copies likely will reach U.S. markets through a large number of different importers and distributors throughout the land. To control the situation, Microsoft will have to institute a wide array of lawsuits against the multitude of resellers all across the country. Clearly, the magnitude of such a task may be daunting.

Section 337   There are various laws and regulations in the United States that allow the Customs Service to block the importation of goods violating U.S. intellectual property rights. These, too, may be viewed as examples of unilateral measures established by the United States. Section 337 of the U.S. Tariff Act offers the most general and far-reaching relief to aggrieved intellectual property owners in the United States. Under Section 337, a U.S. industry may file a complaint with the International Trade Commission (ITC) alleging that pirated goods are being imported. If the ITC, after an administrative hearing, determines that the imported goods do violate U.S. patents, copyrights, mask works, trade secrets, or trademarks, it may effectively prevent further imports of those goods at the U.S. door.[21] This is accomplished by an "exclusion order" which directs the Customs Service to prevent the entry of the offending articles.

The Section 337 route offers a number of advantages to a company such as Microsoft. The most obvious difference is that Microsoft no longer has to chase sellers around the country. As opposed to trial court litigation, which concerns the wrongdoing of the parties being sued, the ITC hearing is aimed at the offending articles. Once the Section 337 proceeding is successfully completed, the ITC and the Customs Service will act as watchdogs for Microsoft, excluding the entry of all offending copies of Excel before they enter the stream of U.S. commerce. In addition, ITC determinations are made within a relatively short period of time. Although Section 337 once required the ITC to make its determinations within 12 to 18 months, it now only must complete them at the earliest practicable time. Nonetheless, the ITC still aims to conclude most cases within 12 months, and expects to resolve even the more complex disputes within 18 months.[22] On the downside, the ITC does not have the power to compensate Microsoft for damages caused by sales made before the exclusion order. Microsoft must use the normal trial court channels for that or use the ITC action as leverage to gain monetary settlements with the offending distributors. Nonetheless, for a company that is being injured in the United States by pirated goods, Section 337 may be an effective weapon indeed.

Actions for Violations Over the Internet

As a general matter, the increased globalization of markets has decreased the effectiveness of unilateral steps, prompting high technology companies to push for stronger foreign laws to protect their investments on an international scale. However, an interesting nuance has developed recently, spurred mainly by the rising importance of the Internet to world trade and affairs. As already explained, a country such as the United States may not directly dictate what the laws of other countries, such as India, will be. Thus, it is up to the government of India to determine the nature and extent of the laws that apply within its borders, whether they be concerned with intellectual property, antitrust, products liability, privacy, gambling, or defamation. On the other hand, the U.S. government does have the ability to protect its citizens when the effects of activities in India are felt within the United States. Therefore, the government of India, through its laws, may allow pharmaceuticals that are patented in the United States to be copied and sold in India. However, the United States government may take steps within its borders to diminish any negative effects on its citizens. This explains why the United States has the ability to prevent sales or imports of those pharmaceuticals into the United States. In essence, India's public policies control the operations within its territory, but the laws of the United States may control their effects when those effects reach into U.S. territory.

The Internet strains traditional concepts of territoriality, since actions that are legal in one country simultaneously may have illegal effects in another. Ordinarily, copyright "pirates" might produce and sell copies of CDs or computer programs in hospitable countries, but later face difficulties if they ever attempted to sell copies in countries having stronger copyright policies. Laws based on territoriality normally can work under this environment, since the actions in one country are discrete and separate from those in another. So, if the U.S. government is concerned about protecting copyright interests in the United States, its laws can challenge those copies of CDs and computer programs entering U.S. borders while ignoring those that are made or sold elsewhere. The Internet, however, changes these dynamics considerably. What happens if an individual in Paraguay uploads a copy of the CD to a server in Paraguay so that it is available worldwide for listening and downloading over the Internet? Perhaps this activity is lawful in Paraguay or the authorities do nothing to prevent it. Whatever its status in Paraguay, the copy on the server in Paraguay may be the source of infringements in the United States and elsewhere. For instance, if people in the United States listen to the CD over the Internet, this possibly could be likened to an illegal transmission of a protected work within the country. Or if copies are downloaded, one might argue that the copies have been imported or distributed into the United States via the Paraguay server in violation of U.S. law. The result is that an action that is allowed in Paraguay may at the same time have effects that are unlawful in the United States. Serious questions thereby might arise about whose public policies should control the activity.

Such problems with the Internet are not limited to copyright. On-line gambling, for instance, has been the source of much controversy.[23] Assume that certain forms of gambling are lawful in Belize. Also, assume somewhat simply that gambling is illegal in most states in the United States and that interstate gambling is unlawful. What if a gambling operator in Belize sets up shop on the Internet, allowing bets to be taken and payoffs made on-line? Does this operator violate U.S. law simply by offering an opportunity for U.S. citizens to gamble? The Belize operator likely will argue that it has done nothing wrong—that gambling is lawful in Belize and those that gamble over the Internet are no different than those who travel to Belize to gamble at a casino. However, U.S. authorities may see this in an altogether different light—that the casino is transmitting gambling information to the United States and collecting bets from those who reside there. Under these circumstances, should U.S. authorities be able to take legal actions against the Belize on-line casino?

Where Can the Lawsuit Be Brought?   Internet scenarios are extremely complex because they raise a set of difficult interrelated issues. For instance, in the gambling situation, what court (or courts) should be able to resolve the matter? Obviously, the Belize gambling operator would desire the case to be decided by courts in Belize, not only because they are more likely to be sympathetic, but also simply because of their proximity. Those in the United States, however, obviously would prefer that the case be heard in their country. And since those actually bringing the case in this example come from the United States, they surely will first ask a U.S. court to resolve the controversy.

The United States has a policy, firmly rooted in its Constitution, that allows defendants to be sued only in courts located where it is fair to make them come and defend.[24] The governing doctrine is whether the court chosen by the plaintiff (the one bringing the lawsuit) has what is called "personal jurisdiction" over the defendant. Within the United States, the question is about which state the court may be in. The answer comes down to two separate criteria. One, it would always be fair to sue the defendant in a state where the defendant resides or has substantial and continuous business operations. This is called *general jurisdiction*, since the defendant generally can be sued in the state no matter what claim is brought against it. The other basis of jurisdiction arises when an out-of-state defendant has sufficient contacts with the state so that under the specific circumstances of the plaintiff's case, it is fair to require the defendant to come into the state to defend the lawsuit. Accordingly, this is referred to as *specific jurisdiction*. Here is one way to consider the difference. If the defendant's actions over the Internet cause the plaintiff harm in the state, then these contacts might serve as the basis for specific jurisdiction. On the other hand, if the plaintiff's grievance is not related to the Internet activities, then a lawsuit still might be appropriate in the state, but, in this instance, only because the defendant conducts enough business in the state over the Internet to support general jurisdiction.

The case that follows, *Hasbro v. Clue Computing*, discusses the complex notion of specific jurisdiction in the context of the Internet. Note that this case does not have international dimensions, but rather evaluates a request by a Massachusetts company to have a Massachusetts court resolve a controversy, even though the defendant resides in Colorado. However, U.S. courts have used similar criteria for determining whether they can exercise personal jurisdiction over defendants from other countries.[25] Also, the issue in this case does not involve gambling, but rather trademarks. As you will learn in Chapter 7, trademark rights are not yet established on a worldwide basis, but rather in regions, such as within countries or states. Although the problem does not really arise in the *Hasbro* case, just imagine what would happen if a company with trademark rights to a name in New Zealand posted an advertisement over the Internet that could be viewed in the United States, where a different company had rights to the same name. Also, think about the many other international contexts in which the Internet will create controversies. One that already has arisen involves defamation, a topic we will consider in Chapter 8. Another involves pornography.[26] Consider what might happen if you were to post a picture on the Internet in the United States that is not morally objectionable there, but that can be viewed in another country where, unknown to you, such a picture is unlawful to display because it is considered lewd and lascivious. Could you face a lawsuit in that remote land for posting the photograph? *Hasbro, Inc. v. Clue Computing* provides insights into how jurisdictional issues regarding the Internet are evaluated by U.S. courts.

HASBRO, INC. V. CLUE COMPUTING, INC.
District Court for the District of Massachusetts, 1997

FACTS: Clue Computing is a computer consulting firm which has its sole office in Longmont, Colorado. Eric Robison is the owner and sole full-time employee of Clue Computing. Clue Computing has served fewer than a dozen clients in its existence, and between 1994 and 1996, had revenues of approximately $170,000. Many of its clients were located in Colorado, but for some Robison had to travel to other states, Canada and Antarctica to perform services. One of Clue Computing's clients was Digital Equipment Corporation, a Massachusetts company. However, Robison never traveled to Massachusetts.

Clue Computing registered the domain name "clue.com" with Network Solutions, Inc. ("NSI") for its Web site, which it uses to advertise its business. On its Web site, Clue Computing states, "Clue will go to any customer site" and notes that Digital is one of its clients. Internet users who view the Web site can e-mail the company by clicking on the page.

Hasbro, Inc., a Rhode Island company that has its largest facility in Beverly, Massachusetts, owns a federal trademark registration for the game, CLUE®. Hasbro notified NSI in 1996 of its trademark registration for CLUE® and requested that NSI freeze use of clue.com by Clue Computing. Due to certain complex litigation reasons, NSI could not comply. Hasbro then sued Clue Computing for trademark infringement in this Massachusetts court. Clue Computing asked the court to dismiss the case for lack of personal jurisdiction.

continued . . .

continued . . .

DECISION AND REASONING: Although traditional approaches dictated by the Supreme Court and our appellate court must be applied in evaluating personal jurisdiction, these concepts should be sensitive to the unique nature of cyberspace, a non-traditional medium through which the contacts between the defendant and the forum state can occur. Since information posted on a Web site becomes available world-wide almost instantaneously, imposing traditional concepts on commercial Internet users might have dramatic implications, subjecting them to nationwide or even international jurisdiction.

The popularity of the World Wide Web is providing courts the opportunity to examine their traditional reaches based on a corporation's computer-based contacts. To date, the case law in this area is limited. Indeed, with the global revolution looming on the horizon, the development of the law concerning the permissible scope of personal jurisdiction based on Internet use is in its infant stages. A review of the cases involving the World Wide Web and personal jurisdiction reveals that the courts that have addressed this issue are reaching conflicting results.

In cases where the courts have conferred jurisdiction, they seem to rely upon facts other than the Web site in making the determination. However, it also appears from the case law that the courts are in dispute as to what type of additional activity, other than the Web site, is necessary to avail a defendant of a forum's laws.

Some courts have relied upon contracts between the two parties. For instance, in *Digital Equipment Corp. v. Altavista*, the judge focused upon the fact that the defendant had a licensing agreement with the plaintiff, a Massachusetts corporation, and had made sales to at least three Massachusetts residents in her decision to exercise jurisdiction. The judge highlighted these additional non-Web contacts, emphasizing that there is no issue of parties being haled into courts of a given jurisdiction solely by virtue of a Web site, without meaningful notice that such an outcome was likely.

In *Zippo Mfg. Co. v. Zippo Dot Com, Inc.*, the defendant used a Web site to advertise and supply applications for its Internet news service. Although the court recognized that the defendant's contacts were almost exclusively over the Internet, it still found them sufficient to allow jurisdiction. The court noted that by entering into contracts with seven Internet access providers in Pennsylvania (the forum state), and selling passwords to 3,000 forum state residents, defendant made a conscious choice to conduct business in Pennsylvania, and thus purposefully availed itself of the forum's laws.

The existence of a contract touching the forum state has not been found necessary for the assertion of personal jurisdiction in other World Wide Web cases. Instead, courts rely upon different contacts. For example, in *Edias Software Int'l v. Basis Int'l Ltd.*, the defendant, in addition to creating an allegedly defamatory web page, regularly e-mailed, faxed and phoned the plaintiff. In cases such as this, the existence of a Web site is simply another piece of evidence demonstrating the defendant's purposeful availment of other states.

A few courts have held that the existence of a World Wide Web site alone is enough to allow for the exercise of personal jurisdiction. In *Panavision Int'l v. Toeppen*, when defendant intended to scam the plaintiff and knew the effects of the harm would be felt in the forum state (where the plaintiff was located), the court based jurisdiction on a Web site contact alone. The court stated that defendant's actions, anything but random, fortuitous or attenuated, justified personal jurisdiction. In *Inset Systems v. Instruction Set, Inc.*, the Connecticut court concluded that advertising via the Internet is solicitation of a sufficient repetitive nature to allow jurisdiction. The defendant, a nearby Massachusetts corporation, used its Web site and a toll-free number to solicit business from Connecticut, the forum state. In *Maritz v. Cybergold*, the court based jurisdiction on an interactive web site that electronically responded automatically and indiscriminately to users of the site regardless of their originating location. The court stated that the defendant, by creating a web site that provide information to and solicited business from individuals in other states, subjected itself to cases in other states.

Yet other cases have not accepted the proposition that the existence of a World Wide Web site automatically confers jurisdiction upon a state. In *Bensusan Restaurant Corp. v. King*, a New York plaintiff brought a trademark infringement case in New York against a Missouri jazz club. The defendant's Web site, advertising the night club, was found to be insufficient contact with the forum state to allow jurisdiction. The defendant, although using the Internet for advertising, only intended to reach a local audience. There was no evidence that the defendant received any business from New York. The court stated, "Creating a site, like placing a product into the stream of commerce, may be felt nationwide—or even worldwide—but, without more, it is not an act purposefully directed toward the forum state."

Most recently, in *Smith v. Hobby Lobby Stores*, an Arkansas court dismissed a case against a Hong Kong defendant who maintained a Web site. The court found that the defendant did not contract to sell any goods or services to any citizens of Arkansas over the Internet, and at most advertisements appeared on the Internet. However, such advertising was not directed to the state of Arkansas.

As the review of the Web site case law suggests, courts currently use traditional jurisdictional analysis models to analyze Web jurisdictional issues. Perhaps the traditional framework most analogous to posting information on the World Wide Web is placing a product into the "stream of commerce." The Supreme Court has indicated that placement of a product into the stream of commerce, without more, is not enough to satisfy the purposeful availment requirement of minimum contacts. Instead the Court focused on

continued . . .

continued . . .

deliberate availment, requiring additional conduct of the defendant which indicates an intent or purpose to serve the market in the forum state. Advertising in the forum state might be one such indication. However, in determining whether the defendant has purposefully availed itself of the benefits of the forum state, courts seem reluctant to base jurisdiction in trademark cases on advertising alone.

In order to establish personal jurisdiction over a non-resident defendant in a way consistent with Constitutional due process, the defendant must either have (1) continuous and systematic activity, unrelated to the suit, in the forum state or (2) certain minimum contacts with the forum state so that the exercise of jurisdiction does not offend traditional notions of fair play and substantial justice. The former confers general jurisdiction; the latter specific. The minimum contacts focus involves weighing the legal sufficiency of a specific set of interactions, and compels the court to examine three distinct components—relatedness, purposeful availment, and reasonableness.

1. *Relatedness:* The trademark infringement claims raised by Hasbro in this action relate directly from Clue Computing's contact with the state.

2. *Purposeful Availment:* The purposeful availment test articulated by members of the Supreme Court requires that the defendant's conduct with the forum state not be due to happenstance. This requirement goes beyond simple "foreseeability" to ensure that only those defendants that willingly and purposefully avail themselves of the benefits of a state will be brought to court there. In this case, Clue Computing purposefully directed its advertising to all the states. It did nothing to avoid Massachusetts. It knowingly worked for Digital. In fact, Clue Computing's work for Digital effectively comprised 33–50% of its 1995 annual income. Indeed, Clue Computing has availed itself of the benefits of doing business in Massachusetts by advertising its work for Digital on its Web site, in an effort to attract more customers. Consequently, Clue Computing not only has taken no measures to avoid contacts in Massachusetts, but rather has encouraged them. It does not appear that Clue Computing has done anything to avoid jurisdiction in terms of its non-Web (non-advertising) contacts with Massachusetts. Additionally, Clue Computing's Web site is interactive, encouraging and enabling anyone who wishes, including Massachusetts residents, to send e-mail to the company. The nature and quality of commercial activity that Clue Computing conducted over the Internet satisfies the "purposeful availment" due process test.

3. *Reasonableness:* In assessing reasonableness, the Supreme Court has directed focus on five gestalt factors: (1) the defendant's burden in appearing in the court; (2) the forum state's interest in hearing the suit; (3)

the plaintiff's convenience and interest in effective relief; (4) the judicial system's interest in obtaining the most effective resolution of the controversy; and (5) the common interests of all interested states in promoting substantive social policies.

a. The first factor relating to the defendant's burden in appearing clearly weighs in the defendant's favor in this case. Here, the defendant will be required to litigate this case in the Massachusetts court despite the fact that Robison, Clue Computing's sole full-time employee and only witness, resides in Colorado. However, the defendant in this case is able and willing to travel, as evidenced by Robison's self-proclaimed frequent and extensive business travel.

b. The second factor relates to the interests of Massachusetts. This factor weighs in favor of keeping the lawsuit in Massachusetts. Hasbro is located in Massachusetts and is an economic entity subject to Massachusetts law. It is the entity that suffers most from the alleged tortious use of the trademark rights in "clue.com." Massachusetts has an interest in preventing trademark infringement against those subject to the protections and requirements of its laws.

c. The third gestalt factor, which relates to the convenience of the venue to the plaintiff, plainly weighs in the plaintiff's favor. Hasbro's witnesses likely will come from its division in Beverly, Massachusetts.

d. The fourth factor relates to the judicial system's interest in the forum. Generally, this factor is considered "a wash." If this case is dismissed, it is unlikely that the parties will be able to resolve the dispute without judicial intervention in some forum. The most efficient path for the judicial system, then, is to move forward with the lawsuit in the present forum.

e. The last factor concerns substantive social policies. In this case, the substantive social policy at issue is the assertion of personal jurisdiction in trademark cases upon Internet activities and the resulting burden of forcing businesses with Web sites to litigate in foreign jurisdictions. While I share the concern of commentators in ensuring some limits to the reach of personal jurisdiction, I do not believe that this is a case that will open a floodgate. I have reservations about decisions such as *Inset* and *Maritz* which found that the existence of a Web site alone is enough to allow jurisdiction in any state. In any event, collection of additional circumstances found here justifies the exercise of jurisdiction in this case.

The gestalt factors taken together weigh in Hasbro's favor. I find the assertion of jurisdiction by this court is reasonable.

Cases such as *Hasbro, Inc. v. Clue Computing* have led many commentators to conclude that the more "interactive" a Web site is with individuals in a state, the more likely it is that the operators will be subject to jurisdiction within that state.[27] Jurisdiction usually is considered fair and reasonable if the Internet operator conducts business over the Internet with customers in a state, such as by selling products or entering contracts. On the other end of the spectrum are passive sites in which information is simply posted without any interchange between the operator and viewers. With these, jurisdiction is much less likely. In the middle are situations where the Internet operator exchanges information with individuals, either over the Net or through traditional channels. Here the level of interactivity and the commercial nature of the information exchange certainly will impact the court's final determination about jurisdiction.[28] In addition, the nature of the laws or rights that may have been violated will be relevant. Exhibit 1.4, on the following page, summarizes the major principles underlying Internet jurisdiction in the United States. Also, the *Matt Drudge* case in Chapter 8, which involves defamation over the Internet, demonstrates further how courts approach jurisdiction issues involving this medium.

None of this should be very comforting to an Internet operator. If a Web page can be viewed anywhere in the world, then one constantly must worry whether unexpected problems may arise in unlikely places. For instance, the Georgia Institute of Technology temporarily ran into some problems in France when its sister institution in France, Georgia Tech Loraine, described its curriculum and invited applications over the Internet using the English language.[29] The issue arose because France has a law that requires the French language to be used in all advertisements in France. Although this law likely does not apply to sites outside of France, it does nonetheless illustrate the kinds of unknown problems that may be lurking for Internet operators.

Of course, throughout this whole discussion of jurisdiction, we have been considering how U.S. courts handle the issue. Thus, if the issue is whether a foreign Internet operator might be hauled into court in the United States, the principles evaluated in *Hasbro* will be determinative. However, courts in other nations may use other principles to judge whether U.S. companies with Internet sites might be subject to suits there. Thus, Internet operators indeed need to be vigilant.

What Law Applies?   Actually, there are even more issues that must be evaluated when determining if U.S. law might apply to foreign activities. So far, we have been discussing where the suit might be brought, but have not focused on which law the court actually might apply to the controversy. For instance, if a U.S. Internet site operator is hauled into a British court based on statements that allegedly defame a U.K. citizen, this does not necessarily mean that the British court will decide that British law should govern the activity. Normally, the court will use complicated "conflict of laws" principles to make this determination.[30] However, as a general rule, if the court sits in a country or region that has laws designed to protect individuals from exactly the harm that the Internet operator allegedly has caused, then the court will apply those laws. Thus, in all the contexts mentioned so far, such as copyright, defamation, gambling, pornography, and trademarks, one should expect that when the plaintiff's local court extends personal jurisdiction over the defendant, it also will apply local laws to the situation.

Exhibit 1.4
Application of U.S. Court Jurisdiction Policies to the Internet

---

BASES FOR COURT JURISDICTION

- General Jurisdiction
  - Defendant has engaged in continuous and systematic business activity within the state.
    - The activity may be unrelated to the subject of the lawsuit.

- Specific Jurisdiction
  - The defendant has sufficient minimum contacts with the state that it is fair to compel a defense within the state.
    - Factors that courts weigh to determine if the contacts are sufficient:
      - The relatedness of the contacts to the claim of the lawsuit
      - The degree that the defendant purposefully directed business within the state
      - The reasonableness of the jurisdiction, based on such issues as the defendant's burden, the plaintiff's convenience, and the state's interest in the suit

APPLICATION TO THE INTERNET

- Business acivity conducted over the Internet within the state
  - Court usually will exercise jurisdiction
- Information exchanged within the state
  - The more *interactive* the Internet site, the more likely the court will exercise jurisdiction
- Passive Web sites to which information is merely posted
  - Court is not likely to exercise jurisdiction

Possibly the greatest exception to this general rule arises in contract disputes, particularly when commercial parties are involved. We will discuss elements of contracts in Chapter 9. But for now, it is enough to recognize that most nations will honor the terms of agreements knowingly made between individuals or companies. If disputes arise between those involved in contractual agreements, then the court usually will look to the contract to determine how the issue should be resolved. Given this, companies involved in Internet commerce now try to control as many variables as possible with on-line contracts. Thus, a U.S. Web site operator might have a customer agree that any dispute arising out of the contract will be decided in a U.S. court. Also, it might establish through mutual agreement that any dispute regarding the terms of the contract should be decided according to U.S. law. As we shall see, the trend in U.S. and European law, as in many other regions, is to support such agreements, at least when they are between sophisticated business parties.[31] However, when ordinary consumers are involved, such agreements usually are more heavily scrutinized, and courts are more likely to exercise jurisdiction and apply local laws to protect citizens when the local laws specifically exist to protect consumers from the harm they allegedly suffered.

Can a Judgment Be Enforced?   Based on personal jurisdiction and conflict of laws principles, Internet operators in Paraguay who upload Bruce Springsteen CDs to their Internet sites without permission may be subject to suits in the United States for violation of U.S. copyright laws if U.S. citizens listen to or download the music. You may think this is a slam dunk, since the Paraguay-based operators very likely will not even travel to the United States to defend the lawsuit. Thus, the court will automatically enter a judgment against them. But, what good is that judgment? The last, and often most critical, question is whether a judgment can be enforced.

If the Paraguayan Web site operators have assets in the United States, then the U.S. court may order that these be used to satisfy the judgment. But, assuming that we are not talking about some large multinational company, which of course we are not, then this is not very likely. Thus, enforcement of the U.S. judgment will be effective only if it is carried out in Paraguay. Within the United States, this is not a problem, since the courts of each state must give what is called "full faith and credit" to the judgments of courts in other states. Therefore, if Hasbro were to win its case against Clue Computing in Massachusetts, then a court in Colorado would enforce the judgment against Clue Computing in Colorado if it failed to comply.[32] However, in the international realm, one may not so readily assume that the judgments in one country will be enforced in other countries.[33] Some countries work under treaties, as do many nations of Europe, providing a mutual framework for enforcing judgments. Many others will enforce a foreign judgment based on a variety of criteria, such as whether the foreign judgment violates a domestic public policy or was rendered in ways violating local notions of due process. Still others will not enforce a foreign judgment unless there is a specific treaty with the foreign country articulating the terms of mutual enforcement obligations. From all this, the only certain conclusion is that when one is forced to go overseas to enforce local judgments, life becomes much more difficult and unpredictable.

Due to the problems of enforcement, it is easy to see why those who are injured over the Internet prefer to sue large multinational companies rather than individual perpetrators. First of all, individuals may not have the money to pay for all the harm they cause, such as when they engage in defamation or post copyrighted materials for worldwide copying. Second, the individuals may be operating in hospitable environments where enforcement against them is virtually impossible. For these reasons, those harmed by Internet activities often attempt to pin responsibility on the Internet service providers, especially those that have assets and operations in their home countries. For instance, Bruce Springsteen might allege that America Online (AOL) or some other relevant service provider is responsible for transmitting the offending materials into the United States, and thus ask a court to enter and enforce a judgment against it. If the suit is successful, not only will AOL be forced to pay, since it certainly has assets in the United States, but it will be motivated to police its files to ensure that other materials do not violate copyrights.

This, in turn, will help Bruce Springsteen and other copyright holders to deter transmissions to the United States in the future. Whether Internet service providers should be responsible for the unlawful activities of their users is an extremely hot and controversial topic that we will explore more fully in Chapters 6 and 8.

Bilateral Arrangements

As U.S. companies have become increasingly dependent on foreign sales and operations, unilateral measures have diminished in their importance and effectiveness. Strong intellectual property laws within the United States no longer are sufficient to satisfy U.S. firms. The potential returns from global markets are simply too great to be ignored. In addition, digital technologies now often make it extremely easy for small foreign operators to easily and cheaply copy the creative works of U.S. nationals and to distribute them in vast quantities across the globe. Such widespread duplication vastly increases the burden on U.S. firms to police infringements even within the U.S. through application of the unilateral measures. Therefore, U.S. firms are committed to global strategies leading other nations to raise the levels of intellectual property protection within their borders. Bilateral and multilateral agreements are designed to achieve these objectives.

Bilateral agreements are promises between two nations to conduct their policy affairs in certain ways. For instance, assume that CD "pirates" in Indonesia are having a significant worldwide negative effect on powerful U.S. music production companies. These companies may appeal to the appropriate U.S. government authorities to negotiate an agreement with the government of Indonesia wherein Indonesia pledges to improve its protection of intellectual property. In order to induce Indonesia to enter such an agreement, the U.S. government likely will have to offer something in return. This may be in the form of a carrot, with the United States agreeing to change certain U.S. practices, resulting in certain benefits to the citizens of Indonesia. Or, as we shall see with Section 301 of the Trade Act, the United States may rely on the stick to coerce an agreement, such as by promising not to carry out trade retaliation threats if Indonesia agrees to U.S. conditions.

Semiconductor Chip Protection Act

Typically, bilateral arrangements are negotiated on a country-by-country basis. However, the Semiconductor Chip Protection Act provides an interesting variant to the standard formula.[34] Over the last couple of decades, the semiconductor industry has become increasingly important to the U.S. economy. Beginning in the late 1970s, U.S. policy makers began to consider ways to ensure that U.S. business investments in semiconductors were sufficiently protected by the intellectual property laws. This was considered necessary because the existing laws were not well suited to this new form of technology. Patents were not viewed as good vehicles for protection, since semiconductor development relies more on hard work than creative invention. Copyright protection also was problematic due to the utilitarian nature of the chip designs. And trade secret laws were ineffective, since one who studies a semiconductor can copy it at a fraction of the original development costs. Therefore, in 1984, the U.S. government passed the Semiconductor Chip Protection Act, which provided a new system of intellectual property protection specially tailored to semiconductors. The U.S. government, however, was not solely concerned with semiconductor protection within the United States. It also wanted foreign nations to take similar actions to protect semiconductors within their borders. Therefore, to motivate foreign counties to adopt these measures, the Semiconductor Chip Protection Act made a special offer. Although this is a simplification, the Chip Act essentially provided protection at first only to chip designs owned by U.S. nationals. Chip designs owned by citizens of other countries did not initially enjoy the benefits of protection within the United States under the act. However, if a foreign country were to adopt laws that provided sufficiently strong semiconductor protection within its borders that applied to designs made by U.S. citizens, then the United States would extend the protection of its semiconductor laws to the citizens of that foreign country. Protection for their citizens within the United States, therefore, was the carrot offered by the United States to those countries willing to agree to protect the semiconductor investments of U.S. nationals. Through this avenue, by 1991, 19 countries had adopted legislation protecting semiconductor chip designs.[35]

Section 301 and Trade Sanctions

More often than not, the United States obtains results in another country through use of the stick, by threatening to impose trade sanctions if that foreign nation does not take steps to improve intellectual property protection for creations of U.S. businesses. Beginning in the 1980s, the importance of intellectual property to the U.S. economy began to skyrocket. As we shall see in the next section on multilateral agreements, there were few, if any, existing agreements upon which the United States could rely to induce foreign governments to suitably protect U.S. intellectual property interests. Most international intellectual property agreements required little in terms of substantive levels of protection and were toothless when it came to enforcement. The General Agreement on Tariffs and Trade (GATT) did not then specifically address the protection of intellectual property, and any alleged harm otherwise related to its missions usually failed to prompt action because GATT's enforcement mechanisms at that time were ineffective. The United States therefore decided to take matters into its own hands with the use of Section 301 of the Trade Act, which was first passed in 1974 but given more prominence with amendments in 1988.

Section 301 authorizes the Office of the United States Trade Representative (USTR), an administrative agency, to take steps to enforce U.S. rights under bilateral and multilateral trade agreements and to respond to unreasonable, unjustifiable, or discriminatory foreign government practices that burden U.S. commerce. Such practices include, among others, providing subsidies to domestic firms, denying market access to U.S. businesses, and failing to adequately protect the intellectual property of U.S. enterprises. In very general terms, Section 301 empowers the USTR to investigate countries suspected of violating trade agreements or engaging in harmful practices, and to attempt resolution of any disputed matters in consultation with the foreign governments. When an international agreement, such as GATT, is involved and consultations fail to satisfy the agency, the USTR must submit the complaint for review according to the dispute resolution procedures provided by the accord. If the controversy is not resolved, either through the mechanisms of the international trade agreement or otherwise through consultation and negotiation, then the USTR is authorized to take retaliatory actions, such as suspending trade agreement concessions or imposing import tariffs or other import restrictions.

Special 301 and Intellectual Property Protection   In 1988, Section 301 was enhanced by what are called the Super and Special 301 provisions of the Omnibus Trade and Competitiveness Act. Super 301 is aimed at those countries that impede U.S. export potential. However, of most interest here is Special 301, which is more particularly concerned with foreign nations that threaten U.S. intellectual property rights. Both of these sections were passed to speed up the time periods of investigations and to limit the discretion of the USTR and the president to begin investigations and take action.[36] In addition, substantial control over implementation of the act was transferred from the president to the USTR. As you might surmise, Congress was motivated to pass these amendments to highlight its resolve in improving international trade matters. Due to the amendments, foreign countries could expect that U.S. trade retaliation for improper behavior would be swift and with little compassion.

Under Special 301, the USTR annually reviews whether the acts, policies, and practices of foreign countries deny adequate and effective protection of intellectual property rights or fair and equitable market access for U.S. citizens who rely on intellectual property protection.[37] By the end of April of each year, the USTR establishes three lists of countries, based on relative levels of concern about their intellectual property protection. The "watch list" consists of those countries to which the USTR wishes to signal that improvement is desired. No immediate tariff action by the United States is contemplated, but that could change in the future if progress toward improvement is not made. In 1999, the USTR placed 37 countries on the watch list. The middle tier is the "priority watch list." It indicates those countries where the need for change is more immediate because their practices are having an especially significant impact on U.S. intellectual property interests. A country on this list is put on notice that its intellectual property laws and practices will be closely monitored for improvement. In 1999, the following 16 countries were placed on the priority watch list: Argentina, Dominican Republic, Egypt, European Union, Greece, Guatemala, India, Indonesia, Israel, Italy, Kuwait, Macao, Peru, Russia, Turkey, and Ukraine. Notably absent from this list was Bulgaria, given that the USTR highlighted it as the most troubling nation on the priority watch list in 1998 based on high levels of CD piracy within its borders. The stern warning motivated Bulgaria to clamp down forcefully and immediately on the production of pirated CDs. In fact, Bulgaria was so successful that the USTR removed it from all the Section 301 lists in 1999.

The third Special 301 level is called the "priority foreign country list." A country is placed on this list when its intellectual property practices have the most egregious effects on U.S. trade, and it has failed to engage in good-faith negotiations with the United States to address the problems. Under the provisions of Special 301, the USTR has 30 days to decide whether to initiate an investigation of a priority foreign country. Assuming the investigation begins, the USTR then is under strict time lines, which may be as fast as six months in some cases, to substantiate its concerns and to impose retaliatory trade sanctions if improvements are not made. In 1999, the USTR did not designate any countries for the priority foreign country list. In 1998, though, the USTR had placed Paraguay on the list due to alarming levels of piracy and counterfeiting as well as inadequate patent, copyright and trademark laws. Although the U.S. government had repeatedly urged the government of Paraguay to take effective actions to crack down on piracy and counterfeiting, the United States believed that Paraguay's efforts had been minimal and clearly insufficient. By putting Paraguay on the priority foreign country list, the USTR demonstrated that the United States was running out of patience. As a result, Paraguay signed a comprehensive agreement with the United States in November 1998, pledging to raise intellectual property standards and to undertake effective enforcement actions. Because of this agreement, Paraguay was taken off the Section 301 lists in 1999 with the understanding that it would be closely monitored for compliance with its promises to combat piracy.

Section 301 can be credited with numerous successes in raising the levels of intellectual property protection across the globe. For instance, in the early 1990s, Taiwan was a focal point of U.S. attention due to widespread piracy of computer software, video and audio recordings, and semiconductor innovations. In 1992, it was designated a priority foreign country, but avoided sanctions in that year by entering a bilateral agreement with the United States promising to adopt new patent and trademark laws and implementing new enforcement procedures for unauthorized exports.[38] Since that time, Taiwan has made substantial progress in improving its intellectual property laws and upgrading enforcement. This does not mean that problems did not continue to persist, especially with pirated and counterfeit CDs, CD-ROMs, and video games. It explains why Taiwan was still listed on the priority watch list in 1998. Nonetheless, the USTR was impressed with Taiwan's dedication in adopting new policies to raise its level of intellectual property protection.

Thailand and Brazil represent two of the many other countries where the recognition of intellectual property rights has been heightened by the application of Section 301. In the 1980s Brazil was hit with trade sanctions on several occasions due primarily to its failure to provide patent protection for pharmaceuticals. For instance, in 1989, 100% surcharges were imposed on pulp and paper exports from Brazil to the United States.[39] Although it made promises that led the United States to quickly lift the sanctions, in 1993 Brazil was again listed as a priority foreign country, indicating that much work still needed to be done, especially regarding patents. By 1996, Brazil had enacted modern patent laws, thereby encouraging the USTR to move it down to the watch list, where the focus shifted to copyright laws. And by 1998, improvements were such that Brazil was no longer even on the watch list. Likewise, Thailand appeared as a priority foreign country in 1991–1993 and was repeatedly threatened with import duties on shoes, garments, and jewelry,

mostly because of widespread copyright piracy in that country of computer programs, videos, and audio recordings. Although these sanctions were averted by
what some observers claim were symbolic piracy crackdowns in 1991 and 1992, in
1993 real progress began.[40] By 1996, U.S. concerns regarding Thailand were reduced to the point that it was placed on the watch list, where it remained at least
through 1999. Thailand passed numerous new intellectual property laws, particularly regarding copyrights, and strengthened its enforcement systems. However, objections remained regarding the consistency of enforcement and the imposition of
sufficient penalties for infringements.

A notable and highly publicized application of Special 301 occurred in 1995 and
1996 when China was designated a priority foreign country and threatened each
year with trade sanctions. In the early 1990s, through at least 1995, China was the
world's leading exporter of pirated optical media products, such as CDs, video
discs, and software CD-ROMs containing software and video games. The country
during this period also was home to a multitude of other intellectual property
problems, such as trademark counterfeiting. In 1994, the USTR designated China a
priority foreign country and, after an investigation, threatened to impose 100%
tariffs on $1.08 billion of imported Chinese products, including cellular telephones,
sporting goods, and plastics.[41] China threatened to retaliate against U.S. exports of
CDs, video games, films, cigarettes, and alcohol. On the day before the U.S. sanctions were to go into effect, China and the United States entered a bilateral agreement under which China promised to (1) implement a detailed enforcement plan,
including an antipiracy task force and increased raids on piracy centers, (2) undertake inspections of suspicious factories, (3) impose more meaningful penalties for
pirating activities, and (4) open greater access to Chinese markets for U.S. movies,
music, and computer software.[42] Nevertheless, China did not tackle these problems
as swiftly and definitively as promised, and the United States therefore threatened
sanctions again in 1996, this time on imports totaling over $2 billion.[43] As in the
previous year, a trade war loomed, and the implementation of U.S. sanctions was
averted only at the last minute. In this round, the United States was pacified by recent Chinese raids on major pirating factories, and by China's renewed promises of
greater enforcement.[44]

Between 1996 and 1998, China shut down 64 CD production lines and largely
reduced exports of pirated intellectual property products. In addition, according to
Chinese government data, over 800 individuals were imprisoned for engaging in illegal pirating activities. Also, Chinese factories began to enter legitimate licensing
arrangements with U.S. copyright owners to obtain rights to produce film and music products in China. During this period, numerous new intellectual property laws
were passed in China, and the courts showed signs that they might order Chinese
violators to compensate foreign victims under them.[45] This is not to say that China
was no longer a problem by 1999. It clearly was, especially regarding the piracy of
business software, the protection of pharmaceuticals, and trademark counterfeiting. However, Section 301 still clearly was responsible for substantial improvements in China's intellectual property protection regime in the 1990s.

Even though Special 301 has proven to be a powerful tool, its role is likely to rapidly diminish. In 1995, many of the world's countries agreed to greatly enhance intellectual property protection and to enforce the agreements using the procedures of the newly formed World Trade Organization. This will be discussed further in the next section. In theory, the United States and developed countries favor multilateral agreements, such as those that formed the World Trade Organization. One problem with bilateral arrangements involves continuity. A concession granted to one country may be demanded by others. Also, bilateral successes may allow other developed countries to enjoy the benefits without paying for the concessions. Finally, the limited scope and hodgepodge nature of bilateral agreements does not promote worldwide trade as well as more far-reaching multilateral approaches.

Multilateral Approaches

Multilateral approaches reach beyond bilateral agreements in that many countries together agree to conform to a policy framework. Currently there are several important multilateral agreements pertaining separately to patents, copyrights, and trademarks. In addition, extensive multilateral negotiations on a comprehensive scale have recently been completed within the General Agreement on Tariffs and Trade (GATT). Exhibit 1.5 provides a list of the most important multilateral agreements affecting the protection of intellectual property. These agreements will be touched on here to establish context for the more detailed considerations this book undertakes in later chapters.

Global Intellectual Property Agreements

Patent Agreements   In the patent arena, the most important multilateral accords are the Convention of the Union of Paris for the Protection of Industrial Property (Paris Convention), the Patent Cooperation Treaty, and the European Patent Convention. The members of the Paris Convention, totaling around 80 nations, have agreed that inventors from foreign signatory countries should be accorded the same rights under a member's patent laws as those enjoyed by citizens of that member. Thus, because the United States and Canada both are members of the Paris Convention, a Canadian inventor receives the same protection under U.S. patent laws as does a U.S. citizen. Likewise, a U.S. citizen enjoys the same rights in Canada as does a Canadian native. Such reciprocity, called *national treatment*, is common to many of the major multilateral intellectual property treaties. Note that national treatment provided by the Paris Convention does not specify any common standards for patentability. Therefore, the patent laws of each member can and do vary widely. For example, when there are two or more creators of the same invention, laws differ on who is entitled to the patent, some granting it to the first to make the invention and others issuing it to the first to file for protection. Also, there are substantial differences in the extent to which certain kinds of inventions, such as biotechnology and computers, can receive patents.

The Patent Cooperation Treaty, which had been signed by 100 countries in 1998, provides for certain procedural advantages in filing patent applications

Exhibit 1.5

Major Multilateral Agreements Governing Intellectual Property

FIELD	AGREEMENTS
Patents	Paris Convention Patent Cooperation Treaty European Patent Convention
Copyrights	Berne Convention Universal Copyright Convention
Trademarks	Paris Convention Madrid Agreement Madrid Protocol
Comprehensive	World Trade Organization (WTO) • General Agreement on Tariffs and Trade (GATT) • Trade-Related Aspects of Intellectual Property Rights (TRIPs) Treaty of Rome and Maastricht Treaty (European Union) North American Free Trade Agreement (NAFTA)

within member nations. Similarly, the more regional European Patent Convention simplifies the task of filing for patents within 19 European nations. However, the European Patent Convention is more ambitious than the Patent Cooperation Treaty because it also requires the participating nations to accept certain substantive principles of patent protection. Indeed, the European Patent Convention has established something very close to a European-wide patent. It therefore serves as a model for future multilateral patent accords.

Since the mid-1980s, the World International Property Organization (WIPO), an agency with over 170 members that is affiliated with the United Nations, has attempted to develop a treaty to harmonize substantive patent policies on a more global scale (Patent Law Treaty). In the early 1990s, negotiators within WIPO made substantial progress in ironing out some of the key differences that existed between the patent laws of various countries. Indeed, the final drafts would have required the United States to change a fundamental principle of its patent system, which awards patents to the first person to conceive an invention. This will be discussed further in Chapter 2. However, the momentum for completing that round of negotiations stalled in 1993, when the United States requested the postponement of a diplomatic conference that was scheduled to finalize the treaty. The United States made this request after the American Bar Association surprisingly voted to oppose the major change to U.S. law.[46] Since that time, efforts within WIPO have resumed, but they have focused on harmonizing more procedural matters such as formalities required in patent applications. Still, there are reasons to be optimistic that a more substantive treaty might someday be completed and signed by a large portion of the international community, including the United States. In fact, the likelihood should only improve as the international community continues to reduce disparities in patent policies via other multilateral accords.[47]

Copyright Agreements   International copyright policy is dominated by two multilateral arrangements: the Universal Copyright Convention and the Berne Convention. Until 1988, these two separate multilateral accords might have been considered of equal importance in terms of world international trade. The Universal Copyright Convention could boast the United States as a signatory country; the Berne Convention was older and had the broader membership. However, on October 31, 1988, the Berne Convention established itself as the dominant multilateral agreement when the United States became its 79th participant.

The fundamental principle of both copyright conventions is the same: Foreigners from signatory countries must be granted national treatment under the copyright laws of any other member country. This is the same philosophy guiding the Paris Convention. The two conventions part ways, however, in that each also requires adherence to a small but differing set of substantive standards. Under the Universal Copyright Convention, participants must comply with certain formalities for protection such as a copyright notice and possibly registration. An important tenet of the Berne Convention, on the other hand, is that "the enjoyment and the exercise of (copyright) shall not be subject to any formality." Historically, notice and registration requirements were such a fundamental component of the U.S. copyright system that the United States shunned the Berne Convention. Indeed, its reluctance to alter its system of copyright protection caused the United States to lead the effort within the United Nations to create the alternative Universal Copyright Convention. In addition, the Berne Convention establishes that authors must have protection for "moral rights" under the laws of the member countries. Such a Hegelian concept of intellectual property protection does not conform well to the more Lockean philosophy underlying U.S. law. This too made Berne somewhat hard for the United States to swallow.

That the United States was so stubbornly unwilling to join the dominant international copyright code raised the hackles of a number of important trading partners. Many nations criticized the United States for not being fully committed to the international protection of copyrights. At the same time, the United States was calling for greater standards for the international protection of intellectual property. The position of the United States on copyrights, however, was seen as a double standard, greatly weakening its international bargaining position. By joining the Berne Convention in 1988, the United States climbed to philosophically higher ground. Its willingness to compromise on copyrights should strengthen its leadership in establishing better international protections across a broad range of intellectual property issues.

Trademark Agreements   International trademark policy is governed primarily by three multilateral agreements. The Paris Convention has provisions that extend the principle of national treatment to trademarks. It also specifies a few substantive minimum requirements for trademark protection and requires signatory countries to provide effective protection against unfair competition. Another important trademark agreement is the Madrid Agreement Concerning the International Registration of Trademarks (Madrid Agreement), joined by 50 nations in 1998 but not the United States. The Madrid Agreement is similar to the Patent Cooperation Treaty in that it provides certain procedural and administrative advantages for protection within member countries. The third major multilateral trademark accord is the Madrid Protocol. The Madrid Protocol is a direct descendent of the Madrid Agreement but is expected to have wider appeal because it deals with certain objections that some nations, such as the United States, have had with the Madrid Agreement. As with the major patent and copyright conventions, these three international trademark arrangements have relatively little to say about the substantive content and enforcement of each member's trademark laws. One important effort to harmonize trademark policies and procedures in a more regional, multilateral context has been developing within the European Union. In December 1993, for instance, the European Union established the Office of Harmonization of the Internal Market in Alicante, Spain to administer a new Community Trademark registration system.

World Trade Organization

For nations such as the United States that are committed to stronger intellectual property protections around the globe, the aforementioned set of multilateral approaches suffers from two glaring defects. First, the promise of national treatment does not require anything in terms of the level of protection within a country. All that is required is that foreigners be treated the same as nationals. If a developing country chooses not to protect the intellectual assets of its citizens, then it can allow substantial copying of foreign products as well. Second, even when the parties to these various agreements pledge to have some protection, as they do with the Berne Convention, there generally is no meaningful multilateral mechanism to ensure that they actually abide by their promises. This means that complying members have to fall back on bilateral methods, such as the threat of Special 301 sanctions, to ensure that other nations meaningfully undertake to fulfill their obligations. For this reason, the United States and other developed countries aggressively pursued the adoption of minimum substantive standards for intellectual property protection within a multilateral body that also had an enforcement structure and procedures capable of forcing members to comply with their promises.[48] The vehicle selected to undertake this important task was the World Trade Organization (WTO).

The WTO governs the operation and implementation of the General Agreement on Tariffs and Trade and other associated multilateral agreements.[49] The GATT was first negotiated in 1947 by 23 nations to establish a new international trading order and to eliminate protectionism. The focus of the GATT at that time primarily was mutual tariff reduction, but the contracting parties also established other fundamental principles of international trade which have only increased in prominence over time. The most important of these guiding principles are:

Elimination of Quotas and Other Nontariff Barriers

The goal of the GATT is to convert quotas and other barriers to tariffs, through a process called tariffication, and then to mutually agree to tariff reductions. Obviously, this goal has never been fully attained, since nontariff barriers continue to exist to protect important domestic industries, especially those related to agriculture, fishing, and clothing. In addition, the GATT expressly provides that countries may use quotas to safeguard their balance of payments.

Multilateral Trade Negotiations

The parties to the GATT have agreed to meet periodically to further eliminate protectionism and liberalize trade. Since the inception of the GATT in 1947, the contracting parties have completed eight major rounds of multilateral trade negotiations, each aimed at reducing tariffs and trade barriers in various sectors of the international economy. The final effort, called the Uruguay Round, was completed in 1994 and resulted in a substantial set of new agreements including the creation of the World Trade Organization to administer them.

Nondiscrimination

a. Most-Favored-Nation Trade (MFN)

Nondiscrimination is furthered primarily by the application of what is called unconditional MFN trade. Unconditional MFN means that when a GATT party extends some privilege to another GATT member (such as a lower tariff rate), then that privilege is automatically extended to all other GATT participants. There are several exceptions contemplated within the GATT, allowing some members to receive better treatment than others because, for instance, they are members of free-trade areas or common markets to which the others do not belong.

b. National Treatment

As discussed earlier, national treatment means that a GATT member will treat the products of other GATT members in the same way it treats those of domestic companies. In other words, it will not discriminate against foreign goods relative to domestic goods.

Dispute Settlement

The members of GATT are to rely on GATT dispute resolution procedures to settle differences (covered by GATT agreements) rather than employ unilateral measures, such as those contemplated by Section 301. Until recently, dispute resolution was the weakest link of the GATT process. At first, GATT did little more than facilitate negotiations between complaining parties. Later, panels were often used to make decisions about improper conduct, but there were questions about impartiality and there was no system of appellate review. Also, delays were interminable and any member ultimately could block the adoption of a panel's recommendation. In addition, the GATT really had no power to compel a country to comply if that country was unwilling. Thus, by the 1960s, members lost faith in the ability of the GATT dispute resolution process to make timely decisions that would be fair and effective.[50] This is one reason that the United States was motivated to pass Section 301 in 1974. Negotiators in the Uruguay Round addressed many of the concerns regarding dispute resolution by adopting major new dispute resolution procedures within the authority of the WTO.

As just noted, the most recent set of multilateral negotiations regarding GATT, called the Uruguay Round, resulted in the most comprehensive set of changes to the accord since its beginnings in 1947. The Uruguay Round took almost eight years to complete, and its successful resolution can be viewed as somewhat of a miracle. For one thing, by 1994, the number of countries that were involved in GATT had mushroomed from the initial set of 23 participants to around 125, and these represented the entire spectrum of global economic development. In addition, each successive set of GATT talks has tackled increasingly complex and divisive issues, a trend that continued with the Uruguay Round, where the primary focus was on nontariff barriers and substantive codes of conduct rather than tariff reduction. Indeed, the United States was committed to forging new agreements regarding agriculture, services, and, of most interest here, the treatment of intellectual property. Also, the United States placed a substantial stake in addressing deficiencies in the GATT dispute resolution process. In the end, the Uruguay round resulted in the adoption of 17 separate agreements. Among these were (1) an updated version of the original GATT agreement that extended the basic philosophies of that accord, (2) new procedures regarding dispute resolution, (3) the creation of the World Trade Organization to serve as the administrative structure, and (4) specific resolutions regarding a host of separate issues, including intellectual property, services, agriculture, textiles, dumping, and import licensing.

The TRIPs Agreement   The agreement regarding intellectual property formally is called the Agreement on Trade-Related Aspects of Intellectual Property Rights, and is known by the acronym TRIPs. The negotiations that ultimately resulted in TRIPs were extremely heated. Developed countries such as the United States considered the adoption of minimum substantive standards of protection and enforcement to be essential to their economies, which increasingly depended on information technologies. However, certain less developed members of GATT, such as India, Brazil, and Argentina, vigorously opposed the adoption of minimum standards. As previously discussed, these countries had philosophical and economic objections to intellectual property reforms within their boundaries. The various members also disagreed on the specific details about the minimum standards that eventually might be adopted. New technologies based on computers and genetic engineering raised a host of vexing issues that divided the members. In addition, several important procedural aspects of protection, especially in the patent realm, proved to be very contentious. Nonetheless, the parties ultimately reconciled their differences, often by making extensive compromises on their initial positions, and adopted a document that is quite impressive in its scope and depth.

Summarized below are many of the more important issues addressed by TRIPs. Since many of these required far-reaching changes to the laws and enforcement procedures of the less developed countries, these countries were given more time to bring their practices up to compliance. Thus, although developed countries had to comply with all the requirements of TRIPs by January 1, 1996, developing countries were given until January 1, 2000, and the least developed members have until January 1, 2005. In addition, developing countries, such as India, were given additional time, specifically until January 1, 2005, to extend patent protection to technologies that were not protected within their borders prior to the year 2000. Although this delay was opposed by the U.S. pharmaceutical industry in particular, it at least gave the industry a defined date when protection is supposed to begin.

In addition, keep in mind that although the membership of the WTO comprises more than 80 percent of world trade, there still remain nations that are not members. For a nation to join, it first must enter acceptable bilateral market access agreements with WTO members. Its application moves next to an accession working party, which formulates the precise terms and conditions for entry into the WTO, and then goes to the General Council for approval.[51] To gain the votes of developed countries, such as the United States, applicants have to show a commitment to intellectual property protection, while making a host of other concessions. In 1999, China signed a bilateral market access agreement with the United States after 13 years of negotiations.[52] Since most observers believed that the United States was the biggest roadblock preventing China's entry into the WTO, this agreement raised expectations that China soon would become a WTO member. Assuming China is admitted, only a handful of important countries, such as Russia, would remain outside the WTO.

WTO Dispute Resolution   As already mentioned, the United States was sorely disenchanted with GATT dispute resolution and enforcement mechanisms prior to the Uruguay Round. Its objections were widespread, and included concerns about due process, unwarranted delays, inexperienced decision makers, and extensive veto powers. The WTO dispute resolution procedures that emerged from the Uruguay Round substantially addressed all of these concerns. The major steps are summarized in Exhibit 1.6 on page 48.

The primary body in charge of dispute resolution within the WTO is the Dispute Settlement Body, or DSB, which is composed of one person from each country that is a member of the WTO. If one member, let's say the United States, feels that its citizens are being harmed because another country, for example India, are not

Major Provisions of TRIPs

1. GENERAL COMPLIANCE DATES
   a. Developed Nations: January 1, 1996
   b. Developing Nations: January 1, 2000
   c. Least Developed Nations: January 1, 2005

2. ADMINISTRATION
   a. The Council on Trade-Related Aspects of Intellectual Property Rights was created to conduct administrative tasks, such as publicizing the laws adopted in member states and monitoring the operation of the TRIPs agreement.

3. PATENT ISSUES
   a. Members are required to comply with the Paris Convention.
   b. Term of patents: Patent protection must last until at least 20 years after the filing date of the patent application. This necessitated a change to U.S. patent law, which previously had provided patent protection for a term of 17 years after the patent was granted.
   c. Subject matter of patents: With certain exceptions, patents must be available for all products and processes, in all fields of technology, subject to the normal tests of novelty, inventiveness, and industrial applicability.
   d. Exceptions. The following may be refused patent protection:
      1) Inventions contrary to "ordre public" or morality. These include inventions that may be dangerous to the lives or health of humans, animals, or plants, or that may seriously harm the environment.
      2) Therapeutic and surgical methods for the treatment of humans or animals.
      3) Plants. However, if denied patent protection, plants must be protected by an effective alternative system of protection.
      4) Animals other than microorganisms. This exclusion was a blow to the genetic engineering industry.
      5) Developing nations may delay extending patent protection to areas of technology, such as pharmaceuticals or agricultural chemicals, that were not protected within their borders before the year 2000. The delay lasts until January 1, 2005. However, these countries must implement procedures under what is called the "mailbox provision" to allow applications to be filed by current inventors so that they can establish priority for patent protection when it finally is allowed.
   e. Nations may still require owners of patented technologies to license them to local businesses (compulsory licensing). However, opportunities for compulsory licensing are circumscribed to make them more acceptable to U.S. interests. For instance, compulsory licenses must be nonexclusive, the licensee must first attempt to secure a negotiated license with the patent holder, reasonable remuneration must be paid under a compulsory license, and the duration of a compulsory license must be limited.
   f. Patents must be available without discriminations as to the place of invention, the field of technology, or whether the products are imported or locally produced. Part of this was aimed at the United States, which, in determining priority under its first-

to-invent system, previously had discriminated against inventions made in foreign countries. This discrimination was eliminated from U.S. law in 1995 to conform to this requirement.

4. TRADE SECRETS
   a. Protection for information is required if the information is secret, has commercial value because it is secret, and has been subject to reasonable steps to keep it secret. This conforms to state trade secret policies in the United States.
   b. Testing data submitted with applications to obtain government marketing approval of pharmaceutical and of agricultural products which utilize new chemical entities must be protected against unfair commercial use.

5. INDUSTRIAL PRODUCT DESIGNS
   a. Protection is required, but may be limited to those designs that are significantly different from known designs. The U.S. design patent laws meet this criterion.
   b. The term of protection must be at least ten years.

6. COPYRIGHT
   a. Members are required to comply with the Berne Convention, except for provisions relating to moral rights. This exclusion benefits the United States, which was concerned that moral rights under GATT might exceed the privileges granted under U.S. law.
   b. Computer programs and compilations of data must be protected by copyright.
   c. Copyright owners of computer programs and sound recordings have the right to authorize or prohibit rentals of their products.

7. TRADEMARKS
   a. Members are required to comply with the Paris Convention.
   b. Use of a trademark may not be a condition for filing an application for registration. However, use may be a requirement for registration. The United States came into compliance in 1988 when it started to allow intent-to-use applications.
   c. Protection must be extended to "signs" which are capable of distinguishing the goods or services from those of others. This requires a "likelihood of confusion" standard as is used in the United States. If the signs are not inherently capable of allowing distinction, then countries may require that such distinction be acquired through use. This conforms to U.S. law, which requires that secondary meaning be proven for marks that are not suggestive or fanciful.
   d. Paris Convention restrictions on the registration or unauthorized use of "well-known" marks are enhanced. First, they apply to services as well as goods. Second, public knowledge may result not only from use of the mark in the member country, but also from other means, such as promotion. Third, protection of a well-known mark extends to uses on dissimilar goods or services if such uses indicate some connection to the owner of the well-known mark. This conforms to U.S. law, which protects famous marks from dilution.
   e. Members may allow limited exceptions to trademark rights, such as for the fair use of descriptive terms.

f. Initial registration must last at least seven years and must be indefinitely renewable.
g. A mark can be cancelled for nonuse only if it is not used for at least three years in the member country.

8. ANTICOMPETITIVE PRACTICES
   a. Member countries may adopt appropriate measures to prevent or control licensing practices that are abusive and anticompetitive, as long as they are otherwise consistent with other TRIPs provisions.

9. ENFORCEMENT
   a. Nations are required to provide in their national laws for "effective" action against infringement of intellectual property rights. The procedures should not be unnecessarily costly or complicated and should not entail unreasonable time limits.
   b. Expeditious remedies are required. These include, with some qualifications, injunctions and preliminary injunctions.
   c. Criminal procedures are required for willful trademark counterfeiting and copyright violations on a commercial scale.
   d. Judicial review of administrative decisions must be provided.

---

abiding by a provision of the Uruguay Round agreements, its first step is to request consultations with India through the WTO to seek a negotiated solution. If the United States does not obtain a satisfactory response from India within 60 days, the United States may request that a panel be formed to hear the case. Panels consist of three to five individuals who are nominated by the Secretariat, the administrative arm of the WTO, but who may be rejected by either party for compelling reasons. Panelists must be well-qualified governmental or private individuals who have demonstrated expertise in trade matters. The panel meets with the parties twice to hear arguments and rebuttals, and ultimately files a report with the parties within six months that provides the basis of its determination.

Let's assume that the report confirms U.S. allegations that India is not abiding by its agreements. If India chooses not to appeal the panel report, then the report is automatically adopted within two months by the DSB unless all the members of the DSB, by consensus, decide not to accept the report. Thus, unlike before, when each member individually had veto power over a report, now the members have veto power only through unanimous consent. Alternatively, India may appeal the panel decision to an Appellate Body, which consists of three experts in law and international trade who are selected by the DSB for four-year terms. The Appellate Body may take up to three months to file its report regarding the matter. As with the panel report, the appellate report is automatically adopted by the DSB unless unanimously rejected by the members.

Once the DSB adopts the report, here specifying that India is not in compliance with WTO agreements, the question naturally arises, so what? What can the WTO do to make India change its practices? After all, the WTO does not have the power

Exhibit 1.6
WTO Dispute Resolution Procedures

- Complaint to Dispute Settlement Body (DSB)

- Consultation

- Panel Convened

- Panel Report Filed

- Possible Appeal to Appellate Body

  - Appellate Report filed

- Panel or Appellate Report Adopted by DSB

  - Unless rejected by unanimous consent

- DSB Recommendations for Compliance

- Authorization for Retaliatory Trade Sanctions

to put any officials of India in prison, nor to take Indian assets to compensate U.S. interests. The only leverage that the WTO has is to give the United States a form of internationally endorsed permission to apply trade sanctions against India. Recall that through GATT, the United States has pledged to grant India most-favored-nation status. This means that the United States may not independently employ trade sanctions against India, for by doing so, it will treat goods or services from India in a fashion that is inferior to how it treats those from other countries. Thus, any independent action to employ sanctions could subject the United States to a legitimate WTO complaint. The DSB adoption of the report starts a process by which the WTO ultimately may grant the United States an exception to its most-favored-nation pledge toward India.

The DSB first will recommend ways for India to come into compliance. If India does not agree to settle the problem, or fails to correct it within a reasonable time, then the panel may authorize the United States to impose retaliatory trade sanctions. Although this may seem no more impressive than measures discussed under Section 301, official endorsement of the action by the accepted international arbiter of trade disputes carries tremendous ethical weight. Clearly, defiance by India would subject it to widespread international scorn. In addition, other countries that might be harmed by India's nonconforming trade practice are likely to bring their complaints to the WTO, leading eventually to trade sanctions from numerous fronts.

In 1997 and 1998, the United States could claim a number of successes with the new WTO dispute resolution processes. For instance, in 1997, a WTO panel agreed with the United States that Japan violated the Uruguay Round agreements with discriminatory taxes on distilled spirits. This was affirmed by the Appellate Body and led to Japan's compliance with DSB recommendations.[53] Regarding TRIPs, the United States brought a complaint against India for failing to adequately protect agricultural chemicals and pharmaceutical inventions in compliance with the TRIPs patent "mailbox provision." In 1997, the WTO panel issued its report, which agreed with the U.S. position. India appealed the panel decision, and the Appellate Body upheld the ruling in December 1997. In February 1998, India pledged to implement the recommendations of the DSB, and in 1999, India passed amendments to its Patent Act that brought it into compliance.[54] The U.S. claimed other TRIPs victories during this period, often through negotiations before a panel had to be convened. For instance, in response to complaints in 1997, Sweden promised to make changes in its intellectual property enforcement processes, and Ireland agreed to step up its efforts to pass new copyright laws. Similarly, Greece and Denmark took steps to fight piracy and strengthen intellectual property laws after the United States initiated WTO proceedings against these countries in 1998.

In the mid- and late-1990s, the United States brought two highly confrontational complaints against the European Union. In one action, the United States charged that the EU violated WTO agreements through a discriminatory banana import regime that gave preference to bananas that originated from Europe's former colonies in the Caribbean and Africa. A WTO panel determined that the U.S. allegations were correct, and this conclusion was affirmed on appeal by the Appellate Body and accepted by the DSB. Although the EU agreed to make changes to comply with its Uruguay Round obligations, the United States complained in 1998 that the EU plan was insufficient to meet its obligations. In response, the DSB authorized the United States to impose higher tariffs on over $190 million of European imports in 1999.[55] In another proceeding, the United States argued that EU laws banning importation of hormone-treated beef violated WTO rules. The European Union stated that the ban was justified because beef injected with growth hormones poses a threat to human health and safety. However, in 1997, a WTO panel dismissed this rationale, finding no scientific substantiation for the health claims. In 1998, the DSB accepted the panel report and recommended that the EU take specific steps to rectify the situation. However, the EU did not satisfactorily meet these obligations, paving the way for a WTO ruling in 1999 that authorized the United States to impose 100% import duties on $116.8 million of EU merchandise.[56]

Although the U.S. position often has been accepted within the WTO dispute resolution process, there have been times when its arguments have been rebuffed. For instance, Venezuela and Brazil complained about a U.S. oil import pollution control law in 1995, and after failing to resolve their differences with the United States by consultation, requested the formation of a panel.[57] The panel determined that the United States had violated its obligations, a ruling that was later affirmed by the Appellate Body. In response, the United States changed the offending law to comply with DSB requests. In another setback, the United States, at the behest of

Eastman Kodak, complained in 1996 that certain Japanese film distribution practices benefited Japanese film companies, notably Fuji, at the expense of U.S. film companies in violation of certain GATT accords.[58] However, in 1997, a WTO panel rejected the U.S allegations.[59] Although the United States was disappointed with the decision, it did note that Japan nonetheless did take some positive steps to correct some of the alleged problems while the proceedings were ongoing.

Failures at the WTO always tug on emotional chords about U.S. sovereignty.[60] There are those who would argue that the United States should independently take retaliatory action under Section 301 whenever the WTO process fails to render the decision or result requested by the United States. Many also believe that the United States should ignore adverse WTO decisions when those rulings are contrary to U.S. policy interests, particularly those designed to protect the environment. Should the United States allow an international body to determine whether the United States may implement pollution control policies or ban imported tuna from countries failing to use dolphin-safe fishing practices? Despite these objections, the United States has been satisfied so far that it has gained, on net, through the Uruguay Round agreements and the WTO dispute resolution process. For the United States to take unilateral actions in the face of defeat, such as against Japan for its film distribution practices, would effectively nullify any credibility that the WTO might enjoy. Thus, for now, one can expect the United States to respect the decisions of the DSB.

Such a posture, coupled with the adoption of the TRIPs agreement, has significant impact on the future use of Special 301. The United States will continue to monitor countries for intellectual property protection and issue annual reports under Special 301 about the worst offenders. However, since most countries belong to the WTO, and since the TRIPs agreement covers most intellectual property aspects that might trouble the United States, it is very likely that the majority of Special 301 investigations will result in complaints to the WTO rather than in unilateral threats of trade retaliation. In addition, it is likely that the United States will not independently retaliate even when the DSB does not agree with the its position. Of course, this does not mean that Special 301 is obsolete or has been completely supplanted. It clearly will continue to provide powerful signals to countries about forthcoming U.S. actions. Now, however, they are more likely to be in the form of WTO complaints. In addition, it still will be a potent weapon against countries, such as Russia, that are not members of the WTO.

Regional Trade Pacts

Even though the Uruguay Round has now been successfully completed, one should not forget the tremendous hurdles that had to be overcome to finalize the agreement. Because of the inherent difficulties in formulating worldwide multilateral accords, smaller sets of countries, often in geographical proximity and/or with similar economic development patterns, strive to reach more regional multilateral agreements.[61]

The European Union (EU)   A substantial number of nations in Europe have made great strides in unifying their policies regarding trade and development through multilateral agreements. The most important European effort began in 1957 when six nations signed the Treaty of Rome, which established the European Community. The original goals of this multilateral agreement were to establish a common market and to promote harmonious development of economic activities. In 1986, the members of the European Community, which by that time numbered 12, signed the Single European Act. The intent of this act was to strengthen the ability of the members to achieve harmonization and to further economic integration. In November 1993, the members of the European Community formed the European Union when they signed the Maastricht Treaty on European Union. Through the European Union, the member nations, which by 1999 numbered 15, hope to achieve greater monetary and political union, as well as further certain social principles.[62]

Since a primary objective of the European Union is economic integration, a governmental structure has been established which strives to harmonize the laws of the different members so that there will be a common legal environment across national borders. The major way that the government accomplishes such harmonization is by passing what are called directives and regulations. A *directive* essentially provides a policy objective and directs each member nation to pass its own laws so that the policy can be attained within that country in ways that are consistent with the terms of the directive. Normally, the directive provides that the separate national governments have a certain number of years, often three, to implement the required measures. A *regulation* is a transnational law that has general application across all the European Union countries. In effect, it is like a federal law in the United States, having direct effect across state borders and requiring no separate legislative action by the individual states.

The major governing bodies of the European Union are the Council of Ministers, the Commission, the Parliament, and the European Court of Justice. The details of how these institutions make and enforce directives and regulations are quite complex. In general, though, initial proposals for legislation begin with the Commission, which is composed of 20 individuals who each serve four-year terms. Each national government nominates one or two individuals to serve on the Commission, but approval is required from the Council of Ministers. This is supposed to ensure that the Commission is motivated more by general European concerns than narrow political objectives. Once legislative proposals are developed by the Commission, they are forwarded to the Council of Ministers, which is the primary legislative body of the European Union. The Council has 15 members, one from each country, although each has different voting rights, weighted according to the relative sizes of the respective countries. Before adopting a measure, the Council of Ministers requests an opinion from the Parliament, a more political body having 626 representatives elected by the citizens of the individual nations. In theory, the Parliament serves mainly as a consultative body in the legislative process, although it does have the power to block legislation by failing to report an opinion back to the Council on a particular proposal. After receiving an opinion from the Parliament, the Council of Ministers then has the power to formulate and pass the directives and regulations of the European Union. The role of the European Court of Justice is to resolve disputes regarding European Union laws. For instance, disputes sometimes arise about whether the laws passed by a particular country to meet the objectives of a directive really do comply with the terms of the directive. In such a circumstance, the European Court of Justice would be the forum to resolve the controversy.

The legislative bodies of the European Union have focused their attentions on numerous topics that are substantially important to those involved with managing technology. For example, they have proposed or passed regulations and directives for such subjects as copyrights and computer software, database protection, information privacy, copyrights on the Internet, trademarks, biotechnology, and semiconductors. Many of these will be discussed in later chapters of this book. For consistency, the text ascribes all directives and regulations to the European Union (rather than the European Community), even though many of them were originally proposed or became effective prior to the formalization of the European Union.

North American Free Trade Agreement (NAFTA)   The United States recently negotiated with Canada and Mexico another regional trade pact called the North American Free Trade Agreement (NAFTA). This agreement, which became effective on January 1, 1994, created the world's largest free trade zone, affecting more than 350 million consumers. Of particular interest for managers of technology, it also provides for greater harmony of patent, copyright, trademark, and trade secret standards in the region, and it obliges member countries to enforce their laws effectively. Technology areas that substantially benefit from the accord include computers, pharmaceuticals, sound recordings, and motion pictures. In 1991, as a prelude to NAFTA, Mexico passed an enhanced intellectual property protection law, which achieved in Mexico much of what NAFTA now requires.[63] However, enforcement of that law, which had been subject to criticism, was a key issue in the NAFTA negotiations.

Acceptance of NAFTA by the United States was initially frustrated by various concerns, especially over environmental issues and possible loss of employment opportunities.[64] One potential stumbling block was averted when an appellate court reversed a lower court decision that had required the Clinton administration to file an environmental impact statement, evaluating the environmental effects of the trade accord. Organized labor opposed the agreement vigorously, claiming that lower U.S. tariffs on imported goods from within the region would induce U.S. manufacturers to relocate, especially to Mexico. After an extremely narrow and contentious vote in the House of Representatives, NAFTA finally was approved by Congress in November 1993. This paved the way for its eventual adoption in all three countries soon thereafter.

PRINCIPLES OF STRATEGY FOR MANAGING TECHNOLOGY

The making of business strategy is an enormously complex task, relying on a wide range of variables.[65] It is highly dependent on the nature of an organization and the environment that surrounds it. For instance, corporations often are built on different core philosophies about how business should be conducted. Looking simply at the computer software industry, one can find companies that advocate and practice the free interchange of ideas as well as others that expect information to be protected at great lengths. The core philosophy of firms can affect what strategic steps executives should take in managing technology. For instance, as will be discussed in Chapter 4, trade secrets must be protected with reasonable security measures. If the core philosophy of a firm is not compatible with such actions, then choosing this form of protection may not be a good strategy for managers to take. Other aspects within the organization that affect strategy formulation are the leadership styles employed by its executives and the flexibility of the internal systems established to implement policies. Looking externally, managers who formulate strategies must account for the social, political, economic, and competitive environments in which the business operates. In addition, they must recognize the constraints of laws, including those that are imposed by nature and created by man. It is here, of course, where this book fits in, by providing insights into the legal aspects affecting management decisions.

With this as a basis, managers devising strategies should be mindful of a number of principles. First, it is important to anticipate what the competition will do, so that appropriate measures can be taken to keep the firm profitable. Second, managers should strive to incorporate the strengths of the competition. This means that they should learn about the core competencies of competitors and assimilate them when appropriate. It also suggests that firms should seek to take advantage of the resources held by competitors. This principle does not instruct managers to steal those resources, but it informs them that working with rivals, through perhaps strategic alliances, can be mutually beneficial. Some attributes of strategic alliances will be explored in Chapter 9.

One also can learn from this doctrine that there may be times when it is better to share information rather than hoard it. This book spends a lot of time discussing various methods that might be used to protect intellectual property. This does not mean, however, that the best strategy always is to use every available means to protect one's ideas. Indeed, it might be a better strategy, depending on the circumstances, to simply give ideas away in the hopes of building a market. To substantiate this, one has only to reflect on a strategy once pervasively used by several computer hardware companies wherein they effectively gave software to the public for free. This made sense at the time because software tied the customers to a particular type of hardware, which then was by far the more profitable aspect of the industry.[66] Likewise, many business strategists suggest that it might be best to give information over the Internet to customers for free rather than to rely on intellectual property laws to protect it. Profits then can be realized from the sale of associated "ancillary" services, such as consulting arrangements, live musical performances or speeches, customer support, and advertising, among other possible arrangements.[67]

There are other key aspects of strategy that should guide how decisions are made. For instance, managers must fully understand the particular business that they are in, including the products, the market, and the competition. A strategy that is appropriate for a tobacco concern may have little relevance for a computer company. Also, strategies must be flexible, having the capability to adapt to changes. Strategies are best when they involve constant planning rather than relying on static long-term plans. Periodic intellectual property audits, for instance, are based on the notion of change and on having the ability to respond to change in ways that best meet the strategic needs of the enterprise.

While reading this book, you should always keep these principles in mind. The book provides the legal framework under which strategies are formulated. As a student of business or technology, it is up to you to use this knowledge to determine the strategy that is best for a company to adopt. This, of course, is highly dependent on the particular situation, as defined by the variables previously discussed. The book provides a lot of information about techniques that are available to carry out business strategies for managing technology. But it is ultimately up to you to determine which techniques are most prudent for a company to adopt and how it should plan to carry them out.

CONCLUSION

This chapter has provided a bird's-eye view of the legal environment affecting those companies managing technology. You now have a preliminary feel for what intellectual property is and why it often is protected by law. You also should be somewhat comfortable with the dynamics of policy making within the United States. Further, you have had a glimpse of the complicated web of international policies shaped by the dynamics of world affairs.

This book proceeds to focus more in depth on the important legal issues and considerations bearing on the management of technology. The orientation chosen is that of a company based in the United States. Therefore, there is a pronounced emphasis on U.S. laws and policies. However, the book does respect the critical importance of international policy aspects to those managing technologies from the United States.

The legal decisions required to manage technology are challenging because there often are numerous options from which to choose. For instance, one may protect a computer program through patents, copyrights, and/or trade secrets. We will see that numerous considerations will guide the best approach to protection. These include:

- The types of features that make the technology valuable;
- The technology's stage of development;
- The expected life of the technology in the market;
- The cost of legal protection;
- The length of time to obtain legal protection; and
- The difficulty of obtaining foreign protection.

On top of this, many technology products can cause substantial physical and economic harms if they malfunction or are used in unusual ways. Often, manufacturers must assess whether they need to make their products safer or more reliable. On the other hand, they may address the issues through contracts, perhaps by having users agree that they will assume those risks. In order to pull some of these concepts together, the book introduces at the beginning of the next chapter a hypothetical new product called the **Audio Enhancement System (AES)**. Throughout the book, the text considers how various legal issues might affect decisions regarding the development and sale of the **AES**. These discussions are highlighted with an **AES** icon in the margin.

The book is organized in the following manner. Chapters 2 through 7 are dedicated to the major fields of the intellectual property system: patents, trade secrets, copyrights, and trademarks. The goal of these chapters is to provide you with sufficient background in intellectual property protection methods so that you can make strategic decisions regarding any new technological development. The book fully evaluates all the modern intellectual property debates arising with computers and the Internet. Nevertheless, the book's focus is broader than these technologies. As we shall see, the legal policies that apply to modern contexts almost always are developed through analogies to more traditional technologies. Thus, these chapters will give you a deeper and more useful understanding of intellectual property concerns than a text that focuses solely on Internet or e-commerce issues.

Chapters 8 and 9 introduce other topics critical to managers of technological products. Chapter 8 deals with the legal responsibilities imposed on companies when their products or behavior harm customers, employees, or others. As you might expect, the chapter discusses various traditional bases of liability, such as negligence and strict liability. However, in addition, Chapter 8 covers the new ways that recent technological developments may cause harm in the information age. Here, the chapter discusses such things as intrusions on privacy and defamation, among other topics. Chapter 9 is dedicated to contract and antitrust issues. Much of the presentation regards sales and warranty concerns. The chapter also tracks the most controversial modern contracting issues, covering the debates over click-wrap licenses and the development of new model laws governing electronic commerce. In addition, Chapter 9 serves to bring together many of the concepts developed earlier in the book by examining the rise of strategic alliances. The text concludes by examining how antitrust considerations might affect the strategic plans of a technology concern. In this regard, there is substantial discussion of the highly publicized antitrust case brought by the Justice Department against Microsoft. Undoubtedly, by the end of this book, you will have a sophisticated and comprehensive understanding of the legal frameworks that guide strategic decisions regarding technology.

Notes

1. J. Hughes, "The Philosophy of Intellectual Property," 77 Georgetown L.J. 287, 302–303 (1988).

2. In a perfectly competitive market, the innovative firm would not be profitable at all. Once the technology

has been introduced, the market would price it at the marginal cost of replication. The price, therefore, would not be sufficient to cover the R&D outlays, yielding a negative net profit for the innovator. *See* K. Maskus, "Intellectual Property Rights and the Uruguay Round," Federal Reserve Bank of Kansas City Economic Review (First Quarter 1993) at 13.

3. For an excellent discussion of the contrasting historical and philosophical justifications for copyright, see P. Goldstein, Copyright's Highway (Hill and Wang, 1994).

4. J. Hughes, "The Philosophy of Intellectual Property," 77 Georgetown L.J. 287, 330–339 (1988).

5. There are other, more specific components of the intellectual property system. For example, federal law protects semiconductor chips, or mask works, under a separate (sui generis) system. 17 U.S.C. §§ 901–914 (1984).

6. For a thorough discussion of the role of trademarks in reducing search costs, see Folsom and Teply, "Trademarked Generic Words," 89 Yale L.J. 1323 (1980).

7. The federal government often regulates contracts and torts within the context of other specific regulatory areas such as drugs, motor vehicle safety, securities, and cigarettes. Also, Congress has for some time debated adopting a more general products liability law.

8. 489 U.S. 141 (1989).

9. The Supremacy Clause does not prevent the federal government from passing laws that protect boat hull designs, however, even when those laws otherwise might seem to conflict with existing patent policies. In 1998, the federal government passed the Vessel Hull Design Protection Act, which does provide some federal protection to boat hull designs. Title V of the Digital Millenium Copyright Act of 1988, Pub. L. No. 105-304, 112 Stat. 2860 (Oct. 28, 1998).

10. Annual Report of the Patent and Trademark Office (1997), available at www.uspto.gov.

11. J. Barton, "Patenting Life," Sci. Am. (March 1991) at 40.

12. Department of Justice Antitrust Guidelines for the Licensing of Intellectual Property (April 6, 1995), available at www.usdoj.gov.

13. T. McCarroll, "Whose Bright Idea?" Time (June 10, 1991) at 45; P. Dwyer, "The Battle Raging over Intellectual Property," Bus. Wk. (May 22, 1989) at 79.

14. We will see in Chapters 5 and 6 that copyright owners have suffered several losses lately. Examples include the extent of copyright protection for databases, the liability of Internet service providers for copyright infringements on their systems, and the judicial trend since 1992 that has reduced the level of copyright protection for computer programs.

15. R. Korman, "Lo! Here Come the Technology Patents. Lo! Here Come the Lawsuits," N.Y. Times (December 27, 1998) at Business 4.

16. T. McCarroll, "Whose Bright Idea?" Time (June 10, 1991) at 44.

17. T. McCarroll, "Whose Bright Idea?" Time (June 10, 1991) at 44. Other studies indicated that the losses, albeit significant, may not have been as high as these estimates suggested. *See* K. Maskus, "Intellectual Property Rights and the Uruguay Round," Econ. Rev. (First Quarter 1993) at 19–20.

18. This estimate was made by a joint study conducted by the Business Software Alliance and the Software Publishers Association. Reuters, "U.S. Software Firms Lost Billions to Pirates in 1997," (June 17, 1998). Some argue that studies such as this may overestimate the extent of revenue loss because they assume that pirates would purchase the software if they did not copy it. C. Mann, "Who Will Own Your Next Good Idea?" Atlantic Monthly (September 1998) at 61 *See also* K. Pope, "Software Piracy Is Big Business in East Europe," Wall St. J. (April 27, 1995) at A10.

19. J. Pitts, "Pressing Mexico to Protect Intellectual Property," Wall St. J. (January 25, 1991).

20. *See* Office of the United States Trade Representative, "USTR Announces Results of Special 301 Annual Review," (May 1, 1998); K. Pope, "Software Piracy Is Big Business in East Europe," Wall St. J. (April 27, 1995) at A10.

21. The president may overrule the determination of the ITC for any reason. Normally, the president invokes this power for international trade and policy reasons, such as when President Reagan rejected an ITC exclusion order of certain semiconductor "DRAMs" in 1987. P. Victor & E. Naftalin, 2 J. of Proprietary Rights (June 1990) at 115.

22. "Section 337 Investigations at the U.S. International Trade Commission: Answers to Frequently Asked Questions," United States International Trade Commission Pub. 3027 (March 1997) available at www.usitc.gov.

23. Some recent newspaper articles on the subject of Internet gambling include the following: W. Leibowitz, "Senate Bans Most Net Gambling; Many Bet on Poor Enforcement,"Nat'l L. J. (August 10, 1998); K. Freeling and R. Wiggins, "Despite Tough Talk from Prosecutors, and Despite Indictments of Those Charged with Internet Gambling, No Court Has Held That U.S. Law Prohibits Such Betting," Nat'l L. J. (March 30, 1998) at B7; P. McGuigan, "Stakes Are High in Battle to Bar Internet Gambling," Nat'l L. J. (November 3, 1997) at B8; B. Berselli, "The Web's Wheel of Fortune," Wash. Post Weekly Ed. (August 25, 1997) at 32. For a case that involves the subject of interstate gambling over the Internet, see State of Minnesota v. Granite Gate Resorts, Inc., 568 N.W.2d 715 (Minn. Ct. App. Sept. 5, 1997).

24. International Shoe Co. v. Washington, 326 U.S. 310 (1945).

25. For two examples, see Smith v. Hobby Lobby Stores, 968 F. Supp. 1356 (W.D. Ark. 1997) and Weber v. Jolly Hotels, 977 F. Supp. 327 (D.N.J. 1997). U.S. courts may be more careful in exercising personal jurisdiction over foreign defendants than other U.S. defendants. This is based on a heightened concern for other nations' sovereignty, and can be analyzed under the reasonableness factor discussed in *Hasbro*.

26. For a case involving Internet pornography within the United States, see United States v. Thomas, 74 F.3d 701 (6th Cir.), *cert. denied*, 117 S.Ct. 74 (1996).

27. *See* J. Ginsburg, "Copyright Without Borders? Choice of Forum and Choice of Law for Copyright Infringement in Cyberspace," 15 Cardozo Arts & Ent. L. J. 153 (1997).

28. Zippo Manufacturing Co. v. Zippo Dot Com, Inc., 952 F. Supp. 1119 (W.D. Penn 1997).

29. Complaint filed by L'Association "Avenir de la Langue Francaise" and L'Association "Defense de la Langue Francaise" (January 1996).

30. For thorough treatments of conflict of laws principles over the Internet, see A. Reindl, "Choosing Law in Cyberspace: Copyright Conflicts on Global Networks," 19 Mich. J. Int'l L. 799 (Spring 1998); J. Ginsburg, "Copyright Without Borders? Choice of Forum and Choice of Law for Copyright Infringement in Cyberspace," 15 Cardozo Arts & Ent. L. J. 153 (1997). For a general discussion of international conflicts of laws principles, see R. August, International Business Law (Prentice-Hall, Inc., 1993) at 130–133.

31. *See* European Community Convention on the Law Applicable to Contractual Obligations, 1980 O.J. (L. 266), commonly known as the Rome Convention; "Uniform Commercial Code Article 2B: Software Contracts and Licenses of Information," National Conference of Commissioners on Uniform State Laws (August 1, 1998 Draft), §§ 2B–107, 108.

32. Hasbro did not prevail at trial in Massachusetts. Hasbro v. Clue Computing, Inc., 66 F. Supp. 2d 117 (D. MA 1999).

33. For a more complete discussion of international enforcement principles see R. Schaffer, B. Earle, and F. Agusti, International Business Law and Its Environment, 3d ed. (West Publishing Co., 1996) at 125–131.

34. For an excellent discussion of the Semiconductor Chip Protection Act, see J. Dratler, Jr., Intellectual Property Law (Law Journal Seminars-Press, 1991 & Supp. 1999) at Chapter 8.

35. *See* 56 Fed. Reg. 32180 (July 15, 1991).

36. *See* W. Sprance, "The World Trade Organization and United States' Sovereignty: The Political and Procedural Realities of the System," 13 Amer. Univ. Int'l L. Rev. 1225 (1998).

37. Much of the following information on Special 301 was based on USTR press releases that report on the results of the annual reviews. These are available at www.ustr.gov.

38. E. Lachica, "U.S., Taiwan Reach Pact on Copyrights, Patents, Ending Unfair-Trade Inquiry," Wall St. J. (June 8, 1992).

39. M. Margolis, "Tougher Patent Law Expected from Brazil," L.A. Times (April 26, 1993).

40. K. Stier, "Thai Piracy Likely to Top U.S. Hit List," L.A. Times (April 26, 1993) at D2, D7.

41. H. Cooper and K. Chen, "U.S. Sanctions, China's Retaliation Start Countdown to a Trade War," Wall St. J. (February 6, 1995).

42. H. Cooper and K. Chen, "China Averts a Trade War with U.S. by Agreeing to Crack Down on Piracy," Wall St. J. (February 27, 1995) at A3.

43. R. Greenberger, "U.S. Sharply Attacks China over Intellectual Property," Wall St. J. (May 1, 1996) at A3.

44. K. Chen and H. Cooper, "U.S. and China Reach an Agreement, Averting Trade Sanctions by Both Sides," Wall St. J. (June 18, 1996) at A3.

45. In 1999, a Chinese court ordered two domestic software companies to pay 800,000 yuan (about $96,000) to Microsoft for infringing Microsoft's copyrights. "Microsoft Wins First China Copyright Cases," Reuters Limited (March 7, 1999) reported on Yahoo! News (www.dailynews.yahoo.com).

46. PTC Newsletter, A.B.A, Vol. 11 (Spring 1993) at 1–2. The American Bar Association's Section of Intellectual Property Law approved the change by a wide margin (102-8), but the House of Delegates narrowly defeated it (99-90).

47. Some of those who opposed a move by the United States to a first-to-file priority system felt that the change shoudl be made only after the international community raised various patent standards. Successful completion of NAFTA and GATT may persuade these opponents that the time is now right for the United States to yield on its adherence to the first-to-invent system.

48. For an excellent discussion about the history of U.S. positions and arguments regarding GATT and the WTO, see W. Sprance, "The World Trade Organization and Unived States' Sovereignty: The Political and Procedural Realities of the System," 13 Am. Univ. Int'l L. Rev. 1225 (1998).

49. For a thorough discussion of GATT and the WTO, see R. Schaffer, B. Earle, and F. Agusti, International Business Law and Its Environment, 3d ed. (West Publishing Co., 1996) at Chapter 10.

50. W. Sprance, "The World Trade Organization and United States' Sovereignty: The Political and Procedural Realities of the System," 13 Am. Univ. Int'l L. Rev. 1225 (1998).

51. For information about entry into the WTO, see the WTO Web site at www.wto.org/wto/about/accgen.htm.

52. See E. Iritani and M. Magnier, "China Trade Pact to Widen Access for U.S. Firms," L.A. Times (November 16, 1999) at A1; C. Hutzler, "China, U.S. Sign Market-Opening Deal," Yahoo! News (November 15, 1999).

53. W. Sprance, "The World Trade Organization and United States' Sovereignty: The Political and Procedural Realities of the System," 13 Am. Univ. Int'l L. Rev. 1225 (1998).

54. The United States had serious reservations regarding certain aspects of this law, but the USTR concluded in 1999 that no further action was required. Office of the U.S. Trade Representative, "USTR Announces Results of Special 301 Annual Review," (April 30, 1999), Press Release 99-41, available at www.ustr.gov.

55. U.S. Trade Representative Press Release, "WTO Authorizes U.S. Retaliation," Release No. 99-38 (April 19, 1999), available at www.ustr.gov.

56. U.S. Trade Representative Press Release, "WTO Finds U.S. Trade Damaged by EU Beef Import Ban," Release No. 99-58 (July 12, 1999), available at www.ustr.gov.

57. W. Sprance, "The World Trade Organization and United States' Sovereignty: The Political and Procedural Realities of the System," 13 Am. Univ. Int'l L. Rev. 1225 (1998).

58. See U.S. Trade Representative, "WTO to Launch Panel on Film Case," Press Release No. 96-86 (October 1996); C. Chandler and P. Blustein, "Cutting Kodak Out of the Picture," Wash. Post Nat'l Weekly Ed. (July 3–9, 1995); W. Bounds and H. Cooper, "Kodak to Spell Out Charges That Japan Conspired to Bar It from Photo Markets," Wall St. J. (November 6, 1995) at A3.

59. B. Bahree, "WTO's Kodak Ruling Heightens Trade Tensions," Wall St. J. (December 8, 1997) at A3. For a discussion of U.S. reaction to the WTO panel ruling, see Office of the U.S. Trade Representative, "USTR and the Department of Commerce Announce Next Steps on Improving Access to the Japanese Market for Film," Release No. 98-10 (February 3, 1998).

60. See E. Iritani, "Trade Pacts Accused of Subverting U.S. Policies," L.A. Times (February 28, 1999) at A1.

61. Examples of existing or proposed regional accords include the Andean Common Market, Mercosur, the African Economic Community, Asia Pacific Economic Cooperation Group, the Association of South East Asian Nations, and the North American Free Trade Agreement. For a full discussion of these regional pacts, see R. Schaffer, B. Earle, F. Agusti, International Business Law and Its Environment, 3d ed. (West Publishing Co., 1996) at 105–109.

62. The members of the European Union are Austria, Belgium, Denmark, Finland, France, Germany, Greece, Ireland, Italy, Luxembourg, Netherlands, Portugal, Spain, Sweden, and the United Kingdom.

63. Ley de Fomento y Protecciùn de la Propiedad Industrial, Diario Oficial (June 27, 1991). For a discussion of how NAFTA affected the adoption of intellectual property laws in Mexico, see J. Cristiani, "Enacted to Comply with NAFTA, Recent Mexican Legislation Strengthened Intellectual Property Protection, Offering Encouragement to Foreign Investors," Nat'l L. J. (June 19, 1995) at B5.

64. *See* T. Robberson, "A Cloud Drifting Over Trade and Texas," Wash. Post Weekly Ed. (June 28–July 4, 1993) at 16–17; M. Lavelle, "Free Trade vs. Law," Nat'l L.J. (March 29, 1993) at 1.

65. I wish to thank Carey Heckman, Co-director, Stanford Law and Technology Policy Center, for these insights, which he based on R. L. Wing, The Art of Strategy (Dolphin, 1988).

66. *See* P. Heckel, "The Software-Patent Controversy," 9 Comp. Law. (December 1992) at 17.

67. E. Dyson, Release 2.0, (Broadway Books, 1997) at 142–157.

The U.S. Patent System: Fundamental Conditions for Protection

2

INTRODUCTION

AES Scenario: You are an electronics engineer who loves music, especially pre-1990s rock and roll. You have made the transition to compact disc technology in your living room, so much so that you no longer can listen to your large assortment of favorite rock and roll LPs. Somehow, the crackles, skips, and hisses of that old JethroTull album now seem to ruin an experience that once was totally enjoyable. It occurs to you that it would be nice if you could use digital technology to filter out the unwanted annoyances and boost the clarity of the desirable material. Then you could appreciate your old classics and not be burdened with investigating whether they have been rereleased on expensive new compact discs.

You and some friends set out to develop a machine that can achieve this goal. You are certain that such a device would be a hot item among the 35 to 60 age bracket and would be extremely profitable if the price were manageable. After two years of effort and experimentation, your team is on the verge of a solution: a machine that uses modified standard digital technologies along with a computer program uniquely suited to identify and eliminate unwanted audio characteristics. As the time for marketing what you have coined the **Audio Enhancement System (AES)** comes near, you begin to wonder whether your efforts should have legal protection.

Like most persons dealing with new and potentially lucrative technological inventions, you are inclined to focus first, if not exclusively, on whether it is possible to obtain patent protection. There are several reasons why most inventors have a heightened level of awareness of patents within the spectrum of intellectual property rights. Of most importance is the somewhat common knowledge that patents provide substantial benefits. Only with a patent, for instance, may an inventor keep others from independently creating and marketing the same invention. Reinforcing this basic awareness of the power of patents are periodic newspaper accounts of huge, multimillion-dollar returns obtained by patent holders in patent infringement lawsuits or from contractual agreements. Polaroid's suit against Eastman Kodak for violating its instant photography patents, for instance, resulted in a highly publicized $909-million judgment against Eastman Kodak. In 1992, a court ordered Minolta to pay $96 million to Honeywell for infringing Honeywell's patents covering autofocus and automatic flash technologies. This ruling quickly motivated 15 other major camera manufacturers who had been sued by Honeywell to seek settlements totaling over $314 million.[1] Honeywell was in the news again in 1993 when a jury found that it infringed Litton Industries' patent for an airplane guidance device and awarded Litton $1.2 billion in damages. As you might expect, the magnitude of this award prompted a series of appeals, and in 1999 a court threw out the award entirely, finding that Honeywell had not even infringed Litton's patent.[2] Nonetheless, it does indicate just how large patent damages can become.

In 1997, the press came alive when Digital Equipment sued Intel, claiming that Intel's Pentium line of processors violated one of its patents. This claim, had it persisted, obviously would have been worth billions of dollars.[3] The parties, however, quickly settled the dispute. Similarly, a patent issued to Compton's New Media in 1993 for a multimedia search-and-retrieval system brought cries of disbelief from industry participants who feared that the breadth of the patent might cover many of their interactive products. In fact, the reaction was so vociferous that the Patent and Trademark Office (PTO) decided to reexamine its decision to issue the patent just months after the patent was granted; it ultimately overturned the patent in 1994.[4]

Undoubtedly, you may derive rich rewards from a patent. However, there are numerous drawbacks to the patent system that also must be considered before you determine if it is the best or only means to protect AES. First, in order to be issued a patent by the PTO, you have to demonstrate that your machine is the type of invention deemed suitable for patent protection and that it meets a variety of criteria, such as novelty and nonobviousness. Second, a patent costs money, possibly lots of money. There are fees to obtain a patent and to maintain it. Specialized attorneys are almost always needed, which can magnify the expenses of getting the patent. Also, if you plan to broaden your horizon to international markets, you can expect those expenses to increase severalfold, with such possible additional categories of expenses as translators, communication, and travel. And then, even after you have the patent, you will bear the burden and expense of tracking down and enforcing your patent rights against alleged infringers. The numbers here are not trivial. The median cost to bring a patent infringement suit is around $1.2 million, according to a 1998 study, and complex trials may cost as much as $6 million or more.[5] Another problem is that when you receive the patent, the public will learn sufficient information about your invention so that those who are skilled in the appropriate technical art may replicate it.[6] If a court later judges that your patent was inappropriately granted by the PTO—an occurrence that is more likely than you might suspect—then your fully informed competitors are free to develop and market their own versions of your creation.

Clearly, an inventor must seriously consider the long-term advantages and disadvantages of patent protection. Chapters 2 and 3 strive to provide a feel for the basic concepts that underlie patent protection, as well as the benefits and pitfalls that attend protection. This can be only the beginning of the inquiry, however. Before reaching a final decision, the inventor must also factor in the pros and cons of alternative methods of protection, such as trade secrets and copyrights. Only then can the inventor arrive at the most suitable comprehensive strategic plan for protecting the valuable elements of the invention.

The two chapters on patents are divided as follows: Chapter 2 focuses on the essential characteristics that make an invention suitable for patent protection in the United States. Here we consider what it takes for an invention to be novel and nonobvious. Also, we will investigate how the envelope of patent protection has expanded recently to cover new forms of technological frontiers, such as computers and biotechnology, and how the extension has led to questions, confusion, and controversy. The chapter also provides a basic understanding of how design patents might apply to technological products.

Chapter 3 provides a feel for the hurdles that an inventor must overcome to obtain and defend a patent in the United States and abroad. The chapter focuses first on the United States by illustrating the essential components of a U.S. patent application, the typical process that one follows to obtain a U.S. patent, and the difficulties one may encounter to prove infringement of that patent. The goal of these discussions is not to enable you to handle the U.S. PTO without an attorney. In fact, just the contrary is intended—you should clearly recognize that the realm of patent protection constitutes highly specialized, technical, and complicated waters that can be navigated only with the aid of an experienced attorney. Following this exposition, Chapter 3 considers the rapidly changing international environment. As the lines of domestic and international economic affairs have become increasingly blurred, so has the ability of the American inventor to concentrate on U.S. laws. This is especially true in the patent arena, where foreign policies not only may be very different from those in the United States but also may form the basis of substantive international patent agreements likely to be achieved through WIPO. Chapter 3 thereby alerts you to the overall strategic implications that foreign laws and international treaties bear on your ultimate decision to pursue patent protection.

OVERVIEW OF PATENT POLICIES AND PROCESSES

The fundamental rationales for patent protection in the United States, as well as in most foreign jurisdictions, are to stimulate research and development of new inventions and to encourage thorough and rapid disclosures. Patent protection can be likened to an agreement with the government wherein the inventor promises to divulge sufficient information about a new invention so that others may readily understand and replicate it and have the opportunity to consider improvements to it. In return for those disclosures, the government provides the inventor a narrowly circumscribed and temporally limited right to exclusively control who makes, uses, and sells the invention within the nation's borders. In effect, the government is bestowing a limited monopoly over particular claims to the invention so that the inventor may be amply rewarded for creative energies. As you might have guessed, patent policy has had a contentious history in the United States, owing to the fundamental antipathy its citizens share toward publicly sanctioned monopoly control in the marketplace. One must always be mindful of that tension when embarking on a patent protection strategy. The tension not only explains many of the difficulties one may encounter in obtaining patent protection but should also raise red flags of caution when deciding to enforce monopoly privileges against alleged infringers.

Basic Requirements

The U.S. patent system is governed by the Patent Act, which was first established in 1790 and has been amended on numerous occasions thereafter. The Patent Act provides that a person is entitled to a patent for an invention if that invention is novel, nonobvious, and a proper subject for protection. As we shall see, the details about meeting the standard of novelty, delineated in Section 102 of the act, are somewhat technical but are based on three principles: The first is that a person may not stake claim to an invention that was publicly available before the person invented it. The second is that if two or more persons allege that they are entitled to patent rights in the United States for the same development, then priority will be given to the person deemed to have invented first. This is the so-called first-to-invent standard of the United States, which differs from the first-to-file system of almost all other countries, wherein priority is granted to the first inventor to file for the patent. The third guiding principle, based on the rapid-disclosure rationale for patents, is that there are reasons not to delay too long after completion of an invention before filing for a patent. Here again, one with an international vision will find differences abroad, where the policies of some countries provide even more incentives to file as early as possible.

The standards for nonobviousness are provided in Section 103 and essentially require that an invention must be something more than that which would be obvious, in light of publicly available knowledge, to one who is skilled in the relevant field. The proper subjects for patent protection are given in various sections of the Patent Act. Section 101 controls utilitarian inventions; here the guiding principle is that all things made by human ingenuity are patentable while those elements that are bestowed by nature are not. This concept is at the center of the debate over the patentability of computer programs and biotechnology. Section 171, which covers design patents, provides that product designs may be patented if they are primarily ornamental. In this regard, important questions are arising in the computer field, for instance about the patentability of screen displays. These basic standards, which will be discussed at length in this chapter, are outlined in Exhibit 2.1.

In contrast to copyrights and trade secrets, an inventor must undertake an

Exhibit 2.1
Conditions for Patentability in the United States

- **Novelty**
  - Section 102
  - Knowledge of the invention was not publicly available at the time of invention
    - — **CASE:** *Dunlop Holdings Limited v. Ram Golf Corporation*
  - The patent application was filed in time
    - — One-year grace period
    - — Experimental use
  - First-to-invent priority

- **Nonobviousness**
  - Section 103
  - Not obvious at the time of invention to one skilled in the art
    - — **CASE:** *Panduit Corporation v. Dennison Manufacturing*

- **Appropriate Subject Matter for Utility Patents**
  - Section 101
  - Useful
  - Anything under the sun made by man
    - — Biotechnology
      - – **CASE:** *Diamond v. Chakrabarty*
  - Not abstract ideas, laws of nature, or manifestations of nature
    - — Mathematical algorithms and computer programs
      - – **CASE:** *Diamond v. Diehr*
    - — Business methods
      - – **CASE:** *State Street Bank & Trust v. Signature Financial Group*

- **Appropriate Subject Matter for Design Patents**
  - Section 171
  - Primarily Ornamental
  - **CASE:** *Avia Group International, Inc. v. L.A. Gear California*

arduous examination and approval process to receive patent protection. The inventor initiates the process by filing a patent application with the PTO. As will be discussed in some detail in Chapter 3, the Patent Act and PTO regulations set out the requirements for the application. The most important components are (1) a description of the invention, which is sufficient to enable one skilled in the art to practice it; (2) an illustration of the best mode of carrying out the invention known to the inventor at the time of filing the application; (3) all information known to the inventor that may bear on the patentability of the invention, such as pertaining to its novelty or its obviousness; and (4) the precise aspects of the invention claimed for patent protection. Until recently, all information presented to the PTO was treated in confidence until a patent was granted, at which time it became publicly available. In 1999, though, Congress passed several amendments to the patent laws in legislation titled the American Inventors Protection Act.[7] The most important changes are listed in Exhibit 2.2, and many will be discussed in this book. The relevant aspect here is that most patent applications now are held in secrecy only for 18 months. The legislation provides an important exception for patent applicants who have not filed for patent protection in foreign countries.[8] Therefore, inventors who seek patent protection only within the United States still may assume that their patent files will remain secret until the patent issues. Others, though, now face publication of their patent applications 18 months after they file with the PTO. As we shall see, the term of secrecy is important to an inventor who may want to rely on trade secret protection if it turns out that the patent avenue is not promising or available.

If the PTO is satisfied from the application and subsequent discussions that the invention is novel, nonobvious, and a proper subject for protection, then it will issue a patent. Currently, it usually takes from one and a half to over three years for a patent to issue, depending often on the type of invention and its complexity. For instance, biotechnology and computer applications take more time for their patents to issue than do those claiming conventional inventions. Once granted, the patent entitles the patent holder to take action against infringers of the patent. Infringers

---

Exhibit 2.2

The American Inventors Protection Act: Major Changes to the Patent Laws

- Rights for companies using a business method in secret before a patentee filed for the patent

- Patent term extensions for administrative delays over three years

- Publication of patent application 18 months after filing if the applicant files in foreign countries or with foreign conventions requiring publication

- Greater public involvement in reexamination proceedings

include those who make, use, or sell the invention in the United States without permission. In addition, when the patented invention is a process, one becomes an infringer by selling articles in the United States that were produced in other countries according to the patented process. A patent holder can challenge alleged infringers in the federal district courts and, if successful, is entitled to a variety of remedies, including injunctions and damages.

Note that the U.S. Patent Act does not require that one actually use an invention to be entitled to a patent or to maintain rights under it. This means that companies are allowed to accumulate patent rights in the United States primarily to prevent competitors from using new technologies. Based on this, big corporate players in several technology-related areas, such as the computer industry, have accumulated extensive portfolios of patent rights, sometimes for technologies that they are not using or developing. The patents, then, can be used as weapons, allowing their owners to have colorable claims against upstart companies that introduce challenging new technological innovations to the marketplace.[9] Patents in the portfolio also can be used as bargaining chips to obtain rights from competitors under patents that they might own, under contractual arrangements called cross-licensing. We will consider these issues further in Chapter 3.

Patent Duration

The duration of utility patent rights in the United States was changed in 1995 so that the United States could comply with its obligations under the TRIPs Agreement of the GATT Uruguay Round. Before this time, the traditional standard in the United States was to measure the utility patent term from the date the patent was granted by the PTO. The length of the patent term was 17 years. The TRIPs Agreement requires that the utility patent term be at least 20 years, with the term measured from the date of filing the patent application. The Patent Act therefore was amended in 1995 to conform to this requirement. Thus, utility patents in the United States now last for 20 years, with that term measured from the date of filing the patent application. The new Patent Act provisions, however, did not change the term of design patents. Therefore, design patents still last for 14 years, and their term begins only after the date of issuance. As mentioned above, others may not make, use, or sell an invention without permission while the patent is in force. Legal protection starts when the PTO actually issues the patent and lasts until the relevant term expires. So, always remember that just because the term of a utility patent begins when the patent application is filed, this does not mean that any legal protection is offered at that time. Rather, patent protection is available only after the patent is granted, which may be years after the application is filed. Thus, the patent laws do not prevent other companies from using an invention while the PTO processes a patent application for it, even though the patent term has begun.[10] Also, after the patent expires, the inventor no longer enjoys the exclusive privileges of patent protection. Anyone else, then, is free to practice the invention, unless some other form of federal protection, such as perhaps copyright or trademark, is found to apply.

The changes in the duration of utility patents may seem minor—and indeed, for most inventions they are—but they still became the source of vigorous objections. Many U.S. inventors and companies clung to the notion that they deserve at least 17 years of actual patent protection, no matter when the clock of the statutory term begins to tick. Of course, none of this matters if the patent is issued within three years of the date that the application is filed. And, as already noted, most patents do issue within that time frame. But, there are times when a patent may be held up for greater periods of time. When the Patent Act was amended in 1995, the new law accounted for certain possibilities for delay, allowing the PTO to extend patent protection for up to five years in particular situations. For instance, some patent applications become subject to what are called "secrecy orders" because they contain information that may have important military or other classified applications. The Patent Act accounts for the possibility that a secrecy order will result in a lengthy delay and thus allows the PTO to extend the term of protection if warranted. Similarly, the Patent Act allows the PTO to extend the patent term for up to five years when delays are caused by specified judicial-style proceedings within the agency.[11] The 1995 amendments, however, did not account for the possibility that extensive administrative delays within the PTO might severely reduce the length of patent protection, causing it to fall somewhat below the preexisting 17-year figure. The biotechnology industry complained bitterly about the detrimental ways that the TRIPs-mandated law often served to diminish its patent protection, arguing that biotechnology patent applications involve such new and complex technological subjects that the PTO sometimes takes as many as five to ten years to evaluate them.[12] In response to these criticisms, amendments were passed in 1999 as part of the American Inventors Protection Act that provide for extensions based on administrative delays, virtually guaranteeing that the actual length of patent protection now will always exceed 17 years. This change clearly represented an important victory for the biotechnology industry, and for other fields, such as computers, that often suffer from lengthy PTO proceedings.

Enforcement Issues

This simplified exposition of U.S. patent protection makes the road appear relatively smooth and clear. However, you will learn over the course of the two chapters on patents that there are pitfalls at every step. The concepts of novelty, nonobviousness, and subject matter raise numerous difficult hurdles. Meeting the requirements of the patent application also may prove challenging. In addition, even after receiving the patent, an inventor may find the task of enforcing the patent against infringers to be troublesome, even overwhelming and economically dangerous.

That final statement may have surprised you. What could be so financially devastating once a patent is granted? Assume that you and your somewhat expensive patent attorney spent nearly two years persuading the PTO that you deserved a patent and you finally obtained one. You then locate a manufacturer in Idaho who you believe is infringing the patent. When your attempts at negotiating with that manufacturer are rebuffed, you decide to defend your patent rights in an Idaho federal district court. This action demands a great deal of your time and will involve your attorney substantially, again at great expense. The manufacturer likely will defend itself on a number of grounds. First, it probably will argue that its products do not infringe the narrow parameters of the patent claims. However, it may also allege that the patent was invalidly granted by the PTO. For instance, it may claim that the PTO erred in its determination that the invention was novel or nonobvious. According to the Patent Act, a patent granted by the PTO is presumed to be valid. Thus, one challenging the patent has the burden of overcoming that presumption. However, one never knows how heavily a court will weigh the presumption. Thus, the Idaho court may look at the invention in light of the history considered by the Patent Office and may determine that the PTO was simply wrong in issuing the patent. Possibly the invention just seems so obvious to the judge reviewing the case that that judge cannot back the PTO's decision. Or the manufacturer may dig up and introduce evidence not even found or reviewed by the PTO. In such an instance, the Idaho court likely will reduce even further its deference to the PTO, given that the PTO's decision was based on an incomplete record of previous information about the invention. Whatever the reason, if the court determines that the patent is invalid, then you have wasted a huge amount of time and money obtaining and trying to defend your patent. But worse, critical information about how to make the invention became publicly available when your patent was issued.[13] A court determination that the patent was invalid, coupled with the disclosure, enables any manufacturer to cheaply learn how to duplicate your efforts.

With the advice of your attorney, you might try to consider which court forum is most likely to respect the validity and breadth of an issued patent, and to bring the case there if possible. However, even this attempt at forum-shopping may be foiled by a potential competitor who is allowed to initiate a court proceeding for the purpose of obtaining a judgment declaring that the patent claims are narrow or invalid (called a declaratory judgment). The competitor, of course, will in turn try to select the forum most likely to doubt the determination of the PTO. And when this action is brought, you and your attorney have to defend it. Needless to say, one cannot breathe easily once a patent is issued. An inventor must be willing to invest time, energy, and resources in defending a patent for it to be meaningful. In addition, one must factor in the very real prospect that the patent could be lost along with all the attendant problems of disclosure.

The Federal Circuit Court of Appeals   In 1982, Congress made a change to the judicial landscape that relieved some of the anxieties faced by patent holders. In that year, it created the Court of Appeals for the Federal Circuit, a new, specialized court with jurisdiction over a limited set of legal matters. One of its duties is to hear appeals by inventors who are dissatisfied with negative judgments from the PTO about patent issues. More important, appeals from district court decisions regarding patents also must be made to the Federal Circuit. Prior to the creation of this court, appeals from the district courts followed the usual routes to their respective regional courts of appeals and, finally, to the Supreme Court. This led to varying standards across the nation about patent matters, which were dependent on the disparate views of the justices sitting on the appellate courts. Some jurisdictions were positively hostile to patent protection and were much more likely to strike down a patent than uphold it. Now all patent appeals go to the same place—the Federal Circuit. Thus, a patent holder who is given an unsatisfactory decision at the district court level, whether from an infringement or a declaratory judgment action, no longer must wonder what principles might be applied by the relevant appellate court. Instead, no matter where the first action took place, the appeal goes to the Federal Circuit. During its first two decades, the Federal Circuit has proven to be a relatively hospitable place for patent holders, upholding patent claims at a rate close to 55% when validity is challenged.[14] Also, the Federal Circuit's regard for patent validity filters down to the district court justices, whose judgments are subject to the unified standards from the sole appellate court. Thus, the creation of the Federal Circuit has greatly reduced the dangers of forum-shopping, even at the initial stages of legal proceedings. None of this means that a patent holder is home free; one still must be financially willing to defend a patent and consider the possibility of losing its protections. However, the forum-shopping risks that used to put a cloud over all patents have now been substantially reduced.

NOVELTY

The concept of novelty in the United States, as well as in most other countries, is based on the principle that patent protection is a reward for disclosing new innovations to the public. This notion can be broken down into two fundamental requirements. The first is that one should not be allowed to receive patent protection for knowledge that is already available to the public. The conferring of patent rights to existing knowledge is contrary to underlying patent philosophy, for it removes from the public something it previously possessed rather than ultimately presenting something new to it. The second principle recognizes that the public stands to gain from the disclosures that attend patent protection, especially when the disclosures are provided as early as possible. To account for this, there are embedded within the concept of novelty disincentives for an inventor to unreasonably delay in filing a patent application.

Another key determinant of novelty, this one somewhat peculiar to the United States, is that when two or more persons have applied for patents covering the same invention, the patent will be granted to that person who invented first. In almost all other countries, patent decisions regarding competing applications for the same invention favor the first person to file a patent application. In the early 1990s, negotiators for the United States within WIPO made it clear that the United States may be willing to abandon its first-to-invent priority system in favor of the first-to-file system if certain other concessions, such as expanding the scope of patentable subject matter, are adopted by other countries.[15] Since many of these issues were addressed with the TRIPs Agreement, it is possible that the United States soon may end its stubborn resistance to changing this feature of its patent system.

The requirements to satisfy novelty in the United States are provided in Section 102 of the Patent Act. Three subsections—102(a), 102(b), and 102(g)—are particularly important, and we will restrict our discussion to those:

Section 102. Conditions for Patentability; Novelty

A person shall be entitled to a patent unless—

(a) the invention was known or used by others in this country, or patented or described in a printed publication in this or a foreign country, before the invention thereof by the applicant for patent, or

(b) the invention was patented or described in a printed publication in this or a foreign country or in public use or on sale in this country, more than one year prior to the date of application for patent in the United States, or

(g) before the applicant's invention thereof the invention was made in this country by another who had not abandoned, suppressed or concealed it. In determining priority of invention there shall be considered not only the respective dates of conception and reduction to practice of the invention, but also the reasonable diligence of one who was first to conceive and last to reduce to practice, from a time prior to conception by the other.

Section 102(a) serves mainly to ensure that patentees do not claim publicly available knowledge as their own, although as we shall see, it also provides some incentive to disclose new inventions rather than maintain them in secrecy. The role of Section 102(b) is to encourage inventors to file patent applications soon after they begin to commercialize or otherwise disseminate information about their inventions. Section 102(g), with some reinforcement from Section 102(a), establishes the first-to-invent priority system within the United States. Section 102(g) also works in tandem with Section 102(a) to dissuade inventors from relying too heavily on trade secret protection in certain situations. As noted, this subsection, as well as Section 102(a), may undergo substantial change in the near future as part of an international patent accord.

Sections 102(a), (b), and (g) are extremely technical, and it is easy to get lost in the statutory verbiage. You should notice first that these sections cover instances when an inventor would **not** be permitted to get a U.S. patent. For that reason, these criteria are often called statutory bars to protection. Sections 102(a) and (g) are drafted so that the pivotal events are in terms of what other people besides the patent applicant knew or had done before the applicant's date of invention. Section 102(b) addresses activities of anyone, including the applicant, more than one year prior to the date the applicant filed the U.S. patent application. Exhibit 2.3 strives to bring some clarity to the nine statutory bars listed in Sections 102(a), (b), and (g) by logically separating them into relevant components.

Is the Invention New?

The thrust of Section 102(a) is to keep a patentee from controlling knowledge that was previously available to the public. Therefore, it prevents an applicant from

---

Exhibit 2.3

Statutory Bars in the United States: Sections 102 (a), (b), and (g)

SECTION 102(a)

Activity	Where	By Whom	When
Publicly known	U.S.	Others	
Publicly used	U.S.	Others	Before the date
Patented	Anywhere	Others	of invention
Printed publication	Anywhere	Others	

SECTION 102(b)

Activity	Where	By Whom	When
Patented	Anywhere	Anyone	More than one
Printed publication	Anywhere	Anyone	year before the
Use	U.S.	Anyone	filing date of the
On sale	U.S.	Anyone	U.S. patent application

SECTION 102(g)

Activity	Where	By Whom	When
Made	U.S.	Others not concealing it	Before the date of invention

---

obtaining a patent if the claimed invention was in the hands of the U.S. public prior to the date of invention. Publicly available information that is printed is considered accessible in the United States, no matter where in the world it is published or in what form it is preserved. However, other demonstrations of public knowledge or use must be within the United States to bar the patent.

Looking solely at Section 102(a), our attempts to acquire a patent for certain aspects of the **Audio Enhancement System** should be unsuccessful if those aspects were previously described by another inventor in a technical journal or even in an obscure paper published in a small foreign nation. The only requirements are that the paper make the information accessible to interested members of the public and that it describe the invention in sufficient detail to enable one ordinarily skilled with the technology to duplicate it without further research or experimentation. An interesting question is whether a description found on the Internet would satisfy the requirement since it is not, strictly speaking, printed. However, this really should not matter. The courts for some time now have recognized that the word "printed" is merely a historic vestige and that its intent is to ensure that the information is in such a form that it is readily accessible to interested members of the public.[16] Based on this reasoning, the courts have interpreted the term "printed" liberally to account for modern storage and retrieval systems.[17] Thus, information stored on an Internet server likely would qualify as a printed publication.

The more difficult issues often are whether use or knowledge is publicly available in the United States. Suppose we claim a specific technique to convert analog signals to digital ones via a computer. Clearly, if another person had made a public demonstration at a convention illustrating how the invention works, then our claim should be barred. However, what if another company had used this process to accomplish tasks within its confines but had taken great lengths to maintain the secrecy of the process? If we later arrive at the same invention, should we be barred because of that previous secret use? What if that company used the process to improve recordings and then distributed the recordings to the public? Does that weaken our position? Or going to the other extreme, what if the company actually sells machines that employ the technology but does not otherwise disclose to the public how the machine operates?

To answer these questions, one must interpret Sections 102(a) and (g) in light of patent policy. Patents are designed to bring forth new knowledge so that it can be shared by the public at the end of the patent term. The issue of protection, therefore, devolves to how much the public knows and how much it is likely to find out if a patent is not granted. If someone already has made the invention, then it can be assumed that, in most instances, information about the invention will naturally spread to those in the public who have an interest in it. Thus, a patent normally is not required to inform the public of those inventions already in existence. However, if the invention were made by someone who does absolutely nothing with it or who actively takes steps to ensure that the public will not learn about it, then the presumption about eventual public disclosure is less compelling. This explains the language of Section 102(g) that forbids the patenting of an invention that was previously made by another who had not abandoned, suppressed, or concealed it. It also helps interpret what public knowledge or use under Section 102(a) entails. Use or knowledge is public, even without specific disclosure about the invention, if the public is likely to learn of the invention based on what is said or done. For example, if the public could study distributed products and thereby understand the invention in less than 20 years, then a patent would not be socially beneficial because the public would be able to share the invention earlier if left alone. Therefore, a patent should be denied in such circumstances. *Dunlop Holdings Limited v. Ram Golf Corporation* discusses these considerations about new inventions.

Dunlop Holdings Limited v. Ram Golf Corporation
Seventh Circuit Court of Appeals, 1975

FACTS: Dunlop received a patent for golf balls with covers made of certain synthetic materials, such as Surlyn. Ram produced and sold golf balls made of Surlyn, and Dunlop sued for patent infringement. Ram alleged that the invention was made and publicly used by a third party named Butch Wagner before Dunlop's date of invention, although Wagner had not disclosed his formula to the public. The trial court agreed and determined that the patent was invalid. Dunlop appealed.

DECISION AND REASONING: The patent covers the discovery that certain synthetic materials, when fabricated by themselves (or with minor amounts of compatible materials), produce a golf ball cover with exceptional cutting resistance. An example of the material described in the patent is Surlyn. The date of invention claimed by Dunlop is February 10, 1965.

In April 1964, Du Pont was trying to find a commercial use for its Surlyn, a recently developed product. Shortly thereafter, Butch Wagner, who was in the business of selling re-covered golf balls, began to experiment with Surlyn as a golf ball cover. He first made some sample balls by hand and then, using a one-iron, determined that the material was almost impossible to cut. He then made several dozen experimental balls, trying different combinations of additives to achieve the proper weight, the proper color, and a texture that could easily be released from an injection molding machine. By November 5, 1964, he had developed a formula he considered suitable for commercial production and had decided to sell Surlyn-covered balls in large quantities.

During the fall of 1964, Wagner provided friends and potential customers with Surlyn-covered golf balls. At least three golfers used these balls that fall for rounds of golf played at a country club in Los Angeles. By February 1965, Wagner had received orders for over 1,000 dozen Surlyn-covered balls, and by the end of 1965, he had ordered enough Surlyn to produce more than 900,000 such balls. Wagner died in October 1965.

Dunlop's patent claims are broad enough to encompass any golf ball cover made principally of Surlyn, and there is no doubt that Wagner had made a large number of such golf balls and successfully placed them in public use. The only novel feature of this case arises from the fact that Wagner was careful not to disclose to the public the ingredient that made his golf ball so tough. Dunlop presented evidence that an acknowledged expert on golf ball construction failed to discover the Surlyn content of the cover in an analysis of Wagner's ball. Dunlop also relies on the secretive manner in which Wagner gave the formula to his daughter "to keep in case something ever happens to me."

Dunlop relies on a case involving a patent on a machine that had previously been developed by a man named Haas. Haas had used the machine in his own factory under tight security. The output from the machine had been sold, but the public had not been given access to the machine itself. In holding that Haas had concealed the invention, Judge Hand drew a distinction

continued . . .

continued . . .

between the secret use of an invention and a noninforming public use. Haas had made only a secret use of his machine.

Wagner's situation involves neither abandonment nor a mere secret use. The evidence clearly demonstrates that Wagner endeavored to market his golf balls as promptly and effectively as possible. The balls themselves were in wide public use. Therefore, at best, the evidence establishes a noninforming public use of the subject matter of the invention.

If Wagner had applied for a patent more than a year after commencing the public distribution of Surlyn-covered golf balls, his application would have been barred notwithstanding the noninforming character of the public use or sale [this is provided by Section 102(b), which will be discussed later], for inventors must exercise reasonable diligence if they are to be rewarded with patent protection. Although Wagner may have failed to act diligently to establish his own right to a patent, there was no lack of diligence in his attempt to make the benefits of his discovery available to the public.

In view of his public use of the invention, we do not believe he concealed or suppressed the discovery, even though the use did not disclose the discovery. There are three reasons for this. First, a noninforming use, such as this, gives the public the benefit of the invention. If the new idea is permitted to have its impact in the marketplace, it surely has not been suppressed in an economic sense. Second, even though there may be no explicit disclosure of the inventive concept, when the article itself is freely accessible to the public at large, it is fair to presume that its secret will be uncovered by potential competitors long before the time when a patent would have expired if the inventor had made a timely application and disclosure to the PTO. Third, inventors are under no duty to apply for a patent; they are free to contribute ideas to the public, either voluntarily by an express disclosure—or involuntarily by a noninforming public use. In either case, although they may forfeit their entitlement to monopoly protection, it would be unjust to hold that such an election should impair their right to continue diligent efforts to market the product of their own invention.

We hold that the public use of Wagner's golf balls forecloses a finding of suppression or concealment. We therefore affirm the decision of the district court that Dunlop's patent is invalid.

The Issue of Secret Prior Uses   *Dunlop Holdings* alludes to some potential strategic dangers from relying too heavily on trade secret protection. After a reading of Chapter 4, it will be clear that there may be instances in which companies will decide to protect their technological investments by preserving their secrecy rather than by pursuing patent protection. Usually when this is done, the company believes that the greatest downside is that the secret may get out, at which time protection is lost. However, by keeping an invention secret, the company risks the possibility that another inventor will develop the invention on its own. If this inventor then files for a patent, the PTO may issue one given the lack of disclosure about the previous use. Although it may seem unfair, this patent then may effectively block the originating company from using what it discovered first, because its continued use would constitute patent infringement. The original company might be able to argue that its invention, although secret, was in public use. Clearly, from *Dunlop Holdings*, it will be better off if its secret is an aspect of distributed products rather than a process used only to manufacture them. In any event, Section 102 potentially raises the stakes for those who choose the trade secret route for protection.

The potential difficulties for trade secret holders motivated Congress in the late 1990s to consider amendments to the Patent Act that would provide some relief. The patent reform packages contained provisions intended to protect companies that previously had made secret commercial uses of inventions in the United States. The proposals did not prevent other companies from obtaining patents for technologies that secretly had been used before by others. The principles related in *Dunlop Holdings*, therefore, regarding public use and the novelty standard for obtaining a patent, remained intact. However, the reform proposals permitted prior users to have a defense against patent infringement claims.

The notion of prior user rights upsets many patent experts and inventors.[18] First, it runs counter to the disclosure principles of the patent laws by protecting those who attempt to maintain their inventions in secrecy. This defense might cause inventors who otherwise would seriously consider patent protection to feel more comfortable with preserving the secrecy of new technologies. This is because they know that they always will at least be able to use the invention without paying a royalty to another inventor. The notion of prior user rights also disturbs some individuals because it carves out an exception to the general rule that a patent provides *exclusive* rights by preventing *all* others from using an invention without permission. Some see such an exception as the tip of the iceberg; a first step on a road to eroding patent protection.

Even in light of these objections, Congress ultimately did add prior user rights to the Patent Act in 1999 as part of the American Inventors Protection Act. The law now provides that a company has a defense to the claim that it infringed a patent under the following circumstances:

1. The patent covers a method of doing business;
2. The company had developed the same method more than one year before the patent application was filed;[19] and
3. The company used the method before the patent application was filed.

This version considerably narrows the extent of the "prior use" defense, since it applies only to business methods, whereas previous proposals extended the defense to manufacturing processes as well. Thus Congress, for the most part, listened to those who objected to prior user rights. Nonetheless, it authorized prior user rights for business methods to address some potential problems that it feared might develop as a result of the Federal Circuit opinion in *State Street Bank & Trust Co. v. Signature Financial Group*, which clarified that business methods are patentable. The landmark *State Street* opinion is presented later in this chapter in the section dealing with patent issues for computer programs. For now, though, it is enough to say that prior to *State Street*, there were substantial doubts whether business methods were patentable. Therefore, many businesses may have tried to keep their business methods secret rather than file for patents. This secrecy, coupled with the decision in *State Street*, might now open the door for other companies to receive patents for the same business methods under the principles of *Dunlop Holdings*. The prior user defense therefore was preserved for business methods to address this possible "unfair" outcome.[20]

The Scope of Prior Art   When examining an invention for novelty under Section 102, the question is whether the previous public source of information completely embodies what the inventor claims for protection. Thus, a slight modification in what is claimed over the previous "art" releases one, strictly speaking, from the statutory bars of novelty. However, one must always be careful to read the novelty provisions of Section 102 with the demands of nonobviousness in Section 103. A good example is provided by the litigation over the patentability of PCR (polymerase chain reaction), a biotechnology process used to locate and regenerate strands of DNA (deoxyribonucleic acid). Cetus Corporation obtained several patents covering the process of PCR in the mid-1980s. When Cetus refused to license the technology to Du Pont, Du Pont challenged the validity of the patents. Du Pont's primary basis for asking the court to strip patent protection was that the invention was predated by both an article published in the *Journal of Molecular Biology* in 1971 and a subsequent report publicly released by the same authors in 1974. Although the PCR process was not exactly that described in these papers, Du Pont argued that it was obvious in light of them.[21]

The Search for Prior Art   The possibility of such challenges, especially with lucrative inventions such as PCR, highlights the potential risks of patent protection. Competitors who wish to use the process will have a tremendous incentive to search aggressively around the globe for information that "anticipates" the prized patented claims. If something is found, as was the case with PCR, then the company owning the patent will face expensive litigation and possibly loss of its patent privilege. The risks will only increase with widespread adoption of the Internet. For instance, Wang Global Inc. claimed in 1997 that Netscape's use of its animated meteor shower violated one of Wang's patents.[22] In response, Netscape posted on its Web site an appeal for evidence of prior art that might be used to defeat the patent. It was reported that within three days, Netscape had received nearly 200 leads. Such developments in information technologies make it increasingly imperative for inventors to diligently perform a patent search prior to obtaining a patent. Otherwise, the PTO, with its somewhat more limited resources, may miss a pertinent piece of prior art, thereby exposing an issued patent to risk of loss.

The Date of Invention   The issue of whether an invention is new raises one final question. You probably have been wondering what date constitutes the date of invention. After all, one does not invent at a particular instance of time. Rather, invention normally is a continuous process beginning with conception of the idea, which leads to drawings, then possibly to models, and through other steps until finally it is reduced to a working prototype. According to Section 102(g), which we will soon look at more closely, the date of invention for patent purposes is the date of conception, as long as the subsequent steps are carried out diligently. Otherwise, the date of invention will be later—either when the invention is reduced to practice or when the patent application is filed.

When dealing with the patent office, or when faced with litigation questioning a patent's validity, determination of the exact date of invention may be crucial. For instance, what if you conceived of **AES** in March 1993 but did not reduce it to practice until April 1997? In the interim, an article describing the technique was published—let's say, on June 14, 1996. The public release of this article will serve to bar your ability to patent **AES** unless you can prove that your conception of the idea for **AES** predated the release and that you diligently put the idea into practice with reasonable and continuous efforts. The importance of such proof means that inventors must clearly document through lab notebooks—or otherwise—all progress made on development of an idea. It also raises a host of uncertainties about patent validity and priority between simultaneous inventors. These issues, which are most troublesome in the context of Section 102(g), explain why other countries reject the first-to-invent standard and rather employ a system based on the filing date, something that is easy to define and prove. These frustrations with the system also may reinforce the willingness of the United States to abandon it in the context of a comprehensive international patent treaty.

Was the Patent Application Filed in Time?

The One-Year Rule

Section 102(b) encourages rapid filings by inventors interested in patent protection. On the one hand, it serves as a wake-up call for an inventor when others enter the field. This is especially true for those inventors who ploddingly develop their ideas and/or who regard patent filing with a lax attitude. The section accomplishes its intended result by giving inventors one year to file their patent applications once other inventors make knowledge of the invention public through performing one of the listed activities in the requisite location (see Exhibit 2.3).

So, consider again the example wherein you conceived of **AES** first and worked on it diligently to reduce it to practice by April 1997. The June 14, 1996, publication of the article describing the invention means that you have to turn on the burners somewhat to complete and file a patent application. If you have not done so before June 14, 1997, you will be barred from receiving a patent. This is true regardless of your ability to prove that you were the first inventor to conceive of **AES** and that you diligently reduced it to practice.

Frequently, the most unrecognized aspect of Section 102(b) is that it also establishes a one-year filing deadline when the inventor discloses the information. This comes especially as a surprise to unsuspecting entrepreneurs who unwittingly learn when discussing the prospects for patent protection with an attorney that they have already blown their chances through their own activities. For instance, engineers who publish articles in academic journals describing recent experiments may be surprised to find that the article will prevent them from getting a patent if they do not file the patent application within one year after publication. Most alarming to uninformed businesspersons, however, is the requirement that they file patent applications within one year of the first public use or sale of their inventions in the United States. These considerations are most insidious because of the wide latitude courts have taken in defining what constitutes a "public use" and a "sale."

Experimental Use When a business is in the process of finalizing a new invention, there ordinarily is a lot of excitement and energy devoted to determining whether the invention works as anticipated, whether customers will want it, how much they will pay, and what aspects they prefer. There also is some degree of urgency to beat competitors to the punch by announcing and demonstrating the invention as early as possible. Thus, when a prototype of **AES** is completed, you probably will send it to an independent lab so that it can conduct a variety of experiments to test its operational characteristics. As part of the testing procedures, the lab may invite a number of typical potential customers to use the machine, possibly in their home, so that certain functional characteristics can be judged in a standard environment. After the bugs in the functional elements have been ironed out, you then may engage a marketing consultant to help determine pricing policies, customer acceptance levels, media techniques, and other strategies to help move the product. As part of this effort, demonstrations may be made at important audio products trade shows to arouse interest and to test potential demand.

Obviously, much of this activity involves a use of the product in a public environment. But a lot of it is not so much to use the invention as to determine what final form it should take when it ultimately is released for use by the public. According to the courts, an inventor, or another person under the inventor's direction, does not make a public use of an invention when the use is made for *experimental purposes* to bring the invention to perfection. In general terms, a use is experimental when the inventor engages in controlled studies of the invention in private so that the invention may be perfected. Courts look at the totality of the circumstances to determine if a use is experimental, but they have found a number of indicia to be useful, such as:

1. the number of prototypes that are tested;
2. the duration of testing;

3. the existence of a secrecy agreement between the inventor and the party performing the testing;
4. whether the inventor received compensation for use of the invention; and
5. the extent of control the inventor maintained over the testing.

Lough v. Brunswick Corporation[23] provides an excellent illustration of how the courts apply these factors to judge if a use is experimental. Steven Lough invented a seal assembly for inboard/outboard motors to prevent corrosion. Lough made six prototypes of the assembly in the spring of 1986. The first prototype was used in his own boat. Three months later, he provided the other prototypes to acquaintances who worked at boat dealerships and marinas to see if the seal assembly worked as well in their boats as it had in his. Lough did not charge anyone for the use of the assemblies, nor did he try to sell the seal assemblies during the period. However, he did not ask for any comments about the operability of the prototypes. In addition, one of the prototypes was lost after the boat in which it was installed was sold.

Lough filed for a patent on June 6, 1988, and the patent issued on July 18, 1989. Brunswick then designed its own improved seal assembly, which Lough alleged infringed his patent. Brunswick asked the court to invalidate the patent on the grounds that the invention was in public use more than one year before Lough filed his patent application (that is, the invention was in public use before June 6, 1987). The lower court determined that the patent was valid and awarded Lough $1.5 million.

The Federal Circuit reversed and vacated the monetary award, ruling that Lough's use before June 6, 1987, was not experimental, but rather was a public use. The court acknowledged that Lough had not commercialized the seal assembly during this time, since he neither received compensation nor tried to sell it. Also, Lough testified that his intent was to distribute the prototypes for experimental reasons. In addition, the public could not see the components because of the way they were installed in the boats. Nevertheless, the Federal Circuit was not persuaded. The court ruled that subjective intent does not carry much weight. Also, the visibility of components is not determinative when they are housed in products that are in public use. Of most importance, though, was the fact that Lough did not maintain sufficient supervision and control over the assembly during the alleged testing. Lough kept no records nor did he inspect the seal assemblies after they were installed. Thus, there was insufficient follow-up during the period for him to assess the success of the so-called experiment. Also, the loss of one of the assemblies demonstrated that he did not maintain the requisite level of supervision and control.

When considering whether any of the **AES** activities constitute a public use, one needs to consider (1) whether the individuals involved are under duties to maintain secrecy, (2) whether the testing is performed to improve the operation of the invention, and (3) whether there is sufficient supervision over the testing. Secrecy normally is not an issue when employees use the product because their position implies a duty to maintain the secrecy of new product developments. In addition, all employees usually sign express contractual agreements promising to maintain the confidentiality of new inventions. Similarly, any outsiders retained to test the product should sign agreements to maintain confidentiality.

Assuming we use confidentiality agreements and appropriate experimental procedures, many of the contemplated **AES** activities should qualify as uses that are not public. This is because they are intended to perfect the invention, such as with beta testing. However, the customer acceptance tests and pricing experiments are designed not so much to improve the invention as to answer marketing questions. Thus, they would be public uses of the invention and would initiate the one-year filing period. Also, the trade show demonstration clearly would be a public use.

Public Use by the Applicant   "Public use" has a broader reach when applied to activities of the applicant rather than the knowledge of third parties. What this means is that a use of an invention by the applicant can be public even if third parties could not figure out how the invention operates. For instance, a secret use of a process or machine to make goods that are then publicly distributed would trigger the one-year filing requirement for the applicant under Section 102(b). However, as we know, this would not be the sort of public use to bar the ability of others to obtain a patent. In this regard, the American Inventors Protection Act provides some protection to those making a secret use of a business method. Although the act does not prevent others from receiving a patent on the secret business method, the prior user has a defense to a patent infringement claim.

What Constitutes a Sale?   The term "sale" also has been given widespread effect. It does not take a completed sales transaction of an invention to start the one-year filing period. The time that the invention is first offered for sale qualifies, even if that offer ultimately is rejected. Nor does the invention have to be physically completed at the time of the "sale." Rather, the invention must only be ready for patenting—meaning that the inventor has described the invention in sufficient detail to enable one skilled in the art to make it.

For example, the Supreme Court determined in *Pfaff v. Wells*[24] that a company that only had completed detailed engineering drawings of a new product made a "sale" when it accepted a purchase order, even though the product had not yet been manufactured. This ruling was devastating for the company, since it filed its patent application less than one year after it shipped the product, but more than one year after the date it signed the purchase order. Clearly, inventors need to begin thinking about patent protection as soon as they engage in any efforts to sell their innovations.

(AES)   If you dealt with **AES** in an unsophisticated fashion and only considered the possibility of patent protection more than one year after making a public use or sale, you probably would experience deep feelings of resentment. Here is another technical rule to trip up the small businessperson! However, from an international perspective, the one-year grace period can seem extremely generous. This is because many countries are more stringent, demanding absolute novelty before a filing. To be eligible for patent protection in these countries, there can be no public use or sale of the invention at any time prior to filing. The one-year period in the United States, assuming one is aware of it, allows inventors to engage in various forms of commercial tests for up to a year before determining if it is worth investing their time and money in patent protection. In several other countries, the decision has to be made before one objectively tests commercial viability. And for some, testing or sales anywhere in the world, not simply within national boundaries, negate the possibility for patent protection. So, given that your vision for **AES** reaches international dimensions, you must thoughtfully consider the countries in which you ultimately might need protection and the requirements of those countries' laws before you engage in any commercial activity putting **AES** in public use or on sale. Ways to simplify the task of preserving overseas rights so that marketing activities can begin as expeditiously as possible will be discussed in Chapter 3. Also, it should be noted that U.S. representatives involved with negotiating a patent harmonization treaty within WIPO have strongly urged that any agreement include a unified novelty standard permitting a one-year grace period before filing.

Who Gets the Patent When There Are Multiple Inventors?

The U.S. First-to-Invent Standard

Section 102(g) states that an inventor is entitled to a patent unless the invention was made first by another person who has not abandoned, suppressed, or concealed it. This establishes the first-to-invent principle in the United States, a standard that is virtually unique in the international community. Nearly all other countries rely on a much simpler formula: the first inventor to file a patent application gets priority. As noted previously, the United States may someday give up its isolating adherence to the first-to-invent scheme, most likely as part of an international agreement providing for elevated substantive patent principles worldwide.

Determining the First Inventor   According to Section 102(g), the determination of the first inventor is based on the dates of conception and reduction to practice. An inventor who conceives the invention at the earliest time is the first inventor if that inventor also reduces it to practice first. The more difficult scenario arises when one inventor conceives the invention first but reduces it to practice subsequent to another. Again, the inventor who conceives the invention at the earliest time is the first inventor, but in this case only as long as the inventor was reasonably diligent in reducing it to practice beginning from a time just prior to the other inventor's conception. Exhibit 2.4 illustrates the pertinent aspects of this analysis. Of course, all of this opens the door to a lot of questions: (1) What is conception? (2) What is reduction to practice? (3) What is reasonable diligence? and (4) How does one prove the timing and existence of each?

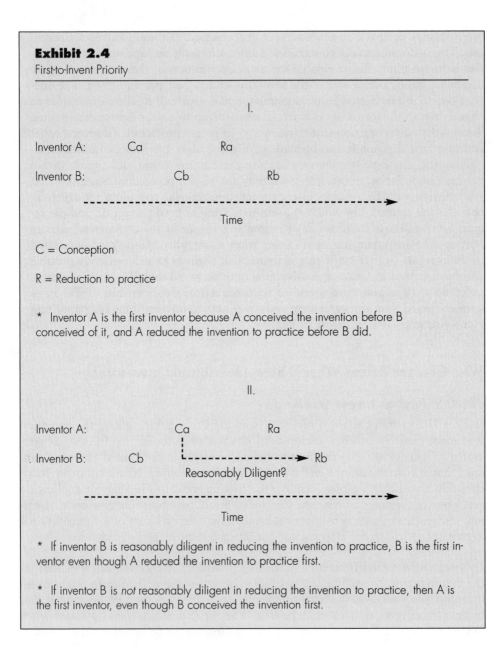

Exhibit 2.4

First-to-Invent Priority

I.

Inventor A: Ca   Ra

Inventor B: Cb   Rb

                    Time

C = Conception

R = Reduction to practice

* Inventor A is the first inventor because A conceived the invention before B conceived of it, and A reduced the invention to practice before B did.

II.

Inventor A: Ca   Ra

Inventor B: Cb   ⌐------------→ Rb
                              Reasonably Diligent?

                    Time

* If inventor B is reasonably diligent in reducing the invention to practice, B is the first inventor even though A reduced the invention to practice first.

* If inventor B is *not* reasonably diligent in reducing the invention to practice, then A is the first inventor, even though B conceived the invention first.

One of the difficult aspects of the first-to-invent standard is the ill-defined nature of the important determinants for priority. The time of conception, for instance, is a nebulous but obviously critical juncture. Clearly, conception is a mental criterion. However, it is not simply the first time the idea for the invention arises. Rather, conception does not occur until the details of the invention are sufficiently advanced so that a person of ordinary skill could make it operational without exercising any further inventive creativity.

Conception, by itself, is not enough to "make" an invention. What normally follow are continuous and deliberate steps to reduce an idea to practice by completing a working finished product, such as a functional prototype or a useful composition. An invention does not have to be in its commercially optimal form for it to be judged reduced to practice. All that is necessary is that it work as expected. Thus, after an invention's reduction to practice, one may still make changes to improve production techniques or to increase customer acceptability.

The Patent Act establishes another way to reduce an invention to practice. One may constructively reduce an invention to practice by filing a patent application that discloses the invention sufficiently to meet the enabling requirements of the statute. These will be discussed in Chapter 3, but essentially the application must describe the invention in enough detail so that a person of ordinary skill could reduce it to practice without undue experimentation. Once again, we see the disclosure rationale at work here, encouraging inventors to file as quickly as possible after conception. This also raises a procedural point about rapid disclosure. Because filing equates with reduction to practice, inventors who file first have a leg up on proving who was first to make an invention. This is because without more evidence, first filers have proven that they completed the invention, albeit constructively, prior to those who later file applications. Subsequent filers therefore will have the burden of demonstrating earlier conception dates and reasonable diligence in reducing to practice.

Reasonable diligence is a very subjective standard, depending considerably on the personal situation of the inventor. The determination often comes down to whether the inventor had the time and financial means to proceed more quickly but chose not to do so. In addition, activity to reduce to practice is more likely to be viewed as reasonably diligent if it is deliberate and continuous.

Proving the Date of Invention   Because patent priority in the United States is held by the first inventor, it is extremely important for a person who desires a patent to have sufficient evidence to prove the date of conception, the date of reduction to practice, and the reasonable diligence used in the effort. Oral testimony by the applicant is not very persuasive in this context. Rather, corroboration through physical evidence and the testimony of disinterested third parties is usually needed. Thus, inventors are well advised to consider techniques that document on a routine basis their efforts to conceive an invention and reduce it to practice. The use of bound and consecutively numbered lab manuals wherein the inventor routinely records and dates inventive activity is very persuasive in the demonstration of key times and reasonable diligence. In addition, having witnesses attest to the documentation and dates presented within the lab book can help eliminate such allegations as that the book was contrived after the fact and backdated.[25]

An interesting example of first-to-invent principles comes from the biotechnology field. In 1996, the PTO granted two patents to Mycogen Plant Science, Inc. for certain specific contributions it had made within the burgeoning new field of using gene-splicing technologies to create pest-resistant plants. The day that the PTO issued the patents, Mycogen sued Monsanto and other major companies, contending that they were making and selling seeds for Bt (Bacillus thuringiensis) pest resistance that infringed the Mycogen patents. Since Bt-resistant seeds are enormously important to agricultural interests, particularly corn growers, patent rights have the potential to be extremely lucrative. Mycogen sued for $70 million in damages and requested an injunction, which would have prevented the other companies from selling any more seed that infringed the patents. Monsanto argued that the patents were invalid because it was the first to invent the technology. In court, Monsanto's witnesses detailed the development of the company's own Bt research efforts, using internal documents and notebooks to illustrate every step of its creative process. According to Monsanto's counsel, the evidence proved that Monsanto conceived of the process first and made it work first.[26] The jury agreed, since it concluded in 1998 that the patents were invalid and that Monsanto therefore was not liable for infringement.[27]

Will the U.S. Adopt a First-to-File System?   That the U.S. patent system rests on the first-to-invent standard has two important drawbacks. First, the system has the tendency to increase litigation expenses, because it raises a host of uncertainties.[28] Under the first-to-file standard, it is easy to determine priority. Also, an inventor who relies on the first-to-invent system to gain priority over those who file more quickly may succeed in the United States but may lose patent rights in almost all other countries in the process. Thus, once again, reliance on U.S. patent law may be commercially hazardous to those with an international vision. On the other hand, the first-to-invent policy does have an underlying sense of fairness to it. The inventor should be rewarded for creative actions and not for technical steps such as filing patent applications. Such a principle applies especially to the small inventor, who often is not fully cognizant of patent requirements until it is time to commercialize the invention. In addition, small inventors are the ones that are most likely to want extra time before deciding if an invention is worth the expense of hiring an attorney and filing a patent application.[29] And as we know, motivating the entrepreneurial spirit of the small businessperson continues to be an important philosophical norm guiding U.S. policy. Advocates of the first-to-invent standard also point out that the system has worked remarkably well in the United States for over 200 years and that it would be a mistake to tinker with success. Finally, supporters argue that establishing a race to the patent office may lead inventors, in their haste, to resort more often to crash development programs and to file less thoughtful patent applications.

Those who advocate that the U.S. change to a first-to-file patent system are not impressed with these arguments, however. They contend that when there is dispute between patent applicants regarding who was first to invent, the applicant who filed the patent application first wins nearly 95% of the time. Thus, the first-to-invent system causes substantial headaches for everyone—by creating uncertainties, inhibiting efforts to achieve international uniformity, and raising litigation expenses—but in the end changes the outcome only in a very few instances.

Thus, they feel that the overall negatives of the first-to-invent system outweigh its benefits.

Recently adopted global and regional trade accords have raised expected levels of patent protection around the world. TRIPs, for instance, ensures that most major commercial trading partners will provide patent protection to a broad range of technologies for a minimum of 20 years after the filing date. We will see in Chapter 3, though, that there still are many differences in international approaches to patent protection. Prior to the signing of the GATT agreements, including TRIPs, the United States was close to signing an international patent harmonization treaty which, among many other things, provided that the first person to file a patent application would be entitled to priority. Those efforts were derailed, and the world now awaits their resurrection. The question is how much motivation the U.S. now has to change its priority system since it gained several of the items it wanted with TRIPs. The first-to-invent system is fundamental to the U.S. patent system, and the U.S. likely will use it as major bargaining chip to gain concessions from other nations. However, the most important concessions may already have been made, and others may not seem sufficient to those who wish to retain the first-to-invent system. On the other hand, major U.S. multinational corporations that are forced to deal with the first-to-file system around the world may lead a domestic effort to adopt the international standard, even without substantial foreign concessions. The only thing that is clear, therefore is that this will be an interesting public policy forum to watch.

NONOBVIOUSNESS

For an invention to be patentable, not only must it meet the standards of novelty under Section 102, but also it must be nonobvious, as defined in Section 103. Section 103 provides:

> A patent may not be obtained though the invention is not identically disclosed or described as set forth in Section 102 of this title, if the differences between the subject matter sought to be patented and the prior art are such that the subject matter as a whole would have been obvious at the time the invention was made to a person having ordinary skill in the art to which said subject matter pertains.

That an invention must be something more than new in order to merit a patent demonstrates the basic antipathy toward the monopoly attributes of a patent. The thoughts of Thomas Jefferson, who served on the first patent commission in the United States, are instructive on deciphering the rationales for the nonobvious requirement. According to Jefferson, a key issue in determining patentability is "drawing a line between the things which are worth the public embarrassment of an exclusive patent, and those which are not.[30] Jefferson did not believe that patents should be granted for small details, obvious improvements, or frivolous devices. Thus, there had to be some decisional means for weeding out those inventions that would not be disclosed or devised but for the inducement of a patent. The condition that an invention be nonobvious is supposed to satisfy those additional concerns.

In contrast to the novelty concept, with its somewhat precise definitions of predisclosure and timing, the nonobviousness requirement is extremely nebulous. The Supreme Court has articulated the thinking process one should follow in reaching a determination about obviousness. However, in reality, its procedure adds little in the way of comfort to those who want greater predictability about the implementation of this standard. In *Graham v. John Deere*, the Supreme Court interpreted Section 103 as requiring that the obviousness or nonobviousness of a particular subject be determined in light of a three-part analysis:

1. The scope and content of the prior art are to be determined;
2. Differences between the prior art and the claim at issue are to be ascertained; and
3. The level of ordinary skill in the pertinent art is to be resolved.

The Supreme Court added that there might also be "secondary considerations," which may serve as relevant indicia to substantiate a determination of nonobviousness, such as commercial success, long felt but unresolved needs, and failure of others.

In terms of predictability, none of this is too helpful for the makers of an invention, such as **AES**. AES is certainly novel, in that no one has written about or made the invention before. And it nicely solves certain problems that audiophiles have with listening to their old records. However, it is hardly an earth-shattering work of extraordinary genius. Rather, the inventors logically integrated a variety of technologies used in different contexts with some personal adaptive measures to produce a machine capable of providing compact-disc-quality sound. Is this enough to be nonobvious? How big do the differences with the prior art have to be? What if all the elements of the invention already existed in the prior art but they were scattered in different contexts? How much skill is ordinary skill? As the Supreme Court indicated, "What is obvious is not a question upon which there is likely to be uniformity of thought in every factual context." So, how does one even begin to approach this standard?

In reality, one can only pull together the factors that shed light on the question of obviousness. For instance, that the invention merely combines concepts, inventions, and principles that were known before does not make for a great start. However, the statute is clear that the invention must be considered as a whole and not element by element in isolation. If there was in the prior art documentation that suggested that the elements might be combined to make an audio enhancement product, this would suggest obviousness. On the other hand, maybe the prior art indicates that audio improvement cannot be achieved with the various technologies. Or possibly the prior art alludes to audio improvement but does not

---

Exhibit 2.5
Nonobviousness

Nonobviousness determined in light of:

- Scope and content of prior art
- Differences between prior art and claims at issue
- Level of ordinary skill in pertinent art

Reference point for nonobviousness is the time the invention is made.

- Problem of hindsight

Aspects that may be persuasive in finding nonobviousness:

- The invention causes disproportionate, unexpected, surprising, or unusual results.
- The prior art relates to an entirely different field.
- There is no suggestion in the prior art to combine the references to achieve the invention.
- Secondary considerations—objective factors
  - Long-standing problem or need in the field solved or satisfied by the invention
  - Failure of others to solve the problem
  - Invention copied by others
  - Infringer's abandonment of prior art machines in favor of patented machine
  - Commercial success

---

contemplate the degree of clarity achieved. Demonstrations of unexpected, unusual, or synergistic results are strong evidence of nonobviousness, although they are not necessarily required.

The statute provides that the point of reference is one ordinarily skilled in the art at the time of making the invention. One trap to which the PTO and judges easily fall victim is the so-called problem of hindsight. In this phenomenon, what appears to be difficult may seem easy and obvious once one knows how to do it. In other words, whoever is deciding the question of obviousness has to be careful not to use the invention against the inventor. Rather, one must forget the solution taught by the inventor and step back to a time before that solution was devised. However, advanced knowledge invariably taints one's perception, and the apparent simplicity of a solution, once learned, may be difficult to ignore.

Often, the best evidence that an inventor will have in order to demonstrate nonobviousness is more objective. Normally, the argument follows the logic of "If this invention is so obvious, then why has X occurred?" For instance, why is this invention selling like gangbusters if it had been so obvious? Of course, it could be because the price is so low, or because of a marketing campaign, but clearly commercial success may be relevant to the value society places on the invention. Or, one might ask how an invention can be perceived as obvious when others in the field had tried to solve the problem but had not reached the inventor's solution. Or, one might inquire why competitors immediately abandoned old technology in favor of the inventor's solution if the new approach were so obvious. These are the factors the Supreme Court called secondary considerations, but often they are the best definitive indicator one has on the issue of nonobviousness. Indeed, the Federal Circuit has embraced the evidentiary importance of these factors. It has done so, first, symbolically by designating them objective factors rather than secondary considerations, thereby placing them on the same plane of importance as the three basic criteria. It has also done so explicitly, both by claiming that such objective factors may constitute the most pertinent, probative, and revealing evidence available to aid the obviousness decision and by requiring them to be considered whenever such evidence is available.[31] Exhibit 2.5, on the previous page, depicts the basic concepts underlying the nonobviousness inquiry.

The review for nonobviousness is a fact-dependent exercise that cannot adequately be appreciated with a simple set of rules or guideposts. *Panduit Corporation v. Dennison Manufacturing* is an important Federal Circuit court opinion that demonstrates the many variables that may bear on the obviousness question and how this key court handled those variables in one particular fact context.

PANDUIT CORPORATION V. DENNISON MANUFACTURING
Federal Circuit Court of Appeals, 1985, 1987[32]

FACTS: Jack Caveney, the founder of Panduit, began a research program in 1961 to develop a one-piece plastic cable tie to be used to bind a bundle of cables or insulated wires. That program lasted nine years and cost several million dollars. Caveney received three patents: the '146 patent (filed in 1968, issued in 1970), the '869 patent (filed in 1969, issued in 1972), and the '538 patent (filed in 1969, issued in 1976), which represents the culmination of his work.

One-piece cable ties have a strap that wraps around a bundle, with one end of the strap passing through an opening in a frame in the other end. Teeth on the strap engage with a locking device on the frame. Optimally, the tie would be easy to engage but difficult to withdraw. However, before Caveney's tie, those ties that took little force to engage also had undesired low withdrawal forces and those that provided high withdrawal forces required a high insertion force. Caveney was first to make a cable that was easy to insert and difficult to withdraw, requiring only a ½-pound insertion force but yielding a withdrawal force of 80 pounds. First sold in 1970, the cable tie achieved annual sales of $50 million by 1984.

Dennison Manufacturing began working on a one-piece cable tie develop-ment program in 1968. This project lasted for ten years at great expense but with no success. Dennison copied the '869 patent in 1976, and soon there-after the '538 patent when it issued. It failed to succeed with its own re-search, but it became the second-largest supplier of one-piece cable ties with its copy of the '538 tie.

Panduit sued, alleging infringement of all three patents. The district court held that the three patents were invalid on the grounds of obviousness. Pan-duit relied heavily on the fact that the prior art did not show any inventions even close to those claimed in its patents. However, the district court stated that Panduit had given insufficient attention to what is taught by general prin-ciples of engineering and physics and by the common experience of mankind.

The district court found the '146 patent to be obvious in light of both a previously patented tie system that used one tooth, and two other references, which disclosed the use of multiple teeth. The court concluded that multiple teeth represented an obvious solution to the disengagement problem of the one-tooth system and that any intelligent reader of that patent would have placed the teeth as did Caveney.

The '869 patent improved compression by changing the orientation of the locking mechanism within the frame and using a ledge to absorb compressive force. The district court cited three references showing a ledge to absorb compressive forces and thus found the invention obvious, indicating that the result achieved was altogether expected.

The '538 patent addressed a problem with the '869 tie—that the teeth tended to break off because of insufficient flexibility. The district court found that the only difference over the '869 patent was the use of a "discrete hinge"—something that was shown in the '146 patent, albeit in a different way, and in four other patents.

Panduit appealed the district court's determinations of invalidity.

DECISION AND REASONING: En route to its decision on obviousness, the dis-trict court made several errors:

1. It employed the benefit of hindsight.
2. It misinterpreted the claimed inventions.
3. It misevaluated the prior art.
4. It misconstrued its role.
5. It applied an improper and impossible standard of obviousness.
6. It gave too little weight to the objective evidence of nonobviousness and the real world story reflected in that evidence.

1. Hindsight. The present record reflects the insidious and powerful phenom-enon known in patent law as the use of hindsight. The test is whether the

continued . . .

continued . . .

subject matter of the claimed inventions would have been obvious to one skilled in the art at the time the inventions were made—not what would be obvious to a judge after reading the patents in suit and hearing the testimony. In this regard, the decision maker confronts a ghost, that is, "a person having ordinary skill in the art," not unlike the "reasonable man" and other ghosts in the law. To reach a proper conclusion under Section 103, the decision maker must step backward in time and into shoes worn by that "person" when the invention was unknown and just before it was made. However, the record compels the conclusion that the district court, having heard many days of testimony from the inventor Caveney, was unable to cast its mind back to the time the invention was made. Instead, the court consulted the knowledge taught by the inventor in his patents and in his testimony, and then it used that knowledge against its teacher.

2. Misinterpretation of the Claimed Inventions. The statute requires that the subject matter of the claimed invention be considered "as a whole." Dissecting claims into individual elements to determine the obviousness of each element in isolation is improper. In the present case, the district court interpreted the claims of the '146 patent as though they were drawn to "multiple teeth," those of the '896 patent as though they were drawn to a "ledge," and those of the '538 patent as though they were drawn to a "hinge." But validity is to be determined on the basis of the claimed subject matter as a whole, not in respect of a single element.

Dennison argued that if the court upheld Panduit's patents, it would be telling the entire industry that you can't have more than one tooth, you can't have a ledge in the frame, and you can't use a hinge inside the frame. This is not true. Upholding the patents in suit will not preclude any worker in the art from employing multiple teeth, ledges, and hinges in whatever combinations the worker may desire, so long as those combinations are distinct from those claimed in the present patents. The sole effect of the grant to Caveney of the property right to exclude others for a limited time from unauthorized use of his inventions is to require that others avoid the claimed structure newly disclosed to the public in the patent documents.

3. Misevaluation of the Prior Art. The well-established rules of law are that each prior art reference must be evaluated as an entirety and that all of the prior art must be evaluated as a whole. Inventions have often been held to have been obvious when no single reference disclosed the claimed invention. That result was compelled because the art as a whole in those cases suggested the combination claimed. At the same time, inventions have been held to have been nonobvious when neither any reference, considered in its entirety, nor the prior art as a whole suggested the combination claimed. Nowhere did the district court indicate where in the prior art there might be a suggestion for combining the teachings of individual references. Rather, it speculated on a "problem" of how prior art devices might be reconstructed to match the claimed structure, with the benefit of hindsight aided by the inventor's engineering testimony about the inventions in suit.

Virtually all inventions are necessarily combinations of old elements. The notion that combination claims can be declared invalid merely upon finding similar elements in separate prior patents would necessarily destroy virtually all patents and cannot be the law under Section 103. Indeed, that the elements noted by the court lay about in the prior art, available for years to all skilled workers without suggesting anything like the claimed inventions, is itself evidence of nonobviousness.

The district court made a fundamental error by refusing to credit the real-world environment surrounding the inventions disclosed in the references and in the patents in suit. The court paid no attention to insertion and withdrawal forces in the reference structures or to the striking differences in the references, treating them as equivalents of each other. The court specifically stated, "I don't need to know all the details about how all these other things work or don't work." But "how things work" is critical to encouragement of every research and development activity and to every advancement of the useful arts.

It was precisely "how things work" that made the prior-art cable ties failures and the cable tie of the patent in suit the most successful in the history of the industry. It was "how things work" that caused Dennison's ten-year development to fail and led Dennison to copy the tie of the patents in suit. It was "how things work" that enabled Caveney alone to achieve a ½- to 80-pound ratio between insertion and withdrawal forces. And it was a refusal to consider "how things work" that caused the court to cite isolated minutiae from various references while ignoring critically important structural distinctions that significantly affect the different achievements of which the reference and claimed structures are capable.

The record is compelling that the inventing of cable ties is not a simple matter. Panduit invested nine years and several million dollars before achieving success. Dennison tried for ten years and failed. Indeed, it was only the district court who believed that cable tie inventing was a simple, obvious, routine matter of finding elements in the prior art and modifying them in accord with "principles of physics" and "common experience." To reach that belief, the court had to ignore what workers of ordinary skill actually did in the real world with that same experience over the years.

4. Misconstruence of the Role of the Court. Courts are not bound by the decisions of the PTO. However, the statute mandates a presumption of

continued . . .

continued . . .

validity, and it places the burden of proving facts compelling a conclusion of patent invalidity on the party asserting invalidity. This court has said the burden of proving facts compelling a conclusion of invalidity must be carried by clear and convincing evidence. Though the district court referred to the presumption of validity, mere lip service is insufficient.

The district court said it had been "going back and forth" on the questions of obviousness. It said that there was room for difference of opinion based on the overwhelming record of objective evidence. The court said it was not easy to reach its obviousness conclusion because the patent was an excellent and preeminent commercial product. Such uncertainty should have ended the obviousness inquiry in favor of the patentee.

5. **Improper and Impossible Standards:**
   a. *General Principles and Common Experience.* The district court in reaching its obviousness conclusion relied heavily on what it thought was taught by general engineering principles, general principles of physics, and the common experience of mankind. It cannot be the law that the only inventions patentable are those that cannot be explained by any known principles of engineering and physics. Whatever the unidentified principles of engineering and physics the court intended, and whatever the nondescribed common experience of mankind the court had in mind, those principles and that experience were fully available to all who tried and failed before Caveney succeeded. They cannot serve as a basis for holding that the claimed inventions in suit would have been obvious under Section 103.
   b. *Unexpected Results.* The district court, in finding the cable tie obvious, stated that Caveney's invention produced no "unexpected result." The Federal Circuit has specifically pointed out that, whereas an "unexpected result," like "synergism," may be evidence of nonobviousness, it is not a requirement. Moreover, if there were a requirement for an "unexpected result," then that requirement would have been fully met here. That the achievement of a ½- to 80-pound ratio between insertion and withdrawal force was unexpected is fully reflected in the totality of the evidence.

6. **Objective Evidence.** That respect is required for the effect to be given objective evidence of nonobviousness, when the evidence is present, has been stated by the Federal Circuit.

The cable tie of the patents in suit was an outstanding commercial success, selling at $50 million a year by 1984 and becoming, early on, the unquestioned leading tie on the market. The district court did not explain why, if

Caveney's superior cable tie had been so obvious, the many inventors who preceded Caveney had not found it so. It is extremely difficult to believe that Panduit and Dennison would have invested years and millions of dollars in an effort to achieve what had been obvious all along to all those with ordinary skill in the art. Dennison's conjectural argument that Panduit's success with the ties is due to other factors besides the invention is refuted by its own handsome success with its copied product.

That many others, including Dennison, had tried for years and failed to create a superior cable tie is virtually irrefutable evidence that the superior tie of the patents in suit would not have been obvious to those skilled in the art when it was invented.

That earlier workers were, as the district court said, "going in different ways" is strong evidence that inventor Caveney's way would not have been obvious.

That Dennison, a large corporation with many engineers on its staff, did not copy any prior art device but found it necessary to copy the cable tie of the claims in suit is equally strong evidence of nonobviousness.

Dennison's suggestion that Panduit's success is due to unclaimed features, its advertising, or sales staff is either unsupported or contradicted in the evidence.

For all of these reasons, the district court was clearly erroneous in its conclusion on obviousness, and its judgment is reversed.

There are mnay lessons from *Panduit*, all of them encouraging to the prospective inventor. Obviousness should not be an impossible hurdle. The PTO and the courts are instructed to be careful with the use of hindsight; what may seem obvious today may have been hard to fathom when the inventive activity occurred. Also, an invention is not obvious simply because it builds on old technologies and employs natural laws of physics. Rather, the inventive enterprise must be reviewed as a whole to judge whether there is a nonobvious result. In addition, the Federal Circuit clearly was impressed by the real-world story. Objective factors that demonstrate that an invention was not obvious now may be a decisive factor in one's favor. Finally, once a patent is received, the patentee can take solace in the due respect that the Federal Circuit now requires the courts to give to the PTO's decision to award that patent. Obviously, a patent based on such a fuzzy notion as nonobviousness may be extremely risky if a judge has a free rein to substitute personal interpretations for those of the PTO. And that was pretty much the state of patent affairs prior to the 1980s. However, as indicated in *Panduit*, the Federal Circuit now has affirmatively articulated that the one who is challenging patent validity is the one who must bear the burden of proof by way of clear and convincing evidence. This turns the tables, for it is difficult to be clear and convincing about something that is not very clear from the beginning.

PATENTABLE SUBJECT MATTER

Introduction

The patent system has been devised to provide incentives for the creation and disclosure of new inventions and commercial designs. Section 101 is the fundamental patent provision governing the types of useful inventions that are proper subjects for patent protection. Section 101 provides:

> Whoever invents or discovers any new and useful process, machine, manufacture, or composition of matter, or any new and useful improvement thereof, may obtain a patent therefor, subject to the conditions and requirements of this title.

The statutory language of Section 101 is extremely broad. Indeed, one might argue that its only restriction is that the invention be useful. However, the courts have not interpreted this provision as having infinite scope. Rather, they have recognized on public policy grounds that there are certain inventions and discoveries over which no person or entity should be entitled to exclusive control. For instance, Albert Einstein is widely credited for discovering that there is a scientific relationship between energy and mass. Should the patent system allow an inventor, such as Einstein, to receive a patent for the discovery of a basic law of nature? If so, then the inventor will control a large spectrum of intellectual and commercial practices, for the application of a law of nature transcends any particular device or field of use. Similarly, a mathematician or scientist may determine that a particular mathematical formula can solve certain problems because it accurately addresses fundamental natural relationships. Can the application of the formula to solve problems be considered the discovery of a useful process under Section 101? Again, exclusive control may have far-reaching implications. What about patent protection for the discovery of a new, exotic tree bark that helps cure cancer? Or—to go to the logical extreme—consider the potential social and economic repercussions of allowing patent protection for abstract ideas. Wouldn't it be nice to have patent protection for, say, the idea of selling sugared cereals by placing them on the lowest shelf in the grocery store?

The courts have determined that patent protection cannot be boundless. Protection would be too broad if it covered the laws of nature, mathematical algorithms, materials common to nature, or unapplied ideas. In a sense, patent protection for these fundamental building blocks of nature would over-reward the patent holder to the detriment of the public welfare. Thus, the courts are careful not to allow inventors to use the patent system to lay claim to the basic physical and theoretical resources of nature. Rather, those resources are bestowed on the public by nature for all to use freely.

The debates over patent protection for biotechnology and computer systems essentially come down to these issues. What are the limits to patent protection? How do we distinguish between what is given by nature and what is made from nature?

Do computer systems do anything more than solve mathematical algorithms? If so, will patent protection for **AES** be excluded because it utilizes computer processes? This book now addresses the evolving patent policies in these realms.

Biotechnology Protection

As technology moves to new frontiers, it inevitably raises questions about the suitability of patent protection for unforeseen discoveries. Nowhere is this debate more heated than in the realm of biological and genetic engineering. The fundamental question is whether it is morally and economically appropriate to grant an inventor exclusive rights to new life forms. Or, in short, should one be able to obtain a patent on living things? The issue is not altogether new. Congress has addressed it previously in the context of plants. But now the issues have risen to higher plateaus—to microorganisms, to proteins that fight human disease, to strands of human DNA, even to new types of animals. The Supreme Court set the stage for the new revolution in biotechnology with its landmark decision in *Diamond v. Chakrabarty*.

DIAMOND V. CHAKRABARTY
United States Supreme Court, 1980

FACTS: In 1972, Chakrabarty filed a patent application that claimed a human-made, genetically engineered bacterium, capable of breaking down multiple components of crude oil. Chakrabarty's patent claims were of three types: first, process claims for the method of producing the bacteria; second, claims for an inoculum composed of a carrier material floating on water—such as straw—and the new bacteria; and third, claims to the bacteria themselves.

The patent examiner allowed the claims that fell into the first two categories but rejected the claim to the bacteria. His decision rested on two grounds: (1) that microorganisms are "products of nature" and (2) that as living things microorganisms are not patentable subject matter under Section 101. Chakrabarty appealed to the Patent Office Board of Appeals, which affirmed the patent examiner's rejection. Chakrabarty appealed to the Court of Customs and Patent Appeals (today, such an appeal would go to the Federal Circuit), which reversed. The Commissioner of Patents and Trademarks appealed to the Supreme Court.

DECISION AND REASONING: The question before this Court is a narrow one of statutory interpretation, requiring us to construe Section 101 of the Patent Act. Specifically, we must determine whether Chakrabarty's microorganism

continued . . .

continued . . .

constitutes a "manufacture" or a "composition of matter" within the meaning of the statute.

In cases of statutory construction, we begin with the language of the statute. Unless otherwise defined, words will be interpreted according to their ordinary meaning. And courts should not read into the patent laws limitations and conditions the legislature has not expressed. In choosing such expansive terms as "manufacture" and "composition of matter," modified by the comprehensive "any," Congress was contemplating that the patent laws would be given wide scope.

The relevant legislative history, too, supports a broad construction. The Patent Act of 1793 embodied Jefferson's philosophy that ingenuity should receive a liberal encouragement. The committee reports that accompanied the 1952 amendments to the act inform us that Congress intended statutory subject matter to "include anything under the sun that is made by man."

This is not to suggest that Section 101 has no limits or that it embraces every discovery. The laws of nature, physical phenomena, and abstract ideas have been held not patentable. Thus, a new mineral discovered in the earth or a new plant discovered in the wild is not patentable subject matter. Likewise, Einstein could not patent his celebrated law that $E = mc^2$; nor could Newton have patented the law of gravity. Such discoveries are manifestations of nature—free to all persons and reserved exclusively to none.

Judged in this light, Chakrabarty's microorganism plainly qualifies as patentable subject matter. His claim is not to a hitherto unknown natural phenomenon, but to a non-naturally occurring manufacture or composition of matter: a product of human ingenuity having a distinctive name, character, and use. A previous case underscores the point. A scientist discovered six naturally occurring root-nodule bacteria that could be mixed into a culture and used to inoculate the seeds of leguminous plants. This court denied patentability, ruling that what was discovered was only the handiwork of nature. The combination of species produced no new bacteria, no change in the six species of bacteria, and no enlargement of the range of their utility. Their use in combination did not improve in any way their natural functioning. They served the ends nature originally provided, and they acted independently of any effort by the scientist.

Here, by contrast, Chakrabarty has produced a new bacterium with markedly different characteristics from any found in nature and one having the potential for significant utility. Chakrabarty's discovery is not nature's handiwork but his own. Accordingly, it is patentable subject matter under Section 101.

The commissioner argues that microorganisms cannot qualify as patentable subject matter until Congress expressly authorizes such protection. Its position rests on the fact that genetic technology was unforeseen when Congress enacted Section 101. The commissioner argues that the legislative process is best equipped to weigh the competing economic, social, and scientific considerations involved and to determine whether living organisms produced by genetic engineering should receive patent protection. In support of this position, the commissioner relies on this court's recent statement that the judiciary must proceed cautiously when asked to extend patent rights into areas wholly unforeseen by Congress.

It is, of course, correct that Congress, not the courts, must define the limits of patentability, but it is equally true that once Congress has spoken, it is the province and duty of the judicial department to say what the law is. Congress has performed its role in defining patentable subject matter in Section 101; we perform ours in construing the language Congress has employed.

Broad, general language is not necessarily ambiguous when congressional objectives require broad terms. This court frequently has observed that a statute is not to be confined to the particular applications contemplated by the legislators. This is especially true in the field of patent law. A rule that unanticipated inventions are without protection would conflict with the core concept of the patent law that requires novelty for patentability. Congress employed broad, general language in drafting Section 101 precisely because such inventions are often unforeseeable.

To buttress their argument, the commissioner and others point to grave risks that may be generated by research endeavors such as Chakrabarty's. Their briefs present a gruesome parade of horribles, suggesting that such research may pose a serious threat to the human race. It is argued that this Court should weigh these potential hazards in considering whether Chakrabarty's invention is patentable. We disagree. The grant or denial of patents on microorganisms is not likely to put an end to genetic research or its attendant risks. Legislative or judicial fiat as to patentability will not deter scientific minds from probing into the unknown any more than King Canute could command the tides. Whether Chakrabarty's claims are patentable may determine whether research efforts are accelerated by the hope of reward or slowed by want of incentives, but that is all.

The choice we are urged to make is a matter of high policy for resolution within the legislative process after the kind of investigation, examination, and study that legislative bodies can provide and courts cannot. Whatever their validity, the contentions now pressed on us should be addressed by the Congress and the executive, but not the courts. Congress is free to amend Section 101 so as to exclude from patent protection organisms produced by genetic engineering or to craft a statute specifically designed for such living things. But until Congress does, the Court must construe section 101 as it stands. And that language embraces Chakrabarty's invention.

Accordingly, the judgment of the lower court is Affirmed.

Chakrabarty received a patent on the genetically engineered bacterium in 1981. However, by 1992, the organism had yet to be used in a commercial application. This is not for want of a practical use, however. Recent studies have shown that living microbes, such as Chakrabarty's, may effectively break up oil by releasing soap-like sulfcants that emulsify oil into droplets small enough for bacteria to convert into carbon dioxide and water. This, of course, could be extremely useful for major oil-spill cleanup efforts, such as that needed after the *Exxon Valdez* spilled its cargo in Alaska. Indeed, the microbes may be less toxic and more biodegradable than traditional methods using chemicals. But the stumbling block for this technology, as with most biotechnology concerns, is fear.[33]

Whenever living organisms are introduced into new environments, public anxiety buttons are pushed. This is true even when living things that have been developed by nature are taken from their natural habitat and moved into new regions. One only has to consider what happened when a few African killer bees were shipped to South America, or when the Mediterranean fruit fly made its way to California. Clearly, the balance of nature is a delicate and complex matter well beyond the total grasp of human understanding. Any human action that would serve to upset the natural chain of life in a region, therefore, is rightly met with concern, hostility, and scrutiny. And obviously, the reaction will be many times as strong when the issue is not simply the displacement of natural life, but rather the introduction of new life forms not yet contemplated in the natural scheme of Earth. For a simple illustration, consider the widespread negative public reaction that emerged in 1999 when a laboratory study indicated that pollen from bioengineered pest-resistant corn might also be toxic to monarch butterflies. Although harms to butterflies do not directly cause widespread damage to humans, and although the dangers had not yet been proven in the field, the study nonetheless mobilized a coalition of national environmental groups to request greater government oversight of biotechnological applications in agriculture.[34]

For these reasons, the difficult issues pertinent to patent protection for living things, of which there are many, may be only the beginning of the frustrations for biotechnology enterprises. Beyond typical patent concerns regarding the propriety and extent of legal control, biotechnology inventions must bear additional social, ethical, and political burdens. Thus, a biotechnology business that successfully navigates the extremely uncertain waters of patent protection typically has only begun its journey through the legal and public policy process. This is particularly true when the newly engineered life forms will be released into the open environment as opposed to being controlled in a laboratory setting. For instance, field tests for evaluating genetically altered crops often engender stiff resistance from environmental groups and require oversight from government regulators. Companies involved with biotechnology therefore must be prepared to contend with regulations from a myriad of administrative agencies, even after a patent is granted.

Patents for Higher Life Forms   As the science of biotechnology advances, the patent issues become increasingly contentious and complex. A primary concern is just how far up the ladder of life proprietary rights through patents should be allowed. It is one thing to grant a patent on genetically altered microorganisms. It may seem quite another to permit ownership of a strain of celery or a breed of mice or cows. But patent protection now clearly extends to such higher forms of life. In 1985, the PTO Board of Patent Appeals and Interferences (the board) held that seeds, plants, and plant tissue cultures are patentable subject matter under Section 101.[35] In early 1987, the board went further, holding that Section 101 covers non-naturally occurring oysters in which polyploidy was induced by hydrostatic pressure.[36] Soon thereafter, on April 21, 1987, the PTO issued a policy statement indicating that it considers all non-naturally occurring nonhuman multicellular living organisms, including higher animals, to be patentable subject matter under Section 101. In 1988, the PTO granted the first patent for a transengenic nonhuman mammal: a mouse—called the Harvard Oncomouse—into which a gene was inserted so that the mouse would be more susceptible to developing cancerous tumors.[37] By 1998, the PTO had issued around 85 animal patents and reportedly was soon to allow nearly 90 more.[38]

So far, the majority of the transengenic animals have been developed to aid in drug research. Human genes responsible for specific diseases or maladies are introduced into the animal, causing it to carry the genetic disorder. For example, researchers have created transengenic animals that are especially susceptible to afflictions such as AIDS, enlarged prostate, sickle-cell anemia, and cystic fibrosis.[39] These animals have great medical potential because they may serve as laboratories for experiments aimed at curing or preventing afflictions. But they also raise hostile objections, particularly from animal rights activists and opponents of genetic engineering. For example, the Foundation on Economic Trends aggressively challenged attempts by scientists at the National Institutes of Health to perform AIDs research on mice that were genetically altered to improve the study, arguing that the experiment posed an undue danger if the animals were to escape.[40] Research on transengenic animals also poses serious ethical questions about creating animals that are purposefully deformed, often with painful and debilitating maladies. Not all research creates diseased animals, however. For example, researchers at Princeton University created mice with better memory by inserting the so-called NR2B gene into the nuclei of fertilized eggs. This research ultimately could yield new drugs and treatments for preventing memory loss in the elderly.[41]

CLONING   In 1997, the world was struck by the announcement that biotechnology research scientists at the Roslin Institute in Scotland had successfully cloned an adult sheep. The birth of the lamb, which was given the name Dolly, was greeted with both tremendous excitement and enormous fears. Traditional gene-splicing methods of creating transengenic animals are frustrating because they are extremely inefficient.[42] Only about one-tenth of 1% of the animals born with these techniques assimilate the desired genetic characteristics. It thus is somewhat of a hit-and-miss approach to creating transengenic animals.

Cloning can make this process much more predictable, since a transengenic animal can provide the resource base to create a large number of identical copies. The key to cloning is that cells contain all the genetic information required to create exact duplicates. The problem is that cells are specialized, so that genes that are not needed for particular functions are, in effect, switched off. In order to clone a complete animal from a cell, therefore, a way had to be found to switch these genes back on. The Roslin scientists discovered a method to make this happen.[43]

Cloning techniques, as they are refined, have the capacity to greatly increase the efficiency of the biotechnology industry. However, they also have raised anxieties regarding biotechnology to new heights. This is particularly because it is not a great leap to begin considering the very real possibility that the technology will soon be available to clone human beings. And from this there emerge all the worries that heretofore were simply the wild notions of science fiction authors, such as multiple duplications of sinister leaders and creations of master races. In the United States, reactions by scientists and public officials were swift. A host of Nobel Prize–winning scientists, among many others, called for voluntary bans on human cloning.[44] In addition, numerous pieces of legislation were rapidly introduced at both the federal and state levels, calling for various kinds of bans on human cloning activities and prohibitions on public funding of human cloning research. The reactions were no less strong in other nations, particularly in Europe, where similar policies were developed in Great Britain, Denmark, Germany, Belgium, the Netherlands, and Spain.[45] In addition, as will be noted below, the European Union added a provision to its Biotechnology Directive preventing patents on human cloning techniques.[46]

The ethical issues surrounding human cloning intensified with the discovery that stem cells from human embryos may have the potential to treat chronic ailments, such as diabetes and Parkinson's disease.[47] In 1999, it was reported that a team of researchers had attempted to clone human embryos. Even more startling, another team was involved in cloning embryos that were part human and part cow. The goal of the research teams was to find ways to produce large quantities of the potentially beneficial human embryonic stem cells, which are harvested from human embryos. Thus, the therapeutic benefits for humans may be substantial. Nonetheless, religious leaders and others who believe that life begins at conception object to the practice. To them it is offensive to create human beings that otherwise would not be born and then to destroy them. Some scientists contend that an embryo does not become a person until it is 14 days old, when there is first evidence of a nervous system. Since the cloning experimentation is performed on embryos that are less than 10 days old, they believe that their work does not involve human life. Legislators in the United States have had a difficult time addressing the issue. On the one hand, they do not want to ruffle the feathers of antiabortion forces, but on the other, they are reluctant to interfere with potentially useful medical research.[48] Some European countries have made a policy distinction between "therapeutic cloning," which is intended to create useful cells, and "reproductive cloning," which is used for creating babies.[49] Clearly, cloning represents a new chapter in the biotechnology saga. How the plot will unfold is still an open question.

Biotechnology and Agribusiness Issues   Genetic engineering may prove to revolutionize agribusiness. Whereas classical crossbreeding of, say, a tangerine and a pomelo to yield a tangelo, is an imprecise science, manipulation of specific genes could allow the creation of an unlimited number of tangelos having a precise selection of desired characteristics. By proper selection and introduction of genes, plants, can be made to be more resistant to normally harmful microorganisms, pests, and weather conditions.[50] For instance, DeKalb has numerous bioengineering patents involving corn and other food products.[51] One covers the so-called Bt corn seed that has a gene inserted into it so that the corn produces a protein that is toxic to the European corn borer. Another deals with a method to make crops produce more lysine, an amino acid used in feed that enhances the development of chickens and hogs. Monsanto also has developed and patented numerous genetically engineered crops, such as soybeans that are resistant to its Roundup brand herbicide, and cottonseed that is resistant to the bullworm.[52] Recently, DuPont has been studying the possibility of using genetic engineering to make food healthier, such as by instructing soybeans to produce cancer-fighting compounds.[53] Animals, likewise, can be tailored to be more efficient for human uses, such as by growing more lean on less food or by producing more milk. In addition, it is now possible to inject into the embryos of animals certain genes that trigger the production of useful human proteins in controlled locations such as in mammary glands. When the animal matures, it then can be used for "pharming," the derivation of drug proteins from animal milk supplies.[54] Clearly, new biotechnological inroads such as these, coupled with the greater efficiency of cloning, will have an immense capacity to radically alter the economics of agriculture and animal husbandry.

BIOLOGICAL DIVERSITY AND SAFETY CONCERNS   In 1992, the United Nations sponsored the Earth Summit in Rio de Janeiro, at which the participants developed the Convention on Biological Diversity.[55] The convention addresses issues regarding the effects of humans on the vitality of natural species, and as you might expect, many of these closely relate to the introduction and use of biotechnogical innovations.[56] For instance, if agriculture comes to depend on a smaller set of bioengineered food products bred for specific superior traits, then the diversity of living plants may diminish. This could render the world food supply extremely vulnerable to disease, pests, or changing weather conditions.[57] The convention also focuses attention on the ways that bioengineered plants and animals might harm natural species, thereby affecting biological diversity. Another important topic addressed by the Biological Diversity Convention regards the extent of control that nations should have on the genetic raw materials that are derived from natural species found within their borders. The United States at first failed to sign the Biological Diversity Convention based, in large part, on objections from the biotechnology industry. However, President Clinton signed the international agreement in 1993. Nonetheless, due to continued objections from the biotechnology industry, the Senate, as of 1999, still had not ratified the treaty, as is required for the United States to be bound by its provisions.[58]

Those opposing the use of bioengineering in agribusiness are not convinced that bioengineering techniques are as safe as the industry claims. In support of their doubts, they point to some surprising issues resulting from the injection of recombinant bovine growth hormone (rBGH) into cows to increase milk production. The rBGH is made through a genetic engineering technique based on a cow gene re-sponsible for growth. Some studies indicate that cows treated with rBGH have a higher incidence of mastitis, requiring treatment with antibiotics. If the additional levels of antibiotics pass into the milk supply, they possibly could result in harmful consequences.[59] As noted in Chapter 1, the United States and the European Union were involved in heated disputes in the late 1990s regarding European import bans on hormone-treated beef. The controversy ultimately landed in the WTO, where a dispute resolution panel determined that there was insufficient evidence of harmful health effects to justify trade barriers. Notwithstanding this decision, fears about the use of growth hormones have not abated.

A large set of other concerns centers on the long-term effects of tinkering with nature. Since life can mutate, reproduce, and migrate, there are a host of contain-ment issues. For instance, a herbicide-resistant plant might pollinate in other areas where that plant is not wanted. Removing it then could necessitate the increased use of more lethal weed killers.[60] Ecological fears also are compelling. As already mentioned, there are constant worries about the delicate balance of nature. A fish that is engineered to achieve greater size may be beneficial for food production, but its introduction into the environment might substantially alter the ecosystem. The 1999 laboratory study indicating that bioengineered Bt corn may have unexpected toxic effects on monarch butterflies serves as a case in point.[61] As of 1998, over 250 field tests or introductions of genetically engineered plants and animals had taken place, including the release in Florida of a predatory mite specifically de-signed to eat insects that plague strawberries.[62] Although such organisms often are expected to be naturally weak and thus have short-term lives in the wild, there is rising concern that this may not always be the case.

One provision in the Biological Diversity Convention requires the participants to consider whether there is a need for a protocol that addresses how organisms modified through biotechnology might affect the safety of the ecosystem.[63] In 1999, some 130 nations participated in a summit at Cartagena, Colombia, to draft a Biosafety Protocol under the ambit of the Convention on Biological Diversity.[64] Since the United States had not yet become an official member of the convention, it attended the meetings and voiced its concerns without having any final say on what the protocol ultimately might require. Many issues were addressed at the summit, and many proved to be extremely controversial. For instance, there were discussions regarding the kinds of products that would be covered by the protocol, ranging from living organisms that are intended to be released into the environ-ment to commodities, such as corn, that have been modified through biotechnol-ogy. Another set of issues were related to disclosures, such as when disclosures have to be made, what kinds of information must be provided, the types of review a country might use, and whether approval or permits might be required. The par-ticipants also debated whether countries might impose significant liabilities for eco-nomic or biological losses caused by the introduction of modified organisms. The Biosafety Protocol ultimately became bogged down by disagreements at the 1999 Cartagena meeting. Nonetheless, the participants expected that there would be re-newed efforts to reach consensus within the next few years.[65]

The Biological Diversity Convention establishes that individual nations have sovereign rights to determine who may have access to their genetic resources.[66] It also provides that nations are entitled to receive a fair and equitable sharing of the benefits arising out of the utilization of genetic resources.[67] Biotechnology depends on locating genes that have potential benefits for human applications and then devising ways to effectively utilize them. For instance, some genes cause cells to manufacture curative proteins. Drug companies that locate these genes can use biotechnology to mass-produce the proteins for drug products. For example, Merck's cholesterol drug, Mevacor, is derived from a fungus found in Japan, and Novartis's transplant-rejection drug, Cyclosporine, depends on genetic material from a Norwegian mountain fungus. In fact, according to one source, seven of the world's 25 top-selling drugs in 1997 were derived from natural products.[68] Likewise, agribusiness firms search the globe for genetic material that can be spliced into the genetic makeup of natural agricultural products, resulting in plants that are hardier or more pest resistant, and foods that are tastier or sweeter.

Many of these useful genetic materials are found in developing regions that are rich with unique varieties of natural species, such as the Amazon and Africa. Members of these communities have become increasingly frustrated. They see multinationals from developed countries reap enormous profits from bioengineered products that depend on original materials found on their lands. Yet, often, the developing countries share little of the return. Indeed, when the drugs and agricultural products are patented, individuals in these regions may not even be able to make the very products that were derived from resources found within their homelands.[69] Thus, developing countries sometimes accuse foreign multinationals of engaging in "bio-colonialism" or "bio-piracy," since the companies allegedly take their resources without paying any compensation.[70]

The Biological Diversity Convention authorizes countries to pass laws that might limit access to genetic materials and require equitable compensation for their use. The first country to enact such a law was the Philippines, which in 1995 passed legislation requiring collaboration with local scientists, informed consent from the indigenous tribes located where samples might be taken, and compensation. Other countries, such as Costa Rica, Bolivia, Colombia, Ecuador, Peru, and Venezuela, soon followed suit. As of 1999, dozens of other countries were considering similar proposals. Scientists and biotechnology companies fear that some countries will overestimate the value of their resources and will prevent access to potentially useful genetic materials. Others lament that these actions merely continue the disheartening trend toward private ownership of genetic resources. Clearly, issues regarding safety, biological diversity, and the ownership of genetic resources will be contentious for years to come.

REGULATORY AND LABELING CONCERNS   In 1992, the FDA issued a policy statement laying out how it would regulate foods derived from new plant varieties, including those designed through bioengineering.[71] Essentially, the policy does not require genetically modified foods to be reviewed by the FDA prior to marketing. Rather, companies are allowed to sell these foods once they are satisfied that the food is safe. Genetically modified foods, therefore, are treated in the same fashion as all other foods, in that they are subject to "postmarket" scrutiny by FDA officials. This means that the foods may be seized by the government if dangers materialize after they are sold. Companies, though, are encouraged to consult with the agency prior to marketing so that they may discuss the nutritional makeup of the products and any safety issues that may exist. The first consultation occurred in 1994 with Calgene regarding the Flavr Savr tomato, which was genetically engineered to soften less rapidly. Over the next five years, over 40 firms consulted with the FDA through this voluntary process.[72]

The 1992 policy also addresses labeling issues. To the dismay of many consumers and environmentalists, the policy does not impose a general labeling mandate on all genetically modified food warning consumers that it has been subjected to bioengineering. Instead, genetically modified food sold in the United States requires a special label only in a few circumstances. One instance is when the food's composition has been significantly changed from the conventionally grown counterpart. For example, a manufacturer that modified canola to produce increased levels of lauric acid in the seed oil had to label it as "laureate canola oil."[73] Labeling also is required when the genetically modified food has fewer nutrients than the traditional food product. In addition, a label is necessary when genes are transferred from foods that are known to cause allergic reactions, such as from peanuts or Brazil nuts.[74] Under the policy, the food has to be labeled so that buyers know that it contains a gene from an allergen, unless the developer can demonstrate with scientific proof that the allergenic properties of the food are not transferred by the gene to the modified product.

During the late 1990s, a global groundswell emerged calling for public controls over genetically modified food products, particularly through labeling. The epicenter of the international antibioengineering movement was Europe, with England and France leading the way.[75] There are many explanations why European sentiment toward bioengineered food products became so antagonistic.[76] Farming interests in Europe, for instance, may have seen bioengineering more as a threat than an opportunity, and so raised fears to lessen competition from U.S. corn and soybean imports. In 1996, Great Britain had to deal with a scare about mad-cow disease, leading to fears about the food supplies and the abilities of public officials to regulate safety. This was reinforced by reports of contaminated chicken in Belgium and tainted cans of Coca-Cola in Belgium and France. Then came U.S. trade duties in 1999 on luxury products, such as foie gras, in retaliation for European restrictions on hormone-fed beef. On top of all this, farmers and others in Europe often portrayed genetically modified food as a symbol of American imperialism. By 1999, bioengineered products were termed "Frankenstein foods" in publications throughout Europe.

In response to these frenzied negative sentiments, the EU Council of Ministers adopted a regulation in 1999 requiring member countries to begin labeling all foods that contain genetically modified ingredients. The laws of some individual countries went even further. For instance, in England, restaurants, caterers, and bakers had to label genetically modified ingredients.[77]

Countries in other regions rapidly followed suit. In 1999, Japan was in the midst of bioengineering schizophrenia.[78] On the one hand, the government was taking steps to stimulate greater development of Japan's bioengineering industry. However, consumers shared similar sentiments to those found in Europe. Kirin Brewery Co, for instance, acquired the Japanese marketing rights to the Flavr Savr tomato and quickly won approval from Japanese authorities to sell the tomato. A Japanese consumer group, though, threatened to boycott Kirin's products if it began selling the tomato, and so Kirin killed the project.[79] As in Europe, some of the objection may have been based on protectionism. Nonetheless, a 1997 government survey in Japan found that 80% of Japanese consumers had reservations about genetically modified foods, and 92% favored labeling.[80] For this reason, despite the government's efforts to build confidence in bioengineering, it simultaneously proposed that mandatory labeling begin in 2001. Experiences in New Zealand and Australia, among other nations, were similar, leading their governments to impose mandatory labeling.[81]

Labeling laws are philosophically easy to support because in theory they require sellers to supply consumers with information they might find important to make informed choices. However, when labeling is required, marketing professionals have found that the safest and most successful course is to promote their products as free from genetic modification. On the one hand, this has led to disputes about the honesty of claims.[82] On a more important level, though, labeling has substantially raised demand for grains and ingredients that are not genetically modified.[83] The effects were felt in the United States as early as 1999. For example, Archer-Daniels-Midland, one of the largest crop purchasers in the United States, told its suppliers to begin separating genetically modified crops from those free of bioengineering. Also, Heinz and Gerber began to remove genetically modified foods from their product lines.[84]

In 1999, the FDA began a series of hearings to address whether the 1992 food policy needed to be revised.[85] Among the questions posed was whether the FDA should be more involved in safety regulation, and whether labeling regulations should be modified and strengthened. Biotechnology interests fear that labeling requirements will lead to the same kind of consumer backlash in the United States that was experienced in Europe.[86] They worry that labels noting genetic modification will be stigmatized with implications that safety or nutrition is being compromised. At the same time, food products heralding that they are free from genetic modification may be perceived as superior. In 1999, members of the World Trade Organization met in Seattle to consider starting a new round of trade negotiations. Although the effort to initiate the new round failed at that meeting, many members, including the European Union and the United States, did agree that a vital area for future WTO trade discussions is the regulation of biotechnology food products.[87]

ISSUES REGARDING THE OWNERSHIP OF PROGENY   An extremely contentious issue is whether plant and animal patents should cover progeny. In the context of traditional machine patents, one who purchases a machine is entitled to use it without restriction. Thus, the buyer is allowed to tear the machine apart or transform it into something else. What the buyer may not do is duplicate the machine. Plant and animal patents strain the traditional constructs because the subject matter of the invention—the plant or animal—can reproduce naturally. May purchasers of a patented plant or animal breed it without permission, or must they contract to pay royalties for the harvested seeds or offspring?[88] Clearly, this is a critical issue for those engaged in agribusiness ventures.

Unless the patent laws are amended to specifically address this issue, it is likely that animal patents will extend to progeny. Otherwise, many inventors of transengenic animals and plants will conclude that their most profitable course of action is to maintain the invention in secrecy and to distribute only the final products. That outcome is contrary to the disclosure principles of patent policy. It also might tend to consolidate the production of agricultural products.[89] Therefore, it is logical to assume that breeding that duplicates the protected features will be covered by a patent. But what if a purchaser of a patented animal breeds the animal with one from another species, resulting in some different variation of life? What if the animal runs loose and mates wildly in nature? Is the purchaser liable to pay royalties for all the resultant offspring? These issues are of such concern to farmers that they have aggressively lobbied Congress to either place a moratorium on animal patents or amend the patent laws so as to allow farmers to breed, use, and sell patented farm animals and their offspring.[90]

The problems escalate when viewed from an international perspective. For instance, suppose that an inventor has a U.S. patent on a strain of corn. If protection for that variety is not obtained or is not available in another country, then purchasers can grow several generations of corn with seedlings. Can imports of the corn be prohibited? What if the corn is legally made into meal or into tortillas? Can these types of indirect products be barred from importation into the United States? Although a strict reading of Section 337 would appear to cover such indirect products, there clearly will be practical problems of enforcement as well as sensitive issues of international relations.

THE ISSUE OF STERILIZED SEEDS   An interesting associated issue regards the development of a recently patented seed technology that essentially enables seed manufacturers to sterilize their products.[91] Normally, seed grows into plants that produce more seed that then can be used to grow more crops in a continuous cycle. If the original seed is patented, then harvesting seed from its plants may indeed be unlawful. However, enforcement is an enormous problem.[92] As mentioned, seed companies face even greater difficulties if the seed does not benefit from patent protection in other countries. A sterilizing process, if effective, would prevent farmers from avoiding payments for subsequent crop cycles. Some argue, though, that this technology may be misused by multinational seed companies, allowing them to exercise excess control over minimally improved seed products. This, they fear, simply will allow large multinational corporations to derive even greater profits from basic human needs for food, especially in third-world countries.

The sterilizing seed technology was patented in 1998 by the Delta & Pine Land

Co. and the Department of Agriculture. Critics swiftly began to use the title "Terminator" to refer to the technology, alluding to the robotic killer played by Arnold Schwarzenegger. Opposition to the seed became so widespread that Monsanto, which entered discussions to buy Delta, pledged in 1999 that it would not use the so-called Terminator sterilizing seed technology.[93] Notwithstanding this statement, one can be sure that numerous eyes will continue to focus on potential future developments and actions regarding sterilized seeds.

Pharmaceutical Patent Issues   That the processes and products of genetic engineering are alive leads to numerous other complicated legal and social issues, especially in the pharmaceutical area. One excellent example is provided by the litigation between Amgen and Genetics Institute over patent rights to erythropoietin (EPO), a hormone secreted by the human kidney, which when purified may be used to treat anemia.[94] Genetics Institute received a patent on the purified hormone in 1987. This alone might surprise you because EPO is a natural product of the kidney. However, there is precedence in the chemical field, indicating that if a chemical can be found in nature only in an unpurified form, then a patent can be received on the purified form. Likewise, if EPO exists in nature only in an unpurified form, then the purified version is eligible for patent protection as an invention made through human ingenuity.

EPO is secreted by human kidneys in such minute quantities that its production from that source is not commercially viable. Therefore, Genetics Institute entered into a race with Amgen to develop the drug through genetic engineering. For genetic engineering to occur, one must locate within the DNA the gene sequence that contains the instructions for a cell to manufacture the desired protein. The gene sequence then is placed into a DNA molecule of an appropriate living cell, which, as it multiplies through natural division, serves as a production factory of the protein. Amgen was the first to discover the appropriate gene sequence, and in 1987 it received a patent on it. Amgen also discovered that a Chinese hamster's ovary cell served well as an EPO factory, and the company received another patent on the transformed version of that cell.

Genetics Institute found a similar way to genetically engineer EPO and used the method to manufacture and sell EPO in the United States. It also licensed a Japanese pharmaceutical company to market EPO worldwide. In the ensuing litigation, Amgen argued that its patents were infringed by Genetics Institute's technique of producing EPO through genetic engineering. Genetics Institute alleged that it had sole rights over purified EPO to treat anemia and that the sale of purified EPO by any unauthorized company infringed its patent, no matter how it was made. In effect, what could have resulted was a standoff, wherein one company owned the useful final product but another owned the only viable way to make it.

If patents on purified proteins take precedence over the biotechnological means to make them, this could have a chilling effect on the biotechnology industry. The Genetics Institute/Amgen litigation did not settle the question, because the appeals court found Genetics Institute's patent to be invalid. Therefore, Amgen could continue to sell EPO using its biotechnology technique. The larger question regarding the precedence of valid purified protein claims thus survived this dispute. The few other cases that have considered this issue have been extremely complex, as was the case with EPO, and the debate still remains somewhat unresolved.[95] However, evidence is mounting that the courts support the priority of the purified protein claims.[96] Clearly, the courts need to reach a definitive consensus on this important issue soon.

Human Genome and Related Issues   A key aspect of genetic engineering is determining the gene sequence that produces an identified useful protein. Human cells each have 23 pairs of chromosomes, which consist of two twisted strands of DNA. The problem is that not all of the DNA is composed of genes that make proteins. In fact, the 100,000 genes that are thought to exist make up only about 3% of DNA. The rest of the DNA logically is called junk DNA. The problem of fully identifying gene sequences is magnified because each gene consists of between 2,000 and 2,000,000 pairs of nucleotides. Therefore, the endeavor to locate and identify the full makeup of all the genes in human cells is a major undertaking indeed. To achieve this understanding, a major multinational effort, called the Human Genome Project, was initiated in 1990 to map and sequence all the human genes.[97] At the same time, scientists in the public and private sectors began to develop new techniques that allowed them to more efficiently zero in on the sequences of genes and gene fragments.[98]

As noted previously, U.S. law allows a gene sequence to be patented. This is based on the same notion that allows purified chemicals to be subject to patents. Since the gene does not exist in nature in an isolated form, it falls outside of *Chakrabarty*'s exclusion for natural things. In 1991 and 1992, the National Institutes of Health (NIH) raised an enormous controversy when it filed patent applications for 2,700 genes and gene fragments that its scientists located through use of a new identification method.[99] The most contentious point of these applications was that although the genes had been located, their function and utility were not yet known. Many experts questioned whether a utility patent is appropriate for an invention before one knows the utility that the invention might accomplish. NIH, on the other hand, worried that if it published its findings without filing for a patent, then scientists who later discovered the function of the genes would be precluded from enjoying patent rights, based on a lack of novelty.[100] The applications caused an international stir, igniting a frantic response by the British government to withhold information on its gene research discoveries and to begin efforts to patent genes located by its scientists.[101] Also, the applications raised substantial speculation that other governments and private companies would join in a global race to file patents for as many genes and gene fragments of the human body as they could locate. In September 1992, the PTO rejected the applications, citing the utility concerns as well as other problems.[102] Tremendous uncertainty remains, however, especially in an international context. Some countries, for instance, may not go so far as to allow the patenting of gene sequences, even when their utility is identified. Rather, a patent may be available only for techniques or organisms that employ the gene in useful ways. Clearly, any international accord dealing substantively with the patentablity of bioengineered inventions will have to approach this issue carefully.

The commercial potential of discovering the location and functions of genes has caused a debate among government scientists engaged in basic research because they believe that the results of privately funded genetic research sometimes are kept under wraps so that patent protection is not jeopardized.[103] For instance, government scientists have placed an enormous priority on learning the genome of the staphylococcus bacteria because new strains are increasingly resistant to antibiotics, raising fears that there someday may be an outbreak of an untreatable infectious disease. They contend that several private companies have uncovered valuable information about the staphylococcus genome but have been unwilling to share it with the public. Consequently, public money is being used to duplicate efforts already undertaken in the private sector. This, they argue, has delayed basic research by up to five years. Those involved in publicly funded research believe that the public sector should be responsible for determining the structure of the genome, while private sources seek ways to make useful products. In their view, patents should not be available for the sequence of the gene, but only for applications derived from it.

Locating human genes and determining their functions will have tremendous medical benefits but may lead to numerous social and ethical problems as well.[104] One exciting application of this new technology is called gene therapy. Many diseases are caused by defects or mutations in genes. If healthy genes can be spliced into cells having such defects, then it is possible that particular diseases may be slowed or halted. The benefits of this form of treatment are so great that the only objections to patents for standard gene therapies are that scientists may put their pursuit of profits above the search for truth.[105] Gene therapies, though, may have an even larger potential, but unfortunately one that does raise ethical objections.[106] Standard gene therapies are directed at what are called somatic cells. Somatic cells affect a person's tissues and organs, but their structures are not passed along to other generations through reproduction. Thus, gene therapies directed at somatic cells may heal the individuals who are being treated, but have no affect on the conditions of their offspring. On the other hand, gene therapies also may be directed at what are called germline cells, which are involved in reproduction. Through germline techniques, one may find permanent treatments to inheritable diseases. However, they also raise the possibility that people may predetermine the characteristics of their children. This has led to substantial moral inquiries and raised questions about the propriety of patent protection, since it would encourage scientists to engage in objectionable pursuits.

Another medical benefit that may result from identifying the structure and function of healthy genes is that tests may be developed to determine defects, thereby indicating whether an individual has some potential susceptibility to specific diseases.[107] Diagnostic genetic tests, for instance, may provide an early warning to those who have an increased predisposition to breast, ovarian, or colon cancers and allow them to take important preventative measures, if any are available. However, these tests also raise various personal and social issues.[108] One set of concerns involves the adequacy of personal counseling that should accompany a test that may reveal the potential for life-threatening conditions, especially if suitable treatments do not exist. Other concerns involve the potential that employers and insurance companies may use such tests to discriminate against those that have a higher statistical probability of requiring medical care in the future.[109] Employers also might use genetic testing to appraise job skills or the potential for harmful medical reactions from environmental conditions in the workplace. Obviously, genetic testing raises a host of privacy concerns, a topic that will be addressed more fully in Chapter 8. Also, greater understanding of genetics raises philosophical questions, such as the nature of free will and its relevance to criminal laws that often require intentional behavior. The list of questions seemingly increases with each new discovery. All that one can say is that patents will play a critical role as these emotional issues regarding genetic inventions unfold.

International Biotechnology Patent Issues   Heated and controversial discussions have erupted in the international arena over the propriety and means of protection for biotechnology inventions. Many would point to Europe as the epicenter of conflicting emotions on these issues. Environmental organizations, such as Greenpeace, have moved aggressively to arouse public passions to oppose biotechnology patents on moral and safety grounds.[110] Europe's biotechnology industries, on the other hand, adamantly warn that insufficient patent protection will lead to their demise, resulting in widespread economic harms throughout the continent.

The language of the European Patent Convention Treaty, and interpretations of it by the European Patent Office, typify the struggle in Europe to find consensus on biotechnology issues.[111] The EPC Treaty prohibits patents on inventions where commercial use would be contrary to public policy. It also explicitly denies patents for plant and animal varieties. In the early 1990s, the EPO's Examination Division at first used this language to deny a patent for the Harvard Oncomouse. However, after receiving instructions from the EPO Board of Appeal that there is a difference between an "animal" and an "animal variety," the division granted the patent. In arriving at its decision, the division also determined that the patent did not violate public policy because the potential benefits to mankind outweighed the environmental risks and the potential for cruelty to animals. Many observers assumed that this determination opened the door for transengenic plant and animal patents in Europe. However, in a subsequent action, the EPO denied patent claims to a genetically modified plant that had a gene inserted specifically to make the plant resistant to an herbicide. Although the disparate treatments may have been defensible based on other less prominent statutory provisions, the public became confused and discontented over the legality of biotechnology patents in Europe. Compounding the controversies were the patent laws and decisions within the individual countries of Europe which often treated biotechnology inventions in very different ways.

In the midst of this hotly contested environment, the European Union has struggled to find consensus through a directive that would harmonize intellectual property rights for biotechnology inventions among its members. In the early 1990s, the council began work on a directive providing for patents on living organisms, including plants and animals, and extending protection to progeny. However, the directive became bogged down in the parliament in 1993 due to proposed amendments allowing farmers to harvest plant seed from patented plants and requiring compulsory licensing in certain situations. After many more years of difficult negotiations, the parliament gave its blessing in 1998 to a revised Biotechnology Directive.[112] The directive states that patents may be granted on plants and animals, unless the claims extend to an entire genome that is distinct from other varieties. The directive also makes it clear that inventions having industrial applications, even when they involve biological materials or processes, are patentable. Gene sequences thereby are patentable in Europe, but only if the function of the sequence is clearly disclosed.[113] The directive does, however, with various limitations, acknowledge some of the fears raised by those who oppose biotechnology patents. For instance, patents are not allowed for procedures to clone human beings, for commercial uses of embryos, and for germline therapies that would transmit genetic changes to a person's descendants. In addition, the directive prohibits patents on genetic engineering inventions that cause animal suffering without substantial medical benefits.

Many other countries, such as Japan and Canada, provide biotechnology patent protection, but there still are nations that do not. As in the European Union, many countries prohibit patent protection for certain forms of biotechnology inventions on moral or economic grounds. For instance, objections to patents related to human cloning and heredity are somewhat common. In addition, many nations are reluctant to issue patents for bioengineering products and processes when they have medical or pharmaceutical applications.[114] The successful conclusion of the Uruguay Round of GATT should improve the situation but will not necessarily end the disparities. The participants of the Uruguay Round agreed that patents must be available without discrimination as to the field of technology. However, member countries are allowed to exclude animals, other than microorganisms, from patentability. Also, they may prohibit patents for inventions contrary to public order or morality, such as was done in the European Union. In addition, certain developing and least developed countries have until the year 2005 to implement new policies regarding biotechnology patent protection.

Other Biotechnology Patent Issues   Many biotechnology companies complained bitterly when the United States changed its policy regarding patent terms to comply with the TRIPs Agreement of the GATT Uruguay Round. With the length of protection beginning with the application date, the industry worried that lengthy review times would eat into the periods of exclusivity after the patent issued. As mentioned previously, Congress initially provided some relief by allowing extensions for up to five years under certain specified circumstances, such as when two companies simultaneously claim the same invention. Nonetheless, the biotechnology industry was not completely satisfied, since Congress did not allow extensions for delays caused by unusually lengthy administrative review times. Therefore, the industry appealed to Congress in the late 1990s to more adequately address its concerns as part of a comprehensive patent reform package.[115] In 1999, the industry received the safeguards that it sought with the enactment of the American

Inventors Protection Act. Under this revision, when a patent application takes over three years for the PTO to review, then the patent normally may be extended for the length of the delay beyond the three-year period.[116] Therefore, the patent terms of most biotechnology inventions now will exceed 17 years, even when there are lengthy administrative delays.

There are many issues regarding the requirements of the patent application. One of the most troubling is that new organisms often cannot be described in words, thereby requiring the deposit of viable living specimens into public facilities. This has led to serious questions about the timing and extent of permissible public access. In this regard, the United States is a signatory of the Budapest Treaty, an international accord administered by WIPO, which prescribes standards for approved locations, maintenance, and replacement of deposited organisms.

The patent application raises other complex issues as well. For instance, there are difficult questions regarding the breadth of patent claims allowed by the PTO and the extent of protection the claims provide against potential infringers.[117] In this regard, the Federal Circuit has been concerned that the outcomes of genetic techniques may be very unpredictable and that the information provided in the application therefore may not enable a skilled scientist to achieve as wide a breadth of results as the inventor claims in the patent. There also are issues regarding utility, not only regarding the function of gene sequences, but also in other contexts, such as when claims to medical treatments for humans are based on tests conducted on animals.[118] Serious issues about obviousness have arisen also. For instance, should patents on genes be denied for obviousness when fragments have been previously disclosed to the public? In addition, biotechnology inventions sometimes rely on the way old processes are applied to new compositions of matter. Should the inventor be able to obtain a patent on the process, since the steps in the process are nothing new? Confusing answers from the Federal Circuit through the early 1990s prompted the biotechnology industry to seek greater certainty through legislation.[119] These efforts ultimately led to amendments to Section 102 in 1995, which specifically provided industry members many of the assurances they desired.

A final fascinating patent issue regards the power of the PTO to deny a patent on the grounds that the invention is morally offensive. In 1998, the news media reported that a patent application had been filed for a method for making research creatures that would be about half human and half animal.[120] The application, which was filed by Jeremy Rifkin and a biologist, was intended to highlight the general immorality of allowing patents on life, including transengenic animals, human genes, and other bioengineering inventions. Bruce Lehman, who was then head of the PTO, assured the public that the patent office would deny patents for monsters and other immoral inventions, stating that the patent laws give the PTO the power to deny patents for inventions that do not meet certain public policy and morality criteria. Patent scholars question whether the PTO actually has this discretion under the law. Notwithstanding the legal debate, there also is the very obvious problem of trying to determine just where the line of immorality may be crossed. Already, the PTO is granting patents for transengenic animals that are tailored to have human diseases. And of course, once morality enters the picture, one has to ask about other technologies, such as effective inexpensive handguns.

In 1999, the PTO refused to patent the creature, stating that the agency would not patent an invention that embraces a human being.[121] Apparently, the PTO will deny patent protection to inventions that are too human based on notions of public morality. After the denial, the inventors stated that they intended to appeal the decision vigorously. This may force the PTO to address the morality of patenting life with more specificity, and in the process may raise public consciousness about the ethics of bioengineering.

In sum, biotechnology promises tremendous human benefits. However, the fact that the technology is relatively new, coupled with the fact that it deals with life, has raised enormous legal and social questions. Patents are at the center of the controversy because they are the means to reward investors for taking the tremendous financial risks that biotechnological inventions require. However, they do so by providing ownership interests in living things. They also are very effective in stimulating the kinds of commercial activities that many wish would never be allowed to move forward. The result is that biotechnology patents have opened a fascinating new international frontier where emotional legal, ethical, and economic debates will unfold for years to come.

Patent Protection for Computer Programs

Another significantly important concern of certain high-technology companies is whether computer programs, and those machines and processes that utilize them, may be patented. The proposed **AES**, for instance, depends on a computer program to properly filter out unwanted noises and to enhance desired frequencies. Within the program, streams of data relayed from various digital sources are run through a logical series of mathematical relationships and decision steps to yield the optimal solutions to the filtering and enhancement problems. Because the laws of nature and the mathematical formulas that explain them are not patentable subject matter, one may reasonably wonder whether a patent may issue on **AES**. In other words, may a system such as **AES** be patented when part of that system consists of nonpatentable subject matter?

Computer Processes Are Patentable   In the 1970s, the Supreme Court reviewed two computer-related patent cases, and in both it determined that the inventions did not involve patentable subject matter.[122] This led to the general view that patents were not the appropriate vehicle to protect this form of technological innovation. For this reason, computer programmers typically relied on other forms of intellectual property protection, notably trade secrets and copyrights, to protect their innovations. In 1981, the Supreme Court clarified in *Diamond v. Diehr* that the sweeping generalization about the nonpatentability of computer processes was inappropriate and that computer-related inventions could be subject to patent protection. *Diamond v. Diehr* thus is a landmark patent decision representing a pivotal point for the protection, within the United States, of inventions utilizing computer programs.

DIAMOND V. DIEHR
United States Supreme Court, 1981

FACTS: The claimed invention is a process for molding raw, uncured synthetic rubber into cured precision products. Achieving the perfect cure depends upon several factors, including the thickness of the article to be molded, the temperature of the molding process, and the amount of time that the article is allowed to remain in the press. It is possible using well-known time, temperature, and cure relationships to use the Arrhenius equation to determine when to open the press and remove the cured product. Nonetheless, the industry had heretofore not been able to obtain uniformly accurate cures because the temperature of the molding press (a key variable in the equation) varied as the press heated up and it could not be precisely measured at any moment of time. The result was that rubber often was overcured and sometimes was undercured.

The invention by Diehr and Lutton (D&L) is a process that constantly measures the actual temperature inside the mold and feeds the data to a computer that repeatedly recalculates the cure time by use of the Arrhenius equation. When the appropriate time from the equation equals the elapsed cure time, the computer signals a device to open the press. According to D&L, the continuous measuring of the temperature, the feeding of the information to a computer that constantly recalculates the cure time, and the signaling by the computer to open the press are all new in the art.

The patent examiner rejected the patent claims on the sole ground that those steps carried out by a computer under control of a stored program are not statutory subject matter under Section 101. The Patent and Trademark Office Board of Appeals agreed with the examiner, but the Court of Customs and Patent Appeals (which has currently been replaced by the Federal Circuit) reversed. The Commissioner of Patents and Trademarks appealed to the Supreme Court.

DECISION AND REASONING: To decide this case, the Court must interpret the meaning of the word "process" in Section 101. In so doing, we must be mindful that Congress intended statutory subject matter to include anything under the sun that is made by man. A process is a mode of treatment of certain material to produce a given result. It is a series of acts performed upon the subject to be transformed and reduced to a different state or thing.

Transformation and reduction of an article to a different state or thing thus constitutes the clue to patentability of a process claim.

That D&L's claims involve the transformation of an article—in this case uncured synthetic rubber—into a different state or thing cannot be disputed. That conclusion is not altered by the fact that in several steps of the process, a mathematical equation and a programmed digital computer are used.

The Supreme Court has undoubtedly recognized limits to Section 101, and every discovery is not embraced within the statutory terms. Excluded from such patent protection are laws of nature, natural phenomena, and abstract ideas.

Our recent holdings in two computer-related cases are consistent with this policy. In *Gottschalk v. Benson*, we determined that an algorithm that is used to convert binary code decimal numbers to equivalent pure binary numbers is unpatentable. We defined "algorithm" as a procedure for solving a given type of mathematical problem, and we concluded that such an algorithm or mathematical formula is like a law of nature, which cannot be the subject of a patent. In *Parker v. Flook*, we held unpatentable claims drawn to a method for computing an "alarm limit." An alarm limit is simply a number, and the application sought to protect a formula for computing the number. The application did not purport to explain how the variables were to be determined, nor did it disclose the chemical processes at work, the monitoring of process variables, or the means of setting off an alarm or adjusting an alarm system.

In contrast, D&L seek to patent not a mathematical formula but a process of curing synthetic rubber. The process admittedly employs a well-known mathematical equation, but D&L do not seek to preempt the use of that equation. Rather, they seek only to foreclose from others the use of that equation in conjunction with all of the other steps of the claimed process. These include installing rubber into the press, closing the mold, constantly determining the temperature of the mold, constantly recalculating the appropriate cure time through the use of the formula and a computer, and automatically opening the press at the proper time. Obviously, one does not need a computer to cure natural or synthetic rubber, but if the computer use incorporated in the process patent significantly lessens the possibility of overcuring or undercuring, the process as a whole does not thereby become unpatentable subject matter.

A claim drawn to subject matter that is otherwise statutory does not become nonstatutory simply because it uses a mathematical formula, computer program, or digital computer. It is commonplace that an application of a law of nature or mathematical formula to a known structure or process may well be deserving of patent protection. That is, although a scientific truth, or the mathematical expression of it, is not a patentable invention, a novel and useful structure created with the aid of knowledge of scientific truth may be.

continued . . .

continued ...

The Arrhenius equation is not patentable in isolation, but when a process for curing rubber is devised that incorporates in it a more efficient solution of the equation, that process is not barred at the threshold by Section 101. In a determination of the eligibility of a process for patent protection, the claims must be considered as a whole. It is inappropriate to dissect the claims into old and new elements and then to ignore the presence of the old elements in the analysis. The novelty of any element or steps in a process is of no relevance in determining whether the subject matter of a claim falls with the Section 101 categories of patentable subject matter. Rather, novelty is of importance only with reference to the requirements of Section 102.

In this case, it may later be determined that D&L's process is not deserving of patent protection because it fails to satisfy conditions of novelty under Section 102 or nonobviousness under Section 103. A rejection on either of these grounds does not affect the determination that the subject matter of D&L's claims was eligible for patent protection under Section 101.

We view D&L's claims as nothing more than a process for molding rubber products and not as an attempt to patent a mathematical formula. We recognize, of course, that when a claim recites a mathematical formula (or scientific principle or phenomenon of nature), an inquiry must be made into whether the claim is seeking patent protection for the formula in the abstract. A mathematical formula as such is not accorded the protection of the patent laws, and this principle cannot be circumvented by attempting to limit the use of the formula to a particular technological environment. Similarly, insignificant postsolution activity will not transform an unpatentable principle into a patentable process. To hold otherwise would allow a competent draftsperson to evade the recognized limitations on the type of subject matter eligible for patent protection. On the other hand, when a claim containing a mathematical formula implements or applies that formula in a structure or process that, when considered as a whole, is performing a function that the patent laws were designed to protect (e.g., transforming or reducing an article to a different state or thing), then the claim satisfies the requirements of Section 101.

Because we do not view D&L's claims as an attempt to patent a mathematical formula, but rather to be drawn to an industrial process for the molding of rubber products, we affirm the judgment of the Court of Customs and Patent Appeals.

Diamond v. Diehr makes it clear that a process does not become unpatentable subject matter simply because a computer program is incorporated within it. The Supreme Court recognized that computer programs achieve their tasks by solving problems based on laws of nature. However, so do all inventions. For instance, a traditional clock depending on gears keeps the correct time only because the gear ratios have been accurately determined based on mathematical and geometric relationships. All inventions work because the laws of nature allow them to work. Thus, it is not enough that an invention simply uses a law of nature for it to be designated unpatentable. Rather, as the Supreme Court indicated, the invention must be little else but a law of nature for it to be designated unpatentable.

Old Standards and the Importance of Physical Transformations   After *Diamond v. Diehr*, the courts and the PTO have struggled with defining the characteristics of particular computer-related inventions that might render them unpatentable due to the use of mathematical algorithms or laws of nature. The most widely used test, coined the Freeman-Walter-Abele test, was developed in a series of Court of Claims and Patent Appeals opinions (this court preceded the Federal Circuit), and was employed until the mid-1990s by the Federal Circuit and the PTO. The Freeman-Walter-Abele test required a two-step analysis to determine the patentability of computer-based inventions. The first step was to determine if the computer process employed a mathematical algorithm. If not, then there logically would be no concern that patent protection of the process would allow the patentee to exercise unwarranted control over a natural law. Therefore, if the answer to this inquiry was that the invention did not rely on a mathematical algorithm, than the invention was considered the appropriate subject matter for a patent without the need for further inquiry.

However, if the computer process did make use of a mathematical algorithm, a second step was required to investigate whether the algorithm was applied in some fashion to physical elements or processes. These extra attributes were considered necessary to ensure that the patent extended only to the use of the mathematical algorithm and not to the algorithm itself. The focus of this inquiry was very much on the ways that the mathematical algorithm was used in the invention to allow certain physical transformations to take place. The test raised few questions when applied to inventions like the rubber curing process in *Diamond v. Diehr*. For in that case, it is very clear that the invention involved a lot of physical activity such as opening and closing a press. In addition, the computer process used the mathematical algorithm to transform an electrical signal representing heat into a signal that activated the press. Thus, the invention entailed more than simply the mathematical equation. Rather, it constituted a technological application of the equation.

To reiterate, the goal of the Freeman-Walter-Abele test was to analytically confirm that a patent was directed to an application of a mathematical algorithm and not to the algorithm itself. The easy cases were those in which the algorithm was merely one of several important attributes of a machine, such as in *Diehr*. However, the courts and the PTO became increasingly reluctant as the invention looked less like a machine and more like a system that merely solved an equation. For instance, one could not get a patent on a computer process that simply displayed the results of its numerical calculations on a screen because the physical aspects of the invention were so inconsequential. From this, it does not take a great leap to understand why there was so much concern whether software programs might be patentable. For one thing, a software program, by itself, does not do anything physical. Rather, the transformations only occur when the program gets the separate computer to operate according to its instructions. This led to the view that software programs, such as might exist separately on a floppy disk, were not patentable, since they did nothing more than indicate a series of logical steps that a computer might use to solve a problem. In effect, software might be viewed as merely a series of unapplied mental steps. For this reason, patent attorneys went out of their ways to claim these inventions not as a separate software process, but in terms of making the computer—the physical machine—do particular things. The feeling was that the more the computer program appeared to be integrated into the physical function of the computer machine, the more patentable it appeared. If this seems to exalt form over substance, your instincts are correct. Yet, this is just what occurred. A related concern with software programs was that they primarily crunched numbers, albeit in complex ways, and then simply recorded the results of those operations on the computer display monitor. For these reasons, application of the Freeman-Walter-Abele test led to continuing concerns that computer-based inventions that did not involve substantial additional physical functions, such as opening a press, were not patentable.

The Modern Trend   Beginning in the early 1990s, the Federal Circuit, in a series of cases, lowered the bar in terms of the physical transformations that are required for a computer process to be patentable subject matter under the Freeman-Walter-Abele test. For instance, in *Arrhythmia Research Technology, Inc. v. Corazonix Corp.,*[123] the court evaluated a method for analyzing electrocardiograph signals to determine the likelihood that a heart attack patient might become subject to a heart arrhythmia condition which is dangerous if not immediately treated with medications. Essentially, the process took a portion of the electrocardiograph signal, processed it through a filter, and performed a mathematical calculation on the output. The process then compared the resultant number with a predetermined level and indicated whether the patient was highly susceptible to arrhythmia based on that comparison. One way to look at the invention is that it merely took a selected input number, performed a calculation, and indicated the risk level based on that calculation. Clearly, this is much closer to simply solving an equation than what took place in *Diehr*. Yet, the Federal Circuit concluded that this was patentable subject matter. It stated that the "claimed steps of converting, applying, determining and comparing are physical process steps that transform one physical electrical signal into another. The view that there is nothing necessarily physical about signals is incorrect."

In 1994, the Federal Circuit decided *In re Alappat*,[124] in which it overturned the PTO's rejection of claims to an oscilloscope. One problem with oscilloscopes is that their waveforms may appear choppy because they are composed of a series of straight lines between two points. The *Alappat* invention made the waveform appear more consistent by increasing the brightness of the pixels that were closest to the waveform. This was achieved through a series of mathematical calculations. The court concluded that the oscilloscope was patentable subject matter. It determined that the transformation from waveform data to pixel illumination intensity data was sufficient to comply with the Freeman-Walter-Abele test. The Federal Circuit also offered some opinions regarding the patentability of computer programs. It stated that under the PTO's reasoning, a programmed general purpose computer could never be viewed as patentable subject matter under Section 101. However, this reasoning, it said, is without basis in the law. According to the Federal Circuit, the Supreme Court had never held that a programmed computer may never be entitled to patent protection. Indeed, the Supreme Court specifically stated in one opinion that its decision did not preclude a patent for every program servicing a computer. For this reason, the Federal Circuit concluded in *Alappat* that "a computer operating pursuant to software may represent patentable subject matter."

PTO Guidelines   In 1996, the PTO issued new guidelines for its examiners to use in evaluating the patentability of computer-related inventions. The likely impetus for these changes was from the Federal Circuit, which was making it pretty clear that any physical activity, required under the Freeman-Walter-Abele test, was minimal. In addition, the court often instructed that inventions had to be evaluated as a whole without undue focus on their reliance on mathematical algorithms. In response, the PTO guidelines now tell examiners to rely less on technical formalities and concentrate more on what the invention really is. They make it clear that the PTO will issue patents for computer software, no matter how they are framed. Thus, one can get a patent for (1) a computer invention that operates under the operation of software, (2) a computer readable memory that directs a computer to operate in a particular manner, or (3) a series of steps to be performed with a computer. In other words, the software may be structured as part of a machine, as instructions on a memory format, such as a disk, or as a process. No longer should patent attorneys feel constrained to make the software appear to be part of a machine. Rather, substance is to take precedence over form. The guidelines also indicate what is not patentable. For instance, a compilation of nonfunctional information or data is not patentable. Also, the guidelines provide that a process consisting solely of steps to solve a mathematical problem is not patentable. Based on *Corazonix* and *Alappat*, this clearly was intended to have little effect. And after the *State Street* opinion, which follows, that role clearly is diminished even further.

Computer Applications of Business Methods   In 1998, the Federal Circuit handed down a landmark decision in *State Street Bank & Trust Co. v. Signature Financial Group*, which addressed the patentability of business software designed to perform financial calculations for an investment system. As you will see, the case effectively rejects the notion that computer-related inventions might not be patentable due to their use of mathematical algorithms, even when there is no physical activity besides calculating and displaying numbers.

State Street also is important because it explicitly deals with another troublesome issue regarding computer systems. As noted earlier, business ideas are not properly the subjects of patent protection; only novel and nonobvious systems implementing those ideas are patentable. Questions naturally arise when computers are used to effectuate these systems, particularly when they rely extensively on numerical calculations. Prior to *State Street*, the leading case addressing this topic dealt with a computer process implementing the Merrill Lynch Cash Management Accounting (CMA) system.[125] Among other things, the system managed up to four types of financial accounts so that idle cash balances were invested promptly in money market funds, and so that credit card liabilities were paid most efficiently for customers according to a schedule indicating the cheapest sources of available funds. The Delaware federal court noted that the CMA method would not be patentable if it were done by hand. However, it determined that the patent on the computer system was valid because it demonstrated a method of operation on a computer to effectuate a business activity. In other words, although the idea was not patentable, the computerized system to implement it was.

The Federal Circuit, in *State Street*, follows this reasoning but makes the argument more strongly. It explicitly rejects the notion that methods of doing business somehow require special consideration when implemented through computer processes. Rather, the inquiry is the same no matter what objective the invention has—does it do something useful in a way that is novel and nonobvious? In this way, *State Street* again slams the judicial door shut on those who argue that computers require special attention under the patent laws.

STATE STREET BANK & TRUST CO. V. SIGNATURE FINANCIAL GROUP
Federal Circuit Court of Appeals, 1998

FACTS: Signature is the owner of the '056 patent which is generally directed to a data processing system for implementing an investment structure. In essence, the system, which is identified by the proprietary name Hub & Spoke, facilitates a structure whereby several mutual funds (Spokes) pool their investments in a single investment portfolio (Hub) allowing for economies of scale in administering investments. The system determines the percentage share that each Spoke maintains in the Hub, while taking into consideration daily changes both in the value of the Hub's investment securities and in the concomitant amount of each Spoke's assets. The system allows for the allocation among the Spokes of the Hub's daily income, expenses, and net realized gain or loss. The system additionally tracks all the relevant data determined on a daily basis for the Hub and each Spoke, so that aggregate year end income, expenses, and capital gain or loss can be determined for accounting and tax purposes for the Hub and for each publicly traded Spoke. It is essential that these calculations be quickly and accurately performed. In large part this is required because each Spoke sells shares to the public and the price of those shares is substantially based on the Spoke's percentage interest in the portfolio. Given the complexity of the calculations, a computer or equivalent device is a virtual necessity to perform the task.

State Street and Signature are both in the business of acting as custodians and accounting agents for multi-tiered fund financial services. State Street negotiated with Signature for a license to use the patented Hub & Spoke system, but these negotiations broke down. State Street brought an action asking the District Court to, among other things, declare the patent invalid, arguing that the patent did not claim statutory subject matter under section 101. The district court found the patent invalid, and Signature appealed the determination to the Federal Circuit.

DECISION AND REASONING: The district court concluded that the claimed subject matter fell into one of two alternative judicially-created exceptions to statutory subject matter. The court refers to the first exception as the "mathematical algorithm" exception and the second exception as the "business method" exception.

The plain and unambiguous meaning of section 101 is that any invention falling within one of the four stated categories of statutory subject matter may be patented, provided it meets the other requirements for patentability. The repetitive use of the expansive term "any" in section 101 shows Congress's intent not to place any restrictions on the subject matter for which a patent may be obtained beyond those specifically recited in section 101. Indeed, the Supreme Court has acknowledged that Congress intended section 101 to extend to anything under the sun that is made by man. Thus, it is improper to read limitations into section 101 on the subject matter that may be patented where the legislative history indicates that Congress clearly did not intend such limitations.

The Mathematical Algorithm Exception. The Supreme Court has identified three categories of subject matter that are unpatentable, namely laws of nature, natural phenomena and abstract ideas. Unpatentable mathematical algorithms are identifiable by showing they are merely abstract ideas constituting disembodied concepts or truths that are not "useful." From a practical standpoint, this means that to be patentable an algorithm must be applied in a "useful" way. In *In re Alappat*, we held that data, transformed by a machine through a series of mathematical calculations to produce a smooth waveform display on a rasterizer monitor, constituted a practical application of an abstract idea (a mathematical algorithm, formula or calculation), because it produced a useful, concrete and tangible result—the smooth waveform. Similarly, in *Arrhythmia Research Technology Inc. v. Corazonix Corp.*, we held that the transformation of electrocardiograph signals from a patient's heartbeat by a machine through a series of mathematical calculations constituted a practical application of an abstract idea (a mathematical algorithm, formula or calculation), because it corresponded to a useful, concrete or tangible thing—the condition of a patient's heart.

continued . . .

continued . . .

Today, we hold that the transformation of data, representing discrete dollar amounts, by a machine through a series of mathematical calculations in a final share price, constitutes a practical application of a mathematical algorithm, formula, or calculation, because it produces a useful, concrete and tangible result—a final share price momentarily fixed for recording and reporting purposes and even accepted and relied upon by regulatory authorities and in subsequent trades. After *Diehr* and *Alappat*, the mere fact that a claimed invention involves inputting numbers, calculating numbers, outputting numbers, and storing numbers, in and of itself, would not render it nonstatutory subject matter, unless, of course, its operation does not produce a useful, concrete and tangible result.

The district court erred by applying the Freeman-Walter-Abele test to determine whether the claimed subject matter was an unpatentable abstract idea. The Freeman-Walter-Abele test was designed by the Court of Customs and Patent Appeals, and subsequently adopted by this court, to extract and identify unpatentable mathematical algorithms. After *Diehr* and *Chakrabarty*, the Freeman-Walter-Abele test has little, if any, applicability to determining the presence of statutory subject matter. As we pointed out in *Alappat*, application of the test could be misleading because a process, machine, manufacture, or composition of matter employing laws of nature, physical phenomenon or abstract idea is patentable subject matter even though a law of nature, natural phenomenon, or abstract idea would not, by itself, be entitled to such protection. The test determines the presence of, for example, an algorithm. However, after *Diehr* and *Alappat*, the mere fact that a claimed invention involves inputting numbers, calculating numbers, outputting numbers, and storing numbers, in and of itself, would not render it nonstatutory subject matter, unless, of course, its operation does not produce a useful, concrete and tangible result.

The question of whether a claim encompasses statutory subject matter should not focus on which of the four categories of subject matter a claim is directed to—process, machine, manufacture, or composition of matter—but rather on the essential characteristics of the subject matter, in particular, its practical utility. Section 101 specifies that statutory subject matter must also satisfy the other conditions and requirements of the Patent Act, including novelty, nonobviousness, and adequacy of disclosure and notice. For purpose of our analysis, the patent claim is directed to a machine programmed with the Hub and Spoke software and admittedly produces a useful, concrete and tangible result. This renders it statutory subject matter, even if the useful result is expressed in numbers, such as profit, percentage, cost, or loss.

The Business Method Exception. As an alternative ground for invalidating the '056 patent under section 101, the district court relied on the judicially-created, so-called "business method" exception to statutory subject matter. We take this opportunity to lay this ill-conceived exception to rest. The business method exception has never been invoked by this court to deem an invention unpatentable. Application of this particular exception has always been preceded by a ruling based on some clearer concept of the Patent Act or, more commonly, application of the abstract idea exception based on finding a mathematical algorithm.

The district court announced the precepts of the business method exception as set forth in several treatises, but noted as its primary reason for finding the patent invalid under the business method exception as follows:

> If Signature's invention were patentable, any financial institution desirous of implementing a multi-tiered funding complex modeled on a Hub and Spoke configuration would be required to seek Signature's permission before embarking on such a project. This is so because the '056 patent is claimed sufficiently broadly to foreclose virtually any computer-implemented accounting method necessary to manage this type of financial structure.

Whether the patent claims are too broad to be patentable is not to be judged under section 101, but rather under sections 102, 103 and 112. Assuming the above statement to be correct, it has nothing to do with whether what is claimed is statutory subject matter. Whether the claims are directed to subject matter within section 101 should not turn on whether the claimed subject matter does "business" instead of something else.

The appealed decision is reversed and the case is remanded to the district

---

With *Diamond v. Diehr* as a springboard, patent policy has now progressed to the point where computer-related inventions no longer are considered a unique class of technology requiring special scrutiny. The fact that they rely heavily on mathematical algorithms or implement methods of doing business is not important in appraising their suitability for patent protection. Nor does their form matter. As the PTO guidelines and court decisions make clear, patent protection is available for software programs in isolation as well as in conjunction with a machine.

Patents for Internet Business Methods With the meteoric rise of the Internet, those with computer expertise are busily developing new inventions that allow business transactions to be carried out in cyberspace. It should come as little surprise that these individuals are looking to the patent system to protect their investments. The PTO issued 1,595 Internet patents in fiscal year 1998, which was more than triple the number allowed in 1997.[126] Some notable examples of Internet patents that were granted by the PTO are:

- A patent for a system to carry out reverse sellers' auctions over the Web (Priceline.com, Inc.).[127]
- A patent for a one-click ordering system that stores a customer's billing and shipping information so it does not have to be reentered on subsequent visits (Amazon.com, Inc.).
- A patent for an on-line frequent-buyer program that rewards Web shoppers with benefits such as American AAdvantage miles (Netincentives, Inc.).
- A patent for a method for delivering advertising on the Internet (DoubleClick, Inc.).
- A patent related to the "shopping carts" which are used to aid on-line purchasing (Open Market, Inc.).
- A patent for a system that pays computer users for responding to on-line advertisements and surveys (Cybergold).
- A patent for a method that permits customers to choose options for a car ordered over the Internet (Trilogy Software, Inc).
- A patent for a system to embed Web addresses in e-mail postings (Thomas Higley).

By 1999, companies owning patents such as these had already begun to bring legal actions against others who allegedly were violating them. For instance, Amazon.com sued Barnesandnoble.com for infringing its one-click ordering system only one month after its patent was issued.[128] In December 1999, a federal district judge in Seattle granted a preliminary injunction, barring Barnesandnoble.com from using its Express Lane service.[129] Preliminary injunctions will be discussed further in Chapter 4 regarding trade secrets. Essentially they are used as an emergency measure based on an abbreviated hearing to stop a practice when the judge is convinced that the plaintiff is very likely to win at trial and will suffer irreparable harm if something is not done immediately. In another action, Priceline.com sued Microsoft, claiming that Microsoft's Hotel Price matcher infringed its reverse auction patent.[130] Also in 1999, Double Click sued L90, Inc., contending that L90's advertisement and tracking software and hardware infringed its Internet advertising patent.[131]

The reactions to many of these patents were little different from the feelings expressed after the PTO first allowed Compton New Media's patent on a multimedia search-and-retrieval system. Numerous industry participants argue that many of these patents cover well-worn business methods that have been applied to the Internet in obvious ways.[132] Perhaps PTO examiners overlook relevant publicly available prior art because they do not have sufficient information about computer technologies and business systems at their fingertips. As will be discussed shortly, this is a problem that continues to plague the patent office, although its resources are improving steadily. Also, there may be firms that used some of these business methods within their internal operations but kept them secret, since, until *State Street*, they may have believed that business methods were not patentable. The American Inventors Protection Act helps alleviate this potential problem.[133] If business methods were used in secrecy, then other companies still may receive patents on them. However, the prior users may be able to continue using the methods without infringing the patents.

One also must keep in mind that a patent is not beyond challenge just because the PTO issues it. We have already noted that the PTO subsequently rejected the Compton patent through its own reexamination, a process we will look at in Chapter 3. In addition, patents may be overturned or narrowed in the courts, usually in the course of infringement actions. But it should be clear that with Internet and computer-related patents, the battleground has shifted from arguments about subject matter to debates regarding the novelty and nonobviousness of the invention.

Other Issues Regarding Patents for Computer Programs   Now that it has been clearly established that patents are available in the United States for computer-related technologies, this does not end the problems and debates in this arena. Clearly, many considerations, such as the cost to obtain a patent, are the same with the computer field as with other more traditional contexts. Nonetheless, computer-based inventions raise their own interesting problems and considerations. In addition, many experts still vociferously argue that it is wrong, from a policy point of view, to grant patents for computer software. We now turn to some of these issues and arguments.

RECEIVING A PATENT FROM THE PTO   While *Diamond v. Diehr* was under review by the Supreme Court, some 3,000 computer-related applications were held by the PTO pending the decision in that case. Ever since the Court announced its decision, the PTO has been playing catch-up with an ever-increasing number of computer-related filings. For instance, in 1997, the PTO estimated that it received close to 37,000 patent applications for software inventions.[134]

Whereas patents in more traditional areas may be received an average of 22 months after filing, the average length of pendency for computer systems, albeit improving, still is closer to 2½ years. Coupled with that fact is the rapidity of technological change in this arena. One relevant question therefore concerns the expected life cycle of an invention, because those who wish to clone computer software may do so without restraint from patent policies until the patent issues.[135] While evaluating this, one must bear in mind that patents on computer systems often extend beyond the confines of a particular program. Thus, the relevant life cycle may not simply be that of a defined software product. Rather, the potential family of products to which the invention might apply must be considered.

Because patent protection for computer processes is a relatively new area, the PTO's data bank of prior art, although improving rapidly, still is not fully developed.[136] The PTO has taken substantial steps to improve its sources of information, especially through on-line commercial databases such as DIALOG, ORBIT, and Mead Data Central. However, patent examiners often do not have the time to make comprehensive searches of these sources, due mainly to the sheer volume of patent applications that they are called upon to evaluate.[137] Therefore, they usually spend the bulk of their time reviewing information contained within previously issued U.S. patents. In established technical fields, this may not be a problem, since most pertinent prior art information has built up over time within the patent files. However, there are not yet sufficient numbers of issued computer-related patents to provide the same level of confidence. In addition, there have been allegations that PTO examiners do not have the proper qualifications to sufficiently understand computer software inventions.[138] Some believe that insufficient information at the hands of, or utilized by, PTO examiners coupled with inappropriate backgrounds cause those examiners to mistakenly grant patents for computer systems that are not novel. As examples, they point to several controversial patents issued by PTO examiners in the mid-1990's, including, (1) the patent originally issued to Compton's New Media for a multimedia retrieval system, (2) a patent received by Software Advertising Corporation covering the use of computer screen savers for advertising, and (3) patents issued for Internet business processes, as noted above, such as the one for shopping carts.[139]

For those computer programmers who are contemplating patents, these alleged deficiencies within the PTO lead to two concerns, which unfortunately are at odds in making the decision about patent protection. On the one hand, an issued patent may be at risk because a challenge could uncover the overlooked prior art. This could lead to a loss of patent rights, thereby freeing the technology for all to use. When this occurs, the better solution may have been to have kept the technology under wraps rather than to have publicly disclosed it through the patent process. On the other hand, a patent does carry a lot of power while in force, and the PTO decision to issue one commands substantial deference from the Federal Circuit. Along with this, one must consider that the decision to maintain an invention in secrecy rather than to obtain a patent might open the way for a competitor to claim the invention. Thus, the decision not to pursue a patent carries substantial risks as well.[140]

DISCLOSURE   A concern with all patents is how public disclosure of the invention might ultimately be used by competitors to their benefit. Possibly competitors can use disclosure to develop products that do not infringe the claims of a patent. Or, if a patent is found to be invalid, they will then be free to use as they wish the knowledge they obtain. An inventor who fully evaluates these risks might determine that another form of protection, such as trade secrets, may be more appropriate.

The discussion of trade secrets in Chapter 4 shows that computer programs and processes can be successfully protected as trade secrets, particularly if the processes are distributed only in limited contexts amenable to controls ensuring that their secrets will be maintained. However, trade secret protection may not be adequate for mass-marketed products, because customers are free to reverse-engineer products (by decompilation and disassembly), thereby allowing them to learn the sets of instructions that make the processes operate.[141] In addition, the critical features of some inventions, such as with graphical user interfaces, are valuable only in a public environment, limiting the applicability of trade secret protection.

There are other negative aspects about trade secret protection. For instance, if a computer program or process is developed in conjunction with university professors, the professors likely will want to publish the details of the work, thereby making the "secrets" publicly available for competitors to use. Also, trade secret protection does not guard against independent creation of the same process, as does patent protection: strong market demand for an invention means that there likely will be a host of competitors working on achieving the same solution. Depending on the circumstances, these deficiencies of trade secrets suggest that patent protection will be superior if the costs are manageable and the required disclosures are not too extreme.

The disclosure requirements for patent applications will be discussed in the next chapter. Essentially, sufficient information must be disclosed to enable one skilled in the art to make the invention. For a computer process, the application may not have to reveal source or object code to achieve this purpose. Rather, a flow chart presenting the logic of the process may suffice, as long as a skilled programmer could in a reasonable amount of time draft a working program based on the flow chart. In addition, if the computer process is not the entire invention, but rather is one aspect of a broader invention, then the inventor may be able to disclose even less about how to implement the process. The risks from disclosure, therefore, depend greatly on the particular circumstances. *White Consolidated Industries v. Vega Servo-Control, Inc.*, presented in the next chapter, provides a good example of how to evaluate the requisite amount of disclosure for computer processes.

THE POSSIBILITY OF COPYRIGHT PROTECTION   The decision to seek patent protection for computer programs carries another wrinkle because, unlike with most other utilitarian inventions, the copyright system represents another viable means of protection. All else being equal, an inventor has reasons to prefer copyright protection because it is much cheaper and easier to obtain, and it enjoys a longer life. However, in theory, everything is not equal, for copyright is designed to protect expressions, whereas patents may protect systems. In addition, copyright protects only against copying, whereas a patent reaches even independent creation of the same invention.

As we will investigate fully in Chapter 6, there is substantial controversy over the amount of protection a computer program may be entitled to enjoy from copyright. The debate comes down to determining just what aspects of the program constitute protectible expression and what parts compose the system to which copyright may not extend. Some courts are willing to grant substantial protection to computer programs through copyright. According to them, a copyright on a computer program may prevent competitors from developing programs having the same "look and feel" as the protected program. Although such protection does not prevent competitors from making programs having the same purposes as the copyrighted work, it does severely restrain the ways competitors may go about achieving those ends. Under some circumstances this may be almost as beneficial as protecting the system under the patent laws. However, one must be cautious here, because a clear new trend has emerged in the courts, which are retreating from such sweeping copyright protection for computer programs. Nonetheless, copyright protection still is clearly applicable. The end result is that managers undertaking to protect computer processes must evaluate how copyright protection might fit into their strategic plans. Depending on the circumstances, copyrights may be used either in lieu of patents, in addition to patents, or possibly not at all.

INTERNATIONAL PATENT PROTECTION OF COMPUTER PROGRAMS   Although patent policies in the United States now clearly provide that inventors may receive patents for computer processes and programs, policies regarding such inventions in other global regions may be less certain. Up to the early 1990s, only a handful of the industrialized nations permitted patents to be granted for computer software. Since then, however, there has been a definite trend to follow the lead of the United States, enabling computer-related inventions to be the subjects of patents. For instance, in 1997, the Japanese Patent Office adopted Guidelines for Computer Software Related Inventions which have many similarities to those used by the PTO in the United States. In general, computer programs are patentable in Japan as long as they possess a high degree of technical creativity and utilize the laws of nature. In addition, computer programs may be patented as processes or as products and may be recorded on machine-readable media, including CD-ROMs and diskettes.[142] In 1995, New Zealand changed its longtime practice of refusing to issue patents for computer software inventions. According to the new policy, a computer program may be patented if it involves the production of some commercially useful effect. As in the United States, mathematical algorithms may not be patented unless they are implemented in some manner to produce a useful result.

Europe is slightly more enigmatic, although the clear trend in that region, too, is to permit software patents.[143] For example, France's patent law states that mathematical methods and computer programs may not be considered patentable inventions. However, the French courts have interpreted this only to mean that programs, by themselves, are not patentable. In a ruling similar to that in *Diamond v. Diehr*, the Paris Court of Appeal ruled that an invention should not be deprived of patent protection merely because a computer controls several of its steps. Similarly, the European Patent Convention declares that "programs for computers" are not patentable subject matter. Nonetheless, the Guidelines of the European Patent Office (EPO) direct that "patentability should not be denied merely on the ground that a computer program is involved." The test used by the EPO is whether the software invention produces a technical or physical effect. Under this standard, the EPO will grant a patent for an invention, even if it is primarily a computer program, as long as it solves a technical problem. For instance, the EPO has issued a patent for an algorithmic method to convert word processing command codes. On the other hand, patent applications for computer programs that involve more intellectual or abstract activities have been rejected. Thus, it might be a stretch to say that patent practice in Europe regarding computer programs is as liberal as that enunciated by the Federal Circuit in the *State Street* opinion. Nevertheless, influential patent practitioners indicated in 1998 that they were satisfied that the European Commission and the EPO were making rapid progress toward allowing the full range of protections for software-related inventions.[144]

One of the international changes sought by the United States in the mid-1990s, when serious negotiations took place through WIPO to formulate a thorough

Patent Harmonization Treaty, was for enhanced patent protection of computer-related inventions. As noted, this effort stalled in 1995, mostly due to U.S. concerns. Since then, efforts have focused mostly on procedural matters, while the more substantive issues have been deferred. Thus, it is unclear how much influence WIPO will have regarding this issue in the near future. The TRIPs agreement of the GATT Uruguay Round indicates that all classes of inventions except certain forms of life must be accorded patent protection. However, it does not specifically address whether software-related inventions must be protected. Thus, a company having an international vision must consider the possibility that a novel and nonobvious computer process may enjoy patent protection in the United States and countries such as Japan but may not receive patent rights in various other important marketing and manufacturing regions. In those countries, protection, if available at all, will have to be achieved through copyright laws. Clearly, international issues must be considered early in the strategic planning process because the issuance of a patent in the United States will make knowledge of the invention publicly accessible. This, of course, may have devastating consequences if the knowledge is then used to manufacture and distribute products in potentially lucrative trading environments wherein patent protection is unavailable.

THE CONTROVERSY CONTINUES: SHOULD COMPUTER PROGRAMS BE PATENTABLE? The availability of patent protection for computer software in the United States does not mean that there has been an end to the controversy over the propriety of such protection.[145] As mentioned earlier, many experts in the field believe that the PTO has sometimes issued "bad" patents because of inappropriate search facilities and routines as well as insufficient expertise. It is true that those bad patents could theoretically be challenged at any time based on their lack of novelty. However, according to the experts, small companies may not be willing to invest resources in such a challenge, especially with the presumption of validity that attends a PTO decision. Rather, it may make more sense for these companies to accept a license fee from the patentee, thereby leaving the inappropriate patent unchallenged.

Opponents to software patents also note that because software clearly was not patentable before 1981, programmers took steps to protect the secrecy of their computer processes. With the change of position by the courts, the door has opened for companies to claim computer processes that, strictly speaking, may have been secret, but yet still were within the common knowledge of many programmers.[146] Another concern of this group is that computer programs may include a host of patentable processes. If just one of these is already patented, then programmers could be sued for infringement, severely jeopardizing their business operations. Therefore, a programmer must conduct patent searches for all these processes—even without the intention to obtain patents—simply to evaluate the risks of infringement. However, patent searches of computer processes are expensive, possibly totalling up to $2,000 per search.[147] In addition, those against patent protection believe that the large stimulus of a patent is unnecessary for computer programs because programmers do not risk large amounts of capital in their creative endeavors. To confirm this argument, they point to the remarkable growth of the industry in an era when patent protection was not even available. Finally, this opposing group is concerned because the confidentiality of the patent process leads to surprise when the patent issues, thereby requiring computer programming firms, some of which are relatively small, to pay unanticipated license fees. In this regard, one only needs to consider the shock waves that reverberated through the computer industry in 1990 when Gilbert Hyatt received a patent on microprocessors after the PTO had spent more than 15 years reviewing the application in secrecy.[148]

Those who approve of patents for computer processes counter these positions with equally compelling arguments.[149] They claim that the PTO must contend with a learning curve for all new technologies. There is nothing particularly special about computer software that makes it more troublesome for the PTO than biotechnology is. Once the PTO identifies its deficiencies in handling new technologies, it takes steps to rectify them. This is currently happening in the computer area. For instance, the PTO is developing a new software classification system, is improving its search facilities, and is increasing its number of software examiners. Proponents also doubt that the industry would continue to advance so rapidly without patents. According to them, the early innovations occurred without patents because the developers were using software to sell hardware. Software now is often extremely complex, making it expensive and risky to develop. In addition, recent court decisions suggest that the copyright system may not be as effective in protecting software as it used to be. Without patents, software developers may be left with little alternative but to rely heavily on trade secrets.

Those supporting patents for software also point out that the United States recently changed its patent system, so that most patent applications now will be published 18 months after they are filed. This will substantially account for the objections raised by confidentiality and surprise. In addition, recent changes to reexamination procedures coupled with early publication will provide computer professionals the opportunity to put more relevant information in the hands of PTO examiners.[150] These measures, therefore, should enable the agency to make more informed decisions. Finally, supporters argue that any move to treat software as a special case in the United States may make attempts to achieve uniform protection standards within the international community impossible. From all this, one can easily see that the controversy continues. Nonetheless, the policy direction is now firmly established. Patents may be used to protect computer software, and there seems little prospect for turning the clock back, no matter how much one fears the consequences.

((AES)) In conclusion, there is no longer any doubt that computer programs may be patented in the United States. Inventions utilizing computers, as well as computer processes and computer software, all are patentable subject matter. Thus, the door is open for patent protection in the United States for an invention such as **AES**. In addition, it is possible to claim isolated features of **AES**, such as the computer process or software. However, the ultimate decision to seek patent protection should be made only after one comprehensively considers the full spectrum of ways to preserve rights in the invention, in terms of both their respective positive attributes and their possible negative consequences.

DESIGN PATENTS

Section 171 of the Patent Act provides, "Whoever invents any new, original and ornamental design for an article of manufacture may obtain a patent thereof, subject to the conditions and requirements of this title." There is little doubt among marketing professionals that a product's design may be one of the most important attributes impacting a consumer's purchase decision. As we shall review in Chapter 6, copyright does not offer much opportunity to protect product designs in the United States, although there have been legislative efforts for change. The discussion in Chapter 7 will demonstrate that trademark protection is a possibility, but with a lot of qualifications. Thus, the primary means to protect innovative product designs in the United States is through design patents. The following Federal Circuit opinion clearly presents the requirements to receive design patent protection and gives the special considerations that are used to determine if there is infringement of such a patent.

AVIA GROUP INTERNATIONAL, INC. V. L.A. GEAR CALIFORNIA
Federal Circuit, 1988

FACTS: The subject of this controversy consists of two design patents owned by Avia. The first, termed the '420 patent, claims an ornamental design for an athletic shoe outer sole. The other, designated the '301 patent, claims an ornamental design for an athletic shoe upper. L.A. Gear sold two athletic shoe models—Boy's Thrasher and Boy's Thrasher Hi-Top. Avia sued L.A. Gear, claiming that Boy's Thrasher infringed its '420 design patent and that the Hi-Top model infringed both patents. L.A. Gear alleged that there was no infringement and requested the court to declare that the two patents were invalid because the designs were both obvious and functional. The district court found for Avia, and L.A. Gear appealed to the Federal Circuit.

DECISION AND REASONING:
Validity of '420 and '301 Design Patents. A patent is presumed valid. The burden is on a challenger to introduce evidence that raises the issue of invalidity. Further, the challenger must establish facts, by clear and convincing evidence, that persuasively lead to the conclusion of invalidity.

The patents in suit are design patents. Under Section 171, a patent may be obtained on the design of an article of manufacture that is "new, original and ornamental" and "nonobvious" within the meaning of Section 103, which is incorporated by reference into Section 171.

continued . . .

continued . . .

Ornamental versus Functional Designs. L.A. Gear correctly asserts that if a patented design is "primarily functional" rather than primarily ornamental, the patent is invalid. When function dictates a design, protection would not promote the decorative arts—a purpose of the design patent statute. There is no dispute that shoes are functional and that certain features of the shoe designs at issue perform functions. However, a distinction exists between the functionality of an article or features thereof and the functionality of the particular design of such article or features thereof that perform a function. Were that not true, it would not be possible to obtain a design patent on a utilitarian article of manufacture or to obtain both design and utility patents on the same article.

With respect to functionality of the design of the '301 patent, the district court made the following observations:

> L.A. Gear took each little aspect of the upper and pointed out that many of the aspects or features in the upper have a function. Even if this is assumed to be true, that would not make the design primarily functional. If the functional aspect or purpose could be accomplished in many other ways than is involved in this very design, that fact is enough to destroy the claim that this design is primarily functional. There are many things in the '301 patent on the upper which are clearly ornamental and nonfunctional such as the location of perforations and how they are arranged, and the stitching and how it's arranged, and the coloration of elements between black and white colors. The overall aesthetics of the various components and the way they are combined are quite important and are not functional.

On the design of the '420 patent, the district court made a similar analysis of various features and drew these conclusions:

> Every function which L.A. Gear says is achieved by one of the component aspects of the sole in this case could be and has been achieved by different components. And that is a very persuasive rationale for the holding that the design overall is not primarily functional. Moreover, there is no function which even L.A. Gear assigns to the swirl effect around the pivot point, which is a very important aspect of the design. This is a unique and pleasing design and its patentability is not offset or destroyed by the fact that the utility patent is utilized and incorporated in this aesthetically pleasing design.

We agree with the district court that the designs in suit have not persuasively been shown to be functional.

Obviousness. Design patents must meet a nonobviousness requirement identical to that applicable to utility patents. Accordingly, Section 103 applies in order to determine whether the designs of the '420 and '301 patents would have been obvious to one of ordinary skill in the art.

Four factors must be considered in determining obviousness: the scope and content of the prior art, the differences between the prior art and the claims at issue, the level of ordinary skill in the art when the invention was made, and secondary indicia, such as commercial success and copying.

With respect to a design, obviousness is determined from the vantage of the designer of ordinary capability who designs articles of the type presented in the application. L.A. Gear argues that the designs would have been obvious because they are traditional ones consisting of features old in the art. That some components of Avia's designs exist in prior art references is not determinative. If the combined teachings suggest only components of the claimed design but not its overall appearance, a rejection under Section 103 is inappropriate. There is no evidence that the overall appearances of the '420 and '301 designs would have been suggested to ordinary shoe designers by the references.

L.A. Gear does not contest the commercial success of Avia's shoes manufactured according to the patented designs, but it argues the success is attributable to factors other than the designs themselves, such as advertising. Although commercial success is relevant only if a nexus is proven between the success of the patented product and the merits, Avia provided evidence tending to prove such nexus, and L.A. Gear has only conclusory statements in rebuttal. In addition, the district court referred to L.A. Gear's products as "copies" of the patented designs. Copying is additional evidence of nonobviousness.

On the basis of its evaluation of the four factors outlined above, the district court held that the ordinary designer would not have found the '420 and '301 designs, considered as whole designs, obvious in light of the differences between the prior art and the claimed designs. We agree.

Design Patent Infringement. In a previous case, the Supreme Court established the test for determining infringement of a design patent.

> If, in the eye of an ordinary observer, giving such attention as a purchaser usually gives, two designs are substantially the same, if the resemblance is such as to deceive such an observer, inducing him to purchase one supposing it to be the other, the first one patented is infringed by the other.

In addition to overall similarity of designs, the accused design must appropriate the novelty in the patented device that distinguishes it from the prior art.

continued . . .

continued . . .

The district court correctly applied this test for infringement. It made the following statements:

> L.A. Gear's soles are virtually identical to the '420 patent. In each instance, L.A. Gear has appropriated the novelty of the patented article. One needs only to look at the two soles to see that the infringement exists. But if it is necessary to particularize it, we have in the accused sole copying of the swirl effect, copying of the separate coloration and configuration of the pivot point, though without the red dot. And we have in the accused sole the whole general appearance, which is almost a direct copy of the patented sole. Similar analysis applies to the '301 upper. It is almost a direct copy—much more than the substantially-the-same standard.

Thus, the district court found that L.A. Gear's shoes had overall similarity to the patented designs and incorporated the novel features thereof. For the '420 patent, those features included the swirl effect and the pivot point; for the '301 patent, the novelty consisted of the combination of saddle, eyestay, and perforations.

L.A. Gear points to undisputed evidence that Avia's shoe, made in accordance with the patent, and L.A. Gear's accused models are intended for different customers. Avia's are for tennis players; L.A. Gear's are for children. That fact, according to L.A. Gear, renders the products not "substantially the same" as necessary under the infringement test. But L.A. Gear is grossly in error. To find infringement, the accused shoes need only appropriate a patentee's protected design, not a patentee's market as well. The products of the parties need not be directly competitive; indeed, an infringer is liable even when the patent owner puts out no product. Thus, infringement is not avoided by selling to a different class of purchasers.

For the foregoing reasons, we affirm the decision of the district court that L.A. Gear infringed Avia's valid patents.

((AES)) This case illustrates the basic requirements for a design patent. The design must be "primarily ornamental." This does not mean that the design cannot have attributes that perform functions. Rather, the design cannot be dictated by the utilitarian purposes of the product. In other words, the design must be only one of several equally suitable ways for the product to achieve its useful functions. In addition, as with all patents, the design will have to be novel and nonobvious. This inquiry, as *Avia* demonstrates, is the same as for utility patents. Therefore, it might be possible to receive a design patent for the "look" of the AES stereo component if the design is novel and nonobvious and is not required to make the system operate. Also, as the case indicates, we may receive utility patents for claims to the **AES** system along with a design patent for its appearance.

In the next chapter, it will be shown that the determination of infringement for utilitarian patents is a complicated affair. *Avia* clearly shows that with design patents, one is on much less technical ground. Essentially, a design infringes a design patent if it looks to an ordinary observer substantially the same as the protected design. This is true even if the design appears on a product sold to an entirely different universe of buyers. Therefore a design patent on **AES** would be infringed by a machine having a similar design, even if that other machine were sold to auto mechanics to test engine performance.

There is substantial speculation that design patents soon will have an increasingly important role to play in the computer industry.[151] As competition in the field intensifies, industry participants likely will take new steps to differentiate their products in the marketplace. One way for these firms to do this is by developing unique product designs, as the introduction of Apple's iMac computer in 1998 clearly demonstrates. Obtaining design patents for computer hardware items is one possible method to protect these designs, although computer firms have yet to make widespread use of this practice. Nonetheless, the variety of patents that have issued for computer hardware—such as for monitors, printers, keyboards, laptop personal computers, disk drive units, and modems—demonstrates the potential of this avenue of protection.

More controversial is the possibility of receiving design patent protection for graphical user interface screen displays. In 1988, the PTO issued 22 design patents to Xerox Corporation for attributes of screen displays such as icons. However, in 1989, the PTO rejected similar applications made by Xerox. The PTO indicated that screen displays are not the proper subjects for design patents because they are transitory and not affixed to a utilitarian article (the computer). On appeal, the Board of Patent Appeals and Interferences upheld the denial of Xerox's design patent applications, but it did so for procedural reasons dealing with how the applications were drafted.[152] More important, however, the board indicated that graphical displays on computer screens are the proper subjects for design patents, as long as the applications provide the required information in the appropriate fashion. Therefore, the way now seems clear for computer firms to receive design patents on screen displays as well as on the ornamental attributes of their hardware.

International Protection of Industrial Designs

The primary way to obtain protection for industrial designs in the United States is through design patents. To issue a design patent, the PTO must examine the design patent application to make sure that the design meets the standards of novelty and nonobviousness. Normally, one can expect the process of receiving a design patent to take about 18 months. Once granted, a design patent in the United States lasts for 14 years after the issue date.

Other countries, such as Japan, are similar to the United States in that a governmental body must examine an application for compliance with substantive standards before a design may receive legal protection. However, a host of other countries do not examine applications before granting protection. Rather, they offer
protection to industrial designs according to a registration system, which simply requires that procedural steps be followed. Therefore, government agencies in countries employing registration systems often can "review" an application and issue
protection much more quickly than can agencies in examination countries, such as
the United States and Japan.

The Hague Agreement   Normally, when designers want to receive protection for
industrial designs in other countries, they have to file applications in every country
in which protection is desired. Since 1934, the World Intellectual Property Organization ("WIPO") has administered the Hague Agreement Concerning the International Deposit of Industrial Designs, a treaty that makes it somewhat easier for designers to obtain protection in those countries that are parties to it. Under the
treaty, an applicant may file an "international" application with WIPO and designate the countries in which protection is desired. The application is made on a
standardized form and may be filed in French or English. A reproduction of the design then is published, and the appropriate governmental bodies in the designated
countries have up to six months to object to protection based on local laws. Design
protection automatically is granted in those countries that do not refuse protection
within the six-month period. Under the treaty, international protection lasts five
years, but it can be renewed for additional five-year periods. The length of protection in any individual countries may vary according to local laws, but it must last
at least ten years (assuming the international application and deposit is renewed for
a five-year extension).

The Hague Agreement facilitates international protection of industrial designs
because it standardizes application formats, centralizes the filing and fee process,
and allows a designer to file the application in one language. However, as of 1999,
only 29 countries had signed the agreement. Notably absent from the list of signatories are the United States and Japan, among many other important countries. The
reason that many countries are reluctant to join the Hague Agreement is that the
six-month period to object is not enough time for substantive examinations. This
explains why most countries that have become members to the treaty have registration systems rather than examination systems.

In the late 1990s, serious negotiations began in WIPO to revise the requirements of the Hague Agreement, mostly to overcome the objections from examina-
tion-based countries. The primary recommendation made by the United States and
Japan was to extend the period that countries have to refuse protection so that they
might have time to at least complete an initial examination. In 1996, the United
States indicated that it might be comfortable with a 12-month period, while Japan
proposed that the term be 18 months.[153] In 1999, the discussions about revising the
Hague Agreement continued at WIPO and optimism mounted that a new treaty,
meeting the needs of countries such as the United States, might soon be completed.

CONCLUSION

This chapter focused on the fundamental conditions that must be fulfilled for one to receive a patent. The United States clearly is taking the lead in expanding the reach of patentable subject matter, especially regarding biotechnological and computer-related inventions. Prompted by the TRIPs Agreement, the international trend is to follow this lead, albeit slowly in some cases. The international picture is somewhat more mixed regarding novelty standards, however. Here, one should anticipate that the United States eventually will give up its first-to-invent standard and embrace the much more widely accepted first-to-file process. On the other hand, it is likely that the international community will accept other U.S. novelty principles, such as the one-year grace period. One thing is clear, though. In the long term, the give and take of international negotiations will slowly but steadily lead to increasing unification of patent standards.

The next chapter presents both an overview of the steps one must take to receive a patent in the United States and the rights a patent provides against alleged infringers. In addition, the horizon is expanded to the international community, giving some insights into the ways that countries have agreed to make it easier for inventors to receive patent protection within their borders. From this exposition, it becomes clear that inventors with more than a domestic vision should understand as early as possible the fundamental principles of international patent protection and should plan their intellectual property strategies accordingly.

NOTES

1. S. Feyder, "Honeywell Reaches Settlement with Fuji in Dispute Over Patent," Minneapolis Star Tribune (September 16, 1993) at 1D; C. Scott, "Honeywell Reaches $124.1 Million Pact with Camera Firms," Wall St. J. (August 24, 1992); P. Tirschwell, "Honeywell Chases 15 Camera Makers after Minolta Win," Nat'l L. J. (July 27, 1992) at 23.

2. In 1996, the Federal Circuit Court of Appeals determined that Honeywell had infringed the patent, but ordered a new trial to determine damages. R. Rundle, "U.S. Court Rules Against Honeywell in Case with Litton," Wall St. J. (July 9, 1996) at B5. Honeywell appealed to the Supreme Court, and the Court vacated the judgment, sending the case back to the appellate court under new instructions. The case then returned to the trial court, which determined that Honeywell did not infringe Litton's patent. See M. Fisk, "A 10-year Legal War Steams On," Nat'l L. J. (October 11, 1999) at B16.

3. J. Auerbach and D. Takahashi, "Digital Files Big Patent Suit Against Intel," Wall St. J. (May 14, 1997) at A3.

4. See P. Lewis, "The New Patent That Is Infuriating the Multimedia Industry," N.Y. Times (November 28, 1993) at F10; C. MacLachlan, "Multimedia Patent Battle Looms," Nat'l L. J. (November 29, 1993) at 3; D. Clark, "Patents May Raise Price of Information Highway," Wall St. J. (November 15, 1993) at B1. In December 1993, the Patent and Trademark Office decided to reexamine the validity and scope of the Compton patent. See also J. Shiver Jr., "Low-Tech Problems with High-Tech Patents," L.A. Times (January 9, 1994) at D1. In March 1994, the PTO overturned its original determination regarding patentability.

5. R. Korman, "Lo! Here Come the Technology Patents. Lo! Here Come the Lawsuits," N.Y. Times (December 27, 1998) at Business 4.

6. For many patents, the PTO will release information about an invention 18 months after the patent application is filed.

7. Congress passed the Intellectual Property and Communications Reform Act of 1999 (S. 1948), on November 19, 1999, as part of a consolidated appropriations package, which was signed by the president on November 29, 1999 (Pub. L. No. 106-113). The relevant title within this act is called the American Inventors Protection Act of 1999.

8. A patent applicant who files for foreign protection either directly or through a patent convention that requires patent applications to be published 18 months after filing—such as the Patent Cooperation Treaty—is not exempt from the U.S. publication requirements. The Patent Cooperation Treaty is discussed in Chapter 3.

9. *See* D. Caruso, "Concern Is Growing Over People and Companies That Are Stockpiling Patents to be Used as Competitive Weapons," N.Y. Times (February 1, 1999) at C4.

10. The American Inventors Protection Act of 1999 provides that patent applicants have "provisional rights" after their applications are published, but while their applications are still under PTO review. An applicant with provisional rights may not prevent others from making, using, or selling the invention before the patent issues. However, if the patent issues, then the applicant has the right to recover royalties from those who used the invention after the date of publication. This will be discussed further in Chapter 3.

11. Patent term extensions may be granted for delays caused by (1) secrecy orders, (2) interference proceedings, and (3) certain successful appeals to the Board of Patent Appeals and Interferences or the federal courts. 35 U.S.C. § 154.

12. V. Slind-Flor, "Patent Boss Hears an Earful," Nat'l L. J. (October 31, 1994).

13. Due to the American Inventors Protection Act, this information will be released prior to patent issuance, if protection is sought in certain foreign countries or through international conventions requiring publication.

14. *See* Allison and Lemley, "Empirical Evidence on the Validity of Litigated Patents," 26 Am. Intell. Prop. L. Ass'n Q. J. (Summer 1998) at 185. Some authorities claim that the Federal Circuit upholds patents 80% of the time. P. Dwyer, "The Battle Raging over Intellectual Property," Bus. Wk. (May 22, 1989) at 79.

15. *See* Annual Report, Section of Intellectual Property Law (1993–1994) at 68–69.

16. In re Wyer, 655 F.2d 221, 226 (Cust. & Pat. App. 1981). For a thorough discussion of the printed publication requirement, see J. Dratler, Intellectual Property Law: Commercial, Creative and Industrial Property, Law Journal Seminars-Press (New York, 1991 & Supp. 1999) at §2.03[1].

17. *In re* Hall, 781 F.2d 897, 898 (Fed. Cir. 1986).

18. K. Day, "A Reinvention of Patent Rules," Wash. Post (April 24, 1997) at E1. *See also* T. Alexander, "Pending Inventors Act," Nat'l L. J. (November 15, 1999) at B12.

19. Under the new law, a prior use qualifies only if the invention actually has been reduced to practice. In earlier versions, the defense could be satisfied by demonstrating effective and serious preparation for use.

20. As will be discussed later, prior users of business methods also might be precluded from enjoying patent rights to their inventions, even after *State Street*, if they used the business methods in commercial applications for more than one year prior to filing for a patent. Others, though, may not be barred from receiving patents on the same methods. *See* S. Alter, "'State Street' Sets Stage for New Patents, Battles," Nat'l L. J. (October 25, 1999) at C8.

21. M. Chase, "Du Pont and Cetus Fight Over Patents on New Genetic Tool," Wall St. J. (December 12, 1989) at A1, 5.

22. P. Judge, "From the Patent Wars, a Patent Medicine," Bus. Wk. (May 25, 1998) at 111.

23. 86 F.3d 1113 (Fed. Cir. 1996).

24. 525 U.S. 55 (1998).

25. If the United States were to change to a first-to-file priority system, it still would be a good idea to keep excellent records of the invention process in lab notebooks. For instance, if a company were sued for patent infringement, its lab notebooks could be used to demonstrate the skill in the art, thereby proving that the invention was obvious to those working or doing research in the field.

26. "Warding off Pests—and Challenges to Patents," Nat'l L. J. (April 19, 1999) at A13.

27. Mycogen Plant Science Inc. v. Monsanto Co., 96-505 (D. Del, February 3, 1998).

28. The legal battle over patent rights to the cancer drug AZT provides an interesting example. See E. Felsenthal, "Who Invented AZT? Big Bucks Are Riding on What Sleuths Find," Wall Street J. (October 21, 1993) at A1.

29. J. Emshwiller, "Patent-Law Proposals Irk Small Inventors," Wall Street J. (April 30, 1992).

30. Bonito Boats, Inc. v. Thunder Craft Boats, Inc. 489 U.S. 141 (1989) quoting 13 Writings of Thomas Jefferson 335 (Memorial ed. 1904).

31. W. L. Gore & Assoc., Inc., v. Garlock, Inc., 721 F.2d 1540, 1555 (Fed. Cir. 1983), *cert. denied*, 469 U.S. 851 (1984), *on remand*, 670 F. Supp 760 (N.D. Ohio 1987).

32. This case was first decided by the Federal Circuit in 1985. The Supreme Court vacated the decision and remanded the case because the Federal Circuit did not adequately address the clearly erroneous standard that must be used to reverse factual determinations on appeal. On remand in 1987, the Federal Circuit restated its previous opinion in terms of the clearly erroneous standard. In the 1987 opinion, it emphasized that its earlier opinion remains on the books and that for a full understanding, both opinions must be read together. This case synopsis is based on language from both opinions.

33. A. Naj, "Scientists Say Alaska Oil Spill Cleanup Would Have Benefited from Microbe Use," Wall St. J. (April 13, 1990).

34. *See* R. Weiss, "Biotech Food Raises a Crop of Questions," Wash. Post (August 15, 1999) at A1.

35. *Ex Parte* Hibbard, 227 U.S.P.Q. 443 (Bd. Pat. App. 1985).

36. *Ex Parte* Allen, 2 U.S.P.Q. 2d 1425 (Bd. Pat. App. 1987).

37. For a good discussion about animal patents in the late 1980s and early 1990s, see M. Cone, "The Mouse Wars Turn Furious," L.A. Times (May 9, 1993) at A16.

38. W. Feiler, "Birth of Dolly Raises Patent Issues on Clones," N.Y. Law J. (March 9, 1998).

39. M. Cone, "The Mouse Wars Turn Furious," L.A. Times (May 9, 1993) at A16.

40. M. Lavelle, "Biotech: The Unknown Frontier for Lawyers," Nat'l L. J. (February 6, 1989) at 1.

41. *See* T. Maugh II, "Genetic Researchers Create Smarter Mice," L.A. Times (September 2, 1999) at A1.

42. *See* R. Holtz and T. Maugh II, "Biotech: The Revolution Is Already Underway," L.A. Times (April 27, 1997) at A1; A. Underwood, A. Rogers and S. McGuire, "Little Lamb, Who Made Thee?" Newsweek (March 10, 1997) at 53; R. Langreth, "Cloning Has Fascinating, Disturbing Potential," Wall St. J. (February 24, 1997) at B1.

43. In 1998, scientists at Advanced Cell Technologies reported that they had cloned genetically engineered calves, with the goal of creating herds that might produce medicinal milk. (This topic is addressed in the agribusiness section). Also, scientists in Hawaii cloned mice and Japanese researchers cloned several calves from a single adult cow. In 2000, researchers at The Oregon Health Sciences University reported that they had successfully cloned a rhesus monkey.

44. W. Feiler, "Birth of Dolly Raises Patent Issues on Clones," N.Y.L.J. (March 9, 1998).

45. A. Underwood, A. Rogers and S. McGuire, "Little Lamb, Who Made Thee?" Newsweek (March 10, 1997) at 53.

46. "Patent Law Passed," Nat'l L. J. (May 25, 1998) at A11.

47. The information for this discussion comes from R. Weiss, "Embryo Work Raises Specter of Human Harvesting," Wash. Post (June 14, 1999) at A1.

48. In December 1999, the National Institutes of Health issued draft guidelines for public comment that would govern the use of human embryonic stem cells by federally financed scientists. The guidelines would require federally funded researchers to obtain the stem cells from private sources. As of 1999, most cells come from excess human embryos created in fertility clinics. See N. Wade, "Government Proposes Regulations for Embryo Cell Research," N.Y. Times (December 2, 1999) at A24.

49. In 1998, the United Nations Commission on Human Rights adopted international guidelines on bioethics and the human genome. The guidelines, which are provided in the "Universal Declaration on the Human Genome and Human Rights," state that "practices which are contrary to human dignity, such as reproductive cloning of human beings, shall not be permitted."

50. J. Welsh, "Tinkering with Genes to Get a Tall, Strong Supertree," Wall St. J. (January 13, 1997) at B1; R. Rhundle, "Bright Future Is Predicted for Pest-Resistant Seeds," Wall St. J. (August 31, 1998) at B4; A. Manning, "Clones May Wilt Use of Pesticides," USA Today (November 26, 1993) at A1; K. Yamada, "Toward Leaner Meat and Celery Sticks without Strings," Wall St. J. (February 24, 1992) at B1; A. Hagedorn, "Suits Sprout Over Rights to Seeds," Wall St. J. (March 5, 1990) at B1; J Adler and L. Denworth, "Splashing in the Gene Pool," Newsweek (March 9, 1992) at 71.

51. S. Kilman, "How Lawyer Made DeKalb a Biotech Star," Wall St. J. (April 3, 1998) at B1. DeKalb Corporation was purchased by Monsanto in 1998.

52. R. Weiss, "Seeds of Controversy," Wash. Post National Weekly Ed. (March 1, 1999) at 8. In 1999, more than one half of the 72 million acre U.S. soybean harvest was planted with Monsanto's Roundup-resistant seeds. Ibid.

53. S. Kilman and S. Warren, "Old Rivals Fight for New Turf—Biotech Crops," Wall St. J. (May 27, 1998) at B1.

54. D. Stipp, "Animals Altered to Make Drugs in Their Milk," Wall St. J. (August 27, 1991) at B1.

55. The European Union and 153 nations signed the Convention on Biological Diversity at the summit in 1992.

56. Article 1 of the Convention provides that its objectives are to support "the conservation of biological diversity, the sustainable use of its components and the fair and equitable sharing of the benefits arising out of the utilization of genetic resources." For a good article describing the basic sections of the convention and the nature of the controversies related to them, see R. Blaustein, "Convention on Biological Diversity Draws Attacks," Nat'l L. J. (October 28, 1996) at C39.

57. J. King, "Breeding Uniformity," Amicus J. (Spring 1993) at 27.

58. C. Zalewski and P. McQuade, "A Stalemate on Biosafety Pact," Na'l L. J. (May 24, 1999) at C1; R. Blaustein, "Convention on Biological Diversity Draws Attacks," Nat'l L. J. (October 28, 1996) at C39.

59. D. Russell, "Miracle or Myth?" Amicus J. (Spring 1993) at 23–24. The Food and Drug Administration, while noting the possibility of a slight increase in mastitis, approved the marketing of a bovine growth hormone called recombinant somatotropin on November 5, 1993. In the wake of this FDA action, a 90-day moratorium was imposed (through a budgetary provision) on the sale of the product so that information regarding budgetary, social, and economic effects could be reported to Congress. M. Levy, "FDA Gives Formal Approval to Drug That Boosts Milk Production in Cows," Wall St. J. (November 8, 1993) at B7.

60. One study indicates that herbicide-resistant canola in Canada is cross-pollinating with wild plants, creating weeds that now are more difficult to eliminate with traditional herbicides. See R. Weiss, "Biotech Food Raises a Crop of Questions," Wash. Post (August 15, 1999) at A1.

61. Other studies indicate that Bt corn also may be inadvertently killing insects that naturally control pests, such as ladybugs and lacewings. See R. Weiss, "Biotech Food Raises a Crop of Questions," Wash. Post (August 15, 1999) at A1.

62. R. Hotz and T. Maugh II, "Biotech: The Revolution Is Already Underway," L.A. Times (April 27, 1997) at A1.

63. Article 19, U.N. Convention on Biological Diversity (June 5, 1992).

64. For an excellent article covering the important and divisive issues debated at the biosafety summit in Cartagena, see C. Zalewski and P. McQuade, "A Stalemate on Biosafety Pact," Nat'l L. J. (May 24, 1999) at C1.

65. An agreement was reached in Montreal, Canada on January 29, 2000. See D. Palmer, "Countries Reach Landmark GMO Food Agreement," Yahoo!News (January 29, 2000).

66. Article 15, U.N. Convention on Biological Diversity (June 5, 1992).

67. Articles 1 and 19, U.N. Convention on Biological Diversity (June 5, 1992). The discussion on access and compensation for genetic resources is based on an excellent article: A. Pollack, "Biological Products Raise Genetic Ownership Issues," N.Y. Times, (November 26, 1999) at A1.

68. A. Pollack, id., stating that the information comes from a book titled The Commercial Use of Biodiversity.

69. An interesting example is provided by a 1986 patent for ayahuasca, a tropical plant derived in the Amazon that has hallucinogenic properties when combined with other components, and is used by indigenous tribes for healing and religious purposes. The patent outraged nations in the Amazon region. Several

groups representing indigenous tribes in the Amazon requested a reexamination based on prior printed publications—plant specimen sheets in herbarium collections—depicting the plant. The PTO rejected the patent in November 1999.

70. A. Pollack, "Biological Products Raise Genetic Ownership Issues," N.Y. Times (November 26, 1999) at A1.

71. Food and Drug Administration, "Statement of Policy: Foods Derived from New Plant Varieties," 57 Fed. Reg. 22984 (May 29, 1992).

72. Food and Drug Administration, "Biotechnology in the Year 2000 and Beyond; Public Meetings," 64 Fed. Reg. 57470.

73. J. Henkel, "Genetic Engineering Fast Forwarding to Future Foods," located at www.fda.gov/bbs/topics/consumer/geneng.html.

74. A study found that soybeans that were genetically modified with genes from Brazil nuts caused positive allergic reactions on skin-prick tests. M. Chase, "Should You Worry About Health Risks from Biotech Food?" Wall St. J. (November 5, 1999) at B1.

75. See J. Barry, "Frankenstein Foods?" Newsweek (September 13, 1999) at 33; R. Weiss, "No Appetite for Gene Cuisine," Wash. Post National Weekly Ed. (May 3, 1999) at 18.

76. These explanations were reported in J. Barry, "Frankenstein Foods?" Newsweek (September 13, 1999) at 33.

77. See S. Stecklow, " 'Genetically Modified' on the Label Means . . . Well, It's Hard to Say," Wall St. J. (October 26, 1999) at A1.

78. See S. Effron, "Japanese Choke on American Biofood," L.A. Times (March 14, 1999) at A1; S. Effron, "In the Land of Sushi, Lab Tomato Strikes Out," L.A. Times (March 14, 1999) at C1.

79. S. Effron, "Japanese Choke on American Biofood," L.A. Times (March 14, 1999) at A1

80. Id.

81. See M. Mansour, and J. Bennett, "Dispute Over Modified Food Hits U.S.," Nat'l L. J. (November 29, 1999) at B11.

82. See S. Stecklow, "'Genetically Modified' on the Label Means . . . Well, It's Hard to Say," Wall St. J. (October 26, 1999) at A1.

83. See R. Weiss, "Food War Claims Its Casualties," Wash. Post (September 12, 1999) at A1.

84. See M. Mansour and J. Bennett, "Dispute Over Modified Food Hits U.S.," Nat'l L. J. (November 29, 1999) at B11.

85. Food and Drug Administration, "Biotechnology in the Year 2000 and Beyond; Public Meetings," 64 Fed. Reg. 57470 (October 25, 1999). A bill also was introduced in Congress that would require labels indentifying whether fresh produce or any ingredient in packaged foods was grown from genetically modified seed. See S. Kilman, "Once Quick Converts, Midwest Farmers Lose Faith in Biotech Crops," Wall St. J. (November 19, 1999) at A1.

86. See R. Weiss, "The Next Food Fight: Listing Genes on Labels," Wash. Post (August 15, 1999) at A1.

87. See M. Fitzpatrick, "WTO Protesters Clash in Seattle's Curfew Hours," Yahoo! News, http://dailynews. yahoo.com (December 2, 1999).

88. Harvested seeds are not protected under the Plant Variety Protection Act, but they may receive protection when the plants are protected under the regular patent act. J. Barton, "Patenting Life," Sci. Am. (March 1991) at 43.

89. Id. at 43.

90. Transengenic Animal Patent Reform Act, S. 387 (February 16, 1993).

91. C. Anderson, "Patent for Seeds Sows Controversy," AP, San Luis Obispo Telegram-Tribune (May 23, 1998) at E5; G. Guidetti, "Seed Terminator Threatens Food and Freedom," Quixote's Horse (July 18, 1998), available at http://king.igs.net/~wacoppin/seeds.htm. According to this source, the patent is titled "Control of Plant Gene Expression" (U.S. Patent No. 5,723,765), and is jointly owned by the U.S Department of Agriculture and the Delta and Pine Land Company.

92. Monsanto, for instance, licenses its patented seeds rather than sell them to farmers. Under the licenses, the farmers agree not to save seed, and they give Monsanto permission to come onto the farm and take

samples for three years after seeds are last purchased. Monsanto uses various enforcement measures, such as providing toll-free tip lines, hiring private investigators, and conducting random DNA tests on plants growing in the fields of farmers who have bought seed in previous years. R. Weiss, "Seeds of Controversy," Wash. Post National Weekly Ed. (March 1, 1999) at 8.

93. C. Farrow, "Monsanto Promises Not to Market 'Terminator' Seeds," AP, San Luis Obispo Telegram Tribune (October 6, 1999).

94. Amgen, Inc. v. Chugai Pharmaceutical Co., Ltd., 706 F. Supp. 94 (D. Mass. 1989), *aff'd in part and rev'd in part*, 927 F.2d 1200 (Fed. Cir. 1991), *cert. denied*, 112 S.Ct. 169 (1991).

95. *See* Scripps Clinic & Research Foundation v. Genentech Inc., 724 F. Supp. 690 (N.D. Cal. 1989), *aff'd in part and rev'd in part*, 927 F.2d 1565 (Fed. Cir. 1991), *clarified on reconsideration*, 18 U.S.P.Q. 2d 1896 (Fed. Cir. 1991) (litigation over Factor VIII:C); Genentech Inc. v. Wellcome Foundation Ltd., 14 U.S.P.Q. 2d 1363 (D. Del. 1990), 798 F. Supp. 213 (D. Del. 1992) (litigation over t-PA).

96. See E. Moroz and W. Feiler, "Biotechnology," Nat'l L. J. (November 1, 1993) at S24, which discusses litigations over EPO, Factor VIII:C, and t-PA and, based on them, concludes that purified natural protein claims cover recombinant processes.

97. For a full discussion of the Human Genome Initiative, see D. Karjala, "A Legal Research Agenda for the Human Genome Initiative," Jurimetrics (Winter 1992).

98. For a discussion of one method, that works backwards from RNA to discover what is called complementary DNA, or cDNA, *see* J. Carey, "The Gene Kings," Bus. Wk. (May 8, 1995) at 72. Another system to track down genes is called SNP (single nucleotide polymorphisms) technology. *See* M. Waldholz and E. Tanouye, "Glaxo to Report It's Closing in on Genes Linked to 3 Diseases," Wall St. J. (October 19, 1999) at A1.

99. R. Herman, "The Great Gene Gold Rush," Wash. Post (June 16, 1992) at H11; E. Andrews, "Dr. Healy's Big Push on Patents," N.Y. Times (February 16, 1992) at C12; H. Stout, "U.S. Pursuit of Gene Patents Riles Industry," Wall St. J. (February 13, 1992) at B1; M. Waldholzf and H. Stout, "A New Debate Rages Over the Patenting of Gene Discoveries," Wall St. J. (April 17, 1992) at A1.

100. H. Stout, "Gene-Fragment Patent Request Is Turned Down," Wall St. J. (September 23, 1992) at B1.

101. M. Waldholz and H. Stout, "A New Debate Over the Patenting of Gene Discoveries," Wall St. J. (April 17, 1992) at A1.

102. H. Stout, "Gene-Fragment Patent Request Is Turned Down," Wall St. J. (September 23, 1992) at B1. *See also* L. Pasahow and A. Kumamoto, "Human Genome Project Raises Patenting Issues," Nat'l L. J. (October 20, 1997). In December 1999, the PTO proposed new examination guidelines for patenting small segments of DNA sequences that allegedly are useful as aids to find other DNA fragments. The proposed guidelines tell examiners to look for specific and substantial utility in these inventions. See V. Slind-Flor, "PTO's New Guide to DNA Info," Nat'l L. J. (January 17, 2000) at B6.

103. M. Cimons and P. Jacobs, "Biotech Battlefield: Profits vs. Public," L.A. Times (February 21, 1999) at A1.

104. For an article describing some of the ethical issues related to genetic research, see R. Rundle, "What Should I Do?: The More We Know About Our Genes, the More Difficult the Ethical Questions We Will Face," Wall St. J. (October 16, 1999) at R16.

105. M. Gladwell, "Rights to Life: Are Scientists Wrong to Patent Genes?" The New Yorker (Nov. 13, 1995).

106. T. Mays, "Biotech Incites Outcry," Nat'l L. J. (June 22, 1998) at C1.

107. For a good overview of genetic testing issues, see R. Langreth, "Early Warnings," Wall St. J. (October 18, 1999) at R7.

108. For a thorough discussion of ethical issues regarding genetic research, see L. Andrews, "Body Science," A.B.A. J. (April 1997) at 44.

109. For an excellent discussion of genetic testing and insurance issues, see N. A. Jeffrey, "A Change in Policy: Genetic Testing Threatens to Fundamentally Alter the Whole Notion of Insurance," Wall St. J. (October 18, 1999) at R15.

110. I. Voelker, "Europe Won't Reverse Controversial EPO Ruling," IP Worldwide (July/August 1997); B. Baggot, "Legislating a Transgenics Revolution," IP Mag. (May 1998).

111. For discussions of the history of animal and plant patents in Europe, see I. Voelker, "Europe Won't Re-

verse Controversial EPO Ruling," IP Worldwide (July/August 1997); B. Baggot, "Legislating a Transgenics Revolution," IP Mag. (May 1998).

112. "Patent Law Passed," Nat'l L. J. (May 25, 1998) at A11; K. Dunleavy and M. Vinnola, "E.U. Biotech Directive Departs from U.S. Practices," Nat'l L. J. (May 24, 1999) at C11.

113. See B. Baggot, "Legislating a Transgenices Revolution," IP Magazine (May 1998).

114. The TRIPs Agreement allows WTO members to exclude from patentable subject matter "diagnostic, therapeutic and surgical methods for the treatment of humans or animals." The United States permits patents on medical and surgical procedures, but a law passed in 1996 limits available remedies. 35 U.S.C. §287(c)(4).

115. See, e.g., "Call to Send Patent Reform to Senate for Full Vote," Marketletter (May 25, 1998), discussing the position of the biotechnology industry regarding S. 507, the proposed Omnibus Patent Act.

116. American Inventors Protection Act of 1999, Subtitle III, "The Patent Term Guarantee Act of 1999" (1999). Applicants will not be compensated when their actions cause the delays.

117. S. Johnston and L. Ben-Ami, "Unpredictability Factor Narrows Biotech Patents," Nat'l L. J. (June 16, 1997) at C2.

118. For an interesting article describing how this issue arose in a dispute about patent ownership of the drug AZT, see E. Felsenthal, "Who Invented AZT? Big Bucks Are Riding on What Sleuths Find," Wall St. J. (October 21, 1993) at A1.

119. For a thorough treatment of this topic, see J. Dratler, Intellectual Property Law: Commercial, Creative and Industrial Property, Law Journal Seminars-Press (1991 & Supp. 1999) at §2.03[3][g].

120. R. Weiss, "What is Patently Offensive?" Wash. Post (May 11, 1998) at A21.

121. R. Weiss, "U.S. Ruling Aids Opponent of Patents for Life Forms," Wash. Post (June 17, 1999) at A2.

122. Parker v. Flook, 437 U.S. 584 (1978); Gottschalk v. Benson, 409 U.S. 63 (1972).

123. 958 F.2d 1053 (Fed. Cir. 1992).

124. 33 F.3d 1526 (Fed. Cir. 1994).

125. Paine, Webber, Jackson & Curtis, Inc. v. Merrill Lynch, Pierce, Fenner & Smith, Inc., 564 F. Supp. 1358 (D. Del. 1983).

126. See J. Aquino, "Patently Permissive," A.B.A. J. (May 1999) at 30. In the first six months of 1999, the PTO issued 1,390 Internet-related patents. S. Hansell, "As Patents Multiply, Web Sites Find Lawsuits Are a Click Away," N.Y. Times (December 11, 1999) at A1.

127. In a reverse sellers' auction, Web shoppers specify the terms of purchase for items and the system finds the sellers.

128. See L. Kaufman, "Amazon Sues Big Bookseller Over System for Shopping," N.Y. Times (October 23, 1999) at B1.

129. See S. Thurm and R. Quick, "Amazon.com Wins an Injunction in Patent Dispute," Wall St. J. (December 3, 1999) at B5.

130. Priceline.com Inc. v. Microsoft Corp., No. 399CV1991 (D. Conn, 10/14/99); See N. Wingfield, "Priceline.com Names Microsoft in Suit, Alleging Violation of One of its Patents," Wall St. J. (October 15, 1999) at A4.

131. DoubleClick Inc. v. L90 Inc., (E.D. Va (11/12/99).

132. See J. W. Gurley, "The Trouble with Internet Patents," Fortune (July 19, 1999) at 118; T. Weber, "Battles Over Patents Threaten to Damp Web's Innovative Spirit," Wall St. J. (November 8, 1999) at B1; B. Wright, "Business Methods," Nat'l L. J. (November 22, 1999) at B9.

133. American Inventors Protection Act of 1999, Subtitle II, "First Inventor Defense Act of 1999" (1999).

134. A. Riddles and B. Pomerance, "Software Patentee Must Conduct Own Search," Nat'l L. J. (January 26, 1998) at C19.

135. With the passage of the American Inventors Protection Act of 1999, those cloning software still may sell their products before the patent issues. However, if the patent is granted, then they must pay royalties for the period of use after the PTO publishes the patent application.

136. *See* R. Van Dyke, "Software Patents Offer Opportunities and Obstacles, " Nat'l L. J. (May 24, 1999) at C19; A. Riddles and B. Pomerance, "Software Patentee Must Conduct Own Search," Nat'l L. J. (January 26, 1998) at C19; J. Shiver Jr., "Low-Tech Problems with High-Tech Patents," L.A. Times (January 9, 1994) at D1.

137. A. Riddles and B. Pomerance, "Software Patentee Must Conduct Own Search," Nat'l L. J. (January 26, 1998) at C19

138. B. Kahin, "The Software Patent Crisis," Technology Review (April 1990). In 1995, the PTO started to allow those with computer science degrees to qualify as patent examiners.

139. *See* M. Groves, "A Patent Dispute: Lawsuit Raises a Hot Issue in Exploding Technology," L.A. Times (February 14, 1994) at D1. The PTO ordered reexaminations of the Compton and Software Advertising Corporation patents. The PTO reversed its decision on the Compton patent in 1994. Likewise, the PTO rejected Software Advertising's patent later in that same year through the reexamination process. Reexaminations will be discussed in Chapter 3.

140. The risk has been reduced for those who use patentable business methods in secret. If others receive a patent because the prior use was a secret, then the prior user of the secret business method may have a defense to infringement. American Inventors Protection Act of 1999, Subtitle II, "The First Inventor Defense Act" (1999).

141. Copyright protection, however, may serve to prevent reverse engineering under certain circumstances. This will be reviewed in Chapter 6 when clean-room techniques are discussed.

142. "Japan Publishes New Examination Guidelines for Computer-Related Inventions," J. of Proprietary Rights (May 1997) at 24; "Japanese Patent Office Proposes Guidelines for Examination of Software Patents," J. of Proprietary Rights (November 1996) at 19.

143. For a nice discussion of trends in Europe, see L. Tellier-Loniewski and A. Bensoussan, "Europe Extends Patent Protection to Software," IP Worldwide (September/October 1996).

144. See P. Garnett, Committee Chair's Report, Electronic and Computer Law Committee, American Intellectual Property Law Association (1998), available at www.aipla.org/rpts/elec&com.html.

145. The following arguments in opposition to software patents appear in "Against Software Patents," The League of Programming Freedom (February 28, 1991); B. Kahin, "The Software Patent Crisis," Tech. Rev. (April 1990).

146. Similarly, opponents argue that computer program developers have not been conditioned to publish their achievements in the traditional sense, since the successful operation of a program demonstrates its validity. *See* J. Shiver Jr., "Low-Tech Problems with High-Tech Patents," L.A. Times (January 9, 1994) at D1.

147. B. Kahin, "The Software Patent Crisis," Tech. Rev. (April 1990).

148. Hyatt received more than $70 million in license fees before the PTO cancelled the patent claims in 1996. See J. Markoff, "For Texas Instruments, Some Bragging Rights," N.Y. Times (June 20, 1996) at 5.

149. *See, e.g.*, P. Heckel, "The Software-Patent Controversy," 9 Computer Law. (December 1992) at 13–23; J. Sumner and S. Lundberg, "Software Patents: Are They Here to Stay?" 8 Computer Law. (October 1991) at 8–13.

150. The PTO uses reexamination procedures to reevaluate patents that the agency previously issued. In 1999, Congress provided for greater public participation in these procedures. Reexaminations are discussed more fully in Chapter 3.

151. *See, e.g.*, K. Liebman, G. Frischling, and A. Brunel, "The Shape of Things to Come: Design-Patent Protection for Computers," 9 Computer Law. (November 1992) at 1; R. Barr and S. Hollander, "Design Patents Revisited: Icons as Statutory Subject Matter," 9 Computer Law. (June 1992) at 13.

152. *Ex parte* Donaldson, Appeal No. 92-0546, 1992 Pat. App. LEXIS 6 (Bd. Pat. App. and Interferences, April 2, 1992); *Ex parte* Strijland, Appeal No. 92-0623, 1992 Pat. App. LEXIS 8 (Bd. Pat. App. and Interferences, April 2, 1992).

153. Information on recent developments at WIPO regarding the Hague Agreement can be found at www.fryer.com.

Patent Policy: Obtaining and Defending Patent Rights

INTRODUCTION

Inventors find patents to be so desirable because they provide a period of exclusive rights during which no one else may make, use, or sell protected inventions without permission. In order to receive the benefits from patents, though, inventors must release thorough information about their inventions to the public. The first part of this chapter is designed to give a basic feel both for the steps one must take to get a patent and, more important, for the types of information that must be presented to the PTO for public disclosure. In this regard, there is substantial focus on Section 112. This section of patent law requires a written description of the invention that is sufficiently comprehensive so that one skilled in the art can make and use the invention. Section 112 also demands that the inventor describe the best mode of carrying out the invention.

The chapter then evaluates the potential reach of patent claims to allegedly infringing activities. Here, we will consider some of the rather mechanical doctrines used to evaluate whether an article or process literally infringes the claims of a patent. In addition, there is an investigation into the more nebulous and controversial doctrine of equivalents, which serves to frustrate those who try to gain unfair advantages from strict application of infringement rules. This portion of the chapter concludes with an examination of the ways that damages are ascertained in patent cases.

The final component of the chapter takes a snapshot of the rapidly changing landscape of international patent protection. Most firms no longer may be content with U.S. patent protection alone. The international commercial environment necessitates patent protection on an international scale. This chapter will review some of the important considerations one must evaluate to preserve patent rights on a global basis.

THE PATENT APPLICATION PROCESS: A BRIEF OVERVIEW

Although the process of obtaining a patent is designed so that the inventor can theoretically accomplish the steps alone, it is normally advisable to retain expert assistance given the somewhat complex and technical requirements involved. It is not the goal of this section to do more than scratch the surface of these demands. There are numerous books and guides available that are devoted solely to providing such assistance.[1] Rather, the purpose here is to raise your understanding of the types of issues involved in the process, so that you can meaningfully evaluate the costs and benefits of patent protection, especially in view of other possible techniques to protect inventions. Exhibit 3.1 summarizes important aspects of the patent application process, which should be recognized by those contemplating patent protection.

Who May File the Patent Application

If you were asked who must file the patent application, your probable initial reaction would be that the inventor is entitled to patent rights to the invention and thus should be the one to file for the privilege of obtaining them. This is precisely the approach taken by the Patent Act. With certain limited exceptions, the inventor (or inventors) must file the patent application with the PTO.

Inventive activity less frequently is within the exclusive domain of individual hobbyists tinkering in their spare time out of a garage. Rather, it usually takes place in the confines of an employment relationship, often while working within an employing company's research and development department. Who has patent rights, for instance, if an employee of IBM develops a novel and nonobvious computer process while at work for IBM in the company labs? You may be surprised that there are situations where the employee will be the owner of the patent rights in the computer process. In fact, the employee will be the owner unless: (1) the employee was hired to create the specific computer process or to achieve its specific objective or (2) the employee signed an agreement assigning the rights in the invention to the employer. Thus, the IBM employee who works without an invention assignment agreement may own the patent rights in the computer process, depending on the specific scope of the employment relationship. This may seem unfair because IBM's facilities were used to develop and perfect the invention. However, the law accounts for this by providing IBM with what are called "shop rights" to the invention. Although the employee is the owner of the patent rights to the invention, through its shop rights, IBM is allowed to make, use, and sell the invention without paying a royalty fee to the employee-inventor. In all other respects, however, ownership and control, in these situations, resides with the inventing employee.

Invention Assignment Agreements Normally, an employer such as IBM will not be content with only shop rights to inventions. Rather, the company will want to

Exhibit 3.1
The Patent Application: Key Considerations

■ **Who May File the Patent Application**

- Inventor
- Employer-employee relationship
  - Employee is inventor who must file
  - Contract clauses assign patent rights to employer
  - Shop rights provide nonexclusive license for employer

■ **When to Apply for the Patent**

- Record events proving conception of invention and diligent reduction to practice
  - Lab notebook: Signed, witnessed, and dated
  - Important for determining priority if others are simultaneously working on the same invention
- Perform a patent search
  - Of existing patents and publications
  - To determine if patentable
  - To improve the invention
  - To save attorneys' fees
  - To facilitate prepatent licensing opportunities
  - To facilitate discussions with PTO patent examiners
  - To strengthen the patent
- File as soon as possible
  - When disclosure requirements of patent application can be met
  - May be important to prove priority over other inventors
    - Confers procedural advantages in the United States
    - In most other countries, the first to file the patent application receives priority
  - Must file within one year of public use or sale
    - For patents in some countries, grace period is less than one year
- Provisional applications facilitate early filing

■ **Important Components of the Patent Application**

- Summary of the invention

continued . . .

Exhibit 3.1 *(continued)*
The Patent Application: Key Considerations

- Enablement
  - Sufficient disclosure so that one skilled in the art can make and use the invention
  - **CASE:** *White Consolidated Industries v. Vega Servo-Control, Inc.*
- Best mode
  - Of the invention contemplated by the inventor at the time of filing the patent application
- Claims
  - Definite statement of patent monopoly
  - Draftsmanship art
- Information disclosure statement
  - Materiality standard

- ■ Confidentiality of Patent Application
  - PTO does not publish information if applicant does not file in foreign country or with foreign convention that requires publication
  - Otherwise, PTO publishes information 18 months after filing date

---

decide when other companies might be allowed to make, use, and/or sell the invention, and it will want to be paid for granting those privileges. IBM can accomplish this result most effectively by entering an agreement with its employees stating that the employees will assign to the company all rights to their inventions. Normally, this is done in the initial employment contract signed by the employees. Of course, the critical question remains concerning exactly what inventions an employee will be expected to assign to the company. Taking the company's point of view, it likely will want to lay claim to all inventions conceived while the employee works for the company, on the assumption that the company's work environment, facilities, and programs were the motivating force behind the invention. Logically, such reasoning extends to inventions allegedly made in the employee's spare time at home and indeed to inventions made shortly after the employee leaves the company. As you can imagine, the employee will often take issue with the latter demand. Inventors often work at home or in their spare time or in new jobs on creations that are totally separate from what they are doing or what they learned on the job. Unfortunately for the employee, the employer often has a greater bargaining position and will have the ability to demand that the employee sign a far-reaching assignment provision in the employment contract. For this reason, certain states, such as California, undertake to equitably balance these valid and competing interests by restricting to some degree the extent of an employer's reach in assignment clauses. California's Labor Code provides:

> Any provision in an employment agreement which provides that an employee shall assign or offer to assign any of his or her rights to an invention to his or her employer shall not apply to an invention for which no equipment, supplies, facility, or trade secret information of the employer was used and which was developed entirely on the employee's own time, and (a) which does not relate (1) to the business of the employer or (2) to the employer's actual or demonstrably anticipated research or development, or (b) which does not result from any work performed by the employee for the employer. Any provision which purports to apply to such an invention is to that extent against public policy and is to that extent void and unenforceable.

Although the complex linguistic form of this provision makes it hard to precisely pin down what is or is not permissible, the intent is clear that an employer may not lay claim to an employee's invention that is totally separate and distinct from the employer's business affairs.

A typical employment contract, mindful of the foregoing language, may contain the following simplified provision:

> I hereby agree to notify the Company about all inventions, discoveries, developments, improvements, and innovations (herein called "inventions"), whether or not made or conceived during working hours, which
>
> a. relate to the existing or contemplated business or research activities of the Company, or
> b. are suggested by or result from my work at the Company, or
> c. result from the use of the Company's time, materials, or facilities
>
> and to assign to the Company my entire right, title, and interest to all such inventions.

> I will, at the Company's request and expense, execute specific assignments to any such invention and take such further action as may be considered necessary by the Company, during or subsequent to my employment with the Company, to obtain and defend patents in any country.

> I agree that an invention described in a patent application filed by me within six months following my employment with the Company shall be presumed to have been conceived or made during my employment with the Company unless I can prove otherwise.

Note that this provision obligates inventors to take such actions as necessary to obtain the patent, even after assigning away their rights. This is because the patent laws require the patent application to be filed by inventors even if they do not own the invention. The normal course of action in this situation, therefore, is for the inventor to file a patent application that indicates for the public record that ownership in the invention and the resulting patent rights have been assigned to the company. As just one example, Chakrabarty's bacterium was developed while he was employed at General Electric Co. As the inventor, Chakrabarty filed the patent application, but the application provided that ownership had been assigned to General Electric.

When to Apply

Even though the United States bases priority on a first-to-invent standard, an inventor should apply as soon as possible for patent rights to an invention in this country. The reasons for this already have been given in Chapter 2. For example, if several inventors are working on the invention at the same time, then the first person to file the patent application has procedural advantages. Also, the statutory bars of Section 102(b) require filing to occur within one year of certain events, such as publication or a sale. In addition, international considerations, which will be further discussed at the end of this chapter, provide reasons to file early. And of course, if the United States converts to a first-to-file system, the need to apply quickly becomes self-evident.

Provisional Applications   In 1995, the United States adopted a change to its patent laws which allows inventors to file an initial application more easily with the PTO. According to the new procedures, an inventor may file what is called a "provisional application" with the PTO. As we will review shortly, the key aspects of a regular patent application are proper disclosure of the invention and the claims, which delineate the specific attributes of the invention that the inventor will control by means of the patent. With a provisional application, the inventor must prepare the proper disclosure but does not have to provide the claims. This enables an inventor to file with the PTO much more swiftly, since the most difficult part of developing a sound patent application often is drafting the all-important claims. Once the provisional application is filed, the inventor has one year to file a regular (nonprovisional) application with the PTO, which must include the claims. If this is done, then the filing date of the provisional application will be considered the filing date of the regular application. This has a number of enormous advantages. For instance, it allows an inventor to comply more readily with Section 102(b). Indeed, the inventor gains an additional year to test the invention in the market before deciding whether to move forward with completing the patent application and working with the PTO to obtain the patent. We also will see in the final section of this chapter that provisional applications may help the inventor deal more smoothly with international patent requirements, such as first-to-file priority and possible shorter grace periods. At the same time, the term of the patent still will be 20 years, measured from the date of filing the regular patent application, which may then turn out to be 21 years after the provisional application filing date.

Important Steps Before Applying   Prior to filing a patent application, an inventor must keep two steps in mind while working on an invention. An inventor should make accurate records throughout the inventive process so as to document the date of conception and to prove that the idea was reduced to practice in a diligent fashion. This normally is accomplished by means of bound lab notebooks, which are signed, witnessed, and dated on a regular, even daily, basis.

The other task worth doing before filing a regular patent application is conducting a patentability search, which essentially is an investigation by the inventor prior to filing in order to determine whether the invention can meet the standards of novelty and nonobviousness. This is accomplished by reviewing prior art references, such as patents, publications, and advertisements, to ensure that the invention complies with Section 102 of the Patent Act. Such a search is not mandatory. The PTO will make its own independent search to determine whether these patentability standards are met. Indeed, conducting a search may potentially be counterproductive, for inventors are required to disclose to the PTO any information they know may be material to the examiner to determine patentability. Without the search, therefore, information damaging to the prospects of obtaining certain patent claims may never be uncovered. However, it still clearly is advisable to perform a patentability search before engaging in the patent application process.

There are several good reasons to conduct a patentability search. First, the inventor may determine from the search that the invention is not patentable. Abandoning the patent project for the modest fee of a search may save the substantial amount of time and resources that otherwise would have gone into preparing and filing the patent application. Second, information gained from the search may actually help the inventor improve the invention. Third, gathering the information can facilitate the dialogue with the PTO. Approaching the PTO with arguments based up front on all the available knowledge will normally be more fruitful than responding to the discovery of prior art by the PTO examiner. Fourth, if the inventor wishes to license the technology prior to receiving the patent, then potential licensees will feel more secure that a patent is likely to be issued if the inventor can demonstrate the results of a thorough patent search. Fifth, a search may help demonstrate that the invention is nonobvious by perhaps indicating that the bulk of previous efforts to solve a problem used a different approach for the task.

Finally, the search may uncover prior art that the patent office otherwise would have missed. Although one might think this is a negative, it normally is not. Remember what happens if the patent issues and then is later challenged based on a prior art surprise, such as an obscure publication. As noted in Chapter 2, those in the computer industry need to be especially wary of this possibility. It is far better to find the proper limits of the patent early—before substantial investments are made. In addition, it makes sense to put all possible prior art references into the hands of the PTO examiner because this helps to strengthen the patent if it is later challenged. When judges review patents, they usually defer to the expertise of PTO examiners, since the examiners are more specifically trained to understand how the parameters of the claims relate to the often very technical aspects of the prior art. At least, this is true if the examiners have had an opportunity to review the prior art. However, when judges must evaluate patents in light of prior art references that were not reviewed by PTO examiners, then the judges are much more likely to make independent assessments based on the newly uncovered evidence.

Dealing with the PTO

Before getting started with the PTO, the inventor should consider how much time and money it will take to receive a patent. The total number of patent applications filed with the PTO rises annually. For example, 164,000 applications were filed in 1990, 168,000 in 1991, and over 170,000 in 1992.[2] By 1997, the PTO reviewed 237,000 patent applications, and it approved 123,000 in that year.[3] Obviously, the enormity of the task facing the PTO is impressive. The PTO, through computerization and other improvements, has managed to keep the average pendency of a patent application at around 22 months.[4] However, applications in certain technological areas such as computers and biotechnology may take between two and four years for a patent to issue, and in some cases the PTO review period may be even longer.

Filing fees and maintenance fees for patents are generally on the rise.[5] The basic fee to file a patent, for instance, rose from $370 ($185 for a small business) in 1989 to $710 ($355 for a small business) in 1994 and to $760 ($380 for a small business) in 1999. By 1999, patent issuance fees had increased to $1,210 ($605 for a small business) and the costs to maintain a patent after it had issued totaled more than $5,700 ($2,800 for a small business). One also should be aware that the PTO has fees for many other technical aspects of the application process. In addition, one obviously should not overlook the costs of attorneys and other experts, which ultimately may make the PTO fees pale in comparison. For example, it has been estimated that a sophisticated patent application for a complex computer software invention may cost as much as $50,000 for it to be prepared and then reviewed by the PTO.[6] This gives added support to the benefits from provisional applications, since many of these costs may be delayed until the invention is further tested in the market. In 1999, the fee to file a provisional application was only $150 ($75 for a small business).

Basics of Disclosure   The types of information that must be in the regular patent application, and the methods that should be used to present the information, are given in the Patent Act and in the Code of Federal Regulations. The regulations provide the proper form, order, and characteristics of the application. According to the regulations, the inventor is to format the application and present information in the following way: (1) the title of the invention; (2) a brief summary of the invention, which often discusses the background of the invention, indicating problems encountered by the prior art and explaining the object and advantages of the invention; (3) descriptions of the drawings if any are included; (4) an enabling description of the invention and the contemplated best mode; (5) a claim or claims; (6) an abstract, which is used by the PTO to quickly identify the nature and gist of the invention; (7) an oath signed by the inventor or inventors; and (8) the drawings if any. In addition, an Information Disclosure Statement should be filed either with the application or at least very early in the evaluation process.

Clearly, proper disclosure and the scope of the claims represent the core ingredients of the application process. The focus of proper disclosure rests on three key aspects of the application. How much information must be provided to enable one skilled in the field to practice the invention? How does one determine what is the best mode that must be disclosed? These two questions are so controversial and important that they are individually treated in the following sections of this chapter.

The third key element of disclosure involves the content of the *Information Disclosure Statement* (IDS). In essence, applicants must present to the PTO all material information within their knowledge that bears on patentability. The function of the IDS is to promote candor by the applicant and to ensure that patent examiners have all the relevant information needed to make a proper determination about patentability. What constitutes "materiality" has been the subject of great debate and has tremendous ramifications, because the withholding of information later determined to be material may invalidate an entire patent. Prior to 1992, the applicant had to disclose any information that would be important to a reasonable examiner in ruling on patentability. This was troublesome because honest applicants sometimes mistakenly forget to reveal information that is relevant to the subject of patentability. Under the old standard, applicants might lose patent rights once the mistake was uncovered, even if the information ultimately would not have changed the examiner's decision to grant the patent claims. In an attempt to alleviate the harshness of this outcome, the PTO amended its rules in 1992 to add greater specificity to what must be divulged. Now, the rules articulate that information is material if the information, by itself or in conjunction with other references, compels the conclusion that a claim is unpatentable or is otherwise inconsistent with a position taken by the applicant.

Claims   The claims specify the boundaries of the legal monopoly created by the patent. Drafting claims is an art for which expert assistance is highly recommended. Decisions have to be made on the breadth of the claims, their form, and their language. Great care must be given here, for the claims ultimately define the rights of the patent holder against alleged infringers.

The usual goal of the applicant is to maximize the breadth of patent rights. As a simple example, consider how one might claim a new form of cup. A broad claim would recite rights to a device with a bottom, sides attached to that bottom, and no top. When we investigate infringement later in this chapter, it will be clear that if this claim were granted, the patent would be extremely lucrative, extending to almost every variety of cup that might be contemplated to be used in any context and to hold any kind of item. The problem for the applicant is that this claim is so broad that it is not novel or nonobvious. Many previous devices have the claimed general elements. To overcome novelty and nonobviousness, therefore, the applicant must be more specific about the limits of the invention. Perhaps a device with a bottom comprising certain characteristics, with sides of certain characteristics, with a handle of certain characteristics, to hold items of certain characteristics, would have more of a chance. And, of course, how broadly those certain characteristics are defined may be critically important. The downside with specificity, naturally, is that the patent rights to exclude are more narrowly circumscribed, thereby making it easier for competitive inventors to develop similar noninfringing items. Fortunately, the PTO allows the applicant to claim the invention in various ways in the application. Thus, it is common practice to formulate a set of claims ranging from the very broad to the extremely specific. In this way, an applicant might fight hard to receive a broad claim but, if unsuccessful, can still be protected by an allowable narrower position.

The form of expressing the claims may be important too. A lawn mower, for example, may be claimed as a machine consisting of various components. Alternatively, it may be claimed as a method for cutting grass consisting of a set of steps. Patent experts in certain fields believe that the form of the claim may affect patentability. For instance, some continue to believe that a computer program is more likely to be viewed as patentable subject matter if expressed as a machine or apparatus rather than as a process or system. The Patent Act also allows drafters the freedom to express a claim as a means for performing a specified function, often called a means-for or a means-plus-function claim. According to the act, if such a means-for claim is used, then the claim is construed to cover the structure, material, or acts described in the disclosure sections and their equivalents. Claims often are drafted in this form in the computer field, among others, and their breadth has been the subject of considerable controversy. Many questions regarding means-for claims were answered by the Federal Circuit in *Pennwalt Corp. v. Durand-Wayland, Inc.*, a case that is presented later in this chapter to illustrate infringement.

Secrecy Orders   Once the application is filed with the PTO, it will first be scrutinized to determine if it is a candidate for a secrecy order. The United States uses the patent process to help it control the dissemination of information about inventions made in the United States that may have national security ramifications. All patent applications filed in the United States are subject to screening to determine if they contain information that may affect national security. If the PTO determines that there is some possibility of national security repercussions, then the application will be sent to relevant government agencies—often the Defense Department and/or the Nuclear Regulatory Commission—for further scrutiny. Within six months, the government must determine if the invention will be subject to a secrecy order, which prohibits public disclosure of the invention.

The secrecy order process raises a number of issues, particularly when it comes to dealing with foreign patent offices. Those who make inventions in the United States may not file for patents overseas (1) unless they obtain a foreign filing license or (2) do not receive a secrecy order within six months of filing a patent application in the United States. We shall see that two important international patent conventions, the Patent Cooperation Treaty and the Paris Convention, allow U.S. inventors to file first in the United States and preserve rights overseas. Thus, most U.S. inventors can take care of the foreign filing license issue by filing their initial patent application in the United States and then waiting at most six months before filing in foreign offices. Often, though, the PTO will issue a foreign filing license earlier—usually in conjunction with the application filing receipt—if it determines that there are no national security grounds for secrecy. If an inventor wishes to file in a foreign office before applying for a patent in the United States, though, then the inventor must follow a special petition process to receive a foreign filing license.

If the U.S. government issues a secrecy order, then, while the order remains effective, the applicant may not receive a U.S. patent nor file for patents in foreign offices. Violation of the secrecy order can result in a permanent loss of patent rights in the United States and may subject the inventor to criminal sanctions. Secrecy orders are limited to one year in duration but may be renewed annually for as long as the national interest requires. A long delay thereby may cause substantial commercial harm, and, as we shall see shortly, may result in a loss of patent rights in other countries. In this event, the inventor may be able to sue the U.S. government for just compensation.

Secrecy of Information Submitted to the PTO   Secrecy orders should be distinguished from the secrecy of information in patent applications, which became a hot topic of controversy in the late 1990s. The patent offices in many countries preserve the secrecy of information contained in patent applications for a limited period of time, usually 18 months after the application is filed. This also is true with major international conventions, such as the European Patent Convention and the Patent Cooperation Treaty. The United States, though, has had a long history of maintaining the secrecy of information contained in patent files until the patent issues. Toward the end of the 1990s, substantial efforts were made to change U.S. laws about secrecy to bring them more into conformity with international standards.

Those opposed to U.S. secrecy policies provided numerous reasons why Congress should change U.S. policies and provide for publication of patent files. One of the primary objections raised against secrecy regarded submarine patents, which get their name because they rise from the patent office without preexisting public knowledge. If the U.S. PTO were to release information in patent files, this would put the public on notice about technologies that soon might be subject to patent rights, allowing users in the field to take appropriate steps without wasting substantial resources. Also, U.S. multinationals complained that U.S. law served only to protect small companies with localized business interests. This is because large companies usually seek foreign patent rights, usually resulting in the public release of information about their inventions, notwithstanding U.S. secrecy policies. In addition, opponents argued that U.S. secrecy laws benefited foreign interests, since the information that foreigners provided was protected in the United States from public release, while U.S. companies that filed overseas faced disclosure.

Small inventors, on the other hand, stated that U.S. law had served U.S. inventors exceedingly well for over two centuries and should not be changed. They feared that publication of patent files would serve foreign interests by giving them access to information about U.S. inventions that they otherwise would not get.

In 1999, Congress amended the patent laws, providing for the publication of patent applications 18 months after filing.[7] However, there is an exception for inventors who do not file in foreign countries or under conventions that require publication. This compromise appeased the small inventors who had worried about foreign access to information in their patent application files, while to a large degree it satisfied those who lobbied for change. You may be wondering what competitors might be able to do with information that is publicly released before the patent is approved. Since there are no patent rights preventing others from using that information, aren't these companies free to use the information, at least until the patent issues? The answer is yes. However, the new patent law allows a patent applicant who ultimately receives a patent to obtain royalties from those that use the information prior to the issue date. This, then, serves as a disincentive for others to use that information unless they are confident that a patent will not be forthcoming. Of course, if the patent is rejected, then the public is free to use the information. This means that the patent applicant has an important decision to make 18 months after the application is filed. If there is some likelihood that the PTO will not approve the patent, the applicant may wish to withdraw the application before the information is published and protect the invention by other means, such as through trade secret polices.

PTO Procedures and Appeals   After the secrecy order hurdle is met, the application is referred to an examiner within a sector specializing in the invention's field. For instance, biotechnology inventions go to Sector 1, which covers biotechnology, organic chemistry, and designs. To carry out a review of the prior art, the examiner performs an independent search of U.S. patents in the relevant field of technology. The examiner also may search on-line databases for other sources of information, such as foreign patents and technical journal articles.[8] In addition, the examiner reviews any prior art information disclosed by the inventor in the patent application or the IDS. After several months, the examiner makes the first Office Action. Although this action may indicate a notice of allowance, normally it indicates objections, concerning such aspects as the breadth of claims, defects in the drawings, or the novelty or nonobviousness of the invention. The applicant typically has three months to make amendments or otherwise respond to the first Office Action.[9] Applicants who do not completely agree with the examiner may formulate arguments to persuade the examiner to withdraw certain objections while conforming with other requests. The examiner will issue either a notice of allowance or another rejection. The applicant then has another period to make amendments or reiterate former positions. This process may go on for several cycles, closing the gaps of disagreement. Eventually, the examiner issues either a notice of allowance or a final rejection.

When the applicant receives a notice of allowance, then the patent will be issued after the appropriate fee is paid. At this time, articles using the invention should be properly marked with the patent number. The reason for doing this is to provide notice for potential infringers, thereby making it easier to recover damages for infringement. Prior to one's receiving the patent, but after the application is filed, it is a common practice to mark articles embodying the invention with the term "patent pending."[10] This notice has no legal effect; because the patent has not issued, the applicant has no rights under patent law to exclude others from using the invention. However, it warns others that a patent may issue soon. Knowing this, competitors may pause before investing resources to produce the invention and rather may choose to reduce the risk by entering into negotiations with the patent applicant.

The applicant who receives a final rejection may file an appeal within six months to the Board of Appeals and Patent Interferences—a tribunal of examiners-in-chief within the PTO. The board may either uphold the examiner's decision to refuse the patent or agree with the applicant and instruct the examiner how to proceed. The board upholds the examiner about 65% of the time. When the board upholds the examiner, the applicant may appeal to the federal court system, usually to the Federal Circuit Court of Appeals.[11] The final possible appeal is to the U.S. Supreme Court. Although appeals rarely go that far, we have seen examples in *Diamond v. Diehr* and *Diamond v. Chakrabarty*. Exhibit 3.2 provides a flowchart to illustrate the steps one can expect to encounter after a patent application is filed with the PTO.

Loss of Patent Rights

Reexamination   Keep in mind that concerns about patent rights do not necessarily come to an end just because a U.S. patent has issued. Although it does not do so too frequently, the PTO has the power to reexamine a patent at its own discretion at any time. According to the Patent Act, the PTO Commissioner may open a reexamination proceeding whenever a substantial new question about the patentability of an invention has been raised. Normally, this order comes after the PTO receives information from an interested member of the public (often a competitor of the patent holder) in conjunction with a request for reexamination. The procedures for the reexamination are little different from those used for an initial application. In essence, an examiner reconsiders patentability in light of any new information.

Although reexaminations do not usually make headlines, they certainly did in 1994 when the PTO seemingly responded to waves of public criticism and invalidated two far-reaching patents—Compton's patent for a multimedia search and retrieval system and Software Advertising Corporation's patent covering computer screen savers used for advertising—shortly after giving them its blessing.[12] These incidents ignited a growing controversy about the capabilities of the PTO to adequately address the patentability of new technologies, particularly in computer fields. Many industry participants argued that the PTO does not have sufficient information at its fingertips to appraise the novelty of computer-related inventions and they called for new approaches to assist the PTO in reaching an informed judgment.

Exhibit 3.2
Patent Application Procedures

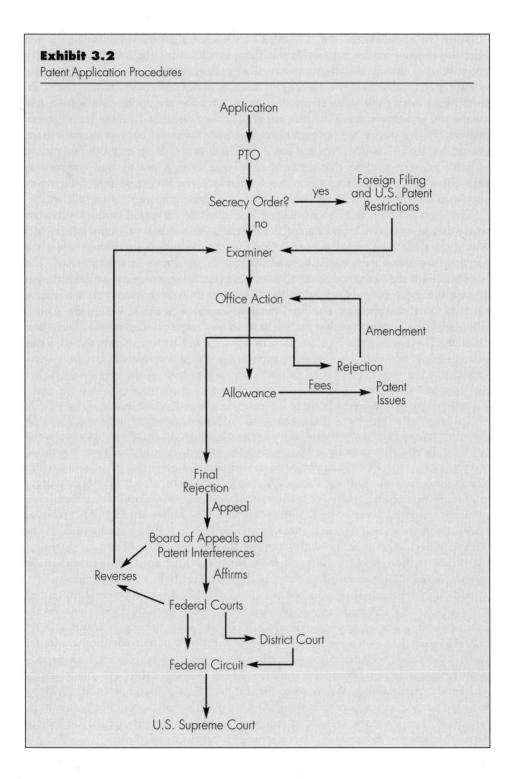

One solution adopted by Congress in the American Inventors Protection Act of 1999 was to authorize the publication of patent files after 18 months. Publication provides members of the public an opportunity to learn about patent applications in the PTO pipeline, allowing them to submit relevant information to the PTO before the agency makes final decisions about patentability. In the same piece of legislation, Congress also provided for new optional "inter partes" reexamination procedures that permit greater participation by the public.[13] Without getting too technical, the PTO, in an inter partes proceeding, must give a public participant copies of the documents filed by the patent owner and the PTO and provide opportunities for the participant to file responses. The PTO still makes the decision to cancel or change the scope of the patent based on the proceeding. The third party, though, may file an appeal with the Board of Patent Appeals and Interferences.

Opposition Procedures in Other Countries   Other countries provide even more formal processes, called oppositions, for third parties to challenge patents within their respective patent offices. There are widely varying procedures for conducting oppositions, but they tend to rely somewhat heavily on the involvement of third parties in dispute resolution proceedings. Some countries allow third parties to initiate opposition proceedings even before the patent is formally granted by the patent office. By strategically filing a series of these so-called pre-grant oppositions, opponents may have the power to delay the final approval of a patent for years. Until recently, Japan employed a pre-grant opposition system, as did China and Australia. These countries changed to the more common post-grant system in response to criticisms about delays. However, other countries, such as South Korea, Norway, New Zealand, and Vietnam still provide for pre-grant proceedings.[14] The majority of nations, as well as the European Patent Convention, allow third parties to file for oppositions only after the patent is granted by the patent office in what are called post-grant opposition proceedings. Patent holders favor post-grant processes because their patents typically remain in force while the disputed issues are being resolved within the patent office.

Litigation   Those wishing to use a patented invention without permission also have recourse to litigate in the courts. For instance, they may file suit against the patent holder and seek a determination by the court that the PTO erred in issuing the patent.[15] If the court is persuaded, it can issue a declaratory judgment and invalidate the patent. Alternatively, they may simply use the invention and wait to be sued for infringement. They then will raise issues of patent validity in their defense, hoping again for an invalidation order. As covered in Chapter 2, patent opponents may raise a variety of arguments to convince a court that the PTO made a mistake, such as improper subject matter, lack of novelty, or nonobviousness. As another tack, however, they may raise deficiencies in the application. The most common points of contention involve whether the disclosure is sufficient to enable one skilled in the art to practice the invention and whether the best mode was revealed. This chapter now looks more closely at these requirements.

DISCLOSURE: ENABLEMENT AND BEST MODE

Section 112 of the Patent Act requires the patent application to contain a written description of the invention and of the manner and process of making and using it, in such full, clear, concise, and exact terms as to:

1. enable any person skilled in the art to which it pertains, or with which it is most nearly connected, to make and use the same, and
2. set forth the best mode contemplated by the inventor of carrying out the invention.

These disclosures often are called the specification in the patent application, although strictly speaking, the Patent Act also includes the claims within the definition of "specification." The amount of disclosure required by Section 112 clearly is the most contested area of the patent application process.

Enablement

The patent application must provide enough information about the invention to enable one skilled in the art to practice it. There are three frequently encountered problems with that standard. First, it is an objective requirement. What the inventor subjectively believes is enough information to allow others to make or use the invention is not determinative. Rather, the information is judged with reference to a reasonably skilled practitioner. Second, inventors often want to withhold as much information as possible regarding their inventions. For instance, an invention might require use of a component, but the inventor might not want to provide production details of it, possibly because they are considered valuable trade secrets. Similarly, inventions could use computer programs. The inventors may be willing to illustrate what the programs must do, but might not want to provide source code listings that will carry out the specifications. Rather, inventors may believe that their versions of the source code, used to implement the patented claims, are separate "inventions" that do not have to be revealed. In their minds, disclosure of requisite tasks, parameters, and logic sequences should be enough for a skilled programmer to practice the invention. A third problem is that inventors typically attempt to write their claims so that they have the broadest reach possible. Questions then arise whether the information provided in the application is sufficient to enable one who is skilled in the art to practice the invention to the full extent of the claims.

Mindful of these considerations, the courts have determined that a disclosure is not insufficient just because some experimentation may have to be performed by a skilled artisan. However, the amount of experimentation needed to practice the invention must not be undue. The Federal Circuit has offered a set of criteria that illustrate the factors one should consider in determining if disclosure is sufficient:

1. The quantity of experimentation necessary;
2. The amount of direction or guidance presented;
3. The presence or absence of working examples;
4. The nature of the invention;
5. The state of the prior art;
6. The relative skill of those in the art;
7. The predictability or unpredictability of the art;
8. The breadth of the claims.[16]

The following case provides a classic example of how the courts handle high-technology cases involving trade secret information.

WHITE CONSOLIDATED INDUSTRIES V. VEGA SERVO-CONTROL, INC.
Federal Circuit Court of Appeals, 1983

FACTS: On June 6, 1972, White Consolidated Industries received a U.S. patent (the '653 patent) for a machine tool numerical control (NC) system. In an NC system, a machine tool, such as a mill head or a drill bit, is placed under the control of a computer program (the "part program") that defines the operations to be performed by the tool in machining a particular part. The computer part program is created either manually, by writing the instructions directly in machine-readable form (called machine code), or with the assistance of a computer. In the latter situation, the part program is written using an English-like programming computer language that is then translated into machine code by another computer program, called a processor or translator. Processors can be developed so that the translation is completed with a two-step process or in a single pass.

White markets a single-pass NC system called Omnicontrol, which is the subject of the '653 patent. The system provides for two-way conversational communication between the operator and the computer so that the operator may modify the controlling part program while the program is running. The system also includes a universal input feature so that a single part program can be used to control several tools, thereby eliminating the need to create a new part program for each tool. This feature allows one to write the part program in a universal language without considering the specific tool to be used. A language translator in the system converts the part program to the machine code needed to operate the requisite tool. The '653 patent describes the language translator as follows:

> The language TRANSLATOR used in the RUN mode may be a known translator capable of converting, in a single pass, a part program in

continued . . .

continued . . .

programming language form into a part program in machine language form, as for example SPLIT (Sundstrand Program Language Internally Translated).

At the time the application for the '653 patent was filed, SPLIT was a trade secret of Sundstrand (Sundstrand subsequently assigned its patent rights to White) and was available only by purchase from Sundstrand.

White sued Vega, charging that Vega manufactured and sold NC systems that infringed the '653 patent. Vega denied infringement and alleged that the patent was invalid. The trial court ruled for Vega, finding the patent invalid for failure to meet the enablement requirement of Section 112 of the Patent Act. White appealed to the Federal Circuit.

DECISION AND REASONING: Section 112 requires that an invention be described "in such full, clear, concise, and exact terms as to enable any person skilled in the art . . . to make and use the same." White does not claim that SPLIT was disclosed, but rather that the specification contains an enabling disclosure notwithstanding its omission. White says (1) that the '653 patent calls for a known or standard single-pass translator—as for example SPLIT—and specifies the characteristics of such a translator, (2) that SPLIT was only an example, and (3) that there were other known single-pass translators interchangeable with SPLIT. White states that because those other translators, such as ACTION and COMPACT, were known to those skilled in the art and available to them, the enablement requirement is satisfied.

We disagree. It is true that one may refer to an element of a claimed invention held as a trade secret by name only and yet satisfy the requirements of Section 112 if equivalent elements are known, are known to be equivalents, and are available to those skilled in the art. However, there is insufficient evidence here from which to conclude that suitable substitutes for SPLIT were known and widely available.

Testimony that ACTION and COMPACT were takeoffs of, or patterned upon, SPLIT does not establish that those translators were known to be suitable substitutes for SPLIT. That other translators were available when the application was filed is unavailing when there is no basis in the record for finding that a person skilled in the art on reading the specification would know that another single-pass processor would be suitable. Indeed, statements made by Sundstrand employees suggest that the inventors, themselves, originally considered SPLIT the only language suitable for operation in the conversational mode of the invention. For instance, Sundstrand announced at a press conference one week after filing, "The system is compatible with programs created by APT or other programming systems; however, we doubt at this time that these systems are compatible with instantaneous reprogramming by use of the 'conversational' part of the system."

White's assertion that SPLIT was itself widely available, albeit only upon purchase from Sundstrand, misses the mark. The sine qua non of a valid patent is a full, clear, enabling description of the invention. Though the language translator by itself is not the claimed invention, it is an integral part of the disclosure necessary to enable those skilled in the art to "make and use the same." Were Sundstrand (now White) to maintain SPLIT as a trade secret, it could theoretically extend its exclusionary rights beyond the 17-year life of the patent by controlling access to SPLIT, a result inconsistent with the objectives of the patent system. Sundstrand was therefore obliged to disclose the details of SPLIT or some other language translator, unless suitable substitutes were known and available to those skilled in the art or unless a suitable substitute could be obtained without undue experimentation.

Respecting the latter alternative, White correctly says a disclosure is sufficient even if it required that one skilled in the art must conduct some experimentation. The amount of required experimentation, however, must be reasonable. Richard Stitt, a skilled programmer in the NC field, testified in this case that development of a single-pass translator would require from 1½ to 2 person-years of effort. This is clearly an unreasonable requirement.

White argues that the estimate is irrelevant because it concerns the development of a commercially profitable single-pass translator and that suitable commercial translators were readily available. However, the language of the '653 patent, "a known translator . . . as for example SPLIT," is insufficient to identify which translators could be satisfactorily used, and there is no evidence that one skilled in the art would be able to select or develop a suitable translator without undue experimentation or delay.

It is immaterial that commercial use made, and publications issued, after the filing date of the '653 patent may have established the suitability of other language translators (e.g., ACTION, ADAPT, APT, AUTOSPOT, COMPACT, and UNIAPT). A sufficient disclosure must exist as of the application filing date. That the listed language translators were not specifically identified at that time as suitable substitutes for SPLIT renders futile their citation by White in this case.

White says that APT's suitability was made known three months before the filing date by the following announcement in Metal Working News:

> In a status report on its Omnicontrol system for on-line computer control of n/c machine tools, Sundstrand Corp., here, discloses that the "conversational" reprogramming feature has been made compatible with APT-created part programs. Omnicontrol conversational reprogramming originally was restricted to Sunstrand's own SPLIT language.

continued . . .

continued ...

That announcement supplies an insufficient basis, however, from which to infer that one skilled in the art would know that APT could be used as a direct substitute for SPLIT, particularly when the specification contains no mention of APT's compatibility. An announcement in a news magazine is inadequate proof of such recognized knowledge in the art as will excuse a failure to supply a fully enabling disclosure in a patent application.

For these reasons, White has not demonstrated that the district court erred in concluding that the '653 patent failed to meet the enablement requirement of Section 112. The judgment that the '653 patent is invalid is affirmed.

This case not only illustrates what information is needed to make a disclosure enabling, but it also indicates how important it is to be forthcoming with that information in the application process. Although the disclosure in the application was not enough to enable those skilled in the art to use the invention, information released to the public soon after the filing date filled the necessary gaps. Nonetheless, the disclosures were judged lacking in the application, and the patent claims were deemed invalid. This, then, serves as a powerful warning about the importance of disclosure in the application.

Enablement and Computer Programs   Those filing patent applications for inventions using computer programs should be careful not to overreact to the decision in *White v. Vega*. White claimed that there were other programs on the market besides the one disclosed in the patent application that would enable the invention to work. However, White did not convince the court that skilled programmers would be able to identify those programs without undue experimentation. Had White introduced such evidence, the case likely would have been resolved in its favor. In addition, the court relied on evidence that it would take a skilled programmer more than one and one-half years to develop the program needed to implement the invention. This amount of time clearly was over the line of what constitutes undue experimentation.

The Federal Circuit has made it clear that patent specifications for inventions utilizing computer programs may not have to provide details about the programs, such as source code, flow charts, or block diagrams. According to the court, the amount of disclosure that will enable one to make an invention incorporating a computer program "may vary according to the nature of the invention, the role of the program in carrying it out, and the complexity of the contemplated programming, all from the viewpoint of the skilled programmer."[17] The Federal Circuit also has recognized that "writing a computer program may be a task requiring the most sublime of inventive faculties or it may require only the droning use of clerical skill."[18] For instance, in *Northern Telecom, Inc. v. Datapoint Corp.*,[19] the court reviewed a patent for a batch data preparation and entry invention that was challenged because the specification did not provide any information about the software program used to make it operate. The court noted that in this particular situation, the claimed invention was not in the details of the program but rather in a process based on a combination of components and steps. In addition, experts testified that experienced programmers could write programs to carry out the computer operations revealed in the specification without unreasonable effort. The court stated that it did not matter that the programmers might work out those programming details in different ways, or that some solutions might be better than others, as long as they could make the invention work without undue experimentation. Therefore, the court determined that the patent specification satisfied the enablement requirements of the Patent Act, notwithstanding its failure to provide source code listings or block diagrams.

Enablement and the Breadth of the Claims   In *White v. Vega*, the inventors had completed the invention to the full extent of the claims and could have disclosed enough information to enable others to practice it had they chosen to do so. However, they attempted to hold back on certain elements, hoping that they could retain an advantage in the marketplace. Sometimes, though, inventors simply claim more than they actually have invented. For instance, the Federal Circuit was faced with a case in 1999 dealing with a machine used to sort PVC plastic containers from PET containers for recycling purposes.[20] The machine relied on the fact that PVC absorbs more electromagnetic radiation than PET, and so transmits less radiation through it when equivalent pieces of PVC and PET are irradiated. The industry encountered two problems, however. First, a thick portion of a PET container may absorb more energy than a thin PVC portion. Also, containers often are folded and squashed, leading to the possibility that the radiation may pass through several layers of PET material. The trick, therefore, is to determine what portions of the containers are not unusually thick or folded, and make the radiation transmittal measurements there. The claimed invention took care of this problem by radiating the containers at several points. For the invention, it was assumed that the portions having the highest readings did not have irregularities or folds. However, the machine still might misclassify the plastic if the plastic was severely deformed, because even the highest readings may have come through irregular portions. The patent, however, claimed an invention that could determine when the radiation did not penetrate regular portions and thereby would classify only those containers where regular portions had been measured.

The Federal Circuit determined that the patent was invalid. The written description in the patent application did not explain how to distinguish between signals that passed through irregular portions of containers and those that did not. The court noted that the scope of the claims must be less than or equal to the scope the enablement. It also reiterated that a claim is not enabled if one who is skilled in the art is not able to replicate the claimed invention without undue experimentation. The problem here was that those skilled in the art did not yet know how to devise a way to determine that none of the signals passed through irregularities. Indeed, even one of the inventors believed that additional research and experimentation was needed to build a device that could selectively identify signals based on whether they had passed through irregularities. Although classifying the plastic based on the highest transmission readings might come close to achieving the goals of the invention, this procedure could not do everything that the patent claimed the invention could do.

A similar type of enablement problem is fairly common in the biotechnology industry.[21] For instance, a scientist may discover a way to integrate a particular sequence of DNA into a particular type of plant cell that causes the plant to produce a useful mammalian peptide. Based on this research, a patent application may claim the process of integrating the DNA sequence into any kind of plant to make the peptide. The problem is that there often are uncertainties whether biotechnological processes will work the same way on different types of cells or species. According to the Federal Circuit, a claim is not enabled when those skilled in the art cannot predict, based on the specification and the scientific knowledge available at the time of filing, that the invention will work to the extent claimed in the application.[22] Thus, scientists in biotechnology—and other—industries must be careful when drafting patent applications to make sure that current research predictably supports the breadth of their claims.

Best Mode

Claims to inventions usually are drafted with sufficient breadth that there will be several ways to carry them out. As a simple hypothetical, pretend that an inventor seeks to patent a method to improve the longevity of CDs by soaking them in a heated bath of diluted soap or bleach. The process is effective with any amount of heat and within a wide range of dilution levels. However, based on experiments conducted before filing the patent application, the inventor believes that a 30% solution of lavender soap heated to 140 degrees achieves the best results. In addition, the inventor has found that the process works even better if the mixture is illuminated with fluorescent lights while the CDs are immersed in it. The inventor, however, does not want to reveal these specific parameters and attributes in the patent application. If the disclosures are not made, then the inventor might maintain an advantage when the patent expires, since members of the public, even 20 years later, still might not know all the preferred techniques and parameters to optimize the invention. The Patent Act, though, prevents the inventor from gaining a valid patent while attempting to strategically conceal from the public the best or preferred embodiment of the invention. It does this by requiring the inventor to reveal the best mode of carrying out the invention in the specification of the patent application.

The best-mode requirement is drafted in terms of what is contemplated by the inventor at the time of filing. Clearly the inquiry must begin with a subjective analysis: did the inventor subjectively know of a mode of practicing the invention that was considered to be better than any other? If the answer is yes, then one must probe further to determine if the disclosure is adequate to allow those skilled in the art to identify and practice that preferred mode. This part of the evaluation is objective, akin to that used for enablement. Indeed, although best mode and enablement are treated as separate requirements, they clearly are interrelated.

Software inventions often raise difficult questions regarding best mode disclosures, such as whether source code must be revealed. A good example is provided by *Fonar Corp. v. General Electric Co.*,[23] which involved Fonar's patent for a magnetic resonance imaging machine capable of performing multi-angle oblique (MAO) imaging. General Electric alleged that the patent was invalid because it failed to disclose two software routines that the inventors testified were the best means they knew to accomplish MAO imaging. Fonar argued that providing a description of the software's functions was more important for a best-mode disclosure than revealing actual source code because the source code was tailored to specific hardware and may not have worked with other hardware. The Federal Circuit agreed. It stated: "As a general rule, where software constitutes part of a best mode of carrying out an invention, description of such a best mode is satisfied by a disclosure of the functions of the software. This is because, normally, writing code for such software is within the skill of the art, not requiring undue experimentation, once its functions have been disclosed."[24] Thus, one often does not have to reveal flow charts or source code to adequately disclose the best mode of an invention.

An interesting aspect about the best-mode requirement is that it rarely is raised by the PTO during the application process. An examiner is not going to investigate whether the applicant subjectively knows of a better mode than that disclosed in the application. Thus, an inventor may well receive a patent while concealing the best mode of an invention. However, this is not a toothless tiger to be routinely ignored. Those who challenge the validity of the patent will be keenly interested in what the inventor both believed and disclosed at the time of filing. Even those who are aware of the best mode may challenge any knowledge-disclosure disparity in the application on the basis that others may not have been so well informed. Therefore, the ultimate strength of a patent greatly depends on fulfilling the best-mode requirement of the Patent Act.

INFRINGEMENT AND REMEDIES

Section 271(a) of the Patent Act provides that "whoever without authority makes, uses or sells any patented invention, within the United States during the term of the patent therefor, infringes the patent." Infringement analysis has three components as illustrated in Exhibit 3.3. First, one must determine if there is *literal infringement*. If so, then infringement is established and that is the end of the inquiry.[25] If there is not literal infringement, then one must evaluate whether the *doctrine of equivalents* applies. If it does not, then there is no infringement. If it is determined that the doctrine of equivalents is applicable, then before concluding that there is infringement, one must investigate further and consider whether *file wrapper estoppel* bars the allegations. These principles first will be reviewed; their application then will be illustrated by the landmark case, *Pennwalt Corp. v. Durand-Wayland, Inc.*

Exhibit 3.3

Patent Infringement

Flow Chart of Infringement Issues

- Is there literal infringement?

  - Yes: infringes.

  - No: Go on.

- Does doctrine of equivalents apply?

  - No: Does not infringe.

  - Yes: Go on.

- Does file wrapper estoppel apply?

  - Yes: Does not infringe.

  - No: Infringes.

Infringement Analysis

- Literal Infringement

  - Rule of exactness: Defendant literally infringes if (s)he makes, uses, or sells (in U.S.) the invention exactly as recited in the claim.

  - Rule of addition: Defendant literally infringes if (s)he makes, uses, or sells (in U.S.) an apparatus, composition, or process having all the elements, compounds, or steps specified in the claims and adds other elements, compounds, or steps.

  - Rule of omission: Defendant does *not* literally infringe if (s)he omits one or more of the elements, compounds, or steps recited in the claims.

- Doctrine of equivalents

  - Device performs substantially the same function in substantially the same way to obtain the same result.

- File Wrapper Estoppel

  - Equivalent arrangement used by defendant was abandoned by the patent holder to overcome PTO objections based on prior art.

- **CASE:** *Pennwalt v. Durand-Wayland*

Literal Infringement

A person literally infringes a claim in a patent by making, using, or selling an item in the United States that contains all the elements of the claim. Literal infringement often is evaluated according to one of three rules: the rule of exactness, the rule of addition, or the rule of omission. According to the rule of exactness, one infringes a claim by making, using, or selling an item that exactly conforms to that claim. By the rule of addition, infringement also is present when one makes, uses, or sells an item that not only has all the elements of the claim but also includes other elements. Under the rule of omission, one does not infringe a claim if the item under review omits any of the elements that compose the claim.

A claim for a chair provides a simple example. A broad claim might read:

A mechanism comprising a level surface, a back, and four legs.

A person who manufactures a chair with a back and four legs will infringe the patent by the rule of exactness. What happens if a person manufactures a four-legged chair on casters? Does this infringe the patent? According to the rule of addition, the answer is yes. Therefore, even an improvement such as the mobile chair is subject to the patent because it cannot be made without the basic elements claimed in the patent. Therefore, the inventor of the rolling chair will need permission from the patent holder before making and selling the new means to relax.

Now, take this concept a step further. Suppose including wheels on the chair is a novel and nonobvious improvement over the current art—the stationary chair. This means that the mobile chair meets the standards for patentability, and thus its inventor could receive a patent for it. The interesting thing is that even with a patent, the inventor of the chair on rollers would not be able to make it, use it, or sell it in the United States. This inventor is effectively blocked by the patent on the regular chair according to the rule of addition. Likewise, the patentee of the regular chair will be blocked from making a rolling chair; by the rule of exactness, such a chair that has exactly the elements of the mobile chair patent will infringe that patent. This scenario of two patents' blocking the production of an improvement is somewhat common, and it requires the respective patentees to come to some agreement to break the deadlock. A typical solution is a cross-license, wherein the inventor of the mobile chair allows the regular chair patentee to make the rolling variety, and the regular chair patentee gives permissions as to the regular model. As indicated in Chapter 2, blocking patents have raised serious questions in biotechnology such as whether a patent on a purified protein might block production of that protein through genetic engineering. Blocking patents also are frequently encountered in the computer field.

The rule of omission indicates that a person has to omit only one of the elements of the claim to escape literal infringement. Thus, a chair with a back and only three legs would escape liability for literal infringement because it omits an element of the claim. Obviously, this can have a pernicious effect if the inventor is not very careful with drafting the claims, since those who want to make the invention must only find some element that might be left out or replaced with a suitable substitute.

Doctrine of Equivalents

Strict application of the rule of omission allows individuals to avoid the spirit of a patent because they can simply omit an element and include an obviously similar feature in its stead. Due to the potential harshness of this result, the Supreme Court approved of an equitable inquiry, called the doctrine of equivalents, in *Graver Tank & Mfg. Co. v. Linde Air Products*. In that case, the patentee claimed an electrical welding compound consisting of silicates of calcium and magnesium. The alleged infringer omitted magnesium and substituted manganese for it. The Supreme Court stated:

> Outright and forthright duplication is a dull and very rare type of infringement. To prohibit no other would place the inventor at the mercy of verbalism and would be subordinating substance to form. It would deprive [the inventor] of the benefit of his invention and would foster concealment rather than disclosure of inventions, which is one of the primary purposes of the patent system.[26]

The doctrine of equivalents evolved to ensure that one could not practice a fraud on the patent by making obvious changes. Even if a device does not literally infringe, a patentee may proceed under the doctrine of equivalents if the device "performs substantially the same function in substantially the same way to obtain the same result."[27] The Supreme Court offered that an important factor in this judgment is whether a person reasonably skilled in the art would have known of the interchangeability of the element omitted with the one substituted. With reference to the issue before it, the Court found equivalency between the uses of magnesium and manganese in welding compositions and thus found infringement. Infringement here was based not on literal infringement, which was avoided by the rule of omission, but rather on the doctrine of equivalents.

The doctrine of equivalents is somewhat controversial because it takes something that is supposed to be definite—the claims—and makes their reach more nebulous. In 1997, the Supreme Court addressed whether U.S. courts should continue to apply the doctrine of equivalents in *Warner-Jenkinson Co. v. Hilton Davis Chemical Co.*,[28] a case opinion that was eagerly awaited by patent professionals. Hilton Davis's patent in that case claimed an improved purification process involving the ultrafiltration of dye through a porous membrane "at a pH level from approximately 6.0 to 9.0." Warner-Jenkinson developed an ultrafiltration process that operated at a pH of 5.0. Hilton Davis sued for patent infringement. It admitted that Warner-Jenkinson did not literally infringe the claim of its patent, but argued that it nonetheless infringed under the doctrine of equivalents. Warner-Jenkinson asked the Court to put an end to the doctrine of equivalents, stating that it had taken on a life of its own, unbounded by the patent claims. The company argued that the doctrine conflicts with the basic purpose of requiring patent claims, which is to provide public notice regarding the precise definition of the invention. The Supreme Court refused this request, however. According to the Court, the doctrine of equivalents, when properly applied, does not enlarge the bounds of the invention beyond what is claimed. Rather, the doctrine refers only to whether elements of the invention have been substituted with equivalents. We will see what this means in more detail in *Pennwalt Corporation v. Durand-Wayland, Inc.* The key point, though, is that every element that one claims is part of the invention is material, and the doctrine of equivalents evaluates only whether any of these key attributes has been swapped with known insubstantial equivalents. Thus, if one were to remove an element altogether, there could not be infringement under the doctrine of equivalents.

Warner-Jenkinson also argued that since the equitable doctrine is aimed at unscrupulous copyists, it should not apply to those who make equivalent inventions without knowledge of the patent or some evil intent to evade it. The Court, however, dismissed this notion and held that intent plays no role in the application of the doctrine of equivalents. Rather, the doctrine is based on the objective standard of whether one skilled in the art would know about the interchangeability of claim elements. The Court also ruled in *Hilton Davis* that the proper time for evaluating the requisite knowledge of interchangeability is at the time of infringement and not at the time the patent issued. Having set these standards, the Court sent the case back to the lower court to determine, among other things, if the lower pH level was equivalent to the levels related in the claim.

The doctrine of equivalents therefore continues to be viable in the United States. The doctrine, however, is not uniformly accepted across the globe, although some important countries, most notably Japan, have recently adopted it.[29] Due to many remaining disparities, though, any effort in the future to harmonize international patent policies likely will have to address the breadth of claims and how they might be infringed.

File Wrapper Estoppel

When an individual makes a substitution that falls under the doctrine of equivalents, an additional issue—file wrapper estoppel[30]—must be considered before finding infringement. Suppose the patent for the chair covered legs made of oak. The alleged infringer makes chairs out of cherry wood, which everyone in the business knows is equivalent for holding a seat above the ground. Thus, this is a good candidate for infringement under the doctrine of equivalents. However, when one looks at the history of the patent application, called the file wrapper, one might find that the patentee took actions that should prohibit extension of rights to cherry wood. For instance, assume that when the patentee filed for the patent, the claims covered legs of oak or cherry wood. However, since the prior art used a lot of cherry wood, the PTO denied these claims as obvious. Ultimately, though, the PTO was persuaded to allow the patent when the claims were narrowed to oak only. Under these circumstances it would be unfair to allow the patentee to take back through the doctrine of equivalents that which the patentee willingly gave up to get the patent in the first place. The doctrine of file wrapper estoppel prevents this unfair result. In effect, the patentee is estopped from claiming rights to cherry wood via the doctrine of equivalents due to conduct in obtaining the patent.

Since *Hilton Davis* involved the doctrine of equivalents, the Supreme Court had to consider the possibility that file wrapper estoppel applied as well. The restriction in the claim that the invention operate "at a pH from approximately 6.0 to 9.0" was added to meet an objection from the PTO that a prior art reference related an ultrafiltration process operating at a pH above 9.0. Since the upper pH limit clearly was added to satisfy the PTO by distinguishing the invention from the prior art, the Court noted that Hilton Davis could not broaden the claim above 9.0 through the doctrine of equivalents. However, the evidence was not so clear why Hilton Davis added the lower limit. Warner-Jenkinson argued that anything given up during the patent prosecution process with the PTO cannot be reacquired by the doctrine of equivalents due to file wrapper estoppel. However, the Supreme Court disagreed. File wrapper estoppel applies only to elements that are given up to avoid PTO objections based on the existence of prior art. However, the patent applicant may add new elements to the claims for reasons unrelated to prior art. If this is the case, then file wrapper estoppel should not be used to limit the application of the doctrine of equivalents. The Court held that the burden is on the patent holder to prove that the reason for the change was not related to objections based on patentability. Accordingly, Hilton Davis must demonstrate that it added the lower limit for some reason other than to distinguish the prior art. If it is unable to do so, then file wrapper estoppel will apply and Hilton Davis will not be able to rely on the doctrine of equivalents to allege infringement by a 5.0 pH ultrafiltration process.

The following case, *Pennwalt Corp. v. Durand-Wayland, Inc.*, demonstrates the difficulty of applying these seemingly simple doctrines to complex, high-technology patent claims. The discussion by the Federal Circuit is enlightening and paints a real-world picture on the entire subject of infringement. The court's evaluation is complicated because the claims at issue use the means-plus-function technique. Although it can be confusing, recall that literal infringement of such claims covers the means indicated in the specification and those means' equivalents. This language has led many observers to believe that the determination of literal infringement with means-plus-function claims simultaneously includes analysis under the doctrine of equivalents. Others take the approach that the two are intimately linked but that the doctrine of equivalents still requires some further considerations. The Federal Circuit, in *Pennwalt*, assumed the latter, but you should notice how this strains the analysis. In 1998, the Federal Circuit acknowledged that the analysis of literal infringement with means-plus-function claims is closely related to the application of the doctrine of equivalents but that the tests nonetheless are not coextensive.[31] Therefore, the Federal Circuit continues to use, although with some hesitancy, the three traditional steps—(1) literal infringement, (2) infringement by the doctrine of equivalents, and (3) file wrapper estoppel—for appraising infringement with means-plus-function claims.

PENNWALT CORPORATION v. DURAND-WAYLAND, INC.
Federal Circuit Court of Appeals, 1987

FACTS: Pennwalt sued Durand-Wayland for infringing certain claims in its patent (the '628 patent) for a sorting invention. The principal object of the invention is to provide a rapid means for sorting items, such as fruit, by color, weight, or a combination of these characteristics.

Pennwalt's invention is claimed using means-plus-function language. The weight sorter recited in claims 1 and 2 conveys items along a track having an electronic weighing device that produces an electrical signal proportional to the weight of the item, along with signal comparison means, clock means, position-indicating means, and discharge means, each of which performs specified functions. The specification describes the details of a hardwired network consisting of discrete electrical components that perform each step of the claims. Essentially, signals from the weighing device are compared to reference signals, and an appropriate signal is sent at the proper time to discharge the item into a container corresponding to its weight. In effect, the invention continuously tracks the positions of the items to be sorted, and it discharges them at the proper times.

The combined sorter of claims 10 and 18 is a multifunctional apparatus whereby the item is conveyed across the weighing device and also carried past an optical scanner that produces an electrical signal proportional to the color of the item. The signals from the weighing device and color sensor are combined, and an appropriate signal is sent at the proper time to discharge the item into the container corresponding to its color and weight.

Durand-Wayland manufactures and sells two different sorting machines: the Microsizer, which sorts by weight, and the Microsorter, in conjunction with the Microsizer, which sorts by weight and color. These machines differ from Pennwalt's in that they use microprocessors and computer programs to store data about weight and color. These machines do not continuously track the position of the items as does Pennwalt's invention; rather, data about the items and the distances to relevant drop points are stored in memory so that, under the direction of software routines, they can be released when the appropriate time intervals have elapsed.

The district court ruled for Durand-Wayland, determining that there was neither literal infringement nor infringement under the doctrine of equivalents. Pennwalt appealed to the Federal Circuit.

DECISION AND REASONING:
Literal Infringement. Pennwalt asserts that all limitations set forth in its patent claims can be read literally on Durand's devices. Pennwalt contends that the district court erred in interpreting the claims by both going beyond

continued . . .

continued . . .

the means-plus-function language of a claim limitation and comparing the structure in the accused device with the structure disclosed in the specification. Such comparison allegedly resulted in the court's reading nonexistent structural limitations in the claims. Pennwalt relies on the statement in *Graver Tank*: "If accused matter falls clearly within the claim, infringement is made out and that is the end of it."

In view of the breadth of means-plus-function language in the claims, that test for literal infringement would encompass any means that performed the function of a claim element. This is not the proper test, however, for means-plus-function limitations. The *Graver Tank* statement predated the inclusion—in the 1952 Act—of the provision specifically permitting means limitations: Section 112, paragraph 6. This paragraph requires that means language be construed to cover the corresponding structure, material, or acts in the specification and their equivalents.

Section 112 rules out the possibility that any and every means that performs the function specified in the claim literally satisfies the limitation. Rather, literal infringement occurs only if the accused device uses means to achieve every claimed function that are the same as or equivalent to the structures disclosed in the specification. Of course, if every function cited in the claim is not performed by the accused device, then there cannot be literal infringement.

Thus it was appropriate that the district court made a comparison between Durand-Wayland's structure and the structure disclosed in the specification for performing a particular function. The statute means exactly what it says: To determine whether a claim limitation is met literally—when expressed as a means for performing a stated function—the court must compare the accused structure with the disclosed structure and must find equivalent *structure* as well as *identity* of claimed *function* for that structure. Thus, Pennwalt is in error when it argues that if an accused structure performs the function required by the claim, then there are structural equivalency and literal infringement.

We need not determine whether the district court correctly found no equivalency in structure because the district court also found that the accused devices, in any event, did not perform all the same functions specified in the claims. For example, the accused devices had no position-indicating means for tracking the locations of the item being sorted. The absence of that function negates the possibility of literal infringement.

Infringement under the Doctrine of Equivalents. Under the doctrine of equivalents, infringement may be found if an accused device performs substantially the same overall function in substantially the same way to obtain substantially the same overall result as the claimed invention. That formulation, however, does not mean one can ignore claim limitations. Each element of a claim is material, and the plaintiff must show the presence of every element or its substantial equivalent in the accused device.

Pennwalt argues that the accused machines simply do in a computer what the patent illustrates doing with hardwired circuitry. If Pennwalt were correct that the accused devices differ only in substituting a computer for hardwired circuitry, it might have a stronger position for arguing that the accused devices infringe its claims. The claim limitations, however, require the performance of certain specified functions, for which the microprocessor in the accused devices was not so programmed.

The district court found that certain functions of the claimed inventions were missing from the accused devices and that those that were performed were substantially different. For example, all of Pennwalt's claims require the function of continuously indicating positions of items. Some language from claim 10 is representative:

> first position-indicating means responsive to a signal from said clock means and said signal from said second comparison means for continuously indicating the position of an item to be sorted while the item is in transit between said optical detection means and said electronic weighing means.

> second position-indicating means responsive to the signal from said clock means, the signal from said first comparison means and said first position-indicating means for generating a signal continuously indicative of the position of an item to be sorted after said item has been weighed.

The district court found that the accused devices do not have any position-indicating means to determine the positions of the items being sorted. Rather, it correctly found that the microprocessor stores weight and color data, not the positions of the items to be sorted.

Pennwalt argues that there is a way to find out where an item is physically located on the track of the accused machine. Thus, Pennwalt asserts that the accused devices have position-indicating means. However, the accused machine simply does not do what could be done. The physical tracking of fruit is not part of the way in which the Durand-Wayland sorter works. Although a microprocessor theoretically could be programmed to perform that function, the district court determined that the function performed by the Durand-Wayland machines was substantially different.

Pennwalt also claims that the memory component of the Durand-Wayland sorter, which stores information as to weight and color of an item, performed substantially the same function as claimed for the position-indicating means. The district court found that a memory function is neither the same nor

continued . . .

continued ...

substantially the same as the function of continuously indicating where an item is physically located in a sorter. On this point the record is indisputable that before the words "continuously indicating" were added as an additional limitation, the claim was unpatentable in view of prior art that, like the accused machines, stores the information with respect to sorting criteria in memories but did not continuously track the location.

Thus, the facts here do not involve later-developed technology, which should be deemed within the scope of the claims to avoid the pirating of an invention. On the contrary, the inventors could not obtain a patent with claims in which the functions were described more broadly. Having secured claims only by including very specific functional limitations, Pennwalt now seeks to avoid those very limitations under the doctrine of equivalents. This it cannot do.

Conclusion. In sum, all of Pennwalt's claims require the function of continuously indicating the positions of the items to be sorted. No means in the accused device performs that function and thus there can be no literal infringement. No means with an equivalent function was substituted in the accused devices and thus there can be no infringement under the doctrine of equivalents. The district court's finding of no infringement is affirmed.

Infringement of Process Patents

A U.S. patent generally protects only against acts of infringement that occur in the United States. Thus, if the patent claims an article of manufacture or a machine, then one who makes, uses, or sells that machine in the United States infringes the patent under the terms of Section 271. Alternatively, a person who makes, uses, or sells the article outside the United States does not infringe the U.S. patent. However, note that one who makes the article in a foreign country will not be able to sell it in the United States without infringing the U.S. patent. In this way, a patent on a machine or an article secures the inventor from direct competition within the United States.

One who has a patent on a process used to manufacture products faces a more complicated international scenario. Prior to 1989, infringement under Section 271 occurred only if someone used that process within the United States. Therefore, strictly speaking, one did not infringe a U.S. process patent by using that process beyond U.S. borders to manufacture products and then selling those products in the United States. Without more, the only possible remedy was through the International Trade Commission (ITC) under Section 337. However, actions through the ITC may be a weak deterrent because the ITC can only grant an order excluding further imports; it has no power to order monetary damages.

Congress adopted the Process Patent Amendments in 1988 to defeat competition within the United States by foreign manufacturers using processes protected by U.S. patents. Section 271(g), which was added by the amendments, reads in part: "Whoever without authority imports into the United States or sells or uses within the United States a product which is made by a process patented in the United States shall be liable as an infringer." The aim of the change clearly is against foreign manufacturers who use a patented process and import the resultant products into the United States. However, the reach of the amendments is not so limited. Anyone who uses or sells products impermissibly developed from the patented process infringes the patent. Thus, even retailers and noncommercial users of the product are theoretically subject to infringement actions. However, the act makes them susceptible only if there is no adequate remedy against the primary manufacturers, importers, distributors, or wholesalers. In addition, when a business has inventories of products that infringe process patents, it nonetheless will not be liable for damages if those products were acquired before the business knew or had reason to know about the infringement. Under circumstances such as these, when the business can establish its innocence, it is free to sell the products, notwithstanding the fact that they infringe process patents.

The details of the Process Patent Amendments are extremely complicated, well beyond the scope of this book. The complexity results from the fact that it is difficult to determine the processes by which a product or its components were made. For instance, what steps should a retailer, such as Sears, be expected to take to reasonably assure itself that its bicycle frames, or any of the frames' integral component parts, were not constructed by means of patented processes? The act establishes due diligence procedures by which retailers and others may immunize themselves from liability. In very simple terms, a business can limit its exposure by writing to other manufacturers of similar products, requesting that they disclose any process patents they hold related to the product. Once that information is received, the business transmits it to the manufacturer or supplier of the product in question. If the manufacturer then provides adequate written assurance that the product is not made through the patented processes, then the inquiring business is relatively safe from liability for infringement. The full impact of these amendments has not yet become clear, but certainly the amendments increase the risks and the paperwork for wholesalers and retailers in the United States.

Remedies for Patent Infringement

One must consider a lot of issues throughout the process of obtaining a patent. Is the subject matter patentable? Is the invention novel and nonobvious? What must be disclosed? How much protection is possible? How much will it cost? The payoff for all this is that a court will enforce the right to exclude others from enjoying the fruits of one's invention. It does this in two ways: by issuing injunctions prohibiting further infringement and by ordering that compensation be paid for the infringing acts that have occurred. Compensation awards potentially can reach staggering amounts, and they often are reported in the popular press. A very notable figure was the $909

million that Kodak was ordered to pay Polaroid for its infringement of instant photography patents.[32] Indeed, monetary awards can be so high as to bankrupt companies, such as occurred after Smith International was ordered to pay Hughes Tool Co.
$134 million for infringement of patents related to rock bit technology.[33] Likewise,
Paragon Trade Brands, Inc., a manufacturer of disposable diapers, sought protection
under the bankruptcy laws after a court ruled that it had violated a Procter & Gamble diaper patent and ordered Paragon to pay $178 million in damages.[34]

Section 284 of the Patent Act provides that a patent holder may recover damages for infringement. In particular, the section states:

> Upon finding for the claimant, the court shall award the claimant damages
> adequate to compensate for the infringement but in no event less than a rea-
> sonable royalty for the use made of the invention by the infringer, together
> with interest and costs as fixed by the court. . . . [T]he court may increase the
> damages up to three times the amount found or assessed.

According to this provision, a patentee is entitled to be compensated for profits lost
by virtue of an infringement. Establishing this figure can be a demanding exercise,
however. The ultimate inquiry for determining lost profits is, "Had the infringer not
infringed, what would the patent holder have made?" Logically, one begins with the
sales made by the infringer. But then one must ask whether the patentee would have
made all those sales had the infringer not used the patented technology. It could be
that the infringer's customers were motivated more by certain unique features on the
infringer's products than by the patented technology. Perhaps the infringer's customers would have purchased products employing other technologies outside the
purview of the patent.[35] Maybe the patentee's sales staff would not have solicited the
customers reached by the infringer. Possibly the patentee could not have manufactured the products sold by the infringer because of deficiencies in capacity.

Once the lost sales are determined, then one must figure what would have been
the cost to produce the goods. Should one base that on variable costs or factor in
fixed costs? And then one can argue that the lost sales resulted in other losses, such
as fewer accessory sales. And on top of that, one might make further points, such
as that the unlawful competition by the infringer caused the patentee to lower its
sales prices below the amount it would have charged without the infringement. All
of these are acceptable arguments if the patentee has sufficient proof.

The Patent Act states that the patentee is, at a minimum, entitled to a reasonable
royalty for use made by the infringer. This usually means that the patentee will receive a reasonable royalty for those sales made by the infringer that it cannot prove it
would have otherwise made. In other words, the patentee normally will receive lost
profits for the infringer's sales it would have made and a reasonable royalty for the
rest. The reasonable royalty will be based on established rates or on a hypothetical
rate determined by the court. In addition to lost profits and a reasonable royalty, the
patentee can receive prejudgment interest equal to the amount of interest lost due to
the delay between the time the profit or royalty should have been earned and the
time it is finally paid by the infringer under court order. Finally, for cases of willful

---

Exhibit 3.4
Damages for Patent Infringement

- Profits from lost sales
  - Based on sales made by the infringer that otherwise would have been made by patent holder
  - Includes lost accessory sales
- Reasonable royalty for sales made by infringer that patent holder nevertheless would not have made
- Price erosion on patented product sales due to unlawful competition by infringer
- Prejudgment interest
- Treble damages and attorneys' fees if willful

---

infringement, the Patent Act provides that the court may treble the damage award and have the infringer pay the patentee's attorneys' fees as well.[36] Exhibit 3.4 summarizes the elements one must consider in calculating damages for patent infringment.

The trend in the courts toward patent protection in the United States is very clear: patentees are increasingly winning patent infringement actions and are being awarded higher sums as compensation. This means that small businesses now have more incentive to bring patent infringement actions against large corporations, since the odds for success and the expected payoffs have increased. However, always remember that patent infringement lawsuits can be extremely expensive to undertake. These costs may serve as insurmountable roadblocks to many small businesses, even when the prospects for recovery look good. Fortunately, insurance is now becoming available which may help cover the expenses of patent infringement suits.[37] Typically, the insurers make an independent review of the patent before issuing a policy to determine its strength and validity. The policies may cover legal bills up to $500,000, or perhaps more. Fees for the policies may be stiff, and they usually have significant copayment requirements. Nonetheless, small businesses that own patents are finding insurance to be an increasingly effective way to level the playing field against larger well-financed corporations.

INTERNATIONAL PATENT PROTECTION ISSUES

The increasing interdependence between the global economies has intensified the need for companies to pursue international business plans. Although patent protection within the United States is an important aspect of a business venture, its protective reach likely will be too limited for the modern corporation. Therefore, most business concerns now must contemplate patent protection on an international scale. Clearly, it would be easiest if an inventor could file for a global patent, which would give worldwide rights once granted. Although this is the ultimate goal of multinational businesses, it does not currently represent reality. Rather, for the most part, each country has its own patent policies, which it enforces in its own way within its own borders. This leads to substantial hardship and expense for inventors seeking global protection. Fortunately, significant strides are being made toward facilitating international patent protection. This is occurring on two fronts: on a substantive level wherein countries are attempting to harmonize their standards for patentability, and in a procedural sense, making it easier for inventors to file applications and receive protection within selected international boundaries.

Substantive Patent Policy Issues

The various patent policies throughout the world, especially among the major developed participants, share significant common ground, although the overlap tends to be overshadowed by important distinctions. Almost all patent systems have subject matter requirements for patents, although they differ on the types of inventions that are permissible. Most nations, too, demand that novelty be a basis for patent protection. However, as we shall see, novelty can have very different meanings that may result in substantial commercial repercussions. Possibly the most consistent similarity has to do with nonobviousness, which most nations assess with principles that are very much like those applied in the United States.

Companies involved with global markets wish that the international community could establish uniform standards for patent protection. In the early 1990s, the World Intellectual Property Organization (WIPO) made substantial progress in ironing out an important agreement, called the Patent Harmonization Treaty. However, this effort bogged down in 1993, due somewhat to objections from the United States. In the late 1990s, WIPO changed course and began to work on a much narrower agreement, termed the Patent Law Treaty. The topics discussed within this round of talks were much less ambitious, focusing on unifying certain technical elements, such as the requirements for obtaining a filing date, procedures for recording a change of address or patent ownership, and certain issues regarding administrative review of patent invalidation decisions. Since these matters do not raise heated disputes, this treaty likely will be accepted by WIPO members early in the twenty-first century.

Patent Terms   As presented in Chapter 1, TRIPs made some significant strides in establishing uniform standards, especially regarding patent terms and patentable subject matter. Prior to TRIPs, many nations had very short patent terms. In addition, most countries measured the terms from the date of filing, a standard with which the United States, of course, was not in accordance. TRIPs relieved these differences, requiring at least a 20-year term measured from the date of filing. Also before TRIPs, many nations, especially those in the early stages of development, did not allow patents for certain important commercial categories, such as agricultural chemicals, pharmaceuticals, computer programs, and biotechnological inventions. By the year 2005, TRIPs requires its membership to extend patent protection to most of these products. However, important exceptions remain, particularly for medical processes, animals other than microorganisms, and inventions contrary to public order or morality. These exceptions likely will have a continued impact on the biotechnology industry, especially in nations where public fears may be heightened, as we have seen in Europe.

First-to-File Priority   There are numerous disparities in the novelty requirements across the globe which raise enormous headaches for those interested in international patent protection. The United States is still the odd country out regarding patent priority principles, relying on the first-to-invent standard rather than first-to-file. This may lead to obvious problems when unsuspecting U.S. inventors decide to internationalize their operations. It also may result in substantial incongruities as to ownership of patent rights for the same invention, depending on the jurisdiction. That the United States ultimately will adopt the first-to-file system is nearly a certainty. The first-to-invent system requires detailed records and can lead to expensive litigation over priority. In addition, sophisticated international corporations already mobilize and file early to protect their patent rights overseas. The first-to-invent standard thus yields little advantage for them, and indeed even raises their risks in the United States. Large companies, therefore, among others, have provided substantial political support for change in the United States. Nonetheless, the opposition, which consists mostly of independent inventors and academics, has been surprisingly effective, often by appealing to cultural and historical attachments to the uniquely American first-to-invent standard. Therefore, those advocating that the Untied States join the international community regarding its priority system may have to wait longer than one otherwise would expect to achieve their goals.

Grace Periods   Novelty raises a host of other dangers for U.S. inventors as they venture into foreign lands. Recall that in the United States there is a one-year grace period for filing after certain triggering events such as a sale or publication. Many other countries are not so lenient, however. Some nations deny patent protection if the triggering events occur within their borders at any time prior to filing. Japan is somewhat like this, although it has a six-month grace period for certain limited acts of the inventor, such as making a demonstration at a trade show.[38] Other countries may be even more stringent, barring patent rights if the triggering events have occurred anywhere in the world prior to filing.[39] In this way, inventors who publish an article believing that they have one year to file may unknowingly jeopardize or relinquish patent rights in many important commercial trading areas around the world.

Related areas of controversy surround the ways that triggering events, such as "sale" and "public use," are defined. The United States tends to be relatively strict here, broadly interpreting what constitutes a sale to cover such activities as test marketing and offers. It also considers certain secret uses by the inventor to be public, such as when a process is used to manufacture goods for public sale. When the more substantive Patent Harmonization Treaty was being seriously negotiated in the early 1990s, U.S. representatives expressed the importance of a grace period, especially as to acts of the inventor, so that technical and market experimentation can be performed. However, they showed much more flexibility on issues regarding the activities that may constitute public uses or sales.[40]

Secrecy of Patent Applications   There are additional differences in foreign patent policies that must be considered by inventors having international visions. One important issue regards the secrecy of patent applications. Many nations, notably in Europe and Japan, retain the secrecy of patent applications only for a defined period of time, generally for 18 months after the application is filed. Also, inventors who file through the Patent Cooperation Treaty, which will be discussed shortly, face publication of their files after 18 months. The rationale for early publication is to accelerate disclosure of new inventions—a primary goal of all patent systems—and to provide information to the public so it can raise objections to the administrative officials making patent decisions.

The United States has had a long history of preserving the secrecy of patent applications until the patent issues. The secrecy of information in the patent files is extremely important to inventors who rely on trade secret laws for protection, especially when the claims eventually are not allowed. Inventors in countries where secrecy is preserved must be careful when they venture into nations where early publication is the rule. This may lead unsuspecting inventors to publicly release information that they otherwise may have wanted to remain private. This is especially true when patent rights are uncertain, and the inventors are testing the patent waters. The lesson is to be very aware of the possible different publication principles that may apply in different regions.

As noted earlier, U.S.-based multinational corporations have had to deal with international publication principles for decades, and so began a concerted drive to change U.S. laws regarding secrecy in the late 1990s. In 1999, U.S. secrecy laws were changed in the American Inventors Protection Act, but only to a limited degree. Now, patent applications filed in the United States will be held in confidence, but only if the applicant has not filed in a country or with an international convention that requires publication. If such a foreign filing is made, then the PTO will publish the application 18 months after it is filed. Thus, U.S. inventors who are relying on the secrecy provisions of U.S. laws have further reasons to be wary when their patent aspirations extend to foreign nations.

Oppositions and Delays   An inventor must note other variations as well. As mentioned earlier, there are different approaches to how the public might get involved in administrative patent decisions. Many countries allow members of the public to bring formal opposition proceedings within the agency. In most cases, the proceedings begin only after the patent is granted, but in some nations, the hearings may begin before the patent office makes a patent determination. This form of opposition procedure was used in Japan until recently, and it irked U.S. inventors since it sometimes led to substantial delays, often spanning several years, before the Japanese Patent Office would issue a patent. Delays are compounded in some countries due to administrative constraints and lax scheduling procedures. Again, Japan has been a focal point, since inventors often have faced relatively long administrative delays there. In response, the Japanese Patent Office announced a new initiative in 1998 to dramatically reduce examination periods for patents by the year 2005.[41]

Other Issues   Many countries have different traditions concerning the breadth of claims that will be approved. The United States tends to allow relatively broad claims, while other nations, such as Japan, tend to issue patents with only narrow claims. Also, nations diverge over their application of a doctrine of equivalents, although the trend, even in Japan, is to allow some form of equitable relief. Many foreign countries, unlike the United States, require that the invention be worked, or put into commercial use, in the country within a prescribed number of years. Otherwise, patent rights will be lost. In addition, there are differences in the amount of control bestowed by patent rights. Some countries, for instance, may require patented inventions to be licensed to other businesses at reasonable royalty rates, a practice called compulsory licensing. In this regard, TRIPs put limits on the use of compulsory licensing, but it did not end the practice. There also are important differences regarding what it takes to prove infringement of process patents. Although the United States recently made it easier for process patent holders to win infringement actions, the burden is still somewhat more difficult in various other countries. One final distinction worth noting here has to do with information regarding the best mode of an invention, which, as we have seen, must be disclosed in the United States but does not have to be revealed in patent applications in many other nations.

Clearly, an inventor who ventures into the international marketplace faces a complex and often divergent web of patent policies. The resultant complexity and frustrations can be averted only through greater international harmonization. The success of the Uruguay Round has given the international community a taste of how progress can be made in this area. It is hoped that the spirit of cooperation engendered though GATT will carry over to negotiations within other multilateral channels, most notably within WIPO.

Procedural Patent Policy Issues

An important variable in any business decision is the degree of transaction costs the decision will entail. For a business contemplating an international patent program, such costs could be overwhelming. This is due to the largely uncoordinated set of diverse national patent procedures, which, with few exceptions, must be followed piecemeal on a country-by-country basis. Imagine the difficulty of receiving patent protection in just a few countries, such as Japan, Germany, Australia, Argentina, and Mexico. An inventor first has to become advised on the substantive patent laws of each nation. This likely will require advice from specialist attorneys in each country. Applications then have to be filed and defended in each jurisdiction, according to each one's respective laws and policies. Translations obviously will be necessary, not only raising financial costs but also jeopardizing the inventor's understanding of the patent applications and resultant patent rights. Then there are costs to business strategy as well. For instance, if test marketing must be curtailed until applications are filed in all desired countries to preserve patent rights, the delay may carry substantial business risk. Fortunately, several international treaties have been negotiated to alleviate some of these procedural problems. The most important are the Paris Convention, the European Patent Convention, and the Patent Cooperation Treaty.

The Paris Convention   The Paris Convention is the oldest and most comprehensive multilateral accord dealing with intellectual property. Almost all the industrialized countries and many developing nations are signatories. One of the provisions of the Paris Convention is crucially important to inventors attempting to overcome the procedural impediments to international patent coverage. Under that provision, the filing date of an application filed in a signatory country will be considered the effective filing date of an application filed in another signatory country if the latter application is filed within one year of the first.

Thus, if a patent application is filed for **AES** in the United States on February 8, 1998, then an application filed in Korea before February 8, 1999, will be treated as if it were filed in Korea on February 8, 1998. This can be extremely important, for instance, when one considers that Korea has no grace period for certain sales or publications.[42] Due to the Paris Convention, we can file a U.S. patent application for the **Audio Enhancement System** and then perform test marketing, release information, and engage in sales. As long as we file in Korea within one year, these actions will be treated as having happened after the effective filing date in Korea. As depicted in Exhibit 3.5, this is a tremendous benefit. Now, we can file in the United States and over the next year decide if we want to seek patent protection in other signatory countries. This allows time to test the product, consider business strategies, and consult with legal experts before investing the energy and resources in making patent applications abroad.

If the inventor files a provisional application in the United States, then the filing date of the provisional application serves as the effective filing date under the Paris Convention, as long as the full U.S. application and the foreign patent applications are filed within one year of that date. In this way, an inventor may receive the benefits of the earlier provisional application date in Paris Convention countries even though claims have not been filed with the original application. Note, though, that when the provisional application route is used, the foreign filings must be made within one year of filing the provisional application. Thus, provisional applications are not a means to gain an additional year over and above the standard Paris Convention year to test products in international markets.

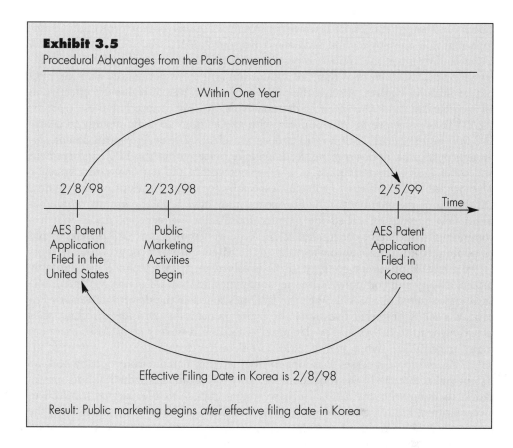

Exhibit 3.5
Procedural Advantages from the Paris Convention

Within One Year

2/8/98   2/23/98   2/5/99
                                                                    Time

AES Patent   Public   AES Patent
Application   Marketing   Application
Filed in the   Activities   Filed in
United States   Begin   Korea

Effective Filing Date in Korea is 2/8/98

Result: Public marketing begins *after* effective filing date in Korea

When relying on the Paris Convention, one must keep foreign patent laws in mind. For instance, if we release a publication about our invention before the U.S. application is filed, relying on the grace period of Section 102(b), then our application in Korea will not be timely, even if it is filed within one year under the Paris Convention. This is because the patent laws of Korea do not permit any publication, even by the inventor, prior to the relevant filing date—in this case, the date the U.S. application is filed. One must be wary of U.S. laws as well. For example, the one-year grace period of Section 102(b) is not affected by the Paris Convention. Therefore, once a publication has been released, a patent application must be filed in the United States within one year (the grace period) of that publication to preserve U.S. patent rights. Filing in a signatory country within the one-year grace period would not give the inventor an additional year under the Paris Convention to file in the United States.

The European Patent Convention   Nineteen nations in Europe have made great strides in establishing the equivalent of a European patent.[43] Under the European Patent Convention (EPC), the participating nations have agreed to a number of substantive patent principles concerning subject matter, novelty, utility, priority, patent length, and interpretation of claims. An inventor seeking patent protection in Europe may file one application with the European Patent Office (EPO), which will search and examine the application under the terms of the convention. One advantage for the U.S. inventor is that the application and correspondences with the EPO can be made in English. Also, if the patent is granted, patent rights are effective in all member countries the inventor designates in the application. For these reasons, the EPC has proven to be very popular, with applications growing steadily to nearly 100,000 in 1997. However, the EPC does not create a truly European patent. Although post-grant opposition proceedings take place within the EPO, enforcement and other judicial actions must be carried out within the national court systems. This has led to a number of problems, especially regarding issues of patent validity. On this score, the members of the European Union have been attempting to hammer out a new agreement, called the Community Patent Convention, under which a community-wide patent court, akin to the Federal Circuit Court of Appeals, would be established to add greater uniformity to the patent enforcement process.

As a matter of patent strategy, firms involved in certain technologies, notably biotechnology and computer software, sometimes approach Europe with a conservative, two-tiered approach. Since the EPC ties together the diverse nations of Europe, the many unsettled questions about the patentability of radical technologies inevitably lead to delays and/or denials of a European-wide patent. Also, there are many uncertainties when a national court determines that the EPC patent is invalid. Therefore, businesses may opt to double-bank patent protection by seeking patent rights directly in the most commercially important individual nations in addition to filing with the EPO. Thus, we might choose to file patents for **AES** in Great Britain, France, and Germany as well as through the EPO. In this way, if the process is held up on the European scale, we may have better success and obtain protection in some or all of the individual countries.

The Patent Cooperation Treaty   The Patent Cooperation Treaty (PCT), which by 1998 had grown to 96 member countries, further facilitates the process of obtaining international patent rights. Under the PCT, an inventor may file an international application (IA), designating all the member countries in which patent protection is sought.[44] The IA uses a standardized format that can be filed in numerous different languages, including English. Under PCT rules, an IA will be published 18 months after the filing date.

An inventor can follow one of two approaches under the PCT. One option is to request that an international search be conducted by an approved searching authority, such as the PTO.[45] The search report contains no comments about the patentability of the invention but lists citations to relevant prior art references. This gives the inventor an opportunity to evaluate the chances that patent rights will be available in the designated national offices. A favorable report may be helpful in the national proceedings. If the report is unfavorable, the inventor may be able to amend the claims or withdraw the application before it is published. Twenty months after the "priority filing date," the search report is sent to the selected countries for independent national examinations and actions.

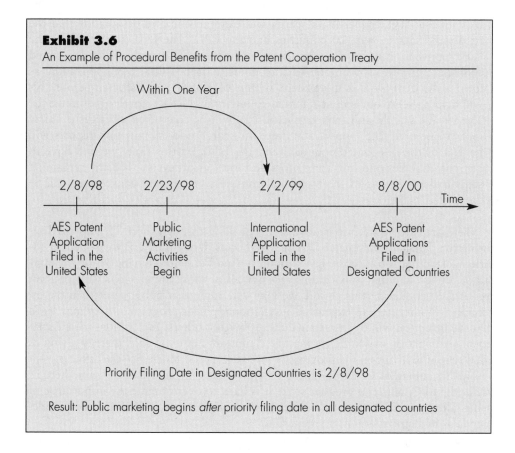

Exhibit 3.6

An Example of Procedural Benefits from the Patent Cooperation Treaty

Within One Year

2/8/98	2/23/98	2/2/99	8/8/00

Time →

AES Patent Application Filed in the United States	Public Marketing Activities Begin	International Application Filed in the United States	AES Patent Applications Filed in Designated Countries

Priority Filing Date in Designated Countries is 2/8/98

Result: Public marketing begins *after* priority filing date in all designated countries

Alternatively, the inventor can request that a preliminary search and examination be conducted at the international level. Under this option, a selected International Preliminary Examining Authority, which again includes the PTO, provides an opinion, based on the international search report, about the validity of the claims.[46] The examination report is very persuasive with the member nations and gives the inventor an even stronger basis for dealing with the designated national offices. If this route is selected, the search and examination reports are sent to the selected nations for their separate actions 30 months after the priority filing date.

The PCT provides us with tremendous flexibility in our attempt to gain international patent protection for **AES**. The following example, illustrated in Exhibit 3.6, is one of several possible options: We can initiate the international process by filing a U.S. patent application with the PTO. The date of that application will serve as our "priority filing date" under the Paris Convention. Since we have an international vision, we will file the application before making public sales or publications of the invention. Within 12 months, we will file an

IA with the PTO, requesting a search and examination and designating that the reports be sent to, say, 20 countries and the EPO. The PCT works within the Paris Convention in such a way that the filing dates for each of the designated countries and regions will refer back to the date of the initial U.S. application, as long as the IA is filed, as it was here, within 12 months. As discussed before, this will help preserve our patent rights in countries with strict novelty requirements. The IA, the search, and the examination all will be conducted in English. Thirty months after the U.S. application date, the search and examination reports will be sent to the designated countries and the EPO. At this time, we will have to pay national fees and hire translators and local attorneys so that any remaining steps under the laws of the individual countries or regional conventions can be completed.

There are three tremendous advantages of filing through the PCT: improved information, language, and deferral of fees and costs. Using the PCT, we gained an additional 18 months to test the invention in the market before having to file the myriad of foreign national applications and pay all of those applications' concomitant fees and costs. During this period, we may determine that public interest in the invention will not merit an expensive international patent program. Or we may learn that the invention will fly in certain cultures but not others. In addition, the international examination may indicate that the claims are not allowable, thereby giving us good reason to abandon the program before sinking too much into the effort.

The advantage of undertaking the patent process in English is the same here as under the EPC, but on a broader scale. It is hard to overestimate the importance of being allowed to communicate in one's native tongue, especially in an area that demands as much precision as a patent.

Finally, the deferral of the separate national stages of the patent program can substantially alleviate financial burdens. These normally outweigh the additional fees required to undergo the PCT examination process, especially if more than three or four countries are targeted for patent protection. If the IA had been filed with the U.S. PTO in 1998, fees for the international search and examination would have run around $2,150, plus $105 per designated country (up to a maximum of $1,050). Although $3,200 may seem like a lot of money, especially to the small inventor, the importance of deferring the substantially higher national fees and costs must be considered. This is particularly true when one considers the cost of hiring translators and local patent attorneys. The popularity of the PCT proves the point. In 1979, some 2,625 applications were filed under the PCT. By 1998, that number had grown to 67,002.[47]

As depicted in Exhibit 3.7, there are innumerable possible options for filing through the PCT. Rather than file a U.S. patent application first, we could have filed the IA first and designated the United States along with the other countries for protection. If this were done, then the date of filing the IA would constitute the "priority filing date." Thus, the reports would be transmitted to designated countries 20 or 30 months after that filing date, depending on whether search only or examination is selected. Notice also that we selected the EPO to receive the reports.

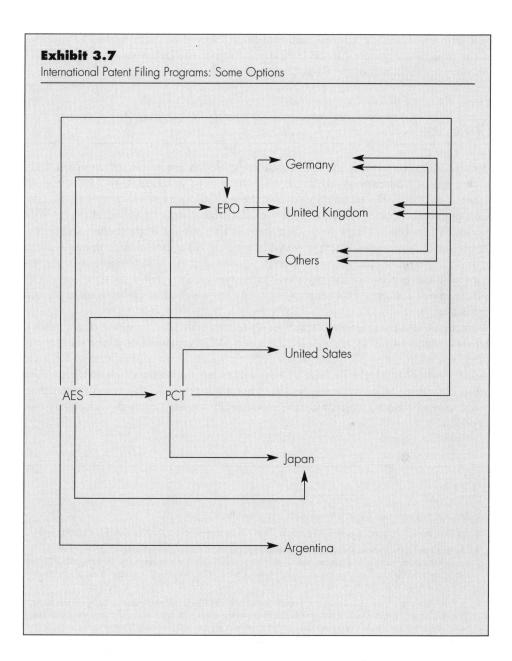

Exhibit 3.7

International Patent Filing Programs: Some Options

Under this option, we are requesting review under the EPC to cover countries in the European Community. Of course, we also could have designated individual European nations as well as the EPO in order to provide greater security in that region. Clearly, the most appropriate strategy to use via the PCT deserves careful attention. Also, one must always remember that not every country is a party to the

PCT. For nonmember countries, national filings should be made within 12 months of the priority filing date (of the U.S. application or the IA), assuming, as is likely, that they are members of the Paris Convention.

CONCLUSION

Decisions about how best to protect new technologies are extremely complex. Balancing the considerations involved with the patent decision alone are difficult enough. Can the PTO be convinced that the technology is novel, nonobvious, and a proper subject for protection? Will the allowable claims be broad enough? Will too much information have to be disclosed? Is the amount of protection worth the patent fees and the costs of experts and attorneys? Is the inventor/company willing to fight in court, if necessary, to preserve patent rights? Is it possible to come to grips with the vagaries of international patent protection? You now have some feel for the major concerns and benefits that must be weighed in an analysis of patent protection.

Evaluation of patent rights, however, represents only the beginning of a comprehensive business strategy for intellectual assets. Maybe patents do make sense for a particular technology. However, trade secret protection or copyright may be even better. Possibly it would be best to rely somewhat on patents but reinforce that protection using other available means. This book proceeds to review these other major considerations, which must be strategically assessed by high-technology enterprises.

NOTES

1. *See, e.g.*, D. Pressman, Patent It Yourself, 6th ed. (Nolo Press 1997).

2. "A New Act . . . A New Challenge," speech by Harry F. Manbeck Jr. in PTC Newsletter (Fall 1991) at 16.

3. Current information about the number of patent applications that have been filed and the number of patents that have been issued may be found on the PTO Web site at www.uspto.gov. In 1998, the PTO issued nearly 155,000 patents, an increase of 26% over the 1997 figure. *See* J. Aquino, "Patently Permissive," A.B.A. J. (May 1999) at 30.

4. In 1997, average pendency increased 1.4 months over the 1996 level, allegedly due to budget constraints. The efficiency of the PTO often is appraised in terms of the average pendency for applications, from filing to final action. The PTO believes the data about pendency do not fully reflect efficiency gains at the agency because the measure includes, among other things, delays caused by the applicant. The PTO thus has begun to use a measure it calls "cycle time," which focuses more precisely on the time used by the PTO to process patents. The average cycle time in 1997 was 16 months.

5. Many patent fees actually were reduced slightly in 1999 from 1998 levels.

6. A. Riddles and B. Pomerance, "Software Patentee Must Conduct Own Search," Nat'l L. J. (January 26, 1998) at C19.

7. American Inventors Protection Act of 1999, Title IV, "The Publication of Foreign Filed Applications Act," (1999).

8. The patent office has a Scientific and Technical Information Center and a Foreign Patents Branch that conduct these searches upon request by examiners. Also, in 1998, the patent office signed a contract with Derwent Information Ltd. that allows each individual examiner to have unlimited access to Derwent's World Patents Index, which is considered the world's most comprehensive database of global patent data. *See* M. Goldman, "High-Tech Customers Turn to Derwent Patent Index," Wash. Bus. J. (March 19–25, 1999) at 38.

9. The PTO may give the applicant from one to six months to respond. 35 U.S.C. § 133.

10. The term "patent pending" also can be used after a provisional application is filed.

11. Certain appeals may go to the D.C. Circuit Court of Appeals. Appeals from this court will then go to the Federal Circuit.

12. In December 1999, the PTO decided to reexamine a controversial patent that claimed a "windowing" system to correct Y2K problems in older computer systems. The system provided a shortcut to translate the typical two-digit years, so that the computer would properly understand them as being in the 1900s or the 2000s. For instance, the programmer might select a window of 30 years, causing all two-digit numbers between 00 and 29 to be preceded with a 20, while all higher numbers would receive a 19. The PTO granted a patent on the system in September 1998. This was followed by a storm of protest arguing that the system was not novel. See R. Chandrasekaran, "Agency to Review Y2K Patent; Facing Large Fees, Firms Say Fix Had Been Known," Wash. Post (December 23, 1999) at E2.

13. The American Inventors Protection Act of 1999, Title V, "The Optional Inter Partes Reexamination Procedure Act" (1999).

14. *See* S. Knowles, C. Doster, and C. Reichman, "Opposition Proceedings Are Alternative to Court," Nat'l L. J. (October 19, 1998) at C45.

15. Other countries have similar court proceedings called revocation or invalidation proceedings.

16. *In* re Wands, 858 F.2d 731, 737 (Fed. Cir. 1988).

17. Northern Telecom, Inc. v. Datapoint Corp., 908 F.2d 931, 941 (Fed. Cir. 1990).

18. *Id.*, quoting *In re* Sherwood, 613 F.2d 809, 817 (CCPA, 1980).

19. 909 F. 2d 731 (Fed. Cir. 1990).

20. National Recovery Technologies, Inc. v. Magnetic Separation Systems, Inc., 1999 U.S. App. LEXIS 1671 (Fed. Cir. 1999).

21. *See* S. Johnston, and L. Ben-Ami, "Unpredictablity Factor Narrows Biotech Patents," Nat'l L. J. (June 16, 1997) at C2.

22. *See, e.g., In re* Goodman, 11 F.3d 1046 (Fed. Cir. 1993).

23. 107 F.3d 1543 (Fed. Cir. 1997).

24. *Id.* at 1549.

25. There is a minor exception to this conclusion, based on what is called the reverse doctrine of equivalents. For an example of this doctrine, see Mead Digital Systems, Inc. v. A. B. Dick Co., 221 U.S.P.Q. 1035 (6th Cir. 1983).

26. Graver Tank & Mfg. Co., v. Linde Air Products Co., 339 U.S. 605, 607 (1950).

27. *Id.* at 608.

28. 520 U.S. 17 (1997).

29. *See* S. Helfgott, "Japanese Supreme Court Accepts Doctrine of Equivalents," American Bar Association, Section of Intellectual Property Law Newsletter (Spring 1998) at 26.

30. This topic sometimes is known as "prosecution history estoppel."

31. Chiuminatta Concrete Concepts v. Cardinal Industries, Inc., 145 F.3d 1303, 1310 (Fed. Cir. 1998).

32. Polaroid Corp. v. Eastman Kodak Co., 16 U.S.P.Q. 2d (BNA) 1481 (D. Mass. 1990).

33. Oil & Gas J. 64 (March 17, 1986).

34. T. Parker-Pope, "Stopping Diaper Leaks Can Be Nasty Business, P&G Shows Its Rivals," Wall St. J. (April 5, 1999) at A1.

35. The question here is whether there are acceptable noninfringing substitutes for the patented technology. If the infringer had not used the patented technology, some of its customers may have purchased these substitutes rather than the patentee's products.

36. Section 285 provides that the court in exceptional cases may award reasonable attorneys' fees to the prevailing party. For an excellent example of how courts address the issue of damages, see Micro Motion, Inc. v. Exac Corp., 761 F Supp. 1420 (N.D.CA, 1991).

37. L. Scism, "Insurance Helps Little Guy Sue Patent Infringer," Wall St. J. (November 25, 1996) at B1.

38. E. Radlo, "The Time to Harmonize Is Now," IEEE Grid (April 1992) at 6.

39. The patent laws of France and Korea provide two examples.

40. See M. Powers and I. Fu, "International Intellectual Property Developments in 1991: A Year of Transformation and Evolution," J. of Proprietary Rights (February 1992) at 7.

41. S. Helfgott, "JPO Proposals for Improving Its Patent System," IPL Newsletter, Vol. 16, No. 4 (Summer 1998) at 39.

42. Korean Patent Law No. 3891, Art. 6(1)(i) (invention anticipated if publicly known or worked in Korea) and Art. 6(1)(ii) (invention anticipated if described in a printed publication distributed in Korea or in a foreign country), reported in Dratler, Intellectual Property Law: Commercial, Creative, and Industrial Property (Law Journal Seminars-Press, 1991 & Supp. 1999) at §2.07[2].

43. The members of the European Patent Convention are Austria, Belgium, Cyprus, Denmark, Finland, France, Germany, Greece, Ireland, Italy, Lichtenstein, Luxembourg, Monaco, the Netherlands, Portugal, Spain, Sweden, Switzerland, and the United Kingdom. In 1999, the members of the European Patent Convention invited eight central and eastern European countries to join the treaty in 2002. These nations are Bulgaria, the Czech Republic, Estonia, Hungary, Poland, Romania, Slovakia, and Slovenia.

44. The IA can be filed in the inventor's national patent office, with WIPO or with the EPO. The office where the IA is filed is called the PCT receiving office.

45. In 1995, the International Searching Authorities were the national patent offices of Australia, Austria, China, Japan, Russia, Spain, Sweden, and the United States along with the EPO.

46. In 1995, the International Preliminary Examining Authorities were the same as the International Searching Authorities, except for Spain.

47. "Patent Applications Rose 23 Percent Worldwide in 98," Reuters (February 12, 1999).

Protection of Secret Information: Trade Secrets and Unsolicited Ideas

INTRODUCTION

As a developer of the **Audio Enhancement System (AES)**, you may now be a little disenchanted with the patent system as a means to protect your valuable creative ideas embedded in the invention. Clearly, the rewards from a patent are significant if its coverage is sufficiently broad. But there are substantial drawbacks as well. The costs of retaining a patent attorney to prepare the patent application and negotiate with the PTO may be hard for a new company to bear. These expenditures are particularly hard to absorb if the PTO eventually decides not to issue the patent. Even if it does, there are the rapidly increasing patent issue and maintenance fees to consider, as well as the enormous costs of seeking protection outside the United States. Further, one must factor in the potentially expensive and exhausting tasks of enforcing the patent.

Then there is the question of whether **AES**, which embodies computer technologies, is patentable subject matter. Also, one must evaluate whether the invention meets the high standards for patent protection. If it is not patentable, how can the invention be protected? What if the PTO determines that **AES** is patentable, but a federal court later disagrees? Then the important attributes of the invention will be thoroughly explained for all to use freely. Do the potential benefits from patent protection for **AES** justify that risk?

Even if we decide to pursue patent protection, what do we do before the invention is sufficiently finalized to file for a patent? Renegade employees entrusted with the project may decide to use the information on their own, possibly hoping to file first in various international patent offices, or simply to market their own versions of the invention. How can we be sure that those entrusted with our valuable information use it properly and maintain its confidentiality?

There are other issues as well. What if we have to approach another company to manufacture and market the system? If we are not careful, that company may attentively learn the essential concepts behind **AES** and thereafter not deal with us. How do we ensure that the company pays us for our valuable ideas? Also, we must consider how rapidly the technologies embedded in **AES** are changing and what the reasonable marketing life of the product may be. For inventions utilizing computer technologies, it may take three years to obtain patent rights in the United States. In foreign jurisdictions, such as Japan, the wait may be even longer. If **AES** will be obsolete before patent rights can be obtained, then there is little point in pursuing that avenue of protection. So, what strategy should we use during the effective life of the product? In the alternative, albeit unlikely for AES, we may desire protection for a longer period of time than provided by a patent on the assumption that the invention could be lucrative for decades. Is there a reasonable way to accomplish that goal?

As noted in Chapter 1, the federal intellectual property system provides three other principal modes of protection. In historical terms, trademarks and copyrights clearly are the most important, while the development of federal trade secret rights are relatively new and limited. The purpose of trademarks is to help consumers identify the sources of products. Although the federal trademark system thereby may protect various external design characteristics of **AES**, it will not be useful for controlling the fundamental concepts behind the invention. Federal copyright protection extends to expressions, but not ideas and processes. Here, again, protection for **AES** likely will be insufficient. The only possible exception is for the system's computer programs. As we shall see in Chapter 6, there currently is substantial controversy over the extent of copyright protection for computer programs. Some courts take a very expansive approach, allowing copyright to protect almost all aspects of computer programs. Other courts, however, believe that copyright should play a more limited role in protecting programs. Depending on the importance of the program to the overall utility of **AES**, copyright protection could be a viable means of protection. At a minimum, it could provide some partial degree of support. However, in all likelihood, we will need something more than copyright to preserve the bulk of our valuable insights from use by competitors.

With all of the foregoing considerations in mind, it is no wonder that businesses turn to trade secret laws to protect some or all of their valuable creative ideas at various stages of development. These laws predominantly derive from governmental policies at the individual state level, although they now have been supplemented by the federal Economic Espionage Act. The popular press certainly has publicized the importance of trade secrets, especially to high-technology enterprises, and the efforts taken by competitors to acquire them. The dispute between Apple Computer and its founder, Steve Jobs, made headlines when Jobs formed a new company called NeXT after leaving Apple. In that situation, which was finally settled, Apple alleged that

Steve Jobs had been improperly using Apple's resources and proprietary secrets to form the new company and its products.[1] More recently, attention focused on IBM's attempts to prevent a former employee from working for Seagate Technology on the grounds that the employee would divulge IBM's trade secrets.[2] Similar accusations arose when AT&T sued Fujitsu to prevent a recently departed software engineer from taking a position at Fujitsu, allegedly for an enormous signing bonus.[3] In 1994, American Airlines sued Northwest Airlines, alleging that it hired 17 managers and technical experts from American so that it could get its hands on American's proprietary computerized fare-setting systems.[4] Likewise Wal-Mart sued Amazon.com in 1998, claiming that Amazon and two related organizations attempted to jump-start development of their customer service software by hiring several employees from Wal-Mart and one of its consulting companies.[5] Silicon Valley also was shocked by two criminal trade secret cases in the 1990s. The more notable involved allegations that an employee of Borland International Inc. stole valuable secrets when he left the company to join Symantec Corp.[6] In the other criminal proceeding, a former employee of Intel Corp., who later joined ULSI Technology Inc., was accused of stealing technical information and materials from Intel regarding Intel's 80387 math coprocessor.[7] Other controversies, such as those between Reebok and Spalding over pump technology baseball gloves and between Invitron and Monsanto over cell culture technology secrets similarly have been newsworthy.[8]

Indeed, attention to trade secrets has risen to the level of international intrigue. In 1982, the FBI arrested employees of both Hitachi and Mitsubishi for allegedly paying hundreds of thousands of dollars for stolen data regarding the IBM 3081 computer.[9] Likewise, in the mid-1990s, a dispute between Cie des Machines Bull and Texas Instruments raised allegations worthy of the best spy novels, including claims that the French government planted moles at Texas Instruments and IBM to steal information about computer chips and other technologies.[10] According to U.S. intelligence sources, foreign governments are taking extreme measures to acquire the secret information that gives U.S. firms their strategic and technological edge. The measures have included intercepting overseas electronic and satellite communications, using electronic bugs, interviewing foreign nationals working for U.S. firms, and having spies serve as maids in foreign hotels to snoop hotel rooms occupied by executives of U.S. companies.[11]

The value of trade secrets has increased markedly over the last ten years, and so have the losses attributed to trade secret theft. Empirical studies indicate that trade secret losses doubled between 1995 and 1996 and had increased by over 300% between 1992 and 1996.[12] By one estimate, U.S. industry was losing $63 billion annually to trade secret misappropriation in the mid-1990s.[13] Indeed, in 1997, a corporate security consultant concluded that U.S. companies lost as much as $250 billion annually to thefts of trade secrets.[14] Also, in a 1996 survey of Fortune 1000 companies, 41% of respondents stated that losses totaled more than $500,000 per incident.[15] Many of these claimed that the losses exceeded $1 million.

High-technology companies, almost without exception, have found trade secret protection to be an important component of their strategic intellectual property protection plans. The purpose of this chapter is to familiarize you with the basic concepts of trade secret protection and to propose methods that will help preserve trade secret rights. In addition, this chapter alerts you to common mistakes inexperienced inventors make when attempting to get established companies to "buy" their ideas. You may be surprised just how careful one must be before disclosing potentially lucrative commercial concepts to a major company.

RATIONALES FOR TRADE SECRET LAWS

(AES) Trade secret policies are concerned primarily with enforcing minimum standards of commercial ethics in the competitive marketplace. These policies developed first through the common law; that is, they were created by judges to address business situations that seemed egregiously unfair and unethical. For example, in developing **AES**, you may have had to entrust certain employees with the novel ideas that will set the invention apart from other types of audio equipment. During the time that these employees worked for you, they may have learned which techniques help make **AES** succeed and which ones are failures. How would you feel if, after making all the necessary investments to perfect **AES**, those employees set up their own company and in order to compete with you, immediately used all they learned at your expense? Clearly, you would feel outraged and violated, as if someone had broken into your house and stolen your valuables. Likely, you would go to court, hope to convince the judge of the inequities, and request a remedy. However, unlike with common theft of objects, misappropriated information cannot simply be returned to the rightful owner. Thus, your only hope is that the judge orders the employees both not to use the information and not to tell others who might use it.

The employees may see the situation in an altogether different light. First, they may argue that they did not take anything that really belonged exclusively to you. They may show that the information used was known by others in the field. Sure, they may have learned the information from your business, but that does not mean you have the right to control it. Many employees learn common technical skills on the job. Just because the employer invested in training the employees does not mean the employees cannot use the acquired skills in other jobs. Also, if others know of the information, who is to say that the employees did not learn it from those other sources? On top of this, employees may question how the information could be competitively valuable if competitors already know it. The bottom line of this defense is that if the information was not secret within your business organization and relationships, then the employees have done nothing wrong by using it.

Another argument the employees might raise is that they did not know they were using information you considered to be your secret and expected to be kept in confidence. Employees are exposed to all kinds of information on the job. It would be unreasonable for you to expect them to know just which information you considered to be proprietary and which you did not. Rather, you had some obligation to inform them. Indeed, how could you expect them to treat information as secret if you did not take particular steps to keep the secrets your-self? If you allow documents containing the information to lie on a receptionist's desk in a public waiting room, for instance, it would be hard for you to claim that you expected the information to be maintained in secrecy.

Trade secret policies attempt to balance the claims of the employers with those who wish to use information. The employers' position is that they will not be adequately compensated for their creative investments if those persons who must be entrusted with it cannot be prevented from using it for their personal benefit. Likewise, if com-petitors can freely use information acquired through inappropriate forms of espi-onage, then employers will have to concentrate inordinately on fortifying the premises rather than on making valuable contributions to society. The counterposition is that the information is not secret, is not treated sufficiently as a secret, or cannot provide a competitive advantage. To balance these concerns, trade secret policies generally pro-tect an employer's information from misappropriation by employees or others if the information is competitively valuable, is secret, and has been the subject of reasonable security measures. Protection is achieved, when appropriate, through court-ordered in-junctions against use or disclosure and through monetary damage awards.

Those who oppose trade secret protection, at least when it is provided by state government policies, also might claim such laws interfere with federal patent policies. After all, patent laws provide a carefully circumscribed right of protection against the backdrop of free competition in ideas and information. If the information is not the subject of a patent, should it not be free for all to use? The answer to this is a quali-fied yes. The fundamental notion of free competition does not necessarily condone unethical competition. It is one thing to acquire a product legitimately and tear it apart to figure out how it works. Such a practice, called reverse engineering, fits within the moral constructs of free competition and must be allowed under state law to conform with patent policies. However, stealing the information or using it in vio-lation of a fiduciary responsibility is a whole different ball game, appropriately sub-ject to state law. This is why state trade secret laws prohibit misappropriation but ex-plicitly permit acquisition of the information through reverse engineering. One also may question whether state trade secret laws, which protect the secrecy of informa-tion, conflict with the disclosure principles of patent policies. The following land-mark Supreme Court case thoughtfully considers the purposes of trade secret policies and addresses why such policies do not conflict with federal patent laws.

KEWANEE OIL COMPANY V. BICRON CORPORATION
United States Supreme Court, 1974

FACTS: In 1949, Harshaw Chemical, a division of Kewanee, commenced re-search into the growth of synthetic crystals, which are useful in the detection of ionizing radiation. At that time, the company was not able to produce a

continued . . .

continued . . .

crystal exceeding 2 inches in diameter. By 1966, as a result of expenditures in excess of $1 million, Harshaw was able to grow a 17-inch crystal, something no one else had done. Harshaw developed many processes, procedures, and manufacturing techniques to accomplish this feat. Many of those techniques it considered to be trade secrets.

The individual defendants were employees of Harshaw. Each of them had signed nondisclosure agreements requiring them not to disclose or use confidential information or trade secrets obtained as employees. These individuals became associated with Bicron, which was formed in 1969 to compete with Harshaw in the production of the crystals. By April 1970, Bicron had grown a 17-inch crystal.

Kewanee sued Bicron and the individuals for trade secret misappropriation under Ohio's state trade secret laws. The district court granted an injunction until such time as the trade secrets had been released to the public or had been obtained by the defendants from sources having the legal rights to convey the information.

The Court of Appeals reversed. Although it found that trade secrets had been misappropriated, it concluded that Ohio's state trade secret laws conflicted with the federal patent laws. The Court of Appeals reasoned that the state of Ohio could not grant monopoly protection to processes that were appropriate subjects for patent protection but that had been in public use for over one year, thereby making them ineligible for patent protection under Section 102(b). Kewanee appealed to the Supreme Court.

DECISION AND REASONING: The protection accorded a trade secret holder is against the disclosure or unauthorized use of a trade secret by those to whom the secret has been confided under the express or implied restriction of nondisclosure or nonuse. The law also protects the holder of a trade secret against disclosure or use when the knowledge is gained, not by the owner's volition, but by some improper means, which may include theft, wiretapping, or aerial reconnaissance. A trade secret, however, does not offer protection against discovery by fair and honest means, such as by independent invention, accidental disclosure, or by reverse engineering, that is, by starting with the known product and working backward to divine the process that aided in its development or manufacture.

Novelty, in the patent law sense, is not required for a trade secret. However, some novelty will be required if merely because that which does not possess novelty is usually known; secrecy in the context of trade secrets thus implies at least minimal novelty.

The question of whether the trade secret law of Ohio is void under the Supremacy Clause involves consideration of whether that law stands as an obstacle to the accomplishment and execution of the full purposes and objectives of Congress. To determine whether the Ohio law clashes with the federal law, it is helpful to examine the objectives of both the patent and trade secret laws.

The patent laws promote progress in science and useful arts by offering a right of exclusion for a limited period as an incentive to inventors to risk often enormous costs in terms of time, research, and development. In return for the right of exclusion—the reward for invention—the patent laws impose a requirement of full disclosure.

The maintenance of standards of commercial ethics and the encouragement of invention are the broadly stated policies behind trade secret law. Trade secret protection is important to the subsidization of research and development and to increased economic efficiency within large companies through the dispersion of responsibilities for creative developments.

Trade secret laws can protect items, such as customer lists and advertising campaigns, which are not proper subjects for patent protection under Section 101. For these items not amenable to patents, there is no reason to apply for patent protection. Abolition of trade secret protection, therefore, would not result in increased disclosure of these nonpatentable discoveries. On the other hand, keeping such items secret encourages businesses to initiate new and individualized plans of operation, and constructive competition results. This, in turn, leads to a greater variety of business methods than would otherwise be the case if privately developed marketing and other data were passed illicitly among firms involved in the same enterprise.

The question remains whether those items that are proper subjects for consideration for a patent may also have available the alternative protection accorded by trade secret law. Certainly the patent policy of encouraging invention is not disturbed by the existence of another form of incentive to invention. Similarly, the policy that matter once in the public domain must remain in the public domain is not incompatible with the existence of trade secret protection. By definition, a trade secret has not been placed in the public domain.

The more difficult objective of patent law to reconcile with trade secret law is that of disclosure. For this analysis, it is instructive to distinguish between three categories of trade secrets: (1) the trade secret for which the owner knows a valid patent cannot be obtained, (2) the trade secret for which patentability is dubious, and (3) the trade secret for which the owner believes a valid patent could be obtained.

As to the trade secret known not to meet the standards of patentability, very little in the way of disclosure would be accomplished by abolishing trade secret protection. The reasoning is analogous to that for trade secrets of nonpatentable subject matter. In this scenario, trade secret protection does not conflict with disclosure policies and has a decidedly beneficial effect on society. Without trade secret protection, innovative individuals would engage in increased self-help to maintain secrecy. Knowledge would be widely

continued . . .

continued . . .

dispersed among the employees of those companies still active in research. Security precautions necessarily would be increased, and officer salaries would have to be made sufficient to ensure their loyalty. Smaller companies would be placed at a distinct economic disadvantage, for the costs of self-help could be great, and the cost to the public to use the invention would increase. Without the ultimate assurance of legal protection against breaches of confidence, innovative entrepreneurs with only limited resources would tend to confine their research efforts to themselves and those few whom they felt they could trust. As a result, organized scientific and technological research could become fragmented and society would suffer.

Another problem that would arise if trade secret protection were precluded is in the area of licensing others to exploit secret processes. The holder of a trade secret would not likely share the secret with a manufacturer who could not be placed under a binding legal obligation to protect the secret. The result would be to hoard rather than disseminate knowledge. Instead of licensing others to use the invention and making the most efficient use of existing manufacturing and marketing structures within the industry, the trade secret holder would either limit the utilization of the invention or engage in the time-consuming and wasteful enterprise of constructing duplicative manufacturing and marketing mechanisms to exploit the invention. The detrimental misallocation of resources and economic waste that would thus take place if trade secret protection were abolished with respect to employees or licensees cannot be justified by reference to any policy that the federal patent law seeks to advance.

The next category consists of trade secrets for which there is a legitimate doubt regarding patentability. In most cases of genuine doubt, the potential rewards of patent protection are so far superior to those of trade secrets that the holders of such inventions will seek patent protection rather than rely on trade secret laws. Some may not wish to undergo the costs and risks of patent protection, even if trade secret protection were not available. Considering them, abolishing trade secret protection would only harm society, as discussed previously. It is true that if trade secret protection were not available, some inventors who are unsure about the patentability of their inventions would more likely give patent protection a try. Some of these would not receive a patent, and the discoveries would remain a secret anyway. Others, however, would receive a patent, and disclosure would take place. Overall, though, we cannot say that this speculative gain outweighs the potential deleterious effect on society that would result from the elimination of trade secret protection.

The final category of patentable subject matter to deal with is the clearly patentable invention. It is here that the federal interest in disclosure is at its peak. If a state law were to dissuade these inventors from relying on the patent system, then the law would have to fall. However, in the case of trade secret law, there is no reasonable risk of deterrence from patent application by those who can expect to be granted patents.

Trade secret law provides far weaker protection in many respects than does patent law. Whereas trade secret law does not forbid the discovery of the trade secret by fair and honest means, for instance by independent creation or reverse engineering, patent law does. The trade secret holder also takes a substantial risk that the secret will be passed on to competitors by theft or breach of confidence in a manner not easily susceptible to proof. Where patent law acts as a barrier, trade secret law functions relatively as a sieve. The possibility that inventors who believe their invention meets the standards of patentability will sit back, rely on trade secret law, and after one year of use forfeit any right to patent protection is remote indeed.

Nor does society face much risk that scientific or technological progress will be impeded from the rare inventor with a patentable invention who chooses trade secret protection over patent protection. The history of the inventive process indicates that even if inventors keep an invention entirely to themselves, there is a high probability that the invention will be independently developed by others. And if the invention, though protected as a trade secret, is put into public use, then the competition is alerted of the inventor's solution to the problem and may be encouraged to make extra efforts to independently find that solution thus known to be possible. We therefore conclude that the extension of trade secret protection to clearly patentable inventions does not conflict with the patent policy of disclosure.

Trade secret law and patent law have coexisted in this country for over 100 years. Each has its particular role to play, and the operation of one does not take away from the need for the other. Trade secret law encourages the development and exploitation of those items of lesser or different invention than might be accorded patent protection, but which still have an important part to play in the technological and scientific advancement of the nation. Trade secret law promotes the sharing of knowledge and the efficient operation of industry; it permits individual inventors to reap the rewards of their labor by contracting with a company large enough to develop and exploit it. Congress, by its silence over these many years, has seen the wisdom of allowing the states to enforce trade secret protection. Until Congress takes affirmative action to the contrary, states are free to grant protection to trade secrets.

The judgment of the Court of Appeals is reversed, and the order of the district court is reinstated.

Kewanee Oil clearly addresses the recognized purposes of trade secret laws. The Supreme Court put substantial weight on the importance of such protection in a limited distribution environment: to research and development, manufacturing, and marketing efforts within organizations or among different companies working on projects. The Court also rested its judgment heavily on the relative weakness of trade secret protection compared to patent protection. In this regard, the ability of consumers or others who legally acquire products to reverse engineer is seen as critical. You should keep this notion in mind when we evaluate "shrink-wrap licenses" in Chapter 9. Shrink-wrap licenses are used particularly by developers of computer software to keep purchasers of their widely distributed programs from discovering trade secrets through reverse engineering. As we shall see in Chapter 9, one court once found that such licenses violate federal copyright policies. In light of *Kewanee Oil*, one also might question their legality in the face of federal patent laws. Having said this, you should note that the recent legal trend regarding shrink-wrap licenses is to give their use the green light. Again, this will be explored in Chapter 9.

IMPORTANT ASPECTS OF TRADE SECRET LAWS

Trade secret policies developed first in the states through the common law. In 1939, the American Law Institute summarized the prevailing common law doctrines of the various states in a treatise called the Restatement of Torts. In 1995, the Institute released an updated analysis of trade secret concepts in a similar authoritative guide, titled the Restatement (Third) of Unfair Competition. Although these documents have no binding legal effect, they greatly influence judges in various state jurisdictions and, over time, have served to unify trade secret principles. In 1979, the Commissioners of Uniform State Laws devised the Uniform Trade Secrets Act (UTSA). The UTSA represents a model for state legislatures to follow in passing statutes that explicitly codify trade secret policies. As of 1996, over 40 states, including California, Connecticut, and Virginia, had passed statutes based on the UTSA. Although there are subtle differences between the Restatements and the UTSA, the overall guiding principles are the same. The general discussion that follows concentrates on the language of the UTSA, but it applies equally well to states relying on the common law principles of the Restatements. We shall see this later in this chapter when reviewing *Integrated Cash Management Services*, a New York case that discusses trade secrets in terms of the original Restatement of Torts and bases its decision on it. Exhibit 4.1 provides a brief overview of the trade secret protection policies that will be considered in this chapter.

Definition of Trade Secret

Under the UTSA, a trade secret holder is entitled to remedies when the trade secret has been misappropriated. Thus, an analysis of one's rights under the UTSA requires an understanding of what information constitutes a trade secret and what type of conduct amounts to misappropriation.

Exhibit 4.1

Important Aspects of Trade Secret Protection Policies in the United States

- **Governing Laws and Policies**
  - State
    - Uniform Trade Secrets Act
    - Restatement of Torts
  - Federal
    - Economic Espionage Act

- **Elements of a Trade Secret**
  - Valuable information
  - Secrecy
  - Reasonable security measures

- **Offense of Misappropriation**
  - Acquisition by improper means
    - Theft, fraud, espionage
  - Breach of fiduciary duties to maintain secrecy
    - Implied through employment relationship
    - Confidentiality agreements
  - Reasonable awareness about trade secrets
  - Reverse engineering is not misappropriation

- **Proving Misappropriation**
  - High investment in trade secret
  - Access by alleged misappropriator
  - Fast development by alleged misappropriator

- **Remedies for Trade Secret Misappropriation**
  - Injunctions
    - For actual or threatened misappropriation
    - Preliminary or permanent
    - Potential impact on employee mobility
  - Monetary damages
  - Criminal remedies
    - State laws
    - Federal Economic Espionage Act

The UTSA defines a trade secret as:

information, including a formula, pattern, compilation, program, device, method, technique or process, that:
(i) derives independent economic value, actual or potential, from not being generally known to, and not being readily ascertainable by proper means by, other persons who can obtain economic value from its disclosure or use, and
(ii) is the subject of efforts that are reasonable under the circumstances to maintain its secrecy.

This definition indicates that there are three essential components of a trade secret. The first concerns the type of information that may constitute a trade secret. This condition is easy to satisfy, since the breadth of the definition seemingly permits trade secret protection to extend to any kind of information, whether it be related to financial, technical, marketing, or organizational topics. Thus, trade secret protection may apply to engineering information, formulas, customer information and lists, sources for raw materials, manufacturing processes, design manuals, operating and pricing policies, market research studies, equipment and machinery, computer software and flow charts, and drawings and blueprints. Indeed, knowledge about negative results—that certain techniques or processes are not effective, for instance—also comes within the ambit of acceptable trade secret information. Clearly, trade secret protection covers a much wider array of business interests than does patent protection, which is limited to useful processes, machines, and compositions.

The second fundamental aspect of a trade secret is that it be economically valuable because it is not known or easily ascertained by those who might benefit from it. Thus, it is not enough that the information have value; it must be valuable because it provides an advantage not yet widely available to others in the industry. For instance, a production technique that improves efficiency may be economically valuable even when those in the industry have thorough knowledge about it and widely use it. However, this form of economic value would not be the type required for a trade secret. Rather, the value has to be derived from the relative secrecy. Also, it is not enough to show that the general public does not know the information. The question is whether those who might profitably use the information know about it. A programming technique, for example, may not be known to the average member of the public, but if it is generally known by computer programmers, or even known by the principal competitor in the field, that will be enough to destroy its trade secret status. Economic value also is a function of how fast others can learn the information by proper means. Here, proper means involve learning about the information through reverse engineering, independent invention, observation in a public forum, or the reading of published literature. For example, if competitors can quickly discern or learn about the unique features of a product once it hits the market, then the secrecy of the information before product release ultimately may yield no commercial benefits. Putting all this in a nutshell, one could say that economic value is simply a function of whether any real advantage can be obtained from secrecy.

The third requirement for trade secret status is that the information be subject to reasonable measures to preserve its secrecy.[16] Since the first two criteria are normally somewhat easy to meet, this factor often is the most important focus of attention. Such a requirement is completely logical. If one does not recognize the importance of secrecy to the value of the information and thus take reasonable steps to maintain that value, then there is no reason to expect the law to come to the rescue. In addition, one cannot expect others to respect the value of secrecy unless one demonstrates a personal commitment to preserving it. Finally, information will not be economically valuable for long if reasonable efforts are not undertaken to maintain its secrecy. The measures one might contemplate to maintain the secrecy of information will be discussed further in the next section.

Misappropriation

The UTSA prohibits misappropriation of trade secrets. The definition of "misappropriation" specifically covers a broad range of unethical acts. However, they are all grounded on similar philosophical principles. Misappropriation occurs (1) when one acquires a trade secret by improper means or acquires it from another person reasonably knowing that the person used improper means to get it, (2) when one discloses or uses a trade secret reasonably knowing that such conduct violates a duty to maintain silence, (3) when one who reasonably knows of the impropriety discloses or uses a trade secret that was received from another person who used improper means to get it, or (4) when one who reasonably knows about the fiduciary breach uses or discloses a trade secret that was disclosed by another under a fiduciary duty to maintain silence.[17] These definitions use convoluted language and admittedly are difficult to wade through. However, they all are bound by a unifying theme: to engage in trade secret misappropriation, individuals must not only do something bad or improper, but also must be aware that what they are doing is wrong.

One useful way to appreciate the philosophy of trade secret misappropriation is to consider how you might deal with a new puppy that has recently become a member of your family. For instance, when the puppy has to do "its business," it invariably will find a comfortable place on the rug for relief. Your instinct is to jump up and scream, "Bad Dog!" However, when you do this, you will have wrongly accused your pet. Your puppy is not a bad dog. How was he supposed to know that he should not piddle on your rug? It certainly is not in his genes to know, nor has he ever been notified that there is a better place to go. The proper response when the puppy uses the rug is to sharply tell him, "No," and then take him to the location outdoors that you prefer him to use. After this lesson has been repeated several times, then there probably has been sufficient communication to the dog that he should know that it is wrong to go potty on the rug. At this point, if he uses the rug, then he truly is a bad dog and deserves to be treated as one. Those dealing with trade secrets deserve the same consideration and should not be called misappropriators unless they have acted like bad dogs. And as with bad dogs, this requires not only inappropriate behavior but a clear understanding that the behavior is wrong.

Improper Means By the terms of the UTSA, improper means include "theft, misrepresentation, breach or inducement of a breach of a duty to maintain secrecy, or espionage through electronic or other means." This definition is probably just what you expected. In general, activities that illegitimately interfere with a person's expectations of privacy are improper. However, one always must keep in mind the interplay of improper conduct and the security measures the trade secret holder reasonably should take to thwart it. So, consider a competitor who takes a public tour of your facilities. While the group is asking questions, the competitor sneaks into a room and takes pictures. Clearly, this is improper. However, you probably should have taken steps to ensure that the competitor could not wander into private areas of particular importance. Thus, although the conduct may have been improper, it may not be unlawful because the information taken may not have been sufficiently protected to be a trade secret. One final point to remember, as explained in *Kewanee Oil*, is that reverse engineering and independent creation are never improper. Some states that have adopted the UTSA, such as California, make this abundantly clear by explicitly excluding such conduct from the definition of improper means.

Reasonable Awareness of Wrongdoing Those who handle trade secrets like bad dogs also must know that what they are doing is improper. Individuals who engage in theft or espionage or who use deceit to obtain the secrets clearly know that they are involved in wrongful conduct and easily can be pegged as bad dogs. However, other situations are not so clear-cut. This is particularly true with employees who have access to corporate information simply as part of doing their jobs. For them to handle trade secrets in unethical ways, they must know which pieces of information constitute trade secrets and that they have obligations to maintain that information in confidence. Given this, employers need to consider how they might make their employees aware of their trade secret obligations. How the employers treat the information is a start. For instance, if the information is strictly controlled in a guarded environment and released only on a need-to-know basis, then the employees should have at least an intuitive sense that the employer values the secrecy of the information. Further, if the employers put written legends on the cover of the information, explicitly stating that it is confidential and proprietary, then the message is even more direct. And knowing that the employer values the secrecy of the information should be enough for employees to recognize that they should not use or disclose it. Really, this is simply a matter of being reasonable. Consider how you would respond if your employer entrusted you with valuable and secret information for the purposes of carrying out your duties. Wouldn't you know from the circumstances that the employer does not intend for you to somehow use it for your own benefit? Indeed, the employer does not have to explicitly tell you to maintain the information in confidence. The duty may be implied merely from the employer-employee relationship.

Reasons for Confidentiality Agreements The employer can take a further step that strengthens an employee's awareness of fiduciary responsibility and focuses attention on the particular information covered by such confidential obligations. This action, which is highly advisable for all business dealing with trade secrets, is to have employees enter explicit confidentiality agreements. Confidentiality agreements make it very clear to new employees that they will be dealing with trade secrets in the business and that they have a duty to maintain the secrecy of that information by not using or disclosing it during and after the employment relationship. In addition, the agreements should indicate with as much specificity as possible the types of information the employer considers sensitive, and to which the confidentiality obligations clearly apply. Express confidentiality agreements, especially in conjunction with other security measures, are very effective in defeating employees' claims that they knew neither their general obligations to maintain the confidentiality of trade secrets nor the specific information they were supposed to keep secret. In addition, they make it clear at the outset of employment that the employer is very serious about maintaining the security of important trade secret information.

Employee Knowledge vs. Employer's Trade Secret Rights   Problems with employees frequently arise when employees use their own knowledge and skills to develop valuable trade secret information. The most pressing question results when an employee leaves the firm and begins work on a similar project elsewhere. The employer has rights to the trade secrets for which it bargained and paid. Valuable secret information developed on the job or under contract rightly belongs to the hiring party. In addition, the employer has trade secret rights to specific information that employees or third parties agree in employment contracts belongs to the employer. The employer does not have rights, however, to the general knowledge and skills that employees originally bring to the job. The problem is that it may be very difficult to determine where the preexisting knowledge ends and the trade secrets begin. In postdeparture disputes, the former employer will claim trade secret misappropriation while the employee will argue that only native skills and abilities are being used in the new project—just as they were for the former employer. This debate is one of the important issues that faced the court in *Integrated Cash Management.*

**INTEGRATED CASH MANAGEMENT SERVICES, INC.
v. DIGITAL TRANSACTIONS, INC.**
United States District Court, New York, 1989

FACTS: Integrated Cash Management Services (ICM) designs and develops computer utility programs. ICM's programs are marketed to banks, which in turn market them to the financial and treasury departments of various corporations. ICM develops generic programs, which may be readily customized to suit a particular client's specifications, thereby reducing the need for computer consultants. The ICM programs at issue are: (1) SEUNIMNT, a generic universal database management system; (2) Telefon, a generic communications program; (3) Menu System/Driver, a treasury workstation program; and

continued . . .

continued . . .

(4) Report Writer, a financial report customizing program. The generic programs are able to work together to form a unified generic utility system.

Newlin and Vafa each worked for ICM. Newlin was employed as a computer programmer between 1984 and March 1987. While an ICM employee, Newlin wrote the Communications and Menu modules of the ICM system. He also assisted in writing the SEUNIMNT program in the computer language called C and in writing an initial version of the Report Writer module for ICM. Vafa was employed by ICM as a computer programmer between 1986 and March 1987. Vafa collaborated with Newlin in creating Report Writer and the C-language version of SEUNIMNT. Vafa and Newlin had particular trouble designing Report Writer so that it would work with the rest of the system. ICM expended substantial time and money with different formulations of the Report Writer before developing a suitable version. Both Newlin and Vafa signed nondisclosure agreements with ICM in which they agreed not to disclose or use any confidential or proprietary information of ICM upon leaving the company's employ.

Newlin and Vafa left ICM on March 13, 1987, and formed Digital Transactions, Inc. (DTI), three days later. Within two weeks, DTI had created a prototype database program. That program, and other generic programs subsequently produced for DTI by Newlin and Vafa, were similar to comparable ICM programs. In addition, the overall architecture of the DTI system, which allows the individual programs to work together, was substantially similar to that developed by ICM. ICM sued DTI, alleging that Newlin, Vafa, and another individual formerly linked to ICM had misappropriated trade secrets.

DECISION AND REASONING: A plaintiff claiming misappropriation of a trade secret must prove (1) it possessed a trade secret, and (2) defendant is using that trade secret either in breach of an agreement, confidence, or duty or as a result of discovery by improper means. DTI contends that the architecture of ICM's system is not a trade secret. This court disagrees.

The most comprehensive and influential definition of a trade secret is that set out in the Restatement of Torts. The definition provides that a "trade secret may consist of any formulation, pattern, device or compilation of information which is used in one's business, and which gives him an opportunity to obtain an advantage over competitors who do not know or use it." In determining whether a trade secret exists, the New York courts have considered the following factors to be relevant:

1. the extent to which the information is known outside the business;
2. the extent to which it is known by employees and others involved in the business;
3. the extent of measures taken to guard the secrecy of the information;

4. the value to the information to the business and competitors;
5. the amount of effort or money expended in developing the information; and
6. the ease or difficulty with which the information could be properly acquired or duplicated by others.

Applying these factors to the software programs at issue in this case, it is evident that ICM retains a protectible trade secret in its product.

The manner in which ICM's generic utility programs interact, which is the key to the product's success, is not generally known outside ICM. DTI presented evidence that the various components of the ICM system are not secret but are available to the public through books, commercially sold products, and scholarly publications. However, a trade secret can exist in a combination of characteristics and components each of which, by itself, is in the public domain but whose unified process, design, and operation, in unique combination, affords a competitive advantage.

Here, the way in which ICM's various components fit together as building blocks in order to form the unique whole is secret. ICM's combination of programs was not disclosed in ICM's promotional literature, which contains merely a user-oriented description of the advantages of ICM's product. Such limited information does not contain sufficient technical detail to constitute disclosure of the product's architecture. The package as a whole, and the specifications used by ICM to make the parts of that package work together, are not in the public domain.

Clearly, ICM has made reasonable efforts to maintain the secrecy of the source code of its programs. The doors to the premises were kept locked. Also, employees, including Newlin and Vafa, were required to sign nondisclosure agreements, which provided that "when employment is terminated, the former employee agrees not to use, copy or disclose any of ICM's secrets, software products, software tools or any type of information and software which belongs to ICM."

The remaining factors to be considered in ascertaining the existence of a trade secret are also satisfied. The court is satisfied about the value of the programs to ICM and its competitors. Also, it is not disputed that ICM made large investments in research and development. In this regard, the court notes that a significant amount of time and money was spent in investigating alternatives that, in the end, were not fruitful. Such a trial-and-error process is also protectible as a trade secret. Finally, expert testimony reveals that the ICM product's architecture could not be readily duplicated without the secret information acquired by ICM through years of research. Therefore, we find that ICM's winning combination of generic utility programs is a trade secret.

Having found the existence of a trade secret, the court must next decide whether the defendants misused that secret information in creating their own

continued . . .

continued ...

system. The difficulty here results from the need to preserve the proprietary information of ICM while at the same time not unduly restricting Newlin and Vafa from utilizing their admittedly extensive skills, experience, and general knowledge. This is especially the case when, as here, there exists a situation in which no direct copying occurred. Certainly, an employee who achieves technical expertise or general knowledge while in the employ of another may thereafter use that knowledge in competition with that former employer, so long as the employee (or ex-employee) does not use or disclose protected trade secrets in the process.

Certain factors help fashion a just result. One important factor is the existence of a nondisclosure agreement, since it puts the employee on notice about the nature and existence of trade secrets. In this case, Vafa and Newlin were well aware of their duties not to disclose secrets of ICM. Defendants assert that the DTI programs were created from scratch and that Vafa and Newlin approached their tasks with fresh minds. It is a well-recognized principle that when a defendant in a trade secret case claims independent development, the burden shifts to the defendant to show that this was in fact the case. Defendants have not sustained the burden here.

The court does not doubt defendants' good intentions and professional integrity. However, it seems impossible for them to develop a competing system for DTI without dwelling upon their experience from ICM and in the process incorporating into any system for DTI many of the valuable, confidential, and proven-workable features in ICM's systems. Newlin and Vafa made use of information learned while at ICM concerning which functions and relationships among the modules would and would not work in the generic program. That information was maintained as a secret by ICM and was valuable to its business. Newlin and Vafa were simply too bright to make the same mistakes twice in writing the programs. Not general experience, but specific experience with, and knowledge of, those particular types of generic programs for banking and financial applications were utilized, perhaps unavoidably, by Vafa and Newlin when they chose to take up the same task at a new company.

ICM does not attempt to prevent defendants from competing with it on a fair basis. It seeks only to prevent them from creating a substantially similar system of utility programs. The four programs at issue are among approximately 1,000 programs or modules created by defendants. ICM has no complaint concerning the balance of these programs. In light of the equities, and the inadequacy of damages to compensate ICM for the misappropriation of its valuable trade secrets, injunctive relief is appropriate.

Defendants are enjoined for a period of six months from the date of this decision from utilizing, as part of DTI's systems, any versions of the database manager, menu, communications, and report writer programs created in whole or in part by either Vafa or Newlin. In addition, and for the same period, Newlin and Vafa are enjoined from contributing to the creation of any new programs embodying these utilities. DTI is otherwise free to develop new programs, provided that it does not rely on the restricted programs during the development. The period of six months has been chosen with a view to the length of time ICM spent in creating its systems, the increased speed of the current hardware available to programmers, and the need to neutralize the head start gained by DTI from the improper use of ICM's trade secrets.

Defendants also are permanently enjoined from distributing any unmodified versions of ICM's four generic utility programs in existence on the date of this decision. This prevents them from simply shelving the misappropriated information for six months, and then distributing the ICM product as their own.

Dealing with Third Parties   Fiduciary obligation to maintain secrecy may extend beyond the employment relationship. As indicated in *Kewanee Oil*, firms often must divulge trade secrets to third parties so that they can efficiently assist in achieving certain mutual goals, such as research and development, manufacturing, or marketing. Express agreements to maintain confidentiality are even more important in this setting because proof of implied obligations is harder to sustain. Thus, in dealings outside the firm, it would be a mistake to assume that the other parties know that you expect certain information to be kept secret. Rather, it is critical to have confidentiality agreements signed before any trade secret information is presented. In addition, as will be explained in the next section, the firm will have to implement additional safeguards as well to preserve the secrecy of its valuable information.

Clearly, it is important that those who work for or directly with the trade secret holder understand the sensitive nature of proprietary information. When this is done appropriately, an employer may seek trade secret remedies against those individuals if they are caught divulging or using the information improperly. However, what if a former employee discloses the information to another party or simply uses it in developing a new product for a subsequent employer? Are there any rights against these recipients? Such an occurrence requires a careful balancing of equitable rights. To understand the complex issues often involved, it is helpful to consider the extremes first. On one end of the spectrum, a competitor who pays a recalcitrant employee specifically to divulge trade secrets is no different from a co-conspirator to the misappropriation. In this situation, it is philosophically easy to treat the competitor as if it had committed the wrongful act and accordingly hold it responsible to the extent of the law. On the other hand, that same employee may simply take another job and, unbeknownst to the new employer, use the information in developing, manufacturing, and/or marketing the new employer's new products. What makes this situation different is the total absence of knowledge. Here, the new employer is just as innocent as the deprived trade secret holder, and it is therefore conceptually difficult to find the new employer legally responsible for what happened. Of course, the equities in most situations are not so clear-cut. For instance, the new employer may hire a technical expert to work on a project knowing the expert had once worked on a similar secret project for a competitor. Although the new employer may not specifically know that secret information is being used, the employer should be on notice of the potential for misappropriation.

The UTSA strives to find the right balance based on the degree of knowledge the recipient should have had under the circumstances. One engages in misappropriation when one acquires, uses, or discloses information knowing that it contains misappropriated trade secrets. An individual also misappropriates if a reasonable person, based on the situation, would have been aware that misappropriated trade secrets were involved. One can apply these standards to the case brought by Minnesota Mining and Manufacturing (3M) alleging that Johnson & Johnson (J&J) had misappropriated secrets from 3M about a new casting tape and had infringed 3M patents.[18] An employee of 3M sent a stolen sample of the new tape to J&J, offering to explain the technology for a fee.[19] J&J did not accept the offer. However, an executive at J&J sent the sample to the J&J laboratory for analysis. J&J chemists were never instructed not to use the results of the analysis in developing J&J products, and so they employed the technology in a competing product.[20] Given these facts, one can conclude that responsible executives at J&J knew or reasonably should have known that J&J's new casting product benefited from trade secret information wrongfully taken from 3M. For this reason, the court ruled that J&J had unlawfully misappropriated trade secrets from 3M. Moreover, the behavior helped persuade the court that J&J willfully infringed 3M's casting tape patents, allowing the court to double the overall damages.[21]

Sometimes, a recipient has no way of knowing about the trade secret status of certain information until the trade secret holder finds out what's going on and then hurriedly brings it to the recipient's attention. If the innocent recipient has done little with the information, it is easy to settle the situation by simply preventing its further use. However, before being informed, the recipient may have invested in new production equipment and begun sales of a new line of products. Now, it might be too harsh to require the recipient to stop manufacturing or sales. To equitably handle this situation, the UTSA allows a judge tremendous flexibility to devise remedies. For instance, rather than issue an injunction, the court may allow the recipient to continue its use of the trade secrets but require it to make reasonable royalty payments for the privilege.

Third parties must be reasonably aware that they are dealing with misappropriated trade secret information before a trade secret holder may have a remedy against them. One technique used by employers is to have employees agree to the following kind of provision in their confidentiality agreements:

The employer may notify anyone employing me or evidencing an intention to employ me as to the existence and provisions of this Agreement.

Now when the employee changes jobs, the employer may notify the new company about the employee's former duties and the employee's obligations to maintain secrecy about certain kinds of information and projects. Alerting the new company in this manner makes it easier, if necessary, to prove that its executives should have known that the employee would use trade secrets. To protect itself, the new company may take its own steps in its employment agreements. For instance, it likely will make employees promise that they will not use or disclose trade secrets of former employers or others. In this way, the new company tries to demonstrate its good faith in attempting to prevent misappropriation on its premises.

Proving Misappropriation

Proving that trade secrets were improperly used or disclosed often is very difficult. For instance, suppose one of your employees quits the job and begins work with a competitor in a similar capacity. Soon thereafter, the competitor comes out with a product that is suspiciously similar to your most important commercial development—one that relies on some carefully guarded secrets. It would be nice if you had direct evidence that the former employee had disclosed or used secret information. Perhaps you could discover a photocopy of a key document in the competitor's files. Or maybe someone will testify how your secrets were used. It is more than likely, however, that such direct proof will be unavailable. Thus, proof will have to be made by circumstantial evidence. Normally, a trade secret holder will try to prove misappropriation circumstantially by showing (1) that it spent large sums of money and spent considerable time developing the secret information, (2) that the alleged misappropriator had access to that information, and (3) that the alleged misappropriator developed its functionally similar product in substantially less time and with fewer resources. The importance of this kind of proof was evident in *Kewanee Oil*, wherein defendants took less than 1 year to produce a crystal that had been developed by the plaintiffs over a 17-year period of expensive trials. We also encountered the same logic in *Integrated Cash Management*, where several years of work was duplicated in a matter of weeks.

Keep in mind the importance of the common employee in these examples to prove access. What if your competitor came out with its similar product but you did not have an explanation such as employee mobility? You are intuitively certain that misappropriation somehow occurred, but you are unable to find the link. Maybe a judge will be persuaded by the similarities alone, if they are sufficiently extraordinary, but that is not likely. Always remember that even if valuable information is misappropriated, trade secret law is not helpful without proof. This is another reason why trade secrets should be closely guarded: not only does such guarding establish the existence of a protectible secret, but it helps ensure that misappropriation, and the associated problems of proof, do not arise at all.

Remedies for Trade Secret Misappropriation

Injunctions   The UTSA provides a trade secret holder with a number of remedies for unlawful misappropriation. Of these, the most potent are court-ordered injunctions preventing use or disclosure of the secrets. According to the UTSA, actual or threatened misappropriation of trade secrets may be enjoined. It should not seem surprising that, when a trade secret holder can prove in court that an individual stole trade secrets through espionage, the judge may use judicial powers to prevent use or disclosure of the unlawfully obtained secrets. Similarly, when an employee forms a competitive company and uses the secrets in its operations, a court may issue an injunction preventing further use of the secrets. Likewise, when the employee joins another company and uses the secrets to aid that competitor, then an injunction is appropriate.

All of these are examples of actual misappropriation, and injunctive relief raises little controversy. In such situations, the debate often involves the length of the injunction, that is, the period of time the misappropriator will be prevented from using the secrets. For instance, suppose a company is subject to an injunction for having misappropriated a trade secret. What happens if that information somehow becomes publicly available? Should the misappropriator still be subject to the injunction even after it could otherwise legally obtain and use the information? According to the UTSA, the misappropriator may apply to the court to remove the injunction once the trade secret has ceased to exist. However, the court may continue the injunction for an additional period if needed to eliminate any head start or other commercial advantage that the misappropriator might enjoy by virtue of the earlier misappropriation.

Judges also have tremendous flexibility to fashion the length of the injunction from the outset depending on the equities of the situation. In one case, for instance, employees who misappropriated confidential customer lists were enjoined for 15 months from soliciting those customers. The length of the injunction was based on the court's determination of the time it would take diligent salespersons to independently discover the valued customer names.[22] *Integrated Cash Management Services* provided another illustration of the flexibility judges have in fashioning injunctions. There, the judge imposed a six-month injunction, a period that was devised in light of the circumstances to remove any unfair advantage that DTI might have obtained from its improper use of ICM's trade secrets.

INEVITABLE DISCLOSURE The UTSA also gives courts the power to enjoin threatened misappropriation. The interesting question here arises when a competitor hires away employees to perform similar jobs with the new company. Employees who know valuable trade secrets have an obligation not to use those secrets in a new position. Indeed, an injunction strengthening that duty might be available. However, even an injunction preventing use or disclosure may not be very comforting to the previous employer. That employer intuitively knows that it will be impossible for the employees to work on similar projects without leaking or using some of the valuable information. And the burden of monitoring and proving such misuse may be very difficult to sustain. Thus, the previous employer may feel that the court should enjoin the employees from working on related projects with the new employer, even before there is any evidence of improper behavior. At the greatest extreme, the previous employer might ask the court to prevent employment of any kind with the competitor for a reasonable period of time. The theory in these situations is that disclosure of important trade secrets is inevitable, given what the employees know and the overall business or specific projects to which they are headed.

One highly publicized example unfolded in the early 1990s when IBM sought an injunction barring Peter Bonyhard from working on Seagate Technology's project to develop magnetoresistive (MR) disk drive heads. Mr. Bonyhard had formerly headed IBM's MR development team. The district court initially granted the injunction, as IBM requested, forcing Seagate to reassign Bonyhard to a division not working on the MR heads. However, this injunction was lifted on appeal.[23]

As the IBM scenario demonstrates, courts have difficulty with injunctions affecting employment because of the serious economic consequences they may create for persons who have yet to do anything wrong. Nonetheless, injunctions restricting employment have been carried out when the courts were more firmly convinced that disclosure was inevitable. For instance, in 1994, Pepsico, Inc. asked a court to prevent William Redmond, the former general manager of Pepsico's California business unit, from taking a position with Quaker to serve as its vice president of field operations of the Gatorade brand.[24] At the time, Pepsico was attempting to bolster its All-Sport brand in a fierce competitive battle with Quaker for control of the sports drink market. Redmond had intimate knowledge of Pepsico's strategic and operating plans for the All-Sport brand, including marketing objectives, financial goals, event calendars, pricing architecture, distribution channels and systems, packaging size, retailer merchandising agreements, and marketing attack plans. The court issued an injunction, preventing Redmond from assuming his duties at Quaker for five months, stating that Pepsico was in the position of a coach, one of whose players had left, playbook in hand, to join the opposing team before the big game. In a similar action, DoubleClick, Inc., an Internet advertising firm, brought suit against two former executives which it had fired after learning that they planned to launch a rival firm. The court enjoined the executives from working in the industry for six months, since it was inevitable that they would disclose and use DoubleClick's trade secrets.[25]

Certain forms of evidence may be particularly persuasive in inevitable disclosure cases.[26] For instance, when a mid-level employee is hired by a competitor for a large salary increase or a disproportionate signing bonus, this logically raises an inference that the company may be seeking something more from that employee than normal business talents. Likewise, suspicions are raised when a company seemingly goes out of its way—often geographically—to hire employees from a rival when equally skilled personnel could be more easily found. For example, in 1998, Wal-Mart alleged that Amazon.com raided several information systems employees from its Arkansas headquarters to work in Amazon's offices in the Pacific Northwest. Although Amazon claimed that it was simply looking for the brightest and most talented people, Wal-Mart noted that with the glut of talented computer-savvy people in the Pacific Northwest and Silicon Valley, the only reason that Amazon went to Arkansas was to acquire Wal-Mart's proprietary information.[27]

It is important to reemphasize that judges are very reluctant to impose injunctions based on inevitable disclosure. You should not get the impression that employers routinely may get court-ordered injunctions whenever their employees decide to take similar jobs with competitors. Rather, judges need to be convinced that disclosure really will take place unless they intervene. As we have seen, when the new employers are particularly aggressive in hiring individuals who have specific knowledge that will benefit their businesses, this may lead to the conclusion that disclosure is inevitable. In fact, application of the doctrine very often is based on evidence that the departing employee and/or the new employer are not to be trusted. Even in *Pepsico*, there was evidence that Redmond had not been forthright with his former employer, leading the court to conclude that he could not be trusted to act with the necessary sensitivity and good faith that was required under the circumstances. Other factors also matter, such as the level of responsibility that the employee had with the former employer over similar projects.[28] In addition, the more immediate the concern due to the time sensitivity of the information, the more likely the court will intercede.

PRELIMINARY RELIEF Given the typical backlog in state courts for civil cases, a trade secret holder may have to wait years before fully presenting its case. In the rapidly changing environment of high technology, such a long deferral may make the lawsuit moot. By the time the case is set for trial, the secret may have become public or the technology may be obsolete. For this reason, the courts have set up a preliminary mechanism to stop illicit behavior before a case comes to trial. A trade secret holder may request that a judge issue a temporary restraining order (TRO) preventing an alleged misappropriator from using or disclosing the information until a preliminary hearing can be scheduled. The TRO usually lasts less than ten days. At the preliminary hearing, the judge will examine the evidence and may issue a preliminary injunction preventing use or disclosure until the completion of a full trial on the merits. To obtain a preliminary injunction, the trade secret holder must prove (1) that it will suffer irreparable harm if the defendant is allowed to use the information before trial and (2) that there is a strong likelihood that it will win when the case comes to trial. These are formidable hurdles, and the trade secret holder often will not have sufficiently compelling evidence to clear them. Nonetheless, a preliminary injunction, once granted, puts the alleged misappropriator in a difficult position. First, the defendant now must endure the wait to compete in the contemplated way. Second, the judge has sent a strong signal that the trial will not yield positive results. Thus, those subject to a preliminary injunction often try to negotiate a settlement rather than wait for trial.

From the perspective of a company trying to protect its valuable trade secrets, pursuing preliminary and permanent injunctions is simply an honest means to further its legitimate commercial interests. However, competitors may take a different view. Many high-technology enterprises, especially small companies in the start-up phase, consider trade secret suits to be standard operating procedure for established firms to keep the new rivals "down on the farm."[29] From their vantage, established companies use trade secret litigation simply to tie up small companies that are gearing up to manufacture and market competitive products. Such suits can absorb enormous energy and funds from the new enterprise as it attempts to fend off court-ordered injunctions. In addition, the lawsuits can have a chilling effect on venture capitalists and other financial backers. Ultimately, the small firm may have to cease operations even though its legal position is relatively strong.

Without commenting on the merits of this argument, one must be aware that litigation can have powerful strategic implications. The expenses of legal disputes can be enormous, and they can have disproportionate impacts on smaller firms. On the other hand, it is likely that most trade secret suits brought by large companies do have substantial factual bases, such as employee defections and rapid development of similar products by the competitor. Indeed, the UTSA gives some protection from spurious suits by requiring one who litigates in bad faith to pay the attorneys' fees of the innocent party.

Monetary Relief   The UTSA also provides that a trade secret holder is entitled to damages, or monetary remuneration, for misappropriation. Damages have two components: (1) the amount needed to compensate the trade secret holder for the losses caused by the misappropriation and (2) the unjust enrichment earned by the misappropriator by virtue of the unlawful use or disclosure. The techniques for determining losses for trade secret misappropriation are very similar to those used for patent infringement. For instance, the trade secret holder may demonstrate that there is an established royalty rate for using the information or that the misappropriation had a demonstrable negative effect on profits. The trade secret holder also is entitled to the profits earned by the misappropriator to the degree that they are not already accounted for in the determination of losses. In addition, as with patents, the court has the power to award a reasonable royalty rate if damages to the trade secret holder cannot otherwise be satisfactorily established. Finally, the UTSA provides for double damages and attorneys' fees for willful and malicious misappropriation.

Criminal Actions   The UTSA does not have any provisions authorizing state governments to bring criminal actions against those who violate trade secret rights. However, many states have separate statutes that make trade secret theft a crime. One of the more visible criminal actions involved allegations that Eugene Wang, an employee of Borland International, conveyed confidential business information to Gordon Eubanks, the CEO of Symantec Corporation, just before Wang left Borland to begin a new job at Symantec. On the date that Wang announced his decision to depart, officials at Borland, who feared that Wang might have conveyed secrets to Symantec, searched Wang's electronic mail files and found several messages sent to Eubanks which they believed contained confidential information belonging to Borland. Borland contacted the local Scotts Valley police, who worked with the Santa Cruz district attorney's office to search Symantec's headquarters and the residences of Eubanks and Wang. The DA ultimately brought criminal charges against Eubanks and Wang, alleging that they were involved in conspiracies to steal trade secrets, receive stolen property and access computer data without permission—activities which violate specific provisions of the California Penal Code. The action raised eyebrows in Silicon Valley in 1992 because employee defections were so common in that culture while criminal proceedings were so rare.[30] To many observers, Borland was using its close association with local government officials to harass Symantec and to inhibit employee defections to a primary competitor. Indeed, Borland did work extremely closely with the DA and even paid for the services of computer specialists who assisted the DA. In November 1996, the California Supreme Court dismissed the charges due to conflicts of interest. In addition, the parties settled separate civil trade secret actions that were brought under the California trade secret act, which is based on the UTSA.[31]

Criminal trade secret proceedings under state law are definitely the exception and not the rule.[32] Many states do not have well-established laws that deal with this area of activity. In addition, numerous procedural obstacles deter state prosecution when information is transferred to individuals and corporations in other states or countries. Thus, criminal charges often have to be handled under federal law if they are to be raised at all. Until recently, though, there was no federal law that dealt specifically with trade secret theft. Thus, federal prosecutors were forced to rely on statutes that primarily addressed associated forms of criminal activity, such as the National Stolen Property Act or the mail and wire fraud statutes. Various limitations in these laws, though, raised hurdles to bringing successful federal prosecutions.[33] The Economic Espionage Act, which was passed in 1996, addresses these problems and provides a new forum for federal criminal proceedings. The details of this new law will be discussed later in this chapter.

TRADE SECRET PROTECTION MEASURES

High-technology companies with trade secrets to protect must implement an appropriate set of security measures to ensure that the information does not fall into public hands. As previously discussed, information does not rise to the protectible status of being a trade secret under the UTSA unless reasonable security measures are undertaken. In addition, one can go only so far in relying on the law to maintain the value of secret information. Suppose, for example, a competitor learns trade secret information through espionage. The competitor then uses the information in its operations and sells it to various organizations. As the use becomes more widespread, some of the informed sources handle the information in a somewhat relaxed manner. Ultimately, the secret gets out, thereby destroying any relative advantage it had previously bestowed. The UTSA provides for injunctions and damages as remedies for misappropriation. But in the case at hand it is too late for an injunction to be effective. Thus, the victim must rely on monetary damages for relief. However, the victim may find that the assets held by the misappropriators are far less than the losses sustained. And, of course, there is the very real possibility that the victim will never even determine who the misappropriators are. Without adequate proof, the law offers little protection. Therefore, for both legal and practical reasons, security is an important consideration for high-technology companies handling trade secrets.

Most sophisticated businesses give trade secret protection high priority. They recognize that a suitable plan requires a formal process of periodic review, called the trade secret audit. Since the auditors will be evaluating all of the company's trade secrets, they must be extremely trusted personnel. Often the audit team will consist of an engineer who understands the technical nature of the secrets, a security expert, an attorney, and a manager who is knowledgeable about the daily operations of the company. The goal of the team is to act in a proactive manner to continually identify trade secrets and match appropriate measures to secure them.[34]

Some companies erroneously assume that once trade secret protection measures are put in place they operate sufficiently on a form of autopilot. Although these companies think they are being diligent by having a plan at all, they really are opening themselves to trouble. Company personnel have to be constantly reminded what the trade secrets are and how they should be handled. It is surprisingly easy for an employee to be careless with, say, a sales brochure, a speech, or a tour of plant facilities. Companies with high turnover have to be especially concerned that new employees learn the required protection steps and that departing personnel understand their continuing obligations and handle them appropriately. Also, trade secrets change over time. There may be new items that should be subject to security measures. Likewise, there may be information that has lost its value but remains subject to security according to an old plan. This is simply wasteful. Generally, companies that treat trade secrets on a static basis act on the defensive, taking new steps only when some crisis arises. Such defensive management rarely substitutes adequately for conscientious planning and monitoring.

A proactive trade secret protection strategy including periodic audits is the best way to consistently dedicate the appropriate resources to the maintenance of trade secrets. Periodic review by the audit team of trade secrets and security measures enhances the prospects that valuable information will be suitably protected. Such continual evaluation substantially reduces the likelihood that secrets will get into the wrong hands. Indeed, the firm's commitment to security may deter competitors and others from even attempting to misappropriate information. In addition, if secrets are misappropriated and litigation ensues, the company will have an easier time proving to the court that the measures used to protect the secrets were sufficient to be deemed reasonable under the terms of the UTSA. Finally, the attention to security may have a positive influence on employee morale, although this is not universal. At some companies, the degree of security may be so high that some may feel the atmosphere is akin to that of an armed camp.[35] Certain employees may react negatively to such scrutiny, feeling that the company engages in Orwellian tactics because employees are fundamentally distrusted. Others, however, may appreciate the importance attributed by the company to the work they perform. Obviously, the audit team must give some attention to the psychological impact that the security, scrutiny, and paperwork have on employee attitudes and performance.

The duty of the audit team is to identify valuable trade secrets and formulate appropriate security measures. One mistake that companies often make is to instruct employees that everything they learn or hear on the job is valuable proprietary information that must be kept in confidence. Identifying everything as a trade secret has no instructive content; indeed, it is counterproductive. Rather than inform the employees about the items that must be handled delicately, a blanket warning sends the message that nothing deserves special treatment. A wide range of financial, organizational, marketing, and technical information may be suitable for trade secret protection. The job of the audit team is to cull through that information and specifically identify the pieces that are sufficiently valuable to be guarded.

The audit team also must determine the appropriate degree of protection merited by the various pieces of information. This decision must consider the UTSA mandate that security be reasonable. As indicated in *Integrated Cash Management*, the courts usually review whether a firm utilized a suitable combination of security measures.[36] Although this does not provide much specific guidance, it suggests a couple of important considerations. First, it probably would be an error to rely on only one form of security measure to protect a secret. That is, locking a formula in a safe is not enough without considering who has the keys and what those key-holders are allowed to do with the information when they retrieve it. On the other hand, the firm does not have to engage in every conceivable form of security to preserve the secrecy of information. Rather, it should engage in a cost/benefit analysis to arrive at that combination of measures that is appropriate under the circumstances.[37] Such an appraisal will indicate the amount and types of security that should be adopted based on the value of the secret, the ways it could be misappropriated, and the costs of the various measures that could be used for deterrence.

The number of possible security measures the audit team should consider is virtually infinite. The following list provides an overview of the variety of general measures that ought to be reviewed. Keep in mind that an appropriate plan does not have to implement all of these techniques, but rather should strike the proper balance based on a cost/benefit analysis.

Use Employee Confidentiality Agreements

Courts often consider employee confidentiality agreements to be a crucial component of trade secret security plans. As discussed before, these agreements explicitly inform the employee about the importance of trade secrets to the company and the employee's duty to maintain them in confidence. The agreements will define the types of information considered trade secrets in as much specificity as possible to avert possible future disputes about the scope of expectations. Also, the agreements may attempt to clarify ownership issues. For instance, with situations such as that in *Integrated Cash Management* in mind, the employer will want the employee to explicitly agree that secret information developed by the employee is owned by the employer. In addition, the agreements may address issues such as the removal of important documents from the premises.

Employee confidentiality agreements generally contain other provisions as well. The employees normally agree that the employer can notify subsequent employers about their duties of confidentiality to thwart any claim that the new employer was not aware of the obligations. Employees also will promise not to use or disclose trade secrets of former employers to substantiate, if necessary, that the employer was unaware of any employee impropriety.

Specifically Inform Employees of Trade Secrets

Employee confidentiality agreements usually can identify only general areas of trade secret concerns. Also, specific trade secrets arise over time. Thus, the employer needs other techniques to continually inform employees about information that must be held in confidence. One prevalent method is to mark sensitive documents with legends that address the trade secret obligations. For example, computer software containing trade secrets may be marked as follows:

> This computer program is proprietary to X Company and contains valuable trade secrets. It is to be kept confidential and not used unless with written consent of the owner.

As mentioned before, the employer should refrain from marking too many documents as confidential, since overuse may lead employees not to take the warnings seriously.

Obviously, employees may be informed in other ways. That information is contained in a high-security area should indicate to a reasonable employee that the employer considers secrecy to be important. Also, the employer should periodically discuss continuing trade secret obligations with employees both to ensure that they do not forget their duties and to update their responsibilities.

Physically Restrict Access to Trade Secrets

If possible, the trade secrets should be physically separated, and access should be granted to those who can demonstrate that they have a need to know the information. The following measures should be considered.

- Keep track of who enters sensitive security areas through written logs, employee badges, and/or electronic-entry security systems.
- Lock gates, cabinets, and doors; establish a routine procedure for checking the locked status, especially at the end of the working day.
- Use security systems such as guards, alarms, and closed-circuit television.
- Have one person be responsible for distributing copies of trade secrets.

Maintain Computer System Security

Computer systems and programs often contain valuable trade secrets that may be easily accessed and copied unless safeguards are taken. Some measures are as follows:

- Use access restrictions such as passwords which are changed regularly.
- Restrict software use to hardware within secure areas.
- Fingerprint data with phony codes so that copying can be more easily proven.
- Limit distribution of source code.
- Carefully label disks with trade secret legends and use physical security measures to restrict unlawful access.
- Scramble data transmissions.

Completely Destroy Written Information

Do not throw old documents into the trash. Competitors have a right to and sometimes do rummage though refuse outside the premises and may be able to learn essential information from seemingly innocuous documents. All written materials should be shredded before disposal.

Do Not Provide Access to Entire Trade Secret

If possible, divide trade secret processes into steps, and have different employees or companies perform the individual procedures. KFC Corporation, for instance, protected its secret chicken recipe by having the seasonings produced in two parts by two separate companies.[38]

Screen Repair and Service Personnel

Service providers should be referenced and proper security enforced to limit their access to key data. This may be especially pertinent to computer service technicians.

Restrict Plant Tours

As part of their civic and community responsibilities, companies will be called upon to demonstrate what they do and how they accomplish it. Plant tours often help serve this important function. Companies must be wary, however, that industrial spies may join these tours to try to learn delicate information. Thus, the public should be restricted from high-security areas. In addition, the tours should be carefully controlled and escorted so that participants do not wander into sensitive areas. Cameras should be forbidden. Also, the escort should be trained in fielding questions so that trade secret information is not unwittingly revealed.

Screen Speeches, Publications, and Trade Show Materials

Executives often need to highlight the latest achievements of the firm while addressing stockholders, finance professionals, or the public. These speeches should be screened to ensure that they do not unnecessarily reveal important trade secret information about the projects. Marketing personnel trying to land deals at trade shows should be given special attention. They need to be adequately trained to deal with "prospective clients" who may pump for information about upcoming secret design specifications or the names of major clients. In addition, marketing literature and publications should be reviewed.

Conduct Employee Exit Interviews

Before employees leave the firm, they should be reminded of their contractual and implied obligations to maintain the confidentiality of trade secrets. In addition, the firm should be careful to collect all secret documents, security passes, keys, and badges in the employee's possession.

Deal with Third Parties Appropriately

It often will be necessary for the firm to share trade secret information with third parties for such purposes as joint research and development or distribution. Third parties should be treated with precautions similar to those applied to employees. Thus, third-party employees who come into contact with the secrets should be required to sign confidentiality agreements defining the ownership of trade secrets and obligations to preserve secrecy. The trade secret holder also will want assurances that the third party's physical security measures are adequate, that its computer systems are secure, and that its employees are monitored.

If the trade secret holder needs assistance from or furnishes services to a third party but does not want that company to learn trade secrets in the process, then additional steps will have to be taken to prevent disclosure. For example, with computer software, the trade secret holder may provide only object code and require the recipient to pledge not to reverse engineer that code through decompilation and disassembly. Some computer software companies have gone so far as to extend these steps to ordinary consumers through shrink-wrap licenses. As suggested earlier, such wide-scale attempts to prevent reverse engineering may run afoul of federal patent and/or copyright policies.

Make Covenants Not to Compete

When employees leave a high-technology company, they often have learned several important trade secrets. Although these employees have implied and contractual obligations not to use or disclose the secrets, many companies find such promises to be insufficient protection. For instance, the employee may never have understood the extent of the promises not to use information, may legitimately dispute whether the alleged trade secret information is owned by the company, or may try to take advantage of the company for personal gain, believing that the betrayal will never be proven. Rather than deal with this uncertainty when employees change jobs, these companies will have their employees promise in their employment agreements that after leaving the company, they will not take competing jobs for a specified period of time within a defined area. Such agreements are often called noncompete clauses or covenants not to compete.

Covenants not to compete are very controversial because of the sweeping ways that they can prevent employees from engaging in their professions and because of their potential effects on legitimate competition. For public policy reasons, courts view the clauses with skepticism and will enforce them only to the extent deemed reasonable under the circumstances. When courts do enforce the covenants, it is only after they have been persuaded that the restrictions are clearly needed to protect the release of trade secrets and are reasonable in terms of their duration and geographic scope.

Courts are more likely to uphold the agreements signed by employees having clear access to trade secrets, such as key executives and scientists, than agreements signed by those less removed from the secrets, such as typists and receptionists. Also, the length of time that the company can keep an employee from competing depends on the circumstances, but it rarely exceeds two years.[39] In addition, courts will enforce the covenant only within the area in which the employer conducts business. This may be as small as a city or county, or it may extend around the world. Finally, courts carefully scrutinize the types of job activities subject to the restriction. A narrowly tailored restriction preventing an employee from working for a competitor only in the same capacity as for the employer is more likely to be upheld than a blanket covenant prohibiting work with the competitor at all.

Some states, notably California, prohibit covenants not to compete. The California code, for example, states that with a few exceptions "every contract by which anyone is restrained from engaging in a lawful profession, trade, or business of any kind is to that extent void."[40] Therefore, in these states, companies must rely much more heavily on confidentiality agreements in conjunction with their other security measures. The only other recourse that companies have in these states is to ask a court to enjoin employees from working for competitors because disclosure of trade secrets is inevitable. As we have seen, courts generally are reluctant to rely on this doctrine to impose injunctions. In states that forbid covenants not to compete, the antipathy likely should be even stronger, given the legislature's express concern about any form of employment restrictions.[41] Thus, one should not expect a court to issue an employment injunction based on inevitable disclosure in states such as California unless there are extraordinary circumstances.

FEDERAL ECONOMIC ESPIONAGE ACT

In 1996, the federal government enacted the Economic Espionage Act (EEA), which for the first time specifically brought the theft of trade secrets under federal jurisdiction.[42] On one level, passage of this new statute has tremendous symbolic importance. Over an extended period of time, the U.S. economy has become increasingly dependent on the value of information and other forms of intangible assets. U.S. firms now often opt to have their manufacturing take place in foreign countries, while relying on the licensing of valuable information to sustain their profitability and growth. At the same time, the rapid emergence of computer technologies, electronic mail, and the Internet have subjected the value of these assets to tremendous jeopardy. Although firms go to great lengths to protect their valuable trade secrets, if certain employees want to make copies of important information residing in computer files, they likely can find a way to do it without detection. And once the information is in their hands, they can rapidly disseminate it over the Internet or transfer it to international bidders. In light of these changing conditions, the EEA makes a clear statement. Trade secret protection no longer is merely a topic for local concern and enforcement. Nor is it simply a private matter. Rather, trade secrets have become so vital to the U.S. economy as a whole that they merit specific protection under federal laws.

One of the primary reasons that Congress passed the EEA was to rectify perceived deficiencies in state and federal enforcement of trade secret misappropriation. In the legislative history of the act, Congress indicated that state civil laws, which dominated the trade secret landscape, did not adequately deter trade secret misappropriation in many situations.[43] Often, the aggrieved party does not have the financial resources to meaningfully undertake the investigations that are required in complex civil trade secret cases. Also, some companies might treat the statistical odds of ultimately paying civil judgments for trade secret misappropriation as a cost of doing business. In addition, Congress was aware that the states did not consistently criminalize trade secret theft, and those few that did rarely brought criminal prosecutions under them.[44] Finally, there were no federal statutes that specifically addressed trade secret theft. Federal prosecutors sometimes tried cases under the National Stolen Property Act, but the provisions of this law are more applicable to goods, wares, and merchandise than intellectual property.[45] Similarly, some actions were brought under the federal mail and wire fraud statutes, but they presented certain obstacles, such as the need to prove a "scheme to defraud."[46]

From the title of the act, it is clear that Congress was seriously concerned that foreign companies and governments were relying more and more on espionage to infiltrate U.S. companies and to steal their most valued trade secret possessions. However, the act is not limited to foreign acts of espionage, and indeed, only a few of the provisions deal specifically with international issues. Rather, the EEA makes it a crime to steal trade secrets either in interstate commerce or in foreign commerce. The act is tailored after the UTSA, and is remarkably similar in most respects. For instance, the EEA defines a trade secret very broadly to include "all forms and types of financial, business, scientific, technical, economic or engineering information." In addition, as with the UTSA, the information must derive its value from the fact that it is not known or readily ascertainable by the public and must be subject to reasonable security measures. Since the EEA is a criminal statute, it defines the unlawful activity as trade secret "theft" instead of "misappropriation." The elements, however, are extremely similar, again patterned on the bad dog theory. Thus, those who take the trade secrets as well as those who knowingly receive them are implicated. One difference is that the EEA requires knowledge or intent, whereas under the UTSA, having reason to know may suffice. This again reflects the fact that the EEA establishes a crime and not merely a civil wrong. In addition, as with many criminal statutes, the act prohibits attempts and conspiracies to engage in the targeted activity, which, here, is trade secret theft.

Although it does not really change anything, the language of the EEA demonstrates that Congress was particularly concerned about the theft of digital information. The definition of a trade secret, for instance, specifically recognizes that information may be stored in various electronic forms. Also, the EEA provides some examples of the kinds of activities that constitute trade secret theft. These include such things as uploading, downloading, transmitting, and replicating.

Since the EEA is a criminal statute, private parties may not bring actions under it. Thus, unlike with the UTSA, one company cannot sue or threaten to sue another company under the EEA. Rather, cases may be brought only by the Justice Department. This means that the number of cases that annually may be filed under this statute will be somewhat limited, reflecting the budgets allocated to the Justice Department for criminal enforcement.[47] In addition, the Justice Department has tremendous discretion in determining the types of activities that it might choose to investigate. Thus, the emergence of the EEA does not mean that one should expect federal policies to rapidly supplant trade secret enforcement under state laws. Rather, the EEA is merely a relatively new arrow in the arsenal of weapons that may be used to deter trade secret misappropriation.

Penalties for violating the EEA may be quite severe. Individuals convicted of stealing trade secrets may be imprisoned for up to 10 years and fined up to $500,000. Corporations and other organizations may be fined up to $5 million. The act ups the ante when the theft is done in concert with, or on behalf of, a foreign government, by increasing the potential prison sentence to 15 years and the maximum corporate fine to $10 million. This is one of the more obvious ways that the EEA demonstrates that Congress had a heightened concern with espionage activities authorized by foreign instrumentalities. The EEA also provides that those found guilty of trade secret theft may be required to forfeit not only the proceeds derived from the misappropriation but also the facilities or property used to carry out the crime. A few other criminal statutes, such as the Racketeer Influenced and Corrupt Organizations Act (RICO) and the Comprehensive Drug Abuse Prevention and Control Act, have similar forfeiture provisions, and experience shows that they have the potential to be extremely onerous.[48] It will be interesting to monitor over the next several years the extent of the remedies that are sought by the Justice Department for trade secret theft and the amounts that actually are allowed by the courts. It also should be fascinating to see how often the Justice Department actually sues agents working with foreign governments, and whether the new law serves to deter international espionage efforts.

INTERNATIONAL TRADE SECRET PROTECTION

Trade secret protection, even in the United States, requires a long-term focused effort to maintain the confidentiality of valuable information. All it takes is a momentary period of inattention to allow a critical piece of information to get into the wrong hands. And once this happens, the competitive value of the information may be compromised, or worse, the secret may be destroyed as it is filtered into public forums. At least in the United States there is a cultural tradition of strong trade secret protection laws coupled with an effective judicial system to come to the assistance of a trade secret holder. Thus, if the owner of a trade secret acts quickly enough in the United States, it may convince a court to grant injunctive relief, preventing further dissemination or use of the valuable information.

Conditions change markedly, however, as one enters international markets.[49] Although one may encounter some countries, such as the United Kingdom, Canada, and Australia, where trade secrets enjoy substantial legal protections, there are numerous other nations where different principles apply. And it is difficult to generalize what may be found in terms of trade secrets as one travels across the globe. Some countries have strongly worded trade secret laws, but their judicial systems lack the authority to provide effective relief. Other nations have laws which provide some protection but with numerous caveats which must be carefully scrutinized. And still other countries do not yet have laws or are only beginning to develop them. As with all other forms of intellectual property, the various world nations have widely different philosophies and cultural traditions regarding the protection of trade secrets. The only certain result, therefore, is that a company needs to be especially vigilant before allowing important information to enter foreign countries. It also generally means that one must be ready to markedly increase investments in physical security measures prior to entering the international arena.

The TRIPs Agreement provides that members of the WTO must protect "undisclosed information." Although the term "trade secret" is not used, the definition of undisclosed information is very similar to that of a trade secret in the United States, being based on limited availability, commercial value, and reasonable security measures. The agreement also provides that companies and individuals shall have the possibility of preventing others from using undisclosed information without their consent in a manner contrary to honest commercial practices. A footnote to the text clarifies that dishonest practices include the same kinds of actions that constitute misappropriation in the United States, such as breach of contract or confidence, and other behaviors of a bad dog.[50] On top of this, WTO members are required to enforce their trade secret laws with effective remedies, including injunctions and money damages. Thus, there is reason to hope that over time, the various members of the WTO will move toward a trade secret protection regime that mirrors the one now available in the United States. Of course, some of the nations may pass trade secret laws that are far weaker but nonetheless argue that they comply with the provisions of TRIPs. These will have to be tested under the WTO dispute resolution system. Similarly, it still needs to be ironed out exactly how comprehensive the enforcement must be to satisfy TRIPs requirements. Then, one also needs to contend with the least developed countries, which have until 2005 to bring their laws up to the minimum standard. Finally, there still are some important trading partners that are not yet members of the WTO. For now, therefore, the best that one should expect is that progress will come, but come slowly, in many nations around the world. It certainly would be a serious mistake to assume that trade secrets are as safe abroad as they are in the United States due to the TRIPs Agreement. A very large number of countries still have serious deficiencies, by U.S. standards, in their trade secret protection schemes. Therefore, one needs to check with local legal counsel about national laws and judicial remedies prior to entering any new foreign markets.

As mentioned, it is very hard to predict the specific kinds of trade secret problems that one might encounter in foreign lands. However, there are a few things worth considering. For instance, the laws of most nations respect the importance of contractual relationships, including the provisions of confidentiality agreements. This at least provides an opportunity to protect trade secrets even in countries that do not yet have adequate trade secret protection regimes. Thus confidentiality agreements should be given the highest priority when dealing with employees, suppliers, manufacturers, and others who are entrusted with confidential information in foreign countries. Unfortunately, there may be complications even with confidentiality agreements. One area of concern may be the judicial process, which in many nations can be very frustrating when the need arises to enforce contractual obligations. Also, it is not unusual to find that a court may award money damages for a breach of contract, but that it will refuse to impose an injunction. Money, though, often will not adequately redress the harms from misappropriation. The first priority of the trade secret owner is to stop the spread of the information in its tracks. Without the power of a court-ordered injunction, control easily can be lost. And when this happens, the amount of damage in money terms becomes almost impossible to calculate, since the misappropriation likely will result in harms to a company's competitive position and its technological lead, among a host of other such variables that are difficult to predict and assess. The problem becomes even more pronounced when the trade secrets are taken by parties that do not even have contractual relationships with the firm. Contracts have no role when secrets are obtained through means such as industrial espionage. In these situations, the trade secret holder must rely more heavily on trade secret laws, which may have been only recently established, if they exist at all, and which may not yet enjoy sufficient cultural legitimacy to support the imposition of adequate remedies, such as injunctions.

There may be other problems with handling trade secrets in foreign countries as well. For example, some countries may have laws which establish a maximum amount of time that local firms must maintain the secrecy of information obtained through technology licenses. Others may have policies that allow native licensees to continue using confidential technologies even after their licenses expire. There also may be concerns with how information is treated during litigation. In many countries, legal proceedings are held in public, and it may be hard to guard against the release of specific information. Litigation, therefore, may cause public disclosure of just the information that one wanted to protect in court. One also needs to be careful with the types of information that must be released to regulatory agencies and how those agencies might then protect that information. In this regard, TRIPs at least requires member countries to protect undisclosed test data that are submitted to regulatory agencies for approval of pharmaceutical and agricultural chemical products.

The major lesson from all this is that one must be extremely careful with trade secrets when venturing overseas. The members of the WTO have agreed to pass laws that protect undisclosed information and that can be enforced through court-ordered injunctions. However, it will take some time before these provisions are implemented on an adequate scale. Therefore, one needs to specifically assess the risks in each country where confidential information might be disclosed. And based on those risks, one must formulate the appropriate mix of measures that are necessary to protect the valuable secrets. As mentioned, confidentiality agreements are a must. But clearly, they need to be a last resort in the plan to protect the secrets. Rather, the company must rely primarily on practical security measures so that misappropriation can never take place. Techniques must be used to determine exactly which companies and individual employees can be trusted with valuable information. In addition, extremely tight physical security measures must be implemented. Information has to be strictly controlled so only the minimum portions that must be viewed are released on a need-to-know basis. Also, safeguards against theft and espionage have to be given the highest priority. And finally, one must be willing to perceive that the legal risks in many countries may simply be too excessive to even contemplate the transfer of state-of-the-art technologies. Investments in these environments, if they are made at all, clearly should reveal only obsolete or last-generation technologies.

CONCLUDING REMARKS ABOUT TRADE SECRET PROTECTION

The decision about whether trade secret protection should be used for **AES** is complicated. The answer, in fact, can be given only with reference to particular types of information, their various stages of development, the possible alternatives for protection, and their relative costs. Some of the technical components of **AES** and some processes that are used to make the system may clearly seem to be patentable. While bearing in mind the pitfalls of patent protection, it would probably be appropriate to file patent applications and embark on a patent strategy for these inventions. There may be other aspects of **AES** for which patentability is more questionable. Here, it might make sense to file patent applications but use a trade secret program while the application is pending just in case the patent does not issue. This strategy is most straightforward, of course, if patent protection only is sought in the United States, since information in the patent application then is held in confidence until the patent issues. However, as we know, the policy in many foreign countries and under the Patent Cooperation Treaty is to open patent files to public scrutiny 18 months after the filing date. Likewise, the United States now often publishes information after 18 months when applicants also file abroad. Thus, we may have to make an election between going for the patent or relying on trade secrets before we know the ultimate disposition about the patentability of AES's features. As will be covered in the next two chapters, we might determine that copyright protection is the best vehicle to protect other attributes of AES, particularly the computer programs. And, of course, there likely will be other types of information and improvements for which neither patents nor copyrights hold much promise. For these, trade secret protection is the only reasonable possibility of retaining a proprietary advantage. Finally, we have to consider that some information simply is not susceptible to trade secret protection. For example, it is hard to use trade secret laws to protect information that can be readily determined through reverse engineering once products are distributed to the public. If we hope to protect these aspects, we have to look to patents, copyrights, or some other specific alternative.

One misconception should now be cleared up; trade secret protection is not necessarily the inexpensive option. The costs of maintaining appropriate security can be staggering, far exceeding the total costs of obtaining patents. Thus, one should resist the initial hesitation to consider a patent strategy due to high filing costs and attorneys' fees. It may seem simpler at first blush just to keep the valuable information a secret, but in the end this can be extremely expensive. In addition, trade secret measures may disrupt normal workplace habits and disgruntle certain employees who will resent the apparent Orwellian style of management. Thus, trade secrets must be viewed as one of several options providing a set of strengths and weaknesses. The strategic challenge is selecting the most appropriate protective tool for particular information at the right time.

PRESENTING UNSOLICITED IDEAS TO THIRD PARTIES

When was the last time you thought of a great idea for a product? A wristwatch, say, that wakes up the wearer gently and silently through pulsing vibrations. Did you just laugh it off? Maybe you thought seriously about it for a moment but did not have the desire to make it, experiment with it, or market it. Or maybe you went so far as to develop it but did not know what business steps to take next. How should a person or company proceed in these situations? A natural instinct is to contact a corporation already established in the field, such as Seiko, present the idea to it, and expect appropriate remuneration if the corporation successfully launches the product. However, as we shall see, one who desires compensation must be more cautious when submitting ideas to third parties.

Generally, when it comes to commercial matters, the law will not require a person to do something the person did not somehow promise or agree to do. Contract law is based on the principle of voluntary agreement. Those who enter an agreement are expected to keep their promise. However, one should expect nothing from someone who has not agreed to do anything. A promise does not have to be made explicitly with words. It may be made through conduct or actions. Either way, though, an agreement must be struck before the law will require action.

Suppose we decide to present the watch idea to Seiko executives. If the executives like the idea and choose to use it, we expect to be paid. If they reject it, however, we at least want them to keep the idea confidential so that we might find an alternative way to make money with it. After we submit the concept at a meeting, the executives indicate they are not interested. However, to our surprise, we learn that within a year, Seiko is selling vibrating watches. We naturally feel that our idea has been stolen; we demand compensation; and when that is denied, we march into court knowing that the law will be on our side. However, as the next case demonstrates, the result will only fuel our righteous indignation.

ALIOTTI v. R. DAKIN & CO.
Ninth Circuit Court of Appeals, 1987

FACTS: Shelley Aliotti, a designer of craftwork and toys, worked for Favorite Things, Inc., from 1976 to 1979. She designed soft pillows, stuffed animals, and other items directed toward the children's market.

In November 1978, Bernard Friedman, the president of Favorite Things, telephoned Harold Nizamian, the president of Dakin, to ask whether Dakin would be interested in acquiring Favorite Things. After the conversation, Friedman sent Nizamian a letter and pictures of various products manufactured by Favorite Things. Upon a request for more information from Dakin's board of directors, Friedman sent a presentation booklet, which included data concerning the production and sale of its merchandise. Friedman also sent a current sales brochure, which included photographs of three stuffed toy dinosaurs—Brontosaurus, Stegosaurus and Triceratops—which had been designed by Aliotti and were marketed as the Ding-A-Saur line.

During a March 1979 meeting at Favorite Things' office, Friedman and Aliotti showed two Dakin executives many of Favorite Things' designs, including many products designed by Aliotti. In addition to the three stuffed dinosaurs already marketed by Favorite Things, Aliotti displayed prototypes of three additional Ding-A-Saurs: Tyrannosaurus Rex, Pterodactyl, and Woolly Mammoth. They did not discuss the possibility that Dakin might purchase any particular design. After the meeting, the Dakin executives told Aliotti to contact them if she were interested in being considered for employment at Dakin.

In April 1979, Dakin's board of directors decided not to acquire Favorite Things. In July or August 1979, Dakin began developing its own line of

continued . . .

continued . . .

stuffed dinosaurs, called Prehistoric Pets, and started marketing them in June 1980. The six stuffed animals offered by Dakin were of the same six species as those presented to Dakin by Aliotti. The dinosaurs within the two lines had similar postures and body designs and were soft and nonthreatening. In each line, the Tyrannosaurus had its mouth open, and the winged Pterodactyl served as a mobile. The main difference was that Aliotti's dinosaurs appeared dingy, whereas Dakin's depictions were more accurate. Favorite Things became bankrupt in 1982 and assigned all its rights to Aliotti's designs to Aliotti.

Aliotti sued Dakin alleging that Dakin (1) infringed her copyrights by copying the total concept and feel of her toys and (2) unlawfully appropriated her design ideas. Dakin claimed that its employees independently developed Dakin's dinosaur line. The district court judge granted summary judgment, indicating that Aliotti could not win on her claims at trial even if all her allegations were true. Aliotti appealed, arguing that the case should have gone to trial. For the appeal, the Court of Appeals assumes that Dakin appropriated Aliotti's idea of producing stuffed dinosaur toys.

DECISION AND REASONING:

Copyright Claim. The court determines that summary judgment was appropriate because there is no substantial similarity of protectible expression between the dinosaurs in the two lines.

State Law Claims. Aliotti claims that Dakin breached an implied-in-fact contract by using Aliotti's designs without compensating her and that it committed a breach of confidence by disclosing her designs without permission.

Under California law, for an implied-in-fact contract, one must show (1) that one prepared the work, (2) that one disclosed the work to the offeree for sale, (3) that under all circumstances attending disclosure it can be concluded that the offeree voluntarily accepted the disclosure knowing the conditions on which it was tendered (i.e., the offeree must have the opportunity to reject the attempted disclosure if the conditions were unacceptable), and (4) the reasonable value of the work. If disclosure occurs before it is known that compensation is a condition of its use, no contract will be implied.

Aliotti made her presentation to Dakin not to sell her designs but to help persuade Dakin to buy Favorite Things. She argues that she disclosed her ideas because she hoped to obtain employment with Dakin, but no contract may be implied when an idea has been disclosed not to gain compensation for that idea but for the sole purpose of inducing the defendant to enter a future business relationship. Aliotti argues that by hiring her, Dakin would have obtained her design ideas and put them to work for the company. However, the evidence indicates that Aliotti displayed the dolls before Dakin executives suggested that their company might consider hiring her. No contract will be implied when an "idea man" blurts out the idea without first having struck a bargain, even if the idea has been conveyed with some hope of entering into a contract. Summary judgment on the implied-in-fact contract claim was appropriate.

To prevail on her claim for breach of confidence, Aliotti must show that (1) she conveyed confidential and novel information, (2) Dakin had knowledge that the information was being disclosed in confidence, (3) there was an understanding between Dakin and Aliotti that the confidence be maintained, and (4) there was disclosure or use in violation of the understanding. Constructive notice of confidentiality is not sufficient.

Because three of the Ding-A-Saurs were already on the market, Aliotti could not have conveyed confidential information concerning those dolls. She presented no testimony that Dakin knew that the information was being disclosed in confidence or that the parties agreed that confidence would be maintained. Only constructive knowledge of confidentiality may be inferred from Aliotti's testimony that she was sure there had been some discussion at the meeting about keeping the ideas confidential because "it was presented to them under . . . that these were our ideas, and we were introducing them because they were considering buying the company." Thus, Aliotti's claim for breach of confidence must fall.

The district court properly granted summary judgment to Dakin on Aliotti's claims for copyright infringement, breach of an implied-in-fact contract, and breach of confidence. Affirmed.

The lessons from *Aliotti* are clear. An inventor cannot simply blurt out the idea to a prospective manufacturer and then expect compensation if that idea is subsequently used or revealed. Rather, the inventor must procure an agreement from the company that it will either pay to use the idea or keep it in confidence if it ultimately is rejected.

The result of *Aliotti* may seem harsh at first. However, from the company's perspective, it is entirely logical. It may be that the company had already been working on the concept before the meeting with the inventor. Imagine if Seiko's engineers were finalizing their version of the vibrating watch before our visit to company headquarters. If we had indicated to the Seiko executives the nature of our invention and indicated that compensation was expected for providing further details, they certainly would have refused to listen. The claim that they are indebted to us simply because, at our request, they reviewed our idea, would be overreaching. Also, although the invention seemed unique to us, it may be that the concept had already been around for a while. Maybe it had previously been written up in some trade journals. We could hardly expect Seiko to be bound not to use or disclose an idea that others, including its competitors, could freely use.

The result is that when an inventor approaches a company with an idea, the parties have to deal with different concerns. The inventor needs to ensure that the company somehow agrees, either through words or conduct, to pay for the idea or keep it in confidence. If necessary, the inventor wants the judge or jury that reviews the temporal order of events leading to the disclosure to recognize that the company implicitly understood its obligations prior to the final revelation of the idea. The company, on the other hand, has to make sure that the judge or jury does not misinterpret the chain of events and then erroneously find it responsible to pay for something it did not want.

How Companies Handle Unsolicited Ideas

Companies often are besieged with letters and phone calls containing ideas from inventors. Some of these ideas actually will be good ones, ones that the company eventually adopts, albeit not necessarily because of the unsolicited communications from the inventors. If the company does not deal with these situations carefully, it may face many lawsuits from outraged inventors who assume that the company took advantage of them. Therefore, most companies have established routine procedures for handling submissions of ideas.

When a company receives a letter containing unsolicited ideas, the letter is immediately forwarded to a clerk in charge of handling such matters. Without reviewing the ideas contained therein, the clerk will return the letter to the sender. Along with the returned letter, there normally will be included an explanation of why the company cannot consider the contents. Here, the company will explain that it does not want any misunderstanding between it and the submitter and that it therefore will deal only after entering an explicit agreement regarding the subject matter. The company will append a written waiver with this explanation. If the inventor agrees to the waiver by signing it, then the company will review the ideas. A sample of such an agreement follows.

Waiver for Unsolicited Idea

Up to this point, your ideas and materials have not been reviewed by any person in the Company qualified to evaluate them. If you wish that the Company evaluate them, it will do so only under the following conditions:

1. In consideration for the Company's evaluating your materials, you agree that the Company is released from any liability in connection with your materials except as may result under valid unexpired patents which may have been granted or hereafter may be issued.
2. No obligations or confidential relationships, either express or implied, are assumed by the Company with respect to any materials submitted.
3. In order to fully evaluate the materials submitted to the Company, it may have to disclose them to persons outside the Company. Therefore, the Company is under no obligation to maintain the materials in secrecy.

4. Copies of all materials submitted to the Company may be kept by the Company to prevent misunderstandings regarding the contents of the submissions.

5. The Company is under no obligation to reveal any information concerning its present or future activities in any field.

If these conditions are acceptable, please sign this form without making changes and return it. Upon receipt of the signed form, the Company will evaluate the materials, and you will be advised of its interest.

By signing this form, the inventor explicitly states that the company is free to do whatever it wants with the ideas without any obligations to pay for them unless the inventor obtains a patent. Unless the inventor has a patent or strongly anticipates that one is forthcoming, the inventor should not sign the form.

Advice for Offering Unsolicited Ideas

The language of the waiver and the attached explanatory material strongly urge the inventor to pursue patent rights before working with the company regarding future business arrangements. From a practical standpoint, this makes sense for the company. It may not want to invest time and resources exploring a new idea unless it knows that the concept cannot be readily copied by competitors once the product comes to market. However, the advice makes sense for the inventor as well. Since the company is not readily willing to act on a confidential basis, the inventor's only proprietary option for remuneration is through patent rights. For now, patent priority in the United States goes to whoever can establish the earliest date of invention; in most other countries, the first to file gets the patent. In either case, the inventor should at least file for a patent prior to dealing with the other company. This will preserve substantial procedural advantages in case the relationship turns sour in the future and there is a dispute over who did what first and who told what to whom. If the inventor chooses to file after disclosing the invention to the other company, the inventor should be aware of how patent rights are secured in various countries. For the United States, complete documentation of invention should be kept; for other countries, filing speed may be the critical element. Keep in mind that no matter when filing takes place, by the terms of the waiver, the inventor will have no rights against the company if the patent does not issue. Therefore, if the inventor is not confident about the ultimate outcome in the PTO, the inventor should consider pursuing a different relationship with this company or with another, more receptive entity.

Of course, the whole reason for contacting the company in the first place may have been that the inventor did not want to go through all the trouble of pursuing a patent. Or maybe the inventor knew that the idea is not patentable but still could be lucrative for the company that comes to market with it first. If this is the case, then signing the waiver form clearly is not the correct approach. Rather, the inventor should embark on a strategy of sufficiently enticing the company so that it wants to hear more.

The goal for the inventor is to so intrigue the company with general descriptions of the invention that the company becomes willing to enter at least a nondisclosure agreement in order to learn the crucial details of the idea. In essence, the inventor will use a dangle-the-carrot approach to arouse the company and motivate it to negotiate on terms more favorable than the waiver form offers. Without hearing all the details of the invention, however, the company still will be reluctant to enter unqualified agreements promising nondisclosure and/or payment. Rather, the most likely outcome is some middle-ground arrangement. For example, the company may become willing to enter the following style of agreement.

> The Company agrees to review the invention and to keep the invention and all materials received in confidence. The Company also agrees to pay a reasonable sum and/or royalty if it uses the invention. However, the Company will not be so obligated with respect to any information that it can document (a) was known to it prior to receipt or (b) is or becomes part of the public domain from a source other than the Company.

This provision can be mutually satisfactory. It protects the inventor as long as the idea is unique. This is normally what the inventor is after. Few inventors expect to receive special treatment when they do not actually contribute something valuable to the company. The company also is protected, for it has no obligations concerning information it already has or can freely obtain. Its only burden is to be able to document its awareness of or access to that information. This is something it would rather not do, especially if it has a secret proprietary program already under development. However, it may be willing to take on that risk in order to hear the specifics of what may be an exciting new project.

CONCLUSION

A trade secret protection program must be contemplated by every high-technology business concern. A thoroughly developed strategy using trade secrets in conjunction with patents provides the best way to protect product ideas and information. The other major forms of intellectual property protection—copyrights and trademarks—theoretically are less suitable for ideas and inventions. Copyrights focus on the protection of expressions, and trademarks assist consumers in locating and identifying goods. However, we will find that copyright policy has reached a level of schizophrenia in the high-technology environment, sometimes blurring the distinctions between expressions, ideas, and information. Trademark policy, as well, has reached into new arenas, allowing protection for a host of product characteristics and forms. The next three chapters explore the importance of copyrights and trademarks to those involved with high-technology projects.

NOTES

1. "Apple Settles Suit Against Jobs," Wash. Post (January 18, 1986) at C1.

2. M. Miller, "IBM Sues to Silence Former Employee," Wall St. J. (July 15, 1992) at B1.

3. J. Cody, "AT&T Keeps Rein on Midlevel Defector," Wall St. J. (October 20, 1993).

4. W. Carley, "Did Northwest Steal American's Systems? The Court Will Decide," Wall St. J. (July 7, 1994) at A1.

5. V. Slind-Flor, "Trade Secret Suit Surprises the Experts," Nati'l L. J. (November 2, 1998) at B1.

6. S. Yoder, "High-Tech Firm Cries Trade-Secret Theft, Gets Scant Sympathy," Wall St. J. (October 8, 1992) at A1.

7. V. Slind-Flor, "Charges Fly in Chip War," Nat'l L. J. (April 12, 1993) at 1.

8. "Reebok Sues Spalding over Glove," San Luis Obispo County Telegram-Tribune (July 20, 1991) at B-3; J. Miller, "Genentech Charges Invitron, Monsanto with Misappropriation of Trade Secrets," Wall St. J. (February 11, 1988) at A10.

9. R. Eels and P. Nehemkis, Corporate Intelligence and Espionage (1984), at 115-16.

10. W. Carley, "A Chip Comes in from the Cold: Tales of High-Tech Spying," Wall St. J. (January 19, 1995) at A1.

11. W. Carley, "As Cold War Fades, Some Nations' Spies Seek Industrial Secrets," Wall St. J. (June 17, 1991) at A1.

12. C. Levin, "Trade Secret Thieves Face Fines, Prosecution," Nat'l L. J. (January 27, 1997) at C12 citing Greenlee, "Spies Like Them: How to Protect Your Company From Industrial Spies," 78 Mgmt. Acct. 31 (December 1996); S. Rep. No. 359, 104th Cong., 2d Sess. 7-9 (August 27, 1996) (noting survey by American Society for Industrial Security International).

13. S. Rep. No. 359, 104th Cong., 2d Sess. 7-9 (August 27, 1996) (noting survey by American Society for Industrial Security International).

14. F. McMorris, "Corporate-Spy Case Rebounds on Bristol," Wall St. J. (February 2, 1998) at B4.

15. C. Levin, "Trade Secret Thieves Face Fines, Prosecution," Nat'l L. J. (January 27, 1997) at C12 (citing News Release by War Room Research L.L.C. (November 21, 1996) at 2).

16. In the Restatement (Third) of Unfair Competition, efforts to maintain the secrecy of information is only a factor in judging whether the information is a trade secret and is not a separate requirement. Restatement (Third) of Unfair Competition § 39, comment g (1995).

17. Misappropriation may come about in another way. When a person acquires information by mistake and learns that it is trade secret information before relying on it in a material way, then that person misappropriates the information by using or disclosing it. Uniform Trade Secrets Act § 1(2)(ii)(C).

18. Minnesota Mining & Manufacturing Co. v. Johnson & Johnson Orthopaedics Inc., 976 F.2d 1559 (Fed. Cir. 1992).

19. When the samples were sent to J&J, 3M had applied for a patent, but one had not yet issued.

20. K. Kelly, "When a Rival's Trade Secret Crosses Your Desk . . . ," Bus. Wk. (May 20, 1991) at 48.

21. Minnesota Mining & Manufacturing Co. v. Johnson & Johnson, 976 F.2d at 1581. The trial court found for 3M and doubled the damages for patent infringement, awarding a total of almost $117 million. The Federal Circuit affirmed this award on appeal.

22. Q-Co Industries, Inc. v. Hoffman, 625 F. Supp. 608 (S.D.N.Y. 1985).

23. M. Miller, "IBM Sues to Silence Former Employee," Wall St. J. (July 15, 1992) at B1.

24. Pepsico, Inc. v. Redmond, 54 F.3d 1262 (7th Cir. 1995).

25. F. McMorris, "Judge Restricts Two Executives Despite Lack of Noncompete Pacts," Wall St. J. (November 25, 1997) at B10.

26. See M. Lynn, "Is 'Team Raiding' Misappropriation?" Nat'l L. J. (February 8, 1999) at C10.

27. *Id.* at C11.

28. *See* M. Levinson and T. Gerend, "New U.S. Doctrine Aids Trade Secrets," IP Worldwide (July/August 1998), located at www.ipww.com.

29. Statement of Robert Swanson, CEO of Linear Technology Corp., quoted in J. Miller, "Big Firms Pursue Start-Ups with Suits," Wall St. J. (March 24, 1989) at B1.

30. S. Yoder, "High-Tech Firm Cries Trade-Secret Theft, Gets Scant Sympathy," Wall St. J. (October 8, 1992) at A1.

31. People v. Eubanks, 14 Cal. 4th 580, 927 P.2d 310 (December 23, 1996).

32. *See* R. M. Halligan, "The Recently Enacted Economic Espionage Act, Which Makes Trade Secret Theft a Federal Crime, Specially Addresses Theft Perpetrated Via the Internet," Nat'l L. J. (December 9, 1996) at B6; 104 S. Rep. 359, 104th Cong., 2d Sess. [S. 1556].

33. R. M. Halligan, "The Recently Enacted Economic Espionage Act, Which Makes Trade Secret Theft a Federal Crime, Specially Addresses Theft Perpetrated Via the Internet," Nat'l L. J. (December 9, 1996) at B6.

34. M. Epstein and S. Levi, "Protecting Trade Secret Information: A Plan for Proactive Strategy," Bus. Law. (May 1988) at 887.

35. G. Zachary, "At Apple Computer Proper Office Attire Includes a Muzzle," Wall St. J. (October 6, 1989) at A1.

36. In 2000, the DVD Copy Control Association brought a trade secret suit against individuals who were involved with cracking its Content Scrambling System (CSS), an encryption system used to prevent copying of copyrighted materials stored on DVDs. The defendants alleged that the CSS was not a trade secret because it used a 40-bit encryption system, which they claimed was not reasonable security. On a motion for a preliminary injunction, the judge stated that the security was reasonable, especially since its limited strength was required by certain international export regulations. DVD Copy Control Association, Inc. v. McLaughlin, Case Nol CV 786804 Sup. Ct., (Jan. 20, 2000).

37. McKeown and G. Wrenn, "The Stakes on Secrecy Are Rising," Nat'l L. J. (February 24, 1992) at 27. See Rockwell Graphic Systems Inc. v. DEV Industries Inc., 925 F.2d 174 (7th Cir. 1993).

38. M. Epstein and S. Levi, "Protecting Trade Secret Information: A Plan for Proactive Strategy," Bus. Law. (May 1988) at 907.

39. For companies involved with the Internet, a reasonable time may be less than one year, given the dynamic and rapidly changing nature of the industry. *See* Earthweb v. Schlack, 1999 U.S. Dist. LEXIS 16700 (S.D.N.Y. 1999).

40. Cal. Bus. & Prof. Code § 16600.

41. *See* R. Gilson, "The Legal Infrastructure of High Technology Industrial Districts: Silicon Valley, Route 128, and Covenants Not to Compete," 74 N.Y.U. L. Rev. 575, 625-26 (June 1999).

42. Economic Espionage Act of 1996, Pub. L. No. 104-294 (October 11, 1996) (codified at 18 U.S.C. §§ 1831–1839).

43. S. Rep. No. 359, 104th Cong., 2d Sess. (August 27, 1996).

44. H. Rep. No. 788, 104th Cong., 2d Sess. 7 (September 16, 1996).

45. R. M. Halligan, "The Recently Enacted Economic Espionage Act, Which Makes Trade Secret Theft a Federal Crime, Specially Addresses Theft Perpetrated Via the Internet," Nat'l L. J. (December 9, 1996) at B6.

46. *Id.*

47. By the beginning of 1999, the U.S. attorney general had brought fewer than a dozen cases under the Economic Espionage Act. *See* D. Rovella, "Trial Nears for Untested Secrets Law," Nat'l L. J. (March 8, 1999) at B1.

48. C. Levin, "Trade-Secret Thieves Face Fines, Prosecution," Nat'l L. J. (Janaury 27, 1997).

49. For good discussions of international trade secret policies and strategies, see J. Forstner, "Globally, Best Trade Secret Protection Is Oneself," Nat'l L. J. (October 19, 1998) at C22; J. Dratler, Intellectual Property Law (Law Journal Seminars-Press [1991 & Supp. 1999]) at § 4.07.

50. Some of the acts contrary to honest commercial practices include "breach of contract, breach of confidence and inducement to breach" and "acquisition of undisclosed information by third parties who knew, or were grossly negligent in failing to know, that such practices were involved in the acquisition."

Copyright Protection: The Basics

Copyright policy has become the most controversial subject in the high-technology legal arena. Federal copyright laws originated in the early 1900s to protect the creative investments of authors and artists from those who otherwise might profit from simply copying their works. This fundamental objective remains the same today, but advances in technology have changed many of the basic parameters for protection. For instance, there are new forms of authorship that were never contemplated in the formative stages of copyright. Clearly, computer programs were not on the minds of legislators in these early periods. Also, the advent of digital technologies has created new ways to store, alter, distribute, and display creative works. There once was a time when the world of artistic creations was very localized, being highly dependent on fragile media such as paper and ink. However, art now can be digitized, essentially freeing it from the bounds of tangible media and allowing it to become virtually universal. In addition, there has been substantial change in the ways that works may be copied, reducing the cost and time of reproduction and increasing the quality. Just think how photocopying was a revolution to traditional typesetting systems. And consider how computer and digital techniques are creating change now. All you have to do is contemplate how easy it would be for you to scan a copyrighted photograph or poem into your computer and then e-mail it to thousands of friends around the world. Or better yet, you could simply post it on an Internet site, enabling literally millions of people to view it or download it.

As in most areas of the law, change creates new questions, which necessitate new legal solutions. The federal copyright statute has been amended repeatedly to accommodate the forces of change. However, Congress tends to react slowly, thereby leaving temporal gaps when the copyright statute does not satisfactorily answer the arising concerns. This is especially true, as now, when the pace of change is so rapid. During these periods, it is up to the courts to fashion equitable solutions by fitting the current issues into the outmoded legislative frameworks.

As we explore how judges address modern issues, we will see how they are influenced by basic human nature. What parts of computer programs should be protected by copyrights? Do Internet service providers have any responsibility when customers upload copyrighted works onto their servers for others to copy? Can Internet framing or linking be the basis for copyright infringement? When disputes about such issues arise in courts, judges do not have the luxury of waiting for Congress to craft legislative solutions, since the parties expect an immediate determination. Thus, judges have to enter uncharted territory based on wisdom and instinct. And to do so, we will find, they look for answers to new questions from those things that are old and familiar, and they seek guidance about intangibles from those things that are concrete and tangible. Unfortunately, the traditional frameworks never fit perfectly, resulting in disagreements about which to use. Is it best to analyze a computer program like an instructional manual, since the program tells a computer how to operate? If so, the program should enjoy substantial copyright protection. However, it may make more sense to regard the program like a gear in a machine. But if this is so, copyright seems much less appropriate. We will see that the struggle in the courts about many of these novel technological issues is to find the proper analogy. And the struggle can be intense, because the uncertainties are so pronounced while the social and economic effects may be enormous. This often means that the debate begins in the courts but does not end there. Rather the court decisions may serve as the springboard for public outrage, media attention, and congressional appeals to redirect the judicial policy choices.

This chapter and the next review the major copyright concepts bearing on the management of high technologies. Chapter 5 provides an introduction to the basic principles of copyright protection. Here, we shall explore the rights provided by copyright, who may own those rights, and what one must do to obtain them. Such topics as the amount of protection afforded to computer databases and the rights of independent contractors are raised in these sections. The chapter also outlines certain key exceptions to the general rights, most notably the fair use exception and its applicability to such high-technology issues as home video recording and digital audio recording. Chapter 5 ends with a discussion of how one proves copyright infringement and its relevance to certain corporate practices, such as "cleanroom" development techniques. Exhibit 5.1 provides an overview of the topics covered in Chapter 5.

Chapter 6 focuses on selected key copyright issues bearing specifically on the management of technology. Obviously, the protection of computer software by copyright is a major component. This includes the so-called look-and-feel controversy and the protection of user interfaces. The discussion then moves into an associated area—the protection of industrial designs and architecture. The chapter next explores how new technological capabilities, such as digital sampling and imaging, have created opportunities and challenges for artists, and considers the role

Exhibit 5.1
Fundamental Aspects of Copyright Protection in the United States

- ■ **What May Be Protected By Copyright**
  - Original works of authorship
    - — Expressions
      - – Not ideas, processes, systems or methods of operation
    - — Not copied from another
    - — Nominal creativity
  - Relevance to databases
  - **CASE:** *Feist Publications v. Rural Telephone Service*

- ■ **Rights Provided By Copyright**
  - The fundamental rights
    - — Reproduce, derive, distribute, perform and display
  - New limited digital audio transmission right
  - Moral rights
  - Fair use
    - — Equitable defense for violating rights
    - — Application to videocassette recorders
      - – **CASE:** *Sony Corp. of America v. Universal City Studios*
    - — Relevance to digital audio recording formats
      - – **CASE:** *Recording Industry Association of America v. Diamond Multimedia Systems*

- ■ **Copyright Ownership**
  - Author
  - Works made for hire
    - — Employees vs. independent contractors
  - Joint works
  - **CASE:** *Community for Creative Non-Violence v. Reid*

- ■ **Obtaining Copyright Protection**
  - No action required
  - Reasons for registration
    - — Prima facie evidence
    - — Statutory damages
    - — Attorneys' fees and costs
    - — Litigation
  - Reasons for including copyright notice
    - — Defeats claim of innocent infringement
  - Trade secret protection issues

continued

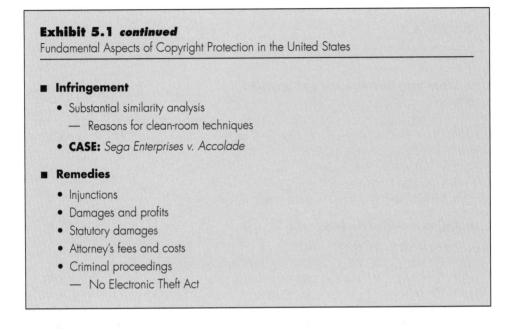

Exhibit 5.1 continued
Fundamental Aspects of Copyright Protection in the United States

- ■ **Infringement**
  - • Substantial similarity analysis
    - — Reasons for clean-room techniques
  - • **CASE:** Sega Enterprises v. Accolade
- ■ **Remedies**
  - • Injunctions
  - • Damages and profits
  - • Statutory damages
  - • Attorney's fees and costs
  - • Criminal proceedings
    - — No Electronic Theft Act

that copyright may play in this changing environment. Finally, Chapter 6 moves specifically to the Internet. The Internet has brought nothing less than a fundamental paradigm shift to the strategic operations of business. Not surprisingly, the new business model is generating winners and losers at astonishing rates, setting the stage for tension and disputes as power is transferred. The law, of course, must serve to arbitrate these disputes, and in so doing, charts the course for the future. The Internet has become all-pervasive, and so too have the legal issues that it has raised. But at the center of the legal maelstrom are certain key participants, and of them, copyrights may be the most crucial. It is therefore fitting that Chapter 6 concludes with an analysis of how copyright policy applies to the Internet.

AES

Within these chapters, we must also consider how copyright might be used to protect certain aspects of the **Audio Enhancement System**. Will copyright protection extend to the computer program within the **AES**, even though that program is an integral component of the product? If so, is the entire program protectible, or just portions of it? Can purchasers of the **AES** tear the system apart and make copies of the program to learn how it works? Who owns the copyright to the program? Is it our company, or possibly another company that made the program for us? Also, can we use copyright protection to keep other companies from duplicating the external appearance of the units? These and other questions regarding copyright protection for the **AES** will be addressed in these two chapters.

What May Be Protected by Copyright

Protection of Original Expressions

By the terms of the copyright statute, one can obtain copyright protection for original works of authorship fixed in any tangible medium of expression. The word "original" is not defined by the Copyright Act, and obviously it could be a substantial hurdle to protection depending on the way it is interpreted. After all, your first inclination probably was that "original" raises some objective standard of novelty, possibly akin to that in patent law. However, the courts have interpreted this word to mean that the work must be original to the author. By that interpretation, a work is original to the extent that it manifests some personal creative effort. This is true, even if the resultant work turns out to be exactly like one that is already existing and publicly distributed. As Judge Learned Hand once described it, if by magic a person were to compose anew Keats's "Ode on a Grecian Urn" without having previously known of its existence, then the work would be original and capable of copyright protection.[1] The word "original," therefore, normally does not present a problem for one contemplating copyright protection as long as the work encompasses at least some very minimal amount of personal creativity. Still, there are contexts in which the originality requirement may have substantial financial ramifications. *Feist Publications v. Rural Telephone Service*, presented in this chapter, provides an important illustration with possibly wide-ranging implications.

The phrase "works of authorship," according to the statute, comprises a wide array of categories. One may receive copyright protection for works that are literary, musical, dramatic, or choreographic. Audiovisual works, such as movies, and sound recordings also are subject to copyright protections. In addition, pictures, graphics, and sculptures may be protected through copyright to the extent that they are not inseparable components of useful products. These categories have been interpreted broadly to cover many new forms of technological products. Video games, for instance, are considered audiovisual works, and computer programs usually are seen as literary works. In addition, to bring the U.S. law into conformity with the Berne Convention, the Copyright Act was amended in 1988 to include architectural works within the protectible realm.

Probably the most critical feature of copyright is that it protects only expressions. This is substantiated by language in the copyright statute that provides that in no case does copyright protection extend to any idea, procedure, process, system, concept, principle, or discovery. Here, then, is an important dividing line between copyrights and utility patents. If one wants federal protection for a product idea, process, or system, then one must look to the patent system rather than copyrights to receive protection. This does not mean that patent protection will necessarily be available. As you know, not every idea is a proper subject for patent protection, and those that are must meet demanding requirements. Still, barring a special federal system of protection such as that for semiconductors, federal protection for publicly disclosed ideas can be derived, if at all, only from a patent. Copyright, on the other hand, never protects ideas. Rather, it covers the ways of expressing them. For example, suppose an author writes a book that describes a new system of accounting, and as part of the book provides various forms necessary to implement that system. A copyright in the book would protect only this author's particular version of expressing how the system works. Any person reading the book can use the accounting ideas so expressed. Also, since the forms are an essential component of the accounting system, they may be freely reproduced and used as well.[2]

As we shall see, distinguishing between the ideas and expressions of any work, even the simplest story, is never an easy task. This book, for example, has a great deal of protectible expression, but it also relates numerous ideas and facts about intellectual property protection. Clearly the copyright in this book cannot give the author the exclusive right to relay these essential matters. However, the analysis can become more complicated. For instance, you might consider whether even the particular organization of this book, including the arrangement and selection of topics, constitutes an unprotectible idea about how best to teach this subject. New types of technologies strain the dichotomy between ideas and expressions even further because they integrate creative expression within useful products. For instance, with a computer program, how does one determine where the protectible expression ends and the unprotectible idea or system begins? Similarly, with an industrial design, how does one determine whether a feature is part of the operational system or simply enhances beauty? The idea/expression dichotomy raises many difficult and substantial questions, which will be pursued later in Chapter 6.

In sum, copyright rewards creativity in expression. Ideas, concepts, facts of nature, and the like are not the subject of copyright; only the ways that they are expressed or communicated are. The expression does not have to be novel; it simply must result from some independent creative process. The following case illustrates the application and interplay of these copyright principles.

FEIST PUBLICATIONS, INC. V. RURAL TELEPHONE SERVICE
United States Supreme Court, 1991

FACTS: Rural Telephone Service (Rural) is a publicly regulated telephone company that solely provides phone service in northwestern Kansas. By law, it is required to issue annually a telephone directory, consisting of white pages and yellow pages. The white pages list in alphabetical order the names, towns, and telephone numbers of Rural's phone service subscribers. Rural obtains this information easily when subscribers sign up for telephone service. Rural distributes its directory free of charge to its subscribers but earns revenue by selling yellow page advertisements. Feist Publications, Inc. (Feist) specializes in area-wide telephone directories that cover much larger geographical areas than do those of the local phone service companies. Feist also distributes its phone books for free but competes vigorously with local phone companies, such as Rural, for yellow page advertising.

Since Feist lacked easy independent access to subscriber information, it offered to pay the local phone companies for the right to use the information in their white page listings. Rural refused to grant this right. Although Feist attempted to gather the information itself, it had to copy certain listings from Rural's directory to complete its directory.

Rural sued Feist for copyright infringement. The district court determined that the listings were protectible by copyright and that Feist unlawfully copied them. The Court of Appeals affirmed. The Supreme Court granted certiorari to determine whether the copyright in Rural's directory protects the names, towns, and telephone numbers copied by Feist.

DECISION AND REASONING: This case concerns the interaction of two well-established propositions. The first is that facts are not copyrightable; the other that compilations of facts generally are. The most fundamental axiom of copyright law is that no authors may copyright their ideas or the facts they narrate. At the same time, however, it is beyond dispute that certain compilations of facts may be protected by copyright. There is an undeniable tension between these two propositions.

The key to resolving the tension lies in understanding why facts are not copyrightable. The sine qua non of copyright is originality. "Original," as the term is used in copyright, means only that the work was independently created by the author (as opposed to copied from other works) and that it possesses at least some minimal degree of creativity. To be sure, the requisite level of creativity is extremely low. Originality does not signify novelty; a work may be original even though it closely resembles other works so long as the similarity is fortuitous and not the result of copying.

Facts may not be copyrighted because they are not created. Rather, they are discovered. All facts, whether scientific, historical, biographical, or news of the day, are part of the public domain and may not be appropriated by any individual through copyright. Factual compilations, on the other hand, may possess the requisite originality. The compilation author typically chooses the facts to include, in what order to place them, and how to arrange the collected data so that they may be used effectively by readers. These choices as to selection and arrangement, so long as they are made independently by the compiler and entail a minimal degree of creativity, are sufficiently original to be protected through copyright.

This protection is subject to an important limitation. Merely because a work is copyrighted does not mean that every element of the work is protected. Copyright protection extends only to those components of a work

continued . . .

continued . . .

that are original to the author. Copyright protection in factual compilations therefore does not extend to the facts themselves. Only the selection and arrangement of those facts, if original, may be protected. Thus, subsequent compilers are free to use the facts listed; they are restricted by copyright only from copying those aspects of selection and arrangement that are original. To this end, copyright ensures authors the right to their original expression but encourages others to build freely upon the ideas and information conveyed by a work. This principle, known as the idea/expression dichotomy, applies to all works of authorship.

Unfortunately, some lower courts have interpreted the copyright statute inappropriately in the past. These courts extended copyright protection to facts based on a faulty "sweat of the brow" theory that copyright should serve as a reward for the hard work that goes into discovering facts. However, this misplaces the role of copyright. Under the copyright statute, facts are never original. Any protectible originality that may exist in a factual compilation is limited to the way the facts are presented.

However, not every selection or arrangement will pass muster. Originality requires that the author make the selection independently and with some minimal level of creativity. There remains a narrow category of works in which the creative spark is utterly lacking or so trivial to be virtually nonexistent.

There is no doubt that Feist took from Rural's white pages a substantial amount of factual information. Certainly, the raw data are uncopyrightable facts. The question that remains is whether Rural selected and arranged these uncopyrightable facts in an original way. The selection and arrangement in Rural's directory is entirely typical and could not be more obvious. It publishes the most basic information and arranges it alphabetically by surname. The end product is a garden-variety white pages directory lacking the modicum of creativity necessary for copyright protection.

Because Rural's white pages lack the requisite originality, Feist's use of the listings cannot constitute infringement. This decision should not be construed as demeaning Rural's efforts in compiling its directory, but rather as making clear that copyright rewards originality, not effort.

The judgment of the Court of Appeals is reversed.

Protection of Databases

Feist is important not only because of its clear exposition of what constitutes copyrightable subject matter but also because of its potential impact on various new, technology-based products. Developers and marketers of computer databases will be particularly affected by this decision. The range of databases has exploded in recent years. A small sample would include databases for or regarding creditworthiness, target marketing, legal and financial research, airline flights, television audiences, hospital patients, and business clients and customers. Clearly, tremendous effort is put into developing these bases. However, *Feist* limits the degree of protection provided through copyright. Now it is clear that the individual pieces of data are not protected by copyright; only the selection and arrangement of that data may be covered, and then only if done in a sufficiently creative way. This ruling will affect the ways that many of the companies providing these services do business and may diminish potential profitability. For example, these companies may have to rely more on state trade secret laws than on copyright to protect the valuable aspects of their bases. But as you know, trade secret protection can be cumbersome and difficult to maintain. In addition, trade secret protection may not be appropriate for widely disseminated products and thus may be preempted by federal patent or copyright policy. We will consider that issue further when we cover shrink-wrap licenses in Chapter 9.

In 1996, the European Union (EU) passed a directive that charts a somewhat different course for the protection of databases in Europe. Under the directive, the role of copyright in protecting databases is very similar to that in the United States. Copyright protection is available for databases, but it extends only to the selection and arrangement of the data and not to the contents themselves. This policy, therefore, conforms to U.S. copyright principles, as articulated in *Feist*. The directive parts ways with U.S. database doctrines, however, by establishing a sui generis right in the contents of databases. The directive creates a "right for the maker of the database to prevent the unauthorized extraction or re-utilization, from the database, of its contents, in whole or substantial part, for commercial purposes." The term of the protection is 15 years from the date the database is made available to the public. According to its preamble, the directive seeks to safeguard the financial and professional investments incurred in collecting data. Therefore, the directive allows the maker of a database to have exclusive rights to facts, based on the sweat-of-the-brow theory that was rejected by the U.S. Supreme Court in *Feist*.

The EU directive identifies a number of exceptions to the sui generis right for data protection. For instance, the user can extract insubstantial portions of the database for commercial purposes as long as the source is acknowledged. Also, the directive provides that a fair and nondiscriminatory license to extract materials must be provided if they cannot be independently collected from any other source. One other aspect of the directive is very important to U.S. database makers. The sui generis right against extraction is available to non-EU nationals only if their home country provides comparable protection to databases produced by EU nationals. Since the United States does not yet provide comparable protection for makers of databases, be they from the EU or from the United States, the proposed EU sui generis right does not apply to U.S. nationals in the EU. However, this needs to be watched closely, since numerous attempts have been made in the United States since 1996 to convince Congress to adopt a sui generis right for data protection. Although these efforts had not resulted in legislation as of 1999, the issue certainly is far from dead in the United States.[3]

In 1996, the World Intellectual Property Organization (WIPO) adopted two treaties intended to deal with certain copyright issues raised by new digital technologies.[4] One provision within these treaties specifies that the copyright laws in the member countries must protect compilations of data, but not the data itself.[5] This conforms to U.S. law as articulated in *Feist*. Interestingly, while the two treaties were being negotiated, the WIPO members also considered a separate proposed Database Treaty that would have created a sui generis right in data akin to that now required under the EU database directive. The proposal raised enormous controversy, pitting database developers against researchers, libraries, scientists, and other database users. Due to the controversy and the perceived lack of sufficient public discussion, the Database Treaty was at least temporarily tabled in 1996. However, it likely will reemerge as WIPO continues to tackle developing copyright issues raised by the digital environment.

RIGHTS PROVIDED BY COPYRIGHT

The Basic Exclusive Rights

Section 106 of the Copyright Act lists six exclusive rights that one enjoys with a copyright. Five of these are traditional in historic terms, while the sixth was only recently adopted to deal with special problems encountered by developers of sound recordings due to new digital technologies. The first, and probably most important, right offered by copyright is the exclusive right to reproduce a work. No one may copy those elements of a work that are protected by copyright without permission. This does not mean that an entire work is off-limits to copying; only the protected expression is. Thus, copyright protection for a database does not give one the right to prevent others from copying the data. Rather the exclusive right to reproduce extends only to the original selection and arrangement of those data. Similarly, as we shall see, copyright protection in computer programs may extend only to certain elements of the program, thereby creating a situation where parts of the program may be reproduced freely while other aspects may be copied only with permission. Keep in mind too that the reproduction right, like all the other rights, may at times be qualified by other provisions of the copyright statute, allowing others to copy even protected expression under certain special circumstances, such as when there is a fair use.

Copyright protection also provides a copyright owner the exclusive right to prepare derivative works. A derivative work is a transformation or adaptation of the protected work, such as a translation, dramatization, motion picture, sound recording, or abridgment. Thus, if one writes a novel, then one has the exclusive right to develop a screenplay based on the novel for television. In addition, copyright law in the United States has for some time now provided three other rights to copyright holders. These are the exclusive right to distribute copies of the work, and the rights to perform and to display the work publicly.

Suppose Harry Hacker develops a BASIC-language computer program, which is protected by copyright. The copyright gives Harry the exclusive rights to make copies and improvements of the program, to distribute them, and to display them publicly. Harry believes that this program could be very popular and might sell for a lot of money. However, Harry's love is programming, not business. Thus, he would like others to market the program for him. Under the Copyright Act, Harry may give others permission through a license to enjoy any or all of his exclusive rights. Thus, he might make a contract with an established software company, granting to it, for a fee, permission to make copies of the work and to distribute those copies to the public. Harry also thinks that there are potential customers who might prefer the program written in another language such as Pascal. He knows that his friend Tammy is more skilled in that language than he. Thus, if he wants, he may enter into a contractual arrangement with Tammy wherein he gives her permission to make the derivative work in Pascal and for which he promises to pay remuneration. He also may grant Tammy permission to make and distribute copies of that Pascal program if he also would like her to be involved in marketing. The key is that Harry has complete control over the set of protected rights. He can retain all the rights, or he may divide them and give others permission to enjoy them. Such permission may be exclusive or nonexclusive, depending on the wishes of the parties. Harry may even completely transfer ownership in any individual right or in the whole program if he so chooses. Clearly, Harry has substantial flexibility to profit from his bundle of protected rights.

The Digital Transmission Right for Sound Recordings

In 1995, a limited new right was added to the Copyright Act for the benefit of copyright owners of sound recordings. Specifically, Section 106 was amended to include a sixth copyright privilege, providing that "in the case of sound recordings," the owner of the copyright has the exclusive right "to perform the copyrighted work by means of a digital audio transmission." In order to understand the basic rationale for this amendment, we need to briefly enter the complex world of how copyrights protect musical creations.

Copyrights in music are more complicated than those in literature because musical recordings encompass not one but two separate copyrights. Consider how an audio recording of a hit song might be developed. First, a musical artist, let's say Paul Simon, must write the composition for the song. As he formulates the song, Paul Simon will memorialize it in some fashion, perhaps by writing the composition on paper. Clearly, at this juncture Paul Simon has copyright privileges in the composition, since it is an original work of authorship and it is fixed in a tangible medium. Therefore, except for one particular important exception specifically provided in the Copyright Act, Paul Simon enjoys the full spectrum of traditional exclusive rights provided by copyright. This means that anyone who wishes to record, distribute, or publicly perform the song, or who wants to arrange a new composition based on it, must receive permission from Paul Simon before proceeding. The notable exception, provided in Section 115, states that after an artist distributes recordings of the song, such as on CDs, any other person may make and distribute separate recordings of that song, as long as a statutorily defined license fee, called a "compulsory license," is paid to the copyright owner of the composition.

After developing the composition for the song, Paul Simon next must have the song recorded to his satisfaction. To do this, he likely will have to hire various band members and singers. He also will need the services of a sophisticated recording studio. The final recording will involve the sounds contributed by the musical artists in conjunction with the creative audio enhancements provided by the recording studio, such as the placement of microphones and the mixing of audio signals. Thus, based on his composition, Paul Simon has given permission for the recording of an original musical session, which has creative elements that are separate from the composition. Or, saying this another way, the musical and technical participants jointly create an original work of authorship that merits its own copyright protection. The Copyright Act recognizes this by granting certain copyright privileges to the creative developers of the particular sound recording. However, prior to 1995, these rights were more limited than those granted to the composition upon which the recording was based. Specifically, Section 114 granted to the copyright owners in the sound recording only the exclusive rights to duplicate the recorded version, to distribute it (for instance in CDs), and to prepare derivative works "in which the actual sounds fixed in the sound recording are rearranged, remixed, or otherwise altered in sequence or quality."

Notably, though, the owner of the sound recording copyright, unlike the composition owner, had no right to keep others from performing the song. This resulted in some interesting consequences. However, to fully appreciate them, consider first the business reality of dealing with recording studios. When Paul Simon and the other musical artists contracted with the recording studio to record, market, and distribute the recorded version of the composition, they almost certainly licensed all their copyright privileges in the sound recording to the studio. Therefore, Paul Simon likely retained his ownership in the composition copyright while the studio became the owner of the copyright in the sound recording. Paul Simon is paid for his creative efforts in two ways. First, the studio remunerated him under some formula for the right to record the composition and to own the copyright in the recording. In addition, radio stations that want to play the song must get permission from Paul Simon to perform the recorded version of the composition publicly over the airwaves. This they likely will do by paying a fee, often negotiated by what are called license rights societies, such as ASCAP or BMI. The deal also makes sense for the recording studio, at least when the sound recording is distributed as part of an album CD through traditional retail outlets. This is because the recording studio will earn compensation through its sales of CDs to the audio retailers.

The emergence of digital transmission technologies, such as cable services and the Internet, threatened the traditional business dynamic. Prior to digital capabilities, the recording studios were not overly dismayed that radio stations did not have to pay them for the rights to play (or perform) sound recordings publicly. After all, sales of CDs often occur because listeners hear selected songs over the radio.

Thus, typical radio airplay is like free advertising for the recording studios. In addition, recording studios rarely lost sales due to radio airplay. It is the unusual listener who might be content to have merely a taped recording of a particular song aired over a radio broadcast rather than the entire CD.

Consider, though, how digital transmission technologies might upset this traditional balance. As one example, I might buy the Paul Simon CD from a retailer, along with hundreds of others, and establish a form of digital jukebox. I might then persuade subscribers to pay me a fee for which I would perform selected albums or songs for them at their request. As the Copyright Act read before 1995, I would have to pay a fee to composition owners, such as Paul Simon, for the right to perform the recording, but not to the recording studio. If the subscribers have new digital audio recording machines, they have the capability to make perfect digital copies of their selections. The legal implications of making such digital duplications will be discussed in the next section. But assuming the practice is legal, then my customers will have no reason to go to the store and purchase CDs. Thus, the recording studios might lose the most important source of income that they have for recording the album.

In 1995, Congress passed the Digital Performance Right in Sound Recordings Act to address this potential problem. The act adds the sixth copyright privilege, specifically granting to sound recording owners the right to perform their works by digital audio transmissions. The act, though, provides for numerous conditions and limitations on this right, which for the most part are too detailed for the purposes of this book.[6] In a nutshell, though, the act separates digital transmissions into three types: (1) subscription transmissions, for which customers pay a fee, but do not select the sound recordings that are delivered over the service; (2) interactive services, which enable customers to request particular selections for a fee; and (3) nonsubscription transmissions (which are like current radio broadcasts), in which no fee is paid to receive the transmission. As you might expect, sound recording studios are most worried about interactive services and least concerned about nonsubscription transmissions. The act, therefore, establishes that a nonsubscription transmission is not an infringement of the new right. This means that nonsubscription services do not have to pay a fee to sound recording copyright owners. Those engaging in subscription services either may negotiate licenses with the studios or, if they meet various conditions, pay a statutorily defined royalty fee. Finally, a business that establishes an interactive service must negotiate individual licenses with the sound recording copyright owner to make the transmission. Again, these provisions are very detailed and should be consulted if you have further interest.

FAIR USE AND OTHER EXCEPTIONS TO COPYRIGHT PROTECTION

The Copyright Act, in Sections 107–120, lists a number of exceptions to the set of protected rights. Most of them are quite specific, applying in only very special contexts. However, one should always refer to these sections to ascertain whether they do or do not apply to a contemplated practice. For example, Section 109 states that one who owns a copy of a protected work may distribute that copy without getting permission from the copyright owner. Thus, when you are finished with this book, you may sell or give it to another without asking for permission from the publisher. This exception, called the first-sale doctrine, therefore qualifies the exclusive right of the copyright owner to distribute copies of that owner's work. Other sections provide exceptions for libraries, for certain performances and displays, for sound recordings, for computer programs, and for a variety of other specialized uses. There are even exceptions to exceptions embedded in these sections. For instance, one who owns a copy of a sound recording or a computer program may not rent that copy to another without obtaining permission from the copyright owner, notwithstanding the provisions of the first-sale doctrine.

The most notable and highly publicized exception to a copyright owner's exclusive rights is the fair-use exception provided in Section 107 of the Copyright Act. Section 107 states that one may, without permission, make a fair use of a copyrighted work for purposes such as criticism, comment, news reporting, teaching, scholarship, or research. What constitutes a fair use is to be determined by the equities of the particular situation, based on an evaluation of four factors:

1. the purpose of the use, including whether the use is of a commercial nature or is for nonprofit educational reasons;
2. the nature of the copyrighted work;
3. the amount and substantiality of the portion used in relation to the whole copyrighted work; and
4. the effect of the use upon the potential market for or value of the copyrighted work.

The Copyright Act provides little explicit direction on how to evaluate these factors or on how much proportional weight to give each of them. Thus, if there is litigation, it is up to the court to fashion the appropriate balance for the situation under review. *Sony v. Universal City Studios*, *Sega v. Accolade*, *Campbell v. Acuff-Rose Music*, and *Religious Technology Center v. Netcom*, four illustrative cases which appear in the copyright component of this book, make it clear that the application of the fair-use doctrine is highly dependent on the equities of a particular situation. Certain general observations about each of the factors can be made, however:

1. **The purpose of the use**
   - An action is more likely to be fair if it is undertaken to further teaching or scholarship or to engage in specially protected forms of speech, such as comment or criticism. But as *Sony* and *Sega* illustrate, it is possible to engage in a fair use when these attributes are totally absent.
   - Use of copyrighted material primarily for private commercial benefit weighs strongly against a finding of fair use. As *Sega, Acuff-Rose,* and *Netcom*

demonstrate, however, a commercial use may nonetheless be fair when the commercial aspect is of minimal significance or is simply outweighed in importance by other relevant considerations.

- The more that the old work was transformed in making the new work, the more likely it is that the new work will be considered a fair use. This principle may be seen in *Acuff-Rose* and *Sega*. In the alternative, as indicated in *Sony*, the less transformation that takes place, the less likely the use will be considered fair, especially if the use is commercial. This is because it is more likely in this instance that the purpose of the new work is to serve as a market substitute for the old work.

2. **The nature of the work**
   - It is very difficult, although not impossible, to make a fair use of copyrighted works that have not yet been distributed to the public.[7] A 1992 amendment to Section 107 clarifies that the unpublished nature of a work does not bar a finding of fair use if the equitable balance of the other relevant factors otherwise supports the determination.
   - It is easier to make a fair use of utilitarian or factual works than of more expressive materials, such as fiction. This is demonstrated in *Sega*.

3. **The amount and substantiality used**
   - The amount of copying should be relatively small, especially if use is made of qualitatively important material. However, this factor is no more controlling than any of the others. *Acuff-Rose* makes it clear, for instance, that a parodist may take enough qualitatively important material as is necessary to conjure up the source of a parody. In addition, *Sony*, *Sega*, and *Netcom* demonstrate that there may be unique situations in which the copying of entire works may be fair uses.

4. **Market effect**
   - The effect on the potential market for the copyrighted work often is the decisive determinant of whether the balance tips toward a fair use. A use that reduces the profitability of the copyrighted work is much more unlikely to be a fair use than one that is monetarily benign. All four cases make this abundantly clear.

The importance of the fair-use exception to the development of high-technology policy cannot be overestimated. As noted in the introduction, the pace of technology has far outstripped the capacity of Congress to specifically address all potential policy conflicts in advance. The old laws deal with old problems. But judges must use the old laws to address the new controversies too. For instance, Internet users must make temporary copies of copyrighted materials in their computers to view them over the Internet. Strictly speaking, such an action may violate the reproduction right. But somehow, in your gut, you are probably thinking that this doesn't feel like it should be unlawful. Numerous issues involving the Internet probably will strike you the same way, such as those regarding linking, framing, and Internet service provider liabilities. With copyrights, the fair-use exception gives judges the flexibility to find behavior lawful when strict application of the statute otherwise might condemn it. *Sony* and *Sega* are particularly striking examples of how this works. Indeed, you may feel in these and other cases that the judges first determined that the disputed action should be lawful and only then did they apply the fair-use exception to make it happen. This may, in fact, be somewhat true. But then, fair use is an equitable test, and thus it should lead to the results that seem fair under the circumstances.

Fair Use and Videocassette Recording

Sony Corporation v. Universal City Studios was the significant Supreme Court opinion that legitimized the videocassette recorder (VCR) industry. The ultimate determination in this case depended on a judgment that VCR time-shifting (the act of taping a television show for the purpose of viewing it once at a more convenient time) at home is a fair use. Note that this case was against a VCR manufacturer rather than the users of the machine. The plaintiffs argued that Sony was responsible for the unauthorized copies made by its customers because it provided the means to make those copies. Also, be aware that the Court of Appeals determined that most of the ways VCR owners use their machines are illegal and did hold Sony responsible. Such a decision, if it had not been reversed on appeal by the Supreme Court, would have given copyright owners substantial leverage to negotiate fees from the sale of VCRs and possibly videotapes. In addition, consider carefully how narrow this opinion really is. Although a popular notion, it is a misconception to believe that any home use of a VCR is legitimate. Finally, this case obviously is relevant to home audio recording, especially with regard to digital audio formats.

SONY CORPORATION OF AMERICA V. UNIVERSAL CITY STUDIOS, INC.
United States Supreme Court, 1984

FACTS: Universal City Studios and Walt Disney Productions own the copyrights on a substantial number of motion pictures and other audiovisual works. Sony is the manufacturer of Betamax, a brand of VCR. The primary use of the machine is time-shifting: the practice of recording a program to view once at a later time, and thereafter erasing it. However, there are other uses of the machine, such as recording tapes to accumulate in a library.

Universal and Disney sued Sony, alleging that individuals used Betamaxes to copy some of their copyrighted works, which had been exhibited on commercially sponsored television. They further contended that these individuals violated their exclusive rights to copy the programs. However, no relief was sought against the individuals. Rather, the studios maintained that Sony was responsible for the wrongful acts of these individuals and as relief sought money damages from Sony and an injunction preventing the further manufacture and sale of Betamaxes. The studios did not raise issues regarding the transfer of tapes or the copying of programs transmitted on pay or cable television systems.

The district court decided that Sony was not liable. It determined that noncommercial home-use recording of material broadcast over the public airwaves was a fair use. It also held that in any event Sony could not be liable for the illegal acts of certain customers since it was not directly involved with them.

The Court of Appeals reversed. It concluded that the home use of a VCR was not a fair use because it did not serve a productive purpose, such as for criticism, comment, teaching, scholarship, or research. The Court of Appeals also determined that Sony was liable for the acts of its purchasers because it knowingly sold Betamaxes for the primary purpose of reproducing television programs, almost all of which were copyrighted.

DECISION AND REASONING: Copyright protection subsists in original works of authorship fixed in any tangible medium of expression. The Copyright Act grants the copyright holder the exclusive right to use and to authorize the use of work in five qualified ways, including reproduction in copies. However, any individual may reproduce a copyrighted work for a "fair use."

Universal and Disney in this case do not seek relief against the VCR users who have allegedly infringed their copyrights. To prevail, they have to prove (1) that users of the Betamax have infringed their copyrights and (2) that Sony should be held responsible for that infringement.

The Copyright Act does not expressly render anyone liable for infringement committed by another. In contrast, the Patent Act expressly imposes vicarious liability on contributory infringers. Although the copyright statute does not mention vicarious liability, it nonetheless exists in this context since vicarious liability is imposed in virtually all areas of law where it is just to hold one individual accountable for the actions of another. And it is appropriate to refer to the patent law cases because of the historic kinship between patent law and copyright law.

The Patent Act provides that the sale of a commodity that is suitable for substantial noninfringing uses does not constitute contributory infringement. Accordingly, the sale of copying equipment does not constitute contributory infringement if it is capable of substantial noninfringing uses. The question is thus whether the Betamax is capable of substantial noninfringing uses. In order to resolve this case we need not give precise content to the question of how much use is substantial, for it is clear that private noncommercial time-shifting in the home meets the standard, however it is understood.

continued . . .

continued . . .

Certain uses of the Betamax clearly are legitimate and noninfringing. Many copyright holders accept private time-shifting. For example, Fred Rogers, president of the company that owns "Mister Rogers' Neighborhood," testified that he had no objection to home taping and expressed that it is a real service to families to be able to record children's programs and to show them at appropriate times. If there are millions of owners of VCRs who make copies of such programs as "Mister Rogers' Neighborhood" and if the proprietors of these programs welcome the practice, then the business of supplying the equipment that makes such copying feasible should not be stifled because the equipment is used by some individuals to make unauthorized reproductions.

Even unauthorized uses of a copyrighted work are not infringing if they constitute a fair use under Section 107. That section identifies various factors that enable a court to apply an equitable-rule-of-reason analysis to particular claims of infringement. The first factor requires that the commercial or nonprofit character be weighed. If the Betamax were used to make copies for a commercial or profit-making purpose, such use would be presumptively unfair. Time-shifting for private home use must be characterized as a noncommercial, nonprofit activity. Moreover, when one considers the nature of a televised copyrighted audiovisual work and that time-shifting merely enables a viewer to see such a work that the viewer had been invited to witness in its entirety free of charge, the fact that the entire work is reproduced does not have its ordinary effect of militating against a finding of fair use.

This is not, however, the end of the inquiry, because one also must consider the effect of the use upon the potential market for or value of the copyrighted work. A challenge to the noncommercial use of a copyrighted work requires proof that the particular use is harmful or that if it should become widespread, it would adversely affect the potential market for the copyrighted work. Universal and Disney raise numerous fears about the potential effects on television ratings, on theater audiences, on television rerun audiences, and on film rentals. However, the District Court found that harm from time-shifting is speculative, and at worst minimal.

When all these factors are weighed in the equitable-rule-of-reason balance, we must conclude, as did the District Court, that home time-shifting is a fair use. The Court of Appeals erred in its determination that a fair use must be a productive use. The distinction between productive and unproductive uses may be helpful in calibrating the balance, but it cannot be wholly determinative. Copying to promote a scholarly endeavor certainly has a stronger claim to fair use than copying to avoid interrupting a poker game. But that does not end the inquiry.

In summary, the Betamax is capable of substantial noninfringing uses because some copyright owners do not object to private time-shifting and because unauthorized home time-shifting is a fair use. Sony's sale of such equipment, therefore, does not constitute contributory infringement. It may well be that Congress will take a fresh look at this new technology. But it is not our job to apply laws that have not yet been written. Accordingly, the judgment of the Court of Appeals must be reversed.

Since there are substantial uses of VCRs that do not violate the exclusive rights of copyright holders, Sony and other manufacturers are free to market these machines. However, it should be clear that not all the ways that individuals use the machines are within the law. For instance, one widespread practice involves making copies to save in a personal library. Do you believe that this is a fair use? Although the first three factors may be no different from the practice of time-shifting, it is probably much easier to prove detrimental economic effects from librarying. After all, one who watches a movie from a personal library might otherwise buy it. Thus, although time-shifting is legal, the act of saving the tape to watch more than once, even at home, probably violates copyrights. You should consider other scenarios too. What about renting a tape and using two machines to make a copy? It is hard to imagine how this could be a fair use. Now think about those video decks with two taping mechanisms built right in. Could a copyright owner prevail in a suit against their manufacturers on the claim of contributory infringement? The answer, of course, comes down to whether there are substantial noninfringing uses of such double decks.

Sony also may have some important ramifications on our ability to sell the AES as well. Since the AES is used to upgrade the sound quality of records, one might allege that the system creates derivative works of the records played through it. If this is correct, then customers would need to get permission from the LP (long-playing-record) copyright owners before using the AES. Otherwise, they would be in violation of the exclusive copyright privilege of those copyright owners to control the making of derivative works. Assuming our customers do not take this step, then we could be held liable as a contributory infringer, given that there would be few noninfringing uses of the AES.

Fortunately, upgrading sound quality likely would not be considered the making of a derivative work. For if it were, then it would follow that all things that consumers do to alter audio or visual aspects of purchased works would infringe copyrights. For instance, reshuffling the order of songs in a compact disc (CD), under the derivative work theory, would be an infringement. So would playing a 33 RPM record at another speed, such as 45 RPM. Likewise, viewing an art object through rose-colored lenses would infringe. Even boosting the treble on an audio recording, or adding special effects, such as surround sound, might then be an infringement.

A scenario similar to the **AES** situation was raised in a lawsuit brought by Nintendo against Lewis Galoob Toys for the sale of Game Genie. Game Genie was a microprocessor-equipped box that plugged into Nintendo game cartridges and allowed players to electronically alter Nintendo video games to create a variety of new rules or special effects for the original games. Nintendo argued that Game Genie allowed users to violate its exclusive rights to create derivative works of its games and that Galoob, by supplying the means for the infringing activity, was a contributory infringer. In 1991, a California district court sided with Galoob, and the court's decision was affirmed on appeal.[8] Thus, it appears that the **AES**, by improving sound quality, does not create a derivative work. Therefore we do not have to fear being charged with contributory infringement for selling the machine.

Fair Use and the Controversy over Digital Audio Recording Formats

The issues raised in the video context are no less real in the audio world. One should now wonder whether it is legal to create a personal library of analog audio tapes copied from records or CDs for use in one's car audio system. Until recently, there was no definitive answer to this query. But then, no one seemed to care too much either, at least enough to raise a legal case about it. Some scholars believed that the legislative history of the 1976 Copyright Act provided an implicit exception for home analog audio taping.[9] Even without special treatment, a fair-use equitable balancing approach very well may have sanctioned the practice. Music recorded on analog tapes has perceptively inferior quality to that on records and CDs. Thus, there generally has been little fear that analog tapes would substitute for the "original." The prospect of playing a recorded tape in the automobile may actually be the decisive factor in convincing one to purchase the CD at all. In addition, recording artists and studios do not worry much about analog "chain-taping" whereby a record is purchased by one individual, who lets a friend tape it, who then lets another friend tape that copy, and so on. This is because analog tape quality deteriorates even more substantially through this process. For these reasons and others, it might have been hard to argue persuasively that home analog audio tape recording could have a negative economic impact on the copyright holders.

Digital audio recording formats (DARs), however, presented a much different picture, and recording artists were not sanguine about the presence of these new technologies. DARs include digital audio tape formats, such as digital compact cassettes, and recordable optical discs, such as MiniDiscs. DARs have the capacity to make identical copies from the original source and can continue to do so from generation to generation in a chain-recording sequence. When DARs hit foreign markets in 1984, the recording industry threatened to bring lawsuits against DAR manufacturers.[10] The theory, of course, was to be contributory infringement: that consumer DAR machines would be used almost entirely to make illegal reproductions of copyrighted albums, which would be saved in private libraries and lent to friends for further reproduction. At the same time, the industry lobbied heavily for legislation requiring all DAR decks sold in the United States to have a "Copy-Code" system, which would prevent them from making copies of copyrighted material. In 1987, the National Bureau of Standards determined that the CopyCode system was unreliable, and the legislative proposals were scrapped. However, the DAR manufacturers still feared lawsuits if DARs were marketed in the United States, and so only a limited number trickled into the country. In 1989, representatives from the recording industry and the DAR industry met in Athens, Greece, and agreed to seek legislation worldwide requiring DARs to have a new technical system, called a serial copy management system, or SCMS, which allows recording of commercially purchased CDs or prerecorded digital audio tapes, but which prevents chain-recording. Nonetheless, in 1990, a contributory infringement lawsuit was filed by certain songwriters in the United States.[11] Finally, in 1992, this chapter in copyright history came to a close in the United States when Congress passed the Audio Home Recording Act.[12] The act essentially requires sellers and importers of digital audio recording devices intended for consumer use to pay a 2% royalty on the sales price to the Copyright Office and to integrate an SCMS into their products. Similarly, sellers of blank digital audio recording media have to pay a 3% royalty. The royalties are to be distributed by the Copyright Office to musicians, vocalists, recording companies, songwriters, and music publishers. In addition, by expressly prohibiting infringement suits against individuals who make private, non-commercial uses of digital or analog audio recording devices or media, the legislation substantially ends the debate about the potential liability of those who copy audio recordings for home use.

Although the Audio Home Recording Act addressed the feared chain-recording problems with consumer DAR machines, its passage has not allowed the music industry to rest easy. As already discussed, advances in digital transmission technologies have been of great concern to recording studios. In fact, the Audio Home Recording Act served to magnify the problems in this area, since the act protects consumers who use DAR machines to record and preserve music that is delivered in this fashion. The music industry, therefore, lobbied for legislation that put restrictions on the sources of these transmissions. Congress responded in 1995 with the Digital Performance Right in Sound Recordings Act, which, as mentioned, entitled the industry to royalties from certain forms of digital transmissions.

The Controversy Over MP3 and Portable Digital Music Players   In 1998, the industry was faced with yet another problem when Diamond Multimedia Systems, Inc. began to market a new digital recording device called the Rio.[13] The Rio is a handheld device that can record and play back what are called MP3 format sound files. Historically, music files were very difficult to transmit over the Internet, since they were extremely large and thus took a huge amount of time to download and occupied a lot of storage. An MP3 file, though, compresses a traditional sound file to 5 to 10% of its original size while maintaining virtually the identical digital sound quality. The advent of MP3, therefore, allowed anyone with the appropriate software to upload an album relatively easily to the Internet; anyone who also has the requisite software could then download it. Individuals who had the Rio could transfer files to the handheld device, allowing them to listen to about 60 minutes of music using headphones. The major concern voiced by the music industry was that the Rio would be used to facilitate unlawful pirating of recorded music. Issues regarding copyrights and the Internet will be explored fully in Chapter 6. But for now, it is probably not hard to assume that when individuals upload copyrighted albums to Web sites without permission, they violate the copyright owners' exclusive right to reproduce. Also, when Internet users download the music to their hard drives, they too make reproductions which may be unlawful. This is because the protection afforded by the Audio Home Recording Act applies only to recording devices that are primarily designed to copy music.[14] Computer hard drives, of course, have far wider purposes. The music industry feared that the Rio would serve to stimulate such unlawful activity, since listeners no longer would be confined to their desks to listen to the pirated music. For this reason, on October 8, 1998, the Recording Industry Association of America (RIAA) sued Diamond Multimedia, asking the court to block the sale of the Rio.[15]

The tricky part for the RIAA was to formulate the theory upon which to bring this suit. One possibility might have been to somehow allege contributory infringement. For instance, if there were no other substantial uses of the Rio besides making unlawful reproductions, then the principles of *Sony* might condemn the sale of the Rio. However, many artists and Internet-based recording companies had already begun to upload their own materials onto the Web and were giving permission for it be downloaded, either with or without a fee. Therefore, there were substantial noninfringing uses of the Rio. Faced with weaknesses in this argument, the RIAA alleged that the Rio was a digital home recording device under the terms of the Audio Home Recording Act, and as such had to incorporate the SCMS system. In addition, RIAA alleged that Diamond owed royalties for the sale of the machine. The 9th Circuit Court of Appeals decided that the Rio is not a digital home recording device, thereby leaving Diamond free to manufacture and distribute the machine without having to make technical changes or pay royalties. The decision provides an instructive look at how courts deal with difficult controversies raised by technological innovations.

RECORDING INDUSTRY ASSOCIATION OF AMERICA V.
DIAMOND MULTIMEDIA SYSTEMS, INC.
Ninth Circuit Court of Appeals, 1999

FACTS: This appeal arises from the efforts of the Recording Industry Association of America and the Alliance of Artists and Recording Companies (collectively RIAA) to preliminarily enjoin the manufacture and distribution by Diamond Multimedia Systems (Diamond) of the Rio portable music player. The Rio is a small device with headphones that allows a user to download

MP3 audio files from a computer and listen to them elsewhere. RIAA brought suit under the Audio Home Recording Act of 1992, alleging that the Rio does not meet its requirements because it does not employ a Serial Copyright Management System (SCMS). RIAA also sought from Diamond payment of royalties that Diamond allegedly owed under the terms of the Act since Diamond is a manufacturer and distributor of a digital audio recording device.

In a preliminary injunction hearing, the plaintiff, here RIAA, must prove (1) that it is likely to win on the merits at trial and (2) that it will suffer irreparable harm if the preliminary injunction is not granted. The District Court determined that RIAA probably could prove at trial that the Rio is a digital audio recording device covered by the Act. However, the court believed that the Rio might not violate the SCMS provision since the machine only can make a copy from a computer, and cannot make a second-generation copy from another Rio device. The court was not satisfied that irreparable injury would result if the preliminary injunction were not granted. Therefore, it denied RIAA's request for the injunction.

DECISION AND REASONING:

I.

The introduction of digital audio recording to the consumer electronics market in the 1980's is at the root of this litigation. Before then, a person wishing to copy an original music recording—e.g., wishing to make a cassette tape of a record or compact disc—was limited to analog, rather than digital, recording technology. With analog recording, each successive generation of copies suffers from an increasingly pronounced degradation in sound quality. For example, when an analog cassette copy of a record or compact disc is itself copied by analog technology, the resulting "second-generation" copy of the original will most likely suffer from the hiss and lack of clarity characteristic of older recordings. With digital recording, by contrast, there is almost no degradation in sound quality, no matter how many generations of copies are made. Digital copying thus allows thousands of perfect or near perfect copies (and copies of copies) to be made from a single original recording. Music "pirates" use digital recording technology to make and to distribute near perfect copies of commercially prepared recordings for which they have not licensed the copyrights.

Until recently, the Internet was of little use for the distribution of music because the average music computer file was simply too big: the digital information on a single compact disc of music required hundreds of computer floppy discs to store, and downloading even a single song from the Internet took hours. However, various compression algorithms now allow digital audio files to be transferred more quickly and stored more efficiently. MPEG-1

continued . . .

continued . . .

Audio Layer 3 (commonly known as "MP3") is the most popular digital audio compression algorithm in use on the Internet, and the compression it provides makes an audio file "smaller" by a factor of twelve to one without significantly reducing sound quality. MP3's popularity is due in large part to the fact that it is a standard compression algorithm freely available for use by anyone. Coupled with the use of cable modems, compression algorithms like MP3 may soon allow an hour of music to be downloaded from the Internet to a personal computer in just a few minutes.

These technological advances have occurred, at least in part, to the traditional music industry's disadvantage. By most accounts, the predominant use of MP3 is the trafficking in illicit audio recordings, presumably because MP3 files do not contain codes identifying whether the compressed audio material is copyright protected. Various pirate Web sites offer free downloads of copyrighted material, and a single pirate site on the Internet may contain thousands of pirated audio computer files.

RIAA represents the roughly half-dozen major record companies (and the artists on their labels) that control approximately ninety percent of the distribution of recorded music in the United States. RIAA asserts that Internet distribution of serial digital copies of pirated copyrighted material will discourage the purchase of legitimate recordings, and predicts that losses to digital Internet piracy will soon surpass the $300 million that is allegedly lost annually to other more traditional forms of piracy. RIAA fights a well-nigh constant battle against Internet piracy, monitoring the Internet daily, and routinely shutting down pirate Web sites by sending cease-and-desist letters and bringing lawsuits. There are conflicting views on RIAA's success—RIAA asserts that it can barely keep up with the pirate traffic, while others assert that few, if any, pirate sites remain in operation in the United States and illicit files are difficult to find and download from anywhere online.

In contrast to piracy, the Internet also supports a burgeoning traffic in legitimate audio computer files. Independent and wholly Internet record labels routinely sell and provide free samples of their artists' work online, while many unsigned artists distribute their own material from their own Web sites. Some free samples are provided for marketing purposes or for simple exposure, while others are teasers intended to entice listeners to purchase either mail order recordings or recordings available for direct download (along with album cover art, lyrics, and artist biographies). Diamond cites a 1998 "Music Industry and the Internet" report by Jupiter Communications, which predicts that online sales for pre-recorded music will exceed $ 1.4 billion by 2002 in the United States alone.

Prior to the invention of devices like the Rio, MP3 users had little option other than to listen to their downloaded digital audio files through headphones or speakers at their computers, playing them from their hard drives.

The Rio renders these files portable. More precisely, once an audio file has been downloaded onto a computer hard drive from the Internet or some other source (such as a compact disc player or digital audio tape machine), separate computer software provided with the Rio (called "Rio Manager") allows the user further to download the file to the Rio itself via a parallel port cable that plugs the Rio into the computer. The Rio device is incapable of receiving audio files from anything other than a personal computer equipped with Rio Manager.

Generally, the Rio can store approximately one hour of music, or sixteen hours of spoken material (e.g., downloaded newscasts or books on tape). With the addition of flash memory cards, the Rio can store an additional half-hour or hour of music. The Rio's sole output is an analog audio signal sent to the user via headphones. The Rio cannot make duplicates of any digital audio file it stores, nor can it transfer or upload such a file to a computer, to another device, or to the Internet. However, a flash memory card to which a digital audio file has been downloaded can be removed from one Rio and played back in another.

II.

The initial question presented is whether the Rio falls within the ambit of the Act. The Act does not broadly prohibit digital copying of copyright protected audio recordings. Instead, the Act places restrictions only upon a specific type of recording device. Most relevant here, the Act provides that "no person shall import, manufacture, or distribute any *digital audio recording device . . . that does not conform to the Serial Copy Management System (SCMS) [or] a system that has the same functional characteristics.*" (emphasis added). The Act further provides that "no person shall import into and distribute, or manufacture and distribute, any *digital audio recording device . . .* unless such person . . . deposits . . . the applicable royalty payments." (emphasis added). Thus, to fall within the SCMS and royalty requirements in question, the Rio must be a "digital audio recording device," which the Act defines through a set of nested definitions:

- The Act defines a **"digital audio recording device"** in section 1001(3) as any machine or device of a type commonly distributed for use by individuals which is designed or marketed for the primary purpose of making a *digital audio copied recording* for private use.

- A **"digital audio copied recording"** is defined in section 1001(1) as a reproduction in a digital recording format of a *digital musical recording*, whether that reproduction is made directly from another digital musical recording or indirectly from a transmission.

continued . . .

continued . . .

- A "**digital musical recording**" is defined in section 1001(5)(A) as a material object in which are fixed, in a digital recording format, only sounds, and material, statements or instructions incidental to those fixed sounds . . .

In sum, to be a digital audio recording device, the Rio must be able to reproduce, either "directly" or "from a transmission," a "digital music recording."

III.

We first consider whether the Rio is able *directly* to reproduce a digital music recording—which is a specific type of material object in which only sounds are fixed (or material and instructions incidental to those sounds).

The typical computer hard drive from which a Rio directly records is, of course, a material object. However, hard drives ordinarily contain much more than "only sounds, and material, statements, or instructions incidental to those fixed sounds." Indeed, almost all hard drives contain numerous programs (e.g., for word processing, scheduling appointments, etc.) and databases that are not incidental to any sound files that may be stored on the hard drive. Thus, the Rio appears not to make copies from digital music recordings, and thus would not be a digital audio recording device under the Act's basic definition unless it makes copies from transmissions.

Moreover, the Act expressly provides in section 1001(5)(B) that the term "digital musical recording" does not include a material object in which one or more computer programs are fixed. Since a hard drive is a material object in which one or more programs are fixed, it is excluded from the definition of a digital musical recording. This provides confirmation that the Rio does not record "directly" from "digital music recordings," and therefore it cannot be a digital audio recording device unless it makes copies "from transmissions."

The district court rejected the exclusion of computer hard drives from the definition of digital musical recordings because it concluded that such exclusion is ultimately unsupported by the legislative history, and contrary to the spirit and purpose of the Act. We need not resort to the legislative history because the statutory language is clear. Nevertheless, the legislative history is consistent with the statute's plain language.

The Senate Report states that if the material object contains computer programs or data bases that are not incidental to the fixed sounds, then the material object would not qualify under the basic definition of a digital musical recording. There are simply no grounds in either the plain language of the definition or in the legislative history for interpreting the term "digital musical recording" to include songs fixed on computer hard drives.

The district court concluded that the exemption of hard drives from the definition of digital music recording, and the exemption of computers gener-ally from the Act's ambit, would effectively eviscerate the Act because any recording device could evade regulation simply by passing the music through a computer and ensuring that the MP3 file resided momentarily on the hard drive. While this may be true, the Act seems to have been expressly designed to create this loophole.

Under the plain meaning of the Act's definition of digital audio recording devices, computers (and their hard drives) are not digital audio recording de-vices because their "primary purpose" is not to make digital audio copied recordings. Unlike digital audio tape machines, for example, whose primary purpose is to make digital audio copied recordings, the primary purpose of a computer is to run various programs and to record the data necessary to run those programs and perform various tasks. In turn, because computers are not digital audio recording devices, they are not required to comply with the SCMS requirement and thus need not send, receive or act upon information regarding copyright and generation status. And MP3 files generally do not even carry codes providing information regarding copyright and generation status. Thus, the Act seems designed to allow files to be "laundered" by pas-sage through a computer, because even a device with SCMS would be allowed to download MP3 files lacking SCMS codes from a computer hard drive, for the simple reason that there would be no codes to prevent the copying.

In fact, the Rio's operation is entirely consistent with the Act's main pur-pose—the facilitation of personal use. As the Senate Report explains, "the purpose of [the Act] is to ensure the right of consumers to make analog or digital audio recordings of copyrighted music for their *private, noncommer-cial use.*" (emphasis added). The Act does so through its home taping exemp-tion, which protects all noncommercial copying by consumers of digital and analog musical recordings. The Rio merely makes copies in order to render portable, or "space-shift," those files that already reside on a user's hard drive. Such copying is paradigmatic noncommercial personal use entirely consistent with the purposes of the Act.

IV.

Even though it cannot directly reproduce a digital music recording, the Rio would nevertheless be a digital audio recording device if it could reproduce a digital music recording *from a transmission.*

While the Rio can only directly reproduce files from a computer hard drive via a cable linking the two devices (which is obviously not a transmis-sion), the Rio can indirectly reproduce a transmission. For example, if a radio broadcast of a digital audio recording were recorded on a digital audio tape machine or compact disc recorder and then uploaded to a computer hard drive, the Rio could indirectly reproduce the transmission by downloading a

continued . . .

continued . . .

copy from the hard drive. Thus, if indirect reproduction of a transmission falls within the statutory definition, as RIAA contends, the Rio would be a digital audio recording device.

RIAA's interpretation of the statutory language initially seems plausible, but closer analysis reveals that it is contrary to the statutory language and common sense. The focus of the statutory language seems to be on the two means of reproducing the underlying digital music recording—either directly from that recording, or indirectly, by reproducing the recording from a transmission. Thus, the most logical reading of the Act extends protection to direct copying of digital music recordings, and to indirect copying of digital music recordings from transmissions of those recordings. Because the Rio cannot make copies from transmissions, but instead, can only make copies from a computer hard drive, it is not a digital audio recording device.

V.

For the foregoing reasons, the Rio is not a digital audio recording device subject to the restrictions of the Audio Home Recording Act of 1992. The district court properly denied the motion for a preliminary injunction against the Rio's manufacture and distribution.

Although the 9th Circuit indicates that the Audio Home Recording Act protects all musical recordings made by consumers for home use, this sweeping statement may be overly broad. The act provides that suit may not be brought against a consumer who makes a noncommerical use of a digital or analog audio recording device. Since the Rio is *not* an audio recording device, the act potentially may not protect consumers who use it. However, as with VCRs, this does not really help musical artists, since it rarely is cost-effective to enforce their copyrights against the individuals engaged in the wrongful actions. As we shall see in the remaining chapters, enforcement is a recurring problem with the Internet, where individuals may violate rights in small ways that taken collectively may cause huge losses. Those with Internet grievances, therefore, usually attempt to locate business interests that they can hold responsible for substantial numbers of violations. These days, VCRs may be far from the cutting edge of technology. Nonetheless, the importance of *Sony* has not diminished in the slightest.[16]

COPYRIGHT OWNERSHIP

Only the owner of a copyright enjoys the privileges of a copyright. The Copyright Act provides that the initial owner of a copyright is the "author" of a work. As you might expect, the author of a work normally is the person who created it. Thus, the general rule is that the one who develops original expression initially owns the copyright to that work and has control over the exclusive rights provided by the copyright. The initial owner may exercise that control in a wide variety of ways. Not only may an owner license to others the right to enjoy any or all of the rights, but an owner also can assign ownership to any or all of the rights. Such assignments serve to transfer complete control over the right or rights to the new owner.

It should be clear that what we are talking about here is ownership in the copyright as opposed to ownership of the material object that "holds" the expression. For instance, when you purchase a book, you own that book. But your ownership extends only to the physical components of the book. The copyright owner of the original expression retains the copyright and all of the benefits from protection. Thus, although you own the book, you may not make copies or prepare derivative works unless you have permission from the copyright owner or such use falls within an exception to the copyright owner's rights, such as fair use.

Works Made for Hire

The general rule is that the person who creates a work initially owns the copyright privileges to it. There is one notable exception to this rule, however, which is critically important for those developing and managing technology. Section 201(b) of the Copyright Act provides:

> In the case of a work made for hire, the employer or other person for whom the work was prepared is considered the [initial owner] for purposes of this title, and, unless the parties have expressly agreed otherwise in a written agreement signed by them, owns all of the rights comprised in the copyright.

So, if one develops original expression under circumstances that fall within the definition of a work made for hire, then the person for whom the work was prepared is the initial owner. Obviously, depending on how "work made for hire" is interpreted, this could have wide-ranging ramifications. For instance, assume that Jack is a computer programmer who works for IBM. If Jack creates a program while on the job for IBM, is this a "work made for hire"? If so, then IBM initially owns the copyright in the program; if not, Jack does. What if Price Waterhouse, an accounting firm, contracts with Jack to develop in his spare time a program that can carry out a specified set of functions and criteria? Is this a work made for hire? Think about the ramifications if this program turns out to be so good that it is desired by a host of other accountants. Who has the right to make copies and distribute them? Price Waterhouse probably thinks it does because it directed and paid for the development of the program. Jack likely believes that he owns the copyright because the program was built on his creative genius. In his mind, Price Waterhouse only purchased a copy of the program and does not own the copyright to it. What if the contract Jack signed stated that the work is a work made for hire? Will this affect the ownership interest? Clearly, the answer to what makes a work a work made for hire will have tremendous financial implications for Jack and Price Waterhouse.

The Copyright Act defines a work made for hire in Section 101 as:

1. a work prepared by an employee within the scope of his or her employment; or
2. a work specially ordered or commissioned for use as a contribution to a collective work, as part of a motion picture or other audiovisual work, as a sound recording, as a translation, as a supplementary work, as a compilation, as an instructional text, as a test, as answer material for a test, or as an atlas if the parties expressly agree in a written instrument signed by them that the work shall be considered a work made for hire.

Courts struggled with the meaning of this definition for years, without much agreement. Different courts could review the same facts and come to opposite conclusions about the copyright owner based on their varying approaches to what constitutes a work made for hire. Finally, the Supreme Court settled the matter in 1989 in *Community for Creative Non-Violence (CCNV) v. Reid.* Although this case dealt with an artist who created for a nonprofit organization a sculpture representing the homeless—a somewhat low-tech scenario—numerous persons and companies involved in high technology and informational pursuits eagerly awaited the Court's decision. Indeed, many tried to influence the Court's rendering by filing with the Court certain briefs that supported their differing perspectives. For instance, IBM, *Time*, AT&T, Dow Chemical, the *Washington Post*, and the *New York Times* supported CCNV; the Graphic Arts Guild and Advertising Photographers of America backed Reid.[17] The ultimate decision that the artist, Reid, was a copyright owner was a tremendous victory for independent contractors who are commissioned to develop works of authorship.

COMMUNITY FOR CREATIVE NON-VIOLENCE V. REID
United States Supreme Court, 1989

FACTS: Community for Creative Non-Violence (CCNV) is a nonprofit association dedicated to eliminating homelessness in America, and Mitch Snyder is a trustee. In 1985, CCNV decided to participate in the annual Pageant of Peace in Washington, D.C., by sponsoring a sculpture to dramatize the plight of the homeless. CCNV members conceived the idea for the nature of the display: a modern nativity scene in which the traditional Holy Family members appear as contemporary homeless people huddled on a steam grate. CCNV also titled the work "Third World America" and settled on a legend for the pedestal: "and still there is no room at the inn."

James Reid agreed to sculpt the three human figures. CCNV agreed to make the steam grate and pedestal. The parties agreed that the project would cost CCNV no more than $15,000, not including Reid's services, which he offered to donate. The parties did not sign a written agreement. Neither party mentioned copyright.

Reid sent CCNV a sketch of the proposed sculpture. Snyder pointed out that homeless people tend to recline on grates, rather than sit or stand. From that time on, Reid's sketches contained only reclining figures. For two months, Reid worked exclusively on the statue, assisted at various times by people who were paid with funds provided by CCNV. CCNV members often visited Reid to check on his progress and to coordinate CCNV's construction of the base.

The statue was displayed for a month. CCNV then returned it to Reid's studio for minor repairs. Snyder made plans for an extensive tour for the work. Reid objected, contending that the materials were not strong enough. He urged CCNV to cast the statue in bronze or to create a master mold. CCNV declined. Reid then refused to return the statue. CCNV sued Reid, seeking both return of the sculpture and a determination of copyright ownership. The District Court ordered Reid to return the sculpture. Since CCNV had paid for the sculpture, it owned that particular copy and had the right to possess it. The district court also determined that the sculpture was a work made for hire and that CCNV therefore owned the copyright. The court reasoned that Reid was an employee within the meaning of Section 101(1) because CCNV was the motivating force in the statue's production. Reid appealed the judgment as to copyright ownership.

The Court of Appeals reversed, holding that Reid was not an employee under strict agency principles and that the work therefore was not a work made for hire. The court remanded to the District Court to determine whether the sculpture was a joint work, authored and owned by both CCNV and Reid. CCNV appealed to the Supreme Court.

DECISION AND REASONING: The Copyright Act provides that copyright ownership vests initially in the author or authors of a work. As a general rule, the author is the party who actually creates the work, that is, the person who translates an idea into a fixed, tangible expression. The act carves out an important exception, however, for works made for hire. The contours of the work-made-for-hire doctrine carry profound significance for freelance creators—including artists, writers, photographers, designers, composers, and computer programmers—and for the publishing, advertising, music, and other industries that commission their works.

CCNV does not claim that the statue satisfies the terms of Section 101(2). Quite clearly, it does not. Sculpture does not fit within any of the nine[18]

continued . . .

continued . . .

categories of works enumerated in that subsection, and no written agreement between the parties establishes that the sculpture is a work made for hire.

The dispositive inquiry in this case is whether "Third World America" is a work prepared by an employee within the scope of employment. The act does not define these terms. In the absence of such guidance, four interpretations have emerged. The first holds that a work is prepared by an employee whenever the hiring party retains the right to control the product. A second, and closely related, view is that a work is prepared by an employee when the hiring party has actually wielded control over the creation of a work. A third view is that the term "employee" within Section 101(1) carries its common law agency meaning. Finally, some contend "employee" refers only to formal, salaried employees.

In the past, when Congress has used the term "employee" without defining it, we have concluded that Congress intended to describe the conventional common law agency relationship. We agree with the Court of Appeals that this is the correct interpretation of "employee" in Section 101(1).

Neither of the first two tests, supported by CCNV, is consistent with the text of the act. Section 101 plainly creates two distinct ways in which a work can be deemed for hire: one for works prepared by employees, the other for those specially commissioned works that fall within one of the nine enumerated categories and are the subject of a written agreement. The right-to-control-the-product test would mean that many works that could satisfy Section 101(2) would already have been deemed works made for hire under 101(1). Also, the unifying feature of the nine enumerated categories is that they are usually prepared at the direction of a publisher or producer. By their very nature, these types of works would be works by an employee under the right-to-control-test. The actual control test presents similar inconsistencies and there is simply no way to milk it from the language of the statute. We also reject Reid's suggestion that Section 101(1) refers only to formal, salaried employees.

We conclude that a work made for hire can arise through one of two mutually exclusive means: one for employees in the traditional common law agency sense, and one for independent contractors. In determining whether a hired party is an employee under the common law of agency, one considers several factors. Amongst factors relevant to this inquiry are the hiring party's right to control the manner by which the product is accomplished, the skill required, the source of the instrumentalities and tools, the location of the work, the duration of the relationship between the parties, whether the hiring party has the right to assign additional projects to the hired party, the extent of the hired party's discretion over when and how long to work, the method of payment, the hired party's role in hiring and paying assistants, whether the work is part of the regular business of the hiring party, the provision of employee benefits, and the tax treatment of the hired party. No single one of these factors is alone determinative.

In light of these factors, Reid was not an employee of CCNV but was an independent contractor. True, CCNV directed enough of Reid's work to ensure that he produced a sculpture that met their specifications. But the extent of control that the hiring party exercises over the details of the product is not dispositive. Indeed, all the other factors weigh heavily against finding an employment relationship. Reid is a sculptor, a skilled occupation. Reid supplied his own tools. He worked in his own studio in Baltimore, making daily supervision practicably impossible. Reid was retained for less than two months, a relatively short period of time. CCNV had no right to assign additional projects. Apart from the deadline, Reid had freedom to decide when and how long to work. CCNV paid Reid a sum dependent on completion of a specific job, a method by which independent contractors are often compensated. Reid had total discretion in hiring assistants. Creating sculptures was hardly regular business for CCNV. Finally, CCNV did not pay taxes, provide any employee benefits, or contribute to unemployment insurance or workers' compensation funds.

Because Reid was an independent contractor, whether "Third World America" is a work made for hire depends on whether it satisfies the terms of Section 101(2). This, CCNV concedes, it cannot do. Thus, CCNV is not the author or owner of the sculpture by virtue of the work-made-for-hire provisions of the act.

CCNV nevertheless may be a joint author of the sculpture if, on remand, the district court determines that CCNV and Reid prepared the work with the intention that their contributions be merged into inseparable or interdependent parts of a unitary whole. In that case, CCNV and Reid would be co-owners of the copyright in the work. We affirm the judgment of the Court of Appeals.

CCNV answers a lot of questions and raises many others. When traditional employees, as determined by standard agency principles, develop works while on the job, these are works made for hire, and ownership resides in the employer. Thus, when Jack created the program for IBM while on the job, the work belonged to IBM, leaving Jack no copyright ownership claims to it. Of course, as the case indicates, the term "employee" is broader than formal salaried personnel, and controversy may result about how to balance the large set of potentially relevant factors (listed in Exhibit 5.2). But it is clear that merely the right to control is no longer sufficient to make one an employee. When independent contractors are engaged, their efforts will not result in works made for hire unless their contributions fall within one of the ten categories enumerated in Section 101(2) and their agreement specifically relates the work-for-hire relationship. Therefore, when Jack worked at

---

Exhibit 5.2
Works Made for Hire

RELEVANT FACTORS TO DISTINGUISH EMPLOYEES FROM INDEPENDENT CONTRACTORS

- Right to control how product accomplished
- Skill of hired party
- Source of tools and instrumentalities
- Location of work
- Duration of relationship
- Right to assign other projects
- Discretion of hired party over working hours
- Payment method
- Regular business of hirer
- Employee benefits paid
- Tax treatment

---

the direction of Price Waterhouse, the final product was not a work made for hire. Be aware that this would have been true even if their contract had stated that the program was a work made for hire; since the program does not fit within any of the nine categories, there can be no work made for hire, even if the parties so agree.

Note also how these principles might be used to determine who owns the rights to copyrightable features of **AES**, such as elements of the computer program. If a salaried employee of our company develops the program, then the program is a work made for hire, thereby yielding ownership for the company. However, if we commission an independent programmer to design the program based on certain parameters and specifications, then initial ownership of the copyright will reside with the programmer. If this is the case, then we will have to account for those rights before making or distributing the **AES**. This can be done by acquiring the programmer's copyright interests, as discussed next, or by gaining permission, through contractual license provisions, to enjoy the necessary copyright privileges.

The *CCNV* decision may have widespread effects on existing works. Many industries depend on the services of outside experts and businesses. In the past, the firms needing assistance often retained these parties under the assumption that they were employees by the terms of the act. Due to *CCNV*, they now face the real possibility that they do not own the copyrights to the works they commissioned. This may hold true even in spite of intentions to the contrary. All of a sudden, this may give independent contractors leverage to demand royalties for the continued use of their creations. It is no wonder that so many companies that frequently hire independent contractors were so interested in the outcome of this case.

There is a technique that can be used by the hiring party to provide it with ownership when a new work is to be developed by an independent contractor. Recall that copyright ownership can be assigned from the owner to another. Therefore, when dealing with an independent contractor, an agreement for services may provide that the contractor will take all necessary steps to assign the copyright upon completion of the work. Since *CCNV*, clauses to this effect in contracts have become much more common. On first glance, one might think that *CCNV* thereby will have little net effect on future business relationships. The hirers will own the copyrights just as they thought they did before *CCNV*. However, there are some differences. The most important effect is on negotiation psychology. Now it will be crystal clear to independent contractors that they are relinquishing all ownership in the work. Before, contracts may not have mentioned ownership, or they may have talked in terms of "works made for hire," a term of art that unsophisticated persons could easily misunderstand. Independent contractors with full knowledge about ownership interests may refuse to sign assignment deals or may demand greater fees. Assignments have other repercussions. For instance, the duration of the copyright is based on the life of the author, rather than the statutory term for works made for hire. Also, the act provides that assignments may be terminated after 35 years. In addition, there is some responsibility to record assignments with the Copyright Office to ensure ownership in case someone else makes a claim.

Joint Works

While *CCNV* clarified the work made-for-hire doctrine, it opened up another can of worms with the "joint-works" scenario. As *CCNV* relates, the act provides for co-ownership when two or more persons jointly develop a work in which they make inseparable contributions. What and how much each must contribute for there to be a joint work is still not clear. Two principles seem to apply, however. First, each person must contribute original expression and not simply ideas.[19] Thus, it is unlikely that Price Waterhouse could claim joint ownership with Jack when it provided him only with the ideas to be embedded in the program. However, as will be explored in the next chapter, it is not always easy to clearly discern what contributions are merely ideas, especially with computer programs. The second principle is that each must contribute more than a de minimis amount of expression. One has to contribute something of substance to be a joint owner, although it can be substantially less than one-half or some other defined percentage. In the event that there is joint ownership, each owner can independently make its own decisions about how to profit from the work but must account to the other owners for the profits made from those endeavors. Therefore, if CCNV and Reid are joint owners, and from the facts it seems likely that they are, then each must pay the other one-half of the profits made through use of the copyrights. So, for example, if CCNV makes and sells prints of the sculpture, it would have to pay 50% of the profits to Reid.

Moral Rights

One other issue was discussed in the *CCNV* litigation, which should be noted before leaving the topic of ownership. The Court of Appeals in *CCNV* raised the possibility that Reid, as an author, might enjoy certain moral rights independent of his ownership stake. This might give him rights, stated the court, both to prevent CCNV or others from distorting or mutilating versions of the work (rights to integrity) and to ensure that he receives proper credit as an author of the sculpture (rights to paternity or attribution).[20]

Moral rights are likely to receive greater attention in the United States now that this country has signed the Berne Convention. Article 6b of the convention states that independent of an author's economic rights, and even after transfer of them, an author has the rights to claim authorship and to object to any distortion or other derogatory action that would be prejudicial to the author's honor or reputation. When the United States passed the Berne Convention Implementation Act in 1988, no explicit changes in the Copyright Act were then made so as to assimilate the concept of moral rights. The drafters believed such moral rights to attribution and integrity were already protected by other state and federal laws. For instance, federal trademark laws prohibit false designations of origin. Also, many states, such as California and New York, have a variety of laws that extend the rights of authors beyond copyright ownership. For example, California protects one's "right of publicity" by preventing the unauthorized commercial use of a person's name, voice, signature, or photograph. Due to state laws such as these, companies that have been given authority from copyright owners to play recordings in commercials nonetheless may be unable to use or even imitate the voices of performers without receiving their permission also.[21] In addition, Congress amended the Copyright Act in 1990 so that it protects the moral rights of visual artists.[22] Section 106A of the act now provides that, independent of the Section 106 ownership rights, authors of certain limited-edition works of visual art have rights of attribution and integrity. The protection of moral rights definitely is on the rise in the United States and around the world, and there likely will be repercussions on those managing copyrighted materials. There will be some discussion of possible implications in the next chapter with respect to digital sampling and multimedia works.

How to Obtain Copyright Protection

Registration and Deposit

Unlike with patents, copyright protection is inexpensive and easy to obtain. Indeed, the two situations are polar opposites in this regard. Ever since the United States joined the Berne Convention in 1988, the actual procedural requirements for copyright protection come down to one word: none. This is because the fundamental tenet of this international agreement is that the enjoyment of copyright protection

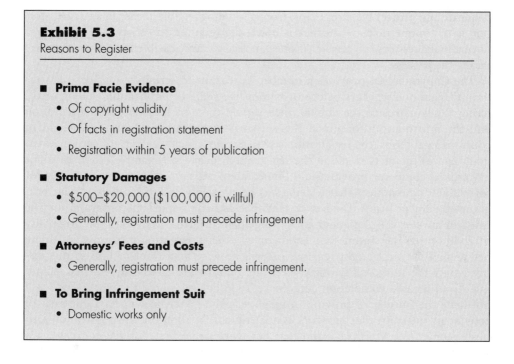

Exhibit 5.3
Reasons to Register

- **Prima Facie Evidence**
  - Of copyright validity
  - Of facts in registration statement
  - Registration within 5 years of publication
- **Statutory Damages**
  - $500–$20,000 ($100,000 if willful)
  - Generally, registration must precede infringement
- **Attorneys' Fees and Costs**
  - Generally, registration must precede infringement.
- **To Bring Infringement Suit**
  - Domestic works only

shall be subject to no formalities. Thus, the mere act of fixing one's creative expression in a tangible form is sufficient to obtain the rights attendant with copyright. However, although no longer necessary, it still is advisable to register one's work with the Copyright Office and to place a copyright notice on the work. These considerations will be reviewed here.

Even before the adoption of the Berne Convention, registration was not required for copyright protection in the United States. Instead, registration essentially was a means to gain certain technical advantages in case a copyright dispute ever materialized. This situation remains the same today, unaffected by the Berne Convention. The fundamental tenet of the convention is satisfied in that registration is optional, yet there are important reasons why one should consider undertaking it. These reasons are outlined in Exhibit 5.3.

Possibly the most significant consideration in deciding whether to register is that the procedure is so simple and cheap. Essentially, only three things are required: (1) completion of a short form, which requests basic information about the author (name, dates of birth and death, nationality) and the work (its nature, completion date, and publication date); (2) deposit of one or two copies of the work; and (3) payment of a $30 fee. The Copyright Office makes only a perfunctory review of the materials to ensure that the information is correctly provided on the form, that the work is suitable for copyright protection, and that the work comprises some expression entailing at least a minimal amount of creativity. The office does not undertake an exhaustive substantive review to confirm the work's originality or to delineate the protectible expression from the unprotectible ideas. In fact, registration is so routine that an attorney is not really required to satisfy it. Therefore, it normally makes sense to register if one can receive any possible benefit from undertaking the process.

The Copyright Act provides a number of reasons to seriously consider registration. First, if one registers before or within five years of publication (selling or offering to sell copies to the public), then should there be a dispute, the registration and the information contained therein carry substantial evidentiary weight in court. In legal terms, the registration serves as prima facie evidence of copyright validity and of the facts stated in the registration form. For example, Todd develops an original computer program and immediately registers it. After marketing it for several years, he notices that Martha has begun selling a substantially similar program at a lower price. Todd is certain that Martha copied his program, and he brings a lawsuit alleging copyright infringement. Martha challenges the originality of Todd's program, stating that Todd copied other preexisting programs, including her own. Todd's copyright registration will be very important to him in this dispute, since the court will strongly accept its validity and factual statements, including the designated completion date. Since Todd has registered the work, Todd will not have the burden of proving originality; rather, Martha will have the task of convincing the court that the work is not original. In addition, the registration seriously jeopardizes Martha's claim that her work came first, for the court will assume that the date provided in Todd's registration is accurate. Although Martha can rebut this assumption with hard evidence, she is still the one who faces the tough burdens of proof rather than Todd. What could have been an unpredictable battle of credibility thereby will likely evaporate in Todd's favor.

Registration also may improve one's ability to be compensated for copyright infringement. The Copyright Act provides that when copyright privileges are infringed, copyright owners may sue not only for their damages but also, to some extent, for the profits derived by the infringer through its violative activities. Even with these substantial remedial rights, however, copyright owners may find it difficult to be adequately compensated. For example, suppose you own the copyright in a new musical composition that has been distributed in the CD format. A radio station, in theory, has to gain your permission before playing that song. However, the damage imposed on you and the extra profits earned by the radio station from playing that song may be relatively little—so little, in fact, that the radio station might risk playing the song without gaining permission, comfortably knowing that you would not go through the effort to sue it for infringement for such a trivial return. However, if radio stations all over the country did this frequently, your losses could become significant. To alleviate this problem, the Copyright Act provides the copyright owner with an alternative to proving damages and profits. The act allows a judge to grant "statutory damages" for an amount between $500 and $20,000 that, in that judge's discretion, is just and fair under the circumstances. In addition, if the copyright owner can prove that the infringement was willful, then the judge may award up to $100,000.

Statutory damages are important not only because they reduce the burden on the copyright owner to prove damages but also because they impose a nontrivial minimum floor that must be paid for infringement, no matter what real damage a violation has caused. In this way, statutory damages are an additional deterrent for those contemplating infringement. Registration figures into all of this because copyright owners are not eligible to sue for statutory damages unless they have registered the work according to certain time limits specified in the Copyright Act. With some exception, the act provides that a work must have been registered before the infringement occurred. This presents a tremendous incentive to register as soon as possible after a work is created.

Another benefit afforded by registration is that it allows a court to require the infringer to compensate the copyright owner for attorneys' fees and costs. As you are probably aware, the prevailing party in a lawsuit is normally responsible to pay for his or her own attorney. This means that even a person who wins a lawsuit may end up with little compensation after the attorney and all the other costs of bringing the suit are paid. Attorneys' fees and costs, thus, are an important special benefit enjoyed by copyright owners. However, as with statutory damages, one must appropriately register, usually before the infringement, to be entitled to them. This, then, represents another good reason to register promptly.[23]

Registration of Materials Containing Trade Secrets   The importance of registration presents a dilemma for one who wishes to enjoy the full benefits of copyright protection for works containing valuable trade secrets. Section 408 of the Copyright Act specifies that those who register an unpublished work that has not yet been offered or sold to the general public must deposit with the Copyright Office one complete copy of that work. This could be devastating if the work contains trade secrets, because material deposited with the Copyright Office is available for public inspection. The act also requires the deposit of two complete copies of the best edition if the work has indeed been published. Although one usually abandons trade secret protection once public sales have been made, sometimes computer software firms attempt to maintain it by distributing their products only in machine-readable form. Given that the "best edition" of a program is source code, deposits of the program definitely would expose whatever trade secrets it contained. Recognizing that deposits might cause problems in certain contexts, Congress empowered the Copyright Office to permit the deposit of identifying portions of a work instead of a complete copy. Based on this, the Copyright Office generally allows one to apply for special relief when the deposit might cause undue hardship. In addition, because of the widespread concern with computer programs, it has established a set of regulations specifically dealing with them.

The computer program deposit regulations promulgated by the Copyright Office automatically allow owners of program copyrights to deposit less than entire copies. For instance, one can deposit only the first and last 25 pages of source code. If those portions contain trade secrets, however, then one can choose between a number of alternatives that allow the deposit of smaller portions, or of portions with the trade secrets blocked out, or of combinations of source code and machine-readable object code. Deposits in one of these manners usually allow the copyright owner of a program to retain all the benefits from registration while protecting trade secrets. If trade secrets still would be jeopardized under any of these alternatives, one even is allowed to simply deposit object code. However, when that option is selected, the registration will not serve as prima facie evidence of copyright validity because the Copyright Office examiners are not able to scrutinize the materials.

Registration of Foreign Works   One other aspect of registration is worth noting. Before adoption of the Berne Convention, all persons had to register their works before instituting infringement actions in court. Because this constituted a procedural step that was needed in order to enjoy one's copyright privileges, it violated the spirit of the Berne Convention. Therefore, this requirement was modified in 1988, when the United States became a participant. However, it was altered only with respect to certain foreign works. Thus, as required by the Berne Convention, foreign works from Berne participant countries now may protect their copyrights in the United States without undertaking any procedural steps, including registration.[24] However, domestic works still must be registered before a suit is filed, although this distinction someday may be changed through legislation.[25] Keep in mind that early registration remains advisable for foreign works so as to retain the other technical benefits such as prima facie evidence, statutory damages, attorneys' fees, and costs. Likewise, if domestic works ultimately are brought into parity, the same advice would apply equally well for them.

Copyright Notice

Although copyright notice once was a critical aspect of copyright protection in the United States, it no longer is required. Again, acceptance of the Berne Convention, and its thesis that protection shall be subject to no formalities, was the reason for the change. Now, one's expression is protected by copyright as soon as it is fixed in tangible form. A copyright notice does not have to be placed on a work at any time, either before or after it is publicly distributed.

The Copyright Act nonetheless provides an incentive to place a proper notice on copies. Those who wrongfully use or copy a work that has no notice might argue that they did not know they were infringing someone's rights. They might genuinely claim that had they known that someone claimed ownership in the expression, they would have refrained from impermissible actions. Under the circumstances, they might ask the court to recognize their innocence in the matter and thus reduce their liability for what they did. The Copyright Act provides that if a notice of copyright properly appears on the copies seen by the defendant, then no weight shall be given to the defendant's claim that actual or statutory damages should be reduced based on the defendant's claimed innocent infringement. Thus, although such notice is not required, it is still good practice to place one on copies of a work to ensure full compensation for acts of infringement.

The Copyright Act specifies what constitutes proper notice: either the letter "c" in a circle or the word "copyright" or the abbreviation "copr.," followed by the year of first publication and the name of the copyright owner. Thus, if William Styron owns the copyright in a book that is publicly distributed for the first time in 1992, then "© 1992 William Styron" is a correct form of notice. The notice should be placed in a location that reasonably may be seen. The Copyright Office has passed regulations that provide guidance as to what are reasonable locations under certain circumstances. For instance, notice on machine-readable copies of computer programs may appear at the beginning or end of printouts, on a user's terminal either at sign-on or continually, or on labels affixed to containers of the copies, such as reels or cartridges.

Suppose you run a company that has just completed a novel software program. Because the program contains many trade secrets, you plan to distribute it on a very limited basis while taking the necessary trade secret protection steps. However, you also want to fully enjoy copyright protection as well. Therefore you will register the work and deposit a copy so as to conceal the important secrets. Should you also place a notice on the copies? On one hand, if the program somehow is wrongfully released to the public, you do not want infringers to claim that they were innocently misled by the lack of notice. On the other hand, the copyright notice for published works indicates the year of first publication. By using the notice, you may thereby admit that your alleged secrets have already been disclosed to the public, making them ineligible for trade secret protection. A common practice to solve this dilemma is to indicate in the notice that the software is unpublished. Thus, a program written in 1992 by Brittany Bee might have as a notice "© 1992, an unpublished work by Brittany Bee." This will be sufficient to inform potential infringers of the copyright interest, without raising the inference that the program's secrets are already publicly available.[26]

Duration of Copyright Protection

One of the reasons that copyright protection is so desirable is that it lasts for a relatively long period of time. The general rule is that the protection endures for as long as the author lives and then for 70 more years thereafter. Thus, as soon as one's expression is fixed, one enjoys a substantial period of copyright protection without having to do anything. Certain works have different protection periods, although they all still are somewhat lengthy. The most important exception is for works made for hire. The copyrights in those works last for 120 years from the date of creation or 95 years from the year of first publication, whichever expires first. For most technological products capable of copyright protection, this period more than suffices given that short life cycles are the overwhelming norm.

INFRINGEMENT AND REMEDIES

A copyright allows its owner to enjoy the fruits of creative energies by providing exclusive control over a bundle of rights to a work's original expression. One who intrudes on any of those rights without permission infringes the copyright unless the use falls within an exception such as fair use. Probably a copyright owner's most important benefit is the right to reproduce a work in copies. But proving infringement of that right is most vexing.

There are several extremely difficult issues in proving infringement of the right to make reproductions. What does it mean to reproduce? The Copyright Act does not define the word. Will only an exact reproduction infringe? What if only ideas are copied, but not any expression? How much copying is too much? Also, how does one prove that another person copied a work? Copyright does not prevent another from independently creating the same expression. So how does one convince a court that one work was used in the preparation of another?

The Substantial Similarity Standard

Proof that the Work Was Copied   Clearly, copying must entail something more than an exact reproduction. Otherwise, one could easily and cheaply take the creative essence of a protected work by making a few minor alterations. Because copyright policy has been designed to preserve the incentives to create original expressions, it should not be so simple to subvert it. Thus, the right to reproduce must be somewhat broader. However, it cannot be so broad to effectively prohibit other persons who see a work from creating works of the same genre.

The balance struck by the courts is that a reproduction is made when one uses a work to make something that is substantially similar. Thus, a work does not have to be an exact replica to be a copy; it only must be substantially similar to the original. The analysis of similarities is not confined to comparisons of notes or words but also extends to plots, structures, and organizations. So, to prove infringement, one step is to provide sufficient evidence that convinces the court that the alleged copy is substantially similar to the protected work. At this point, the issue is whether the entire works, in terms of both their ideas and their expressions, are substantially similar.

A complicating factor in the preceding analysis is that copyright infringement requires copying. One must demonstrate, therefore, that the similarities in the works were not the result of two artists independently arriving at the same creations. It would be nice if alleged infringers admitted that their pieces were derived from that of the copyright owner. But one is not often so fortunate.

When one cannot directly prove that the similarities in the works resulted from copying, then proof must come circumstantially. What would it take to convince you that the similarities in two works did not occur from independent efforts? Of course, if the works are almost exact, then that alone might be sufficient. In such a case, you likely would think it to be unfathomable for such literal duplication to happen by chance. However, when the similarities are more nebulous, you might require something more to be persuaded. One aspect that should strongly affect your determination is whether the alleged infringers had access to the copyrighted work before creating their piece. Previous exposure to the work along with the resultant substantial similarities should be sufficient to convince you that the creation of one work was tied to the other. Thus, in infringement actions, one often demonstrates copying by showing that there was access to the copyrighted work as well as substantial similarity. For this investigation, the courts allow experts in the field to present their opinions as to whether copying occurred.

Proof that Expression was Illicitly Copied   The infringement inquiry does not end, however, with proof that a copyrighted work was reproduced. As you know, copyrights do not protect ideas, facts, and the like. Only expression is protected. Thus, one is allowed to reproduce portions of a copyrighted work and may do so exactly, as long as only the unprotected features are so copied. Proof that one work is substantially similar to another, therefore, may indicate copying but does not necessarily mean there was illicit copying. To satisfy this task, the copyright owner must show that the expression in the allegedly infringing work is substantially similar to the expression in the protected work. Given that the rationale for copyrights is to reward creative expressions through market incentives, one focuses this inquiry on consumers to determine whether the similarities are sufficient to affect their purchase decisions. Therefore, to judge whether unlawful appropriation of protected expression has occurred, only testimony by laypersons in the purchasing public is normally relevant. Also, recognize that it is not always necessary to draw upon large segments of expression to create a substantially similar piece. Usurpation of qualitatively vital creative elements, even if quantitatively only a small portion of the work, can be sufficient.

Of course, before asking the lay audience to determine the existence of substantial similarity in expression, one must adequately factor out the unprotected ideas. This often is the most controversial task in copyright infringement disputes, and it clearly dominates the computer copyright field. Because this specific issue will be considered in depth with the computer materials in the next chapter, we will defer its treatment until then. However, clearly understand that infringement results when one makes a reproduction that is unlawful. The finding of substantial similarity of the entire works is only the beginning. One then must distinguish the ideas from the expressions and ask ordinary consumers to evaluate the similarity of those expressions. Exhibit 5.4 summarizes these points.

Figures 1 and 2 together provide a simple example that may help to clarify these points. Assume that the creator of Figure 1 alleges that Figure 2 violates the copyright in Figure 1. The first question is whether Figure 2 is a reproduction of Figure 1. To make this determination, one has to judge whether Figure 2, in its entirety, is substantially similar to Figure 1. For this analysis, one likely will take into account that both figures have the following characteristics: (1) Five shaded triangles, (2) that are located in the corners and in the middle, (3) with the top two triangles pointing down, (4) and with the middle triangle pointing up, and (5) where the middle triangle is surrounded by three natural objects. Art experts may be helpful for this analysis, since they may have opinions about the importance of these

Exhibit 5.4
Infringing Reproductions: Elements of Proof

■ **Proof that Copyrighted Work was *Copied***
  • Direct evidence
  • Circumstantial evidence
    — Access
    — Substantial similarity
      – Substantial similarity determined by comparing the entire works, including both the ideas and the expressions in the works
      – Experts in the field may offer opinions.

■ **Proof that Copyrighted Work was *Illicitly Copied***
  • One may legally copy the ideas of a copyrighted work.
  • Substantial similarity of expression
    — Distinguish ideas of work from the expression.
    — Would an ordinary observer in the market audience consider the expressions of the two works to be substantially similar?
      – Total concept and feel

similarities. Assuming that the two works in their entirety are appraised to be substantially similar, one must assess whether Figure 2 might have been created independently. Although one might suspect that copying took place, there are enough differences in the works that one cannot reasonably rule out independent creation. Of course, if the creator of Figure 1 can prove that Figure 2's artist had seen Figure 1 before making Figure 2, then one can conclude with confidence that Figure 1 was used to make the substantially similar reproduction in Figure 2.

Although one may determine that Figure 2 is a reproduction of Figure 1 based on the substantial similarity of the entire works, one still needs to assess whether there has been an illicit reproduction of protected expression. To do this, one needs to factor out the ideas and ask consumers whether what is left is substantially similar. Again, we will review the difficult notion of separating ideas from expressions in the next chapter. But be aware how it might matter. The idea of Figure 1 might be to make a picture based on five shaded triangles and three natural objects. And if this is the case, then much of what originally appeared to be similar between the figures will be taken out of the analysis, and what remains may begin to seem somewhat different. Keep in mind, though, that the idea may be as simple as making a picture. If this is so, then everything about Figure 1 is part of the expression.

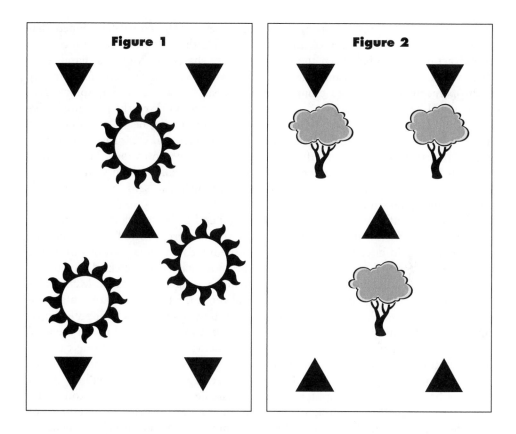

This means that nothing needs to be factored out, and one therefore may merely ask those who normally view or purchase the works whether Figure 2 appears to be much like Figure 1.

The "Total Concept and Feel" Infringement Standard   *Sid & Marty Krofft Television v. McDonald's Corp.* has served as a fundamental precedent for the substantial similarity analysis later used in computer copyright disputes.[27] The Kroffts created *H. R. Pufnstuf*, a children's television show, which included several fanciful, costumed characters who lived in a fantasyland inhabited by moving trees and talking books. The show was very popular, and the characters were licensed to various manufacturers of children's products as well as to the Ice Capades. The Kroffts discussed the concept of a McDonald's advertising campaign based on the Pufnstuf series with the advertising agency serving McDonald's, but a deal was not completed. McDonald's then independently launched its McDonaldland campaign. Licensing revenue from the Pufnstuf series fell dramatically, and the Kroffts sued McDonald's for copyright infringement.

McDonald's admitted in this case that it copied from the Pufnstuf show, so this controversy, as is so often true, centered on whether McDonald's had unlawfully appropriated the expression from the Pufnstuf series. The court determined that the idea of *H. R. Pufnstuf* was a fantasyland filled with diverse and fanciful characters in action. If this had been the only similarity shared by McDonaldland, then there would not have been infringement. However, both worlds were inhabited by anthropomorphic plants and animals, and they shared similar topographical features such as trees, caves, a pond, a road, and a castle. Both works presented talking trees with human faces and characters with large round heads and long wide mouths. Both also had crazy scientists and a multiarmed evil creature. McDonald's argued that there were still significant differences in the expressions. For instance, Pufnstuf wore a yellow and green dragon suit and a medal, which said "mayor." McCheese wore a pink formal coat with a sash, which also said "mayor" but began with the golden arches.

The court found the expression in McDonaldland to be substantially similar to that in *H. R. Pufnstuf*. It noted that since the shows were directed to children, the comparison would have to be made through the minds and imaginations of young people. The court recognized that children are not inclined to detect disparities in details. In the end, the Kroffts won the infringement action because McDonaldland, although certainly not an exact or literal replica, had captured the total concept and feel of the Pufnstuf show. We will see how some of the computer copyright cases, particularly early ones such as *Whelan v. Jaslow*, picked up on the total concept and feel language of *Krofft*. Always remember, though, that one can rely on the notion of total concept and feel only when most, if not all, elements of the work are considered expression. This was the case in *Krofft*, but we will see that it may not be so true with computer programs. The next chapter presents four landmark cases dealing with copyright protection of computer software. Together they provide detailed examples of how these principles are applied in infringement actions and show how the principles might be misapplied in technology contexts.

Clean-Room Techniques

The importance of proving access to copyrighted expression has led many computer software firms to develop so-called clean-room techniques to isolate programmers from any copyrighted expression they wish to emulate. Suppose that Sonny's Software, Inc. (Sonny's) wishes to develop a product to compete with Sally Software's popular A-B-C program. Sonny's splits its development personnel into two groups, occupying two separate rooms. The first group occupies what is called the dirty room. The group thoroughly studies A-B-C and determines what ideas make up the program. Those ideas, and only the ideas, are then transmitted to the other group, at work in the clean room. The group in the clean room then develops an alternative program based on these ideas. The process is shown in Exhibit 5.5.

This technique may protect Sonny's if the resultant programs have substantially similar expressions. Sonny's will admit that its dirty-room programmers had access to Sally's A-B-C but will maintain that they did not illicitly reproduce copyrighted expression, since they recorded only unprotected ideas. Sonny's also will claim that

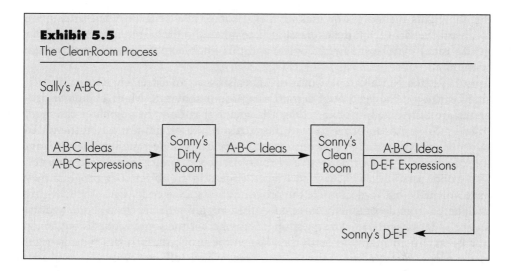

Exhibit 5.5
The Clean-Room Process

Sally's A-B-C

A-B-C Ideas
A-B-C Expressions → Sonny's Dirty Room → A-B-C Ideas → Sonny's Clean Room → A-B-C Ideas D-E-F Expressions

Sonny's D-E-F ◄

its clean-room personnel could not have reproduced any protected expression from Sally's A-B-C program because they never had access to any of the program's expression. Sonny's will argue that any similarities between its program and the expression in A-B-C did not occur because it copied A-B-C's expression, but rather resulted from chance or from the application of standard programming techniques to the unprotected ideas. Sally thereby may be frustrated by the clean-room technique because she will not be able to prove that the clean-room programmers had access to the A-B-C expression.

Clean-room procedures are routinely used and can be very effective. In a notable application, Compaq Computers used clean-room techniques to make its first clone of the successful IBM personal computer. The key proprietary element of the IBM PC was its so-called ROM BIOS (basic input-output system), since most of the other components, such as the microprocessor from Intel, could be purchased off the shelf. Compaq's dirty-room computer experts studied the ROM BIOS and deciphered the unprotected ideas and systems. They then passed these along to clean-room personnel, called "virgins," who had never had contact with the IBM ROM BIOS. Through its clean-room procedure, Compaq was able to successfully reverse engineer the all-important IBM ROM BIOS, thereby allowing it to become a serious contender for the PC market.

When using clean-room techniques, however, one must be mindful of certain inherent pitfalls. As we shall see in the next chapter, it is not always easy to distinguish the ideas of a computer program, or of any type of work for that matter, from its expression. Therefore, what the dirty-room personnel believe to be ideas may turn out to be elements of expression. Since these parts will be given to the clean room, one now can prove that the personnel in the clean room had access to the expression. Also, the personnel in the dirty room must be careful not to violate the copyrights themselves by making illegal copies in that room while attempting to dissect the ideas from the expression. The notes and program listings carried out in this room may be unlawful copies, and this illicit activity may taint the entire procedure.

In 1992, the Ninth Circuit Court of Appeals issued an extremely important decision bearing on the legality of certain clean-room activities. Many computer programs are distributed in object code, a language that only the computer can read. In order for a human being to read the program, the program must be translated into source code, usually by means of a machine called a decompiler. The resultant source code is a copy or derivative of the object code. Under many circumstances, dirty-room personnel who wish to learn the ideas in an object code program may have no choice but to decompile the program into source code. Once the ideas are deciphered from decompiled source code, they are given to the clean room, and the source code is destroyed. The question arises whether the source code listing, made in the dirty room simply to learn the ideas in the program, infringes the copyright in the program. *Sega Enterprises v. Accolade*, which follows, deals with this very important topic.

SEGA ENTERPRISES, LTD. V. ACCOLADE, INC.
Ninth Circuit Court of Appeals, 1992

FACTS: Sega develops and markets video entertainment systems, including the Genesis console. Accolade is a developer, manufacturer, and marketer of computer entertainment software, including game cartridges that are compatible with the Genesis console. Sega licenses its copyrighted computer code to a number of independent developers of computer game software so that they can develop games that can operate in the Genesis console. Accolade has never been one of those licensees.

Accolade used a two-step process to render its video games compatible with the Genesis console. First, it transformed the machine-readable object code contained in commercially available copies of Sega's game cartridges into human-readable source code using a process called disassembly or decompilation. Accolade purchased a Genesis console and three Sega cartridges, wired a decompiler into the console circuitry, and generated printouts of the resulting source code. Accolade engineers studied and annotated the printouts in order to identify areas of commonality among the three game programs. They next loaded the disassembled code back into a computer and experimented to discover the interface specifications for the Genesis console. Accolade then created a development manual that incorporated the information it had discovered about the requirements for a Genesis-compatible game. The manual contained only functional descriptions of the interface requirements and did not include any of Sega's code.

In the second stage, Accolade created its own games for Genesis. In this stage, it did not copy Sega's programs; it relied only on the information concerning interface specifications for the Genesis that was contained in the development manual. Accolade maintains that with the exception of the interface specifications, none of the code in its own games is derived in any way from its examination of Sega's code. Indeed, many of the programs had been developed and marketed for other console systems prior to being adapted for the Genesis console.

Sega sued Accolade for copyright infringement and requested a preliminary injunction. [It also sued for trademark infringement based on facts not provided in this synopsis.] The district court determined that Sega was likely to succeed on the merits and granted preliminary relief. Accolade appealed.

DECISION AND REASONING: Accolade raises four arguments in support of its position that disassembly of the object code in a copyrighted computer program does not constitute infringement. Three will be considered here. First, it maintains that intermediate copying does not infringe the exclusive rights granted to copyright owners unless the end product of the copying is substantially similar to the copyrighted work. Second, it argues that disassembly of object code in order to gain an understanding of the ideas and functional concepts embodied in the code is always lawful. Finally, Accolade contends that its disassembly of object code was a fair use. Copyright law does not support the first two arguments. However, the third argument has merit. We conclude, based on the policies underlying the Copyright Act, that disassembly of copyrighted object code is a fair use of the work if such disassembly provides the only means of access to those elements of the code that are not protected by copyright, and the copier has a legitimate reason for seeking such access.

Intermediate Copying. The Copyright Act does not distinguish between unauthorized copies of a copyrighted work on the basis of what stage of the alleged infringer's work the unauthorized copies represent. Section 501 provides that "[a]nyone who violates any of the exclusive rights of the copyright owner . . . is an infringer." On its face, that language unambiguously encompasses and proscribes intermediate copying. We hold that intermediate copying of computer object code may infringe the exclusive rights granted in Section 106 regardless of whether the end product of the copying also infringes those rights. If intermediate copying is permissible under the act, authority for such copying must be found in one of the statutory provisions to which the rights granted in Section 106 are subject (such as fair use).

The Idea/Expression Dichotomy. Accolade next contends that disassembly of object code does not violate the Copyright Act because disassembly is always necessary to gain access to the ideas and functional concepts embodied in the

continued . . .

continued . . .

code. Because humans cannot comprehend object code, it reasons, disassembly of a commercially available computer program into human-readable form should not be considered an infringement of the owner's copyright. Insofar as Accolade suggests that disassembly of object code is lawful per se, it seeks to overturn settled law.

Accolade's argument, in essence, is that object code is not eligible for the full range of copyright protection. However, the act makes no distinction between the copyrightability of those programs that directly interact with the computer user and those that simply manage the computer system. Nor does the act require that a work be directly accessible to humans to be eligible for copyright protection. Thus, the copyright in a computer program extends to the object code version of the program.

Our refusal to recognize a per se right to disassemble object code does not lead to an absurd result. The ideas and functional concepts underlying many types of computer programs, including word processing programs, spreadsheets, and video game displays, are readily discernible without the need for disassembly because the operation of such programs is visible on the computer screen. The need to disassemble object code arises, if at all, only in connection with operations systems, system interface procedures, and other programs that are not visible to the user when operating—and then only when no alternative means of gaining an understanding of those ideas and functional concepts exists. In our view, consideration of the unique nature of computer object code thus is more appropriate as part of the case-by-case equitable-fair-use analysis authorized by Section 107 of the act.

Fair Use. Accolade contends that its disassembly of copyrighted object code is a fair use privileged by Section 107. Because, in the case before us, disassembly is the only means of gaining access to unprotected ideas and functional concepts and because Accolade has a legitimate interest in gaining such access (to determine how to make its cartridges compatible with the Genesis console), we agree with Accolade.

Fair-use analysis requires an equitable balance of the factors noted in Section 107: the purpose of the use, its market effect, the nature of the work, and the amount copied. We proceed to evaluate these factors.

Purpose. We observe initially that the fact that copying is for a commercial purpose weighs against a finding of fair use. However, the presumption of unfairness can be rebutted by the characteristics of a particular commercial use.

As we have noted, the use at issue was an intermediate one only, and thus any commercial exploitation was indirect and derivative. Accolade's direct purpose in copying Sega's code was simply to study the functional requirements for Genesis compatibility. There is no evidence that Accolade sought to avoid performing its own creative work. Indeed, most of the games that Accolade released for the Genesis console had been originally developed for other hardware. Nor did Accolade simply copy Sega's code; rather, it wrote its own procedures based on what it had learned through disassembly. On these facts, we conclude that Accolade copied Sega's code for a legitimate, essentially nonexploitive purpose and that the commercial aspect of its use can best be described as of minimal significance.

We further note that we are free to consider the public benefit resulting from a particular use notwithstanding the fact that the alleged infringer may gain commercially. In this case, Accolade's identification of the functional requirements for Genesis compatibility has led to an increase in the number of independently designed video game programs offered for use with the Genesis console. It is precisely such growth in creative expression, based on the dissemination of other creative works and the unprotected ideas contained in them, that the Copyright Act is intended to promote. We conclude that given the purpose and character of Accolade's use of Sega's video game programs, the presumption of unfairness has been overcome and this first statutory factor weighs in favor of Accolade.

Market Effect. We must inquire whether there will be an adverse effect on the potential market for the copyrighted work (by way of diminishing potential sales, interfering with marketability, or usurping the market) if the challenged use should become widespread. Accolade sought only to become a legitimate competitor in the field of Genesis-compatible video games. Within that market, it is the characteristics of the game program as experienced by the user that determine the program's commercial success. There is nothing in the record that suggests that Accolade copied any of these elements of Sega's game programs.

By facilitating the entry of a new competitor, Accolade's disassembly of Sega's software undoubtedly affected the market for Genesis-compatible games in an indirect fashion. However, there is no basis for assuming that Accolade's Ishido has significantly affected the market for Sega's Altered Beast, because a consumer might easily purchase both; nor does it seem unlikely that a consumer interested in sports might purchase both Accolade's Mike Ditka Power Football and Sega's Joe Montana Football, particularly if the games are, as Accolade contends, not substantially similar. In any event, an attempt to monopolize the market by making it impossible for others to compete runs counter to the statutory purpose of promoting creative expression and cannot constitute a strong equitable basis for resisting the invocation of the fair-use doctrine. Thus, we conclude that this factor weighs in Accolade's, not Sega's favor, notwithstanding the minor economic loss Sega may suffer.

Nature of the Work. Not all copyrighted works are entitled to the same level of protection. Works of fiction receive greater protection than works

continued ...

continued...

that have strong factual elements, such as historical or biographical works or works that have strong functional elements such as accounting textbooks. Works that are merely compilations of facts are copyrightable, but their copyright protection is thin. Similarly, since computer programs essentially are utilitarian articles, many aspects of such programs are not protected by copyright.

Sega argues that even if many elements of its video game programs are not protected by copyright, Accolade still copied protected expression. Sega is correct, since disassembly involves wholesale copying. But computer programs are unique: The unprotected aspects of most functional works are readily accessible to the human eye. The systems described in accounting textbooks, for example, can easily be copied without also copying any of the protected expressive aspects of the original works. Computer programs, however, typically are distributed for public use in object code form, embedded in a silicon chip or on a floppy disk. For this reason, humans often cannot gain access to the unprotected ideas and functional concepts contained in object code without disassembling that code, meaning, making copies. Because Sega's video game programs contain unprotected aspects that cannot be examined without copying, we afford those programs a lower degree of protection than more traditional literary works. In light of all these considerations, we conclude that this statutory factor weighs in favor of Accolade.

Amount Copied. Accolade disassembled entire programs written by Sega. Accordingly, this factor weighs against Accolade. However, as the Supreme Court explained in *Sony*, the fact that an entire work was copied does not preclude a finding of a fair use.

Summary. We are not unaware of the fact that to those used to considering copyright issues in more traditional contexts, our result may seem incongruous at first blush. To oversimplify, Accolade, a commercial competitor of Sega, engaged in wholesale copying of Sega's copyrighted code as a preliminary step in the development of a competing product. However, the key to this case is that we are dealing with computer software, a relatively unexplored area in the world of copyright law. We must avoid the temptation of trying to force the proverbial square peg into a round hole.

Sega argues that the considerable time, effort, and money that went into development of the Genesis and Genesis-compatible video games militate against a finding of fair use. In *Feist*, however, the Supreme Court unequivocally rejected the sweat-of-the-brow rationale for copyright protection.

We conclude that when disassembly is the only way to gain access to the ideas and functional elements embodied in a copyrighted computer program and when there is a legitimate reason for seeking such access, disassembly is a fair use of the copyrighted work. Our conclusion does not, of course, insulate

> Accolade from a claim of copyright infringement with respect to its finished products. Sega has reserved the right to raise such a claim, and it may do so.
>
> Accordingly, we hold that Sega has failed to demonstrate a likelihood of success on the merits of its copyright claim. Thus, the preliminary injunction issued in its favor must be dissolved.

Sega v. Accolade is one of a series of cases decided since 1992 that mark a possible reversal of policy respecting the degree of protection afforded computer programs by copyright. Two other such cases are *Computer Associates v. Altai* and *Lotus Development Corp. v. Borland International, Inc.*, which are presented in the next chapter. Prior to *Sega*, a developer of mass-marketed computer software could effectively protect trade secrets embodied in its programs by distributing them only in object code. Since copying is required to decipher trade secrets written in object code, copyright effectively could prevent reverse engineering of the code to learn the valuable secrets. *Sega*, however, clouds the issue. According to *Sega*, reverse engineering of object code through copying is a fair use if (1) there are no other means to access the program ideas and functional aspects and (2) there is a legitimate reason for seeking access. Although *Sega* provides that one legitimate rationale for decompilation is to achieve interoperability of game programs with consoles, the case does not clearly identify other reasons that may be acceptable. One can expect that more defined guidance will be available only after numerous and diverse cases are decided by the courts. For now, therefore, purveyors of computer programs containing trade secrets must at least consider whether additional measures should be utilized to protect their secrets. One possibility is to form agreements with customers limiting the ways customers may use programs. As we shall see in Chapter 9, however, there is quite a bit of controversy when distributors of mass-market programs use such agreements.

The degree to which copyright laws may prevent the reverse engineering of computer programs has received international attention as well. The European Union, for instance, has passed a directive providing that reverse engineering of computer programs is not copyright infringement and cannot be barred by contract if it is necessary to obtain information to make interoperable products, and that information is not otherwise available.[28] This conforms to the policy laid down in *Sega*, although it may go further than U.S. law with its restrictions on contract provisions. In 1994, Japan's Ministry of Education, which oversees copyright policy, caused anxiety for several major software development companies, such as IBM, Apple Computer, Microsoft, and Lotus, when it began a review of copyright policies for software.[29] These companies were concerned that the review might lead to a relaxation of Japanese policy regarding reverse engineering, allowing the practice to be used more extensively than merely to achieve interoperability. Indeed, they were able to enlist help from the U.S. Trade Representative and the Department of Commerce secretary to put pressure on Japanese policy officials. Interestingly, the position of the U.S. government angered a coalition of other U.S. software firms, such as Sun Microsystems and Broderbund Software, since these companies believed that some easing of restrictions on reverse engineering might help them enter the Japanese markets. In the end, Japanese officials decided to move cautiously, and their copyright laws regarding reverse engineering have remained in conformity with U.S. and European Union policies.

(AES) All of this, of course, impacts our ability to protect the computer program used within the AES. We may have decided that since the program is distributed in a form that cannot be read by humans, it could somewhat easily be preserved as a trade secret. Any attempt by other companies to reverse engineer the program by decompiling or chip-peeling would require a translation into source code. If these actions were to violate the copyright in the program, then we could use copyright policy to help us preserve the secrecy of our program ideas. However, after *Sega*, reverse engineering of the program by methods such as decompilation might be considered a fair use, depending on the rationale for gaining access and whether there are other ways to determine the ideas used within the programs. Thus, although *Sega* was formally a case about copyright protection, its most important impact will be on the viability of trade secret protection strategies used by firms distributing computer programs and the products utilizing them.

In 2000, *Sega*'s importance to reverse engineering of computer programs became increasingly evident in a legal action brought by Sony against Connectix, alleging that Connectix unlawfully copied Sony's copyrighted PlayStation BIOS to develop software, called Virtual Game Station, that enabled users to play authorized PlayStation games on Macintosh computers.[30] The case shared many similar facts with *Sega*. For instance, the PlayStation BIOS could not be accessed without intermediate copying, and Connectix's end product did not use any copyrighted expression from the PlayStation BIOS. The purpose, though, was different, for in this instance, it was to allow PlayStation games to be played on new platforms, rather than to allow new creative games to be played on the existing console. Nonetheless, the court held that this still was a transformative purpose that deserves heightened weight under the fair-use factors. The court again noted that computer programs that cannot be observed without copying receive lower copyright protection than traditional literary works. The court also acknowledged that there might be a negative effect on the sales of Sony PlayStation consoles, but that copyright law does not confer monopoly control over the market for game-playing devices. Thus, following in the footsteps of *Sega*, the court determined that Connectix did not violate Sony's copyrights by developing its Virtual Game machine through reverse engineering.[31]

Remedies

Once infringement has been proven, the copyright owner may choose from a wide arsenal of remedies. First, the successful copyright claimant may benefit from court-imposed injunctions—orders requiring the infringer to stop engaging in the infringing activity. Not only can one receive a permanent injunction after proving infringement at trial, but one can also obtain a preliminary injunction before trial if the judge is persuaded that the likelihood of success at trial is high and that irreparable harm will result if the allegedly offending activity is not stopped immediately. Second, the copyright owner may sue for actual damages and the infringer's profits. As previously discussed, these may be hard to prove, so the claimant may opt for statutory damages instead, assuming the work was appropriately registered. In addition, the copyright owner may be able to receive attorneys' fees and court costs, again assuming that registration was timely.

No Electronic Theft Act   Violation of the Copyright Act also may lead to criminal penalties. Until 1997, the copyright statute provided for criminal prosecution only when infringement was willful and undertaken for private financial gain. However, a case against an MIT student who posted software programs on the Web for others to freely download demonstrated to some that criminal provisions of the Copyright Act were deficient.[32] Since the MIT student did not post the programs for private financial gain, he was not subject to the criminal provision of the Copyright Act, yet his actions, which willfully defied the copyrights in the posted programs, had the potential to cause the copyright owners tremendous harm. The case demonstrated to members of Congress that widespread reproduction and distribution of copyrighted works may be implemented so easily on the Internet that an infringer no longer need be motivated by financial returns to potentially engage in very damaging behavior. Therefore, in 1997, Congress passed the No Electronic Theft Act, which expanded criminal remedies for copyright violations to certain instances where the infringements are not motivated by private financial gain.[33] Specifically, it is now criminal infringement for a person to infringe a copyright willfully not only for private financial gain, but also "by the reproduction or distribution, including by electronic means, during any 180-day period, of 1 or more copies or phonorecords of 1 or more copyrighted works, which have a total retail value of more than $1,000." The Copyright Act provides for a sliding scale of remedies, depending on the number and retail value of the infringements. For instance, willful reproduction or distribution of ten or more copies of one or more copyrighted works having a total retail value exceeding $2,500 can land one in prison for three years with fines up to $250,000. The penalties for one or more copies having a total value of between $1,000 and $2,500 is up to one year in prison with fines up to $100,000. When the infringement is for private financial gain, potential prison terms are even longer.

A number of commentators fear that the new criminal provisions added by the No Electronic Theft Act may be overextensive. For instance, suppose you post to a newsgroup a quote from a magazine having a value of one cent. If the message is distributed to over 100,000 readers via the newsgroup, then the minimum $1,000 threshold for criminal liability will be reached. Thus, one now needs to be careful whenever any copyrighted material is posted on the Web, no matter how trivial, since the reach of the Web is potentially so broad. What happens, though, if you believe that the inclusion of the magazine quote in your newsgroup message is protected as a fair use? Perhaps you are taking a small portion of the article to make some comment about the author. Could this subject you to criminal liability if your judgment about the fair use is wrong? The answer will come down to how "willfully" is defined; that is, whether it is enough to willfully put the material on the Web, or whether the infringement must be willful. Although it is not yet firmly decided, it seems likely that the act will require some intentional violation of the copyright laws, and that a good-faith belief regarding fair use will protect one from criminal enforcement. Nonetheless, many worry that the new sweeping criminal penalties might chill one's willingness to engage in lawful discourse.

CONCLUSION

Copyright protection seems almost too good to be true. Absolutely nothing needs to be done to acquire it. Even those steps that provide extra benefits are extraordinarily inexpensive and easy to perform. And protection may last for over 100 years. Compared to the patent system, therefore, with its expensive and tedious procedures and relatively short period of protection, copyrights are a bargain. Given these enormous disparities, how can patents and copyrights coexist?

The answer is rooted in the different roles played by the two systems. A patent protects an idea embedded in a product. In a limited sense of the word, a patent provides an owner monopoly control over a product concept. The market dominance legally bestowed by a patent thereby may be extremely lucrative. A copyright, on the other hand, does not protect an idea, but only a means of expressing it. Normally, there will be a large number of equally suitable ways to convey a concept, and one would expect a host of competitors to adopt them. Therefore, a copyright theoretically gives something less than monopoly power and consequently should provide a lower return than a patent. Also, a copyright, unlike a patent, does not prevent independent creation. This further weakens the market posture of a copyright. In sum, then, copyrights are easier to obtain and last longer than patents but should provide lower economic returns for their owners. Overall, this is a reasonable and balanced trade-off.

The next chapter features some of the most current and controversial copyright issues affecting the management of technology. As copyrights extend to components of useful articles, such as computer programs, one needs to be careful that they do not overstep their rightful bounds. One clear benchmark is that copyrights never should be the basis for market dominance. That would be the best of both worlds—easy protection and monopoly returns—a result that would seriously upset the proper relationship between patents and copyrights. Unfortunately, this basic concept often is overlooked or forgotten.

NOTES

1. Sheldon v. Metro-Goldwyn Pictures Corp., 81 F.2d 49 (2d Cir.), *cert. denied*, 298 U.S. 669 (1936).

2. Baker v. Seldin, 101 U.S. (11 Otto) 99 (1879).

3. For instance, the "Collections of Information Antipiracy Act" was introduced in the House of Representatives in October 1997, but it was not enacted by the end of 1998. It would have provided civil and criminal remedies for the misappropriation of databases and other collections of information compiled by "sweat of the brow" investment. The act was introduced again in January 1999.

4. One is the "Treaty on Certain Questions Concerning the Protection of Literary and Artistic Works," which is commonly known as the "Copyright Treaty." The other is the "Treaty for the Protection of the Rights of Performers and Producers of Phonograms."

5. The Copyright Treaty, Art. 5.

6. For an excellent discussion of the Digital Performance Right in Sound Recordings Act, see J. Garcia, "An Analysis of the Digital Performance Right in Sound Recordings Act of 1995," J. of Proprietary Rights (February 1996) at 13–18.

7. Harper & Row Publishers, Inc. v. Nation Enterprises, 471 U.S. 539 (1985).

8. Lewis Galoob Toys, Inc. v. Nintendo of America, Inc., 964 F.2d 965 (9th Cir. 1992).

9. For thorough discussions, see Seth Greenstein, "Contributory Infringement the Second Time Around: The Copyright Case against Digital Audio Tape Recorders," 3 J. of Proprietary Rights (July 1991) at 2; Leete, "Betamax and Sound Recordings: Is Copyright in Trouble?" 23 Am. Bus. L.J. 551 (1986).

10. The initial disputes centered on digital audiotape formats.

11. Cahn v. Sony Corp., 90 Civ. 4537 (S.D.N.Y. 1990). This lawsuit was settled and the case was dismissed by the court in July 1991.

12. 17 U.S.C. § 1001 et seq. (1992).

13. *See* M. Mensik and J. Groulx, "From the Lightweight Rio Flows Heavyweight Battle," Nat'l L. J. (December 14, 1998) at B5; M. Colton, "More Piracy of the High C's?" Wash. Post (November 1, 1998) at G5.

14. Audio Home Recording Act of 1992, 17 U.S.C. § 1001(1) and § 1001(3) (The act defines a digital audio recording device as a consumer device with a digital recording function, the primary purpose of which is to make digital copies of a digital music recording.) *See* M. Mensik and J. Groulx, "From the Lightweight Rio Flows Heavyweight Battle," Nat'l L. J. (December 14, 1998) at B6.

15. Recording Indust. Ass'n of America, Inc. v. Diamond Multimedia Systems Inc., 29 F. Supp. 2d 624 (C.D. Cal. 1998).

16. For a recent example, you should follow the progress of a lawsuit filed in 2000 by the Recording Industry Association of America (RIAA), alleging that the distribution of Napster violates the copyrights of RIAA members. Napster is software that facilitates the sharing of MP3 files that reside on individual hard drives. In effect, when Napster is downloaded, it locates all the MP3 music files on the hard drive and publishes that information in a directory on the Napster.com Web site. Visitors to the Web site can search for the music they want, and download the MP3 file directly from the individual's hard drive. Many of the MP3 files are distributed without permission from the copyright owners. However, Napster is not directly involved with the illegal transactions, nor does it have control over them. Therefore, following the principles of *Sony*, the case may hinge on whether there are substantial noninfringing uses of Napster. *See* A. Kover, "Who's Afraid of This Kid?" Fortune (March 20, 2000) at 129; A. Harmon, "Potent Software Escalates Music Industrys' Jitters," N.Y. Times (March 7, 2000) at C1.

17. Kastor, "Whose Art Is It Anyway?" Wash. Post (March 27, 1989) at C1.

18. There are now ten categories, since "sound recordings" was added to Section 101(2) after the decision in *CCNV*.

19. Ashton-Tate Corp. v. Ross, 728 F. Supp. 597 (N.D. Cal. 1989).

20. CCNV v. Reid, 846 F.2d 1485, 1498 (D.C. Cir. 1988).

21. Midler v. Ford Motor Co., 849 F.2d 460 (9th Cir. 1988).

22. The Visual Artists Rights Act of 1990, Pub. L. No. 101-650.

23. In the 1990s, bills were introduced in Congress that would have allowed copyright owners to recover statutory damages, attorneys' fees, and costs without registering their works. As this book goes to press, these changes have not yet been adopted.

24. In 1998, the Copyright Act was amended to exempt all foreign works from the requirement that works be registered prior to the initiation of a lawsuit. Digital Millennium Copyright Act of 1998, § 102(d), amending § 411(a) of the Copyright Act.

25. For instance, in 1993 bills were introduced in Congress to remove the distinction in registration requirements for foreign and domestic works. 17 U.S.C. § 411. H.R. 897, S. 373, the Copyright Reform Act of 1993.

26. *See* Cooper, Law and the Software Marketer (Prentice-Hall, 1988), at 46–47.

27. 562 F.2d 1157 (9th Cir. 1977).

28. Directive 91/250 on Legal Protection of Computer Programs. OJ 1991 L122/42 (May 14, 1991).

29. T.R. Reid and P. Behr, "A Software Fight's Blurred Battle Lines," Wash. Post (January 11, 1994) at D1.

30. Sony Corporation Entertainment, Inc. v. Connectix Corporatioin, 2000 U.S. App. LEXIS 1744 (9th Cir. 2000). Connectix also was developing a version of Virtual Game Station for the Windows operating system.

31. The reasoning of this case might have some relevance to other situations, such as with the development of software to allow DVDs to run not only on DVD players, but also on computers.

32. United States v. LaMacchia, 871 F. Supp. 535 (D. Mass. 1994).

33. Pub. L. No. 105-147, § 2(b), 111 Stat. 2678 (December 16, 1997). For a discussion of two cases brought under the No Electronic Theft Act, see B. Miller, "Giveaways Costly for Web Pirate," Wash. Post (December 23, 1999) at B1.

6

Copyright Policy: Specific Technology Applications

INTRODUCTION

There once was a time when copyright policy did not garner the public attention that it now commands. To be sure, copyrights were extremely important to artists, musicians, authors, and publishers. Nevertheless, for the vast majority of people and businesses, copyrights were not a prominent area of concern. The situation changed markedly, however, with the rapid rise of computer-related technologies beginning in the 1980s. The first wave of issues dealt with copyrights and computer programs. Does copyright protection extend to computer programs? Should it? What parts of the program are subject to copyright protection? And in what form? What if the program is "written" on a chip or other component of the machine? This chapter addresses many of these issues. In so doing, the chapter demonstrates how computer programs have required judges and other policy makers to undertake substantial soul searching about the proper role of copyrights in the development of this critical industry.

The 1990s and the rise of the Internet truly brought copyrights home to everybody. What can be put on a Web page? Are there any problems with linking or with framing? Who is responsible for copyright infringements on the Web? Can material be downloaded off the Web? Can pictures be taken off the Web and used in other documents? The questions go on and on, and the public is vitally interested, since the Internet rapidly has become an integral component of so many lives, just like television and the telephone. We shall see that on one level, the answers to these questions are not all that difficult, since they generally rely on much of the basic material already covered. However, we also shall see that the sheer ease of copyright infringement, coupled with problems of enforcement, have led many commentators to question whether copyright can or should survive in the digital world.

As the overview provided in Exhibit 6.1 demonstrates, the chapter does not focus only on computers and the Internet. Concerns about copyright protection have

Exhibit 6.1
Overview of Copyright Issues in the Technological Environment

- ■ **Copyright Protection of Computer Programs and User Interfaces**
  - Determination of expressions and ideas
    - — Abstraction analysis
  - The First Line of Cases
    - — **CASE:** *Whelan Associates v. Jaslow Dental Laboratory*
      - – Protection of structure, sequence and organization of computer program
      - – Expression is everything within the program that is not necessary to carry out the function or purpose of the program
      - – "Look-and-feel" protection
    - – **CASE:** *Lotus Development Corp. v. Paperback Software Int'l.*
      - – Broad protection for user interface
      - – Standardization and compatibility not relevant.
  - Modern Line of Cases
    - — **CASE:** *Computer Associates Int'l. v. Altai*
      - – Abstraction—Filtration—Comparison analysis
      - – Reduces the degree of copyright protection for computer programs
    - — **CASE:** *Lotus Development Corp. v. Borland Int'l.*
      - – Menu command hierarchy is not protected by copyright because it is a "method of operation"
      - – Importance of standardization and compatibility
      - – Analogy to designs of useful products

- ■ **Copyright Protection of Product Designs**
  - Protection only for elements not conceived with function in mind
  - Special treatment for architecture
  - **CASE:** *Brandir Int'l. v. Cascade Pacific Lumber*

- ■ **Copyright and Artistic Media**
  - Digital audio sampling
  - Digital imaging
  - Protection of multimedia works
  - **CASE:** *Campbell v. Acuff-Rose Music*

- ■ **Copyright and the Internet**
  - Copyright management systems
  - Internet service provider liability for users' copyright infringements
    - — Contributory infringement principles
    - — **CASE:** *Religious Technology Center v. Netcom On-line Communications*
  - Caching
  - Digital Millennium Copyright Act
  - Linking and framing issues

a wide scope. With increasing frequency, design and style constitute the creativity that sells products. Can copyright protect product designs? Should it? New technologies now have the capacity to easily manipulate traditional art forms. Digital sampling and computerized photograph scanning equipment are two examples. What does copyright policy have to say about the futures of these industries? Interactive CD-ROM technologies now are firmly entrenched in the marketplace. Through this technology, individuals can selectively view and adapt databases of existing works. What hurdles does a manager in the CD-ROM-technology industry face? This chapter investigates some of the important questions arising in these developing contexts.

COPYRIGHT POLICY AND COMPUTER PROGRAMS

When the computer industry was in its infancy in the mid-1960s, there was tremendous uncertainty about whether computer programs could be protected under the copyright laws. On one hand, such programs, especially when written in high-level source code, have all the earmarks of a creative literary-style document. On the other, computer programs are an integral part of an operational machine—just the type of thing excluded from the reaches of copyright. In 1976, Congress substantially revised the Copyright Act after an almost 20-year process of debating the parameters of change. Although Congress was aware of various problems that new technologies such as computers posed to copyright policy, it recognized that it would not be able to adequately address them in the pending legislative effort. Therefore, it created the National Commission on New Technological Uses of Copyrighted Works (CONTU) to make recommendations about changes to copyright policy that might be required in order to accommodate new technological developments.

In 1978, after almost three years of deliberations, CONTU released its final report. CONTU's most definitive recommendation was that copyright protection should be available to computer programs. It stated:

> The cost of developing computer programs is far greater than the cost of their duplication. Consequently, computer programs . . . are likely to be disseminated only if . . . [t]he creator can spread its costs over multiple copies of the work with some form of protection against unauthorized duplication of the work. . . . The Commission is therefore satisfied that some form of protection is necessary to encourage the creation and broad distribution of computer programs in a competitive market, . . . [and] that the continued availability of copyright protection for computer programs is desirable.

The final report made clear that, consistent with copyright principles in traditional contexts, protection should be offered only to the expression of computer programs. However, the report was ambiguous about what aspects of the programs should be considered expression. Likewise, when Congress adopted this recommendation in 1980 by amending the Copyright Act, it failed to reveal its intentions about the limits of copyright protection for computer programs. Thus, the 1980 revisions made it clear that programs were to be protected by copyright but left it to the courts to determine the appropriate parameters for protection. How the courts have wrestled with this critical issue is illustrated by the landmark cases *Whelan v. Jaslow, Lotus Development v. Paperback Software, Computer Associates v. Altai,* and *Lotus Development v. Borland International* presented later in this chapter.

The Importance of Distinguishing Ideas from Expressions

The debate over the proper extent of copyright protection for computer programs is enormously important. Program developers, of course, want the widest possible protection. Thus, they advocate that almost all aspects of their programs constitute protectible expression. This would include not only the code used to implement a program but also the more conceptual aspects, such as the program's basic organization, file structures, and user interface. On the other side, those companies involved in making compatible software, program improvements, and/or clones argue that most aspects of a program should be considered unprotectible ideas, processes, or systems. Their position is that copyright protection of expression should be limited to the literal code only.

Many of the most important copyright disputes in the computer industry have come down to the basic issue of distinguishing protectible expression from unprotectible ideas. The two Lotus cases were very high profile litigations that both centered on the extent of copyrightable expressions in the user interfaces of that company's 1-2-3 program. Similarly, when Intel sued NEC over use of its 8086 and 8088 chip microcodes, the resolution depended on differentiating expressions from ideas.[1] Apple Computer's historic lawsuit against Microsoft and Hewlett-Packard alleging improper use of its graphical computer command system also boiled down to the scope of protectible expression.[2] These, and a huge array of other lawsuits, have held billions of dollars and entire industries in the balance. The problem is that courts have had to make judgments about expressions and ideas without guidance from Congress and with little comfort or familiarity with computer technology. As one court so honestly put it, "The challenge . . . to make comprehensible for the court the esoterica of bytes and modules is daunting."[3] Therefore, the judges have taken the approach that is most natural in such circumstances: they work from familiar territory, such as traditional books and movies, and they filter their considerations through the general principles of copyright policy.

Distinguishing between ideas and expression is a task that can never be taken lightly, even in the context of literature, and even the simplest literature at that. Consider the following children's story about a kitten that wants to find its ball of string. The reader helps the kitten search by physically opening flaps on the book to see what is behind them.

Playtime

A kitten asks, "Where is my ball of string? I want to play. Could it be inside the suitcase?" Under the flap is a lamb who says, "Naaah." "Maybe I left it in the toy box?" In the box are two mice who squeak "No" and "Way." "Is the string under the covers?" Behind the flap depicting the covers is a snake who says, "Ssss-sorry." "I know, it's in the drawer!" After opening the drawer-flap, one finds a hamster who says, "Nope." "Hey, wait, I see something in that shopping bag—That must be my ball!" Behind the flap this time is a duck who quacks, "Look in the bowl behind the plants." The kitten finds the ball of string in the bowl and exclaims in delight, "Play Ball!"

What is the idea of this story? What is the expression? A substantial amount of money may rest on your decision. So how do you decide? Although your first impulse may have been that this is a trivial matter, further reflection surely demonstrates that it is not. Here are just a few of the potentially infinite number of ways to differentiate the idea of this story from its expression:

Playtime
LEVELS OF IDEAS AND EXPRESSIONS

I.
Elements of the IDEA include:

a. A kitten searches for her ball of string because she wants to play.
b. She asks if it is inside the suitcase, and after the reader pulls up a flap, a lamb indicates in the negative.
c. She asks if it is in the toy box, and after the reader pulls up a flap, two mice indicate in the negative.
d. She asks if it is under the covers, and after the reader pulls up a flap, a snake indicates in the negative.
e. And so on until a duck is informative.
f. The kitten is very excited when she finds her ball of string.
g. Some of the animals make appropriate responses to the questions by making their natural animal sounds.

Elements of the EXPRESSION include:

a. The exact words only.

II.
Elements of the IDEA include:

a. An animal searches for something.
b. It ultimately finds what it is looking for.
c. It looks by having the reader open flaps covering the prospects.
d. When asked, animals indicate that the sought-after item is not at that location.

e. Some of the animals make appropriate responses to the questions by making their natural animal sounds.

f. The last animal knows where the item is.

Elements of the EXPRESSION include:

a. A kitten is searching.

b. She is looking for her ball of string.

c. The animals solicited are a lamb, two mice, a snake, a hamster, and a duck.

d. The kitten looks behind, in, or under a suitcase, a toy box, covers, a drawer, a shopping bag, and plants.

III.
Elements of the IDEA include:

a. An animal searches for something.

b. It ultimately finds what it is looking for.

c. It looks by having the reader open flaps covering the prospects.

Elements of the EXPRESSION include:

a. A kitten is searching.

b. She is looking for her ball of string.

c. Animals are questioned about the location.

d. The animals solicited are a lamb, two mice, a snake, a hamster, and a duck.

e. The kitten looks behind, in, or under a suitcase, a toy box, covers, a drawer, a shopping bag, and plants.

f. Some of the animals make appropriate responses to the questions by making their natural animal sounds.

g. None of the animals except the last knows where the ball of string is.

IV.
Elements of the IDEA include:

a. An animal searches for something.

b. It ultimately finds what it is looking for.

Elements of the EXPRESSION include:

a. The animal searches by having the reader open flaps covering prospects.

b. A kitten is searching.

c. She is looking for her ball of string.

d. Animals are questioned about the location.

e. The animals solicited are a lamb, two mice, a snake, a hamster, and a duck.

f. The kitten looks behind, in, or under a suitcase, a toy box, covers, a drawer, a shopping bag, and plants.

g. Some of the animals make appropriate responses to the questions by making their natural animal sounds.

h. None of the animals except the last knows where the ball of string is.

V.
Elements of the IDEA include:

a. To tell a story.

Elements of the EXPRESSION include:

a. Everything in the story is expression including that there is a search, an animal is searching, it opens up flaps, and it finds what it is looking for.

This list was formulated so that the idea is most concrete at level I and increasingly abstract as one moves down to level V. Which is the proper formulation? Courts have tried for decades to answer that question, but without success. The decision will be largely arbitrary and ad hoc. But the choice may be dramatically important.

Following is a hypothetical story about a puppy that searches for its bone. The puppy looks with the help of the reader, who pulls up flaps where the puppy wants to search. Assume that this account was published after *Playtime* and that access can be proven. If there is a lawsuit, can one establish copyright infringement?

The Hunt

A puppy states, "I wonder where my bone could be? Is it under this leaf?" Under the leaf-flap is a snake that says, "Sssssscram." "Is it in this pile of hay?" Under the hay-flap is a squirrel that says, "No." "Is it in the barn?" Behind the barn door–flap is a horse that says, "Naay." "Is it under this pail?" Under the pail-flap is a frog that says, "Go away." "Is it in the burlap bag?" Behind the bag-flap is a duck who says, "I saw it in the mailbox." The puppy opens the mailbox-flap, finds the bone, and screams, "Yummy."

Remember that to prove infringement, one must demonstrate substantial similarity of the works and of the protectible expression. If level I is selected, there is no infringement. Not only are the ideas of the two stories somewhat different but, more important, the expression, which constitutes no more than the words, is not at all similar. At level II, there is more chance of infringement. Now the stories have the same ideas. Also, some elements of the expression are similar. Of all the possible animals to conduct the search, a puppy may seem substantially similar to a kitten. Also, the duck in the bag is the same, and there is a snake in both stories. But still, there are a lot of differences. Most of the places searched, the animals that are questioned, and how they respond are not similar given the idea from which they were derived.

At level III, infringement becomes more likely. A number of things could be found behind the flaps besides different animals, such as people or objects. That a selection of different animals is used in both stories is somewhat similar. Also, the snake and the horse in *The Hunt* answer, to some degree, in their native tongue, just as did the snake and the lamb in *Playtime*. In addition, the last animal in both stories knows where the missing item is. Indeed, this key animal in both stories is a duck. At level IV, one is very likely to conclude that there has been unlawful copying, because the stories share even more similarities in expression. This is especially true because the flap-opening characteristic is a salient attribute of expression that is presented by both books in the same way. Finally, moving to level V, which contains the most abstract version of the idea, one finds so many substantially similar elements of expression that the only possible conclusion is that *The Hunt* infringes *Playtime*.

It is disheartening that an ad hoc decision will determine whether *The Hunt* unlawfully appropriates protected expression from *Playtime*. Courts generally are not content with abstraction level I because it provides so little protection to the work. Likewise, they are not likely to rest with level V because that gives too much: the author of *Playtime* should not have a lock on the entire genre of happy-ending stories involving animals.

Without being too definitive, and recognizing that there is tremendous variability depending on the particular facts, courts seem most inclined to select abstraction level III or IV for literary works of this kind. For example, recall that in the H. R. Pufnstuf litigation, discussed in Chapter 5, the court assumed that the idea was a fantasyland filled with diverse and fanciful characters in action. What this means is that a large part of a novel, play, or movie likely will be considered protectible expression. And be very clear that this extends well beyond the literal words. The plot, organization, characters, mood, and many other aspects often will be viewed as elements of expression capable of copyright protection.

The Availability of Alternative Expressions   Although the determination of proper abstraction levels remains essentially ad hoc, courts still are guided by the underlying principles of copyright. Thus, they are mindful that copyright should provide sufficient incentives to develop and distribute works of authorship without overly stifling creativity. Clearly, level I provides too little protection from copyright. Conversely, level V grants too much in that it might allow an author to have exclusive control of an artistic market. As noted in Chapter 1, copyright never should allow one to enjoy a monopoly position in the marketplace. Rather, copyright protection acts appropriately when it bestows exclusivity to one of several suitable ways to reach the relevant consuming audience. This, then, serves as one guidepost for selecting an abstraction level. If the chosen abstraction level serves to allow the copyright owner to enjoy monopoly-like power in the marketplace, then that level is not a proper level.[4] Such power may be realized when there are not several alternative ways of expressing the chosen idea that would be marketable to a recognized set of consumers. Thus, at any level of abstraction, one must ask whether sufficient alternative expressions are available that would allow others to successfully compete in the marketplace. If the answer is no, then that selected level is too abstract. The following example should help clarify this complicated concept.

A. A. Hoehling wrote a historical account of the Hindenburg disaster based on exhaustive research. In the book, he argued that all previous theories about the disaster (static electricity, St. Elmo's fire) are unconvincing except sabotage. He concluded that the saboteur was a rigger who was influenced by his communist girlfriend to place a bomb in a gas cell. Michael Mooney wrote a literary version of the Hindenburg disaster using Hoehling's sabotage theory and then sold to Universal Studios the rights to make a motion picture version of the book. After the movie was made, Hoehling sued Universal for copyright infringement. He alleged that the movie copied protectible expression from his book, including the specific sabotage plot and various scenes such as those depicting German beer hall revelry, the singing of the German national anthem, and the use of certain German greetings.[5]

Hoehling's story could be abstracted as follows.

1. The IDEA is the particular sabotage theory, embellished with a German beer hall scene, German greetings, and the singing of the German national anthem. The EXPRESSION comprises the exact words only.

2. The IDEA is to relate a theory of the Hindenburg disaster. The EXPRESSION includes Hoehling's particular theory, as well as his use of the beer hall scene, the singing, and the greetings.

3. The IDEA is to tell a story. That the story focuses on the Hindenburg disaster is part of the EXPRESSION.

In his case, Hoehling was asking the court to accept something like abstraction 2 to distinguish the idea from the expression. Obviously, level 3 would be overreaching. If the Hindenburg topic, itself, were an element of expression, then the first account might control the market, since all subsequent versions likely would seem substantially similar by virtue of the common theme. Thus, there would be no alternatives available for competitors to sell to those interested in the Hindenburg incident. For this reason, that level is not proper, and a less abstract one must be selected.

There are substantial problems with level 2 as well, however. Hoehling depicts his theory as the truth, based on historical facts. Those persons interested in the Hindenburg obviously would prefer the most accurate account of the disaster. Thus, if Hoehling can obtain exclusive rights to his theory by virtue of its being protectible expression, then he will dominate the marketplace because there are no other equally suitable expressions available to competitors. For this reason, the theory must be a part of the unprotectible idea, as illustrated in abstraction level 1. This demonstration indicates another reason why facts are not copyrightable, as discussed in *Feist Publications*.

Similarly, the typical German scenes cannot be part of the expression. Although they likely were fictitious embellishments to the factual account, it would not be appropriate to allow Hoehling exclusive rights to them. Such standard literary accounts, called *scènes à faire*, are indispensable to others who wish to compete in that genre of German stories. Thus, they too must be part of the unprotectible idea. Again, abstraction level 2 provides too much market power. One must move the analysis to a less abstract level, therefore, as represented by level 1.

The case of *Aliotti v. Dakin*, presented in Chapter 4, provides another example. Not only did Aliotti allege that Dakin had usurped her confidential disclosure, but she also charged violation of her copyrights in the dinosaur dolls. The court concluded that there had been no copyright violation because most of the items copied by Dakin were part of the unprotectible idea. That both lines of dinosaurs were soft and cuddly, for instance, was deemed irrelevant because such features are indispensable to sell dolls to children. Also, the similar postures and body designs were considered indispensable to depict the various dinosaurs. Other similar characteristics, such as that the winged pterodactyls were used in mobiles also were dismissed because they were natural and expected uses of the dolls. By the end of the analysis, all that was left as protectible expression were the eye styles and the stitching—items that were not substantially similar in Dakin's dinosaur dolls.

This is the familiar terrain upon which courts tread when they review computer copyright cases. The distinction between the ideas of computer programs and their expressions is based on the same set of guiding principles. The courts deal with an array of potential abstractions, and they make decisions that are essentially ad hoc but tailored by the basic underlying policy objectives of copyright.

In very simple terms, a word processing program could fall within the following list of abstractions:

WORD PROCESSING PROGRAM: LEVELS OF IDEAS AND EXPRESSIONS

I.
Elements of the IDEA include:
a. The purpose of the program—to conduct word processing.
b. All the particular functions to be carried out by the program.
c. All the ways the program causes the computer to interact with the user (the user interface).
d. All the subroutine functions selected to carry out the program.
e. The exact structure of commands used within each subroutine.
f. All the ways the subroutines are organized and interact within the program.

Elements of the EXPRESSION include:
a. The exact code only.

———————

II.
Elements of the IDEA include:
a. The purpose of the program—to conduct word processing.
b. Some of the functions to be carried out by the program.
c. Some of the ways the program causes the computer to interact with the user.
d. Some of the subroutine functions selected to carry out the program.
e. Some of the subroutine command structures used within certain subroutines.
f. Some of the ways the subroutines are organized and interact within the program.

Elements of the EXPRESSION include:
a. Code.
b. Some selected functions of the program.
c. Some parts of the user interface.
d. Some of the selected subroutine functions.
e. Some of the subroutine command structures.
f. Some of the ways subroutines are organized and interact.

———————

III.
Elements of the IDEA include:
a. The purpose of the program—to conduct word processing.
b. Elements of the program necessary to do word processing.

Elements of the EXPRESSION include:
a. Code.
b. The selected functions of the program.
c. The user interface.
d. The subroutine functions selected.
e. The subroutine command structures.
f. The ways subroutines are organized and interact.

IV.
Elements of the IDEA include:
a. A computer program that causes a computer to do something.

Elements of the EXPRESSION include:
a. Everything about the program, including that it performs word processing.

The level that programmers would prefer depends on the programmers' type of creative activity. Those who develop new programs argue that the correct level should be very abstract, such as that represented by level III or IV. Those who wish to build upon developments in previous programs believe that the industry is best served by level I or II.

The Original Approach in Computer Copyright Cases

Protection for Computer Programs   The following two cases—*Whelan v. Jaslow* and *Lotus v. Paperback Software*—are landmarks in the field. The opinions illustrate how the courts first handled computer copyright issues by drawing on their experience with literary works. This led the courts to select a somewhat abstract interpretation of a computer program's idea—similar to level III in the example above.

WHELAN ASSOCIATES, INC. V. JASLOW DENTAL LABORATORY, INC.
Third Circuit Court of Appeals, 1986

FACTS: Jaslow Lab manufactured dental devices. Jaslow hired Strohl Systems Group, Inc., to create a computer program that would make its bookkeeping more efficient. Whelan, who worked for Strohl, developed the program after

continued . . .

continued . . .

exhaustive research on Jaslow's business operations. The program was called Dentalab and was written in EDL language. Soon thereafter, Whelan left Strohl, and Strohl assigned its entire interest in Dentalab to Whelan's new company.

Whelan entered an agreement with Jaslow under which Jaslow was to market the new program for 35% of the gross sales price. After two years, Jaslow learned more about computers and determined that many businesses would want a program capable of achieving the same functions as Dentalab, but written in BASIC language. He developed this program and called it Dentcom. Jaslow then canceled the Dentalab agreement with Whelan and independently marketed both Dentalab and Dentcom.

Whelan charged Jaslow with copyright infringement. Jaslow Lab maintained that it owned the copyright because Dentalab had been created for it by Strohl. It also alleged that it did not copy Dentalab in creating Dentcom. The district court found for Whelan on the copyright claim. First, it concluded that Whelan owned the copyright. Second, it found that there was substantial similarity of expression based on the testimony of experts. Whelan's expert claimed that although Dentcom was not a translation of Dentalab, the programs had almost identical file structures and screen outputs, and that five particularly important subroutines performed almost identically. Jaslow's expert argued that there were substantive differences in programming style, structure, algorithms, and data structures, but that there were overall structural similarities. Third, the court ruled that there was unlawful reproduction based on clear access along with the similarities. Jaslow appealed the determination of copyright infringement to the court of appeals.

DECISION AND REASONING: In this case of first impression, the court must determine whether the structure, sequence, and organization of a computer program is protectible by copyright or whether the protection of copyright law extends only as far as the literal computer code.

The coding process is a comparatively small part of programming. By far the larger portion of the expense and difficulty in creating computer programs is attributable to the development of the structure and logic of the program and to debugging, documentation, and maintenance, rather than to the coding. Because efficiency is a prime concern in computer programs (an efficient program being obviously more valuable than a comparatively inefficient one), the arrangement of modules and subroutines is a critical factor for any programmer. The evidence in this case shows that Ms. Whelan had spent a tremendous amount of time studying Jaslow Labs, organizing the modules and subroutines for the Dentalab program, and working out the data arrangements and had spent a comparatively small amount of time actually coding the Dentalab program.

To prove that its copyright has been infringed, Whelan must show two things: that it owned the copyright and that Jaslow copied Dentalab in making Dentcom. Ownership is not contested on appeal. Copying may be proven inferentially by showing that the defendant had access to the work and that the allegedly infringing work is substantially similar. It is uncontested that Jaslow had access so the sole question is whether there is substantial similarity between the two programs.

To prove substantial similarity, a two-part process is used. First, one must decide whether there is sufficient similarity between the two works to conclude that the alleged infringer used the copyrighted work in making the infringer's own. For this test, expert testimony is admissible. Second, one must decide from the perspective of the lay observer only whether the copying was an unlawful appropriation of the expression from the copyrighted work. The court believes that with complex cases involving computer programs, reliance on ordinary observers alone is too limiting, and it thus concludes that expert testimony is relevant to determine if there is unlawful copying as well.

It is well established that copyright protection extends to a program's source and object codes. In this case, however, there is no copying of these codes. Rather, there is only substantial similarity of the overall structure. One can violate the copyright of a play or book by copying its plot. Also, as in *Krofft v. McDonald*'s, substantial similarity may be established by comparing the total concept and feel of two works. By analogy to other literary works, it would appear that the copyrights of computer programs can be infringed even absent copying of the literal elements of the program.

A Rule for Distinguishing Idea from Expression in Computer Programs. It is frequently difficult to distinguish the idea from the expression since the decision is inevitably ad hoc. Because the line between idea and expression is elusive, we must pay particular attention to the pragmatic considerations that underlie copyright policy.

A previous Supreme Court case—*Baker v. Selden*—suggests that the line between idea and expression may be drawn with reference to the end sought to be achieved by the work in question. In other words, the purpose or function of a utilitarian work would be the work's idea, and everything that is not necessary to that purpose or function would be part of the expression of the idea. When there are various means of achieving the desired purpose, the particular means chosen is not necessary to the purpose; hence there is expression, not idea. Also, just as with literary works, those aspects that as a practical matter are indispensable to the treatment of a topic are afforded no protection. Thus, anything necessary to effect the function is part of the idea.

The rule proposed here would provide the proper incentive for programmers by protecting their most valuable efforts while not giving them a

continued . . .

continued . . .

stranglehold over the development of new computer devices that accomplish the same end. The principal economic argument against this position (and supporting that only the literal code is protectible) is that computer programs are so intricate, each step so dependent on all of the other steps, that they are almost impossible to copy except literally. Some also argue that the concept of structure in computer programs is too vague to be useful in copyright cases. In addition, others believe that computer technology is achieved by stepping-stones, a process that requires the use of much of the underlying copyrighted work. Protection of computer programs beyond the code thereby will retard progress in the field. But we are not convinced by any of these arguments.

The rule proposed here has its greatest force in the analysis of utilitarian or functional works, for the purpose of such works is easily stated and identified. Here, it is clear that the purpose of the utilitarian Dentalab program was to aid in the business operations of a dental laboratory. It is also clear that the structure of the program was not essential to that task: there are other programs on the market, competitors of Dentalab and Dentcom, that perform the same functions but have different structures and designs. The conclusion is thus inescapable that the detailed structure of the Dentalab program is part of the expression, not the idea, of that program.

We hold (1) that copyright protection of computer programs may extend beyond the programs' literal code to their structure, sequence, and organization and (2) that the district court's finding of substantial similarity is not erroneous. We therefore affirm.

"LOOK-AND-FEEL PROTECTION"   *Whelan v. Jaslow* was the first of the so-called look-and-feel computer cases. This designation was derived from the court's willingness to have copyright protect the structure, sequence, and organization (SSO) of a program and its reference to the total-concept-and-feel language from *Krofft v. McDonald's*. However, those who wrote about computer copyright protection, especially in the popular press, often were analytically imprecise when they said that the look and feel of computer programs was protectible. In a sense, it was true, but only by using a backdoor determination based on the expansive protection offered in cases such as *Whelan*. The look and feel was not really protected; rather, it was the expression of the program that was protected by copyright. However, if just about everything about the program, including its SSO, were judged to be expression subject to copyright protection, then *Krofft* taught that one might determine infringement by comparing the look and feel of the two works. Therefore, in the special situations where programs in their entirety were judged to be protected by copyright, the look-and-feel designation was appropriate. And given the judicial copyright decisions during this period, this may not have been an inaccurate depiction by the press. Nonetheless, it is important to recognize that the look-and-feel designation works only when virtually all elements of the program are considered protectible expression. If one determines that certain significant elements of the program are not protected by copyright, either because they are indispensable to the purpose or for some other reason, then it no longer will be true that copyright protects the program's look and feel.

The 1994 appellate court opinion in the historic lawsuit brought by Apple Computer against Microsoft and Hewlett-Packard illustrates this point.[6] Apple sued these companies essentially alleging that Windows was substantially similar to the graphical user interface Apple used in its computers, thereby violating its copyrights. We will look more closely at copyright protection for user interfaces shortly with two cases involving Lotus 1-2-3. For now, though, it is only important to know that the court ruled that many aspects of Apple's graphical user interface were not protected by copyright. Apple, for instance, had given Microsoft and Hewlett-Packard permission to use many of the visual displays in a license agreement. The court also determined that several other aspects could not be protected by copyright because they were ideas. These included (1) use of windows to display multiple images on the computer screen and to facilitate user interaction, (2) iconic representation of familiar objects from the office environment, (3) manipulation of icons to convey instructions and to control operations, (4) use of menus to save space and to store information in a place that is convenient to reach, and (5) opening and closing objects to retrieve, transfer, and store information. Nonetheless, Apple argued that the test for substantial similarity required the court to compare the total concept and feel of the works as a whole, without dissecting the unprotectible elements from the analysis. The court denied that this was the correct approach. Rather, it determined that those elements not protected by copyright had to be filtered from consideration prior to any comparison. In this situation, the court concluded that so little of Apple's user interface was protected by copyright that substantial similarity of what was left could be proven only if the works were virtually identical. Based on this reasoning, Apple lost the case.

You should begin to question the simplicity of the court's decision in *Whelan v. Jaslow*. Why is it so clear that the purpose is merely to aid in the business operations of a dental laboratory? Is it also part of the purpose to achieve this goal efficiently? The court noted that other programs can help a dental lab, but can they do so as efficiently as Whelan's program? When efficiency is part of the idea, if there is a most efficient SSO, then this SSO must be part of the idea also. In other words, one must move the analysis up to a less abstract level.

The court also did not evaluate the marketability of alternative programs. What if there were some aspect of Whelan's program that buyers preferred so much that they would not consider buying the alternative dental lab assistance programs? When screen displays are at issue, what if consumers prefer the layout of one more than others? Logically, part of the idea of the program should be that consumers will buy it. Thus, if only one expression appeals to consumers, then that expression should be subsumed within the idea at a less abstract level. Unbelievably, many courts have determined that marketability is not an aspect of the idea. For instance, in a lawsuit between Apple Computer and Franklin Computer, the Court of Appeals stated that commercial and competitive objectives do not enter the metaphysical issue of whether particular expressions serve as ideas.[7] So, if only one program is marketable to consumers, it still may be protected by copyright as long as other programs can achieve the same basic purpose.

One is left in an absurd quandary by this notion. The proper level of abstraction to distinguish ideas from expressions is supposed to limit the possibility that the copyright will yield a market monopoly. Yet, some courts in computer cases ignore the very commercial realities that determine the ultimate market power from copyright protection. This, of course, leads to the issue of standardization in the computer industry. If one expression becomes such a standard in the industry that consumers refuse or are unable to adopt alternatives, hasn't that expression become an idea? Think of it this way: You develop a word processing program which is very widely adopted. Other programs may conduct word processing, but those persons who have learned and invested in your program do not wish to take the time to learn how to use them. Wasn't your solution to the word processing "puzzle" simply a great idea, which has become extremely profitable? Shouldn't competitors now be able to share that idea and thus compete on other dimensions that aren't indispensable to their survival? Now you should really be troubled because to follow this through, one's success in marketing may mean one's demise in terms of copyright protection. Courts, obviously, are cautious with evaluating market realities for just this reason. But as we shall see in the next chapter, successful trademarks may be lost by virtue of their success. Welcome to the twilight zone of intellectual property.

Do not get the impression that courts always ignore market or technical realities. For instance, one court refused to extend copyright protection to a cotton information computer system because it presented cotton information in the manner that the relevant purchasers most desired.[8] Also, in litigation between NEC and Intel, the court determined that if only one set of instructions can feasibly achieve a task within the technical constraints of the hardware, then that set must be considered part of the unprotectible idea.[9] Similarly, the court in *Apple v. Microsoft* determined that the power and speed of computers along with ergonomic factors may limit the creative options for programmers.[10] To this author, all forms of competitive realities, be they based on market conditions or technical constraints, should be relevant to the determination of what constitutes protectible expression. However, one never knows for sure whether a court will agree.

Protection for User Interfaces   Not only did courts provide very broad copyright protection to computer programs, but they also extended it to the various tangible forms in which such programs were found. Programs are protectible if written in source code, object code, and even microcode. In addition, such codes may be protected even if they are embodied within the hardware of the computer, such as with read-only memories. Although it may seem inconsistent for copyright to protect a component of a machine when the statute provides that systems and processes are off-limits, this did not stop the courts. *Lotus Development Corp. v. Paperback Software International*, which first sanctioned copyright protection for user interfaces, is a classic example of how the logic from *Whelan v. Jaslow* was extended to new domains by certain courts.

LOTUS DEVELOPMENT CORPORATION V. PAPERBACK SOFTWARE INTERNATIONAL
District Court, Massachusetts, 1990

FACTS: This case concerns two competing application programs—Lotus 1-2-3 and VP-Planner—which are primarily electronic spreadsheet programs but which also support other tasks such as limited database management and graphics creation. Like manual spreadsheets, the electronic spreadsheet presents a blank form on which numerical, statistical, financial, or other data can be assimilated, organized, manipulated, and calculated. In many spreadsheet programs, a highlighted element of the basic screen display resembles an "L" rotated 90 degrees clockwise with letters across the top to designate columns, and numbers down the left side to designate rows.

The idea for an electronic spreadsheet was first rendered into commercial practice by Daniel Bricklin, who developed VisiCalc. Although VisiCalc was a commercial success, implementational characteristics limited the scope and duration of its marketability as a spreadsheet product. Mitchell Kapor and Jonathan Sachs, the original authors of 1-2-3, exploited the opportunity. Building on Bricklin's idea for an electronic spreadsheet, they expressed the idea in a different, more powerful way, taking advantage of the IBM PC's more expansive memory and its more versatile screen display capabilities and keyboard. Built on the shoulders of VisiCalc, 1-2-3 was an evolutionary product. Microsoft later developed a different powerful spreadsheet program, called Excel, which could handle the characteristics of the Apple Macintosh.

Dr. James Stephenson formulated VP-Planner. The original version of the program had a different user interface than did 1-2-3 or VisiCalc. Stephenson and Adam Osborne then created Paperback Software in 1983 to market VP-Planner. In 1984, they recognized the success of 1-2-3 and reached the conclusion that spawned this litigation: VP-Planner, in order to be a commercial success, would have to be compatible with 1-2-3. The only way to accomplish this, they believed, was to ensure that the arrangement and names of commands and menus in VP-Planner conformed to those of 1-2-3. Such compatibility would allow users to transfer spreadsheets created in 1-2-3 to VP-Planner without loss of functionality for any macros (a series of instructions designed by the user that can be implemented with one command stroke) in the spreadsheet. Also, such compatibility would allow users to switch from 1-2-3 to VP-Planner without requiring retraining in the operation of VP-Planner.

continued . . .

continued . . .

Lotus, the copyright owner of 1-2-3, sued Paperback Software, alleging that it had unlawfully copied the user interface of 1-2-3 in developing VP-Planner. According to Lotus, the user interface of 1-2-3 includes such elements as the menus (and their structure and organization), the long prompts (which provide additional information about a selected command), the appearance of the screens, the function key assignments, and the macro commands and language.

DECISION AND REASONING: The expression of an idea is copyrightable. The idea itself is not. When applying these two settled rules of law, how can a decisionmaker distinguish between an idea and its expression? Answering this riddle is critical to determining the issues of this case: (1) whether and to what extent 1-2-3 is copyrightable and (2) whether VP-Planner is an infringing work containing elements substantially similar to the copyrightable elements of 1-2-3.

The parties agree that literal manifestations of a computer program—including both source code and object code—if original, are copyrightable. Defendants vigorously dispute, however, the copyrightability of any nonliteral elements of computer programs. Plaintiff, on the other hand, maintains that copyright protection extends to all elements of computer programs that embody original expression, whether literal or nonliteral, including any original expression embodied in the program's user interface.

Like all other works of authorship, computer programs are not entitled to an unlimited scope of copyright protection. Section 102(b) makes it clear that the expression adopted by the programmer is the copyrightable element in a computer program and that the actual processes or methods embodied in the program are not within the scope of copyright law.

With respect to such things as musical works and works of literature, it is well settled that a copyright may be infringed even if the infringer has not copied the literal aspects of the work. Infringement may be found if there is copying of the work's expression of setting, characters, or plot with resulting substantial similarity.

The court's task is governed by the object and policy of copyright law. Courts should not draw the line between copyrightable and noncopyrightable elements of computer programs in such a way as to harm the public welfare, nor should courts ignore the accommodation struck by Congress in choosing to advance the public welfare by rewarding authors. Drawing the line too liberally in favor of copyright protection would bestow strong monopolies over specific applications upon the first to write programs performing those applications and would thereby inhibit other creators from developing improved products. Drawing the line too conservatively would allow a programmer's efforts to be copied easily, thus discouraging the creation of all but modest incremental advances.

Defendants suggest that the user interface of Lotus 1-2-3 is a useful, functional object, like the layout of gears in an "H" pattern on a standard transmission, the functional assignment of letters to keys on a standard QWERTY keyboard, and the functional configuration of controls on a musical instrument. This court concludes that defendant's contentions are inconsistent with the legislative history of the Copyright Act. The bulk of the creative work is in the conceptualization of a computer program and its interface rather than in its encoding. Defendants' contentions would preclude from protection the most significant creative elements of the process, a result inconsistent with statutory mandates.

Defendants contend that useful articles are not protected by copyright [see discussion in following section]. It is true that the utilitarian aspects of useful articles are not copyrightable and that things that merely utter work, such as the cam of a drill, are not copyrightable. This does not mean, however, that every aspect of a user interface is not copyrightable. The mere fact that an intellectual work is useful or functional—be it a dictionary, directory, map, or computer program—does not mean that none of the elements of the work are copyrightable. Elements of expression, even if embodied in useful articles, are copyrightable if they may be recognized and identified separately from the functional ideas that make the article useful.

Three concepts are embedded in the idea/expression dichotomy. The first, noted previously, is that expression must embody more than functional elements in the utilitarian sense. The second is that expression must go further than the obvious. The third is that the expression must be one of several possible ways of expressing the idea for it to be copyrightable. If the expression of an idea has elements that go beyond all functional elements of the idea itself, and beyond the obvious, and if there are numerous other ways of expressing the noncopyrightable idea, then those elements of expression, if original, are copyrightable.

In making a determination of copyrightability, the court first must conceive a scale of abstractions along the scale from the most generalized conception to the most particularized and then choose some formulation for distinguishing the idea from its expression. Next the court must decide whether the alleged expression is one of only a few ways of expressing the idea.

In the context of computer programs, nonliteral elements have often been called the look and feel of a program. One may argue that the phrase is analogous to the total-concept-and-feel test developed in *Krofft*. In this case, however, the test was not invoked to determine what nonliteral elements were copyrightable. Rather, the court used the concept in applying the substantial similarity test to determine whether forbidden copying of copyrightable material had occurred.

continued ...

continued . . .

The user interfaces of 1-2-3 and VP-Planner have many similarities. They both have the rotated "L" characteristic. They utilize a two-line moving-cursor menu structure, which presents the user with a list of command choices and a moving cursor to use in entering the choice. With each, the menu is called up to the screen by pressing the slash ("/") key. The top line of the two-line menus contains a series of words representing different commands, and the second line displays a long prompt, which contains further information about a selected command. In addition to having the option of selecting commands with the cursor, a user may instead press the key representing the first letter of the command word. VP-Planner uses the same words or words beginning with the same letters to designate commands, and their placements are identical to 1-2-3 in the menu structure. Function keys are also utilized similarly by the two programs to make command selections. Both programs also utilize macros, which by their nature are related to the structure, sequence, and organization of the menu structures and the first letters of the command choices. Although there are some differences in the menu structures and displays of the two programs, VP-Planner is designed to work like Lotus 1-2-3, keystroke for keystroke.

As the starting point, the idea is a computer program for an electronic spreadsheet. A two-line moving-cursor menu also is part of the idea since it is functional, obvious, and used in various types of computer programs. Nevertheless, not every possible method of designing a menu system that includes a two-line moving cursor is noncopyrightable. The rotated "L" characteristic is also part of the idea since there is a rather low limit on the number of ways of making a computer screen resemble a spreadsheet. In addition, the use of the slash key to invoke the command system is part of the idea. There are not many keystrokes available to perform this task because letters and numbers are used to input spreadsheet cell values. Also, since this function is used so often, it should be easily accessible without the need to hit two keys. Only the slash and the semicolon fit these requirements. Because it is one of only two options, the slash key cannot be expression. Finally, certain commands are obvious such as the use of the "+" key to indicate addition.

The court concludes that a menu command structure is capable of being expressed in many if not an unlimited number of ways and that the command structure of 1-2-3 is an original and nonobvious way of expressing a command structure. Accordingly, the menu structure of 1-2-3 taken as a whole—including the choice of command terms, the structure and order of those terms, their presentation on the screen, and the long prompts—is expression. This is made clear because there are several other spreadsheet programs with different structures, including VisiCalc and Excel. Obviously, 1-2-3's particular expression of a menu structure is not essential to the electronic spreadsheet idea. The order of commands in each menu line; the choice of letters, words, or symbolic tokens to represent each command; the method of presentation of the symbols on the screen; and the long prompts could be expressed in literally unlimited number of ways. Also, the fact that some command terms are obvious does not preclude copyrightability if they have been brought together in an original way.

Comparison of VP-Planner with the copyrightable expression of 1-2-3, from the perspectives of both experts and ordinary viewers, demonstrates that the similarities overwhelm any differences. Even though there are some differences, there are substantial similarities in the qualitatively important aspects of protectible expression. Therefore, defendant has impermissibly copied 1-2-3, and its liability has been established.

Defendants argue that the computer industry requires more legal certainty than the foregoing method of analysis provides. However, hard-and-fast rules, despite their initial attractiveness and false promises of certainty, have consequences that offend one's sense of justice. Defendants also argue that if copyright protection is extended to user interfaces and other nonliteral elements of computer programs, then there will be disastrous consequences for the computer industry. However, this prediction was disregarded by Congress in 1980, has not been proven by the evidence, and therefore is disregarded here as well.

Finally, defendants maintain that needs for compatibility and standardization in the industry require a less expansive role for copyright protection. They state that some expressions may be so effective or efficient that they become standardized throughout the field, even though the idea is capable of being expressed in other ways. However, this court is not persuaded that this is relevant to the issue of copyright protection. Defendants also argue that 1-2-3 is pervasively used and that users who have been trained on it and have written elaborate macros to run on it would be unwilling to switch to VP-Planner unless the task were simplified. Again the court is not persuaded. First, defendants ignore the success of Excel, an innovative spreadsheet that is not compatible with 1-2-3. Also, defendants could have achieved compatibility without copying. For instance, translation devices could have been used to read and convert macros written for 1-2-3 into those that could run on VP-Planner.

Defendants' standardization argument is flawed for another reason as well: By arguing that 1-2-3 was so innovative that all should be free to copy its expression, defendants flip copyright on its head. Copyright protection would be perverse if it protected only mundane increments while leaving unprotected those advancements that are more strikingly innovative.

For all of these reasons, defendants are liable for infringement of Lotus 1-2-3.

Lotus v. Paperback Software makes it clear that some courts have been willing to extend copyright protection to almost all aspects of computer programs. Regrettably, this court, like so many others, intelligently discussed the role of copyrights in the intellectual property system but overlooked it when making its ultimate decision. A copyright should provide incentives to support creative activities. However, since copyright generates its stimulus within the private marketplace, its effects must be policed according to market realities. This is what the defense tried to illustrate to the court in *Lotus*, but without success.

Apparently, the courts were worried that if copyrights did not provide sufficient protection for software and other computer-related creations, then these developments would not be forthcoming. The stunning gap in this logic, however, was that it ignored the emergence of patent protection for software inventions. The various components of the intellectual property system are not mutually exclusive. Under proper circumstances, one can simultaneously protect the ideas of a particular program with trade secret laws, and its expressions by copyright. Similarly, there is no restriction on obtaining protection for a computer program through both patents and copyrights. Thus, one can immediately protect software expression via copyright and protect the software idea through the patent procedures discussed in Chapters 2 and 3.

Before the 1981 decision of *Diamond v. Diehr*, patents provided little coverage for computer programs. However, since that case, the PTO has shown greater willingness to issue patents for an ever-widening range of software inventions, and the courts have upheld them. For instance, utility and/or design patents have issued for business application programs, operating systems software, expert systems, user interface systems, and data processing programs. At times, however, some courts in copyright cases seemed stuck in pre-1981 patent law, thereby ignoring the role that patents legitimately should play in stimulating computer-related inventions. By allowing the subject matter of copyright to extend to what was almost undeniably software systems and processes, these courts merged the roles of patents and copyrights. For this reason, during the 1980s and early 1990s, many legal scholars asked courts to step back and more carefully scrutinize those aspects of computer systems for which patent protection might be appropriate and available. Courts then might feel more free to include these aspects within the unprotectible ideas or processes of the program, comfortably knowing that creative incentives could be properly maintained through the patent process.

The Modern Approach in Computer Copyright Cases

Protection for Computer Programs For some time, there seemed to be little chance that courts would heed this advice and retreat from the sweeping expanse of copyright protection in the computer industry. However, starting in 1992, some courts charted what may be a more sophisticated approach to copyrights in the computer field. The 2nd Circuit Court of Appeals, in *Computer Associates v. Altai*, was the first to take this important step.

COMPUTER ASSOCIATES INTERNATIONAL, INC. v. ALTAI, INC.
Second Circuit Court of Appeals, 1992

FACTS: Both of the firms Computer Associates and Altai design, develop, and market various types of computer programs. CA-SCHEDULER is a job-scheduling program designed by Computer Associates for IBM mainframe computers. Its functions are first to create a schedule specifying when the computer should run various tasks and then to control the computer as it executes the schedule. CA-SCHEDULER contains a subprogram entitled ADAPTER, which was also developed by Computer Associates. ADAPTER is an operating system compatibility component. The IBM System 370 family of computers, for which CA-SCHEDULER was created, is designed to contain one of three operating systems (DOS/VSE, MVS, or CMS). ADAPTER's function is to translate the language of a given program, in this case CA-SCHEDULER, into the particular language that the computer's own operating system can understand. In this way, ADAPTER allows a computer user to change or use multiple operating systems while maintaining the same software. This is highly desirable since it saves the user the costs, in both time and money, that otherwise would be expended in purchasing new programs, modifying existing systems to run them, and gaining familiarity with their operation.

Starting in 1982, Altai began marketing its own scheduling program, entitled ZEKE. The original version of ZEKE was designed for use in conjunction with a VSE operating system. By late 1983, in response to customer demand, Altai decided to rewrite ZEKE so that it could be run in conjunction with an MVS operating system. At that time, James Williams, an employee of Altai, approached Claude Arney, a computer programmer who had worked for Computer Associates. Arney was a programmer who had worked on ADAPTER for Computer Associates and was intimately familiar with various aspects of ADAPTER. Arney left Computer Associates in 1984 to work for Altai and took copies of ADAPTER's source code with him. He did this in knowing violation of employee confidentiality agreements that he had signed.

Rather than redesigning ZEKE, Arney convinced Williams that the best way to make the switch to MVS was to introduce an operating system compatibility component into ZEKE. Arney created the component program, which was called OSCAR 3.4. To this end, Arney copied 30% of the OSCAR 3.4 code from Computer Associates' ADAPTER program. In late July 1988, Computer Associates first learned that Altai may have appropriated parts of ADAPTER, and it brought suit for copyright infringement and trade secret misappropriation. It was at this time that Williams first received actual knowledge that Arney had copied much of the OSCAR 3.4 code from ADAPTER.

Williams initiated a project to rewrite OSCAR so as to preserve as much as could be legitimately saved and to excise those portions copied from

continued . . .

continued . . .

ADAPTER. Arney was excluded from the project, and his source code locked away. The rewrite was entitled OSCAR 3.5. From this time on, Altai shipped only OSCAR 3.5 to new customers and offered it as a free upgrade for its previous customers using OSCAR 3.4.

The district court determined that Altai infringed Computer Associates' copyrights with its OSCAR 3.4 program and awarded $364,000 in damages. However, it found that Altai was not liable for copyright infringement in developing OSCAR 3.5. In addition, the district court determined that Altai was not liable for trade secret misappropriation in developing either program. Computer Associates appealed the copyright decision involving OSCAR 3.5 and the dismissal of the trade secret claims.

DECISION AND REASONING: In recent years, the growth of computer science has spawned a number of challenging legal questions, particularly in the field of copyright law. As scientific knowledge advances, courts endeavor to keep pace, and sometimes—as in the area of computer technology—they are required to venture into less than familiar waters. The copyright law seeks to establish a delicate equilibrium. On one hand, it affords protection to authors as an incentive to create, and on the other, it must appropriately limit the extent of that protection so as to avoid the effects of monopolistic stagnation. In applying the federal act to new types of cases, courts must always keep this symmetry in mind.

Computer Program Design. A computer programmer works from the general to the specific. The first step in programming is to identify a program's ultimate purpose. Next, a programmer breaks down the ultimate function into simpler constituent subtasks, which are also known as subroutines or modules. A programmer then arranges the subroutines into flow charts, which map the interactions between the subroutines. To accomplish these interactions, the programmer must pay careful attention to the form and content of information, called parameter lists, that is passed between modules.

The functions of the modules in a program together with each module's relationships to other modules constitute the structure of the program. In fashioning the structure, a programmer normally attempts to maximize the program's speed, efficiency, and simplicity for user operation while taking into consideration certain externalities such as the memory constraints of the computer upon which the program will be run. This stage of program design often requires the most time and investment.

Once all the necessary modules have been identified and designed and their relationships to the other modules have been laid out conceptually, then the resulting program structure must be coded. After coding is completed, the program is tested for errors. Once these are corrected, the program is complete.

Copyright Infringement. After OSCAR 3.4 was rewritten into OSCAR 3.5, none of the ADAPTER source code remained. Computer Associates argues that OSCAR 3.5 remained substantially similar to the structure of its ADAPTER program. As discussed before, a program's structure includes its nonliteral components such as general flow charts as well as the more specific organization of intermodule relationships and parameter lists. In addition, Computer Associates contends that OSCAR 3.5 is also substantially similar to ADAPTER with respect to the list of services that both programs obtain from the operating systems.

Congress intended computer programs to be considered literary works. A powerful syllogism therefore emerges: Since the nonliteral structures of literary works are protected by copyright and since computer programs are literary works, as we are told by Congress, then the nonliteral structures of computer programs are protected by copyright. We have no reservation in joining those courts that have already ascribed to this logic.

Idea-versus-Expression Dichotomy. It is a fundamental principle of copyright law that a copyright does not protect an idea, but only the expression of the idea. Drawing the line between idea and expression is a tricky business. The essential utilitarian nature of a computer program further complicates the task of distilling its idea from its expression. In the context of computer programs, the Third Circuit's noted decision in *Whelan* has, thus far, been the most thoughtful attempt to accomplish this end.

So far, in the courts, the *Whelan* rule has received mixed reception. Whereas some decisions have adopted its reasoning, others have rejected it. *Whelan* has fared even more poorly in the academic community, where its standard of distinguishing idea from expression has been widely criticized for being conceptually overbroad. The crucial flaw in *Whelan*'s reasoning is that it assumes that only one idea underlies any computer program and that once a separable idea can be identified, everything else must be expression. As we have already noted, a computer program's ultimate function or purpose is the composite result of interacting subroutines. Since each subroutine is itself a program and thus may be said to have its own idea, *Whelan*'s general formulation that a program's overall purpose equates with the program's idea is descriptively inadequate.

Substantial Similarity Test for Computer Program Structure: Abstraction— Filtration—Comparison. We think that *Whelan*'s approach to separating idea from expression in computer programs relies too heavily on metaphysical distinctions and does not place enough emphasis on practical considerations. The following approach breaks no new ground; rather it draws on such familiar copyright doctrines as merger, *scènes à faire*, and public domain. In as

continued ...

continued . . .

certaining substantial similarity, a court should first break down the allegedly infringed program into constituent structural parts. Then, by examining each of these parts for such things as incorporated ideas, expression that is necessarily incidental to those ideas, and elements that are taken from the public domain, a court would then be able to sift out all nonprotectible material. Left with a kernel, or, possibly, kernels, of creative expression after following this process of elimination, the court's last step would be to compare the material with the structure of an allegedly infringing program. The result of that comparison will determine whether the protectible elements of the programs at issue are substantially similar so as to warrant a finding of infringement.

Step One—Abstraction: A court should dissect the allegedly copied program's structure and isolate each level of abstraction contained within it. This process begins with the code and ends with an articulation of the program's ultimate function.

Step Two—Filtration: Filtering entails examining the structural components at each level of abstraction to determine whether their particular inclusion at that level was indeed idea or was dictated by considerations of efficiency so as to be necessarily incidental to that idea; required by factors external to the program itself; or taken from the public domain and hence is nonprotectible expression.

In the context of computer program design, the concept of efficiency is akin to deriving the most concise logical proof. Thus, the more efficient a set of modules is, the more closely it approximates the idea or process embodied in that particular aspect of the program's structure. Although, hypothetically, there may be a myriad of ways in which a programmer may effectuate certain functions within a program (i.e., express the idea embodied in a given subroutine), efficiency concerns may so narrow the practical range of choice as to make only one or two forms of expression workable options. A court must inquire whether the use of a particular set of modules is necessary to implement efficiently that part of the program's process being implemented.

In many instances, it is virtually impossible to write a program to perform particular functions in a specific computing environment without employing standard techniques. This is a result of the fact that a programmer's freedom of design choice is often circumscribed by extrinsic considerations such as (1) the mechanical specifications of the computer on which a particular program is intended to run, (2) the compatibility requirements of other programs in conjunction with which a program is designed to operate, (3) computer manufacturers' design standards, (4) the demands of the industry being served, and (5) widely accepted programming practices within the computer industry. We conclude that a court must examine the structural content of an allegedly infringed program for elements that might have been dictated by external factors.

In addition, material found in the public domain is free for the taking and cannot be appropriated by a single author even though it is included in a copyrighted work. Thus a court must also filter out this material from the allegedly infringed program before it makes the final inquiry in its substantial similarity analysis.

Step Three—Comparison: Once a court has sifted out all elements that are ideas, or are dictated by efficiency or external factors, or are taken from the public domain, there may remain a core of protectible expression. At this point, the court's substantial similarity inquiry focuses on whether the defendant copied any aspect of this protected expression, as well as on an assessment of the copied portion's relative importance with respect to the plaintiff's overall program.

Policy Considerations. Computer Associates argues against the type of approach that we have set forth on the grounds that it will be a disincentive for future computer program research and development. It claims that if programmers are not guaranteed broad copyright protection for their work, they will not invest the extensive time, energy, and funds required to design and improve program structures.

Feist teaches that substantial effort alone cannot confer copyright status on an otherwise uncopyrightable work. Despite the fact that significant labor and expense often go into computer program flowcharting and debugging, that process does not always result in inherently protectible expression. Thus, *Feist* implicitly undercuts the *Whelan* rationale, which allowed copyright protection beyond the literal computer code in order to provide the proper incentive for programmers by protecting their most valuable efforts.

Furthermore, we are unpersuaded that the test we approve today will lead to the dire consequences for the computer program industry that Computer Associates predicts. To the contrary, serious students of the industry have been highly critical of the sweeping scope of copyright protection engendered by the *Whelan* rule, in that it enables first comers to lock up basic programming techniques as implemented in programs that perform particular tasks.

Generally, we think that copyright registration is not ideally suited to deal with the particularly dynamic technology of computer science. Thus far, many of the decisions in this area reflect the courts' attempt to fit the proverbial square peg into a round hole. The district court suggested that patent registration, with its exacting up-front novelty and nonobviousness requirements, might be the more appropriate rubric of protection for intellectual property of this kind. However, Congress has made clear that computer programs are literary works entitled to copyright protection. Of course, we shall abide by these instructions, but in so doing we must not impair the overall integrity of copyright law.

continued . . .

continued . . .

The District Court Decision. We agree with the district judge's systematic exclusion of nonprotectible elements in ADAPTER. The judge found that virtually no lines of code were identical after the rewrite of OSCAR. The judge also determined that most of ADAPTER's parameter lists were either in the public domain or dictated by the functional demands of the program. A few of OSCAR's parameter lists were similar to some of the remaining protectible lists from ADAPTER, but the amount of similarity was *de minimis* and not enough for infringement. The judge also concluded that the overlap exhibited between the list of services required for both programs was determined by the demands of the operating system and of the applications program to which it was linked through OSCAR and ADAPTER. Finally, the district judge accorded no weight to the similarities between the two programs' organizational charts because the charts were so simple and obvious to anyone exposed to the operation of the programs. This is but one formulation of the *scènes à faire* doctrine, which we have endorsed as a means of weeding out unprotectible elements.

We emphasize that infringement cases that involve computer programs are extremely fact specific. The amount of protection due structural elements will vary according to the protectible expression found to exist within the program at issue. The judgment by the district court that OSCAR 3.5 does not infringe the copyright in ADAPTER is affirmed.

Trade Secret Issues. The district court determined that the state trade secrets claim was preempted by the federal copyright statute. We disagree.

With respect to OSCAR 3.4, Altai may have had constructive notice that Arney had misappropriated trade secrets. For OSCAR 3.5, which was written after Altai received actual notice of the misappropriation, it must be determined if any trade secrets were incorporated.

The trade secret claims are remanded for determination of these trade secret issues.

Computer Associates is important for several reasons. Its most important contribution probably is the recognition that the idea of any computer program likely comprises a host of features and attributes of the program rather than simply a generalized statement of the program's purpose. The court's discussion of abstractions in *Computer Associates* may seem a little confusing, since it does not exactly follow the treatment used earlier in this chapter. However, the philosophical intent and the result are the same. The goal of abstraction analysis is to lay out the numerous ways that a work may be conceptualized and in the process weed out those elements that are not protected by copyrights. *Computer Associates* makes it very clear that the idea of a program should be viewed in far less abstract terms than it was in *Whelan*. According to the 2nd Circuit, elements of the program dictated by efficiency and market demand are part of the idea. In addition, standard programming techniques must be filtered out as a component of the idea before the expressions are compared. Indeed, by using terms such as "kernel" and "core" to describe what might be protected as expression, the court gives a pretty good idea about how many elements it believes will be filtered out as ideas.

The case also clearly states that copyrights may not be the most appropriate medium to protect the dynamic aspects of computer science. Rather, patents may be more suitable. Although *Computer Associates* by no means sounds a death knell for copyright in the computer realm, it clearly demonstrates that the courts are willing to swing the pendulum back in the other direction, thereby reducing the extent of copyright protection.[11]

Soon after *Computer Associates* was decided, other courts adopted its philosophy about the role of copyrights in protecting computer programs. The Federal Circuit, for instance, explicitly relied on the case in 1992 to resolve a dispute between Atari and Nintendo.[12] Also, in 1992, the district court completed its evaluation of the case brought by Apple Computer against Microsoft and Hewlett-Packard.[13] Although much of that case ultimately was decided on the basis of contract provisions, the judge also evaluated the degree of protection that copyright afforded to graphical user interfaces. The overriding tone of the judge focused on the functionality of the user interface and the realistic needs of other companies wishing to compete. The judge determined that the arrangement of attributes in Apple's visual screen displays was designed to make the computer more utilitarian, in the same way that the interface of a car, which includes the dashboard displays, steering wheel, gear shift, and accelerator, allows a driver to operate a car.[14] As will be discussed in the next section, this analogy helps lead to the conclusion that copyright is an inappropriate means of protection. In addition, the judge put substantially more weight on the importance of standardization than did the court in *Lotus v. Paperback Software*.

Protection for User Interfaces   In 1995, the 1st Circuit Court of Appeals issued a landmark decision regarding the menu command hierarchy of the Lotus 1-2-3 program. As you read the case, consider how much the philosophical tone has changed since the days of *Whelan* and *Paperback Software* regarding the role of copyrights in protecting elements of computer programs.

LOTUS DEVELOPMENT CORPORATION V. BORLAND INTERNATIONAL, INC.
First Circuit Court of Appeals, 1995

FACTS: Lotus 1-2-3 is a spreadsheet program that enables users to perform accounting functions electronically on a computer. Users control the pro-

continued . . .

continued . . .

grams through menu commands, such as Copy, Print and Quit. Users choose commands either by highlighting them on a screen or by typing their first letter. In all, Lotus 1-2-3 has 469 commands arranged into more than 50 menus and submenus. Lotus 1-2-3 allows users to write macros, enabling the users to designate a series of command choices with a single keystroke.

Borland spent nearly three years developing its Quattro program, which was designed to have enormous innovations over existing spreadsheet products. Borland determined that compatibility with Lotus 1-2-3 was important so that spreadsheet users who were already familiar with Lotus 1-2-3 would be able to switch to Quattro without having to learn new commands or rewrite their Lotus macros. To achieve compatibility, Borland offered its users an alternative user interface called the Lotus Emulation Interface. By activating the Emulation Interface, Borland users would see the Lotus menu items on their screens and could interact with Quattro as if using Lotus 1-2-3, albeit with a slightly different looking screen and with many Borland options not available on Lotus 1-2-3. In effect, Borland allowed users to choose how they wanted to communicate with Borland's spreadsheet programs; either by using menu commands designed by Borland, or by using the commands and command structure used in Lotus 1-2-3. Quattro also had a feature called Key Reader which allowed the program to understand and perform some Lotus 1-2-3 macros even when the Emulation Interface was not being used. In designing these compatibility features, Borland did not copy any of Lotus's underlying computer code; it copied only the words and structure of Lotus's menu command hierarchy.

The district court determined that the menu command hierarchy of Lotus 1-2-3 constituted copyrightable expression, and that Borland infringed Lotus's copyrights with its Emulation Interface and its Key Reader. The district court concluded that the user interface was copyrightable because literally millions of satisfactory spreadsheet menu trees could be constructed using different commands and different command structures than those of Lotus 1-2-3. Borland appealed this ruling, arguing that the Lotus menu command hierarchy that it copied is not copyrightable under section 102(b) because it is a system, method of operation, process or procedure.

DECISION AND REASONING: Whether a computer menu command hierarchy constitutes copyrightable subject matter is a matter of first impression in this court. While some other courts appear to have touched on it briefly, we know of no cases that deal with the copyrightability of a menu command hierarchy standing on its own (i.e., without other elements of the user interface, such as screen displays, in issue). Thus we navigate in uncharted waters.

Before we analyze whether the Lotus menu command hierarchy is a system, method of operation, process or procedure, we first consider the applicability of the test the Second Circuit set forth in *Computer Associates Int'l v. Altai*. The Second Circuit designed its test in *Altai*, which involves abstraction, filtration and comparison, to determine whether one computer program copied nonliteral expression from another program's code. However, in this appeal, we are not confronted with alleged nonliteral copying of computer code. Rather, we are faced with Borland's deliberate, literal copying of the Lotus command hierarchy. While the *Altai* test may provide a useful framework for assessing the alleged nonliteral copying of computer code, we find it to be of little help in assessing whether the literal copying of a menu command hierarchy constitutes copyright infringement. We think that abstracting menu command hierarchies down to their individual word and menu levels and then filtering idea from expression at that stage, as both the *Altai* and district court tests require, obscures the more fundamental question of whether a menu command hierarchy can be copyrighted at all. The initial inquiry should not be whether individual components of a menu command hierarchy are expressive, but rather whether the menu command hierarchy as a whole can be copyrighted.

We think that "method of operation," as that term is used in section 102(b), refers to the means by which a person operates something, whether it be a car, a food processor, or a computer. We hold that the Lotus menu command hierarchy is an uncopyrightable "method of operation." The Lotus menu command hierarchy provides the means by which users control and operate Lotus 1-2-3. If users wish to copy material, for example, they use the "Copy" command. If users wish to print material, they use the "Print" command. Users must use the command terms to tell the computer what to do. Without the menu command hierarchy, users would not be able to access and control, or indeed make use of, Lotus 1-2-3's functional capabilities.

The Lotus menu command hierarchy does not merely explain and present Lotus 1-2-3's functional capabilities to the user; it also serves as the method by which the program is operated and controlled. The Lotus menu command hierarchy is different from the Lotus long prompts, for the long prompts are not necessary to the operation of the program; users could operate Lotus 1-2-3 even if there were no long prompts. The Lotus menu command hierarchy is also different from the Lotus screen displays for users need not "use" any expressive aspects of the screen displays in order to operate Lotus 1-2-3; because the way the screens look has little bearing on how users control the program, the screen displays are not part of Lotus 1-2-3's "method of operation." The Lotus menu command hierarchy is also different from the underlying computer code, because while code is necessary for the program to work, its precise formulation is not. In other words, to offer the same capabilities as Lotus 1-2-3, Borland did not have to copy Lotus's underlying code (and indeed it did not); to allow users to operate its programs in substantially

continued . . .

continued . . .

the same way, however, Borland had to copy the Lotus menu command hierarchy. Thus the Lotus 1-2-3 code is not an uncopyrightable "method of operation."

The district court held that the Lotus menu command hierarchy, with its choice and arrangement of command terms, constituted an "expression" of the "idea" of operating a computer program with commands arranged hierarchically into menus and submenus. Under the district court's reasoning, Lotus's decision to employ hierarchically arranged command terms to operate its program could not foreclose its competitors from also employing hierarchically arranged command terms to operate their programs, but it did foreclose them from employing the specific command terms and arrangement that Lotus had used.

Accepting the district court's finding that the Lotus developers made some expressive choices in choosing and arranging the Lotus command terms, we nonetheless hold that that expression is not copyrightable because it is part of Lotus 1-2-3's method of operation. If specific words are essential to operating something, then they are part of a "method of operation" and, as such, are unprotectable. This is so whether they must be highlighted, typed in, or even spoken. The fact that Lotus developers could have designed the Lotus menu command hierarchy differently is immaterial to the question of whether it is a "method of operation." In other words, our initial inquiry is not whether the Lotus menu command hierarchy incorporates any expression. Rather, our initial inquiry is whether the Lotus menu command hierarchy is a "method of operation." Concluding, as we do, that users operate Lotus 1-2-3 by using the Lotus menu command hierarchy, and that the entire Lotus menu command hierarchy is essential to operating Lotus 1-2-3, we do not inquire further whether that method of operation could have been designed differently. The "expressive" choices of what to name the command terms and how to arrange them do not magically change the uncopyrightable menu command hierarchy into copyrightable subject matter.

In many ways, the Lotus menu command hierarchy is like the buttons used to control, say, a video cassette recorder ("VCR"). Users operate VCRs by pressing a series of buttons that are typically labeled "Record, Play, Reverse, Fast Forward, Pause, Stop/Eject." That the buttons are arranged and labeled does not make them a "literary work," nor does it make them an "expression" of the abstract "method of operating" a VCR via a set of labeled buttons. Instead, the buttons are themselves the "method of operating" the VCR. When a Lotus 1-2-3 user chooses a command, either by highlighting it on the screen or by typing its first letter, he or she effectively pushes a button. Highlighting the "Print" command on the screen, or typing the letter "P," is analogous to pressing a VCR button labeled "Play."

Just as one could not operate a buttonless VCR, it would be impossible to operate Lotus 1-2-3 without employing its menu command hierarchy. Thus, the Lotus command terms are not equivalent to the labels on the VCR's buttons, but are instead equivalent to the buttons themselves. Unlike the labels on a VCR's buttons, which merely make operating a VCR easier by indicating the button's functions, the Lotus menu commands are essential to operating Lotus 1-2-3. Without the menu commands, there would be no way to "push" the Lotus buttons, as one could push unlabeled VCR buttons. While Lotus could probably have designed a user interface for which the command terms were mere labels, it did not do so here. Lotus 1-2-3 depends for its operation on use of the precise command terms that make up the Lotus menu command hierarchy.

That the Lotus menu command hierarchy is a "method of operation" becomes clearer when one considers program compatibility. Under Lotus's theory, if a user uses several different programs, he or she must learn how to perform the same operation in a different way for each program used. Consider also that users employ the Lotus command hierarchy in writing macros. Under the district court's holding, if the user wrote a macro to shorten the time needed to perform a certain operation in Lotus 1-2-3, the user would be unable to use that macro to shorten the time needed to perform that same operation in another program. We think that forcing the user to cause the computer to perform the same operation in a different way ignores Congress's direction in section 102(b) that "methods of operation" are not copyrightable.

In holding that expression that is part of a "method of operation" cannot be copyrighted, we do not understand ourselves to go against the Supreme Court's holding in *Feist*. We do not think that the Court's statement that "copyright assures authors the right to their original expression" indicates that all expression is necessarily copyrightable; while original expression is necessary for copyright protection, we do not think that it is alone sufficient. Courts must still inquire whether the original expression falls within one of the categories foreclosed from copyright protection by section 102(b), such as being a "method of operation."

Our holding goes against the Tenth Circuit's reasoning in *Autoskill Inc. v. National Educational Support Systems, Inc.*, in which that court rejected the defendant's argument that the keying procedure used in a computer program was an uncopyrightable "procedure" or "method of operation" under section 102(b). The Ninth Circuit has also indicated in *Brown Bag Software v. Symantec Corp.* that "menus and keystrokes" may be copyrightable.

Because we hold that the Lotus menu command hierarchy is uncopyrightable subject matter, we further hold that Borland did not infringe Lotus's copyright by copying it. The judgment of the district court is Reversed.

As the court indicates in *Borland*, not all appellate circuits agree with its conclusion that the entire menu command hierarchy is an uncopyrightable system of operation. Many commentators believe that the time has come for the Supreme Court to step in and provide uniform guidance. In fact, the Supreme Court did agree to hear an appeal of the 1st Circuit opinion in *Borland*, and its decision was eagerly awaited by the computer industry. Unfortunately, one of the justices disqualified himself from hearing the case, and the others split 4–4 on the outcome.[15] Therefore, the 1st Circuit opinion survived without comment from the Supreme Court. At this time, it is not clear when the Supreme Court will get another opportunity to hear such a case, and obviously, one cannot predict how the justices will rule. However, one should not expect the clock to turn all the way back to the era before *Computer Associates*. As depicted in Exhibit 6.2, the glory days of copyright protection for computer programs are likely over. For this reason, computer companies now are looking more to patents and trade secrets to protect the key aspects of their programs.[16]

(AES) The new directions offered by *Computer Associates* and *Borland* may have far-reaching implications for the protection of the computer program embedded in the **Audio Enhancement System**. As with many other classes of products, computer programs may be protected in a variety of ways. As discussed in Chapter 2, patent protection may be a viable means to protect a computer program. But assume that we have strong reservations about the prospects for meaningful patent protection for the **AES** program. Thus, our preference is to use trade secret protection, even though the **AES** will be a widely distributed consumer product. We now know, following the principles of *Sega*, that under certain circumstances found to be legitimate, competitors may be able to legally decompile the program in order to determine its ideas. Prior to *Computer Associates*, this might not have posed too severe a problem because the idea probably would have been viewed quite abstractly, as perhaps to alter the digital characteristics of audio information to improve sonic qualities. Such an interpretation would have kept most of the program in the realm of protectible expression, thereby keeping it out of the hands of any clean-room personnel instructed to design a competing product. With the advent of the *Computer Associates* line of reasoning, however, those who reverse engineer the **AES** program may be able to use substantially more of what they learn through decompilation. For instance, those elements that are dictated by the mechanical specifications of the **AES**, or that are required to make the system work with other components, or that allow the system to operate more efficiently, now may be fair game for competitors. Thus, our trade secret protection program, implemented in conjunction with copyright, ultimately may not protect the commercially valuable aspects of the **AES** program. If this is the case, then maybe we should reconsider our initial decision to forgo patents.

International Copyright Protection of Computer Programs

The debate about copyright protection for computer programs becomes even more heated when one peers into the international environment. Some countries rely on

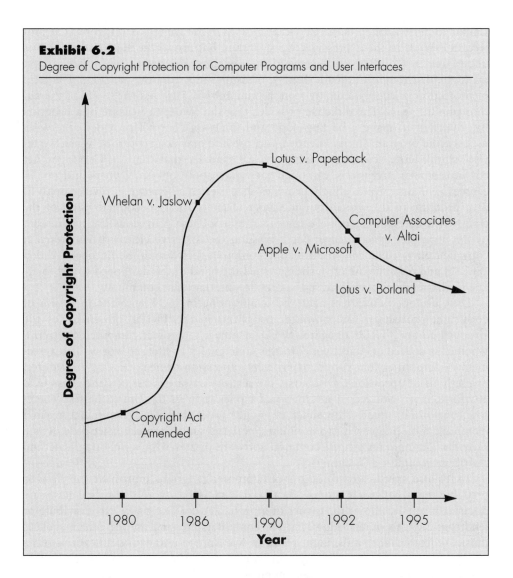

Exhibit 6.2
Degree of Copyright Protection for Computer Programs and User Interfaces

duplicating software to enhance their economic status. Thus, they have been reluctant to pass or enforce laws that extend copyright protection to programs in any meaningful way. Although controversy continues in the United States regarding the degree that copyright should protect computer programs, there is little disagreement that exact code should be covered. Thus, it has been a primary goal of the United States and other developed countries to ensure that copyright laws across the globe apply to computer programs.

In 1991, the European Union Council adopted a comprehensive directive designed to harmonize copyright policies regarding computer programs among the EU nations.[17] With some exceptions, the guiding principles of this directive are very similar to those applied in the United States. As in the United States, copyright protection extends to the expression of a program, but not to the ideas and principles underlying it. Copyright privileges include exclusive rights to reproduce, adapt, translate, distribute, run, load, display, transmit, and store the program. The term of protection is lengthy, ranging from a minimum of 50 years to the life of the author plus 50 years. The directive provides that the owner or licensee of a program has the right to make a backup copy and, unless a contract provides otherwise, may use the program for its intended purpose and may correct errors. When we review shrink-wrap licenses in Chapter 9, we shall see that the U.S. Copyright Act contains similar provisions, although they may apply only to owners and not licensees. The directive explicitly provides that users may engage in reverse analysis of a program to determine its underlying ideas and may decompile parts of the code when necessary to achieve interoperability. These provisions are reminiscent of the principles articulated in *Sega*. In sum, the directive clearly articulates that copyright plays a key role in protecting computer software in the European Union (EU). In addition, the directive strengthened the hand of the developed world to argue for harmonized standards in the broader international community.

The developed countries achieved a milestone in 1994 with the inclusion of copyright protection for computer programs in the TRIPs Agreement of the Uruguay Round. TRIPs obligates WTO members to protect computer programs, whether in source or object code, to the same extent as literary works. The agreement also specifies that copyright protects expressions, but not ideas, procedures, or methods of operations. Of course, the distinction of expressions and ideas is, if anything, more clouded in international circles than in the United States. Therefore, one cannot predict how much copyright protection a program might get in a member nation. However, at a minimum, copyright must protect exact code, which provides ammunition against common software pirates who simply duplicate and distribute commercial programs.

TRIPs also specifies that authors of computer programs must have the right to prohibit rentals of their works. As noted in Chapter 5, the so-called first-sale doctrine normally allows the owner of a particular copy of a work to distribute or lend that copy to others. However, the computer industry, among others such as music, worries that rentals might result in widespread unlawful duplications of its members' works. Given how easy it often is to duplicate programs, the fear is that many users simply may find the temptations to be too great if they can get their hands on the programs cheaply, even if just for a day or two. This likely would be especially true in cultures where copyright protection does not have a strong and lengthy heritage. Therefore, the inclusion in TRIPs of the antirental provision for computer programs was considered an important weapon in the war against software piracy.

As discussed in Chapter 1, most WTO members must abide by these provisions as of January 2000. Some may wait until 2005. Although laws are likely to be on the books within the required time limits, enforcement is another matter. Estimates for software piracy rates in many Eastern European and Asian countries are staggering, sometimes exceeding 90%.[18] Two major computer software industry groups estimated that international software piracy cost the U.S. economy over $11 billion in revenue and 130,000 jobs in 1997.[19] The members of the WTO are supposed to effectively enforce the intellectual property laws mandated by TRIPs. However, it probably is foolish to expect anything more than painfully slow progress in international efforts to combat software piracy. In fact, the rapid rise of the Internet will serve to exacerbate the enforcement problems. This is something we will look at further at the end of this chapter.

COPYRIGHT PROTECTION OF PRODUCT DESIGNS

Consumers buy products to satisfy needs. Most products appeal to customers because they present an appropriate balance of critical factors, including utility, appearance, warranties, and price. There are occasions when purchase decisions are made solely with utilitarian considerations in mind without regard to aesthetics. However, more typically, customers are concerned not only with how a product works but also with how it looks. Thus, a lighting fixture will be selected by reviewing its ability to illuminate a driveway along with its potential appearance to those passing by. Similarly, an exercise bicycle may be chosen as much for its dynamic shape and ergonomics as its ability to provide an aerobic workout. Likewise, purchasers of audio equipment, such as the **AES**, are motivated to some degree by the stylish appearances of competing components.

Marketers of many kinds of products, including those in technology industries, are focusing increased attention on the designs of their goods. As companies have channeled more and more investment dollars into the design aspects of product sales, however, concern has arisen over their protection. Design patents have always been a possibility, but they require one to hurdle the expensive and time-consuming obstacles discussed in Chapter 3. We will also see in the next chapter that trademarks offer another possible opportunity for protection, but there are a number of troubling concerns with that avenue as well. Therefore, product designers have begun looking seriously at copyright or copyright-like protection for their creative investments.

Those who advocate the application of copyright protection to product designs emphasize that some products have reached the status of being works of art and should be treated as such by copyright. If a sculpture may be protected by copyright, why should a stunning-looking exercise bike or light fixture be treated any differently? The problem is that the Copyright Act has an explicit condition that brings protection of useful items into doubt. Section 102 provides that pictorial, graphic, and sculptural works are capable of copyright protection. However, this is qualified in Section 101 by the definition of what constitutes pictorial, graphic, or sculptural works under the act. Section 101 states:

The design of a useful article, as defined in this section, shall be considered a pictorial, graphic, or sculptural work only if, and only to the extent that, such design incorporates pictorial, graphic, or sculptural features that can be identified separately from, and are capable of existing independently of, the utilitarian aspects of the article.

The meaning of these words has sparked a substantial debate and confusing precedents in the courts. For instance, statues that served as bases for lamps were held to be protectible by copyright.[20] However, a modern outdoor lighting fixture was denied protection because of the intimate and inseparable association with being a useful article.[21] On the other hand, belt buckles with sculptured designs cast in precious metals were deemed suitable for copyright.[22] Although they were clearly useful articles, and the artistic elements could not be physically separated from the belt-attaching mechanisms, the court determined that the act requires only that the artistic aspects be "conceptually separable" from the utilitarian ones. The notion of "conceptual separability" opened the door to a host of puzzling questions about the reach of copyright. *Brandir International v. Cascade Pacific Lumber* is an important case that thoughtfully considers conceptual separability and the limits to copyright protection under the existing terms of the Copyright Act.

BRANDIR INTERNATIONAL, INC. v. CASCADE PACIFIC LUMBER CO.
Second Circuit Court of Appeals, 1987

FACTS: David Levine created wire sculptures shaped like sine waves, or continuous undulating ribbons, and displayed them at home. A friend who was a bicycle buff suggested that the sculptures would make excellent bicycle racks, by allowing the bikes to be parked below the overloops and on top of the underloops. Levine modified the designs slightly to accommodate the task of holding bicycles and changed the materials to heavy-gauged, tubular, rust-proof galvanized steel. His company, Brandir, began marketing the bike rack, called the RIBBON Rack, in September 1979. By 1982, the bike rack had been heavily advertised, had been featured in several design and architecture magazines, and had won awards and recognition from industrial design organizations. By 1985, sales were in excess of $1.3 million.

In November 1982, Levine discovered that Cascade Pacific was selling a similar product. In December 1982, Brandir filed an application for copyright registration, but the Copyright Office refused to register the rack, stating that the sculptural aspects were not capable of independent existence apart from the shape of the useful article. Brandir sued Cascade and the Register of Copyrights, alleging that registration was improperly denied, that

Cascade infringed copyright protection in the rack, and that Cascade was confusing consumers. The district court found for the defendants on all points and Brandir appealed.

DECISION AND REASONING: In passing the Copyright Act of 1976, Congress attempted to distinguish between protectible "works of applied art" and "industrial designs not subject to copyright protection." The courts, however, have had difficulty framing tests by which the fine line establishing what is and what is not copyrightable can be drawn. Once again we are called upon to draw such a line, this time in a case involving the RIBBON Rack.

In a previous case involving belt buckles, this court accepted the idea that copyrightability can adhere in the conceptual separation of an artistic element. Conceptual separability is thus alive and well, at least in this appellate circuit. The problem, however, is determining exactly what it is and how it is to be applied. One possible test, termed the "temporal displacement test," proposes that aesthetic features are conceptually separable if the article stimulates in the mind of the beholder a concept that is separate from the concept evoked by its utilitarian function. However, this court previously rejected that test as a standard so ethereal that it would be impossible to administer or apply. Other possible tests include (1) whether the primary use is as a utilitarian as opposed to an artistic work, (2) whether the aesthetic aspects of the work can be said to be "primary," and (3) whether the article is marketable as art. But again, none of these is very satisfactory.

We are impressed by a recently published article written by Professor Denicola, who views the statutory language in Section 101 as an attempt to identify elements whose form and appearance reflect the unconstrained perspective of the artist. Professor Denicola suggests that the dominant characteristic of industrial design is the influence of nonaesthetic, utilitarian concerns and he hence concludes that copyrightability ultimately should depend on the extent to which a work reflects artistic expression uninhibited by functional considerations. Where design elements can be identified as reflecting the designer's artistic judgment exercised independently of functional influences, conceptual separability exists. We believe that this approach provides the best test for conceptual separability and accordingly adopt it.

Applying this test to the RIBBON Rack, we find that the rack is not copyrightable. It seems clear that the form of the rack is influenced in significant measure by utilitarian concerns, and thus any aesthetic elements cannot be said to be conceptually separable from the utilitarian elements. This is true even though the sculpture that inspired the RIBBON Rack may well have been copyrightable.

Brandir argues correctly that a copyrighted work of art does not lose its protected status merely because it subsequently is put to a functional use.

continued . . .

continued . . .

This explains why statues made into lamp bases retain their copyright protection. Thus, the commercialization of the rack is not relevant to determining the status of copyright protection.

Had Brandir merely adopted one of the existing sculptures as a bicycle rack, neither the application to a utilitarian end nor commercialization of that use would have caused the object to forfeit its copyrighted status. Comparison of the RIBBON Rack with the earlier sculptures, however, reveals that whereas the rack was derived from works of art, it is in its final form essentially a product of industrial design. The design clearly was adapted for utilitarian purposes. The upper loops were widened to accommodate bikes more efficiently, vertical elements were straightened to improve installation, and the materials were altered for strength and to sustain the weather.

Brandir argues that its RIBBON Rack can and should be characterized as a sculptural work of art within the minimalist art movement, which is marked by simplicity and clarity. It is unnecessary to determine whether to the art world the RIBBON Rack properly would be considered an example of minimalist sculpture. The result under the copyright statute is not changed. Using the test we have adopted, it is not enough that the rack may stimulate in the mind of the observer an artistic concept separate from the bicycle rack concept. While the RIBBON Rack may be worthy of admiration for its aesthetic qualities, it remains nonetheless the product of industrial design. Accordingly we affirm the decision that the RIBBON Rack is not protected by copyright.

Contrary to the decision of the lower court, however, we find that this rack could possibly be protected by federal and state trademark laws, and we remand to the lower court for further proceedings on this issue alone.

This decision rendered by the very influential 2nd Circuit Court of Appeals substantially shut the door on whatever life the conceptual separability notion may have had. Design elements of useful products are not protectible by copyright unless those elements were conceived without function in mind. Few product characteristics beyond merely external artistic flourishes will satisfy this test. Thus, the prospects for using copyrights to protect external visual characteristics of the AES seem remote.

Copyright Protection for Architecture

Before 1991, limitation on the protection of industrial designs had a curious effect on the application of copyright to architecture. Architectural blueprints and models can be protected by copyright as pictorial, graphic, or sculptural works. Thus, one who copies a protected blueprint in drafting another blueprint infringes the copyright. However, that was about the extent of the protection afforded architects. A blueprint basically depicts an idea for a functional article: a house or a building. Thus, without some special statutory exception, the copyright in the blueprint could not extend to the construction of the functional architectural idea. This means that although one could not make a copy of a blueprint to help construct the depicted structure, one still would be free to erect the structure if one only took a permissible glance at that blueprint.[23] In addition, once a building is constructed, it falls within the definition of an industrial design. Thus, there would be nothing to stop an architect from viewing a home and then creating an identical abode.

In June 1989, the Copyright Office issued a special report on copyright protection for works of architecture. The report indicated that the United States had to afford greater protection to architectural works to stay in conformity with the Berne Convention. Based on this study, Congress passed the Architectural Works Copyright Protection Act of 1990, which became effective in June 1991. The amendment specifically added architectural works to the Section 102 list of protectible subject items. A definition of what constitutes an architectural work also was included within Section 101, which now states:

> An architectural work is the design of a building as embodied in any tangible medium of expression, including a building, architectural plans, or drawings. The work includes the overall form as well as the arrangement and composition of spaces and elements in the design, but does not include individual standard features.

In addition, the 1991 amendments added Section 120 to the Copyright Act, which limits the scope of protection for architectural works in certain instances. For example, a person is allowed to take a picture of a building that can be viewed from a public place without gaining permission from the copyright holder (often the architect). Also, the owner of the building may make alterations or destroy the work without obtaining permission from the owner of the copyright.

Legislative Proposals for Designs of Useful Articles

Computer programs and architectural works both are specific exceptions to the rule that copyright protection does not extend to expressions that are intimately related to functional or utilitarian articles. For instance, computer programs certainly are functional, and the expressions cannot be physically separated from the functional aspects. Also, following the conceptual separability approach of the 2nd Circuit, it is hard to imagine that program codes are written without functional considerations in mind. This has led designers of other functional articles to push for legislation that would similarly extend copyright protection to their creative endeavors. Why, for instance, should the user interface of a computer program be protected by copyright, as some courts still allow, while the layout, controls, and shape of a radio are not? What logical rationale is there for this seeming act of discrimination? Indeed, designers point out that industrial designs are protected in several other countries.

For over a decade, bills have been introduced in Congress to extend copyright-like protection to the designs of useful articles. Under most of these proposals, designs of useful articles would be treated very much like computer programs. For instance, the bills state that protection would not extend to any idea, process, system, or method of operation. Also, designs that are dictated solely by utilitarian functions are not covered. In addition, protection would not be given to ordinary and standard features. The main difference is that these bills would provide only ten years of protection to such designs. However, in the world of rapid technological change, the markedly shorter term of protection usually would not be consequential. Although these bills are introduced annually, none with general application has yet reached the president's desk. One primary reason is opposition by automobile replacement-part manufacturers, insurance companies, and consumer groups, which fear that original-equipment automobile manufacturers would be given a lock on the aftermarkets for their cars if the designs of their components were protected. By the late 1980s, those advocating copyright-like protection for industrial designs seemed to be gathering momentum, and the prospects for passage of sweeping legislation appeared promising. However, by 1994, the momentum stalled. In 1998, Congress passed a specialized design protection law as part of the Digital Millennium Copyright Act, but its application is limited to ship vessel hull designs.[24] Whether this legislation will serve as a springboard for more generalized amendments is an open question.

As a final note, those who oppose broad copyright protection for computer programs and user interfaces have gained ammunition from the industrial design debate. After all, copyright protection for computer programs really is evaluated in a way similar to the temporal displacement test considered by the 2nd Circuit in *Brandir*. Interestingly, in the design context, the court called that test so ethereal as to be almost impossible to apply. One thereby can draw analogies from ordinary everyday products, concrete things that judges understand very well, and demonstrate the misguided paths sometimes being taken in the less understood realm of computer technology. In fact, some courts now seem to be following this approach, as demonstrated in *Lotus v. Borland* and in Apple's case against Microsoft and Hewlett-Packard.

COPYRIGHT AND ARTISTIC MEDIA: SAMPLING, IMAGING, AND MULTIMEDIA WORKS

Even before the Internet revolution, some policy experts began to wonder whether advances in digital technologies might require fundamental changes in copyright policy. New technologies have made it increasingly easy to take and transform small pieces of artistic works, allowing others to reuse them in their creations. In addition, new methods have been developed to store, view, and interact with artistic and literary works. This section briefly looks at three technological contexts-digital audio sampling, digital imaging, and multimedia works—that have raised vexing legal and policy questions.

Digital Audio Sampling

Digital audio sampling is a technique whereby prerecorded sounds are manipulated to form new sounds.[25] Digital samplers have the capabilities to slow down or speed up rhythms, hold notes, lower or raise pitch, change the order of notes, patch different sounds together, and layer different sounds simultaneously. Digital samplers break down analog recordings into discrete, equally spaced segments of time, called samples. The samples are translated into binary digital units of information and stored in the memory system of a computer. At this point, the information can be adjusted and manipulated electronically before being translated back to analog form. Those who use the technique claim that sampling is a new instrument of creativity, but those whose sounds are used often regard the practice as blatant theft of their copyrights. Numerous lawsuits, aimed particularly at rap music artists, have been filed challenging the practice. Notable disputes include those between Jimmy Castor and the Beastie Boys and between the Turtles and De La Soul. The debate raises far-reaching intellectual property questions, not only as to copyrights but regarding other realms as well.

Before we specifically address the copyright concerns of digital sampling, it is important to recall how the Copyright Act protects audio artists. In the discussion in Chapter 5 of the new digital audio transmission right, we reviewed how audio works consist of two separate copyrights. A recorded performance is based on a creative composition that itself enjoys copyright protection. In a sense, the recording is a derivative work based on the original composition, not unlike a movie that is developed from a book. Thus, the maker of the recording needs permission from the composition copyright owner. In addition, anyone who intends to make further use of the recording must mind the rights of the composition owner. The sound recording, though, also adds the creative talents of the performers and technicians to the original composition. These too merit copyright protection. As noted in Chapter 5, the Copyright Act provides more limited rights to the sound recording. However, for the purposes here, one needs only to note that the sound recording copyright owner does have the right to make copies and derivative works "in which the actual sounds fixed in the sound recording are rearranged, remixed or otherwise altered in sequence or quality."

For the following discussion, assume that Jon Anderson writes a musical composition and grants Bonnie Raitt the right to make a recording of it with her recording company. Jon Anderson, therefore, is the owner of the composition copyright and, for simplicity, we will make Bonnie Raitt the owner of the sound recording copyright. We also will assume that a new rock group, called the Retreads, makes a new song, titled "I'm Lazy," that incorporates a sampled portion from Bonnie Raitt's recording of Jon Anderson's song.

A good place to start is to ask whether "I'm Lazy" violates any of the rights granted to either Jon Anderson or Bonnie Raitt in Section 106 of the Copyright Act. Regarding Jon Anderson's composition, one must ask whether "I'm Lazy" is a reproduction (or derivation) of Jon Anderson's song. Since access likely is easy to prove, infringement therefore will come down to a determination of whether

"I'm Lazy" is substantially similar to Jon Anderson's song. Therefore, if only a very small portion of the recording is sampled, and it is sufficiently transformed so that its source is very hard to identify, then there may be no infringement of Jon Anderson's recording, even though the new work uses it through digital sampling. However, as we know, most musicians use sampling techniques because they want their songs to reflect the original to some degree. Although the portion used may be small, it usually consists of a qualitatively important element that makes it easy for the listener to identify the original version. When this is the case, a finding of substantial similarity becomes much more likely. Thus, we can assume that if "I'm Lazy" incorporates an important phrase from Jon Anderson's composition, it infringes unless it falls under special protection, such as from fair use.

Since the Retreads sampled Bonnie Raitt's recording of the song, they need to be concerned about her rights also. The analysis is not really all that different from that for Jon Anderson's composition. However, the Retreads may have slightly less wiggle room to argue that they do not infringe. This is because a strict reading of Bonnie Raitt's right to make derivative works seems to encompass all uses of her actual sounds, no matter how similar they end up after the sampling. In other words, if the Retreads alter the sounds from Bonnie Raitt's recording enough, they may avoid infringement of Jon Anderson's composition due to lack of substantial similarity. Yet, they still may violate Bonnie Raitt's right to rearrange and remix without some other protection, such as fair use. All this means is that as important as fair use likely is regarding the composition copyright owner, it may be more important when considering the rights of the sound recording owner.[26]

The Application of Fair Use to Sampling   Clearly, a fair-use analysis is likely to be important to anyone interested in sampling music. Given that the Retreads hope to sell their new song, they need to be concerned that they are making a commercial use. *Sony v. Universal City Studios*, of course, notes that a commercial use is presumptively unfair, which should cause the Retreads great concern unless that appraisal can be qualified in some way. In addition, they are making use of an artistic work, which makes the situation different from *Sega*, where a utilitarian work was at issue. On the other hand, the Retreads may argue that they are not taking all that much of Bonnie Raitt's recording and that they are not in any way financially hurting Bonnie Raitt or Jon Anderson. They also may state that the purpose of their sampling is to engage in social commentary or criticism, which they may claim gives them favored status under fair use.

Campbell v. Acuff-Rose Music Inc. is an important Supreme Court case that deals with fair-use arguments in the context of music. It thus has direct relevance to the issues of digital audio sampling. However, possibly of more significance, the Supreme Court gives important lessons in *Acuff-Rose* about the application of the fair-use defense in general. Given the increasingly vital role of fair use to emerging technologies, these insights are valuable indeed.

CAMPBELL v. ACUFF-ROSE MUSIC, INC.
United States Supreme Court, 1994

FACTS: In 1964, Roy Orbison and William Dees wrote a rock ballad called "Oh, Pretty Woman" and assigned their rights to Acuff-Rose. In 1989, 2 Live Crew wrote a song entitled "Pretty Woman," which it claimed to be a parody of "Oh, Pretty Woman." For "Pretty Woman," 2 Live Crew copied the characteristic opening bass riff and the first line of the lyrics of "Oh, Pretty Woman." After the opening, 2 Live Crew's version quickly degenerates into a play on words, substituting predictable lyrics with shocking ones. The 2 Live Crew manager informed Acuff-Rose of the group's song, stating that the group would credit Acuff-Rose with ownership of the original song and would pay a fee for the use the group wished to make of "Oh, Pretty Woman." Acuff-Rose refused to grant permission. Nonetheless, 2 Live Crew released records, cassettes, and CDs of "Pretty Woman" in 1989 in an album titled "As Clean as They Wanna Be."

In 1990, Acuff-Rose sued 2 Live Crew for copyright infringement. The district court judge granted summary judgment for 2 Live Crew based on fair use. This means that given certain uncontroverted facts, the judge determined that a trial was not necessary to reach the judgment that 2 Live Crew did not violate the copyright in "Oh, Pretty Woman." The Court of Appeals reversed, ruling that 2 Live Crew's use of material from "Oh, Pretty Woman" could not constitute a fair use. The group 2 Live Crew appealed to the Supreme Court.

DECISION AND REASONING: It is uncontested that 2 Live Crew's song would be an infringement of Acuff-Rose's rights in "Oh, Pretty Woman" but for a finding of fair use through parody. The task of evaluating fair use is not to be simplified with bright-line rules, for Section 107 calls for case-by-case analysis. The statute employs the terms "including" and "such as" in the preamble to indicate the illustrative function of the examples given. Also, the four statutory factors are not to be treated in isolation, one from another. All are to be explored, and the results weighed together in light of the purposes of copyright.

Purpose and Character. The first factor in a fair-use inquiry consists of the purpose and character of the use, including whether such use is of a commercial nature or is for nonprofit educational purposes. The inquiry here may be guided by the examples given in the preamble to Section 107, looking at whether the use is for criticism or comment or news reporting and the like. The central purpose of this investigation is to see whether the new work

continued . . .

continued . . .

merely supersedes the objects of the original creation or instead adds something new with a further purpose or different character. In other words, it asks whether and to what extent the new work is transformative. Although such transformative use is not absolutely necessary for a finding of fair use, the goal of copyright is generally furthered by the creation of transformative works. The more transformative the new work, the less will be the significance of other factors, such as commercialism, that may weigh against a finding of fair use.

Parody has an obvious claim to transformative value. Parody can provide social benefit by shedding light on an earlier work and in the process creating a new one. We thus believe that parody, like other forms of comment and criticism, may claim fair use under Section 107.

For the purposes of copyright law, the heart of the parodist's claim to quote from existing material is the use of some elements of a prior author's composition to create a new one that, at least in part, comments on the original author's work. If the commentary has no critical bearing on the substance or style of the original composition, and the alleged infringer merely uses it to get attention or to avoid the drudgery in working up something fresh, the claim to fairness in borrowing from another's work diminishes accordingly (if it does not vanish), and other factors, such as the extent of its commerciality, loom larger. Parody needs to mimic the original to make its point, and so has some claim to use the creation of its victim's imagination, whereas satire can stand on its own two feet and so requires justification for the very act of borrowing. Still, looser forms of parody, and perhaps even satire, may come within the scope of fair-use analysis. For instance, when there is little or no risk of market substitution for the original (or licensed derivative works), whether because of the large extent of transformation of the earlier work, the new work's minimal distribution in the market, the small extent to which the new work borrows from the original, or other factors, then taking parodic aim at the original is a less critical factor in the analysis.

The fact that parody can claim legitimacy for some appropriation does not, of course, tell the parodist or judge where to draw the line. The suggestion by 2 Live Crew that any parodic use is presumptively fair is not justified. Parody, like any other use, has to work its way through the relevant factors and be judged case by case in light of the ends of the copyright law.

The district court held and the Court of Appeals assumed that 2 Live Crew's "Pretty Woman" contains parody, commenting on and criticizing the original work, whatever it also may have to say about society at large. The district court found that 2 Live Crew's song demonstrates how bland and banal the Orbison song seems to the members of 2 Live Crew. The dissenting judge in the Court of Appeals concluded that "Pretty Woman" was clearly intended to ridicule the white-bread original and to remind us that sexual congress with nameless streetwalkers is not necessarily the stuff of romance and is not necessarily without its consequences. Although the majority in the Court of Appeals had difficulty discerning any criticism of the original, it assumed that there was some.

We have less difficulty in finding the critical element in 2 Live Crew's song than the Court of Appeals majority did, although having found it, we will not take the further step of evaluating its quality. Whether parody is in good taste or bad does not matter to fair use. However, one still must assess whether the parodic element is slight or great and whether the copying is small or extensive in relation to the parodic element, for a work with only slight parodic element and extensive copying will be more likely to merely supersede the objects of the original. While we might not assign a high rank to the parodic element here, we think it fair to say that 2 Live Crew's song reasonably could be perceived as commenting on the original or criticizing it, to some degree: 2 Live Crew juxtaposes the romantic musings of a man whose fantasy comes true with degrading taunts, a bawdy demand for sex, and a sigh of relief from paternal responsibility; the later words can be taken as a comment on the naivete of the original of an earlier day, as a rejection of its sentiment that ignores the ugliness of street life and the debasement it signifies.

The Court of Appeals cut short the inquiry into 2 Live Crew's fair-use claim by confining its treatment of the first factor essentially to the commercial nature of the use and then by overinflating its significance. In giving virtually dispositive weight to the commercial nature of the parody, the Court of Appeals erred.

The mere fact that a work is educational and not for profit does not insulate it from a finding of infringement, any more than the commercial character of a use may bar a finding of fairness. The fact that a publication is commercial as opposed to nonprofit is a separate factor that tends to weigh against a finding of fair use. But that is all. One should see that a bright-line rule forbidding commercial use is not sensible, for the negative weight of this aspect depends on its context. For example, the use of a copyrighted work to advertise a product, even in a parody, will be entitled to less indulgence under the first factor than the sale of the parody for its own sake.

Nature. The second factor, the nature of the copyrighted work, recognizes that some works are closer to the core of intended copyright protection than others. We believe that Orbison's original creative expression for public dissemination falls within the core of the copyright's protective purposes. That fact, however, is not much help in this case, nor is it ever likely to help much in separating the fair-use sheep from the infringing goats in a parody case, since parodies almost invariably copy publicly known, expressive works.

continued . . .

continued . . .

Amount and Substantiality. The third factor asks whether the amount and substantiality of the portion used in relation to the copyrighted work as a whole are reasonable in relation to the purpose of the copying. Here, attention turns to the persuasiveness of a parodist's justification for the particular copying done, and the inquiry will harken back to the first of the statutory factors, for we recognize that the extent of permissible copying varies with the purpose and character of the use.

The Court of Appeals is correct that this factor calls for thought not only about the quantity of the materials used but about their quality and importance, too. Where we part company with the lower court is in applying these guides to parody, and in particular to parody in the song before us. Parody presents a difficult case. Parody's humor, or in any event its comment, necessarily springs from recognizable allusion to its object through distorted imitation. When parody takes aim at a particular original work, the parody must be able to conjure up at least enough of that original to make the object of its critical wit recognizable. What makes for that recognition is quotation of the original's most distinctive or memorable features, which the parodist can be sure the audience will know. Once enough has been taken to ensure identification, how much more is reasonable will depend, say, on the extent to which the song's overriding purpose and character are to parody the original or, in contrast, the likelihood that the parody may serve as a market substitute for the original.

We think the Court of Appeals was insufficiently appreciative of parody's need for the recognizable sight or sound when it ruled that 2 Live Crew's use was unreasonable as a matter of law. It is true, of course, that 2 Live Crew copied the characteristic opening bass riff, and true that the words of the first line copy the Orbison lyrics. But if quotation of the opening riff and the first line may be said to go to the heart of the original, the heart is also what most readily conjures up the song for parody, and it is the heart at which parody takes aim. If 2 Live Crew had copied a significantly less memorable part of the original, it is difficult to see how its parodic character would have come through.

This is not, of course, to say that those who call themselves parodists can skim the cream and get away scot-free. In parody, context is everything, and the question of fairness asks what else the parodist did besides go to the heart of the original. It is significant that 2 Live Crew not only copied the first line of the original but thereafter also departed markedly from the Orbison lyrics for its own ends; 2 Live Crew not only copied the bass riff and repeated it but also produced otherwise distinctive sounds, interposing scraper noise, overlaying the music with solos in different keys, and altering the drum beat. This is not a case in which a substantial portion of the parody itself is composed of a verbatim copying of the original.

As to the lyrics, we think that no more was taken than necessary, even though that portion may be the original's heart. As to the music, we express no opinion whether repetition of the bass riff is excessive copying, and we remand to permit evaluation of the amount taken in light of the song's parodic purpose and character, its transformative elements, and considerations of the potential for market substitution.

Market Effect. The fourth fair-use factor concerns the effect of the use upon the potential market for or value of the copyrighted work. The inquiry must take account not only of harm to the original but also of harm to the market for derivative works. The Court of Appeals assumed such harm because 2 Live Crew's intended purpose of its song was for commercial gain.

No presumption of market harm is applicable to a case involving something beyond mere duplication for commercial purpose. When a commercial use amounts to mere duplication of the entirety of an original, it clearly supersedes the objects of the original and serves as a market replacement for it. But when the second use is transformative, market substitution is at least less certain, and market harm may not be so readily inferred. Indeed, as to parody pure and simple, it is more likely that the new work will not affect the market for the original in a way cognizable under this factor, that is, by acting as a substitute for it. This is because the parody and the original usually serve different market functions. The market for potential derivative uses includes only those that creators of original works would in general develop or license others to develop. Yet the unlikelihood that creators of imaginative works will license critical reviews or lampoons of their own productions removes such uses from the very notion of a potential licensing market. On the other hand, we make no opinion here as to the derivative markets for works using elements of an original merely as vehicles for satire or amusement, without making comment or criticism of the original.

Although there is no recognizable derivative market for critical works under this factor, 2 Live Crew's song is more complex, comprising not only parody but also rap music—and the derivative market for rap music constitutes a proper focus of inquiry. Although 2 Live Crew submitted uncontroverted affidavits on the question of market harm to the original, neither the group nor Acuff-Rose introduced evidence addressing the likely effect of 2 Live Crew's parodic rap song on the market for a nonparody rap version of "Oh, Pretty Woman." Although another rap group sought a license to record a rap derivative, there is no evidence that a potential rap market was harmed in any way by 2 Live Crew's parody rap version. Since the court record is silent on this subject, 2 Live Crew is not entitled to summary judgment in its favor. This evidentiary hole doubtless will be plugged on remand.

We reverse the judgment of the Court of Appeals and remand for further proceedings consistent with this opinion.

Acuff-Rose is an important victory for parodists because it instructed lower courts to apply a more flexible approach to the fair-use doctrine than some theretofore were using. The case, therefore, does give digital samplers some breathing space, but their latitude is carefully circumscribed. The Supreme Court's direct pronouncement that the commercial nature of the work does not negate a possible finding of fair use obviously is critical, since most sampling exercises have a commercial objective. However, the rest of the opinion may not be so helpful to many digital samplers. Some key aspects are worth keeping in mind. Probably the most central proposition of the opinion is that the more the sampled work serves to comment on or criticize the original work, the more liberty the sampler will have to copy the original without permission. As the sampler's critical aim broadens to elements that are not specifically tied to the work utilized, the fair-use arguments weaken. And of course, if the sampler is simply trying to create a new work from preexisting materials without having any particular social commentary function in mind, the Supreme Court makes it clear that the fair-use argument virtually disappears. Because such may indeed be the objective of many digital samplers, they have to be careful indeed.

The other major fork of *Acuff-Rose* instructs that the more the sampled work serves as a substitute in a market that the original copyright owner would be willing to tap, the less persuasive the fair-use arguments will be. This principle also does not bode well for digital samplers who wish to use preexisting material without permission for purposes other than criticizing the original. Seemingly, in these situations, the sampler will have to rest on the small amount of material taken and the degree of transformation that ultimately results.

Acuff-Rose helps answer the question whether the song "I'm Lazy" infringes Jon Anderson's and Bonnie Raitt's copyrights. Clearly, the degree to which "I'm Lazy" serves as a parody will be critical, along with other elements, such as the amount and importance of the sampled snippets. However, sampling raises another issue not explored in *Acuff-Rose*. In order to engage in sampling, even to make a highly tranformative parody, a sampler first must copy the protected work into the sampling machine. Of course, the copy consists of 1's and 0's, and maybe that is enough to say that an unlawful reproduction has not been made. In addition, the copy will be held only temporarily while the music is altered into the final form. This, too, may serve to protect the sampler. Yet these are additional issues which the sampler must address.

The digital nature of the copy probably does not protect individuals engaged in sampling. When a recording is transferred into the memory of a digital sampler, it is hard to say that an actual copy has been made, because the machine translates the information into digital bits prior to storage. Clearly, the 1's and 0's look and feel substantially different from the original song. However, this is also true when an English version of a novel is translated into another language, such as French. The only difference is that whereas typical language translations are made so that other people can read compositions, samplers make translations so that works can be understood by computers. Logically, copyright law treats both forms of translations in the same way—as derivative works. And, equally in both cases, the right to make derivative works is held exclusively by the copyright owners unless a special exception, such as fair use, applies.

The temporary condition of the digital copy may not provide much protection either. This is made clear from *Sega*, where the court determined that intermediate copying of copyrighted material may infringe even if the end result does not. Following the spirit of *Sega*, one will have to argue that the temporary copy in the sampler is a fair use. In *Sega*, the fair-use argument was successful because the temporary copy was the only way to obtain unprotected ideas, and they were sought for a legitimate purpose. Thus, with sampling, one might argue that the purpose of the sampling is legitimate, such as to ultimately create a lawful transformative parody of the original. In addition, though, one might have to argue that sampling is the only way to achieve this goal. However, this may not be persuasive, since the new artists could recreate what they need without sampling, just as 2 Live Crew did with "Oh, Pretty Woman." Still, there is some intuitive logic to the judgment that if "I'm Lazy" is a fair use, then the use of the sampler to make that fair use also should be a fair use. And as already suggested, application of the fair-use defense often seems to follow intuition more than logic. Thus, it is hard to predict how courts ultimately will rule on this issue.

From this entire discussion, one should recognize that digital sampling raises difficult copyright issues. Individuals who sample preexisting material are strongly advised to obtain appropriate copyright licenses from the copyright owners in the musical composition and the sound recording. Without doing so, there are substantial risks of infringement. It is no wonder that most persons who use sampling techniques in their songs gain the necessary copyright permissions in advance.

Digital sampling raises other intellectual property issues besides those from copyright. For instance, if you heard a David Bowie riff within a sampled song, you might believe that David Bowie had been involved in the creation and production of that song. This brings up issues of trademark and unfair competition, based on the possible confusion that listeners will have about the source or sponsor of the song. One example is provided by a dispute between Chuck D, of the band Public Enemy, and McKenzie River Corporation, which marketed St. Ides malt liquor. An advertisement for St. Ides used a recognizable sampled segment of Chuck D's voice without the rapper's permission.[27] Chuck D was then an outspoken opponent of malt liquors because they targeted black consumers. It can be argued that the association of his voice with the malt liquor product might have confused listeners into believing that he endorsed the St. Ides product.

Various other state laws also may protect the artists who perform in songs that are sampled. For instance, California, New York, and a host of other states have statutes protecting personal rights, such as the "right of privacy" and the "right of publicity." Generally, the right of privacy protects an individual's interest in avoiding public scrutiny, and the right of publicity protects a person's right to profit from such attention. In California, a right-of-publicity statute provides that anyone who knowingly uses another person's name, voice, signature, photograph, or likeness in any manner on products or for the purpose of advertising or selling without first gaining consent is liable for damages.[28] Such terms clearly apply to Chuck D's form of dispute with McKenzie, given the commercial nature of his claim. One might try to avoid liability for violating personal rights by imitating an artist's voice before sampling, rather than sampling the exact version. However, certain state courts broadly protect the right of publicity, allowing it to cover a vocalist's distinctive and recognizable voice even when imitated by another singer.[29] Therefore, even if a sampler is so careful as to license or purchase the copyrights to both the underlying composition and the sound recording, permission may still be required from the vocalist under certain circumstances. And this may even be true if the sampler goes so far as to imitate the voice prior to digitally manipulating it. Clearly, one should give great attention to the wide spectrum of rights of various copyright owners and artists before engaging in digital sampling. We will take another look at these personal rights in Chapter 8.

Digital Imaging

The revolution in digital technology has not been restricted to the audio spectrum; visual media have been greatly affected as well. Any person who has seen the movie *Terminator 2* has an excellent feel for the power that this new technology bears. Called digital imaging, the technique utilizes digital equipment to scan film images and to convert the images into electronic signals. These then can be manipulated by graphic artists via computers to alter the shape, color, and density of images and to combine various images in virtually limitless ways. Combinations can even be made with images that are invented totally within the computer. On a simpler level, but using the same technology, single photographs can be scanned into computers and similarly manipulated to create altogether new pictures. One prominent example is the cover of *A Day in the Life of America*, which depicts a cowboy scene. The editors faced a problem when deciding on the dramatic scene for the cover because it was shot horizontally but had to appear vertically for the book. The dilemma was solved through computer technology, which altered the scene so that it emerged vertically without loss of any important elements in the scene.[30]

Digital imaging raises numerous legal and moral issues. Not surprisingly, many of these mirror those with digital sampling, given that the techniques are so similar. In terms of copyright, the photographer stands in the same position as the musical composer. Therefore, when an image is scanned into computer memory, an illegal derivative work probably has been made. As with digital sampling, one might argue that the "copy" stored in the computer is only transitory or will be erased, but these positions become credible only if the final piece of art is lawful. And as we saw with digital sampling, it is not altogether clear that making an interim copy within a digital imaging device is lawful just because the end result is lawful.

The resultant altered version may be infringing also, if it is substantially similar to the original photo. This may be a difficult issue to resolve. One can create a seascape by taking bits and pieces from different photographs—a sail from one, a boat from another, a rainbow from still another—altering their respective characteristics and merging them. The result may be a picture that is very different from the originals. Still, if qualitatively important and recognizable elements are pulled from a photograph, there likely will be substantial similarity. Under these circumstances, one would have to rely on the fair-use defense by, for instance, arguing that the new composite picture integrates no more of the preexisting copyrighted works than is necessary to comment on or criticize the original works. Again, the complicated equitable balance articulated in *Acuff-Rose* likely will come into play.

One other copyright issue pertains more to digital imaging than to audio digital sampling. Many photographs, especially those depicting natural objects and scenes, are somewhat akin to literary works based on factual information. A photograph of a sunset taken from a remote location in Tibet, for example, may be copyrighted. However, the copyright protection does not extend to the elements given to the public by nature. Rather, the copyright protects only the individual creative aspects added by the photographer, such as composition, filtering, exposure, film selection, camera placement, and lighting. Therefore, a direct copy of the Tibetan sunset photograph infringes not because the natural sunset or landscape is reproduced but because the photographer's creative components are taken. With digital imaging, this analysis becomes complicated because the natural elements of the Tibetan scenery may be digitally appropriated while all the creative elements can be digitally altered or removed. If such steps were taken by digital imaging with the Tibetan sunset, then the photographer, who likely invested a huge amount of time and effort to reach the remote locale, may rightfully feel angry that the digital imager could access the scene simply by scanning the image into a machine. However, as we learned in *Feist v. Rural Telephone*, copyright does not protect information, facts, or natural elements even when tremendous energies are devoted to acquiring them. Although the Supreme Court recognized that the result may be harsh in some circumstances, copyright does not provide protection simply because of the sweat of the brow involved in the enterprise. This doctrine is directly applicable to the nature photographer. Therefore, the emergence of digital imaging could change the incentives to engage in nature photography expeditions. In addition, as with databases, the technology may require photographers to reconsider the techniques they use to distribute their works.

Photographers also worry that computer technology will remove their control over their pictures. If a photo is sent to a magazine for review but is rejected by the editors, how can the photographer be sure that the image was not scanned into computer memory so that portions could be used later? Unfortunately, enforcement problems may only increase as digital technologies take hold. For instance, independent photographers were alarmed when Kodak purchased Image Bank, the largest stock-photo house in the United States. Kodak announced plans to use its new photo CD technology to put Image Bank's entire photo library on compact discs so that customers might view and edit the library's contents on computers and television.[31] Such simple access to so many photographs in digitized form magnifies the problems photographers may have in policing copyright violations. However, many of the concerns may be relieved by technical means. For instance, compact discs may be encoded so that customers are billed each time an image is downloaded.

The issue of moral rights may be relevant here also. Even if the copyright to a photograph is owned by someone other than the photographer (copyright owner-ship, for instance, may have been assigned), the photographer still may retain per-sonal moral rights to ensure proper attribution and to protect the integrity of the original photographic work of art. Those engaged in digital photo manipulation cannot disregard these claims. The adoption of the Berne Convention by the United States should elevate the status of moral rights in this country. Indeed, the Copy-right Act was amended in 1991 to explicitly protect the moral rights of an author of a work of visual art, which, under the act, includes among other things "a still photographic image produced for exhibition purposes only, existing in a single copy that is signed by the author, or in a limited edition of 200 copies or fewer that are signed and consecutively numbered." Although most practices involving digital imaging likely do not infringe moral rights as they are currently protected under the terms of the Copyright Act, one still needs to be mindful of future develop-ments to these rights as they become further assimilated within U.S. copyright poli-cies. In addition, one must be aware that legal principles involving moral rights are substantially more developed in various other regions of the globe, such as Europe.[32]

Digital imaging also raises a host of other ethical issues. For instance, ethical concerns are raised when viewers believe that an altered photograph depicts reality. For instance, *Time* magazine, for a cover shot, electronically merged pictures of Nancy Reagan and Raisa Gorbachev under the heading "Nancy Meets Raisa," al-though the two had not yet ever met.[33] Similarly, a cover photograph for *New York Newsday* run prior to the 1994 Winter Olympics made it appear that figure skaters Tonya Harding and Nancy Kerrigan were skating side by side when in fact they had not done so.[34] Digital imaging also may run afoul of other personal rights, such as publicity and trademark rights. For example, Dustin Hoffman sued *Los Angeles Magazine* for publishing a picture in 1997 that merged his head, taken by digital imaging from the movie *Tootsie*, with the body of a model wearing a Richard Tyler designer dress and Ralph Lauren shoes. A caption read, "Dustin Hoffman isn't a drag in a butter-colored silk gown by Richard Tyler and Ralph Lauren heels." A federal trial judge awarded Hoffman $1.5 million in damages in 1999, stating that "the photographs were manipulated and cannibalized to such an extent that the celebrities were commercially exploited and robbed of their dignity, professionalism and talent."[35] Clearly, those engaged in manipulating photos must be concerned with the potential personal effects that their resultant work may have on artists, viewers, and subjects. One can only speculate whether these issues ulti-mately will be addressed through further litigation, ethical codes, or state and fed-eral legislation.

Multimedia Works

The 1990s brought a wave of new multimedia interactive computer products us-ing CD-ROM technology.[36] These products utilize computer database management systems that allow one to control large data banks of textual, audio, and visual images in an interactive manner. Multimedia works differ from traditional ones in that (1) the information is stored digitally; (2) the format allows one to instantaneously jump from one point to another in a work or to merge various portions of a work, rather than being forced to review it from beginning to end; (3) multimedia works are interactive—the product is capable of answering and refining questions about the existence of data; and (4) the appearance of multimedia works is likely to differ substantially each time the work is used.[37] Since so much copyrighted material is being gathered for use in potentially so many ways, the developing and offering of these products can be a legal nightmare.[38] A brief look at some of the difficult issues for multimedia works serves to demonstrate the significant legal and practical hurdles such new technologies face.

Suppose you want to market a multimedia product dealing with education in the United States. The product will offer customers interactive access to huge banks of textual, visual, audio, and statistical information dealing with the subject. For instance, a large number of books will be available, such as *Piaget for Teachers*. There will be photographs of all kinds of things related to education such as schools, great teachers, and facilities. *Blackboard Jungle*, *Goodbye Mr. Chips*, and *Stand & Deliver*, among other movies, will be provided. Music, such as "School's Out" and "Another Brick in the Wall" also will be included. In addition, you plan to collect and offer as much data as you can about education from almanacs and other sources.

Without question, every item that you want to collect requires a large array of copyright permissions. However, this also would be true if you were compiling a traditional collection of these various works. What makes multimedia works different is the various unpredictable ways in which the material may be viewed and used. For instance, one who licenses a photograph for a book knows the single location that the photograph will appear in the book. However, when photographers license a photograph for storage on a CD-ROM, they do not know how many times the picture will be called up by a user or with what material it might appear. This raises difficult contractual questions about fee structures, amounts, and technical monitoring. In addition, users may be able to manipulate the photo, as discussed earlier, raising legal and ethical concerns not only for them, but possibly for you too if you may somehow be blamed for their unlawful actions.

Use of the music and films raises even more problems. For the audio material, licenses will have to be negotiated with copyright owners of the compositions and the recordings. Since the audio portions may be synchronized with video images, you will need to be careful about the extent of the rights obtained in the contract. Owners of audio copyrights often demand greater fees for such uses. If there is a chance that the product will be shown in a public setting, then performance rights will also have to be negotiated with the composition's copyright owners or one of the performance societies, such as ASCAP, BMI, or SESAC. And, of course, there may be legal risks if the music can be sampled by the user.

Films can be very tricky because so much copyrighted audio and video material may be combined in them. Determining exactly what parties have the rights to license particular activities may be troublesome. Also, the actors may have rights, either through their contracts, or based on moral principles, to control the uses of their names and likenesses.

The pitfalls of using databases was covered in *Feist v. Rural Telephone*. If you plan to integrate a database that was collected by someone else and is displayed in an original way, then you will need permission for it. Again, lack of knowledge about how the base will ultimately be used by customers may make negotiations intriguing.

Other issues abound. Since films and pictures will be used, you have to be careful about the potential for invasions of privacy and rights of publicity. What happens if your product is capable of merging sights and sounds in such a way that a person's reputation is harmed? Will you be subject to a defamation charge? The copyright owners of the material you use very likely will demand credit for their works. Given that you do not know when or in what order users will call up various works, where should you include such credits? The list of potential legal issues in this important area is staggering. Obviously, one needs the very careful advice of an experienced attorney before embarking on such a venture.

COPYRIGHT PROTECTION ON THE INTERNET

Copyrights are about money. They are legally sanctioned monopolies. True, they may be limited to creative expressions, but for works of art and literature, that limitation does not account for much. Copyright provides the incentive to create and distribute knowledge. Keep in mind that creation is only part of the process; the public does not benefit unless those involved in distribution are willing to put creative works in public hands. Thus, copyright has always been as much about compensating distributors as paying artists and authors.[39] It is possible that before the printing press, copyrights were not needed. The sheer difficulty of manually transcribing a book was sufficient to provide control over the work. The introduction of the printing press, though, began a long-term process of change.

Consider how books traditionally have been distributed. Authors convince publishing companies to assume substantial risks. The publisher is required to invest in printing equipment, paper, and transportation, among many other things. Many works, though, do not catch on with the public, causing publishers to take losses, which can be made up only through the winners that they sell. If other publishing companies have the legal ability to make copies, however, then they might siphon off the cream without risking investments in unknown works. The interesting result is that publishers will be reluctant to make investments in potentially great books, for these are the ones that surely will be copied.[40] Rather, they may redirect resources into quick-hit pamphlets that are relatively cheap to produce and generate sufficient returns before they can be reproduced.

The monopoly of copyright, therefore, historically has been as much about distribution as creation. However, distribution is becoming increasingly inexpensive.

Publishing no longer requires trees and presses and trucks. With the Internet, all one needs is access to the Web. In fact, with the Internet, authors can become worldwide distributors without the need of publishing companies at all. Certainly, I need an established publisher if I want this book to be distributed on paper with bindings. I also can benefit from a publisher's established distribution networks through universities. Nonetheless, I now could fairly easily choose to post this book on my own personal Web site for professors and students to download. My reluctance has much to do with traditions and compensation schemes. But as systems and habits are established to make this practice more palatable, authors surely will do it. Thus, the time is near when copyrights will not be meaningful in terms of ensuring distribution. Copyright soon will be predominantly about content.

The dilemma posed by the Internet, though, is that the same forces that make content proportionately more valuable also make piracy extremely cheap and easy. Unlawful copying has always been possible. Books could be photocopied and videotapes could be duplicated with two VCRs. The problems were limited in scope, though, due to the cost of the physical media and the machines needed to carry out the process. Digital technologies and the Internet, however, change this dynamic. Anyone with a scanner and a modem can be an instant international pirate. Millions of copies of copyrighted works can be distributed across the globe with virtually no costs.

These forces have stirred a vocal philosophical debate about the future of copyright. In one camp are those who advocate ending copyright protection altogether.[41] To them, copyright was never really about stimulating knowledge or creativity. People naturally are curious and creative, and do not need copyright to engage in these pursuits. The role of copyright primarily was to reward publishers and distributors, a role, as we have seen, that is rapidly diminishing. Of course, artists and authors require some remuneration to engage in their crafts, but copyright is not needed to compensate them. Rather, creators of artistic and literary works may rely on ancillary services to fund their operations.[42] Thus, rock groups might give their music away for free over the Internet to entice listeners to attend live concerts.[43] Or computer scientists might give software away for free while charging for maintenance or other tangible services. In this way, the information is given away for free while compensation is derived from other sources. And to those who find no role for copyright on the Web, this is totally appropriate. Many individuals who take this position believe that information wants to be free. And according to these advocates, there is nothing that one can do, even with copyrights, to prevent the free flow on the Web. Piracy simply is too easy, and enforcement impossible.

Those on the other side of the debate accept that the Internet will radically change the way works will be distributed to the public. But that does not alter the fact that authors and artists need to be paid for their investments in creativity. Ancillary services may work for some. But most creative individuals need assurances that they will be paid when others enjoy the fruits of their creative energies.[44] In their minds, copyrights still provide the only viable incentive, but this incentive is threatened by the ease of piracy on the Web. Therefore, they believe not only that the copyright system must be preserved, but that the laws must be strengthened to facilitate effective enforcement against Internet pirates.

The philosophical debate has not escaped government scrutiny. In the mid-1990s, the U.S. government formed the Information Infrastructure Task Force (IITF) Working Group on Intellectual Property Rights, headed by the commissioner of the PTO, which was charged with making policy recommendations regarding "intellectual property and the national information infrastructure." The Working Group conducted numerous public hearings, circulated a draft for public comment in 1994, and issued its final report in 1995.[45] The Working Group concluded that a strong copyright system is a necessary condition for international commerce on the Web. The final report thoroughly discussed the role of intellectual property on the Internet, but in the end made few recommendations for change. Essentially the IITF Working Group validated the current intellectual property system, including copyright, and thus requested that Congress do little more than tinker with the current laws. For instance, the group suggested that certain copyright terms, such as "distribution," be more clearly defined to cover new practices such as transmissions. It also recommended the adoption of additional measures within the copyright laws to assist those who use copyright management information systems to privately enforce their copyrights. In the final analysis, the Working Group clearly demonstrated its belief that the role of copyrights should be strengthened and not diminished in the Internet environment.

In December 1996, the international community adopted a copyright treaty, negotiated through the World Intellectual Property Organization (WIPO), that was intended to provide solutions to economic, social, cultural, and technological developments in information and communication technologies.[46] In the end, the treaty participants did not agree to far-reaching provisions. But that is always to be expected when diverse nations and cultures attempt to find common ground. Nonetheless, the treaty called for enhanced copyright protections in cyberspace, somewhat in lockstep with the recommendations of the IITF Working Group. For example, the treaty states that authors have the exclusive right of distribution via the Web. It also requires that countries provide adequate legal protection against the circumvention of technological protection methods used by authors to prevent unauthorized copying of their works.

Predictably, there have been some negative reactions to these national and global efforts to strengthen copyright protection. Opponents fear that the world is moving toward lock-and-key solutions to Internet concerns, which is in polar contrast to where they would like to see it go. For instance, new technologies, such as digital watermarking, allow music publishers to embed coded information within digital recordings.[47] Through this technique, publishers may be able to track such information as the computers used to download music files and the names of customers who order material. Watermarking aids enforcement, since it helps identify who is passing around pirated material. In addition, Internet search spider programs can use the codes to locate unlawful sound files that might reside on the Web.[48]

Other private enforcement ideas depend on encryption, contracts, and/or new hardware components. As each year passes, there are improvements in these technologies, allowing copyright owners to more securely guard their works and re-coup payments for their use. The following is one example that was developed in the late 1990s.[49] A movie distributor, for instance, might enter a license agreement over the Web in which the customer clicks what kind of use he wants to make of the movie. He might, for example, have the choice to view it once or make a copy. When the customer makes his choice, he electronically sends the appropriate pay-ment to the movie distributor, let's say $2 to view or $20 to copy. The license agree-ment then is stored on the customer's computer and is encrypted so that others may not "use" it on their computers. Next, an encrypted version of the movie is sent to the customer's computer, with "header" information that identifies the movie. A program in the customer's computer decrypts the license agreement, reads the au-thorization, and matches it with the header information on the encrypted movie. If the license agreement specifies that the movie is to be seen once, then the program will decrypt it for one viewing. After that, the computer will store only a scrambled file, requiring a new agreement and additional fees for it to be viewed again.

There are an enormous number of variations to the above scheme, usually de-pending on specialized computer programs or hardware components. The serial copy management system built into DAR machines is a primitive example of what may soon be commonplace to help police the distribution of copyrighted works. Licenses might become quite sophisticated, allowing multiple viewings, storage for established periods of time, or transfers to other designated computers—all for the appropriate fees, of course. In fact, in December 1998 the Recording Industry As-sociation of America launched a project, named the Secure Digital Music Initiative, having the goal of establishing uniform software standards to facilitate the distrib-ution and control of music over the Internet.[50] Viable technological security and compensation methods, though, depend on copyright management information systems and encryption to protect the works and account for their proper usages. If customers could interfere with these systems, they might then be able to gain access without paying the fees expected by the copyright owners. This is why the WIPO copyright treaty requires nations to pass laws prohibiting circumvention of these management systems. In 1999 the EU was in the final stages of adopting a directive to achieve this goal, allowing copyright owners to take actions against persons who delete, alter, or falsify copyright management information without permission. In 1998, the United States included similar prohibitions in its Digital Millennium Copyright Act. That legislation creates civil and potentially criminal penalties for those who circumvent certain kinds of antipiracy protections.[51] It also forbids the manufacture, sale, or distribution of devices or technologies intended to circumvent copyright management information systems.[52] Coupled with these new policies are separate initiatives that legitimize the use of license agreements over the Web. These so-called click-wrap licenses raise serious questions, much as do shrink-wrap licenses when used with computer programs. But we will see in Chapter 9 that the courts now generally accept the practice of using click-wrap licenses and enforce their terms. In addition, a new set of computer contract licensing standards may soon be prevalent in the United States, and they explicitly authorize use of click-wrap licenses.

These developments in U.S. law, especially the anticircumvention provisions of the Digital Millennium Copyright Act, generated vocal objections, particularly from librarians, educators, and computer scientists.[53] A tremendous fear is that the new technologies will allow copyright owners to have total control over the uses of their works. As a simple example, a business law professor in a university might want to show a segment of a movie in class to demonstrate jury deliberations. Right now, the professor could do so without permission, either due to the fair-use provision or based on other exceptions in the Copyright Act. However, in the future, the copyright owners might encrypt the film, and allow the film to be shown in a class only if fees are paid. In this way, management information systems may supersede copyright, preventing what copyright otherwise would allow the public to freely enjoy. For these reasons, there were substantial requests to allow exceptions to the anticircumvention provisions, so that the systems could be lawfully disabled for various kinds of fair uses. Congress addressed several of these concerns in the Digital Millennium Copyright Act by providing very specific exceptions for nonprofit libraries and educational institutions, law enforcement, computer security testing, encryption research, and reverse engineering of computer programs for interoperability.[54] It also delayed the effective date of the anticircumvention provisions for two years, giving the librarian of congress and the commerce secretary time to suggest whether other exceptions should be included.[55]

At this time, all we know is that the Internet continues to strain accepted philosophical justifications for copyright. Fundamental change rarely comes quickly, however, and this apparently will hold true with copyright policy. So far, those who advocate a reduced role for copyright in the digital world have not made much headway. Rather, the trend is to fortify the copyright system within the Internet by legitimizing technological protection systems and enhancing penalties for misbehavior. The Digital Millennium Copyright Act and the No Electronic Theft Act are just two examples of this trend. On the other hand, copyright owners continue to face hard times on the Internet. Copyright management technologies are only in their infancy, and piracy still runs rampant through the Web. The International Intellectual Property Association estimates that foreign copyright infringement alone costs U.S. firms nearly $20 billion a year.[56] In addition, copyright owners have not always been completely successful in the courts and legislatures. The debate about Internet service providers and whether they should be liable for the copyright infringements of their customers is a case in point.

Internet Service Provider Liability

Responsibility for Copyright Violations by Users The ease of copyright enforcement depends heavily on who may be held responsible for the unlawful acts. Before the digital age and the Internet, those who wished to make widespread distributions of copyrighted materials, either lawfully or unlawfully, had to make substantial investments in duplication machinery, materials, and transportation. The financial and technical requirements thereby limited the number of distributors for copyrighted materials. This, in turn, allowed copyright owners to focus their enforcement efforts on the major distributors, as long as they could be held liable for copyright infringement under the copyright laws. And so they could. Since publishers take an active role in selecting the materials that they publish, there is little debate that they should be held responsible for copyright violations when they copy and distribute copyrighted materials without permission. For this reason, the publisher of this book had to be careful to ensure that the author did not violate any copyrights in its pages. Similarly, photofinishers must take appropriate steps to be certain that they do not duplicate copyrighted photographs, since they have an opportunity to inspect what they copy for customers.[57] What all this means is that in the traditional noncyber world, copyright owners generally have suitable targets for copyright infringement lawsuits, since there usually are large hubs in the distribution process that can be held responsible for the violations of their copyrights

The decentralized nature of the Internet changes the dynamic, however. Now, it is easy for a lone individual with Internet access to make millions of copies and distribute them all over the world. Of course, all of this does not happen without some help. Internet Service Providers (ISPs) are needed to store and route the materials to their destinations. But most often they do their tasks mechanically for millions of customers. In a sense, the ISPs are taking over the roles of the large distributors on the Web, but without the same level of human intervention. The question, then, is whether they should be held to the same degree of responsibility for copyright infringements as traditional publishers. For if they are not, then they may have little incentive to police the Web for copyright infringements, as the publisher of this book certainly did before releasing it to the public. This means that the great weight of copyright enforcement on the Web would rest almost entirely on the shoulders of copyright owners, a burden that some believe would prove too much to bear.

THE KNOWLEDGE REQUIREMENT   One positive thing assisting copyright owners is that the terms of the Copyright Act do not mention that "intent" or "knowledge" is required for one to infringe an owner's rights. Rather, the act simply states that there is infringement when a person violates one of the exclusive rights provided in Section 106. The only reference to knowledge or intent in the act regards "innocent infringers," but even they are not absolved from liability; rather, they may be allowed to pay a reduced amount of statutory damages to copyright owners. Since ISPs copy, display, and distribute materials to carry out their functions, the express terms of the Copyright Act appear to implicate them whether they know about the violations or not. In fact, the earliest cases seemed to follow this reasoning, finding ISPs to be liable for copyright infringements. Perhaps the most noted opinion was *Playboy Enterprises, Inc. v Frena*, in which a subscriber uploaded copyrighted Playboy pictures to a bulletin board service provider for others to view and download.[58] The court held that the bulletin board provider was liable for the infringements, even if it were not aware that copyrighted material unlawfully resided on its system, since intent is not needed to find a violation of rights. ISPs understandably were alarmed by this opinion. Substantial judicial relief, though, came in 1995 with *Religious Technology Center v. Netcom On-Line Communication Services, Inc.*, an opinion that thoughtfully evaluates when ISPs should be held responsible for copyright infringements.

RELIGIOUS TECHNOLOGY CENTER V.
NETCOM ON-LINE COMMUNICATION SERVICES, INC.
District Court, California, 1995

FACTS: Religious Technology Center (RTC) and Bridge Publications, Inc. (BPI) own copyrights in works of L. Ron Hubbard, the founder of the Church of Scientology. Dennis Erlich, who was a former minister of the Church but later became a vocal critic, posted portions of these copyrighted works on an Internet newsgroup dedicated to discussion and criticism of Scientology. Erlich gained access to the Internet through Thomas Klemesrud's bulletin board service ("BBS"), which is run out of his home and has approximately 500 paying users. Klemesrud's BBS is not directly linked to the Internet, but gains its connection through the facilities of Netcom. More specifically, Erlich transmits his messages to Klemesrud's computer, where they are briefly stored. According to a prearranged pattern, these messages are automatically copied onto Netcom's computer and onto other computers on the Usenet. In order to ease transmission, Usenet servers maintain postings from newsgroups for a short period of time—eleven days for Netcom's system and three days for Klemesrud's system. Netcom's local server makes its postings available to a group of Usenet servers, which do the same for other servers until all Usenet sites worldwide have obtained access to the postings

After failing to convince Erlich to stop posting the works, RTC and BPI asked Netcom and Klemesrud to keep Erlich's postings off the system. Klemesrud asked RTC and BPI to prove they owned the copyrights to the posted works, but they refused. Netcom also refused to bar Erlich from the system, arguing that it would be impossible to prescreen Erlich's postings. Netcom admitted, however, that although its system was not configured to do so, it might be able to reprogram its system to screen postings containing particular words or that come from particular individuals. Netcom also contended that it could not kick Erlich off its system without also kicking off the other users of Klemesrud's BBS. However, RTC and BPI disputed this contention.

RTC and BPI, the plaintiffs, sued Erlich for copyright infringement and trade secret misappropriation. They also sued Netcom and Klemesrud for copyright infringement. This case involves the allegations against Netcom and Klemesrud only. Netcom and Klemesrud moved for summary judgment, meaning that they asked the court to dismiss the actions against them, arguing

continued . . .

that the facts, even if true as alleged by plaintiffs, could not result in legal liability. The discussion below only deals with the action against Netcom, but the conclusions apply equally to Klemesrud.

DECISION AND REASONING: This case concerns an issue of first impression regarding intellectual property rights in cyberspace. Specifically, this order addresses whether the operator of a computer bulletin board service and the large Internet access provider that allows that BBS to reach the Internet, should be liable for copyright infringement committed by a subscriber of the BBS. Plaintiffs argue that, although Netcom was not itself the source of any of the infringing materials on its system, it nonetheless should be liable for infringement, either directly, contributorily or vicariously. Netcom disputes these theories of infringement, and further argues that it is entitled to a fair use defense.

Direct Infringement. There is not a question here that copies were made. Even though the messages remained on their systems for at most eleven days, they were sufficiently "fixed" to constitute recognizable copies under the Copyright Act. Also, direct infringement does not require intent or any particular state of mind, although willfulness is relevant to the award of statutory damages. Accepting that copies were made, Netcom argues that only Erlich, and not Netcom, is directly liable for copying.

The court believes that Netcom's act of implementing a system that automatically and uniformly creates temporary copies of all data sent through it is not unlike that of the owner of a copying machine who lets the public make copies with it. Although some of the people using the machine may directly infringe copyrights, courts analyze the machine owner's liability under the rubric of contributory infringement, not direct infringement. Plaintiffs' theory would create many separate acts of infringement and, carried to its natural extreme, would lead to unreasonable liability. It is not difficult to conclude that Erlich infringes by copying a protected work onto his computer and by posting a message to a newsgroup. However, plaintiffs' theory further implicates a Usenet server that carries Erlich's message to other servers regardless of whether that server acts without human intervention beyond the initial setting up of the system. It would also result in liability for every single Usenet server in the worldwide link of computers transmitting Erlich's message to every other computer. There is no need to construe the Act to make all of these parties infringers. Although copyright is a strict liability statute, there should still be some element of volition or causation which is lacking where a system is merely used to create a copy by a third party.

Plaintiffs argue that Netcom is liable for distribution and display of their works, relying on a district court opinion (*Playboy Enterprises, Inc. v. Frena*)

continued . . .

continued ...

which held that a bulletin board was directly liable when copyrighted works owned by Playboy were uploaded by customers and then viewed and downloaded by others. The court notes that this case has been much criticized. The finding in *Playboy* of direct infringement perhaps was influenced by the fact that there was some evidence that the bulletin board operators in fact knew of the infringing nature of the works. Also, the BBS there kept an archive of files for its users. Although the Internet consists of many different computers networked together, some of which may contain infringing files, it does not make sense to hold the operator of each computer liable as an infringer merely because his or her computer is linked to a computer with an infringing file. It would be especially inappropriate to hold liable a service that acts more like a conduit, in other words, one that does not itself keep an archive of files for more than a short duration. Billions of bits of data flow through the Internet and are necessarily stored on servers throughout the network and it is thus practically impossible to screen out infringing bits from noninfringing bits. Because the court cannot see any meaningful distinction (without regard to knowledge) between what Netcom did and what every other Usenet server does, the court finds that Netcom cannot be held liable for direct infringement.

Contributory Infringement. Liability for contributory infringement will be established where the defendant, with knowledge of the infringing activity, induces, causes or materially contributes to the infringing conduct of another. Netcom argues that it did not possess the necessary type of knowledge because (1) it did not know of Erlich's planned infringing activities when it agreed to lease its facilities to Klemesrud, (2) it did not know that Erlich would infringe prior to any of his postings, (3) it is unable to screen out infringing postings before they are made, and (4) its knowledge of the infringing nature of Erlich's postings was too equivocal given the difficulty in assessing whether the registrations were valid and whether Erlich's use was fair.

Netcom cites cases holding that there is no contributory infringement by the lessors of premises that are later used for infringement unless the lessor had knowledge of the intended use at the time of signing the lease. However, providing a service that allows for the automatic distribution of all Usenet postings goes well beyond renting a premises to an infringer. It is more akin to radio stations that have been found liable for rebroadcasting an infringing broadcast. Netcom allows Erlich's infringing messages to remain on its system and be further distributed to other Usenet servers worldwide. It does not completely relinquish control over how its system is used, unlike a landlord. Thus, the relevant time frame for knowledge is not when Netcom entered into an agreement with Klemesrud. It should be when Netcom provided its services to allow Erlich to infringe plaintiffs' copyrights. It is fair, assuming

Netcom is able to take simple measures to prevent further damage to plaintiff's copyrighted works, to hold Netcom liable for contributory infringement where Netcom has knowledge of Erlich's infringing postings yet continues to aid in the accomplishment of Erlich's purpose of publicly distributing the postings.

Netcom argues that its knowledge after receiving notice of Erlich's alleged infringing activities was too equivocal given the difficulty in assessing whether copyright registrations are valid and whether use is fair. Although a mere unsupported allegation of infringement by a copyright owner may not automatically put a defendant on notice of infringing activity, Netcom's position that liability must be unequivocal is unsupportable. Where works contain copyright notices within them, as here, it is difficult to argue that a defendant did not know that the works were copyrighted. To require proof of valid registrations would be impractical and would perhaps take too long to verify, making it impossible for a copyright holder to protect his or her works in some cases. The court is more persuaded by the argument that it is beyond the ability of a BBS operator to quickly and fairly determine when a use is not infringement where there is at least a colorable claim of fair use. Where a BBS operator cannot reasonably verify a claim of infringement, either because of a possible fair use defense, the lack of copyright notices on the copies, or the copyright holder's failure to provide the necessary documentation to show that there is a likely infringement, the operator's lack of knowledge will be found reasonable and there will be no liability for contributory infringement for allowing the continued distribution of the works on its system. Since Netcom was given notice of an infringement claim before Erlich had completed his infringing activity, there may be a question whether Netcom knew or should have known that such activities were infringing.

Vicarious Liability. A defendant is liable for vicarious liability for the actions of a primary infringer where the defendant (1) has the right and ability to control the infringer's acts and (2) receives a direct financial benefit from the infringement.

The first element of vicarious liability will be met if plaintiff's can show that Netcom has the right and ability to supervise the conduct of its subscribers. Netcom argues that it could not possibly screen messages before they are posted given the speed and volume of the data that goes through its system. Netcom further argues that it has never exercised control over the content of its users' postings. Plaintiffs' expert opines otherwise stating that with an easy software modification, Netcom could identify postings that contain particular words or come from particular individuals. Plaintiffs further dispute Netcom's claim that it could not limit Erlich's access to Usenet without kicking off all 500 subscribers of Klemesrud's BBS. The court thus finds

continued ...

continued . . .

that plaintiff's have raised a genuine issue as to whether Netcom has the right and ability to exercise control over the activities of its subscribers, and of Erlich in particular.

On the other hand, plaintiffs cannot provide any evidence of a direct financial benefit received by Netcom from Erlich's postings. Where a defendant rents space or services on a fixed rental fee that does not depend on the nature of the activity of the lessee, courts usually find no vicarious liability because there is not direct financial benefit from the infringement. Also, there is no evidence that infringement by Erlich, or any other user of Netcom's services, in any way enhances the value of Netcom's services to subscribers or attracts new subscribers. Thus, plaintiffs' claim of vicarious liability fails.

Fair-Use Defense. Assuming plaintiffs can prove a violation of one of the exclusive rights guaranteed in section 106 of the Copyright Act, there is no infringement if the defendant's use is fair under section 108. The proper focus here is on whether Netcom's actions qualify as a fair use, not on whether Erlich himself engaged in fair use.

Netcom's use, though commercial, also benefits the public in allowing for the functioning of the Internet and the dissemination of other creative works, a goal of the Copyright Act. Because Netcom's use of copyrighted materials served a completely different function than that of the plaintiffs, this factor weighs in Netcom's favor notwithstanding the otherwise commercial nature of Netcom's use.

Plaintiffs rely on the fact that some of the works transmitted by Netcom were unpublished and some were arguably highly creative and original. However, because Netcom's use of the works was merely to facilitate their posting to the Usenet, which is an entirely different purpose than plaintiffs' use, the precise nature of those works is not important to the fair use determination.

Plaintiffs have shown that Erlich's postings copied substantial amounts of the originals. However, as the Supreme Court found in *Sony*, the mere fact that all of a work is copied is not determinative of the fair use question where such total copying is essential given the purpose of the copying. Here, Netcom copied no more of plaintiffs' works than necessary to function as a Usenet server.

Netcom argues that there is no evidence that making accessible plaintiffs' works, which consist of religious scriptures and policy letters, will harm the market for these works by preventing someone from participating in the Scientology religion because they can view the works on the Internet instead. However, plaintiffs point out that groups in the past have used stolen copies of the Church's scriptures in charging for Scientology-like religious training. This evidence raises a genuine issue that Erlich's postings, made available to the public by Netcom, could hurt the market for plaintiff's works.

In balancing the various factors, the court finds that there is a question as to whether there is a valid fair use defense. The court cannot conclude that Netcom's use was fair without further inquiry.

Conclusion. The court finds that plaintiffs have raised a genuine issue regarding whether Netcom should have known that Erlich was infringing their copyrights after receiving a letter from plaintiffs, whether Netcom substantially participated in the infringement, and whether Netcom has a valid fair use defense. Accordingly, Netcom is not entitled to summary judgment on the plaintiffs' claim of contributory copyright infringement. However, plaintiffs' claims of direct and vicarious infringement fail.

Netcom was extremely important to ISPs because, unlike *Frena*, it states that ISPs are not directly and absolutely liable when customers use their systems to engage in copyright infringements. According to *Netcom*, an ISP should be no more liable for copyright infringements than should the owner of a photocopying machine when customers use it unlawfully to reproduce copyrighted works. The court, though, does not give ISPs total protection, as Netcom requested. Rather, ISPs may be liable as contributory infringers when they reasonably have knowledge that there are copyrighted materials on their systems that are infringing and they have the ability to remove them. Regarding Netcom, the judge was not willing to dismiss all the allegations raised by the plaintiff without a trial because (1) there was at least one instance where Netcom might have reasonably been aware about infringing materials on its system, and (2) it may have had the technical ability to remove those materials. In addition, the judge could not rule on Netcom's fair-use argument without gaining more facts in a trial. Thus, although ISPs viewed the case as a positive development, it did not result in a total and immediate victory for Netcom.

The major concern resulting from *Netcom* was about the information ISPs must receive to be reasonably aware of copyright infringement. According to *Netcom*, the information does not have to be unequivocal. On the other hand, if the ISP has reasonable doubts about the validity of the copyright claim, or if it might reasonably believe that the use of the materials is a fair use, then the ISP has sufficient grounds to argue that it reasonably does not have knowledge of infringement. Of course, no ISP wants to be in the position to have to make these difficult determinations. This is especially true when groups representing copyright owners, such as the Software Publishers Association, are willing to aggressively request that ISPs remove allegedly infringing materials.[59] For instance, what should an ISP do when the subscriber claims that its allegedly infringing work is a parody? Or what if the subscriber argues that it independently created a computer program that relies only on uncopyrightable ideas from the complainant's program? Who should the ISP believe, and how should it make an independent determination? The ISP is put in a huge Catch-22 dilemma. If the ISP leaves the material on its system and the copyright owner then sues it, the ISP might lose because the court may rule that it received reasonable notice. On the other hand, if the ISP erroneously removes the material, then its subscriber may sue, alleging perhaps that the ISP breached its subscriber agreement or engaged in some other wrong.

FEDERAL LEGISLATION PROTECTS ISPS FROM COPYRIGHT INFRINGEMENT   Pleas from all sides reached Congress, and it therefore included in the 1998 Digital Millennium Copyright Act a legislative solution that strikes a balance between the interests of copyright owners, subscribers, and ISPs. First, the act totally absolves an ISP that is merely involved in technical routing functions. This generally applies when the ISP uses a totally mechanized process that stores the material only for the short transient period that is necessary to carry out transmissions, routings, or connections to recipients.

When information is stored on the ISP's system at the direction of a user, however, more complicated procedures take over. The act provides that if the ISP knows that material on its system is infringing, it must work expeditiously to remove that material. It is more likely, though, that the ISP simply will receive a notice from a complaining party alleging infringement. In this event, the act states that the ISP must take action only if the notice contains certain specified forms of information. The notice, for instance must (1) identify the copyrighted works alleged to have been infringed, (2) identify and locate the materials that allegedly infringe, and (3) state that the complaining party has a good-faith belief that the materials infringe. If the notice is sufficient, then the ISP may remove the materials without liability to the subscriber. This protection is qualified, however. The ISP must notify the subscriber that it has disabled access to the materials. If the ISP then receives a counter notice from the subscriber stating that the subscriber has a good-faith belief that the materials were withdrawn by mistake, then the ISP must tell the original complaining party about this counter notification and indicate that the material will be put back on the system in 10 days, unless the original party in that time files suit in court requesting an injunction against the subscriber. If suit is not filed, an ISP that replaces the previously removed material in 10–14 days is protected from liability to the original copyright complainant. All these notification procedures may seem burdensome, but they allow the ISP to disassociate itself from the task of determining infringement. Rather, it has a straightforward process to follow, while the parties must take any continuing copyright dispute to court for a decision on the merits. Of course, all of these protections also presume that the ISP is not making money directly from the posting of the allegedly infringing materials. In such a case, the ISP would be subject to the normal rules on vicarious liability, as discussed in *Netcom*.

The Digital Millennium Copyright Act has at least put some temporary closure on the debate about the liability of ISPs for copyright infringements on their systems. Unless the ISP earns some direct financial benefit when a subscriber infringes a copyright, the ISP will be treated under the rubric of a contributory infringer, as discussed in *Netcom*. Although *Netcom* raises several reasons for ISPs to be insecure, these are rectified by the Digital Copyright Millennium Act, which provides a safe harbor for ISPs when they follow its rules regarding notifications and access to allegedly infringing materials. In the final analysis, this must be seen as a defeat for copyright owners, who certainly were better off in the world of *Frena*, where ISPs were directly liable for copyright infringement. If this situation had survived, copyright owners would have been able to focus their enforcement efforts on ISPs. This, in turn, would have given the ISPs substantial incentives to police their systems for copyright violations so that they could minimize lawsuits from copyright owners. However, with the protections provided to ISPs by *Netcom* and the Digital Millennium Copyright Act, the burden of enforcement shifts markedly back to copyright owners. This will give copyright owners all the more reason to use technical measures to protect their works from unauthorized uses.

Caching   The Digital Millennium Copyright Act also deals with a slightly different copyright issue that had plagued Internet service providers. For efficiency reasons, ISPs sometimes engage in the practice of "caching," whereby they retain copies of on-line material for a limited time so that they can satisfy repeated requests for the material without having to retrieve it from the original source. Caching is a sensible practice because customers often want to go back to a site they only recently left, and the material on the site has not changed during that time. If the ISP had to retrieve the information from the original site, it would merely obtain an exact duplicate of what it only recently had in its possession. Caching therefore reduces the ISP's bandwidth requirements and reduces waiting times for customers.

The Web sites may appreciate the faster response times for customers. However, they may not be so happy with caching when their pages transmit time-sensitive information, since the cached data may be out of date when subsequently retrieved by customers. For the same reasons, caching may affect the advertisements that reach customers, especially if the site regularly changes the ads it displays with its materials. Also, caching may interfere with attempts by Web sites to maintain accurate accounts of the numbers of times customers hit their pages, because the sites no longer directly receive subsequent requests for information. This may hurt Web site owners financially, since hit counts are important determinants of the revenue they receive from advertisers.

Because the practice of caching involves a copy of copyrighted material, and the copyright owners potentially could suffer financial harm, ISPs have to be worried about their exposure to copyright suits. This may be especially true because the ISP's behavior most likely would be analyzed under the rubric of direct infringement rather than under contributory or vicarious principles. The Digital Millennium Copyright Act provides a safe harbor, allowing ISPs to engage in caching without having to fear copyright suits. To benefit from the safe harbor, however, ISPs must meet various conditions dealing with refresh rates and the use of "hit" technologies. Although the act requires ISPs to set up systems to ensure compliance with these conditions, it does give them the opportunity to engage in caching without fear of lawsuits. At the same time, the act suitably protects the interests of Web site owners. The Digital Millennium Copyright Act, therefore, illustrates how the legislative process sometimes can yield effective compromises to conflicting positions.

Linking, Framing, and Other Internet Copyright Issues

The evolving environment of electronic communication raises new questions on almost a daily basis. Since the issues are so new and often have not yet been directly addressed by the courts or legislatures, it is fun to anticipate what the solutions might be. As we just saw in *Netcom*, policy makers rely substantially on analogies to guide their decisions when faced with novel situations. Therefore, you should anticipate that they will continue to base their decisions on the traditional copyright doctrines already covered in these chapters.

Linking Just the simple act of using hypertext links on the Internet raises a host of questions.[60] For instance, clicking on a link causes material from a designated site to be copied on the user's computer so that it may be viewed. Since much of this material likely is creative expression owned by the operator of the designated site, there may be copyright issues when it is transmitted and copied to other locations. So do you think you should get in trouble for placing a link to the designated site on your own Web page, since by doing so, you will cause copyrighted material to be copied by others? Likely, your gut feel is that the answer has to be no. After all, the copyright owner placed the material on the Web with the intent that others would view it. All you are doing is guiding others to the location to view the material that the owner of that site wants to be viewed. Sure, copyrighted material is being copied in the process, but there is a strong implication that the copyright owner consents, given that it is so obviously necessary to achieve the goal of the site. Thus, most analysts believe that basic hypertext linking does not raise copyright issues due to implied consent by the owner of the linked site.[61] In the alternative, one might argue that linking is a fair use, since it usually does not reduce the value of the copyrighted materials.

Of course, the questions are not always this easy. What if you link to a site that has posted material that unlawfully infringes the copyrights of others? Those copyright owners clearly do not consent to the distributions of their works. What is your responsibility in this situation? Likely, the principles of contributory infringement will be relevant. Therefore, if you know or reasonably should know that the linked site contains unauthorized works, then you ought to be liable. On the other hand, if you are totally unaware of the copyright infringements, perhaps you should not be held responsible. The same principles should apply to the ISP that houses your site. In fact, the Digital Millennium Copyright Act explicitly protects ISPs in those situations when it has no knowledge that the linked site contains infringing materials.[62]

What if your link does not go to a home site, but rather takes the user to what is called an embedded site? This was the subject of a dispute brought by Ticketmaster against Microsoft in 1997.[63] At that time, Ticketmaster marketed and sold tickets to entertainment events through the use of a Web site on the Internet. Like many sites, it had a home page that contained a directory of other links, which could be clicked by users, leading them to embedded sites that contained more specific types of information. Ticketmaster sold advertising on its home page to organizations such as MasterCard. The embedded pages either did not have advertising or had advertising that was different from that on the home page.

Microsoft offered an Internet guide to entertainment and restaurants in Seattle that it called Seattle Sidewalk. The home page for Seattle Sidewalk contained advertising from companies such as Visa and Citibank. As part of its Internet service, Microsoft placed on Seattle Sidewalk a link using the Ticketmaster name that led not to the home page, but rather to a relevant embedded page. Ticketmaster sued Microsoft, primarily raising trademark issues and complaining about unfair business practices.

Although this case is not really about copyrights, it does show how complicated these issues may become.[64] Ticketmaster first claimed that it did not want its name to be associated with Microsoft. The implication was that Ticketmaster should be able to dictate who used its name in links. Possibly a more persuasive complaint was that the Ticketmaster name was being used in conjunction with less than Ticketsmaster's total package of services, since Seattle Sidewalk's link led only to an embedded page. We will look at trademark issues such as these more closely in the next chapter. However, neither trademark argument seems very persuasive. Microsoft used the Ticketmaster name to refer to Ticketmaster services. This seems little different from a store hanging a sign that indicates that it has legitimate products from specified companies. Or to use another analogy, one might envision a bus station that lists the business locations to which it is willing to take customers. As for the embedded sites, the problem is that Ticketmaster still freely offered these sites to the public on its own, as long as one knew how to get there. Therefore, the trademark, again, is only being used to indicate the legitimate source of the services.

Analogies help with appraising the unfair business practice claims also. Ticketmaster argued that it lost advertising revenue because Microsoft caused customers to avoid Ticketmaster's relatively expensive home page advertisements. To make matters worse, it noted that Microsoft made money through advertising sold for Seattle Sidewalk based on expenses incurred by Ticketmaster in developing its own sites.

To address this issue, one might compare Ticketmaster's site with a commercial display tent at a trade show. Often these tents have a preferred starting point where visitors are greeted and general information is provided. Also, there may be advertising banners around this main entrance of the tent. However, there is no requirement that visitors access the information and displays within the tent solely by entering through the main entrance. Rather, a person who is familiar with the tent simply could enter the tent from a side and directly see any preferred items. And, of course, the person could bring friends along and show them the shortcut, thereby saving precious time by avoiding the main entrance.

It is hard to understand how a vendor who has set up a service tent allowing easy access from multiple points can complain when certain members of the public actually use those routes. The equities might seem different, however, if the perimeter of the tent were roped off and contained signs informing visitors that access is permitted only through the main entrance. In other words, the more obvious that the tent owner makes its expectations of privacy concerning side entry, the more such entry would become akin to unlawful trespass. Indeed, such technical precautions were always available to Ticketmaster, but it did not at first use them. Later on, visitors from Seattle Sidewalk were denied access and greeted with a notice that read: "Ticketmaster does not have a relationship with Sidewalk. You have been directed to a restricted area. You may go directly to Ticketmaster by pointing your browser to http://www.ticketmaster.com." Given these considerations, it is hard to sympathize with Ticketmaster just because it failed to use these precautions at an earlier juncture.[65] Microsoft, though, allegedly took steps to avoid these precautions after they were implemented.[66] If true, then one could be much more sympathetic to Ticketmaster's complaint. In February 1999, the parties settled the lawsuit.[67] Thus, we will have to wait until another bitter dispute is brought to court before we learn how the judiciary will deal with these linking issues.

Framing Framing may raise more complicated issues than traditional linking.[68] In 1997, several major news publishers sued Total News, Inc., alleging that its use of framing processes violated their copyrights and trademarks, among other things.[69] Since this dispute was settled, it too did not provide definitive guidance on the legality of the practice. Nonetheless, the facts of the case are a good vehicle to discuss the relevant concerns.

Total News provided a service on the Internet that organized news content from over 1,300 sources on the Web and allowed customers to quickly link to the information sources they desired. For instance, a visitor to the Total News Web site could click on the "National" link and find another list of links to publications such as the *Washington Post* and the *Wall Street Journal*. Total News utilized Internet framing techniques in providing these links. By so doing, Total News effectively could maintain elements from its site, such as advertising and other information, and integrate the content from the publication site within them. In this way, Total News might reposition and reduce the size of the advertising and content normally found at the publication site so that they could fit within the advertising and information displayed in the Total News frames. Alternatively, Total News might not even show certain advertising ordinarily displayed on the publication site, but instead substitute it with its own advertising or information. In addition, when the link was made to the publication site, such as the *Washington Post*, the Total News uniform resource locator (URL) was maintained.

An instructive way to consider the equities with framing is to analogize the *Washington Post* Web site with a *Washington Post* newsstand in the tangible world. Patrons are permitted to come to this newsstand and read various *Washington Post* newspapers and publications at the newsstand for free. The newsstand has a large *Washington Post* sign at the top and is surrounded by advertising from several organizations.

When a traditional link is made to the *Washington Post* home page, viewers are provided a shorthand way to visit a site that is offered to the public for free. Assume, for instance, that Total News did not use framing techniques with its list of links to Internet news sources. When Total News customers select the *Washington Post*, they are actually transferred to the *Washington Post* address. Thus, this can be likened to being put on a very short bus ride from the Total News service center to the *Washington Post* newsstand. Once there, the customer can read the information and view the advertisements just like individuals who go to the *Washington Post* site directly by typing the address themselves. Although the linking procedure technically uses copying to reach this result, the analogy with traditional copyright contexts makes it clear that there should be no copyright infringement, since Total News did nothing more than indicate the availability of the site and provide transportation to it.

The use of framing by Total News, however, changes this scenario significantly. Assume first that the Total News advertising and information frames replace the advertising seen at the *Washington Post* home page. This situation no longer can be compared with a simple bus ride to the *Post* newsstand, since customers now see something different than they would if they traveled independently to the newsstand. The more appropriate analogy would be to assume that Total News reproduces the newspapers at the *Washington Post* site and brings those copies back to the Total News service center for customers to view there. In this way, Total News maintains the continuity and control of the advertising seen by the customers at its site. And, indeed, the Total News URL is retained through the process, thereby substantiating the claim that the information is brought back to its home site. Since Total News must reproduce copyrighted materials to carry out this service, copyright infringement logically results, unless the practice can be defended as a fair use. However, a fair-use argument may be difficult to sustain because framing in this manner likely will have negative effects on advertising revenues received by the *Washington Post* for its copyrighted articles.

If the entire *Washington Post* page, including its advertising, is framed, the legalities become even murkier, but the practice probably still would be viewed as unlawful when undertaken without permission. On the one hand, the only material change is that the *Washington Post* home page, which is available to the public for free, might be reduced in size. This seems little different from stopping on the curb in the Total News transportation bus and viewing the *Washington Post* newsstand from that distance through the bus window. This practice would not violate any laws, even if the bus were lined with advertising. On the other hand, when Total News frames in this way, it appears that Total News is shrinking copyrighted materials from the *Washington Post* and pasting them within its own collage. Total News thereby creates a derivative work, which is lawful only if there is implied consent or if the practice is a fair use. One might argue that there is implied consent because the *Washington Post* places its materials on the Internet knowing that framing is possible and common. However, magazine photographers do not necessarily give implied consent to developers of collages simply because they know that most buyers have scissors and glue. The fair-use argument, though, might have potential, despite the commercial nature of the Total News enterprise. This is because Total News will increase the number of customers who will view *Washington Post* materials and advertising. Thus, the market effect on the value of the *Washington Post* copyrights may indeed be positive. On the other hand, the *Washington Post*'s advertising may be overshadowed by advertising within the Total News frames, thereby reducing its value. Courts therefore might have to address this form of framing on a case-by-case basis. In doing so, they need to pay attention to *Acuff-Rose*, in which the Supreme Court factored the willingness of the plaintiff to enter the alternative market into the fair-use calculus. Since the *Washington Post* might be willing to license its sites for framing, this might not bode well for the defense.

Other Internet Issues   There are far too many copyright issues on the Web to consider them all here. Possibly the most important lesson is to make analogies with more common scenarios with which you are more comfortable, for they may clarify the equities of the situation. This will help you predict how courts may address any new Internet concern, since, contrary to some public opinion, courts do try to reach fair and equitable results. Those who use Internet materials often end up copying or distributing copyrighted works, so they often must rely on the fair-use defense or implied consent to legitimize their actions.[70] These doctrines, particularly fair use, usually give courts the flexibility to make decisions that seem appropriate. So, if you want to know if you can view materials on the Web, the answer is probably yes, likely due to implied consent. If you want to know if you can copy articles from a Web site to your bulletin board so that others may read them there, you may have to consider several fair-use variables. For example, does the bulletin board have educational purposes? How long is the article that you copied? Did the Web site from which you copied the article have advertising? If so, then you may deprive the copyright owner of revenue, and your actions seem less fair. Similar considerations apply if you want to know if it is legal to make a hard copy of an article that you found on the Web. Again, you will have to rely on fair use, since implied consent does not seem to be a viable argument. Thus, the type of article, its length, and the reasons that you copied it all are relevant. Also, if making the hard copy somehow deprives the copyright owner of revenue by, for instance, reducing the number of times you or others now may "hit" the Web site to read the article, then the fair-use defense is weakened. For many of these issues, too, you need to consider whether you formed any understandings with the copyright owner, through perhaps a click-wrap license, which expressly governs what you lawfully may do with the works on the site. Contracts such as these will be addressed in Chapter 9. Copyright on the Internet is an interesting and exciting new area of legal policy. You now have the fundamental tools to be a knowledgeable player in this emerging field.

CONCLUSION

This chapter covered several important legal controversies surrounding copyright protection of technological products. Be very aware, though, that it did not provide exhaustive coverage of all copyright topics. For example, there are many copyright issues regarding telecommunications that were not explored. Also, this chapter primarily dealt with the nature and ownership of legal rights in technological developments. One must always keep practical realities in mind, though. Creative individuals are not always winners just because the law is on their side. For example, it is clearly unlawful to purchase copyrighted software and make a copy for a friend. But only a fool would believe that the law has stood as a substantial impediment to those who want inexpensive software. And, as noted in Chapter 1, one can depend even less on legal systems when doing business in several other commercial regions around the globe. As the uses of copyrighted material become more decentralized and the costs of duplication continue to fall, copyright enforcement becomes increasingly difficult. As we have seen, the Internet may be the ultimate threat in this regard. The challenge facing managers of technology is determining how to market their creations effectively and profitably in light of the new state of affairs. Likely, there will be new technical solutions, which will prevent uncompensated access to information or bill users for access.[71] Maybe there will be new legal solutions. The only thing that is certain is that change will come to this arena, and it will happen soon.

NOTES

1. NEC Corp. v. Intel Corp., 10 U.S.P.Q. 2d (BNA) 1177 (N.D. Cal. February 6, 1989).

2. Apple Computer, Inc. v. Microsoft Corp. and Hewlett-Packard Co., 35 F.3d 1435 (9th Cir. 1994).

3. Q-Co Industries, Inc. v. Hoffman, 625 F. Supp. 608, 610 (S.D.N.Y. 1985).

4. An important aspect of judging the power of the firm is defining the marketplace in which it competes for sales. For example, if the marketplace consists of all books, then *Playtime* will not have monopoly power, no matter what level of abstraction is selected. As the marketplace narrows, however, the relative size and power of *Playtime* grow. Under antitrust law, the appropriate competitive market is called the relevant market. Here, one must decide if the relevant market is (1) all recreational products, (2) all books, (3) all fictitious books, (4) all children's books, (5) all children's books with flaps, (6) all children's books with flaps and animals, and so on. The relevant market is determined by considering such things as customer buying habits and the willingness of purchasers to buy alternative types of products in response to price changes.

5. Hoehling v. Universal City Studios, Inc., 618 F.2d 972 (2d Cir. 1980).

6. Apple Computer, Inc. v. Microsoft Corp. and Hewlett-Packard Co., 35 F3d 1435 (9th Cir. 1994).

7. Apple Computer, Inc. v. Franklin Computer Corp., 714 F.2d 1240, 1253 (3d Cir. 1983).

8. Plains Cotton Co-op v. Goodpasture Computer Service, 807 F.2d 1256, 1263 (5th Cir. 1987).

9. NEC Corp. v. Intel Corp., 10 U.S.P.Q. 2d (BNA) 1177 (N.D. Cal. 1989).

10. 35 F.3d 1435, 1444–45.

11. The abstraction-filtration-comparison procedure used in *Computer Associates* is open to criticism. For instance, once an idea is identified, it might not be appropriate to filter it out of the comparison analysis completely. *Feist* makes it clear that the selection and arrangement of ideas may be protectible. *Computer Associates* does not deal clearly with this possible complication.

12. Atari Games v. Nintendo, 975 F.2d 832 (Fed Cir. 1992).

13. Apple appealed the decision of the district court to the 9th Circuit Court of Appeals. The Court of Appeals affirmed the district court opinion in 1994. 35 F.3d 1435 (9th Cir. 1994).

14. Apple Computer, Inc. v. Microsoft Corp. and Hewlett-Packard Co., 799 F. Supp. 1006 (N.D. Cal. 1992).

15. 516 U.S. 233 (1996).

16. J. Moses, "When Copyright Law Disappoints, Software Firms Find Alternatives," Wall Street J. (May 4, 1993) at B6.

17. O.J. Eur. Comm. (No. L 122) 42 (1991). For a thorough discussion of the directive, see H. Pearson, C. Miller, and N. Turtle, "Commercial Implications of the European Software Copyright Directive," 8 Comp. Law. (November 1991) at 13–21.

18. See K. Pope, "Software Piracy Is Big Business in East Europe," Wall St. J (April 27, 1995); J. McClean, "Microsoft Starts Thai Software Anti-Piracy Drive," Reuters (November 10, 1998); C. Mann, "Who Will Own Your Next Good Idea?" 57 Atlantic Monthly (September 1998) at 61.

19. "U.S. Software Firms Lost Billions to Pirates in 1997," Reuters (June 17, 1998); "Clinton Sets Government Software-Piracy Measures," Reuters (October 2, 1998).

20. Mazer v. Stein, 347 U.S. 201 (1954).

21. Esquire, Inc. v. Ringer, 591 F.2d 796 (D.C. Cir. 1978).

22. Kieselstein-Cord v. Accessories by Pearl, Inc., 632 F.2d 989 (2d Cir. 1980).

23. Demetriades v. Kaufmann, 680 F. Supp. 658 (S.D.N.Y. 1988).

24. Digital Millennium Copyright Act, Title V, the Vessel Hull Design Protection Act, Chapter 13 (1998).

25. For thorough discussions of the legal issues involved with digital sampling, see J. Brown, "They Don't Make Music the Way They Used To: The Legal Implications of Sampling in Contemporary Music," 1992 Wisc. L. Rev. 1941; T. Bryam, "Digital Sound Sampling and a Federal Right of Publicity: Is It Live or Is It Macintosh?" 10 Comp. L. J. 365 (1990); T. C. Moglovkin, "Original Digital: No More Free Samples," 64 S. Cal. L. Rev. 135 (1990); B. McGiverin, "Digital Sound Sampling, Copyright and Publicity: Protecting against the Electronic Appropriation of Sounds," 87 Columbia L. Rev. 1723 (1987).

26. One way to avoid infringement of the copyright in the sound recording is to record an independent version that sounds the same and then sample from that. The copyright in the sound recording extends only to uses of the sounds fixed by that owner (Section 114[b]). This will relieve the sampler from having to deal with the owner of the sound recording, but the sampler still will need permission from the copyright owner in the musical work, unless the resultant sampled song is not substantially similar to the original version.

27. Harrington, "Rapper Sues Malt Brewer," Wash. Post (August 28, 1991) at D7.

28. Cal. Civ. Code § 3344.

29. Midler v. Ford Motor Co., 849 F.2d 460 (9th Cir. 1988). See Marks, "An End to Judicial Resistance toward Vocal-Imitation Claims?" Nat'l L. J. (February 20, 1989) at 20.

30. Ansberry, "Alterations of Photos Raise Host of Legal, Ethical Issues," Wall St. J. (January 26, 1989) at B1.

31. "Photographers Call for Boycott of Kodak Film," Wall St. J. (November 5, 1991) at B1.

32. For an excellent discussion of moral rights, see P. Goldstein, Copyright's Highway (Hill and Wang, 1994).

33. C. Ansberry, "Alterations of Photos Raise Host of Legal, Ethical Issues," Wall St. J. (January 26, 1989) at B1.

34. K. Sawyer, "Down to a Photo Refinish," Wash. Post Nat'l Weekly Ed. (February 28–March 6, 1994) at 38.

35. A. Kuczynski, "Dustin Hoffman Wins Suit on Photo Alteration," N.Y. Times (January 23, 1999) at A30.

36. For a thorough discussion of new media works and the important legal and contractual issues related to them, see A. Grogan, "Acquiring Content for New Media Works," Comp. Law. (January 1991) at 2. See also Burgess, "Mixing Up a Revolution?" Wash. Post (July 28, 1991) at H1.

37. A. Grogan, "Acquiring Content for New Media Works," Comp. Law. (January 1991) at 3.

38. The difficulty of handling intellectual property issues when developing multimedia products has not escaped the popular business press. See M. Cox, "In Making CD-ROMs, Technology Proves Easy Compared with Rights Negotiations," Wall St. J. (June 28, 1993) at B1.

39. For an excellent discussion of the purposes of copyright and how they relate to digital environments, see C. Mann, "Who Will Own Your Next Good Idea?," 57 Atlantic Monthly (September 1998). *See also* R. Coleman, "Copycats on the Superhighway," 68 A.B.A.J. (July 1995).

40. Mann, *id.*, at 72–76.

41. *Id.*, at 66–72; V. Slind-Flor, "If It's Online, Why Pay?" Nat'l L. J. (November 18, 1996) at A1; R. Coleman, "Copycats on the Superhighway," 68 A.B.A.J. (July 1995).

42. E. Dyson, Release 2.0 (Broadway Books, 1997).

43. Indeed, as early as 1999, an example showing that this strategy might be successful was provided by the rapid growth of MP3 Internet music sites, such as MP3.com, which allowed musical artists who had not been signed by major recording studios to post their songs on the sites so that consumers could download them for free. *See* N. Croal and A. Murr, "Rockin' the Boat," Newsweek (March 22, 1999) at 63.

44. J. Gleick, "I'll Take the Money, Thanks," N.Y. Times (August 4, 1996) at F16.

45. Intellectual Property and the National Information Infrastructure, the Report of the Working Group on Intellectual Property Rights (September 5, 1995). This document can be accessed through the President's Information Infrastructure Task Force home site at www.iitf.doc.gov.

46. World Intellectual Property Organization, Diplomatic Conference on Certain Copyright and Neighboring Rights Questions (December 20, 1996). The Copyright Treaty can be found through the WIPO home site at www.wipo.org.

47. S. Haar, "Watermarks to Deter Music Theft," Interactive Week (May 12, 1997) at 25; M. Dorney, "New High-Tech Solutions for High-Tech Infringement," Nat'l L. J. (May 17, 1999) at B5.

48. S. Zeidler, "Performing Rights Group Unleashes Robot to Police Web," Reuters (October 17, 1997).

49. E. Corcoran, "Protecting the Ownership Right to Copyright," Wash. Post (February 23, 1998) at Washington Business 5.

50. The Secure Digital Music Intitiative likely will depend on watermarking systems and SDMI compliant software. For instance, music that is copied—or ripped—without permission would not be playable on SDMI-compliant devices. SDMI-compliant devices would be able to play and make copies—perhaps four—of songs that are lawfully obtained from Web sites or are on purchased CDs. The system, though, may allow the copies to be played only from a single device. For discussions of the developing technology in 1999, see S. Robinson, "Recording Industry Escalates Crackdown on Digital Piracy," N.Y. Times (October 4, 1999) at C5; M. Musgrove and R. Thomason, "The Format Frenzy in Digital Music," Wash. Post (October 1, 1999), at E1.

51. The Digital Millennium Copyright Act makes a distinction between technological measures that prevent unauthorized access to copyrighted works and those that prevent unauthorized copying, distribution, or performance. The act prohibits the circumvention of the technological access measures only. Digital Millennium Copyright Act of 1998, § 1201.

52. The act covers devices and services intended to circumvent both kinds of copyright management measures: those that prevent access and those that prevent copying, distribution, or performance. Circumvention devices are defined in Section 1201 as those that (1) are primarily designed or produced to circumvent; (2) have only limited commercially significant purpose or use other than to circumvent; or (3) are marketed for use in circumventing. In 2000, the Motion Picture Association of America sued individuals involved with distributing software called DeCSS, which allegedly was designed to crack an encryption-based security and authentication system used on DVD movies to prevent unauthorized access and copying. A New York court issued a preliminary injunction, finding that DeCSS violated the Digital Millennium Copyright Act. The judge determined that DeCSS was a technology primarily produced for the purpose of circumventing an access control measure since it decrypted an encrypted work without the authority of the copyright owner. He thus granted a preliminary injunction. University City Studios, Inc. v. Reimerdes, 00 Civ. 0277 (LAK), N.Y. Sup. Ct. (February 2, 2000).

53. *See* P. Samuelson, "The Copyright Threat in Bits and Bytes," Wash. Post Nat'l Weekly Ed. (November 9, 1998) at 23; R. Samuelson, "Meanwhile, Back on the Hill . . . ," Wash. Post (September 17, 1998) at A21; J. Schwartz, "House Passes Copyright Bill," Wash. Post (October 13, 1998) at C3.

54. The exceptions include the following categories: (1) nonprofit library, archive, and educational institutions, for the purpose of making a good-faith determination as to whether they wish to obtain authorized access to a work; (2) reverse engineering of computer programs when necessary to achieve interoperabil-

ity; (3) encryption research—to identify flaws and vulnerabilities of encryption technologies; (4) protection of minors; (5) personal privacy, when the work is capable of collecting or disseminating personally identifying information, (6) securtiy testing of computer systems and networks; and (7) law enforcement.

55. The exceptions and the two-year delay apply to the act of circumvention only. They do not apply to prohibitions against the manufacture, import, or sale of devices needed to circumvent encryption technologies.

56. C. Mann, "Who Will Own Your Next Good Idea?" 57 Atlantic Monthly (September 1998) at 61.

57. *See* Olan Mills, Inc. v. Linn Photo Co., 23 F.3d 1345 (8th Cir. 1994).

58. 839 F. Supp. 1552 (M.D. Fla. 1993).

59. J. Kuester and D. McClure, "Internet Service Providers Face Contributory Infringement Suits from Software Copyright Owners Based on the Infringing Activities of Service Subscribers," Nat'l L. J. (January 20, 1997) at B6.

60. There are three methods to link content on the Web. Hypertext Reference (HREF) links are most common and establish a new connection with a new site. Inline image (IMG) links take text and graphics that originate from a different source and make them visible on-screen as part of a Web page's main body. With frames, Web designers may divide Web pages into multiple, scrollable regions and windows that operate independently of each other. Among other things, frames allow Web authors to incorporate remote sites into their pages, allowing viewers to view the remote sites without ever terminating the original connection. In this way, site developers can surround information from remote sites with their own advertising, logos, and information.

61. Some Web sites may place a notice that they do not authorize links to the site. *See* R. Quick, "Can't Get There From Here May Be the Web's New Motto," Wall St. J. (July 2, 1997) at B6. Provisions such as these likely would defeat claims that there is implied consent to link.

62. Copyright Act § 512(d), added by the Digital Millennium Copyright Act of 1998. This protection is subject to the same notice and takedown provisions that apply to materials residing on the ISP's system.

63. Ticketmaster Corp. v. Microsoft Corp., Civ. 3055 (C.D.C.A. April 28, 1997).

64. See S. Pokotilow and M. Siegal, "Controversy Heats Up Over Whether Hotlinks Can Get You in Hot Water," Intellectual Property Strategist (June 1977) at 1; S. Schiesel, "In Ticketmaster vs. Microsoft, It's Tough to Know Whom to Root For," N.Y. Times (May 5, 1997).

65. A case decided in Great Britain, *Shetland Times Ltd. v. Wills*, 1 EILPR 723 (Scot. Sess. Ct. Oct. 24, 1996), suggests that links to embedded pages are unlawful. Some experts agree. See D. Sovie, "Downloading from the Net Is Dangerous," Nat'l L. J. (December 14, 1998) at B5.

66. C. Macavinta, "Sidewalk Sidesteps Ticketmaster," CNET News.com (May 19, 1997).

67. "Short Take: Ticketmaster, Microsoft Settle Linking Suit," CNET News.com (February 15, 1999).

68. See B. Weiss, "Metasites Linked to IP Violations," Nat'l L. J. (July 21, 1977) at B9; A. Hartnick, "Framing: Internet Equivalent of Pirating?" N.Y.L.J. (April 4 & 11, 1997) (published in two parts).

69. The Wash. Post Co. v. Total News, Inc., 97 Civ. 1190 (PKL), (S.D. N.Y. February 20, 1997).

70. An interesting recent example involves a search engine that locates pictures on the Web and displays them as thumbnail images. *See* V. Slind-Flor, "Thumbnail Not Even a Tiny Infringement," Nat'l L. J. (December 6, 1999) at B7.

71. See E. Corcoran, "Protecting the Ownership Right to Copyright," Wash. Post (February 23, 1998) at Business 5; J. Evans, "Copyright Comes to the Internet," Wash. Post (May 10, 1996) at F1; P. Goldstein, "Copyright in the Information Age," Stanford L.J. (1991).

7

Trademark Policy: Protecting Identification Symbols and Product Designs in International Markets

---

INTRODUCTION

Before distributing the **Audio Enhancement System** to the public, we have to consider how consumers will identify our product. If we are the only seller of such a system, maybe this issue is not of great immediate concern. Perhaps we obtained an extremely broad patent covering the entire audio improvement process. However, even in the unlikely event of such comprehensive patent protection, it would be foolish to assume that competition will not appear. If the product is at all successful, engineers will find other ways to improve audio quality. And, of course, the patent will someday expire, allowing competitors to freely use the technology in their products.

Trademark protection for high-technology goods should not be taken lightly. Trademarks are an integral part of the marketing and distribution strategy. Our investments in developing and producing a high-quality product will pay off only if consumers are able to identify such quality in the marketplace. With complex technological products, such as computers or advanced audio equipment, it is not always possible to recognize the value of superior components and processes until after the product is used for some time. However, if the product carries an identifier exclusively associated with a source known for consistently high standards, then a consumer who desires that quality can easily find it. "IBM," for instance, is a classic example of the assurances a trademark can provide.

We also must consider whether there are strategic implications to the identifier we select. The phrase "Audio Enhancement System" has interesting marketing possibilities because it provides information about the purpose of the product. However, there are pitfalls that must be considered in staking one's reputation on such a descriptive designator. We might even consider whether the overall shape of the product and the arrangement of external features might be a suitable means of identification. If we can get consumers to associate a unique ergonomic design of the control panel with our company, for instance, then maybe we can use trademark policy to keep competitors from using similar displays. This might even be advantageous if the arrangement is important for using the equipment easily.

This chapter provides a feel for how trademark considerations fit within the overall strategic plan of marketing technological products. We will consider the fundamental purposes of a trademark and evaluate the range of names and characteristics that may serve in that capacity. The chapter also reviews how one obtains trademark rights and what limitations there may be to protection. The focus then moves to the international arena. Here, we will look at gray market issues as well as international mechanisms to facilitate foreign trademark protection. Finally, we will examine some of the fascinating and contentious new trademark controversies that have been spawned by the Internet.

FUNDAMENTAL PRINCIPLES OF TRADEMARK PROTECTION

Trademark policies coexist at the federal and state levels. The federal trademark statute, which is called the Lanham Act, protects words, names, symbols, or devices that serve to distinguish the sources of goods or services. One of the main attributes of the Lanham Act is the availability of federal registration, which, among other things, provides nationwide notice of the use and ownership of a trademark. However, federal protection extends to unregistered trademarks as well.

Trademark protection at the state level is very similar to federal protection, but with more limited geographical reach. For this reason, companies involved in interstate commerce usually concentrate on obtaining federal rights. However, the laws of some states may sometimes provide more extensive trademark rights than those protected at the federal level. One example that we will explore regards the protection of trademarks from "dilution," a right that historically has been available in many states but only became available under federal law in 1996. In addition, state trademark laws obviously are essential for localized businesses that are not involved in interstate commerce.

As discussed in Chapter 1, the conceptual bases for trademark protection are somewhat different from those for the other components of the intellectual property system. With patents, trade secrets, and copyrights, legal rights are provided to stimulate creative energies. The primary goals of trademark policies, on the other hand, are to combat unethical marketing practices, protect goodwill, and enhance the efficient distribution of goods and services. These are presented in Exhibit 7.1.

Exhibit 7.1
Fundamental Purposes of Trademark Protection

- **Promote Business Ethics by Preventing Palming Off**
  - Symbol or device identifies source
  - Knowledge about the prior use of the symbol or device
  - Similarity creates a likelihood of confusion

- **Protect Goodwill**
  - Reward for investments in quality

- **Promote Market Efficiency**
  - Reduction of search costs
  - Consideration of potential negative effects on competition
    - Generic marks
    - Descriptive marks
    - Functional marks

Trademarks and Competitive Ethics

Federal and state trademark policies are rooted in principles of unfair competition that originally were developed through the common law by state courts. As the name suggests, unfair competition is aimed at competitive practices that unfairly take advantage of honest businesspersons. Let's suppose that we have developed a high-resolution computer monitor that is extremely reliable and will not cause eye fatigue. We stamp the name "HiLiter" on all the monitors so that consumers can readily differentiate our monitors from others in the marketplace. After a successful advertising campaign, sales begin to rise rapidly. But to our misfortune, we are then beset with a menacing competitive presence. Another company begins to sell a substantially inferior computer monitor that from external comparisons looks just like ours. Indeed, the competitor had the nerve to go so far as to stamp the name "HiLiter" on its monitors in exactly the same way as we do. Sales growth falls off dramatically; apparently customers who wanted our product are buying the competitor's product by mistake. By copying our name and design, the competitor is engaging in a deliberate and conscious scheme to palm off its inferior monitors to unsuspecting consumers who believe they are purchasing our reputable product. Even worse, we find that buyers of the competitor's monitors are calling us to complain that our screens do not function as we promised. All of a sudden, the trust and goodwill that we worked so hard to establish for our monitors are severely jeopardized.

Unfair competition doctrines are aimed at preventing the unfair consequences that arise when competitors make it difficult for consumers to locate the goods they want. Normally, when courts review business behavior to determine if it amounts to unfair competition, they look for three characteristics:

1. the product or service of the first company employs a symbol or device—a trademark—which consumers use to identify its source;
2. a competitor uses a symbol or device that is so similar that consumers might confuse it with that of the first company; and
3. the competitor adopted that symbol or device having known, or under circumstances that it should have known, about the prior use by the first company.

The most important remedy for unfair competition usually is an injunction, preventing the competitor from using the identifying trademark. In essence, this means that unfair competition policies legally entitle the first company, such as ours with selling "HiLiter," to have exclusive rights to use that identifier—be it a name, symbol, or product attribute—in its competitive region.

Let's see how application of the three unfair competition factors may work in practice. To make things interesting, assume that our company is rather small and that we decided to advertise and sell the HiLiter monitor only in the Greater San Francisco, California, region. The competitor this time adopts the slightly revised name "HiLighter." Now, consider four scenarios:

Scenario 1: the competitor sells in San Francisco and we can prove it knew about our previous use of "HiLiter;"

Scenario 2: the competitor sells in San Francisco but it alleges that it adopted its name innocently;

Scenario 3: the competitor sells in Reno, Nevada, and we can prove it knew about our previous use of "HiLiter;"

Scenario 4: the competitor sells in Reno, Nevada; it alleges it adopted the name innocently; and we cannot prove otherwise.

SCENARIOS 1 AND 2   The first two situations are the easiest to assess. Scenario 1 is the classic case of palming off in which the company clearly intends to deflect customers by purposely adopting a confusingly similar identifying mark. Scenario 2 really is little different. Although we may not have concrete evidence that the competitor knew about our previous use, it's hard to believe that the competitor entered our region using such a similar name without knowing about our presence. After all, the most simplistic marketing research effort likely would have uncovered that we were already using the name in the region. Even if the competitor is given every benefit of the doubt, logic dictates that we still should prevail in asking for an injunction. Consumers will be confused if two companies have such similar names. Since we were in the area first, it is only fair that we be given priority to use that name. Thus, the results of scenarios 1 and 2 are the same. The first user in the region gets to use the mark and can prevent competitors from subsequently adopting confusingly similar marks in that same competitive area.

SCENARIO 3   Scenario 3 is somewhat different because the subsequent user is not really a competitor. We do not yet sell in the Reno area and thus none of our prospective customers will be misled by use of the similar name. At the same time, one has to be suspicious of the manufacturer's motivations for employing the term "HiLighter," having known about our success with "HiLiter" in San Francisco. Although no immediate harm may come to us, it's hard to say that the maker of "Hi-Lighters" was acting in good faith. With the infinite number of possible names to use as a mark for identification, why did this manufacturer select a name that it knew was being used by another company elsewhere? Likely, the "HiLighter" company opted for the name, hoping that it might benefit in the future if we should someday decide to expand into Reno. Courts will balance the equities of this situation in the following way. As long as we do not intend to sell in Reno and consumers are not being confused, the subsequent user will be allowed to use the "Hi-Lighter" name in that region. However, as soon as we can prove that we intend to expand into that region, we will be able to have a court enjoin the use of "Hi-Lighter" in order to prevent customer confusion. Thus, we ultimately have rights not only in regions where we first used the name but also in others where potential competitors used the name first, but with knowledge of our previous use in another area.

SCENARIO 4   In the fourth scenario, the other business adopted the name "Hi-Lighter" in Reno without knowledge of our usage in San Francisco. This is not totally unbelievable. The Reno company may argue, for instance, that the term was chosen to provide insights into the high-resolution and superior lighting features of the computer screen. This is probably no different from what we were thinking when we selected our name. This business, which acted in good faith, soon will build up its own goodwill in the Reno area. If we later decide to sell "HiLiters" in Reno, customers might be confused by the presence of two trademarks that are so similar. This time, though, the equitable balance leans toward the Reno company, and it will be able to prevent our use of the name "HiLiter" in that region. The result is that we are allowed to use the name in the competitive regions where we first used the name, and the Reno company has priority where it was first. In other words, assuming good faith, unfair competition is a regional doctrine, granting trademark rights to the first user in a competitive area so as to prevent consumer confusion.

Federal Registration and Constructive Notice   Federal registration under the Lanham Act is designed to turn scenario 4 into scenario 3 for the first to use a mark in interstate commerce in the United States. According to the Lanham Act, registration of a mark provides *constructive notice* of the registrant's rights, which among

Exhibit 7.2
Advantages of Federal Trademark Registration

- **Constructive Notice of Trademark Rights**
  - Knowledge about prior use of the trademark assumed
  - Without registration, must prove other had notice of prior use

- **Nationwide Priority**
  - As of the date of filing the trademark application
  - Without registration, priority only in regions where there is actual knowledge of prior use

other things includes nationwide priority to use the registered mark as of the date that the trademark application was filed. In other words, registration notifies everybody in the United States that there already is a user of a particular mark for certain types of goods or services. The notice is considered constructive, because the awareness is assumed no matter if one actually knows of the registration or not. Thus, if we had filed the registration application for "HiLiter" before the Reno company used "HiLighter," and we ultimately were granted the registration, then the Reno company could not claim that it unknowingly adopted the confusingly similar name. This is true even if the company otherwise was acting in good faith and really did not know about our use of, or application for, "HiLiter." Therefore, the situation will be treated the same as scenario 3, in which the subsequent adoption takes place with knowledge. The benefit for us is that now, when we intend to roll into the Reno area, we can demand that the Reno company take whatever steps are required to alleviate customer confusion. Remember that without the registration, the burden was on us to make the necessary changes. The advantages of registering a federal trademark are shown in Exhibit 7.2.

Trademarks and Market Efficiency

Besides enforcing standards of marketing ethics, trademark policies also further economic goals of efficiency. Trademarks provide consumers a shorthand way for finding the goods or services they desire. If the law did not protect a company's exclusive right to an identification mark, then consumers might have to contend with a marketplace where products from different sources look identical, at least from a quick visual inspection. Customers who want our computer screens might have a hard time locating them if there are competitive screens that have copied to the minutest detail our external features, including any names, colors, or symbols that we attached. Some buyers will not realize that the screens originate from different sources—those who buy monitors from competitors by mistake simply will attribute any performance differences to poor quality control. Those purchasers who are aware of the competition in the market will have to undertake measures to "search" for our monitors. They might, for instance, negotiate for trial-use periods or, together with the retailer, trace down the sources of particular shipments. Whatever method is used, consumers are forced to spend additional time and possibly money to locate the goods they desire.

In its purest form, trademark protection relieves consumers from search expenditures and guards a firm's reputation without interfering with free competition. Competitors are free to copy a product along any dimension they choose except for the exclusive identification mark. Assuming that this mark has no intrinsic value to consumers and is used by them only for identification, other companies will not suffer any competitive disadvantages. The only thing they may want but cannot have is the ability to deceive consumers about the sources of products. To put this another way, trademarks enhance market efficiency by lowering the costs of getting desired products to consumers. As long as their role is solely for identification, trademarks will have no negative effect on the efficiencies resulting from free competition. The result can be only a net plus to the competitive marketplace.

Unfortunately, trademarks are not always selected with such pure identification motivations in mind. Even our choice of the name "HiLiter" was not entirely innocent. Clearly we did not arrive at this word solely for identification purposes. Rather we carefully picked the word so that it would provide some information about the qualities of the product as well. When focusing on the net effect of trademark protection on economic efficiency, the question then becomes whether adding this informational component may negatively impact competition. If so, then it becomes less clear that trademark protection must be beneficial. Under these circumstances, one will have to be more cautious before extending trademark protection.

Generic Marks

Suppose that instead of "HiLiter," we desired trademark protection for the word "monitor." If we obtained rights to this name, then we might obtain a competitive advantage in the marketplace. Due to our trademark rights, competitors now would have to market their products as, say, "screens," "terminals," "pads" or some other term. What they will not be able to do is to refer to their products as monitors, since we have exclusive rights to use that word. Most purchasers of computer products know what a monitor is, since that is the word ordinarily used for the display component. However, some may be uneasy with designations such as "pads," and may be reluctant to buy them because they are not absolutely sure that they have the same functions and features as monitors. Thus, although the products are the same, customers may lean toward our offerings simply because the products are clearly identified as computer monitors, just what they knew they wanted. To offset that advantage, competitors will have to engage in additional expenditures to educate consumers that a "pad" is the same as a "monitor."

This example demonstrates that one cannot always perfunctorily assume that there are no social costs from trademark protection. In this instance, in which we selected the generic term for the product, it is clear that protection raises barriers to competition. In addition, one might wonder whether consumers really could associate a generic term, such as "monitor," with only one particular source of products. Trademarks are distinctive identifiers that point to one provider of a kind of product. How can the generic name, which refers to the entire product class, refer only to one provider in the class? Would you ever be willing to conclude that the word "football" might distinctively identify a particular manufacturer of that sports product? Undoubtedly, the answer is no. For both of these reasons—competitive advantage and lack of distinctiveness—unfair competition policies do not allow protection for generic words. Likewise, one may not register a generic term under the Lanham Act. It is for this reason that protection was not available for "shuttle" to identify an airline route, for "cola," for "Swiss Army" knife, and for "386" with respect to a computer chip. Similarly, trademark protection for the phrase "You Have Mail" was denied because it was judged to be a generic way to notify users of electronic communication services that they had received a correspondence.

Genericide   What is perhaps more interesting and dangerous is a corollary: marks that become generic over time will lose their protected status. This policy, coined "genericide," is premised on the same unfairness as before; the only thing different is the timing. For example, Bayer originally chose the somewhat creative term "aspirin" for its headache pain reliever. At first, customers recognized that aspirin was one brand of a type of pain reliever (salicylic acid). However, for a variety of reasons, consumers started to think that "aspirin" referred to the entire class of those pain relievers rather than to one particular brand in that class. This placed other makers of that headache medicine at a disadvantage—they could not call their product "aspirin," yet that is the product that customers wanted. To correct such unwarranted market power, Bayer's trademark registration for aspirin was canceled. Other notable fatalities to genericide include "thermos," "trampoline," "monopoly," "escalator," and "buddy list."

Obviously, genericide can be devastating to a company that has built years of goodwill in a name. All of a sudden, what once was the company's exclusive trademark is available for competitors to use. Compounding the problem is that many customers recognized that the word had brand significance and thus will be confused by the presence of new users of that term. The trademark "Rollerblade" provides a good example. Many people seeking "rollerblades" simply want the new version of roller skates that look like ice skates. To them, the term is generic, representing the name of the product class. Others, however, understand that "Rollerblade" is a brand of in-line skates. If a decision were made to allow competitors to refer to their in-line skates as "rollerblades," these consumers might be confused. For this reason, courts are reluctant to remove trademark protection and will do so only when convinced that the set of those likely to be confused is not substantial.

The reasons that a trademark might become generic vary depending on the circumstances. However, the trademark owner does have some ways to control the situation. For instance, the way in which a product is marketed can affect consumer understanding of a mark. If the makers of "Rollerblade" skates tell the public to try "Rollerblade" brand in-line skates, then they have made it clear that "Rollerblade" is only one brand within its product class, clearly defined as in-line skates. However, if the slogan simply is to try "Rollerblades," then customers may interpret and use the term more broadly. The problem is especially acute for a company that introduces a new class of products. Until competition materializes, consumers often use trademarks in a generic fashion, since there is no need to be specific about the desired source. Just think a few years back, and consider whether you ever asked to go windsurfing, a term derived from the first brand of sailboards. As you can imagine, a company with a patented product must be very careful, because there may not be any competitors for 20 years. The makers of shredded wheat learned the hard way. By the time their patent expired, the name had long since entered the general vocabulary for that type of cereal.

All of this bears directly on our introduction of the **Audio Enhancement System**. Since this will be a new product introduction, we have to be very careful to ensure that consumers distinguish between our brand name and the common name for the product class. Indeed, since the product class does not yet exist, it is incumbent on us to develop both names. This is especially true if we receive a patent on the invention, for competitors will not be introducing similar offerings for a long time. The term "audio enhancement system" probably is not a good choice for a brand name, for if it is so used, what should we call the product class? Do we market our product as the **Audio Enhancement System**, the new breed of LP crystalizers? It seems very likely that **Audio Enhancement System** will be the generic term of choice. Therefore, it is probably better to rely on another term to represent our brand of audio enhancement system. "AES" or "StatFree," for example, should have more longevity. In addition, we should take steps to ensure that retailers and publishers do not use our brand name in a generic fashion. This will require us to scan major newspapers and magazines and to hire investigators to police how retailers treat our brand name. The Coca-Cola Company, for instance, must periodically check to make sure that when a customer asks for a Coke, Coca-Cola is provided rather than just any brand of cola. This measure is designed to prevent retailers from legitimizing the tendency of some consumers to use that trademark as a generic term for cola.

Descriptive Marks

Trademark policies are intended to prevent consumer confusion without imposing unwarranted barriers to free competition. The restraint that could be imposed by allowing exclusivity to generic marks is too great to ever justify trademark protection. Since generic terms are more valuable for marketing purposes than other options open to competitors, the result would be an undue competitive advantage. In effect, the company would profit because it had rights to the best, or one of the very few optimal, trademark choices.

From this, we recognize that generic marks are off-limits for naming our computer monitors. However, we still want our mark to provide information by describing its attributes. Thus, we decide to use the name "Clearvision," a word that directly indicates that our screens have high resolution. As with our choice of a generic term, this selection is meant to do more than simply allow consumers to distinguish our product. However, the selection of "Clearvision" will be less of a burden to competitors. This is because there probably are several equally informative ways to describe high-resolution monitors, such as "Crystalview" and "Focus-Free." Still, the various ways to describe the product are not endless. Thus, there may be competitive dangers, but they are not as great and definite as with generic marks.

Another aspect of descriptive marks is that consumers may not readily recognize that they serve as identifiers. At first, consumers may focus more on the descriptive qualities and not be sensitive to the identification function. For instance, when "Clearvisions" are first introduced, consumers may wonder how many companies make the monitors that provide clear visions. But assuming that we are the only company to sell "Clearvisions," over time consumers will come to understand that there is only one source of "Clearvisions." At this point, "Clearvision" serves to distinguish our product, and consumers would be confused if other companies were allowed to use it.

The Lanham Act does not allow protection of descriptive terms unless they have become distinctive of the goods from a particular source. Once they become distinctive, the terms are said to have secondary meaning—the first meaning is the descriptive information, and the secondary meaning, which comes later, is the identification function. Once secondary meaning is proven, then one can register the mark or otherwise protect it through unfair competition policies. Also, under the Lanham Act, proof that a company has been the only user of a term for five years is prima facie evidence that the descriptive term has secondary meaning.

That descriptive terms may receive delayed protection under the Lanham Act conforms to economic analysis. Exclusivity to a descriptive term may raise some competitive barriers simply because the available number of equally suitable descriptive words may not be enough to satisfy every potential competitor. However, there are enough to ensure substantial competitive recourse. Thus, the dangers are lower than from generic marks. Once secondary meaning arises, customer confusion may result if others use that descriptive term to identify their goods. Using an equitable balancing test, the economic inefficiency resulting from the confusion here outweighs the potential competitive dangers from allowing only one company to have access to the word.

The next case, *Abercrombie & Fitch v. Hunting World*, clearly presents the different ways that marks are treated by the Lanham Act. The opinion provides that trademarks can be divided into four categories that lie along a spectrum of protection, ranging from generic marks, which may never be protected, to fanciful marks,

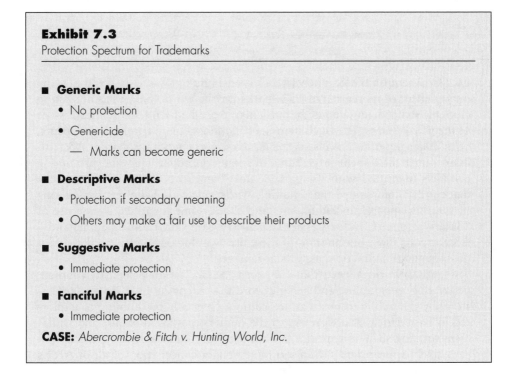

Exhibit 7.3
Protection Spectrum for Trademarks

- **Generic Marks**
  - No protection
  - Genericide
    - Marks can become generic

- **Descriptive Marks**
  - Protection if secondary meaning
  - Others may make a fair use to describe their products

- **Suggestive Marks**
  - Immediate protection

- **Fanciful Marks**
  - Immediate protection

  CASE: *Abercrombie & Fitch v. Hunting World, Inc.*

which may always be protected. Exhibit 7.3 lists the four categories and the degree of protection afforded to each.

Abercrombie & Fitch discusses two other aspects of the Lanham Act that must be clarified to fully appreciate it. One involves the ability to challenge the propriety of registered marks. Later in this chapter, we will review registration procedures. For now, it is enough to know that the PTO's decision to register a mark may be reviewed by a court. For instance, a company wanting to use a registered word may believe that protection is improper because the mark is descriptive and does not have secondary meaning. Most challenges to registration, such as this, must be made within five years of registration. Otherwise, according to the Lanham Act, the registration becomes incontestable. One of the few exceptions to a mark's incontestable status after five years is based on genericism. That is, one can challenge a registration at any time on the grounds that the mark always was or has become generic.

The other issue raised in the case involves fair use of a registered mark. When a company registers a descriptive mark, competitors may want to use the term, not to take advantage of consumers, but rather simply to describe their goods or services. For example, a business that had registered the term "Larvacide" for bug spray could not prevent another company from using the term "larvicide" to describe the larvae-killing properties of its product.[1] Rather, the law only would forbid the competitor from using the word in a trademark sense to identify its goods.

ABERCROMBIE & FITCH V. HUNTING WORLD, INC.
Second Circuit Court of Appeals, 1976

FACTS: Abercrombie & Fitch (A&F) sued Hunting World in 1970 alleging infringement of its registered trademarks for the word "Safari" as applied to clothing and sporting goods. In particular, A&F had ten federal registrations of the word "Safari" for such items as hats, shoes, swim trunks, shirts, pants, belts, luggage, grills, ice chests, tents, axes, and smoking tobacco. A&F alleged that it had spent large sums of money in advertising and promoting products identified with its mark "Safari" and in policing its right in the mark. A&F complained that Hunting World engaged in the retail marketing of sporting apparel, including hats and shoes, some identified by the use of "Safari" alone or by expressions such as "Minisafari" and "Safariland." A&F argued that continuation of these uses would confuse the public, and it thus sought an injunction, as well as damages.

Hunting World alleged that the word "Safari" is an ordinary, common, descriptive, geographic, and generic word that is commonly used and understood by the public to mean an expedition, especially for hunting or exploring in East Africa. It also refers to the hunters, guides, animals, and equipment forming such an expedition. Hunting World alleged that A&F may not exclusively appropriate such a term and sought cancellation of all of A&F's registrations using the word "safari."

After lengthy judicial proceedings, the district court ruled broadly in Hunting World's favor. The judge determined that "safari" is merely descriptive and does not serve to distinguish A&F's goods from anybody else's. The district court dismissed A&F's complaint and canceled all of A&F's registered "Safari" trademarks. A&F appealed.

DECISION AND REASONING: The cases, and in some instances the Lanham Act, identify four different categories of terms with respect to trademark protection. Arrayed in an ascending order that roughly reflects their eligibility to trademark status and the degree of protection accorded, these classes are (1) generic, (2) descriptive, (3) suggestive, and (4) arbitrary or fanciful. The lines of demarcation, however, are not always bright. Moreover, the difficulties are compounded because a term that is in one category for a particular product may be in quite a different one for another (e.g., "ivory" is generic for a product made from elephant tusks, but arbitrary for soap), because a term may shift from one category to another in light of differences in usage through time (e.g., "elevator" originally was suggestive but became generic), because a term may have one meaning to one group of users and a different one to others ("aspirin" is generic for consumers but not for druggists), and because the same term may be put to different uses with respect to a single product (e.g., a term, such as "joy," may be used by one detergent company for identification, but by another to describe the product). In various ways, all of these complications are involved in this case.

A generic term is one that refers, or has come to be understood as referring, to the genus of which the particular product is a species. No matter how much money and effort the user of a generic term has poured into promoting the sale of its merchandise and no matter what level of success it has achieved in securing public identification, it cannot deprive competitive product manufacturers of the right to call an article by its name. The persuasiveness of this principle is illustrated by a series of well-known cases holding that when a suggestive or fanciful term has become generic as the result of a manufacturer's own advertising efforts, trademark protection will be denied.

A descriptive term forthwith coveys an immediate idea of the ingredients, qualities, or characteristics of the product. Such a term stands on a better basis than one that is generic. Although Section 1052(e) of the Lanham Act forbids the registration of a mark that is "merely descriptive," Section 1052(f) removes a considerable part of the sting by providing that such a mark may be registered if the mark has become distinctive of the applicant's goods (i.e., attains secondary meaning). For generic terms, any claim to an exclusive right must be denied because this in effect would confer a monopoly not only of the mark but of the product by rendering a competitor unable effectively to name what it was endeavoring to sell. However, for descriptive terms, the law strikes the balance between (1) the hardships to a competitor in hampering its use of an appropriate word and (2) the hardships of the owner, who, having invested money and energy to endow a word with the goodwill adhering to that owner's enterprise, would be deprived of the fruits of the enterprise's efforts.

A term is suggestive if it requires imagination, thought, and perception to reach a conclusion as to the nature of the goods. The reason for restricting protection accorded descriptive terms, namely, the undesirability of preventing an entrant from describing a product, is much less forceful when the trademark is a suggestive, because the ingenuity of the public relations profession may supply new words and slogans as needed. If a term is suggestive, it is entitled to registration without proof of secondary meaning.

It need hardly be added that fanciful or arbitrary terms, which are chosen solely for identification, enjoy all the rights accorded to suggestive terms— and without the need of debating whether the term possibly is only "merely descriptive."

We have reached the following conclusions: (1) applied to specific types of clothing, "safari" has become a generic term, and "minisafari" may be used for a smaller-brimmed hat; (2) "safari" has not, however, become a generic term for boots or shoes: it is either suggestive or merely descriptive and is a valid trademark even if merely descriptive, because it has become

continued . . .

continued ...

incontestable under the Lanham Act; (3) "Camel Safari," "Hippo Safari," and "Safari Chukka" were used by Hunting World in a purely descriptive way on its boots, and based on fair use, it thus has a defense against infringement.

It is common ground that A&F could not apply "Safari" as a trademark for an expedition into the African wilderness. This would be a clear example of the use of "Safari" as a generic term. What is perhaps less obvious is that a word may have more than one generic use. The word "Safari" has become part of a family of generic terms, which, although deriving from the original use of the word and reminiscent of its milieu, have come to be understood not as having to do with hunting in Africa, but as terms within the language referring to contemporary American fashion apparel. These terms name the components of the safari outfit, well-known to the clothing industry and its customers: the "safari hat," a broad, flat-brimmed hat with a single, large band; the "safari jacket," a belted bush jacket with patch pockets and a buttoned shoulder loop; and the "safari suit," the name given to the combination when the jacket is accompanied by matching pants. Typically, these items are khaki colored.

This outfit and its components were doubtless what the district court judge had in mind when he found that the word "safari" is widely used by the general public and people in the trade in connection with wearing apparel. It is clear that many stores have advertised these items despite A&F's attempts to police its mark. In contrast, no one besides A&F and Hunting World uses the term "Safari" on the other kinds of merchandise subject to A&F's registrations.

The foregoing supports the dismissal of A&F's complaint with respect to many of the uses of "safari" by Hunting World. Describing a publication as a "Safariland Newsletter," containing bulletins as to safari activity in Africa, was a generic use. A&F also was not entitled to an injunction against Hunting World's use of the word in advertising goods of the kind included in the safari outfit. And if Hunting World may advertise a hat of the kind worn on safaris as a safari hat, it may also advertise a similar hat with a smaller brim as a minisafari. Although the issue may be somewhat closer, the principle against giving trademark protection to a generic term in turn sustains the denial of an injunction against Hunting World's use of "Safariland" as the name of a portion of its store devoted to the sale of clothing for which the term "Safari" has become generic.

A&F stands on stronger ground with respect to Hunting World's use of "Camel Safari," "Hippo Safari," and "Safari Chukka" as names for boots imported from Africa. There is no evidence that "Safari" has become a generic term for boots. Since A&F's registration of "Safari" for use on its shoes has become incontestable, it is immaterial whether A&F's use of "Safari" for boots was "suggestive" or "merely descriptive."

Hunting World contends that even if "Safari" is a valid trademark for boots, it is entitled to the defense of fair use provided in Section 1115(b)(4) of the Lanham Act. This section offers such a defense even against incontestable marks when the term charged to be an infringement is not used as a trademark "and is used fairly and in good faith only to describe to users the goods or services of such party, or their geographic origin."

The parent company of Hunting World has been engaged in arranging safaris to Africa since 1959. The president of both companies has written a handbook on safaris, booked persons on safaris, and purchased clothing in Africa for resale in America. These facts suffice to establish, absent a contrary showing, that Hunting World's use of "Safari" with respect to boots was in the context of hunting and traveling expeditions and not as an attempt to garner A&F's goodwill. The district court judge found that Hunting World's use of the term on its boots was intended to apprise the public of the type of product by referring to its origin and use. A plaintiff who has chosen a mark with some descriptive qualities cannot altogether exclude some kinds of competing uses, even when the mark is properly on the register. It is significant that Hunting World did not use "Safari" alone on its shoes, as it doubtless would have done if confusion had been intended. We thus hold that the district court was correct in dismissing the complaint.

We find much greater difficulty in the district court's broad invalidation of A&F's trademark registrations. When a term becomes the generic name of a product to which it is applied, grounds for cancellation exist, even if the registration is otherwise incontestable. The relevant registrations of that sort are Nos. 358,781 and 703,279. The whole of registration No. 358,781, which covers "safari" apparel was properly canceled. With respect to registration No. 703,279 only a part has become generic (to wit, pants, jackets, coats, and hats), and cancellation on that ground should be correspondingly limited.

Some of A&F's other trademark registrations, including the portions of No. 703,279 that are not generic, have become incontestable by virtue of the filing of affidavits indicating five years' continuous use after the respective registrations. There is nothing to suggest that the uses included in these registrations are the generic names of either current fashion styles or African expeditions. The generic term for A&F's "safari cloth Bermuda shorts," for example, is "Bermuda shorts," not "safari"; indeed one would suppose this garment to be almost ideally unsuited for the jungle, and there is no evidence that it has entered into the family for which "Safari" has become a generic adjective. The same holds for luggage, portable grills, and the rest of such suburban paraphernalia, from the swim trunks and raincoats to the belts and scarves included in these registrations.

We also hold that the other registrations, which have not become incontestable, should not have been canceled. "Safari" as applied to ice chests,

continued . . .

continued . . .

axes, tents, and smoking tobacco does not describe such items. Rather, it is a way of conveying to affluent patrons of A&F a romantic notion of high style, coupled with an attractive foreign allusion. Such uses fit into the category of suggestive marks.

The district court is instructed to enter a new judgment consistent with this opinion.

TRADEMARK PROTECTION OF PRODUCT CHARACTERISTICS

The basic purpose of trademark law is to help customers identify the products and services they desire through the protection of distinctive marks. Typically, companies select words to serve as their marks. However, as you are well aware, customers often rely on other kinds of characteristics to distinguish items offered in the marketplace. For instance, customers easily can identify Nike shoes even without seeing that name as long as the shoes bear the characteristic Nike "swoosh." The question for high-technology companies is how far one can take this. If distinctive symbols may be protected because they identify source, does it matter if the symbol is not stationary? This may prove to be important on the Internet, since it is easy to display a moving image on a Web page. Just consider the images one sees on two popular Web browsers: the spinning globe on Microsoft's Explorer and the shooting stars that appear with Netscape's Navigator. What if a Web page or the display of a computer program uses distinctive colors or patterns in the background? Or what if one hears sounds when arriving at a Web site or opening a computer program? May these characteristics be protected as trademarks? May one obtain rights to the distinctive layout of a user interface? And what about the designs of hardware components? Could Apple, for instance, protect the appearance of its iMac computer as a trademark?

The Lanham Act defines a trademark to include "any word, name, symbol, or device, or any combination thereof" and provides protection when the trademark may be used to distinguish goods or services. This language, especially the word "device," potentially has a broad reach, and the PTO and the courts have over time allowed this potential to be fully realized. The PTO, for instance, has registered (1) sounds, such as the NBC chimes and the Lone Ranger theme; (2) smells, such as the plumeria fragrance of a yarn; (3) moving images, such as Tri-Star Pictures winged horse; (4) product colors, such as pink for home insulation; and product shapes, as for instance, faucet designs. Recall, too, that companies do not have to register their marks for them to be protected under federal or state law. And often they do not, choosing instead to rely on general principles of unfair competition to protect them when necessary. Typically, a company will sue a competitor for copying prominent but unregistered features, alleging that customers use those attributes to identify and distinguish the products they desire. The action may be brought under state unfair competition laws or under Section 43(a) of the Lanham Act, which, among other things, extends federal protection to unregistered marks according to basic unfair competition principles. In these situations, the reach of trademark protection is no less than with registration. The main thing that changes is that the company has additional obligations to prove that the competitors were aware of the company's previous use.

So, let's assume that our **Audio Enhancement System** is designed with two extralarge control dials in the center of the front panel. At the time of the product's introduction, this placement was unique to stereo equipment. It also made the equipment easy to use and gave the product a modern technological flair. We decided not to pursue the possibility of a design patent for this arrangement. Could we use the trademark laws to prevent competitors from copying it?

As trademark law moves into the arena of protecting product designs and attributes, it creates additional tension with the basic notions of design patent policies and the underlying principles of free competition. When product designs are not protected by a design patent, then they are supposed to be available for competitors to use freely. However, there is a limited exception to this basic notion, allowing trademark protection when necessary to protect consumers from confusion and under circumstances that will not yield competitive barriers. This, of course, is the same philosophy used to analyze names and words. However, the analysis with product features is more complex because the features may be intimately connected to functioning products. Trademark protection of such nontraditional features, therefore, requires special scrutiny in terms of two underlying trademark concerns. One has to do with the amount of evidence, if any, that companies must dig up to prove that the features may be used by consumers to distinguish source. The other issue regards how trademark protection of the features may serve to disadvantage competitors, an inquiry that relates to what is called "functionality." Exhibit 7.4 indicates how these issues are relevant to those seeking to enforce trademark rights in product characteristics.

Distinctiveness of Product Characteristics

According to *Abercrombie & Fitch*, trademark protection for a word depends on where that word lies on a distinctiveness continuum. Generic terms cannot be protected while descriptive ones can be protected only after secondary meaning can be proven. Suggestive and fanciful terms are so distinctive that they may be registered immediately without any obligation to prove that they identify source. One question with which courts have struggled is whether other potential identification devices should be analyzed according to similar criteria. Words and names are clearly separate from the product—they are merely appended to help consumers identify

---

Exhibit 7.4
Trademark Protection of Product Characteristics: Requirements

---

■ **Identification of Source**
- Product characteristic is inherently distinctive
  - Trademark protection allowed without any proof of secondary meaning
  - A product design cannot be inherently distinctive
  - Product "packaging" may be inherently distinctive
- Product characteristic is common or expected within product class
  - No trademark protection allowed
- All other product characteristics
  - Trademark protection allowed only with proof of secondary meaning

■ **Lack of Functionality**
- Utility supply functionality
  - Cheaper to produce than potential alternatives
- Utility demand functionality
  - More useful than potential alternatives
- Aesthetic functionality
  - More attractive than potential alternatives
  - Controversial standard
- **CASE:** *W. T. Rogers Company v. Keene*

---

and distinguish the product. It may not be so easy, though, to discriminate elements of "trade dress" from the product. Trade dress is a broad term of art. As you might expect, it includes the ways a product may be dressed up, such as with its packaging and labels. However, the term also refers to the total image of the product, including its size, shape, or color.

The courts have had difficulty handling trade dress because the line between identifier and product often is hard to discern, especially when the alleged trademark is part of the product itself. Consider, for example, a stylish new chair with a very tall back. Does the tall back serve as a trademark for the chair? If so, then consumers must somehow be able to conceptually separate the tall back from the product it represents. Some courts have had a hard time believing that consumers approach new products with this form of thinking. In their view, consumers at first perceive that all the attributes of a product are nothing more than parts of the product, even if they are somewhat novel. In other words, consumers would not immediately recognize any aspect of the trade dress as identifying source. Over time, though, consumers possibly might come to understand that certain attributes always come from one source, maybe due to advertising or experience with the product. Following this logic, these courts did not allow trademark protection for any elements of trade dress until secondary meaning could be demonstrated.

The Initial Confusion Regarding Inherent Distinctiveness   In 1992, the Supreme Court first entered the fray and instructed that trade dress should be accorded the same degree of trademark protection as the law provides to words and names. In *Two Pesos, Inc. v. Taco Cabana, Inc.*,[2] the Supreme Court evaluated trademark protection for the trade dress of a restaurant chain. Just to give you an idea of the elements that might make up the trade dress of a product or service, the Court, in this case, accepted that the trade dress was:

> a festive eating atmosphere having interior dining and patio areas decorated with artifacts, bright colors, paintings and murals. The patio includes interior and exterior areas, with the interior patio capable of being sealed off from the outside patio by overhead garage doors. The stepped exterior of the building is a festive and vivid color scheme using top border paint and neon stripes. Bright awnings and umbrellas continue the theme.

The lower courts ruled that the trade dress was "inherently distinctive" but nonetheless denied trademark protection because the restaurant had not proven secondary meaning. The Supreme Court reversed, stating that there is no basis under law for treating trade dress any different from other marks. According to *Abercrombie & Fitch*, suggestive, arbitrary, and fanciful marks—those that are inherently distinctive—are entitled to trademark protection without any need to demonstrate secondary meaning. Therefore, since the lower courts determined that the trade dress of the restaurant was inherently distinctive, it too merited trademark protection without any requirement to prove secondary meaning.

The Supreme Court in *Taco Cabana* held that inherently distinctive trade dress elements merit immediate trademark protection. It did not, however, provide any guidance on how to evaluate when features are inherently distinctive. The Court, though, did suggest that the *Abercrombie & Fitch* distinctiveness spectrum is relevant to the analysis. Some lower courts, however, were reluctant to accept this notion fully, leading to wildly inconsistent approaches. For instance, a few courts held firmly to the notion that product features are different than other marks.[3] According to them, one might treat packaging like words, since one can at least conceptually separate them from the product. Thus, one might conceive of packaging as inherently distinctive and provide immediate protection. However, one never could conclude that product features are inherently distinctive. Other courts focused on another criterion—whether the primary reason that the manufacturer included the product element was to serve as an identifier of source rather than for aesthetics.[4] Despite these approaches, the more significant trend in the courts was to treat all trade dress, whether packaging or product designs, in the same fashion according to the *Abercrombie & Fitch* spectrum.[5] These courts, thus, had to appraise whether product characteristics were generic, descriptive, or inherently distinctive. This, of course, led to interesting problems, for how should one decide if a feature is generic, and what does it mean for an element to be descriptive?

If you think about it, defining the basic product class must be a metaphysical art, very much like that used for determining the idea of a work in copyright analysis.[6] For example, suppose a manufacturer markets a cylindrical trash receptacle with a cone inside and wants trademark rights to the cone and cylindrical shape. Hearkening back to abstracting ideas in copyright, the generic product class might be defined in any of the following ways:

1. A cylinder with a cone inside that holds trash
2. A cylinder that has an interior three-dimensional shape and that holds trash
3. A cylinder that holds trash
4. Something that holds trash

Intuitively, you probably judged that the definition should be no more abstract than level 3, since cylinders are such common shapes for trash receptacles. In fact, the courts have always accepted that common, natural, or expected features may not serve as trademarks. Thus, the cylindrical shape could not be protected, but perhaps the cone might be, depending on how the generic product ultimately was defined. For example, if level 3 were selected, then one might consider the cone to be inherently distinctive since it would be a unique and unexpected addition to the basic product class. However, if the generic product were defined according to level 2, then the cone would be too closely related to the generic product to be considered unique. Rather, it would make more sense to treat the feature like a descriptive mark, necessitating proof of secondary meaning for trademark protection. Of course, if level 1 were deemed appropriate, then the cone could not be protected as a trademark at all, since it then would be regarded as merely a generic product feature.

Distinctiveness of Product Colors Until recently, there was some debate whether a single product color ever could be capable of designating source. In 1995, the Supreme Court resolved the issue in *Qualitex Co. v. Jacobson Products Co., Inc.*,[7] ruling that the green-gold color of pads used in dry cleaning presses could serve as a trademark. Once again, the decision was based on the *Abercrombie* spectrum analysis. The court analogized color in this instance to a descriptive mark, and thereby held that trademark protection was appropriate since there was proof of secondary meaning. The court distinguished this situation from one in which a color was common in its particular context, such as the color "orange" for orange marmalade. Likewise, a company should not be able to appropriate the color green for mint mouthwash, because this feature is generic for the product. On the other hand, pink is not a common color for fiberglass home insulation, and so it did receive trademark protection with a showing of secondary meaning.[8] Interestingly, the Supreme Court implied in *Qualitex* that a single color never could be inherently distinctive. Apparently, the Court believed that the application of a single color always would at least be related to the generic product class.

Inherent Distinctiveness of Product Designs   In 2000, the Supreme Court brought some closure to the controversy regarding the inherent distinctiveness of product designs. In *Wal-Mart Stores, Inc. v. Samara Brothers, Inc.,*[9] the Court evaluated whether designs of children's clothing might be inherently distinctive, thereby allowing the designs to be protected under the trademark laws without proof of secondary meaning. The Court noted that names, symbols, and elements of trade dress are inherently distinctive when they are selected primarily to identify source and signal almost automatically to a consumer that they refer to a brand. The Court believed, however, that even the most unusual of product designs almost invariably are selected not to identify source, but rather to enhance the product. Thus, the Court doubted that there would be many circumstances where product designs might be inherently distinctive.

Based on this conclusion, the Court determined that it would be best if manufacturers never were given the opportunity to convince a jury that their designs are inherently distinctive. For if this door were open, then manufacturers always could mount credible lawsuits against new competitors because the tests for judging the inherent distinctiveness of product designs are so vague and metaphysical that they yield uncertain results. New companies thereby might be deterred from legitimately competing simply because the risks and costs of defending threatened lawsuits are too high. Although a blanket prohibition against proving inherent distinctiveness might disadvantage a few companies, the Court stated that "the game of allowing suit based upon alleged inherent distinctiveness seems to us not worth the candle."

The Supreme Court's decision in *Samara* follows in the footsteps of *Qualitex*: Companies seeking trademark protection for the designs or colors of their products now must demonstrate secondary meaning. However, the ruling in *Samara* is difficult to square with *Two Pesos*, in which the Court allowed an inherently distinctive restaurant decor to be protected without any proof of secondary meaning. According to the Court, restaurant décor is not comparable to a product design. Rather, it is more akin to product packaging, which still is capable of being inherently distinctive. Clearly, the Court was uncomfortable with making this assertion. It also seemingly paves the way for manufacturers to argue that their trade dress should be treated as packaging. This, or course, again raises the specter of metaphysical analyses, since one may have to distinguish the design elements that make up the "product" from those that are part of the separate packaging. Although the Court acknowledged this possibility, it concluded that such arguments would not be raised convincingly very often.

Functionality

In addition to analyzing distinctiveness, one also must address whether product designs or features are functional before concluding that trademark protection is appropriate.[10] The concept of functionality is not consistently treated by the courts and is the subject of much confusion. There is no debate that the doctrine is intended to ensure that trademark protection does not unduly interfere with the free availability of unpatented product designs. However, some courts address this goal in a more limited fashion than others.

Utility Supply Functionality Almost all courts would agree that a product design should not be protected as a trademark if that design allows the product to achieve its function in a way that is cheaper to produce than other possible methods. This was the reason, for example, that Schwinn was denied protection for a bicycle rim design that was simpler and less expensive than other possibilities.[11] Protection would be unfair in this instance because the manufacturer would have a cost advantage in supplying useful aspects of the product. For that reason, this type of functionality may be properly called "utility supply functionality."

Utility Demand Functionality There is also widespread agreement that a product feature or design is functional and not protectible as a trademark if it enables the product to function better than a large set of alternative arrangements. Thus, Bose was denied trademark protection for the hexagonal shape of its speakers because that arrangement was important to the superior performance of that system.[12] On the other hand, the spray bottle design used by Morton-Norwich for such products as Fantastik was not considered functional because there were a large number of spray bottle forms that were equally suitable to perform the function of discharging liquid ingredients.[13] Similarly, a court ruled that the exterior shapes and appearances of two Ferrari automobile models were not functional because they did not contribute to performance.[14] In all of these situations, the focus of the inquiry is whether trademark protection of a design will cause consumers to demand the product more than competitive offerings because the design is more useful to them for achieving their tasks. For this reason, one might properly call this type of functionality "utility demand functionality."

Aesthetic Functionality The most debated aspect of functionality involves the relevance of what is called aesthetic demand functionality. This doctrine prohibits trademark protection for a product design that increases customer demand because it makes the product more aesthetically pleasing. The rationale behind the aesthetic functionality doctrine is no different from that covering the other aspects of functionality: it is intended to ensure that trademark protection does not bestow a competitive advantage. Those who support application of the doctrine perceive no reason to distinguish between protecting utilitarian advantages and protecting aesthetic ones. In both instances, trademark protection empowers the owner with more than a means to distinguish its goods. The only difference is that with utility functionality, the inquiry is on the capabilities of the product, whereas with aesthetic functionality, it is on the product's beauty.

The conceptual difficulty with aesthetic functionality is that the doctrine was misapplied by some courts, leading to what appears to be an overreactive backlash by others. Aesthetic functionality is a problem if it makes the product more desirable. Based on this, the approach taken by some courts was to deny protection to a design if consumers purchased the product in part because they liked and wanted that design. In other words, aesthetic functionality came down to whether the design contributed to the commercial success of the product.[15] As recognized by other courts, this approach meant that one could not get trademark protection for anything attractive, since appearance frequently is an important aspect for commercial success. However, to make manufacturers rely solely on design patents to introduce interesting new designs might make the marketplace extremely dull. Thus, these courts rejected the doctrine. Where they went wrong, at least in the opinion of this author, is by denouncing aesthetic functionality entirely, rather than simply this incorrect application, for the proper methodology is not simply to determine whether a design makes the product more attractive, but whether the design enhances attractiveness more than other designs that might possibly be adopted by competitors. *W. T. Rogers v. Keene* provides a thorough and intelligent exposition of the functionality doctrine, as well as the legitimacy of aesthetic functionality when approached in the correct manner.

W. T. ROGERS COMPANY V. KEENE
Seventh Circuit Court of Appeals, 1985

FACTS: Rogers and Keene are competing manufacturers of office supplies. In 1969, Rogers began to manufacture a molded plastic stacking office tray for letters and documents. The sides of the tray are hexagonal and have little holes on the top and "feet" on the bottom so that trays can be clamped together with other trays to form a stack. The Rogers tray was for long the only tray with hexagonal end panels; competing trays had rectangular panels. Whether because the hexagonal design was pleasing to customers or for other reasons, the Rogers tray was a big success, and by 1985 Rogers had sold about a million of the trays each year.

Wendell Keene worked for Rogers before he founded his own company in 1983. When he went to a plastics firm to get a mold made for his company's plastic stacking trays, he gave the molder a Rogers tray to make a virtually identical tray. Before Keene began competing with Rogers, Rogers had not affixed a trade name to its tray, but afterward it stamped "Stak-Ette" on the tray.

Rogers never tried to get a design patent for the hexagonal end panels that are the most distinctive feature of its tray; nor did it ever try to register the feature as a trademark. Nevertheless, it contends that the feature identifies stacking office trays made by Rogers. Rogers sued Keene under Section 43(a) [15 U.S.C. 1125(a)] of the Lanham Act.

The case was tried in the district court before a jury. The district judge asked the jury to answer two questions: (1) whether the hexagonal end

continued . . .

continued . . .

panels on Rogers's tray were nonfunctional and (2) if nonfunctional, whether they served to identify the Rogers trays. The jury determined that the end panels were functional, and the district judge entered judgment for Keene. Rogers appealed.

DECISION AND REASONING: Functionality is a defense to a suit under Section 43(a). The importance of recognizing a defense of functionality is to head off a collision between trademark law and patent law. The concept of functionality is intended to screen out from the protection of trademark law certain design features even if they have become so far identified with the manufacturer of a particular brand that consumers may be confused about the origin of the good if another producer is allowed to adopt the feature.

The purpose of trademark law is to reduce the cost of information to consumers by making it easy for them to identify the products or producers with which they have had either good experiences, so that they want to keep buying the product (or buying from the producer), or bad experiences, so that they want to avoid the product or the producer in the future. This purpose is achieved by letting a producer pick an identifying name or symbol for a brand and by forbidding competing producers to use the same or a confusingly similar name or symbol on their brands. Since the supply of distinctive names and symbols usable for brand identification is very large, competition is not impaired by giving each manufacturer a perpetual "monopoly" of an identifying mark; such marks are not a scarce input into the production of goods. But if instead of picking some distinctive mark for a brand a manufacturer tries to appropriate the generic name of the product, then it is trying to monopolize a scarce input. In such a case, trademark protection is denied.

The same principle applies if the trademark is part of the design of the product rather than a word or logo affixed to the product. Ornamental, fanciful shapes and patterns are not in short supply, so appropriating one of them does not take away from any competitor something it needs in order to make a competing brand. But if the feature is not ornamental or fanciful or whimsical or arbitrary but is somehow intrinsic to the entire product consisting of this manufacturer's brand and the rivals' brands, trademark protection will be denied. Thus, the first company to make an airplane cannot use the characteristic shape of an airplane as its trademark, thereby condemning its rivals to build planes that won't fly. A firm that makes footballs could not use as its trademark the characteristic oval shape of a football, thereby forcing its rivals to find another shape for their footballs; since they wouldn't be able to sell any round or hexagonal footballs, the firm would have, not an identifying mark, but a product monopoly, and a product monopoly not for a term of years as under the patent laws but forever.

A functional feature is unlike those dispensable features of a particular brand that rivals do not need in order to compete effectively. If the feature asserted to give a product distinctiveness is the best design, or one of a few superior designs, for its de facto purpose, it follows that competition is hindered.

The difficult cases, and this is one, are cases in which the feature sought to be trademarked can be said to be functional by giving aesthetic pleasure. It is apparent that trade names, symbols, and design features often serve a dual purpose, one part of which is to make the product attractive along with identifying the brand to the consumer. On one hand, it would be unreasonable to deny trademark protection to a manufacturer who had the good fortune to have created a trade name, symbol, or design that became valued by the consuming public for its intrinsic pleasingness as well as for the information it conveyed about the maker of the product, unless the feature in question had become generic and therefore costly to engineer around. But it would also be unreasonable to let a manufacturer use trademark law to prevent competitors from making pleasing substitutes; yet that would be the effect of allowing the manufacturer to appropriate the most pleasing way of configuring the product.

Before Rogers began selling its tray, molded plastic office stacking trays came with rectangular end panels rather than hexagonal ones. So evidently, the hexagonal shape was not something intrinsic to the product, as the oval shape of a football is. Of course, products change, and if the hexagonal end panel made the tray substantially more useful, or substantially cheaper to produce, competing manufacturers would be entitled to copy it. But there is no suggestion here of this. The hexagonal shape does nothing to enhance the tray's utility in holding papers. And there is no suggestion that it makes a tray cheaper to produce; if anything, it makes it more expensive, albeit trivially.

It is only when the term "functional" is expanded to embrace the aesthetic that it becomes possible to argue that the hexagonal shape is functional. An identifying mark does not get thrust into the public domain just because the buying public finds it pleasing. If effective competition is possible without copying that feature, then, by analogy to the distinction between arbitrary and generic brand names, it is not a functional feature. That may well be the case here since Rogers is outsold by Eldon, the maker of a rectangular tray—though, of course, other factors could explain Eldon's success while Rogers could have the superior design.

Even if competing manufacturers of molded plastic stacking office trays could not use any form of hexagonal end panel without infringing Rogers's trademark, that would not confine them to the rectangular shape, which we may assume is too drab to be a good substitute for a fancier shape. For even with the hexagon appropriated, an infinity of geometrical patterns would remain open to competitors. Keene could have chosen an oval, a pentagon, a trapezoid, a parallelogram, an octagon, a rectangle covered with arabesques, or machicolated, or saw-toothed.

continued . . .

continued . . .

To summarize this discussion, the jury has to determine whether the feature for which trademark protection is sought is something that other producers of the product in question would have to have as part of the product in order to be able to compete effectively in the market or whether it is the kind of merely incidental feature that gives the brand some individual distinction but that producers of competing brands can readily do without. A feature can be functional not only because it helps the product better achieve the objective for which the product would be valued by a person indifferent to matters of taste, charm, elegance, and beauty but also because it makes the product more pleasing to people not indifferent to such things. But the fact that people like the feature does not by itself prevent the manufacturer from being able to use it as a trademark. The manufacturer is prevented only if the feature is functional as defined earlier, that is, only if without it other producers of the product could not compete effectively.

Though a producer does not lose a design trademark just because the public finds it pleasing, there may come a point where the design feature is so important to the value of the product to consumers that continued trademark protection would deprive manufacturers of competitive alternatives, and at that point protection ceases. This situation is no different from that of the producer of a brand that is so popular that the brand name has become the generic name. Because trademarks do not have fixed time limits like copyrights and patents, other and vaguer methods are used to cut them off at the point where their value as information about product origin is exceeded by their cost in impeding competition. It is just another example of how firms that have the good fortune to succeed may find themselves put under restrictions; but the successful firms have at least the consolation of success. It is not a disaster for the owner of the trademark; should Rogers lose this case in the end and have to share its hexagonal design with competitors, it can (as it has begun to do) imprint a verbal or other trademark more emphatically in order to identify its brand to consumers who can no longer look to the hexagon for identification of source. What Rogers may fear of course is not the loss of an identifying mark but the loss of a competitive advantage stemming from the exclusive possession of a popular design, but for this a manufacturer must seek the aid of the design patent law, with its stringent requirements and its 14-year limitation, and not the aid of the trademark laws.

The case is remanded to the district court for a new trial with jury instructions consistent with this opinion.

We now can return to the issue of whether the exterior design of our **Audio Enhancement System**, especially the placement of the two control dials, may be protected by federal and/or state trademark laws. We need to show, first of all, that when consumers are confronted with products having that control panel design, they believe those products all come from the same source. The more unique and distinctive the design, the easier this will be for us to prove. However, we must keep one possibility, alluded to in *Rogers v. Keene*, in mind. Consumers, over time, may come to believe that a product can be an **Audio Enhancement System** only if it has two control dials such as ours. In other words, that feature, albeit unique, may become generic to the entire product class. Clearly, this is most likely to happen if we are the only seller of the system for a long period of time. However, as with words and names, our marketing and distribution strategies may also be pertinent.

The other set of relevant issues involves questions of functionality. Utility supply functionality likely will not be of concern unless the two-dial design is somehow the cheapest way to have the system perform the functions of those dials. Utility demand functionality may be of some concern, especially if the layout is the most ergonomically sound approach. Perhaps the location of the two dials is most convenient for proper adjustments and tuning. However, this seems very unlikely. On the other hand, we may claim that consumers associate the mere existence of two large wheels, no matter where located, with us. We may encounter more resistance if we try to extend trademark protection this far because large tuning wheels may be the best way for consumers to make the proper adjustments. Or, consumers may become so conditioned to make adjustments with two wheels that their very existence becomes a necessary standard that all companies must use to effectively compete. Just as words may become generic, so too can designs become functional by serving as industry standards. Under these circumstances, trademark protection is inappropriate, since competitors would be forced to retrain customers in order to sell their products.[16] Finally, aesthetic demand functionality also may be a factor on the theory that our layout is one of the only ways to make the product attractive, either in and of itself or in conjunction with other components. As with utilitarian supply functionality, though, this possibility seems very remote.

Trademark Protection and Computers

These same principles can be applied in any high-technology context. The computer industry provides just one example. Trademark protection is available for the shape and appearance of a computer hardware product, for instance, if the design is used to identify the source and is not functional. The analysis for hardware essentially mirrors that just used for the **Audio Enhancement System (AES)**. As with the **AES**, the important issues likely will be whether the hardware has sufficiently unique features to allow customers to distinguish it and whether those attributes are somehow superior for the ways customers use the product.[17] Again, one also must consider whether the product has been accepted by customers as an industry standard. For instance, a unique computer keyboard design, although initially based primarily on aesthetic considerations, was denied trademark protection because it had become an industry standard.[18] In spite of this example, there clearly are situations in which computer hardware products can satisfy all the relevant concerns, especially when they include unique ornamental features. Thus, unlike with copyrights, wherein protection for computer hardware designs is next to impossible, trademarks offer at least some realistic possibility for coverage.

Apple Computer's introduction of the iMac computer in the late 1990s demonstrates how important product design may be in the computer industry. The iMac design was an enormous public relations hit and was partially credited for Apple's resurgence during this period. It is no wonder, therefore, that Apple took the offensive in 1999 when it learned that Future Power, Inc. intended to sell a new product, called the E-Power PC, that allegedly shared strong similarities with the iMac design.[19] Apple filed suit in a California district court, claiming trade dress infringement. If this suit does not end with a settlement, then the relevant issues, as always, will concern the iMac's distinctiveness and functionality. Regarding distinctiveness, one might surmise that Apple could prove secondary meaning. Future Power might argue that the design is generic for a new class of unified computers, but that doesn't seem very compelling. Future Power also would have a hard time claiming that the iMac is functional. The only credible argument would be based on aesthetic functionality, but certainly there are other ways to manufacture attractive computers. Therefore, Apple likely could prove that it has trademark rights in its iMac design. This resolution of this case, therefore, would depend on whether the E-Power PC actually infringes the iMac design. As we shall see later in this chapter, the question of infringement comes down to whether the E-Power design is sufficiently similar to the iMac so that it causes a likelihood of consumer confusion or possible dilution of the iMac design.

Controversial questions also have arisen in the computer field regarding the potential application of trademark protection to the graphical user interfaces of computer software. The analysis for an interface should involve the same principles, thereby leading to the conclusion that it may be protected by trademarks under the right circumstances. As always, the first question will be whether the interface actually serves an identification function. The more nearly unique the look of the interface, the easier will be the burden to prove that this requirement is satisfied. For example, some have argued that when Apple first introduced its user interface for the Macintosh system, it was sufficiently unique to serve as a trademark.[20] However, whatever special attributes it may have originally had were lost over time as other companies introduced interfaces with similar visual appearances. The utility demand functionality concerns may be the real challenge for graphical user interfaces because of the serious potential that they may become standards in the industry. As mentioned before, when this happens, trademark protection should not be available. Computer software companies now are beginning to assert trademark rights in the graphical displays of their products.[21] It will be interesting to see if any special problems arise as the PTO and the courts appraise them in terms of distinctiveness and functionality principles.

Product Design Protection in the EU

Always keep in mind that there are various routes one might consider to protect product designs. In the United States, design patent protection is the obvious choice, while trademark protection may be available if the design is distinctive and not functional. As we have seen, copyright protection for product designs is not readily available in the United States. When venturing into other countries, one will face even more diversity in the ways that designs might be protected. In fact, many nations, especially in Europe, have specialized (sui generis) systems for the protection of product designs in addition to the coverage that may be available under patents, copyrights, or trademarks. In this regard, the European Union passed a directive in 1998 intended to unify the design laws of the member nations.[22] At the same time, the EU was finalizing a regulation that would establish a "Community Design Registration System" allowing union-wide protection based on the same principles. Under the directive, a product design may be registered if it is novel and has individual character at the time of registration. A design is novel if it is not identical to, or differs only in immaterial details from, a preexisting publicly available design. To have individual character, the design must produce an overall impression on an informed user that differs from that of any other publicly available design. The design may have functional attributes, but registration is not available if the design is dictated solely by its technical function. Protection lasts for a five-year term, which may be renewed for up to four additional five-year terms. A registered design is infringed by another design that creates the same overall impression on an informed user.

As discussed in Chapter 6, there have been efforts to expand product design protection in the United States. However, opposition from certain groups, such as the automobile replacement parts manufacturers, has prevented passage so far. The EU directive faced similar struggles, and it provides for various exceptions, reflecting some of the concerns of these groups. For instance, the directive excludes protection for most designs that must be copied exactly to allow interchangeability with products made by other manufacturers. The most heated debates, though, involved the degree of protection afforded to component parts, especially in the automobile industry. The auto industry strongly lobbied for full design protection, while the replacement parts industry called for a complete exemption from protection for purposes of repair. Compromises were introduced, calling for limited periods of protection followed by compulsory license provisions. In the end, the directive put the decision off, instructing member nations to continue whatever policies they currently had regarding component parts and repair. This was done with the expectation that the directive would be amended later to specifically deal with the issue.

FEDERAL REGISTRATION: STANDARDS AND PROCEDURES

As previously discussed, federal trademark registration is desirable primarily because it provides constructive notice of the registrant's rights to exclusively use the mark. However, it carries other benefits as well. For instance, registration is prima facie evidence of the validity of the mark, its ownership, and the registrant's exclusive rights to use the mark. What this means is that a person wishing to challenge the propriety of protection has the burden of proof. In addition, once a mark has been registered for five years, a person may no longer contest the validity or ownership of the mark, except in certain special situations, such as that the mark had become generic. Registration also entitles one to take advantage of enhanced remedies for trademark counterfeiting, a topic to be taken up later in this chapter. Finally, trademark registration provides certain advantages in the international arena, such as by deterring infringing imports and by providing priority in foreign trademark applications.

The Lanham Act states that "no trademark by which the goods [or services] of the applicant may be distinguished from the goods [or services] of others shall be refused registration" unless it falls in particular categories. The criterion for trademark protection, thus, is provided in terms of what may not be protected. For instance, immoral and deceptive marks are impermissible.[23] Also, as discussed before, descriptive marks may not be registered until they become distinctive of the applicant's goods, which requires proof that they have obtained secondary meaning. On this score, the act further provides that five years of exclusive and continuous use of a descriptive mark is prima facie evidence of secondary meaning.

Likelihood of Confusion   The most essential negative condition is provided in Section 2(d), which disallows registration when the mark "so resembles a mark registered in the Patent and Trademark Office or a mark or trade name previously used in the United States by another as to be likely, when used on or in connection with the goods [or services] of the applicant, to cause confusion, or to cause mistake, or to deceive." There are two essential elements to this provision. The first relates to trademark priority. Since one cannot register a mark after there is evidence of previous use by another, the first to use a trademark has the upper hand in terms of registration priority. The second key aspect is based on the likelihood-of-confusion standard, the fundamental cornerstone of trademark policy. Since trademarks are supposed to help consumers clearly distinguish the sources of products and to deter palming off, registration is not allowed when it might result in two or more companies' legitimately providing products with such similar marks that customers are likely to be confused. As we shall see later, likelihood of confusion also is the standard by which infringement is measured. Thus, the same issue is raised in both contexts: what are the circumstances and factors that are relevant in determining whether two marks are likely to cause confusion? How likelihood of confusion is analyzed, both for registration and for infringement, will be demonstrated later in this chapter in *AMF, Inc. v. Sleekcraft Boats.*

Use Requirements   Prior to the Trademark Revision Act of 1988, a person could apply for trademark registration only after using the trademark in interstate commerce. Now, however, a business may file for trademark registration under the

Lanham Act without having actually used the mark as long as there is a bona fide intention to use the mark. Assuming the application eventually results in a registered trademark, then nationwide priority to use the mark is provided from the time of filing the trademark application. Thus, the trademark registrant has rights against anyone who adopts a confusingly similar mark after the filing date of the registration application.

Issues sometimes arise when two companies have innocently used confusingly similar trademarks in distinct trading areas prior to an application for registration. Here, the nationwide notice of registration must interface with common law unfair competition principles. The basic rule in this situation is that the first user is allowed to register the mark. However, the subsequent user retains exclusive rights in the areas where it did business prior to the application for federal registration. The Lanham Act even provides for the possibility of concurrent registrations of similar marks in these situations when consumer confusion is not likely to result.

Trademark priority based on use raises an interesting and important issue for foreign companies that may be planning to someday enter U.S. markets, but have not yet begun to conduct business there. For example, Impressa Perosa, an Italian company, opened a bar with a cafeteria called the Fashion Café in Milan in 1987. Impressa registered the Fashion Café name in Italy in 1988. The principal owner of the Fashion Café made several trips to the United States and distributed free merchandise bearing the Fashion Café name and logo to members of the fashion industry. He also may have had some discussions about someday opening a restaurant in New York. In 1993, Tommaso Buti opened a restaurant in Miami Beach with a fashion industry theme, which he named the Fashion Café. In 1994, Buti planned to open several more Fashion Café restaurants in cities such as New York, and so filed a trademark registration application in the United States and began a widescale publicity effort featuring well-known models. When Impressa learned about Buti's planned opening of the New York restaurant, a bitter lawsuit ensued, which considered whether Impressa's use of the name in Italy along with the promotional efforts in the United States were sufficient to prevent Buti from registering and using the name in the United States.[24]

The court determined that Impressa had no rights to the name in the United States, and that Buti was entitled to a U.S. trademark registration. According to the court, promotional efforts usually are not sufficient to constitute use in the United States. The primary exception to this rule is when the foreign trademark is well known and famous, having received considerable publicity and recognition in the United States.[25] However, the Fashion Café in Milan had not attained the requisite degree of recognition to be considered famous. In addition, it did not matter whether Buti knew of Impressa's use of the name in Italy or not. In this regard the court noted a previous decision by the Federal Circuit in *Person's Co., Ltd. v. Christman*.[26] In *Person's*, a U.S. citizen named Christman, who had visited a Person's Co. retail store in Japan in 1981 and purchased clothing there bearing the Person's logo, soon thereafter manufactured clothing in the United States using the

Person's logo. Christman initiated sales in the United States in early 1982 and filed for a trademark registration for "Person's" in 1983, which issued in 1984. The Japanese company sold some merchandise in the United States toward the end of 1982, but began a concerted effort to sell Person's merchandise in 1985. The Japanese company sued to cancel Christman's registration, claiming that it used the mark first and that Christman acted in bad faith. However, the Federal Circuit determined that knowledge about previous use of a mark in other countries does not constitute bad faith, and that Christman therefore had priority, since the Person's name was not "famous" at the time Christman applied for a U.S. registration. Obviously, the regional nature of trademark rights causes enormous problems for those wishing to expand into international markets. We will take a wider look at international issues later in this chapter.

Reasons to Conduct a Trademark Search   Although it is not required, it is a good idea to conduct a trademark search prior to filing an application for registration. A trademark search reviews prior trademark registrations and other sources, such as trade periodicals, to determine whether any other company is using a similar trademark. A thorough search also should check whether a similar word is being used as an Internet domain name. Although in one sense, a domain name is simply an address, it also may serve as a trademark if the public associates that name with goods or services provided at the site.[27]

One reason to recommend a search is that applicants must allege in their application that to their information and belief, there are no confusingly similar marks being used in commerce. A thorough search can go a long way to demonstrate the good faith of the applicant. The more important reason, though, is to ensure the strength of the mark prior to making substantial investments in goodwill around it. Companies using similar marks have opportunities during the application process to oppose registration; after registration, they are entitled to contest the validity, at least for five years. In a worst-case scenario, a business could actually receive a registration and build substantial goodwill in a name, only to face cancellation several years later because another company can prove that it was the first user of the mark.

Basic Registration Procedures   An application for registration may be based on interstate use or a bona fide intent to use. The basic parameters of the registration process are the same, no matter which path is used, although there are some procedural differences. In 1999, the basic fee to file a trademark application with the PTO was $245. The first part of the registration process involves an examination by the PTO to ensure that the mark meets the statutory mandates. In this regard, the PTO evaluates whether registration should be denied because the mark is confusingly similar to one previously registered at the federal level. In addition, it considers whether registration should be refused for other reasons, such as because it is immoral, deceptive, generic, or descriptive without secondary meaning. The initial review by PTO examiners normally takes around six months, a period that may seem long until one realizes that the PTO evaluates over 220,000 applications per year.[28] As with patents there is a procedure in which the applicant defends or amends its application to satisfy objections by the PTO. In addition, the applicant has the right to appeal decisions by PTO examiners to the Trademark Trial and Appeal Board and ultimately to the federal courts.

Currently, one can expect the total examination process with the PTO to take about 17 months, although the time can be somewhat longer for complex applications.[29] Once the PTO is satisfied that registration is appropriate, the mark is published for four weeks in the Official Gazette of the PTO so that any person who believes that damage might result from the registration may oppose it. Since the PTO reviews only prior registrations, this is the opportunity for those who are using similar marks but who have not sought federal registrations to be part of the process. Assuming the mark makes it through the opposition process, it is then ready for registration. At this juncture, there is a difference depending on whether the application was based on use or a bona fide intent to use the mark. In the former situation, when the application is based on actual use in interstate commerce, the mark will be routinely registered by the PTO.

Intent-to-Use Applications   The other method now available for registration is to file an application before actual use, when one has only a bona fide intention to use the mark in interstate commerce in the future. The main advantage of this course is that a company may stake a claim to a mark and complete the examination process before investing resources into product packaging and distribution. Because the filing date is interpreted to be the constructive date of first use, the application effectively grants nationwide priority to the mark unless it is rejected by the PTO or successfully opposed by a member of the public. Thus, the name is reserved on the date of filing while its suitability for registration is being tested. Assuming it overcomes the usual examination and opposition hurdles, the PTO issues a Notice of Allowance. After receiving the Notice of Allowance, the applicant effectively has 12 months to file a Statement of Use with the PTO, wherein the applicant certifies that the mark is being used in interstate commerce in a way that is commercially typical for that product or service. The filing period for the Statement of Use may be extended for up to 24 additional months upon sufficient showing of good cause. According to PTO regulations, a good cause request for an extension must demonstrate ongoing efforts to make use of the marks, such as research and development, market research, manufacturing activities, promotional activities, steps to acquire distributors, steps to obtain governmental approvals, or other similar activities. Once the Statement of Use is filed, the registration usually will be issued in due course by the PTO, although the statute provides for further examination and acceptance of the Statement of Use. Given the advantages of the intent-to-use registration method, one can predict that the proportional number of intent-to-use applications will rise markedly in the near future.

Loss of Registration Rights A trademark owner cannot totally relax once registration is obtained. As mentioned before, the registration may be canceled on various grounds for up to five years after registration. Someone might allege, for instance, that the mark is descriptive and has insufficient secondary meaning to support registration, or that there was prior use of the mark. In addition, the mark can always be canceled if it becomes generic. In this regard, a trademark owner always has to police advertising and usage of the mark to ensure that it not be used in a generic fashion. Companies with brand names such as Xerox, Band-Aid, Coca-Cola, and Kleenex have to be constantly vigilant about how their marks are being used. Finally, registered trademarks have to be renewed every ten years, verifying that they are still being used in commerce. Exhibit 7.5 summarizes the most important requirements for federal trademark registration.

TRADEMARK INFRINGEMENT AND REMEDIES

Likelihood of Confusion

The essence of a trademark infringement action is proving that consumers are likely to be confused about the sources of products or services in the marketplace. Suppose that we adopt the word "StatFree" as the trademark for our **Audio Enhancement System**, and we obtain a federal registration for it. Another company then uses "HissFree" as the mark for its line of digital audio-tapes. If we bring an infringement action, we will have to show that we own the StatFree mark and that consumers are likely to be confused because a tape manufacturer is using a confusingly similar name. The maker of HissFree likely will put forward a number of arguments in its defense.

For instance, it may claim that "StatFree" is a descriptive name with insufficient secondary meaning to permit trademark protection. Or it may allege that it used the name before we did. Since this is a registered mark, these arguments have to be raised within five years of registration; otherwise, the validity of the mark becomes incontestable on these grounds. Possibly the company will raise the argument that the word "free" or "statfree" is generic for background noise removal equipment. Or, it may establish some inequitable conduct that makes our actions in this matter look as bad as what it did. Maybe we knew about the company's use of "HissFree" for a long time but did not bring suit until after it made a huge investment in marketing and distributing the product.

The most likely position that the other company will take, however, is that customers are not likely to be confused. In other words, the company will deny that purchasers of "HissFree" digital audiotapes are likely to believe that the tapes come from the same source as "StatFree" **Audio Enhancement Systems**. The analysis of whether customers are likely to be confused is unexpectedly complex, depending on a number of pertinent variables. *AMF v. Sleekcraft* provides a comprehensive discussion of the issues involved in a likelihood-of-confusion analysis.

Exhibit 7.5
Fundamental Purposes of Trademark Protection

■ **Identification Symbol or Device**
  - Words or names
  - Colors
  - Smells
  - Sounds
  - Shapes
  - Designs
  - Moving images

■ **Distinctive of Source and Not Functional**
  - According to *Abercrombie & Fitch* spectrum
  - According to *W. T. Rogers v. Keene* principles

■ **Not Likely to Cause Confusion with Other Marks Previously Registered or Used in the U.S.**
  - Likelihood of confusion standard
    — **CASE:** *AMF Inc. v. Sleekcraft Boats*
  - Priority based on use in the U.S.
    — Filing of intent-to-use application qualifies as use

■ **Use Requirements for Application**
  - Actual use in interstate commerce
  - Bona fide intent to use in interstate commerce

■ **Registration Process**
  - Application
  - Examination by PTO
  - Publication
  - Opposition
  - Registration
    — Intent-to-use application
      – Notice of allowance
      – Statement of use in interstate commerce
        * Within 12 months of notice of allowance
        * Extension for good cause
    — Nationwide priority from the date of filing the application

■ **Renewal of Trademark Registration**
  - Every ten years

AMF Incorporated v. Sleekcraft Boats
Ninth Circuit Court of Appeals, 1979

FACTS: AMF's predecessor used the name "Slickcraft Boat Company" from 1954 to 1969, when it became a division of AMF. The mark "Slickcraft" was federally registered on April 1, 1969. Slickcraft boats are distributed and advertised nationally. From 1964 to 1974, promotional expenditures averaged $200,000 annually, and gross sales approached $50 million.

In 1968, Nescher Boats adopted the name "Sleekcraft" for its high-performance boats. The name was selected without knowledge of AMF's use of "Slickcraft." After AMF notified Nescher of alleged trademark infringement, Nescher adopted a distinctive logo and added the identifying phrase "Boats by Nescher" on plaques affixed to the boat and in much of its advertising. The Sleekcraft mark still appears alone on some of Nescher's stationery, signs, trucks, and advertisements. Nescher's gross sales of Sleekcrafts grew quickly—to over $6 million in 1975.

Slickcraft boats are advertised primarily in general circulation magazines. Nescher advertises primarily in racing enthusiast magazines. Both exhibit product lines at boat shows, sometimes the same show.

AMF sued Nescher for trademark infringement and requested that the court issue an injunction prohibiting use of the term "Sleekcraft." Nescher did not argue at trial that it was entitled to the limited geographical defense available to those who innocently adopt an infringing mark after the trademark owner begins use but prior to registration. The district court found that Nescher had not infringed AMF's trademark and denied AMF's request for injunctive relief. AMF appealed this ruling.

DECISION AND REASONING: When the goods produced by the alleged infringer compete for sales with those of the trademark owner, infringement usually will be found if the marks are sufficiently similar that confusion can be expected. When the goods are related but not competitive, several other factors are added to the calculus. If the goods are totally unrelated, there can be no trademark infringement because confusion is unlikely.

AMF contends these boat lines are competitive: Both lines comprise sporty fiberglass boats often used for waterskiing, and the sizes of the boats are similar as are the prices. Nescher contends his boats are not competitive with Slickcraft boats because his are true high-performance boats intended for racing enthusiasts.

The district court found that although there was some overlap in potential customers for the two product lines, the boats appeal to separate submarkets. Slickcraft boats are for general recreation, such as fishing, waterskiing, pleasure cruises, and sunbathing. Sleekcraft boats are low-profile racing boats designed for persons who want high-speed recreation. The district court thus concluded that competition between the lines is negligible. We affirm this ruling that the two lines are not competitive. Accordingly, we must consider all the relevant circumstances in assessing the likelihood of confusion.

Factors Relevant to Likelihood of Confusion. In a determination of whether confusion between related goods is likely, the following factors are relevant:

1. Strength of the mark
2. Proximity of the goods
3. Similarity of the marks
4. Evidence of actual confusion
5. Marketing channels used
6. Type of goods and the degree of care likely to be exercised by the purchaser
7. Defendant's intent in selecting the mark
8. Likelihood of expansion of the product lines

We discuss each serially.

1. *Strength of the mark*

   A strong mark, one that is arbitrary or fanciful, is inherently distinctive and will be afforded the widest ambit of protection from infringing uses. AMF asserts that "Slickcraft" is a fanciful mark that is entitled to wide protection. This is incorrect. Whether "Slickcraft" is suggestive or descriptive is a close question. The distinction is based somewhat on how immediate and direct the thought process is from the mark to the particular product. From the word "Slickcraft," one might readily conjure up the image of AMF's boats, yet a number of other images might also follow. Another criterion is whether the mark is actually viewed by the public as an indication of the product's origin or as a self-serving description of it. We think buyers probably understand that "Slickcraft" is a trademark, particularly since it is used in conjunction with the mark "AMF." We thus hold that "Slickcraft" is a suggestive mark when applied to boats.

   Although AMF's mark is protectible and may have been strengthened by advertising, it nonetheless is a weak mark entitled to a restricted range of protection. Thus, only if the marks are quite similar and the goods closely related will infringement be found.

2. *Proximity of the goods*

   For related goods, the danger presented is that the public will mistakenly assume there is an association between the producers, though no such association exists. The more likely the public is to make such an

continued . . .

continued . . .

association, the less similarity in the marks is required to a finding of likelihood of confusion. Thus, less similarity between the marks will suffice when the goods are complementary (such as drill bits and drill bushings), the products are sold to the same class of purchasers, or the goods are similar in use and function.

Although these product lines are noncompeting, they are extremely close in use and function. Their uses overlap in some aspects. Their functional features, for the most part, are also similar: fiberglass bodies, outboard motors, and open seating. Even though the Sleekcraft boat serves a different submarket, the two product lines are so closely related that a diminished standard of similarity must be applied when comparing the marks.

3. *Similarity of the marks*

Similarity of the marks is tested on three levels: sight, sound, and meaning. Each must be considered the way each is encountered in the marketplace.

Standing alone, the words "Sleekcraft" and "Slickcraft" are the same except for two inconspicuous letters in the middle of the first syllable. To the eye, the words are similar. Nescher points out that the distinctive logo on his boats and brochures negates the similarity of the words. We agree: the names appear dissimilar when viewed in conjunction with the logo, but the logo is often absent, such as when used in trade journals, stationery, and various advertisements.

Another argument pressed by Nescher is that we should disregard the common suffix "craft" and compare "Slick" and "Sleek" alone. Although these are the salient parts of the two marks, we must consider the entire mark. "Craft," a generic term frequently used in trademarks on boats, is not itself protectible, yet the common endings do add to the marks' similarity.

Sound is also important because reputation is often conveyed by word-of-mouth. We recognize that the two sounds can be distinguished, but the difference is only in a small part of one syllable.

The final criterion reinforces our conclusion. Closeness in meaning can itself substantiate a claim of similarity of trademarks. Here, the words are virtual synonyms.

Despite the district court's findings, we hold that the marks are quite similar on all three levels.

4. *Evidence of actual confusion*

Evidence that use of the two marks has already led to confusion is persuasive proof that future confusion is likely. The district court found that in light of the number of sales and the extent of the parties' advertising, the amount of past confusion was negligible. Because of the difficulty in garnering such evidence, the failure to prove instances of actual confusion is not dispositive. Consequently, this factor is weighed heavily only when there is evidence of past confusion.

5. *Marketing channels used*
Convergent marketing channels increase the likelihood of confusion. The boat lines were not sold under the same roof except at boat shows. However, the marketing channels are parallel. Each sells through authorized retail dealers. The same sales methods are employed. The price ranges are almost identical. Different national magazines are used for advertising, yet the retail dealers use similar local means. Although different submarkets are involved, the general classes of boat purchasers exposed to the products overlap.

6. *Type of goods and care by purchaser*
Both parties produce high-quality, expensive goods. The boats are purchased only after purchasers make thoughtful, careful evaluation of the product and the performance expected.

In assessing the likelihood of confusion to the public, the standard is the typical buyer exercising ordinary caution. When the buyer has expertise in the field, a higher standard is proper. When the goods are expensive, the buyer can be expected to exercise greater care in purchasing. Here, the care exercised by the typical purchaser, though it might virtually eliminate mistaken purchases, does not guarantee that confusion as to association or sponsorship is unlikely. The district court also found that trademarks are unimportant to the average boat buyer. Common sense and the evidence indicate that this is not the type of purchase made only on general impressions. This inattention to trade symbols does reduce the possibilities for confusion.

The hallmark of a trademark owner's interest in preventing use of that owner's mark on related goods is the threat such use poses to the reputation of the owner's own goods. When the alleged infringer's goods are of equal quality, there is little harm to the reputation earned by the trademarked goods. Yet this is no defense, for present quality is no assurance of continued quality.

7. *Intent*
Nescher was unaware of AMF's use of the Slickcraft mark when he adopted Sleekcraft, and he designed a distinctive logo after notification by AMF. Nescher's good faith cannot be questioned.

continued ...

continued ...

When the alleged infringer knowingly adopts a mark similar to another's, the courts presume that the defendant can accomplish its purpose, that is, to deceive the public. Good faith is less probative of the likelihood of confusion, yet may be given considerable weight in fashioning a remedy.

8. *Likelihood of expansion*
A strong possibility that either party may expand its business to compete with the other will weigh in favor of finding that the present use is infringing. The evidence shows that both parties are diversifying their product lines. The potential that one or both of the parties will enter the other's submarket with a competing model is strong.

Remedy. Based on the preceding analysis, we hold that Nescher has infringed the Slickcraft mark. A complete prohibition against Nescher's use of the Sleekcraft name is unnecessary to eliminate public confusion. Rather, a limited injunction will suffice.

AMF has a substantial investment in the Slickcraft name, but Nescher also has expended much effort and money to build and preserve the goodwill of its mark. Nescher adopted the Sleekcraft name in good faith and has taken steps to avoid confusion. Use of the Nescher logo in all facets of the business would ensure that confusion would not occur.

In balancing the conflicting interests both parties have in the unimpaired continuation of their trademark use, and the interest the public has in avoiding confusion, we conclude that a limited mandatory injunction is warranted. Upon remand, the district court should consider the foregoing interests in structuring appropriate relief. At minimum, the logo should appear in all advertisements, signs, promotional materials, and business forms. A specific disclaimer of any association with AMF or Slickcraft seems unnecessary, nor do we think it necessary to enjoin Nescher from expanding the product line. In its discretion, the district judge may allow Nescher sufficient time to consume supplies at hand and to add the logo to more permanent assets, such as business signs.

The decision of the district court is reversed.

Exhibit 7.6 lists the factors that are important to consider when analyzing the likelihood of confusion. *AMF v. Sleekcraft* demonstrates that application of the likelihood-of-confusion standard is not susceptible to hard-and-fast rules. Rather, the evaluation is dependent on the commercial realities of particular situations. It is not possible, a priori, to determine which factors are most important or which ones

Exhibit 7.6
Likelihood of Confusion Factors for Registration and Infringement

- Strength of the Mark

- Proximity of the Goods

- Similarity of the Marks

- Evidence of Actual Confusion

- Marketing Channels Used

- Degree of Purchaser Care

- Likelihood of Expanding the Product Line

- Intent in Selecting Mark

should be controlling. This explains, somewhat, why this issue is almost always a point of contention.

As you might expect, likelihood of confusion usually is measured with reference to purchasers. However, there are times when effects on nonpurchasers may be relevant also. For example, a competitor that makes an audio enhancement system that looks very similar to ours might put removable tags on the equipment clearly explaining to purchasers that the product does not come from the company making "StatFree." This tag may successfully keep purchasers from being confused, but others who come in contact with the audio equipment after the explanatory labels are removed may be confused about the source of the product. Assuming that those subsequent listeners are potential future customers, such confusion could negatively affect our goodwill, especially if the competitor's product is inferior.

Application of Likelihood of Confusion Factors to Registration   Likelihood of confusion not only is an issue after the fact in infringement actions, but it also is pertinent on the front end in registration decisions. The evaluation that the PTO must conduct depends on a similar case-by-case analysis of the applicant's mark in light of marks that were previously registered or used. This often leads to similar frustrations and arguments. Just as an example, litigation ultimately resulted when Kenner Parker Toys, owner of the registered trademark "PLAY-DOH," opposed another company's registration of the mark "FUNDOUGH" for children's modeling clay. The Trademark Trial and Appeal Board dismissed the opposition, but the

Federal Circuit, on appeal, analyzed the facts differently. Based on the strength of the PLAY-DOH mark, the low cost of the product, the similar meanings of the words "fun" and "play," the identical sounds of the suffixes, and the identity of the products and channels of distribution, the Federal Circuit determined that there would be a likelihood of confusion and that registration of FUNDOUGH therefore should be denied.[30]

Dilution

Likelihood of confusion is the cornerstone of trademark infringement analysis, since the basic purpose of trademark policy is to prevent the public from being confused about the sources of goods and services. However, there has been a progressive movement over time to protect certain marks not only from uses that might cause confusion but also from applications that might result in dilution of the marks. Dilution potentially occurs when a very distinctive and well-known mark, such as Kodak, is used by another company on an unrelated service or product, such as stereo speakers. Likelihood of confusion is not a central issue because the products and their distribution channels are so dissimilar. In other words, those buying or hearing the Kodak speakers are not likely to believe that the photography company made them. However, Kodak still may be injured by the dilution of its name. For one thing, if enough companies start using the Kodak name in various commercial contexts, then the distinctiveness of the name may become blurred or whittled away. This may lead Kodak to lose control of the overall high-quality image of its name. As one commentator has suggested, there is need to protect "the immense but fragile commercial magnetism values of trademarks."[31] Dilution may be especially relevant if the other companies make inferior goods or services, or are involved in unsavory business practices, such as pornography. In effect, the name "Kodak" will be tarnished by these inferior or undesirable uses, despite the fact that they may be unrelated to cameras and film.

Federal Trademark Dilution Act   Before 1996, trademarks were not protected from dilution under federal law. However, more than one-half the states, including California, New York, and Illinois, had adopted dilution principles either through statutes or by application of the common law. In 1988, there was a concerted effort to add dilution protection to the federal trademark laws. However, that attempt failed, due substantially to concerns from participants in media-related industries that dilution principles might impair free speech and artistic freedom. A number of factors changed in the early 1990s, especially in the international environment, which sufficiently tipped the balance of attitudes regarding dilution to permit passage of a federal statute in 1996. For instance, the European Union adopted a regulation in 1993 that protected trademarks with substantial reputations from dilution.[32] A more important impetus, though, came from TRIPs, which requires WTO members to protect well-known and registered trademarks from uses on dissimilar goods that indicate a connection to the well-known marks. Thus, some argued that the United States had an obligation to provide at least some protection for trademarks against dilution at the federal level. In addition, several members of Congress believed that passage of a federal dilution statute at home would assist U.S. treaty negotiators in their efforts to convince foreign countries to better protect famous marks of U.S. companies.[33] Based on these developments, Congress passed the Federal Trademark Dilution Act (FTDA) in December 1995, and the president signed it in January 1996.[34] Since the federal law has wider geographic scope than state policies, one should expect that the FTDA will become the primary instrument of dilution protection in the United States, while state laws will diminish in importance.

The FTDA defines dilution as the "lessening of the capacity of a famous mark to identify and distinguish goods or services, regardless of the presence or absence of (1) competition between the owner of the famous mark and other parties, or (2) likelihood of confusion, mistake or deception." An important limitation on federal protection, therefore, is that it applies only to marks that are *famous*. Although the statute does not actually define what it means for a mark to be famous, it does list eight nonexclusive factors that courts may consider in determining the fame of a trademark. These are:

1. the degree of inherent or acquired distinctiveness of the mark;
2. the duration and extent of use of the mark in connection with the goods or services with which the mark is used;
3. the duration and extent of advertising and publicity of the mark;
4. the geographical extent of the trading area in which the mark is used;
5. the channels of trade for the goods or services with which the mark is used;
6. the degree of recognition of the mark in the trading areas and channels of trade used by the mark's owner and the person against whom an injunction is sought;
7. the nature and extent of use of the same or similar marks by third parties; and
8. whether the mark is federally registered under the Lanham Act.

The first thing worth noticing here is that federal registration may be considered a positive factor when courts evaluate whether the mark is sufficiently famous to receive federal protection against dilution. Although registration is not required, this provision definitely provides another important reason to seriously consider federal registration of trademarks. Also, dilution principles do not merely apply to famous names; all kinds of famous marks, including the trade dress of products, equally come within the terms of the statute.[35] However, many firms often do not register distinctive elements of trade dress, relying on general unfair competition principles. Those interested in having federal trademark law fully protect product designs, therefore, may now have a reason to reconsider the importance of federal registration.

Another aspect of dilution is that the allegedly damaging use does not have to exactly replicate the mark. Instead, that use must only be sufficiently similar so that it causes an association in the mind of the consumer with the famous trademark. Therefore, an audio company likely would not be relieved from dilution simply by using the brand name "Kodack" on its speakers. Still, always remember that the mark must be famous according to the relevant criteria. For instance, in the late 1980s, there was a highly publicized dilution battle that pitted Mead Data Central, which owns LEXIS computer database services, against Toyota, maker of the Lexus automobile. The district court in New York, on a dilution rationale, enjoined Toyota from using the Lexus name. However, the appellate court reversed this decision, reasoning that most members of the general public were not aware of LEXIS, even though lawyers were familiar with it.[36]

Dilution and Free Speech Dilution principles concern artists and other media interests that use trademarks in their works. Based on dilution principles, owners of famous marks can argue that almost every conceivable commercial use of their marks may whittle away their distinctiveness or tarnish their images. Owners of famous trademarks, therefore, no longer simply possess powerful identification symbols; they now have substantial control over how others may use those symbols in a wide variety of contexts. Prior to the adoption of the FTDA, media interests worried that they might not be able to even report about a company without being accused of diluting its trademark. Advertisers also wondered if they could lawfully engage in comparative advertising, since they might have to mention a competitor's trademarked name in the process. To account for these concerns, the FTDA makes it clear that all forms of news reporting and news commentary are exempt from potential liability. Also, a company is protected when it makes a fair use of a famous mark for purposes of comparative advertising. In addition, dilution does not cover noncommercial uses of a trademark.

Commercial interests that engage in parodies and other forms of social commentary, however, still have reasons to be concerned. As with copyrights, courts must engage in a delicate balancing act, weighing the public's interests in free expression with the benefits it receives from efficient markets. As explained by one court, "[t]o prevent filmmakers, novelists, painters and political satirists from including trademarks in their works is to cordon off an important part of modern culture from public discourse."[37] On the other hand, courts understand that there must be limits to poetic license to preserve the integrity of the trademark system.[38] As we saw in *Acuff-Rose*, courts fashion the appropriate balance with copyrights in terms of a fair use analysis. For trademarks, the courts closely scrutinize the degree to which the use might lead to confusion or dilution. As with copyrights, parodies often fare better in the analyses. For example, a court allowed a clothing manufacturer to sell jeans designed for larger-sized customers and bearing the name Lardasche, finding that the name, although obviously reminiscent of the Jordasche mark, did not raise a likelihood of confusion or dilution.[39] On the other hand, a court enjoined the use of the Dallas Cowboys cheerleaders' uniforms in a pornographic movie.[40] Similarly, a court determined that dilution resulted from the sale of a poster that read "try cocaine," written in Coca-Cola's characteristic stylized lettering format.[41] Thus, courts may be less inclined to appreciate free speech concerns, even those involving parody, when the marks are used in unwholesome or unsavory contexts. This does not

---

Exhibit 7.7
Principles for Evaluating Trademark Dilution under Federal Law

---

- ■ **The Potential Harms from Dilution**
  - • Blurring—The distinctiveness of the mark is whittled away.
  - • Tarnishment—Association with inferior or unsavory products.

- ■ **Requirements to Prove Dilution**
  - • The mark is famous
    - — Eight factors to appraise the fame of a trademark
    - — A reason for federal registration
  - • Sufficiently similar use to cause association with famous mark in the minds of consumers

- ■ **Freedom of Speech and Dilution**
  - • Balance of Competing Interests
    - — Free speech rights
    - — Commercial integrity
  - • Evaluation in terms of long-term potential for dilution
    - — Case-by-case determination
    - — News reporting and commentary protected
    - — Noncommercial uses protected
    - — Fair uses for comparative advertising protected
    - — Parody often, but not always, protected
    - — Unsavory uses less likely to be protected

---

mean, however, that companies necessarily are free to make fun of marks in socially tasteful ways. For example, a court found dilution when a competitor of Deere & Co. produced a commercial in which it animated Deere's well-known "leaping deer" logo and showed it fleeing the competitor's tractor.[42] From all this, it is probably fair to say that one cannot reduce these situations to hard-and-fast rules. The balance simply depends too heavily on highly individualized facts and circumstances. Exhibit 7.7 summarizes the principles involved with dilution analyses.

Dilution and the Internet There is no question that dilution will have an important role to play on the Internet. Since the Internet has quickly become an enormously important information medium, there undoubtedly will be substantial litigation in the future when unflattering remarks are associated with famous trademarks. For example, a disgruntled customer of Bally's Total Fitness set up a web page featuring complaints about the company and displaying Bally's stylized logo with the word "sucks" emblazoned over it. Bally's sued, but a district court judge dismissed the complaint in 1998, finding that the trademark was used to engage in consumer commentary and not for a commercial purpose.[43] Another set of issues involves rights to register domain names. For example, should a ceramic tile company have the right to register the domain name "kodak.com"? If you think the answer is no, you probably will have to reach that conclusion based on dilution, since you will have a difficult time making a strong argument in terms of confusion. Controversies also arise when trademarks are used for hypertext linking or when they are embedded in Internet search codes, called metatags. We will take a closer look at several of these Internet issues in the final section of this chapter.

Remedies for Infringement

Injunctions The most powerful remedy available to trademark owners for infringement is the injunction. The Lanham Act provides that a court "shall have the power to grant injunctions, according to the principles of equity and upon such terms as the court may deem reasonable." Injunctions may take many forms. The most typical is a prohibition against the infringing use. These may vary in strength depending on the equities of the circumstances. For instance, as mentioned in *Sleekcraft*, the court may allow the infringer to use up existing stock of offending items before making corrections, or it may require their immediate destruction. Other types of injunctions include product recalls, corrective advertising, and disclaimers of association.

Monetary Relief The Lanham Act also provides for monetary relief. As with patents and copyrights, monetary relief may be calculated in various ways. The act states that the trademark owner can recover, subject to the principles of equity, (1) the infringer's profits, (2) actual damages suffered by the trademark owner, and (3) the costs of bringing suit. For profits, the trademark owner need prove only the infringer's sales; it is up to the infringer to prove its costs and deductions. Damages may be measured in a variety of ways such as by the extent that sales did not live up to reasonable marketing forecasts or in relation to reasonable royalties. The court also has the discretionary power to increase the actual damages by up to three times, not as a penalty but because the amount of damages the trademark owner could prove seems inadequate given the harm sustained. Indeed, punitive damages ordinarily may not be recovered under the Lanham Act, although they may be under some state laws for egregious conduct. The final item, court costs, are routinely given; however, attorneys' fees are provided only in exceptional cases involving deliberate infringement.

Seizure of Imports Another remedy available to federal trademark owners is having the U.S. Customs Service seize infringing merchandise. As mentioned in Chapter 1, being able to bar imports at the door is a powerful tool, since otherwise, actions may have to be brought in several courts. To benefit from this remedy, a trademark must be recorded with the Customs Office according to regulations issued by that agency.

There is no question that the Customs Office can and should seize infringing merchandise manufactured overseas by totally unrelated companies that have no authority to sell goods using the trademark. However, international commerce is not always so clean and easy, often involving subsidiaries and foreign licensed companies. Whether importation of goods produced by these entities should be barred is a subject of considerable controversy. This issue, which deals with what is called the gray market, will be discussed further in the next section.

Counterfeiting Penalties   In 1984 and again in 1996, Congress amended the Lanham Act to attack what it perceived to be an explosive rise in trademark counterfeiting.[44] Counterfeiting is considered the most egregious form of trademark infringement because it involves the deliberate intent by unscrupulous businesses to mislead consumers. Acts of counterfeiting are not simply situations in which consumers are likely to be confused because similar marks are applied to related goods. Rather, businesses engaged in counterfeiting purposefully capitalize on the reputations, development costs, and advertising efforts of honest businesses by employing nearly identical marks on virtually the same types of goods and services. Testimony provided at congressional hearings indicated that the normal civil remedies were too weak to deter the counterfeiting of a vast array of products such as chemicals, watches, luggage, sporting goods, electronic equipment, computer components, automobile parts, and medical devices.[45] By some estimates, business losses from counterfeiting rose from $5.5 billion in 1982 to over $200 billion in 1996.[46] Substantial evidence showed that the enormous profit potential of counterfeiting far exceeded the magnitude of harm that ultimately might be imposed by a court if a case were ever brought. In this way, the prospect of damage awards and even injunctions were viewed by counterfeiters as merely acceptable costs of engaging in their unlawful businesses.

The 1984 and 1996 amendments were designed to raise the stakes for trademark counterfeiters by making them subject to mandatory treble damage and attorneys' fees awards. They also provide for statutory damages, enabling courts, at their discretion, to award between $500 and $1 million per counterfeit mark. In addition, counterfeiting became a criminal offense, subjecting an offender to fines of up to $15 million and to prison terms of up to 20 years. In addition, those found guilty of counterfeiting may be subject to even greater criminal sanctions under RICO, such as the seizure of nonmonetary personal and real estate assets connected with the conuterfeiting enterprise. Thus, unlike the remedies that are available to be used against more typical trademark offenders, punishment is an explicit characteristic for dealing with counterfeiters.

The Lanham Act defines a counterfeit as a "spurious mark which is identical with, or substantially indistinguishable from, a registered mark." Thus, the additional remedial actions against counterfeiters are available only if a mark is registered. This aspect, therefore, provides one more reason to seek federal registration.

There are other requirements under the act that must be sustained before counterfeiting penalties can be applied.[47] For instance, the counterfeit mark must be used with the same type of goods or services for which the legitimate mark is registered. In addition, the registered mark must actually be in use at the time the counterfeit merchandise appears. Also, a mark can be a counterfeit only if it is applied without the authority of the trademark owner. As we shall see in the next section, this is principally designed to distinguish counterfeit goods from gray market goods. Finally, to be subject to counterfeiting penalties, one must intentionally use a mark knowing that it is a counterfeit. If all of these elements are shown to exist, then the Lanham Act requires a court to impose treble damages and attorneys' fees, barring certain unusual extenuating circumstances. In addition, the counterfeiter potentially is subject to a vast array of other civil and criminal remedies, including certain sweeping penalties available under RICO.

INTERNATIONAL ASPECTS OF TRADEMARK PROTECTION

The internationalization of the business environment now requires most high-technology companies to take steps to protect their goodwill in several countries outside the United States. What companies find is that trademark protection often follows different principles in those countries, sometimes jeopardizing their investments if the proper steps are not taken with the utmost urgency. Also, since trademark rights are strengthened by, if not dependent on, registration, the business has to contend with the procedural demands of registering in all the selected foreign regions. In addition, once trademark rights are established in a foreign country, the product may be altered or priced differently to meet particular local conditions or needs. The question that often arises is whether the trademark owner may prevent those goods from entering the United States. This section reviews developments in these key areas of international trade.

International Trademark Registration

Although steps are being taken to harmonize the trademark protection policies of individual countries, especially within the European Union and through WIPO and GATT, the current reality is that trademark laws vary considerably among the various jurisdictions. One mistake that managers of U.S. companies often make is assuming that they will ultimately have rights to their trademarks in foreign countries because they were the first in the international trading arena to use them. However, their complacency may have serious consequences. Unlike in the United States, where priority is based on use (or intent to use), in most countries, trademark rights are granted to the first person to file for registration. Coupled with this, one must consider that protection in the majority of countries does not depend on use, or even an intent to use. Thus, in many countries, the first to file a trademark registration obtains trademark rights, no matter whether that person has used or intends to use the mark within those borders.

So, assume that the introduction of our StatFree **Audio Enhancement System** is a tremendous success. A substantial advertising campaign, excellent quality control, a thoroughly informed sales staff, and top-flight product features all lead to StatFree's wide acceptance in the United States. When we finally make the decision to expand distribution outside the United States, we may have a rude awakening. Persons or companies in certain countries where we want to do business may have already registered the name "StatFree" for audio equipment, even though they have never made an audio product. What motivated their registration? Given the use and priority rules of those countries, some companies simply register names they might like to use on products if they ever decide to manufacture them. Such a practice, called warehousing, is not possible in the United States because one must have a bona fide intent to use the name in the near future. Another explanation is that the registrant perceived the success of our product in the United States and anticipated that we would soon want to internationalize operations. By registering the name "StatFree," this person now holds us hostage if we want to do business in the person's country. Our choice is to use a different name in that region, or to buy the registrant out. Given the tremendous goodwill built in the name, the first option is not very attractive. Thus, we ultimately are forced to negotiate with the foreign trademark holder simply to use our name on our product in that country.

In addition, we must consider the possibility that our trademark may be registered in certain countries by companies that intend to manufacture counterfeit goods for worldwide distribution. If we register in those countries first, then we can focus enforcement at the counterfeiting source, assuming we can get the local authorities to police their laws. Otherwise, we will be forced to block the counterfeit merchandise through all the distribution channels in nations where we have ownership rights in the mark. Thus, it may be a good idea for a company to consider registration in certain nations where counterfeiting prevails, even if it has little intention of doing business within those borders.[48] The bottom line from all of this is that international trademark strategies must be considered early in product life cycles.

The essential steps for obtaining registrations in foreign countries are similar to those in the United States. It makes sense to perform a search before filing to see if the name is available. Searching normally is less extensive overseas than in the United States because only prior registrations and applications are relevant, whereas in the United States, any use must be considered. There are numerous private commercial sources that can aid in carrying out these searches. In addition, a search can be conducted at WIPO for international registrations that have been obtained under the Madrid Agreement, an important multilateral treaty that facilitates the registration process. Confusing similarity is the guiding principle in all regions, but one must be wary of the peculiar local customs. For instance, in

Germany, vowel sequences have elevated importance, even if the marks do not sound or look alike.[49] In addition, at least with well-known marks, one must consider that dilution principles may apply in many locales as well. If, after conducting a search, a firm uncovers conflicts in important trading areas, then the firm must consider either purchasing the rights to the mark in those locations or developing another mark.

In some countries, there is no examination for registration. Rather, almost all marks filed will be registered, leaving parties with similar registrations to fight it out in court later to determine who filed first. Most nations, though, provide for some examination followed by opposition periods. Also, as in the United States, most foreign registrations have limited terms but may be renewed indefinitely. The real obstacles in this process are similar to those encountered by businesses pursuing international patent strategies. Because individual applications must be filed for each separate country, an international strategy requires a flock of agents, lawyers, and translators to faithfully protect trademark rights in foreign lands. This, of course, not only presents a procedural nightmare but becomes very expensive in time and money as well.

The international community is becoming increasingly sensitive to the headaches that regional trademark policies create for international business operations. Some steps toward unifying trademark principles and procedures already have been made. Others are in the works. Although there is still a lot to be accomplished, the international environment slowly is becoming more hospitable for high-technology companies that need to protect their valuable investments in trademarks. Exhibit 7.8 lists the most important international trademark agreements, and indicates the major advantages that each offers to companies seeking protection in foreign markets.

The Paris Convention As noted in Chapter 1, the United States is a member of the Paris Convention, which applies to trademarks as well as patents. The Paris Convention requires member nations to provide "national treatment," meaning that U.S. citizens must be accorded the same trademark rights in any signatory country as the nationals of that country. This provision, of course, does little to unify international standards and thus does not serve to alleviate the burdens of an international trademark strategy. However, the Paris Convention does include some substantive and procedural requirements that may indeed be helpful. For instance, the convention states that every member country must prohibit the registration, and even the use, of trademarks that would cause confusion with unregistered marks that are well known in the country. We have already seen how this provision might apply in the United States in the discussions of the Fashion Café and Person's garments. Remember that in both those situations, the trademarks were not sufficiently well known in the United States to prevent others from using or registering the same names. Thus, these instances were different from when the owner of a New York restaurant adopted the name Maxim's, hoping to capitalize on the fame of the world-class restaurant in Paris.[50]

Similarly, U.S. companies have rights in other countries if they can demonstrate that their marks are well known within the foreign borders. Kmart, for instance,

---

Exhibit 7.8
Important International Trademark Agreements

■ **Paris Convention**
- Six-month filing window
- Some protection for marks that are well known in a country

■ **TRIPs**
- Fairly broad definition of a trademark
- Infringement if a likelihood of confusion
- Restrictions on registering or using well-known marks
  — Promotion within a country may make a mark well known
- Registration for at least seven years and renewable
- A country may not require use to file a trademark application
  — A country may require use for registration, but it does not have to
- Cancellation only if at least an uninterrupted three-year period of nonuse
  — Countries may have longer periods or may never require use

■ **Madrid Agreement and Madrid Protocol**
- File International Trademark Application with WIPO
- Automatic extension of trademark registration to any designated country unless the country refuses the registration within the allotted time period

■ **Trademark Law Treaty**
- Streamlines some registration procedures

■ **Community Trademark System**
- Allows central filing of one application
- Trademark rights extend throughout EU

---

was able to prevent a Jamaican company from using the name "Kay Mart," even though Kmart had no physical presence in that country, because the store was well known to Jamaicans.[51] This was particularly easy to prove, since many Jamaicans had traveled to the United States and had become familiar with the name there. Likewise, McDonald's was found to have trademark rights in South Africa and Whirlpool had them in India due to the special recognition that is given to well-known marks.[52] Unfortunately, the Paris Convention does not define the criteria for determining whether a mark is well known, leading to inconsistencies and frustration. On this score, TRIPs provides that in determining whether a trademark is well known in a member country, one should take into account the knowledge that has been obtained in the relevant sector of the public as a result of the promotion of the trademark. Based on this provision, the owner of the Fashion Café in Italy might have been able to make a more convincing argument about its rights to the name in the United States had its promotion been substantial and widespread prior to Buti's use of the name.

AES The Paris Convention also provides an important procedural advantage that helps companies gain registration priority in the other member nations. Assume that we filed a trademark application (or an intent-to-use application) for "StatFree" on January 1, 1999. According to the Paris Convention, if we file for trademark registration in a Paris Convention country within six months, then the filing date in that country will be considered the U.S. filing date. Thus, if we file in Japan on, let's say, June 15, 1999, then the Japanese trademark office will treat the application as having been filed with it on January 1, 1999. This give us some breathing room to prepare an application for Japan without having to worry that another company might try to gain the upper hand in that country.

TRIPs The members of the WTO have agreed to several trademark principles that will add some uniformity to the international forum. Under TRIPs, any sign that is capable of distinguishing the goods or services of one business from those of another shall be eligible for trademark protection and registration. An important element here is that members are required to protect service marks, something that the trademark laws of a number of countries previously did not do. The agreement further provides that the owner of a registered mark shall have the exclusive right to prevent others from using similar signs in ways that would result in a likelihood of confusion. TRIPs also incorporates the provisions of the Paris Convention. As just noted, this means that owners of well-known marks can prevent others from registering or using their marks in particular WTO member countries even if the owners have not actually used the marks within those borders. In addition, TRIPs provides that promotion in a member country may be a factor that makes a mark well known among the relevant population there.

TRIPs provides for some uniformity in the registration process. Registrations must be for terms of at least seven years and must be renewable. In addition, although a country may require that use be a requirement for registration, use may not be a prerequisite for filing an application for trademark registration.[53] This solution allowed the United States to continue relying on a use-based priority system in an international realm where first-to-file priority systems are the clear norm. TRIPs also states that registered marks can be cancelled for nonuse only if there has been an uninterrupted period of nonuse for at least three years. Rapidly growing companies have some mixed feelings about policies requiring cancellation due to lack of use, but on balance they tend to support them. The positive attribute is that they inhibit warehousing by firms that have little intention to use the marks. On the other hand, they may force companies to enter markets to protect trademark registrations that were filed in a defensive fashion to prevent pirates from gaining strategic footholds for their operations. Some countries never require use to maintain a trademark registration. Most, though, provide for cancellation if the mark has not been used for a period of time, commonly three to five years. For instance, in the United States the period is three years, while in Europe it normally is five.

Madrid Agreement Two major international trademark accords greatly facilitate the procedures for filing trademark applications in signatory countries, in ways similar to the Patent Cooperation Treaty. The original version of these two accords is the Arrangement of Madrid Concerning the International Registration of Trademarks ("Madrid Agreement"), which by 1999 had been joined by 51 nations, but not the United States. Under the Madrid Agreement, after a trademark registration is received in its home country, a business may file centrally with the International Bureau of the World Intellectual Property Organization (WIPO) in Geneva for an international registration. The international trademark application, which must be filed within two months of receiving the national registration, designates any or all of the signatory countries in which protection is sought. The extension of protection to each selected member state is automatic, unless the country refuses the registration within one year based on its own examination and opposition procedures. For this phase, local agents and attorneys may be required if objections are raised. The principal advantage, therefore, is that one may obtain trademark priority in several nations based on the filing of a single international registration.

The United States has refused to sign the Madrid Agreement principally because the treaty requires that an international application be based on an issued national registration. The United States views this provision as discriminatory because national registrations are easier to obtain in other countries. This is because use is usually not required in order to receive foreign registrations. Even after the 1988 intent-to-use changes, the United States does not actually register marks until they are used. Thus, under the Madrid Agreement, foreign firms have a substantial advantage in gaining international priority. The United States also believes that the 12-month response period authorized by the Madrid Agreement is not sufficient time for the PTO to examine international applications. As noted earlier, the average examination period in the United States is around 17 months.

Madrid Protocol On April 1, 1996, WIPO effectuated a new agreement, called the Madrid Protocol, to address the concerns with the Madrid Agreement that were shared by the United States and other countries, such as Japan, Canada, and Great Britain. Under the Madrid Protocol, international registrations may be granted on the basis of pending applications in the home country. Coupled with the intent-to-use provisions now available under U.S. law, this change substantially erases the primary U.S. concern about discrimination. The protocol also provides national trademark offices 18 months, instead of 12, to advise WIPO of any objection they might have to registration. This time period is more palatable to the PTO. In addition, the protocol allows international trademark applications to be filed in English, whereas the Madrid Agreement required that applications be filed in French. As noted with reference to the Patent Cooperation Treaty, it is always advantageous to be able to file an application in one's native language.

Another important issue addressed by the protocol involves the effect upon the international registration (and the national registrations based thereupon) when the home country either rejects the application to register a mark or cancels a registered mark. According to the protocol, an international registration will lapse (as will the territorial extensions) if the home country application or registration is rejected or canceled within five years of its date. By itself, this basic provision would be unfair to U.S. registrants because the use requirement of U.S. law makes rejections much more likely there than in other countries. Lack of use, therefore, by causing the international application to totally lapse, would wipe out all the advantages, including the priority date, of the international application for U.S. applicants. For others, because use does not affect their home registrations, the only repercussion from nonuse is that they would not obtain an extension of protection to the United States. The protocol alleviates this problem, however. It provides that when a home country application is rejected or canceled, the owner of the international application may file, within three months, national applications in the countries to which the international application extended and may claim the priority date of the international application for them. Thus, although the international registration will lapse, there will be no loss of substantive rights. Given that the Madrid Protocol has resolved the major concerns of the United States, there is little question that the United States will become a member, maybe even by the year 2000.[54] This will be a tremendous procedural step for owners of U.S. trademarks, since the protocol, which had already been joined by 37 nations as of 1999, is expected to involve as many as 100 nations in the near future.[55]

Trademark Law Treaty   Other changes are occurring on the international front that ultimately may yield positive benefits. For instance, in 1994, WIPO adopted the Trademark Law Treaty, which streamlines some of the trademark registration procedures used by the trademark offices of the participating nations. The United States passed legislation in 1998 to bring U.S. processes into conformity with the Trademark Law Treaty.[56]

Community Trademark System (EU)   The European Union (EU) also has been very active in unifying trademark laws and procedures in that region. In 1988, the Council of the European Union adopted a Trademark Law Harmonization Directive, which strives to unify the national laws of the members in the union.[57] Specifically, the directive specifies the types of symbols and devices that can be registered as trademarks, establishes the grounds on which member nations may refuse or invalidate registrations, and defines the rights conferred by registration upon trademark owners.[58] In addition, the EU Council approved a more far-reaching regulation in December 1993 that established the Community Trademark System.[59] Under this regulation, a trademark applicant may centrally register for a Community Trademark with the Office of Harmonization of the Internal Market (OHIM), which, if granted, provides trademark rights throughout the EU.[60] The Community Trademark System works concurrently with the existing national systems in a way that is analogous to the interplay between the federal and state trademark systems in the United States. Given its breadth, one should expect that the Community Trademark System will be very popular. Indeed, more than 40,000 applications were received by the OHIM in just its first nine months of operation in 1996.[61]

The Gray Market

Suppose that our StatFree **Audio Enhancement System** is so well accepted in the United States that we decide to expand our operations into Europe. We, of course, take all the appropriate steps to obtain patent rights within the EU and to register our mark there. While investigating the strategic ways to penetrate the European markets, we begin discussions with a manufacturer in Spain that is willing to pay royalties for the rights to make and distribute StatFrees in Spain. Ultimately we enter a contract allowing the Spanish firm to manufacture and market StatFree **Audio Enhancement Systems** in Spain only. In the contract, we license to this company the rights to use our patented technologies, copyrighted computer programs, and certain necessary trade secrets. In addition, we grant the company the rights to attach the trademark "StatFree" to the goods.

For a number of reasons, StatFrees may be sold in Spain at a relatively cheaper price than in the United States. The laws and customs of Spain may require less warranty protection. Competitive conditions in the wholesale and retail audio markets as well as labor practices may be different in Spain from those in the United States. Also, relative national economic conditions such as interest rates and growth may lead to fluctuations in exchange rates, making goods from Spain relatively attractive. Whatever the reason, any resultant price differentials between Statfrees in Spain and Statfrees in the United States will lead to profitable opportunities for those importing StatFree **Audio Enhancement Systems** from Spain into the United States. These goods are called parallel imports and lead to what is called the gray market.[62]

The problem is that we never intended those StatFrees to compete with our distribution and marketing system in the United States. In a sense, they are not the legitimate StatFrees for the U.S. market. In addition, those selling the Spanish Statfrees in the United States are taking advantage of our investments in promotion, distribution, and service within the United States without sharing in those costs. Their free-riding could have a detrimental impact on our goodwill, especially if there are any differences in the product, such as with warranty terms. On the other hand, we did authorize the manufacture and sale of these goods with our trademark, and we did exercise control of the manufacturing process. Thus, these goods clearly are different from counterfeit goods made by unscrupulous parties. The question is whether the sale of these StatFrees in the United States violates our trademark rights, allowing us either to block their importation or to sue for infringement.

The foregoing situation demonstrates only one of several possible ways that foreign-manufactured products legitimately carrying U.S. trademarks might compete with their U.S. counterparts in the United States. Another scenario is somewhat the reverse from that just described. A foreign manufacturer sells to an independent U.S. distributor the exclusive rights to register its foreign trademark and market its goods in the United States. If the foreign goods bearing that trademark make their way into the United States through other channels, then the domestic firm's goodwill in the U.S. mark may be jeopardized.

Even another set of possibilities occurs when there is an affiliation between a foreign manufacturing firm and a U.S. distributor that owns the U.S. trademark registration for the foreign-manufactured product. For instance, a foreign manufacturer may incorporate a subsidiary in the United States and license to it the U.S. trademark rights so that the subsidiary can distribute the foreign-made products in the United States. Or, a U.S. company that has a registered U.S. trademark could establish a foreign subsidiary or division to manufacture goods that are intended to be sold in the United States by the U.S. firm. In either case, if third parties buy the goods in the foreign nations and then export them to the United States, there will be unwelcome gray market competition with the products distributed by the U.S. trademark owner. All of these situations are set forth in Exhibit 7.9.

Section 526 of the Tariff Act   Two laws empower the Customs Service to block imports that infringe trademarks registered in the United States: Section 526(a) of the Tariff Act and Section 42 of the Lanham Act. Section 526(a) prohibits unauthorized imports into the United States of "merchandise of foreign manufacture" that bear a U.S. registered trademark that is "owned by" a U.S. citizen or organization. Until 1988, the Customs Service interpreted Section 526 very narrowly with respect to gray market goods, blocking parallel imports only when an independent U.S. distributor purchased the rights to the U.S. registration for the foreign trademark (Scenario II in Exhibit 7.9). In 1988, the Supreme Court determined that this reading was too restrictive.[63] The statute also requires the Customs Service to stop imports when the U.S. trademark owner has authorized an independent foreign firm to manufacture goods bearing the trademark (Scenario I in Exhibit 7.9). However, the Court found that ambiguities in certain terms in the statute, such as "of foreign manufacture" and "owned by," adequately supported the Customs Service's policy of allowing gray market imports of goods manufactured by affiliated foreign firms. In other words, gray market imports will not be blocked by the Customs Service under Section 526 if the foreign firm that manufactures the goods is affiliated with the owner of the registered U.S. trademark (Scenario III in Exhibit 7.9).

Section 42 of the Lanham Act   Section 42 of the Lanham Act requires the Customs Service to block imports of articles that copy or simulate trademarks registered in the United States. The Customs Service has interpreted Section 42 in the same way as Section 526 of the Tariff Act; that is, if the foreign manufacturer is affiliated with the U.S. trademark owner, then the gray market goods will not be denied entry into the United States. However, in 1989, the Circuit Court of Appeals for the

Exhibit 7.9
Gray Market Scenarios

***

DEFINITION

A foreign-manufactured good, bearing a valid U.S. trademark, imported into the U.S. without the permission of the U.S. trademark holder.

I.

A domestic U.S. trademark holder authorizes an independent foreign manufacturer to use its trademark, and the manufacturer agrees not to export to the U.S. A gray market is created when:
1. The foreign manufacturer exports to the U.S.
2. A third-party purchaser exports to the U.S.

II.

An independent foreign manufacturing company sells the U.S. trademark rights to a domestic U.S. company. A gray market is created when:
1. The foreign manufacturer exports to the U.S.
2. A third-party purchaser exports to the U.S.

III.

A foreign manufacturing company is affiliated with a domestic U.S. company that owns the U.S. trademark rights.
A. The foreign firm incorporates the U.S. subsidiary to distribute products in the U.S., and the U.S. subsidiary owns the U.S. trademark rights. A gray market is created when:
   1. The foreign manufacturer exports to the U.S.
   2. A third-party purchaser exports to the U.S.
B. The domestic U.S. trademark owner establishes a foreign manufacturing subsidiary or division. A gray market is created when:
   1. A third-party purchaser exports to the U.S.

District of Columbia questioned whether this exception for affiliated firms could be read into Section 42 of the Lanham Act. In that case, Lever Brothers Co. requested that the court order the Customs Service to block imports of Shield soap and Sunlight dishwashing liquid, which were made by its British affiliate, Lever Brothers Ltd. The British products had the same names and appearance as the U.S. products but had different fragrances and colors and produced fewer suds. The circuit court stated that the "natural, virtually inevitable reading of Section 42 is that it bars foreign goods bearing a trademark identical to a valid U.S. trademark but physically different, regardless of the trademark's genuine character abroad or affiliation between producing firms."[64] In 1992, the district court ordered the Customs

Service to block the imports made by the affiliated British firm. That the products were physically different was an important aspect leading the court to reach its conclusion. Whether the affiliate exception would apply to Section 42 if the goods were substantially identical was not resolved in this litigation.

Possible Application of the Copyright Laws   Another potential way to fight the importation of gray market goods is through the application of the copyright laws. Some gray market products primarily consist of copyrighted materials, such as CDs or computer programs. Other products often include copyrightable elements, though. The instructions about how to use products, for instance, may comprise some copyrighted expression. Even product labels may have expressive characteristics that are subject to copyright protection. The Copyright Act has two provisions that potentially apply to the importation of copyrighted materials. Section 602(a) states that the unauthorized importation of copyrighted materials constitutes infringement. This, by itself, seems pretty straightforward. However, the first-sale doctrine, which is provided in section 109(a), states that the owner of a lawfully made copy is entitled to sell or otherwise dispose of that copy without the authority of the copyright owner. This leads to some issues regarding copyrighted gray market goods, since they are lawfully made with authorization from the trademark owner. The only thing that is not authorized is their distribution channel into the United States, but, according to the first sale doctrine, that authorization may not be necessary. The interplay of these two sections leads to three possible solutions regarding the legality of unauthorized imports:

1. all imports of copyrighted materials may be excluded by virtue of section 602, no matter if they are first made in the United States or abroad;
2. no parallel imports of copyrighted materials may ever be barred because they have been lawfully made under the terms of the first-sale doctrine; or
3. the importation of copyrighted materials may be excluded if made overseas, but not if they were lawfully made in the United States and sold from the United States to foreign distributors.

In 1998, the Supreme Court addressed this issue in *Quality King Distributors, Inc. v. L'Anza Research International Inc.,*[65] and determined that the proper formulation definitely is not number 1, above, and likely is number 3. In *L'Anza*, a U.S. manufacturer of hair care products sold its merchandise to foreign distributors (for foreign sales only) at substantially lower prices than those charged to U.S. distributors. When some of the foreign products made their way back into the United States, the U.S. manufacturer sued under the copyright laws, based on the protected expressions in its labels. The Supreme Court held that the first-sale doctrine applied, since the goods were lawfully made in the United States. Therefore, the manufacturer could not use the copyright laws to bar the imports. The Court did not specifically address, however, what the result would have been had the products been lawfully manufactured overseas exclusively for foreign distribution.[66] It implied, though, that the importation of foreign-manufactured gray market goods bearing copyrighted materials might constitute infringement under section 602.[67] Therefore, although the result may seem anomalous, companies wishing to tightly control U.S. distribution channels for their products may have more success under the copyright laws if they manufacture their products outside, rather than within, the United States.

Debate about the gray market is heated, leading to the confusion about its legality and propriety in various contexts. U.S. trademark owners, of course, want all imports bearing similar marks to be blocked. Certain discount retailers and consumers, on the other hand, find the lower prices of gray market goods to be very attractive. As just illustrated, the courts have not provided clear direction. Questions about affiliations, the physical similarity of the goods, and manufacturing locations still need to be resolved. There have been periodic attempts in Congress to clarify existing laws. For instance, in 1991 and 1992, bills were introduced to add a section to the Lanham Act explicitly prohibiting importation of all gray market goods.[68] Since gray markets can have substantial impact on high-technology companies doing business in the United States, prompt resolution of these issues is imperative.

TRADEMARK ISSUES ON THE INTERNET

Since the Internet is rapidly becoming an essential medium of international commerce, it should come as little surprise that it has raised several controversial issues regarding trademark policies. The most contentious involves rights to domain names. Trademark protection is very regional in character. Even with federal registration in the United States, the right to prevent others from employing similar marks only arises from use in localized commercial areas. In addition, the U.S. judicial system is based on courts with regional jurisdiction, allowing trademark disputes to be resolved only in districts with sufficient contacts with the underlying transactions. As one moves into the international sphere, the regional qualities of trademark policies and enforcement only become increasingly magnified. Internet domain names greatly tax the regional traditions of trademark protection because domain names are global in reach. Trademark and domain name policies also clash because trademark rights often extend only to a limited set of goods or services while domain names effectively are exclusive, covering every conceivable offering. These contrasts raise a host of questions. Who has priority in registering a domain name? Who gets to decide? What laws apply when there are disputes? Where can these disputes be resolved? This section will explore some of these contentious issues, to lay a foundation for the solutions that likely will be forthcoming as the twenty-first century unfolds.

Although the international community is most interested in solving the domain name problems, there are other trademark concerns as well. Linking and framing, for instance, may raise trademark issues. Trademark owners also may find certain practices related to search engines to be offensive. In addition, individuals with Web sites often have unflattering things to say about companies, pitting free speech concerns against trademark rights. This section concludes by looking at these emerging issues.

Trademark Rights and Domain Names

In 1992, the U.S. government authorized the National Science Foundation (NSF) to commercialize the computer network that now is known as the Internet. In very simple terms, the Internet links millions of individual computer servers together through telecommunication lines. Every server has a unique address, which is known as its domain name. One component of the domain name is the top-level domain name (TLD). As the Internet emerged in the 1990s, there were five generic top level domain names: .com, .org, .net, .edu, and .gov. There also were over 200 national or country-specific TLDs, such as .us for United States, .de for Germany, and .ne for the Netherlands. In a domain name, the TLD is preceded by a second-level and maybe even lower-level domain names. Often, these are personal or company names or some other memorable phrase. Thus, if we were to register the name statfree.com, "statfree" would be the second-level domain name and ".com" would be the TLD.

NSF contracted with another U.S. government-based organization called the Internet Assigned Numbers Authority (IANA) to take overall responsibility for managing the Internet, including the allocation of domain names. IANA, in turn, assigned the authority over domain names to the Internet Network Information Center, which in 1993 entered a five-year contract with a private company, Network Solutions, Inc. (NSI), to register domain names under four of the generic TLDs. Since .com was the only generic TLD that was intended for commercial enterprises, this TLD quickly became by far the most popular registry sought by businesses. For instance, in 1998, NSI reported that 84% of the domain names registered used .com as the generic TLD.[69]

Given that commercial establishments were predominantly interested in the .com TLD, questions arose when two or more companies had an interest in the same second-level domain name. On the one hand, a domain name is simply an address, merely providing a way to get to a desired location on the Internet. With that understanding, it may be most equitable to allocate domain names on a first-come first-served basis. On the other hand, domain names are not arbitrary, like numerical street addresses. Instead they often are directly related to the goods or services provided at a Web site, leading consumers to view them as designators of source. Thus, although domain names are addresses, they have the attributes of trademarks. This means that a company selecting a domain name may have to be careful, since the use of that name in conjunction with a Web site may infringe trademark rights owned by another firm. Following this logic, one then must consider the circumstances under which infringement may take place. In addition, it raises the issue whether NSI has some duty to ensure that it does not register names that might run afoul of the trademark laws.

As a very simple example, suppose that we sell StatFree audio enhancement systems in California and Oregon. At around the same time, a different company sells Statfree anti-static dryer cloths in the Washington, D.C., metropolitan area, including Maryland and Virginia. If neither company has a federal trademark registration, which should have the right to obtain the domain name Statfree.com.? Suppose the other company used the name Statfree before we did, but we nevertheless obtained a federal trademark registration for the name for use with audio products. Does that change your thinking? What if we used the name first and received a federal registration for the name, but they filed for the domain name before we did? What if our name is really well known for audio products? Should the prospects for trademark dilution enter the decision about who is entitled to the domain name registration? You can begin to see why NSI at first did not want to address the trademark issues when registering domain names, and thus doled out the names on a first-come, first-served basis.

The scenarios above all were concerned with legitimate companies making reasonable claims to register the domain name Statfree.com. However, the intentions of some firms may not be so pure. For example, the other company also may make audio equipment, but sell it under a trademark that is not as well known as StatFree. That company may want to register the domain name Statfree.com to lure to its site those customers who are seeking information on our StatFree brand. What if this company makes counterfeit StatFree audio equipment in violation of our U.S. trademark rights and registers the domain name to assist it in its pirating activities? Does the domain name registrar have a responsibility to prevent this? What if Statfree.com is sought by a pornography site? Should the registrar have some obligation to review the activities of the domain name applicant and consider the possibilities for tarnishment? This is not a far-fetched example. Many adult entertainment sites did register names having clever innuendos, such as Candyland.com and Adultsrus.com.

When the domain name registration rule is first-come, first-served, the door also is open for an individual to rapidly register as many famous and emerging brand names as possible, knowing that many of the legitimate trademark owners soon will desperately want to acquire those domain names for their respective businesses. For instance, an individual may register the Statfree.com domain name for a Web site that merely shows a picture of a lightning bolt with the word "free' emblazoned over it. That individual then may have the nerve to contact us and demand a large payment to relinquish the registration. Depending on the amount that domain name registrations cost, and when those fees are due, this could be a lucrative business having little financial risk. This practice has been given the name, *cybersquatting*, since the domain name registrants merely sit on desirable names until those with legitimate claims buy them out. In 1996, a California court addressed the issue of cybersquatting in *Panavision International v. Toeppen*. This was one of the first cases to consider the respective rights of domain name and trademark holders, and the opinion represented an important victory for owners of famous trademarks.

PANAVISION INTERNATIONAL V. DENNIS TOEPPEN
District Court for the Central District of California, 1996

FACTS: Panavision is involved in photographic camera and equipment businesses, and owns several federally registered trademarks, including "Panavision" and Panaflex." In December 1995, Dennis Toeppen applied for and received registration from Network Solutions, Inc. of the Internet domain name, "panavision.com." After registering the "panavision.com" domain name, Toeppen established a Web site displaying aerial views of Pana, Illinois. Shortly thereafter, Panavision attempted to establish a Web site under its own name, but it discovered that Toeppen had already registered "panavision.com." Therefore, Panavision was unable to register and use its trademark as an Internet domain name. When Panavision notified Toeppen of its desire to use the "panavision.com" domain name, Toeppen demanded $13,000 to discontinue his use of the domain name. Panavision refused Toeppen's demand. Toeppen then registered "panaflex.com" as a domain name for a site that contained only the word "hello." Toeppen never used either domain name in connection with the sale of any goods or services.

Panavision sued Toeppen for, among other things, trademark infringement, unfair competition and dilution. Network Solutions placed both domain names "on hold" pending the outcome of this litigation.

DECISION AND REASONING: In recent years, businesses have begun to use the Internet to provide information and products to consumers and other businesses. Every computer that has access to the Internet has a unique address. All Internet addresses consist of four groups of digits separated by periods that indicate the network, subnetwork and local address. For example, an Internet address might read "231.35.1.19". This address is referred to as the "IP address." Every Internet address also has a unique alphanumeric equivalent to its IP address referred to as its "domain name." Domain names consist of a string of "domains" separated by periods. Most business domain names consist of two domains. First, there is the "top-level" domain, which indicates the type of organization using the name. Commercial entities use the ".com" top-level domain name, while other top-level domain names include ".net," which is used by networks, and ".edu," which is used by educational organizations. Next, there is the "second-level" domain, which is frequently the name of the company (or a derivative thereof) that maintains the Web site. In short, one purpose of domain names is to identify the entity that owns the Web site.

The other primary purpose of domain names is to allow Internet users to locate Web sites quickly and easily. If an Internet user knows the name of another user's Web site, he or she can easily contact the site. If the user does not know the domain name, the user can search for the site using an Internet "search engine." Search engines search the Internet using "key words" selected by the searching party. A key word search will typically produce a list of the Web sites that use the key words. Key word searches will frequently yield thousands of Web sites. The user can access the web sites through programs called "web browsers." The length and success of this process is dependent upon the searching party's ability to deduce the correct key word or words and the number of other web sites that use the same key words.

Because users may have difficulty accessing web sites or may not be able to access web sites at all when they do not know (or cannot deduce) the proper domain name, businesses frequently register their names and trademarks as domain names. Therefore, having a known or deducible domain name is important to companies seeking to do business on the Internet, as well as important to consumers who want to locate those businesses' web sites.

Traditionally, trademark law has permitted multiple parties to use the same mark for different classes of goods or services. Trademark law only prohibited use of the same mark on competing or related goods or services where there was a likelihood of consumer confusion as to the origin of the goods or services with which the user associated the mark. Trademark dilution laws, however, changed the traditional trademark analysis since they protect "distinctive" or "famous" trademarks from certain unauthorized uses of the mark regardless of a showing of competition or likelihood of confusion.

The Internet will leave its imprint on trademark law, and vice versa. An area in which trademark law will have an impact on the Internet involves disputes over the right to use particular domain names. Trademark law permits multiple parties to use the same mark for different classes of goods and services; however, the current organization of the Internet permits only one use of a domain name, regardless of the goods or services offered. That is, although two or more businesses can own the trademark "Acme," only one business can operate on the Internet with the domain name "acme.com." Such a limitation conflicts with trademark principles and hinders the use of the Internet by businesses. Many of the issues, both legal and technical, that arise from the intersection of trademark law and the Internet are difficult to resolve. Ultimately, Congressional action seems necessary.

Prior to the recently enacted Federal Trademark Dilution Act of 1995, trademark dilution was a creature of state law, but the Dilution Act created a federal cause of action. The Dilution Act provides that "the owner of a famous mark shall be entitled . . . to an injunction against another person's commercial use in commerce of a mark or trade name, if such use begins after the mark has become famous and causes dilution of the distinctive quality of the mark." In applying the Dilution Act, the court must be guided by the

continued . . .

continued . . .

policies underlying trademark law. The basic policy is to prevent deception of the public. Trademark law also protects the interests of the trademark owner in not having the value of their marks misappropriated. Finally, trademark law encourages competition and economic efficiency from which the public benefits.

1. *The Panavision Marks are Famous*

   The statute sets forth eight nonexclusive factors the courts "may consider" when determining whether the mark is a "famous" mark. Based on these, the court finds that the Panavision marks are famous. Panavision owns the federal registration of the Panavision marks. The distinctiveness and fame of the Panavision marks are well established and undisputed. The Panavision mark in particular has developed strong secondary meaning because of Panavision's long period of exclusive use of the mark and its status as a major supplier of photographic equipment. Panavision also extensively advertises its marks. In addition, Panavision's "filmed with Panavision" credit appears in the "end titles" of many television shows and movies on a daily basis.

2. *Toeppen's Use of the Panavision Marks is a "Commercial Use" of the Marks*

   Toeppen's "business" is to register trademarks as domain names and then to sell the domain names to the trademarks' owners. Toeppen's business is evident from his conduct with regard to Panavision and his conduct in registering domain names of many other companies. His "business" is premised on the desire of the companies to use their trademarks as domain names and the calculation that it will be cheaper to pay him than to sue him.

   The Dilution Act specifically excludes certain conduct from the coverage of the Act: "[1.] fair use of a famous mark by another person in comparative commercial advertising or promotion to identify the competing goods or services of the owner of the famous mark; [2.] noncommercial use of a mark; [3.] all forms of news reporting and news commentary." The exclusion for non-commercial use of a famous mark is intended to prevent courts form enjoining constitutionally-protected speech. That is, the exclusion encompasses conduct such as parodies and consumer product reviews. Permissible, non-trademark uses stand in sharp contrast to Toeppen's use of the Panavision marks. Toeppen traded on the value of the marks as marks by attempting to sell the domain names to Panavision. This conduct injured Panavision by preventing Panavision from exploiting its marks and it injured consumers because it would have been difficult to locate Panavision's Web site if Panavision had established a Web site under a name other than its own.

3. *Toeppen's Use of the Panavision Marks
as Domain Names Dilutes the Marks*

The precise scope of the conduct included with the definition of "dilution" as used in the federal Dilution Act has not yet been established. Traditionally, state dilution statutes have been concerned with the conduct that dilutes a trademark either by tarnishing the mark or blurring its distinctiveness.

"Tarnishment" occurs when a famous mark is linked to products of poor quality or is portrayed in an unwholesome manner. An example of tarnishment is seen in a case where an adult entertainment group diluted Hasbro's "Candy Land" mark by using the name Candyland to identify a sexually explicit Internet site and by using "candyland.com" as the domain name for the site. "Blurring" involves a "whittling away" of the selling power and value of a trademark by unauthorized use of the mark. Examples of blurring would be "Pepsi" in-line skates or "Microsoft" lipstick. Both prohibitions act to preserve the value of the trademark representing the owner's goods and services and the ability of the trademark to serve as a unique symbol to consumers of the source of goods or services.

As a result of the current state of Internet technology, Toeppen was able not merely to lessen the capacity of a famous mark to identify and distinguish goods or services, but to eliminate the capacity of the Panavision marks to identify and distinguish Panavision's goods and services on the Internet. The court finds that Toeppen's conduct, which prevented Panavision from using its marks in a new and important business medium, has diluted Panavision's marks within the meaning of the statute.

The court holds that Toeppen has violated federal and state dilution statutes and enjoins Toeppen from further violations of these laws. This holding will not impede free competition or lead to any of the "parade of horribles" suggested by Toeppen. This case does not grant trademark owners preemptive rights in domain names. This decision merely holds that registering a famous mark as a domain name for the purpose of trading on the value of the mark by selling the domain name to the trademark owner violates the federal and state dilution statutes.

Exhibit 7.10
Trademarks and Domain Names

- **Domain Names May Infringe Trademark Rights**
  - Likelihood of Confusion
  - Dilution
  - **CASE:** *Panavision International v. Dennis Toeppen*

- **Difficult Issues**
  - How many top-level domain names should there be?
  - Who should be allowed to register domain names?
  - How should registrars assess domain name applications in light of trademark rights?
    - — Registrars not likely to be liable for registering domain names that infringe trademark rights
  - What procedures should be followed to register domain names?
  - How should disputes be resolved?
  - How extensive should protection be for famous marks?
  - Should there be special rules or more extensive penalties for cybersquatting?

- **Authorities Involved with Establishing Domain Name Policies**
  - Internet Corporation for Assigned Names and Numbers (ICANN)
  - World Intellectual Property Organization (WIPO)
  - U.S. Department of Commerce

Panavision makes it clear that the trademark laws apply to domain names. Thus, a person or company contemplating the adoption of a domain name for a Web site should perform a trademark search to determine if use of the domain name might dilute or cause confusion with existing trademarks. Even unregistered marks that are used in relatively small regional areas need to be considered if, as is very likely, there are Internet users in those areas who might view the site and possibly conduct business with its operator. One should not invest goodwill into a domain name without some assurance that the name will stand up in court, if challenged. The decision of the domain name registrar carries no special weight, at least not at this time. This may change, though, if domain name registration policies become more integrated with trademark laws in the future.

The trademark laws raise many challenging issues for those registering domain names. Exhibit 7.10 lists several important considerations. Many of these are discussed in the following pages.

NSI's Dispute Resolution Policy   The recognition that trademark policies govern domain names does not address whether the domain name registrar should take any steps to minimize potential trademark disputes. If the registrar does not screen for trademark infringement, then legitimate trademark holders may suffer if other applicants beat them to the registration window. This is because they will have to wait for the results of a court proceeding before they can use their trademarks as second-level domain names. On the other hand, if the registrar does have certain trademark screening rules, then those with legitimate rights to own domain names may be denied access if the registrar's rules do not suitably conform to the trademark laws.

In 1996 and 1998, NSI adopted some modifications to its first-come, first-served registration policy. Under the new policy, NSI may potentially put a registered domain name on "hold" if a trademark owner presents NSI with a certified copy of a U.S. or foreign trademark registration for a word that is *identical* to the second-level domain name. There are several intervening steps and requirements, however. First, the trademark registration must predate the issuance of the domain name. Second, the complaining trademark owner must present NSI a copy of a written document that it previously had sent to the domain name holder, notifying the domain name holder that the domain name violates its trademark rights. If these conditions are satisfied, then NSI will seek to find out from the domain name owner whether it, too, has a trademark registration for the word. If so, then NSI will not put the domain name on hold. However, if the domain name owner does not have a trademark registration, then NSI will encourage the domain name holder to use certain transition procedures under which it relinquishes its registration for the disputed name and adopts a new domain name. If the domain name holder refuses to relinquish the name, though, then NSI will put the domain name on "hold," thereby not allowing either party to use it until NSI receives a court order or arbitration award specifying the proper owner.

NSI's dispute resolution system has raised a wide variety of complaints. Although trademark registrants believe that the policy is better than when NSI did nothing, they complain that screening only for identical uses leaves them wide open to abuse. For instance, many Web sites, especially those engaged in pornography, simply change or add a letter or phrase to famous trademarks, hoping to attract customers who make simple mistakes. For example, Newswek.com, Nytime.com, wwwpainewebber.com, and www.porschecar.com were registered domain names for pornography sites. Through this process, pornography sites, among other benefits, attract "hits" which translate into higher advertising dollars. Under NSI's policy, the trademark owners have no choice but to sue in court, arguing that the domain name dilutes their trademarks and requesting an order that NSI freeze the use of the domain name. In the meantime, though, use of the domain name can be profitable for the infringing site. Trademark owners believe that NSI has an obligation to screen not only for identical uses, but also those that may cause a likelihood of confusion or dilution. NSI, though, claims such screening would place an undue burden on it.

A case decided in 1999 raised an interesting development in this debate. The owner of the trademark "Worldsport" sued a company that had registered the domain name "worldsports.com." At first, the court not only required that NSI freeze use of the domain name, but ordered it also to screen all future applications for substantially similar variations. However, the judge later recognized the burden that this would place on NSI, and so substantially limited the order, requiring NSI only to screen for two other variations of the trademark in applications from that same defendant.[70] Although, in the end, this disposition does not give trademark owners much solace, it does at least indicate that judges are becoming sensitive to the frustrations felt by trademark owners.

On the other hand, courts have not been willing to hold NSI responsible for registering names that might infringe under the trademark laws. For instance, Lockheed Martin operates an aircraft design and construction laboratory called Skunk Works, and it has a federal trademark registration for that name. Lockheed sued NSI for registering several domain names that were simple variants on its trademark, such as skunkworx.com, theskunkworks.com, and skunkwurks.com. As we have seen in the context of copyright infringement, Lockheed's theory of liability was contributory infringement. The court, though, determined that NSI was not liable for contributory infringement, stating that the volume of Internet registrations was so high that NSI could not be expected to monitor them.[71]

Domain name applicants have objections as well. They argue that NSI's policy is overextensive, allowing trademark owners to block others from using their names in ways that the trademark laws otherwise would permit. As noted above, companies that used the name before the trademark was registered, or who use it for different classes of goods or services, may have equal claims to use the domain name. In the latter situation, the fame of the trademark needs to be taken into account before the registrar assumes that the trademark registrant has superior rights. Thus, domain name holders sometimes believe that trademark registrants engage in what has been called "reverse domain name hijacking," by using their registrations to lay claim to domain names to which they have no legal entitlement.

Cybersquatting Legislation   In November 1999, Congress passed the Anticybersquatting Consumer Protection Act, which aids trademark holders by increasing the penalties for cybersquatting—the practice of registering or using domain names with a bad faith intent to profit from legitimate trademarks.[72] Although such legislation does not increase the responsibility of registrars, it should deter those having underhanded motives for seeking domain name registrations. The act does not precisely define "bad faith," leaving the determination up to the court, but it does provide nine factors that might be considered.[73] As you would expect, these factors appraise the actions of the alleged cybersquatter from two angles: (1) its intent to take advantage of the legitimate rights of trademark owners and (2) its own legitimate rights to register or use that name. The act should serve as a strong deterrent from cybersquatting because it not only provides for domain name cancellations, but it allows courts to assess statutory damages ranging from $1,000 to $100,000 per domain name as the court considers just under the circumstances. In fact, less than two weeks after the president signed the legislation, there were reports of several cases brought under the new act, including suits by the New Zealand America's Cup team, Harvard University, and the National Football League.[74]

International Domain Name Issues Domain name problems only magnify as one enters the international environment. This is particularly true because it is significantly more likely that multiple companies will have rights to, and registrations for, the same words in different countries. We have already seen how easily this might occur with the Person's and Fashion Café cases. And think how complicated issues can become. For example, after we introduce the StatFree audio enhancement system, assume that another individual rushes to NSI and registers the domain name statfree.com. Under the NSI policy, we might easily recover that name if we had registered StatFree as a U.S. trademark before the domain name was registered. However, what happens if that individual had already gone to, let's say, Egypt and registered the name Statfree as a trademark for paper? Remember how easy this may be, since most countries do not have a use requirement for registration. Now, if we show NSI our U.S. trademark registration, the other individual only has to show its Egyptian registration to prevent NSI from putting the domain name on hold. This means that we have to sue that company, claiming that its Web site infringes our trademark rights in the United States. But as we saw in Chapter 1, if the site is passive, then U.S. courts may not even have jurisdiction to hear the case. If we decide, therefore, to travel all the way to Egypt to bring the case, the Egyptian courts may not be willing to apply U.S. law, but rather will evaluate infringement under Egyptian trademark principles. And these may have some important differences, such as in terms of dilution.

In the international sphere, many entities adopt identical or similar names, not for nefarious reasons, but rather from independent good faith intentions to create brand identification. For instance, in 1995, Prince Sports Group, Inc., a U.S. manufacturer of tennis racquets and other sporting goods, had a dispute with Prince, PLC, a British computer services company that registered the domain name prince.com with NSI.[75] Consider also that a beer brewed for over 100 years in the Czech Republic is sold as "Budweiser" and "Budweiser Budvar" in several countries.[76] Although the U.S. beer product is far better known in international circles, the Czech brewery claims to have longstanding trademark rights in the Czech Republic and in other regions. In fact, Anheuser-Busch has been involved in numerous legal battles with Budweiser-Budvar over rights to use the Budweiser name in various European countries.[77] So, if there were a dispute about which company should have rights to the domain name budweiser.com, who should have the power to decide, where should the decision be made, and what principles should guide the outcome?

Proposed Solutions to Domain Name Controversies
INCREASED NUMBER OF REGISTRARS   On top of these difficult questions, there was a growing sentiment in the late 1990s that NSI should no longer exclusively control the allocation of domain names.[78] Prior to 1995, the NSI received funding from the

National Science Foundation to register domain names. However, beginning in 1995, NSF stopped providing taxpayer dollars to the enterprise and instead gave NSI permission to charge fees for its services. Although for two years NSI lost money in these operations, the profitability picture turned around radically in 1997, fueled by the explosion in the Internet. Coupled with alleged dissatisfaction with NSI's prices and operations, a coalition called the International Ad-Hoc Committee (IAHC) was formed to consider changes to the domain name registration system. This group proposed that an international domain name registration system should be established under the direction of a Swiss-based Council of Registrars, called CORE, which would support competition among several different registrars. Other elements of the IAHC proposal included the development of at least seven new generic TLDs (.firm, .shop, .web, .arts, .rec, .info, and .nom) and various expedited dispute resolution systems, including WIPO-administered challenge panels, mediation, and on-line arbitration mechanisms.

INCREASED NUMBER OF TLDS   All along, you probably considered that the majority of the Internet domain name conflicts arise because of the almost exclusive reliance on the .com TLD. If, for instance, there were separate TLDs for music and computers, then perhaps Apple Records could register apple.mus and Apple Computer could use apple.cpu. The IAHC proposed that there be a greater set of meaningful TLDs for just this reason. However, there are fears that multiple TLDs might cause greater consumer confusion and make it difficult for trademark owners to police their rights.[79] Thus many advocate a go-slow approach to the expansion of TLDs.

USE OF COUNTRY-BASED TLDS   Others believe that there should be more reliance on country-based TLDs, which currently are registered under the authorities of the respective governments.[80] With them, the U.S. trademark owner of Person's might register the domain name persons.us, while the Japanese owner could register persons.jp. There even could be separate TLDs which also are differentiated by countries, such as with persons.com.us. The idea with country-based domain names is that they solve at least the legal conflicts about the appropriate law to apply when different companies lay claim to the same domain name, since the law of the designated country should control. In addition, there should no longer be conflicts between legitimate trademark owners from separate countries, since each can use the second-level domain name with its specific country-based TLD. On the other hand, U.S. viewers of persons.jp might believe that the site is associated with the Person's in the United States. Thus, although country-based domain names may facilitate the allocation of domain names, they still may not end trademark disputes. In addition, now that the public is accustomed to international TLDs, such as .com, it may be difficult for Internet users to accept country-based TLDs. Also, some fear that heavy reliance on country-based TLDs might substantially increase registration and policing burdens for companies engaged in international operations.

DIRECTORY SYSTEMS   Other solutions besides, or in addition to, multiple TLDs also are possible. One example involves a directory system. For instance, an Internet user who typed "apple.com" could be shown a directory, which might then list Apple Records, Apple Computer, and any other Apple companies, such as Apple Bank, that may apply for domain names. The list might include explanatory notes about each Apple company to help users identify the site they want. In addition, the list could be set up with hyperlinks to make access easy for customers.

ICANN and WIPO In July 1997, President Clinton directed the secretary of commerce to privatize the domain name system in a manner that increases competition and facilitates international participation in its management. One stimulus for this action, again, was based on NSI's dominant position in registering domain names. In addition, though, the international community increasingly objected to U.S. governmental control over the Internet. Although the Internet began as a limited U.S.-based research vehicle, by the late 1990s it had developed into a crucial international medium of communication and exchange. In response, the U.S. Department of Commerce published a statement of policy in June 1998, dealing with the management of Internet names and addresses.[81] Under this policy, the United States transferred oversight responsibility over Internet administration from IANA to a new private nonprofit organization titled the Internet Corporation for Assigned Names and Numbers (ICANN). The policy statement put ICANN in charge of developing criteria for and selection of new domain name registrars. Pursuant to that authority, ICANN made its first selections in April 1999, when it authorized five new registrars to register domain names under the .com, .net, and .org TLDs.[82] The policy also recommended a plan under which domain name holders would agree that disputes regarding their domain names could be litigated in a variety of jurisdictions, such as where the registrar is located. In addition, the policy requested that WIPO involve the international trademark community in discussions to do the following things: (1) develop recommendations for a uniform approach to resolving trademark/domain name disputes involving cyberpiracy (as opposed to conflicts between holders with legitimate competing rights), (2) recommend a process for protecting famous trademarks in the generic top-level domain names, and (3) evaluate the effects of adding new generic top-level domain names and related dispute resolution procedures on trademark and intellectual property holders.

In July 1998, WIPO commenced the process of soliciting comments so that it could make recommendations to ICANN regarding these concerns.[83] WIPO broke the issues into four categories and requested opinions about particular measures related to each.[84] A few of these are listed below to give you a flavor for the breadth of issues raised by domain names in the international arena.

A. **Dispute Prevention**
   1. The information and elements that should appear in a domain name registration contract, such as
      (i) the registrant's name and address, and
      (ii) an agreement to submit disputes relating to the status of the domain name to the jurisdiction of particular courts and/or to particular alternate dispute resolution procedures.

2. The desirability of imposing waiting periods prior to the activation of new domain name registrations.

3. The desirability of suspending the activation of domain names until payment of registration fees has been received.

4. The desirability of requiring measures to mitigate the warehousing of names.

5. The desirability of requiring certain trademark or similar searches to be performed prior to the registration of a domain name. If so, how would they be performed and by whom?

6. The requirements of any domain name databases that may be developed to allow domain name applicants and other interested parties to search for information regarding intellectual property rights. These requirements may include the need to link the databases and make them accessible through a common interface.

7. The possible use of directory and listing services or other methods aimed at avoiding trademark and domain name conflicts by allowing identical names to coexist.

B. Dispute Resolution

1. The desirability of approaches, other than court litigation, for the resolution of domain name disputes. Such approaches may include various forms of administrative procedures, mediation, and arbitration.

2. Whether some or all of the alternative dispute resolution approaches should be restricted to cases involving cyberpiracy or be available also for conflicts between bona fide parties with legitimate competing rights. If the approaches are to be restricted to cyberpiracy, what range of activities should be deemed to be covered by the term?

3. The extent to which appeal procedures should be incorporated in any alternative dispute resolution approaches.

4. The role of on-line dispute resolution systems for domain name disputes.

C. Protection of Famous Marks in Top Level Domains

1. The desirability of providing protection to famous marks.

2. The processes and criteria for determining whether marks are famous.

3. The relationship between any protection for famous marks under the domain name policy and the protection for famous marks under the Paris Convention and TRIPs.

4. The administration and content of any databases listing the status of any marks determined to be famous.

5. The desirability of providing special measures of protection for famous marks upon the introduction of new generic TLDs to prevent such marks from being registered as domain names by persons other than their owner.

6. The desirability of extending such protection to country-based TLDs.

D. Addition of New Generic Top-Level Domains

1. The extent of problems derived from the interface between Internet domain names and intellectual property rights. Particular attention should focus on the degree and nature of problems with existing TLDs, such as the relative frequency of issues involving cybersquatters as opposed to those with legitimate competing concerns.

2. The extent that such problems have been addressed by current practices.

3. The potential effects from adding new TLDs on trademark rights.

4. Whether any new additional substructures should be introduced to generic TLDs or country-based TLDs to indicate a category of activity or region of a country.

In April 1999, a 15-member multidisciplinary WIPO panel presented recommendations to ICANN.[85] These were based on over 1,300 comments received from individuals, companies, and governments located in more than 74 different countries. Among its initial recommendations were:

a.   A set of "best practices" to be adopted by registration authorities, including contact details for applicants.

b.   A uniform and mandatory administrative dispute resolution system to address abusive domain name registrations (cybersquatting).[86] Panels of three experts should apply streamlined, quick, and cost-effective procedures.

c.   A system by which owners of globally famous marks can prohibit others from registering the marks as domain names in generic TLDs.[87] A WIPO-administered panel of experts should determine the status of famous marks.

d.   The addition of any new TLDs in a slow and controlled manner to ensure that impacts are monitored and assessed.

In response to these recommendations, ICANN approved a uniform domain name dispute resolution policy on October 24, 1999.[88] The policy provides that a domain name registrant is required to submit to an administrative procedure when another party asserts that:

1. the domain name is identical or confusingly similar to a mark owned by the other party,

2. the domain name holder has no rights or legitimate interests in the domain name; and

3. the domain name was registered and is being used in bad faith.

Clearly, the mandatory administrative provisions are aimed at cybersquatting. It therefore should come as little surprise that the types of evidence listed in the policy indicating "bad faith" are very similar to the factors provided in the U.S. cybersquatting legislation. The policy provides rules of procedures for appointing administrative panels and conducting the proceedings.[89] The policy also allows either party to take their dispute to court. To account for this possibility, ICANN will wait ten business days before acting on an administrative panel determination that a registration should be cancelled. If a suit is filed within that 10-day period, ICANN will wait until the lawsuit is resolved or dropped, and then act accordingly.

New domain name practices undoubtedly will unfold rapidly as the twenty-first century gets under way. Solutions will have to be found so that the international character of the Internet may coexist satisfactorily with the regional orientation of trademark policies. Although the timing is not clear, it seems likely that in the end, the Internet will require more uniformity in international trademark policies and possibly more integration in how they operate. To some, it may seem like the domain name tail is wagging the trademark system dog. Nonetheless, companies operating in international markets will find reasons to be pleased by the outcome.

Other Internet-Related Trademark Issues

"Suck" Sites and Critical Commentary   Although the predominant trademark concern on the Internet involves the selection and use of domain names, the Internet has raised other interesting trademark-related issues. One nagging problem for trademark owners is that the Internet is like a global soapbox, from which an infinite number of individuals may voice their concerns to a virtually unlimited audience. Most companies are accustomed to isolated incidents of negative commentary. However, the Internet allows individuals to create, collect, and disseminate huge volumes of hostile remarks and opinions. This ability has led to the birth of what are called "suck" sites, such as AOLsucks.org, Microsoftsucks.org, Cokesucks.com, and Nikesucks.com, which, among other things, allow visitors to read the complaints that others have about the named companies and to share their own negative experiences.[90] For obvious reasons, companies would prefer that these sites not exist, since they have the capacity to pervasively spread negative comments. However, trademark laws usually do not come to their rescue, at least in the United States, because of the high value placed on principles of free speech.

One prominent incident that was touched on previously involved the suit by Bally Total Fitness against an individual who operated a Web site dedicated to complaints about Bally.[91] The Web page displayed Bally's stylized logo with the word sucks superimposed over it. Bally argued that this use of its trademark caused a likelihood of confusion and dilution. However, the court was not persuaded by either argument. To analyze confusion, the court used the *Sleekcraft* factors. Although the court found the Bally mark to be strong, it determined that all the other factors were either neutral or cut against Bally. Regarding dilution, the court doubted that the site made a "commercial" use of the Bally mark, since it was not used to sell services but rather only to express a point of view. Also, the court was not persuaded that marks may be "tarnished" simply by being the subject of unflattering commentary. Although the owner of the site also ran a pornographic site within the same domain, the court did not find the association to be sufficiently direct to tarnish the Bally mark. Therefore, the court ruled that the "suck" site did not infringe the mark.

A related issue regards the registration of the domain names that contain a famous mark followed by the word "sucks." Clearly there is no likelihood of confusion, but dilution may be a tougher call. Following the logic of the Bally case, however, one might determine that the domain name is not a "commercial" use if the site is only involved in commentary. Also, *Panavision* might be distinguished, since registration of the "sucks" domain name does not deprive the trademark owner of the logical means to represent its own goods and services on the Internet. A trademark owner might take steps to preempt use of derogatory words in domain names, by either registering those words in its own domain names or as trademarks before others try to use them. The first route could get very expensive, especially if the number of TLDs begins to proliferate. Also, it is nearly impossible to anticipate all unflattering verbs and adjectives. Trademark registration raises numerous problems also. Clearly the trademark owner would not want to actually use the mark in commerce, as is required in the United States. But it might receive trademark registrations in foreign countries and use those registrations, at least under the 1998 NSI rules, to block identical domain name registrations. Nonetheless, this option really is not palatable, given the sheer number of derogatory options, as well as the cost of trademark registration. Trademark owners are probably just going to have to learn to live with "suck sites." In the next chapter, we shall see that trademark owners may have some possible recourse from libel law, by arguing that the site contains untruthful statements that harm their reputations. However, free speech principles, once again, may make these cases difficult to win.

Metatags Another rather unique trademark issue concerns the use of codes called "metatags," which are not visible to Web site visitors but are used by search engines to help inquirers find information on the topics they list.[92] Metatags serve many useful purposes, such as assisting the operation of programs that screen for content that is not appropriate for children. However, some Web sites have embedded the names of famous trademarks, such as Playboy, in metatags so that search results will list links to their domains. In this way, they hope to increase the number of people who access the site. Although these people may quickly leave once they realize that some mistake has been made, their visit may still be valuable, since advertising rates often are related to the number of "hits" received by a site.

Trademark infringement rests on a likelihood of confusion or dilution. In traditional contexts, this often means that the infringer uses a symbol that appears, through human senses, to be similar to the trademark. Sometimes the similarity is based on other sensory characteristics, such as sound or smell. But the human element remains. With metatags, though, the similarities are not sensed by individuals, but rather are only read by computers. Nonetheless, visitors may be confused if they wonder why a search of the selected trademark took them to the alternative site. That is, they may think there is some affiliation, although they cannot figure out what it may be. The deception may be particularly harmful if the search lands the visitor in pornographic sites, because there also may be dilution. Trademark owners, so far, have won rulings when the trademarked word used in the metatag has no connection whatsoever to information provided within the site.[93] The equities in these situations are not all that difficult to balance, since there is such a clear intent to use the trademark in a deceptive way. However, what if a pornographic site contained a brief comment about the Coca-Cola Corporation or the taste of Coke, and so placed the word "coke" in its metatag to inform search engines that the site does, indeed, have some information on Coke. Would the metatag, in this situation, infringe the Coke trademark? Or is this a fair use, since the mark is used in the metatag to describe information contained at the site?[94] Would it matter if the comment were drafted for the sole purpose of making the metatag appear to be lawful? Clearly, metatags raise numerous questions that still need to be resolved.

Linking and Framing   As was mentioned in Chapter 6 with reference to the *Ticketmaster* and *Total News* cases, linking and framing raise potential trademark issues in addition to the copyright claims. For instance, trademarked names or stylized logos often are used as hypertext links to the trademark owners' home pages. It would be hard to argue that this practice infringes trademark rights, since the mark is used to refer to the goods or services of the legitimate trademark holder. Possibly, one could raise a dilution argument on tarnishment grounds if the Web site groups the trademark link with a set of pornographic sites so that the trademark appears to be associated with pornography. But frankly, this argument does not seem compelling. Linking to embedded pages, as was done in the *Ticketmaster* situation, raises stronger trademark claims, because clicking on the trademark no longer takes the visitor to the beginning of the Web experience, as intended by the trademark owner. This, in turn, may harm the reputation of the trademark owner. However, the harm is caused not so much due to the link, but because the trademark owner allows the public to have free access to its own embedded pages. Thus, again, the equities do not seem to favor the trademark owner. For there to be trademark infringement, the linking Web site likely would have to do something that is considered much more underhanded—such as taking affirmative steps to disable technical security measures that were adopted by the trademark owner to prevent links to the embedded pages.

Framing may raise more difficult trademark issues. The typical trademark case involves a company that attempts to pass off its own products as if they were from the trademark owner. Framing potentially raises a slightly different kind of trademark situation—one in which an unauthorized company passes off the trademark owner's products as if they were its own. For example, a person may buy Tropitone brand chairs, rip off the Tropitone labels, and then resell the chairs with its own labels instead. This is called reverse passing off, and it also is condemned by the trademark laws. However, with framing, Web site users normally are informed about the legitimate sources of the information they receive because they click on hypertext links that designate those sources. Thus, in these situations, the reverse passing off argument does not seem extremely persuasive. On the other hand, if the frames contain advertising for pornographic sites, or feature other degrading materials, then the simultaneous presentation of these items with the trademarked products may serve to tarnish the image of the trademark. This is because some Web users may believe that the trademark owner of the framed Web site somehow approved of the materials that are featured along with its site. As of the late 1990s, the courts have had little opportunity to comment directly on the trademark complaints involving linking and framing. The *Ticketmaster* and *Total News* complaints raised many important issues, and the legal community eagerly awaited court decisions in those cases. However, both disputes were settled. Therefore, this area continues to be clouded with uncertainty.

Internet Searches and Advertising Banners   The Internet has created other trademark-related controversies, and many more are bound to arise. Some may be quite unusual. For example, Internet search engines make their money by selling advertising space. Let's say you type in the word "Yonex" at the Lycos Web "portal" page to search for sites related to that tennis racquet manufacturer. When the search results are displayed, there may be an advertising banner on that page for Wilson tennis racquets. This might occur if Wilson buys the advertising "space" opposite search results that use the name Yonex. Some trademark owners have been upset with this practice—which effectively may prevent them from using the advertising banner spaces accompanying requests of their own trademarks because they are sold to other companies. In fact, in 1999, Estee Lauder and Playboy complained that Excite had sold advertising banner spaces under their names to competitors in their respective business fields.[95] Some argue that this practice does not infringe trademarks, since there is no likelihood of confusion or dilution. They analogize the situation to the supermarket coupons that customers often receive at the checkout line for competitive products. On the other hand, one also might analogize the practice to the unfairness perceived in Panavision, since in a way, it prevents a company from using its own mark in an important new medium of commerce. This controversy will have to be resolved in the courts. So too will the large number of other trademark disputes that the Internet undoubtedly will foment.

CONCLUSION

We have now covered the main components of the intellectual property protection system. Keep in mind that there are other laws and statutes in the United States that protect more specific aspects of intellectual property in various high-technology contexts. The Semiconductor Chip Protection Act is a case in point. In addition, many high-technology industries, such as computers, telecommunications, and biotechnology, are specifically regulated by various government agencies. Thus, you should always consider whether there are specific laws and regulations that apply to your particular type of technology. Having stated that, however, you should feel satisfied at this point that you have a solid grounding in fundamental high-technology intellectual property protection principles.

This book now proceeds to cover two other important legal areas of concern for high-technology companies. Chapter 8 deals with liabilities for accidents, injuries, and other forms of unwanted personal intrusions caused by high-technology products. That chapter considers how careful one must be in designing, marketing, and using high-technology equipment. It also addresses the growing degree of concern over privacy that has been spawned by new methods of electronic commerce and communication. Chapter 9 changes the focus to certain important contractual aspects, such as warranties, which one should consider when developing or distributing high-technology goods. It also evaluates many of the problems encountered in electronic commerce, such as with click-wrap licenses and digital signatures. In addition, Chapter 9 reviews other issues, such as antitrust, which are important to high-technology companies.

NOTES

1. Soweco, Inc. v. Shell Oil Co., 617 F.2d 1178 (5th Cir. 1980), *cert. denied*, 450 U.S. 981 (1981).

2. 505 U.S. 763 (1992).

3. *See* Duraco Products, Inc. v. Joy Plastic Enterprises, Ltd., 40 F.3d 1431 (3d Cir. 1994).

4. *See* Knitwaves, Inc. v. Lollytogs Ltd., 71 F.3d 996 (2d Cir. 1995).

5. *See, e.g.*, Stuart Hall Co. v. Ampad Corp., 51 F.3d 780 (8th Cir. 1995); Landscape Forms, Inc. v. Columbia Cascade Co., 113 F.3d 373 (2d Cir. 1997); I.P. Lund Trading ApS v. Kohler Co., 163 F.3d 27 (1st Cir. 1998).

6. For a thorough discussion, see L. Burgunder, "Trademark Protection of Product Characteristics: A Predictive Model," 16 J. of Pub. Pol'y & Marketing 277 (Fall 1997).

7. 514 U.S. 159 (1995).

8. *In re* Owens-Corning Fiberglas Corp., 774 F.2d 1116 (Fed. Cir. 1985).

9. 2000 U.S. LEXIS 2197 (March 22, 2000).

10. The concept of functionality arose through the common law in court decisions. In 1998, Congress specifically added language to the Lanham Act providing that one has a defense to infringement by claiming that "the mark is functional." Pub. L. No. 105-330, 105th Cong., 2d Sess. (1998) amending section 33(b)(8) of the Lanham Act.

11. Schwinn Bicycle Co. v. Murray Ohio Mfg. Co., 339 F. Supp. 973 (M.D. Tenn. 1971), *aff'd.*, 470 F.2d 975 (6th Cir. 1972).

12. *In re* Bose Corp., 772 F.2d 866 (Fed. Cir. 1985).

13. *In re* Morton-Norwich Products, Inc., 671 F.2d 1332 (C.C.P.A. 1982).

14. Ferrari S.P.A. Esercizio v. Roberts, 944 F.2d 1235 (6th Cir. 1991).

15. Pagliero v. Wallace China Co., 198 F.2d 339 (9th Cir. 1952).

16. *See* U.S. Golf Assn. v. St. Andrews Systems, 749 F.2d 1028, 1034 (3d Cir. 1984).

17. For a full discussion of trademark protection for hardware, see K. Liebman, G. Frischling, and A. Brunel, "The Shape of Things to Come: Trademark Protection for Computers," 9 Comp. Law. (December 1992) at 1–8.

18. Digital Equip. Corp. v. C. Itoh and Co., 229 U.S.P.Q. (BNA) 598 (D.N.J. 1985).

19. D. Hamilton, "Apple Sues Future Power and Daewoo, Alleging They Copied Design of iMac," Wall St. J. (July 2, 1999) at B4.

20. V. Slind-Flor, "Trade Dress Seen to Protect Trademarks: Computer Software Producers Seek Additional Safeguards," Nat'l L. J. (May 17, 1993) at 29.

21. *See* Engineering Dynamics, Inc. v. Structural Software Inc., 26 F.3d 1335 (5th Cir. 1994).

22. Directive 98/71/EC, 1998 OJ L 289 (October 13, 1998).

23. 15 U.S.C. § 1052(a). In this regard, an interesting controversy has developed over the registration of names for sports teams that allegedly disparage Native Americans. In 1999, for instance, the PTO ordered the cancellation of seven trademarks previously registered by the Washington Redskins.

24. Buti v. Impressa Perosa, S. R. L., 139 F.3d 98 (2d Cir. 1998).

25. According to the court, another dubious but possible exception is if the promotional activities are used in advance of a specific "test market" plan to begin operation in the United States.

26. 900 F.2d 1565 (Fed. Cir. 1990).

27. *See* G. Gundersen, "Effect of Domain Name on Searches Is Uncertain," Nat'l L. J. (May 12, 1997) at C12.

28. In 1997, some 188,080 trademark applications were filed with the PTO. However, applications sometimes request registration of a mark for several different classes of goods or services. In 1997, the applications requested registration for marks in 224,355 classes. Data from the 1997 PTO Annual Report, Table 15 (Summary of Trademark Examining Activities) provided at the PTO Web site, www.uspto.gov.

29. 1997 PTO Annual Report (Summary of Trademark Examining Activities) provided at the PTO Web site, www.uspto.gov.

30. Kenner Parker Toys, Inc. v. Rose Art Industries, Inc., 963 F.2d 350 (Fed. Cir. 1992), *cert. denied*, 113 S.Ct. 181 (1992).

31. Pattishall, "Dawning Acceptance of the Dilution Rationale for Trademark–Trade Identity Protection," 74 Trademark Rep. 289, 290 (1983).

32. Regulation on the Community Trademark (EC) 40/94 (December 20, 1993).

33. Congressional Record, 104th Cong., 1st Sess., Vol. 141, pt. 211 (December 29, 1995) S. 19310.

34. Federal Trademark Dilution Act of 1995, Pub. L. No. 104-98, 109 Stat. 985 (January 16, 1996).

35. *See* Nabisco, Inc. v. PF Brands, Inc., 1999 U.S. App. LEXIS 20786 (2d Cir. 1999); I.P. Lund Trading ApS v. Kohler Co., 163 F.3d 27, 51 (1st Cir. 1998).

36. Mead Data Central, Inc. v. Toyota Motor Sales, U.S.A., Inc., 875 F.2d 1026 (2d Cir. 1989).

37. Girl Scouts of the U.S.A. v. Bantam Doubleday Dell Publishing Group, Inc., 808 F. Supp. 1112, 1119 (S.D.N.Y. 1992).

38. Ginger Rogers v. Alberto Grimaldi, 875 F.2d 994, 997 (2d Cir. 1989).

39. Jordasche Enterprises, Inc. v. Hogg Wyld, Ltd., 828 F.2d 1482 (10th Cir. 1987).

40. Dallas Cowboys Cheerleaders, Inc. v. Pussycat Cinema, Ltd., 604 F.2d 200 (2d Cir. 1979).

41. Coca-Cola Co. v. Gemini Rising, Inc., 346 F. Supp. 1183 (E.D.N.Y. 1972).

42. Deere & Co. v. MTD Products, Inc., 41 F.3d 39 (2d Cir. 1994).

43. Bally Total Fitness Holding Corp. v. Faber, 29 F. Supp 2d 1161 (C.D. Cal. 1998); *see* D. Segal, "Leaving Bally Fit to be Tied," Wash. Post (February 22, 1999) at F9.

44. Anticounterfeiting Consumer Protection Act of 1996, Pub. L. No. 104-153, 110 Stat. 1386 (July 2, 1996); Trademark Counterfeiting Act of 1984, Pub. L. No. 98-473, 98 Stat. 2178 (October 12, 1984).

45. S. Rep. No. 526, 98th Cong., 2d Sess. 4–5 (June 21, 1984), reprinted in U.S. Code Cong. and Admin. News 3627, 3630–31.

46. H.R. Rep. No. 556, 104th Cong., 2d Sess. 2 (May 6, 1996).

47. For a thorough discussion of these factors, see J. Dratler, Intellectual Property Law: Commercial, Creative and Industrial Property, Law Journal Seminars-Press (1993) at § 11.09[3].

48. *See* B. Keller, A. Haemmerli, and A. Hsuan, "National Laws Play a Role in International Protection," Nat'l L. J. (December 14, 1992) at 19.

49. M. Feldman, "Trademark Hazards Are Varied," Nat'l L. J. (June 17, 1991) at 18. It is prudent to consider the meaning of trademarks in different languages as well. For instance, "No va" means in Spanish "Does not go," which may make the name unattractive for a car. B. Keller, A. Haemmerli, and A. Hsuan, "National Laws Play a Role in International Protection," Nat'l L. J. (December 14, 1992) at 19.

50. Vaudable v. Montmartre, Inc., 193 N.Y.S. 2d 332 (N.Y. Sup. Ct. 1959).

51. *See* D. Kostello, "Where Goodwill Is Established, Rights May Follow," Nat'l L. J. (May 18, 1998) at C8.

52. McDonalds Corp. v. Jobergers Drive-Inn Restaurant (Pty) Ltd., Supreme Court of South Africa, App. Div. (1996); Dongre (NR) v. Whirlpool Corp., Supreme Court of India (August 30, 1996).

53. TRIPs states that an application cannot be rejected for lack of use unless the mark has not been used within three years of filing the application. The U.S. intent-to-use process provides for extensions for up to three years, thereby complying with this provision.

54. Legislation to adopt the Madrid Protocol was pending in the U.S. Congress in 1999. Madrid Protocol Implementation Act, H.R. 671/S. 769, 106th Cong. (1999). The legislation was being held up because of objections that the European Union has undue voting rights under the organizational structure.

55. W. Cohrs, "Trademark Bar Looks to Accords," Nat'l L. J., (May 11, 1992) at S11.

56. Trademark Law Treaty Implementation Act, Pub. L. No. 105-330, 105th Cong. (October 30, 1998).

57. First Council Directive to Approximate the Laws of the Member States Relating to Trademarks, EEC (89) 104; O.J. 1989 (l40) 32.

58. For a thorough analysis of the Trademark Law Harmonization Directive, see B. Neelman, B. Ezring, and C. Shore-Sirotin, "Trademark Rights in Europe: The EC Moves to Uncomplicate the Process," 5 J. of Proprietary Rights (April 1993) at 11–21.

59. Regulation on the Community Trademark (EC) 40/94 (December 20, 1993).

60. To be eligible to register for an EU Trademark, one must be a national or domiciliary of (1) an EU member nation, (2) a country that is a party to the Paris Convention, or (3) a country that affords national treatment to the EU and that recognizes the EU Trademark. Businesses also are eligible if they have commercial establishments in the EU or in a nation that is a party to the Paris Convention.

61. M. Davis, "Uniformity Flows from IP Treaties and EU Law," Nat'l L. J. (May 12, 1997) at C13.

62. Strictly speaking, *parallel imports* are identical to the goods manufactured while *gray goods* have some material differences. The two terms often are used interchangeably, however, and the distinction is not used in this text.

63. K Mart Corp. v. Cartier, Inc., 486 U.S. 281 (1988).

64. Lever Bros. Co. v. United States, 877 F.2d 101 (D.C. Cir. 1989).

65. 118 S.Ct. 1125 (1998).

66. Justice Ginsburg, in her concurrence in *L'Anza*, stated, "this case involves a 'round trip' journey, travel of the copies in question from the United States to places abroad, then back again. I join the Court's opinion in recognizing that we do not today resolve cases in which the allegedly infringing imports were manufactured abroad." L'anza, 118 S.Ct. at 1135.

67. *See* J. Dratler, Intellectual Property Law: Commercial, Creative and Industrial Property. Law Journal Seminars-Press (1991 & Supp. 1999) at § 6.01[3].

68. For an example, see the Trademark Protection Act of 1991, S. 894, 102nd Cong. (introduced April 23, 1991).

69. J. Berger, "Master of Your Domain?" San Francisco Examiner (April 11, 1999) at B5.

70. *See* W. Leibowitz, "E-Litigation A New Legal Domain," Nat'l L. J. (May 17, 1999) at B16.

71. Lockheed Martin Corp. v. Network Solutions, Inc., 1999 U.S. App. LEXIS 26771 (9th Cir. 1999).

72. Congress passed the Intellectual Property and Communications Omnibus Reform Act of 1999 (S. 1948), on November 19, 1999 as part of a consolidated appropriations package, which was signed by the President on November 29, 1999 (Pub. L. No. 106-113). The relevant title within this act is called the Anti-cybersquatting Consumer Protection Act.

73. The nine nonexhaustive factors are: (1) the trademark rights of the mark's owner; (2) the domain-name holder's intent to divert consumers in a way that could harm the goodwill represented by the trademark, either for profit or with the intent to tarnish or disparage the trademark, by creating a likelihood of confusion; (3) the nameholder's offer to transfer, sell, or otherwise assign the domain name to the trademark owner or a third party for financial gain without having an intent to use the domain name to offer goods and services; (4) the nameholder's providing false information when applying for registration of the domain name; (5) the nameholder's registration of multiple domain names that he or she knows are identical or confusingly similar to the trademarks of others; (6) the protectibility as a trademark of words used in a domain name; (7) the extent to which the domain name consists of the legal name of the name holder; (8) the nameholder's prior use of the domain name in connection with the bona fide offering of goods or services; and (9) the nameholder's bona fide noncommercial or fair use of the mark in a site accessible under the domain name.

74. *See* J. Clausing, "New Law Touches Off Suits Over Names in Cyberspace," N.Y. Times (December 9, 1999) at C2.

75. Prince Sports Group v. Prince PLC, No. 97cv03581 (D.N.J., filed July 3, 1997).

76. *See* W. Leibowitz, "Internet Jurisprudence," Nat'l L. J. (January 25, 1999) at A18. Budweiser Budvar is brewed in Ceske Budejovice in the Czech Republic. The German name for the town is Budweis, and Budweiser was the German name for the beer.

77. A discussion of these legal battles can be found at Budweiser-Budvar's Web site, www.budweiser.cz.

78. *See* G. Simpson & J. Simons, "A Little Internet Firm Got a Big Monopoly: Is That Such a Bad Thing?" Wall St. J. (October 8, 1998) at A1.

79. Testimony of David Stimson, president of the International Trademark Association, before the House Subcommittee on Courts and Intellectual Property for the Hearing on Internet Domain Name Policy, available at www.house.gov/judiciary/41152.htm.

80. J. Moskin, "Domain Name 'Reforms' Will Inflame Internet Problems," IP Worldwide (July/August 1998).

81. U.S. Department of Commerce, Statement of Policy, "Management of Internet Names and Addresses," 63 Fed. Reg. 31741 (1998).

82. As of September 1999, ICANN had accredited 76 registrars to register domain names. *See* "ICANN Accredits 12 New Domain Name Registrars," ICANN Press Release (September 21, 1999) available at www.icann.org.

83. Request for Comments on Terms of Reference, Procedures and Timetable for the WIPO Internet Domain Name Process, WIPO RFC-1 (July 8, 1998).

84. Request for Comments on Issues Addressed in the WIPO Internet Domain Name Process, WIPO RFC-2 (September 16, 1998).

85. Final Report of the WIPO Internet Domain Name Process, WIPO FINAL REPORT (April 30, 1999).

86. WIPO defined an "abusive domain name registration" as one meeting all the following conditions: (1) the domain name is identical or misleadingly similar to a trade or service mark in which the complainant has rights; (2) the holder of the domain name has no rights or legitimate interests in respect of the domain name; and (3) the domain name has been registered and is used in bad faith."

87. WIPO suggested that the following criteria be used to determine if a mark is famous: (1) the degree of knowledge or recognition of the mark in the relevant sector of the public; (2) the duration, extent, and geographical area of any use of the mark; (3) the duration, extent, and geographical area of any promotion of the mark, including advertising or publicity and the presentation, at fairs or exhibitions, of the goods and/or services to which the mark applies; (4) the duration and geographical area of any registrations, and/or any applications for registration, of the mark, to the extent that they reflect use or recognition of the mark; (5) the record of successful enforcement of rights in the mark—in particular, the extent to which the mark was recognized as famous by courts or other competent authorities; (6) the value associated with the mark; and (7) evidence of the mark being the subject of attempts by nonauthorized third parties to register the same or misleadingly similar names as domain names.

88. The ICANN Uniform Domain Name Dispute Resolution Policy may be found at its Web site, www.icann.org/udrp/udrp-policy-24oct99.htm.

89. The ICANN Rules for Uniform Domain Name Dispute Resolution may be found at its Web site, www.icann.org/udrp/udrp-rules-24oct99.htm.

90. *See* M. Murphy, "Developments on the Internet Frontier: Internet Metatags, Beavis and Butthead, and Suck Sites," Bulletin of Law/Science & Technology, American Bar Association Section of Science and Technology (April, 1999) at 5.

91. Bally Total Fitness Holding Corp. v. Faber, 29 F. Supp. 2d 1161 (C.D. Cal. 1998).

92. *See* R. Schmitt, "Terminix Suit Aims to Mute a Web Critic," Wall St. J. (December 3, 1999) at B1; M. Jun, "Metatags: The Case of the Invisible Infringer," N.Y.L.J. (October 24, 1997); W. Leibowitz, "Firm Sues for Invisible Use of Its Trademark on the 'Net," Nat'l L. J. (September 8, 1997).

93. *See* Playboy Enterprises Inc. v. Calvin Designer Label, 985 F. Supp 1220 (N.D. Cal. 1997); Playboy Enterprises Inc. v. Asia Focus International Inc., Civ. No. 97-734-A, (E.D. Va. April 10, 1998); Instituform Technologies, Inc. v. National Envirotech Group, L.L.C., Civ. No. 97-2064 (E.D. La. August 27, 1997). *See also* Oppedahl & Larson v. Advanced Concepts, Civ. No. 97-Z-5192 (D. Colo., July 23, 1997).

94. Playboy Enterprises v. Welles, 7 F. Supp 2d 1098 (S.D. Cal. 1998); Brookfield Communications, Inc. v. West Coast Entertainment Corp., 1999 U.S. App. LEXIS 7779 (9th Cir. 1999); Bally Total Fitness Holding Corp. v. Faber, 29 F. Supp. 2d 1161 (C.C. Cal. 1998).

95. *See* W. Leibowitz, "Rules of the Domain-Name Game," Nat'l L. J. (March 1, 1999) at A16.

8

Tort Liability and Intrusions on Privacy

INTRODUCTION

One cannot be involved in a high-technology enterprise without being concerned about possible tort liability. The term "tort" has a wide umbrella, covering a number of personal harms. In fact, it is hard to phrase a concise definition that would capture the entire spectrum of what a tort may entail. However, as a starting point, one may consider a tort an unwanted intrusion on a protected personal right that causes physical, economic, or psychological injury.

For those conducting business with new technologies, the potential for tort liability is tremendous. Some technologies use or harness substantial power, thereby increasing the possibility for significant physical harm if something goes wrong. In addition, when society becomes dependent on the continuing operation of technological devices, such as it has with computers, the economic effects of even a temporary shutdown can be substantial. Also, new technologies may create new and previously unknown ways to intrude on the rights of individuals. Modern methods to record, store, and transmit personal data, for instance, have raised emotional debates about the future of privacy rights in the United States and around the world.

This chapter reviews the fundamental concepts of tort liability, and it highlights some interesting new tort issues raised by developing technologies. We will first take a brief look at negligence policies and how they apply to the management of technology. Negligence issues arise when one is less careful than a reasonable person should be, and harm to another results. We then will move on to strict products liability, an area that is now especially important to all purveyors of products. Here, we will focus special attention on the difficult controversies regarding tort liability for product designs that allegedly are more dangerous than they should be. In addition, we will consider some new areas that are of particular concern to those in the computer field, such as liabilities for defective programs, poor advice from expert diagnostic systems, injuries from repetitive keyboard practices, and Year 2000 (Y2K) concerns.

We then will take a hard look at privacy rights. New information technologies, particularly the Internet, reach into our everyday lives in ways that are nothing short of revolutionary. Although members of the public clearly enjoy the benefits from using these modern communication tools, they also are very concerned about what they must give up in the process. The Internet and e-mail challenge accepted notions about the kinds of information and behaviors that are protected from public scrutiny. This has led to public pressure on the industry to adopt practices allowing individuals to have more control over information that they expect to be kept in confidence. It also has led to heated disputes, litigation and new laws regarding practices that intrude on areas that many people still feel should remain private.

The chapter concludes by reviewing other torts that may be important to businesses involved with technological developments. Defamation, for instance, is pervasive on the Web. The question is who might be liable for false statements that harm members of the public. Other issues that are discussed here include computer viruses, spamming and intrusions on publicity rights.

NEGLIGENCE

Suppose that in advance of the 1998 Christmas holiday season, our **Audio Enhancement System (AES)** company was barraged with orders for the **AES**.

In order to meet this unexpected surge in demand, we hired several temporary factory personnel so that we could add another production shift. We quickly trained them on their respective jobs and put them to work. Our rapid response apparently was successful, since we increased output by 30% and filled all of our orders by Christmas.

In March, we were notified that one of our customers received a serious electrical shock when moving the **AES** from one location to another. The incident occurred because the unit, which was picked up from its underside, had a loose metal bottom plate. This plate had come into contact with an uninsulated portion of the AC power cord, resulting in electrical shock. Several other similar incidents arose before we were able to recall the products and correct the problem. We determined that the accidents must have occurred because one of our new employees failed to verify the torque on the electronic screwdriver one evening, thereby yielding insufficient pressure on certain screws, including some of those on the bottom of the units.

The foregoing scenario demonstrates a classic case of negligent behavior. Our company and the new employee clearly were not as careful as one would expect. It may be hard to pinpoint exactly why the employee forgot to check the screwdriver torque. Possibly our procedures for checking were not sufficient given the potential severity of the repercussions. Maybe we overloaded the employee with excessive information in insufficient time for the person to assimilate it all. Or maybe it's more simple. Possibly the employee got too little sleep the previous night or was talking while working. Whatever the reason, the company and/or its employee was negligent that evening by failing to take reasonable steps to protect users of the AES.[1] The negligence became tortious when the carelessly screwed bottoms caused the shocks that injured certain users.

Negligence and the Restatement of Torts

Liability for negligence, for the most part, is governed by state law. Fortunately, there is some degree of uniformity in the ways negligence principles are applied from state to state due to the efforts of the American Law Institute, an organization composed of lawyers, judges, and teachers, which has distilled the basic common law principles of tort liability into a treatise called the Restatement of Torts. The Restatement of Torts deals with a number of specific tort topics such as negligence and strict products liability. The American Law Institute drafted the original Restatement of Torts in the 1930s and subsequently published revisions in the mid-1960s. In the 1990s the Institute started the revision process again, and by the late 1990s, began to release third editions of the Restatement. For instance, a third edition dealing specifically with products liability was published in 1998. As of 1999, the Institute was still debating changes regarding general principles, including negligence. Therefore, you would be wise to check whether the third edition covering negligence has now been finalized and published. Although the Restatement itself is not law, the principles enunciated in it are frequently followed by judges to decide cases and by state legislatures in enacting statutes. In this way, the policies of the Restatement are translated into state laws by legal authorities within the various states, leading to a high degree of consistency among the states.

The second edition of the Restatement defines negligence as "conduct which falls below the standard established by law for the protection of others against unreasonable risk of harm." Accordingly, the key issues for evaluating negligence are determining the proper standard of care required under the circumstances and whether the conduct met that standard. If a person was not as careful as the law deems the person should have been, then there has been negligence. Negligence alone is not a tort, however. For tort liability to arise, three other aspects are required: (1) the negligent conduct must cause injury; (2) social policy must make the person responsible for the harm caused by the negligence; and (3) there must be no defenses that limit tort liability. These issues are summarized in Exhibit 8.1.

Causation Issues in Negligence

It is normally easy to determine that the negligent conduct caused injury. In the **AES** situation, for example, the negligence led to the bottom plate's striking the power cord, resulting in the shock and injury to the user. Intuitively, you concluded that the negligence caused the injury because the user

Exhibit 8.1
Negligent Analysis Issues

- **Duty of Care**
  - Reasonable person standard
  - Community standards
  - Legal standards
  - Professional standards
  - Economic formulations
    - Prevention costs vs. expected losses from injuries
    - Cheapest cost provider
  - **CASE:** *Vuono v. New York Blood Center, Inc.*

- **Causation**
  - But-for analysis
  - Joint and several liability

- **Proximate Cause**
  - Liability extends to persons and property to which harm from negligence is reasonably foreseeable

- **Defenses**
  - Assumption of risk
  - Comparative fault

would not have been shocked had the negligence not occurred. In other words, causation is established because the injury would not have happened but for the negligent act. Just to make this clear, assume again that the screws were inappropriately tightened, but that this time injury resulted when an infant pulled off a knob and swallowed it. In this scenario, the negligence regarding the screws did not cause the injury to the baby. That is, the baby would have swallowed the knob even if the screws had been tightened with sufficient care. This is not to say that we may not be responsible for what happened to the baby. Possibly we were negligent in installing the knobs or by making them too small. Nonetheless, the negligence regarding the loose screws was not the cause of what happened to the baby.

Another important issue regarding causation of damage arises when the negligence of two different parties causes the injuries to an innocent victim. For instance, assume that although the loose screws caused the shock, the injuries would not have been so dramatic had there not been a power surge at the same time, resulting from negligent conduct at the electrical utility. Under the laws of many states, the injured user may sue either or both of us for the entire extent of the damages, based on a doctrine called joint and several liability. Our fear, of course, is that if the utility is not sufficiently solvent to pay for its share of the responsibility, then we will have to pay for all the damages, even though they were not all our fault. That possible result, which may be extremely onerous on businesses in certain situations, has led some states, in the name of tort reform, to limit liability to the proportionate extent of one's fault only. In those states, we therefore would be relieved from paying for the utility's share of the fault, even when the utility is unable to sufficiently compensate the user for the additional harms caused by the power surge. To the innocent user, this likely will seem unfair. From the user's vantage, none of this would have happened had we tightened the screws appropriately. Yet the user will not be totally compensated for losses, even though we may have the financial means to cover them.

Proximate Cause: Responsibility for Negligence

Social policies recognize that humans are not infallible—all people make mistakes. Every time you wake up, you surely recognize that there is a good chance that you will do something during the day without being totally careful. Perhaps this will be the day that you don't close the door after UPS arrives with a package while your untrained dog watches from the stairs. Clearly, this is negligent; you even considered the possible repercussions while you carried the package inside. But little did you know that the dog would run outside, chase a cat down the sidewalk, cross the street in front of a fire engine, and cause it to swerve and hit a pole, resulting in the total destruction of the home to which it was bound.

People in their everyday lives take calculated risks with their behavior, including negligent behavior. Think how you would act if you were forced to pay for all the repercussions of negligent conduct, no matter how unpredictable or remote they might be. Likely, you would prefer to sit in your room wearing a straitjacket. So that normal social behavior can be undertaken, the law will not hold a negligent person responsible for all the consequences resulting from negligence. Rather, liability extends only to the persons and property to which harm from the negligence is reasonably foreseeable. Under negligence law, the principle of reasonable foreseeability is called "proximate cause." In the dog situation, you might thus be liable for the harm to the fire truck because it was reasonably foreseeable that your untrained dog would dart across a street and disrupt traffic, resulting in damage to vehicles. However, you would never reasonably consider that the dog might cause the destruction of a home. Therefore, you would not be liable to pay for those damages, even though your negligence caused it to burn down. This policy makes sense because you reasonably should have considered the risk to those on the streets when deciding to leave the door open. However, the harm to the home clearly should not have entered your intuitive risk analysis.

The issue of proximate cause might arise with the loose **AES** screws. Suppose that the user who is shocked is thrown back against a plastic water pipe and drops the unit on a couch. The electrical sparks ignite the couch, causing the home and the neighboring water utility station to burn. The broken pipe starts a flood, which becomes uncontrollable due to the fire next door at the utility. The flood enters the underground subway, wreaking havoc within the city before the situation is contained. Our little **AES** company could be sued by just about everybody in the city for harms to them and their properties. After all, none of this would have happened but for the loose screws. However, our negligence is not the proximate cause of all that occurred, and our liability will be appropriately limited. In this situation, injury to the user is reasonably foreseeable. Also, since sparks and fire are a distinct possibility, damage to the house and its contents likely would be considered reasonably foreseeable. Even damage to the neighboring utility may be in the zone of reasonable danger. However, that should be the outside reach of our responsibility. We likely will not be liable for most, if any, of the damages caused by the flood. Clearly, this provides a good reason for all of those property owners to carry insurance.

Defenses to Liability for Negligence

The issue of defenses often is important in negligence situations as well. Typically the negligent party will disclaim some or all responsibility for harms to the plaintiff (the person bringing suit) because the plaintiff was negligent too, thereby contributing to the harm. For instance, maybe we placed a warning on the **AES** alerting users not to hold the unit from the bottom due to the risk of shock. When the user who was shocked ignored this warning, we might allege that the user assumed the risk of harm or at least deserves some of the blame for what happened. Even without a warning, we might claim that it is negligent to pick up an electrical unit from the bottom while it is plugged in, because most careful people understand the potential for shock. The legal systems of different states vary widely on how they treat defenses to negligence. In most situations, however, the usual result is that the comparative fault of the parties is assessed, with the damage recovery being reduced by the degree of one's blame. So, assume that a jury determines that a person is negligent for picking up the unit from the bottom after reading the warning, but not as negligent as we are for not screwing the bottom as tightly as we should have. The jury weighs the relative faults and concludes that we are 75% negligent and the user is 25% negligent. If the user suffers $60,000 of damages, we will be liable for 75% of that, or $45,000. Had the jury thought that the user was totally at fault for ignoring the warning, then we would have been totally relieved of liability for negligence.

What Is Negligent Conduct?

We have yet to address how it is determined whether conduct is negligent in the first place. Recall that actions are negligent if they fall below the applicable standard of care. How does one determine the proper standard of care? The simple answer, and the one that generally applies, is that one should exercise the care that a reasonable person would use under the same circumstances. However, such a statement somewhat begs the question, because it does not address what a reasonable person would do. The following case struggles with this issue.

VUONO V. NEW YORK BLOOD CENTER, INC.
U.S. District Court, Massachusetts, 1988

FACTS: On May 16, 1983, Frank Vuono was hospitalized at the New England Deaconess Hospital in order to undergo coronary bypass surgery. On May 22 and 23, Vuono received an infusion of serum albumin, which is a fractionated blood plasma derivative. One vial of the serum albumin administered to Vuono was contaminated at the time of the infusion, and as a result, he became ill, suffered both septic shock and herpes simplex, and subsequently was prevented from undergoing open heart surgery. The contaminated vial had been processed by New York Blood Center (the Blood Center), a federally licensed blood fractionation facility.

Fractionation at the blood processing facility involves separating the serum albumin from the blood plasma, dispensing the serum albumin into glass vials, sealing the vials with rubber stoppers, covering the vials with protective aluminum foil, and packaging the vials in a series of cardboard containers. This process also includes filtering out any bacteria in the blood plasma and subjecting the serum albumin to a heat bath for the purpose of killing any contaminants that may elude the filtration procedure. The vial that is the subject of this lawsuit was part of the Blood Center's lot number 5D33A and was processed in August 1982.

Although there is no evidence that the Blood Center failed to follow its standard procedures for processing the serum albumin in this case, there is evidence that the particular glass vial, manufactured by Wheaton Industries, contained a flaw. Specifically, there was a narrow fold in the glass surface, known as a line over. Evidence also exists that this flaw is visually identifiable and that the glass fold in the vial is sufficient to catch a fingernail. Further, there is evidence that this defect interfered with the integrity of the sealed vial and thus permitted contamination from ambient sources.

Vuono sued the Blood Center and several other parties, alleging numerous contractual violations and torts, including negligence. In this proceeding, the Blood Center asked the court to dismiss before trial the action against it for negligence, by way of a procedure called summary judgment. Under the standards for summary judgment, the court is to dismiss the negligence count if the evidence that Vuono hopes to show at trial is insufficient to prove negligence.

continued . . .

continued ...

DECISION AND REASONING: In the law of torts, negligence is commonly recognized as either the omission of doing something that a prudent and reasonable person, guided by those considerations that ordinarily regulate the conduct of human affairs would do or the commission of doing something that a prudent and reasonable person would not do. In other words, the standard of conduct in determining the existence of negligence is whether the actor exercised the duty of care that an ordinarily prudent person would exercise under the same or similar circumstances. There is, however, no absolute liability for all harmful conduct; an actor is not an insurer for all of one's acts.

Applying the negligence standard often requires that the actor's conduct be tested against a background of ordinary usage and custom. The customs of the community, however, although relevant on the issue of negligence, are not conclusive, especially when such customs are clearly dangerous and careless. Judge Learned Hand eloquently explained:

> There are, no doubt, cases where courts seem to make the general practice of the calling the standard of proper diligence; we have indeed given some currency to the notion ourselves. Indeed, in most cases reasonable prudence is in fact common prudence; but strictly it is never its measure; a whole calling may have unduly lagged in the adoption of new and available devices. It never may set its own tests, however pervasive be its usages. Courts must in the end say what is required; there are precautions so imperative that even their universal disregard will not excuse their omission.

In this respect, the negligent standard of the ordinarily prudent person may be a higher standard of care than the standard followed by a particular community or industry. The fact that a certain device or practice is in common use is evidence that its use is not negligent, but such a fact is not conclusive evidence of due care because a large number of persons may fail to exercise due care in their usual practices. The plaintiff may still try to show that the practice of the entire industry is unreasonable; that the community custom lacks ordinary care.

In the present case, Blood Center argues that Vuono's negligence claims cannot survive on the grounds that Vuono fails to set forth facts demonstrating that the Blood Center breached the prevailing standard of care applicable to blood product manufacturers. Specifically, the Blood Center contends that the standard of care that the Blood Center owed to Vuono is that standard established by the blood products manufacturing industry and the applicable FDA regulations. Moreover, the quality control procedures used in testing lot 5D33A, the batch that contained the vial of serum albumin administered to Vuono, equaled or exceeded both the standard of care of the industry and FDA regulations.

As previously discussed, however, conformity with the customs and standards of the industry does not establish conclusively the absence of negligence. Rather, the court must evaluate any evidence that either the industry custom or the Blood Center's conduct was unreasonable under the circumstances. Given all the facts presented by Vuono, the court rules that a genuine issue exists concerning the Blood Center's duty to inspect and test the glass vials containing the serum albumin.

The court's opinion is founded on two sources. First, Dr. Martin Stryker testified in a deposition that:

1. When it's time to fill the vials, the person who loads the vials onto the conveyor belt going into the vial washing and sterilization equipment is instructed to look at the vials.
2. The defect in the glass vial that contained the serum albumin administered to Vuono existed at the time of the visual inspection.
3. The defect in the vial is fairly apparent if you look closely at it.
4. The Blood Center had experienced problems with the quality of the Wheaton glass vials, problems which initially occurred in 1980 and resurfaced in April 1983.
5. The Blood Center ceased purchasing the Wheaton 250-milliliter vials for packaging of serum albumin in late 1983.

Second, the Wheaton report on the glass vial stated, "the bottle . . . did have a line over which is a narrow fold in the glass surface. The line over extended across the top of the finish and on the inside past the sealing contact areas of the rubber stopper. . . . Depth of the glass fold was sufficient to catch a fingernail *which is the factory guideline for rejection of this defect*" (emphasis supplied by the court).

Since the attendant dangers of manufacturing and packaging serum albumin may constitute a hazard to human life, the standard of care required of the Blood Center in this case is extremely high. In this context, the Blood Center's duty of care may be viewed as a matter of the following variables:

1. The probability that a defective vial will be used in packaging serum albumin
2. The resulting injuries if such a vial is used
3. The burden of adequate precautions

Given the facts that (1) in late 1980, the Blood Center was dissatisfied with the quality of Wheaton vials; (2) an unsterile product caused by a defective vial may constitute a hazard to human life; (3) the person who loads the vials onto the conveyor is instructed to look at the vials; and (4) the defect in this

continued . . .

continued . . .

vial is allegedly "fairly apparent if you look closely," this court cannot rule, as a matter of law, that the Blood Center was not negligent in testing and inspecting the glass vials that contain the serum albumin. Accordingly, the court denies the motion of the Blood Center for summary judgment on the negligence claim.

As *Vuono* makes clear, negligent conduct cannot be defined in terms of hard-and-fast rules. What a reasonable person should do under the circumstances depends on a number of factors particular to the situation. Behaving as others do when faced with the same situation is evidence that one is acting like a reasonable person. This is why industry custom is so relevant. In addition, complying with state or federal laws, as the Blood Center did, suggests that one is being reasonable. However, the case makes it clear that these considerations are not conclusive. If industry custom were an absolute standard, then industry participants might have incentives to collectively act irresponsibly, comfortable with the knowledge that they protect themselves with a low industry standard. Legal standards, too, can be only a minimum benchmark of what should be expected from reasonable persons. That is, failure to follow legal requirements may conclusively show negligent behavior, but compliance is merely evidence of reasonableness.

Other formulations of what a reasonable person should do have more of an economic foundation. One of these, which also was raised in *Vuono*, was formulated by Judge Learned Hand in 1947 in a case dealing with a barge that broke from its moorings.[2] In that case, Judge Hand stated that negligence depended on three variables: (1) the probability that the boat would break away, (2) the gravity of the resulting loss if it did, and (3) the burden of adequate precautions. Putting this into algebraic terms—with the probability called P, the loss called L, and the burden called B—liability depends on whether B is less than L multiplied by P. In other words, one acts unreasonably and is negligent if $B < L \times P$. Alternatively, one's conduct is reasonable if $B > L \times P$.

Another economic formulation weighs both the conduct of the person causing the injury and that of the victim. In very simple terms, this analysis asks which of the two parties could have avoided the accident with fewer social costs. Saying this differently, the party who was in the best position to avoid the accident with the cheapest cost should be responsible to pay for the damages created from it.[3] Hypothesizing with Learned Hand's barge, assume that the probability of breaking away is 10%, the expected injury to a dock when it is smashed is $30,000, and the burden to moor the boat more securely is $2,000. Under Learned Hand's test, the boat owner would be negligent if the boat breaks away and causes damage because the burden of prevention ($2,000) is less than the risk-adjusted expected injury

($3,000 = $30,000 × 10%). However, if the dock could have been protected with a rubber wrap costing $200, then under the alternative formulation, the dock owner would bear the responsibility, since the dock owner's cost of prevention is less than that required of the boat owner. This makes economic sense because society is better off with a decision rule that motivates people to incur $200 of prevention costs rather than $2,000 of prevention.

Negligence and Computer Programmers

Negligence is a growing concern for computer software and database developers. For example, an airline inadvertently corrupted its database of passenger reservations while using new software that turned out to have bugs. Eventually, the programmers fixed the bugs, but the false reservations were not eliminated. As a result, the airline had planes flying partially empty for several months because of the false bookings.[4] Given society's growing dependence on computers, there now are tremendous possibilities that huge economic and physical injuries could result from systems that do not perform adequately.

The standard of care owed by computer programmers in developing software and databases is a controversial and critical issue. In some professions, such as law and medicine, the professionals are held to a high standard of care because clients rely so heavily on their expertise. Many argue that computer programmers should be treated similarly, given that individuals and businesses now often entrust their livelihoods to the alleged computer experts. Certainly following Learned Hand's formulation, there is reason to expect programmers to exercise extreme care in software design, because the potential repercussions from system failure often will outweigh the burdens of thoroughly testing the software. As we shall see in the next chapter, many (but not all) of software developers' concerns regarding possible negligence can be handled with clients through contractual provisions. However, these measures will not be effective against third parties who suffer harm. Therefore, computer specialists must be wary of the extreme care that now may be expected from them in developing and testing their wares.

STRICT PRODUCTS LIABILITY

For those companies involved in the manufacture or distribution of products, as opposed to services, the development of strict products liability principles has somewhat usurped the importance of negligence. The area of strict liability is where most of the current controversies lie and the source of most of the large, publicized money judgments. Just think of the public attention given to the defective design of the Ford Pinto gas tank. And consider how staggering the liability can be. For instance, in 1999, a jury awarded six plaintiffs $4.9 billion in a strict liability action against General Motors.[5] Although this amount subsequently was reduced to $1.1 billion, the example illustrates just how high strict liability awards might reach.[6] Strict liability is so far-reaching because liability does not depend on the propriety or reasonableness of a person's conduct. Rather, the focus is on the condition of the product. In a nutshell, under principles of strict products liability, a seller of a product will be liable for damages resulting from an unreasonably dangerous product defect, whether that seller was negligent or not.

Policy Reasons for Strict Products Liability

Why public policy has moved from negligence to strict liability principles can be understood from the following simple example. Suppose the Coca-Cola Company uses the most advanced bottling techniques, employing more state-of-the-art equipment than any competitor worldwide. Although the machinery and systems used are the best available, 1 bottle per 10,000 produced will have a flaw that creates a weakness that possibly could cause an explosion when the bottle is pressurized. Assume that one of these bottles explodes while being lifted by a consumer, causing severe injuries to the face. If the consumer sues Coca-Cola alleging negligence, the consumer will lose because the company, if anything, exceeded its standard of care in bottling its beverages. Therefore, this consumer, even though an innocent victim, will be forced to absorb the losses under negligence principles.

There are a number of policy reasons for creating a legal system requiring Coca-Cola to compensate the consumer for injuries even though the company has not been negligent. Simply out of a sense of justice, we might yearn for a policy that favors the victim over the manufacturer. After all, Coca-Cola has derived profits from its business and thus should be liable for any negative consequences from its operations. This is especially compelling when compared to the situation of the innocent victim, who did not even derive the benefits expected from the product because it proved to be defective. Economic efficiency also may favor placing liability on the company. Under negligence principles, all those who might come near Coca-Cola products, which admittedly are conscientiously made, must take out insurance if they want to be protected from the possible tragic consequences of an exploding bottle. However, if legal rules required Coca-Cola to be responsible for the defective bottles, the company could protect itself by taking out one insurance policy to cover the less than 1 in 10,000 chance that an accident might occur. The cost of this policy, then, could be spread over the millions of bottles of soda sold. Another benefit from holding Coca-Cola strictly liable without fault is that there is a constant incentive for the company to continue improving its manufacturing systems to reduce the risks to customers. The fundamental negative from holding Coca-Cola strictly liable is the traditional cultural antipathy in the United States and elsewhere for making someone take responsibility for a tragedy when that person is not blameworthy for what occurred. Yet, this is just what strict products liability does. More than anything, the notion of liability without blame may be what continually fuels the flame that calls for products liability reform.

Products Liability and the Restatement of Torts (Second Edition)

As with negligence, the Restatement of Torts provides guidance on when product sellers should be liable without fault. Much of the current law regarding strict products liability derived from the statements contained in the second edition of the Restatement. Section 402A of the second edition stated:

1. One who sells any product in a defective condition unreasonably dangerous to the user or consumer or to his property is subject to liability for physical harm thereby caused to the ultimate user or consumer, or to his property, if (a) the seller is engaged in the business of selling such product, and (b) it is expected to and does reach the consumer without substantial change in the condition in which it was sold.
2. The rule stated in Subsection 1 applies although (a) the seller has exercised all possible care in the preparation and sale of his products, and (b) the user or consumer has not bought the product from or entered into any contractual relation with the seller.

The key component of this provision directed that a seller was liable for harm resulting from a product that was in a defective condition unreasonably dangerous to the user. The most difficult aspect was determining what constituted a product defect, something we will consider at some length shortly. That the defect had to make the product unreasonably dangerous may have struck you as akin to a negligence standard, and indeed, as the next case, *Barker v. Lull Engineering*, demonstrates, many commentators and courts questioned what it meant. The best explanation is that the manufacturer is not to be an insurer for every harm that may result from product use. For instance, it is common that users of hammers smash their thumbs. Without some clarification, one might conclude that a hammer is defective when it imparts injury to user. The term "unreasonably dangerous" was included to indicate that something more than harm is required to judge a product defective. Thus, with the hammer, the fact that the product performs as safely as the ordinary consumer expects clearly should be relevant in concluding that the product is not defective. However, as explained in *Barker v. Lull Engineering*, this may not be the end of the inquiry.

Before evaluating what it means for a product to be defective, it is worth noting some of the other components of strict products liability mentioned in the Restatement. First, the Restatement does not confine liability to manufacturers; rather, liability attaches to sellers of the defective product. Thus, any business in the distribution chain is a potential target of a strict products liability suit. Second, the doctrine applies only to sellers who are regularly engaged in distributing the product. This conforms to the risk-spreading and profit-making aspects of strict liability by ensuring that the seller is significantly involved with and derives sufficient revenues from the product. Third, the condition of the product must not be substantially changed by another party before the injuries take place. Thus, if an automobile purchaser makes substantial alterations to a car to jack it up, for instance, this may relieve the seller-manufacturer from liability for injuries caused by problems with the rear axle. This makes sense because the buyer's actions are totally out of the control of the seller. Strict products liability provides substantial incentives to ensure the safety of the product, but those incentives obviously can extend only to elements within the seller's control. Fourth, any person who sustains injury from a product defect may sue any seller of that product within the distribution chain, whether that person has dealt directly with the particular seller or not. Thus, sellers may be sued by purchasers, other persons who use the product, and bystanders. Also, as mentioned before, any seller in the distribution chain who is regularly engaged with the product, including the manufacturer, wholesalers, and retailers, may be liable for product defects.

Forms of Product Defects

Manufacturing Defects The Coca-Cola scenario provides the easiest and least controversial form of product defect that subjects sellers to strict products liability. The bottle is easily identified as defective since it did not leave the manufacturing facility in the condition that the manufacturer intended. This form of product defect therefore is called a *manufacturing defect*.

(AES) When the **AES** machines were sold with loose screws on the bottom, this also constituted a manufacturing defect, since we did not intend for the models to be distributed in that condition. Consider now how much more powerful strict products liability is for the injured consumer. Although they likely would win a negligence suit under the facts provided, the customers who received electric shocks would have to prove that we breached our duty of care in making their particular machine. Under strict products liability, their job is much simpler, since all they must do is demonstrate the defective condition of their machine. Clearly, this should be easy under the circumstances, for all they must do is present their **AES** unit with the insufficiently torqued screws. This process thus skips the often difficult task of delving into the reasonableness of the business behavior that led to the deficiencies in the units.

Design Defects The reach of strict products liability may begin with manufacturing defects, but it definitely does not end there. A product may be defective—even when manufactured exactly as intended—if the design of the product is not adequately safe. In other words, a product may be defective because it should have been designed with more attention to user safety. Logically, this form of defect is termed a *design defect*. The famous Ford Pinto case is a clear example of the design defect situation. The location and condition of the gas tank, which was subject to exploding in a rear-end collision, was manufactured exactly as Ford intended. However, its susceptibility to explosion made the automobile unreasonably dangerous, thereby leading to the conclusion that it had a design defect.

Design defect situations are more difficult than those involving manufacturing defects for two reasons. First, they are harder to identify. Manufacturing defects are readily apparent because the particular unit deemed defective is different from others being produced. With design defects, the allegedly defective unit is no different from any other being made. The second difficulty, which is much more troubling, is determining the standards that should be used to judge a design defective. Is it defective only when the product is more dangerous than expected by an ordinary consumer, or is there more to it? Also, can a product be defective only when used as intended, or must it be designed safely for unintended uses as well? For example, if a ladder manufacturer is aware that some painters will bounce on their ladders to move them from one location to another, must the ladder be strong enough to sustain such use/abuse? The following case comprehensively discusses how strict products liability has been handled in California for design defects.

BARKER V. LULL ENGINEERING CO.
State of California Supreme Court, 1978

FACTS: Barker sustained serious injuries as the result of an accident that occurred while he was operating a Lull High-Lift Loader at a construction site. The loader is designed to lift loads up to 5,000 pounds to a maximum height of 32 feet. It is designed so that the load can be kept level even when the loader is being operated on sloping terrain. The leveling of the load is controlled by a lever that is positioned between the operator's legs and is equipped with a manual lock to prevent accidental slipping of the load level. The loader was not equipped with seat belts or a roll bar. A wire-and-pipe cage over the driver's seat afforded the driver some protection from falling objects.

On the day of the accident, Barker, who had previously had only limited instruction and practice on the loader, was filling in for the regular operator. The accident occurred while Barker was attempting to lift a load of lumber to a height of approximately 20 feet and to place it on the second story of a building. The lift was particularly difficult because the terrain was sharply sloped in several directions. During the lift, Barker felt some vibration. When it appeared to several coworkers that the loader was about to tip, they shouted to Barker to jump from the loader. Barker heeded these warnings, but while scrambling away, he was struck by a piece of falling lumber and was seriously injured.

Barker alleged that the accident was attributable to one or more design defects of the loader. An expert testified at trial that the loader was unstable

continued . . .

continued . . .

due to its narrow base and had a tendency to roll over when lifting loads to considerable heights. The expert stated that the loader should have been equipped with outriggers to compensate for its instability. Cranes and some high-lift loader models are equipped with outriggers or offer them as optional equipment. Also, the expert testified that the loader was defective since it was not equipped with a roll bar or seat belts. In the absence of this equipment, according to the expert, Barker had no reasonable choice but to leap from the loader as it began to tip. In addition, pointing to the absence of an automatic leveling device and the placement of the lever such that it is vulnerable to inadvertent bumping, the expert stated that the accident may have been caused by the defective design of the leveling mechanism.

Lull denied that the loader was defective, and it claimed the accident resulted from Barker's lack of skill with or misuse of the loader. Lull's experts testified that the loader was not unstable when utilized on the terrain for which it was intended. If the accident did occur as a result of the tipping of the loader, then it happened because Barker had operated the loader on terrain that was too steep. The experts stated that outriggers were not necessary when the loader was used for its intended purposes and that no competitive loaders with similar-height lifting capacity were so equipped. They testified that a roll bar was unnecessary because the loader could not roll over completely given its bulk. They also stated that seat belts would have increased the danger by impairing the operator's ability to leave quickly in emergencies. As for the leveling device, they testified that the position was the safest and most convenient for the operator and that the manual lock provided adequate protection.

Lull argued that the accident probably was caused by Barker's own inexperience. If the lumber had begun to fall during the lift, it was because Barker had failed to lock the leveling device prior to the lift. In addition, Lull hypothesized that the lumber had fallen off only after Barker had leaped from the machine and that he was responsible because he had failed to set the hand brake, thereby permitting the loader to roll backward.

The trial court instructed the jury that strict liability for a defect in the design of a product is based on the finding that a product was unreasonably dangerous for its intended use. Based on this instruction, the jury returned a verdict in favor of the defendant. Barker appealed.

DECISION AND REASONING: California courts have frequently recognized that the defectiveness concept defies a simple, uniform definition applicable to all sectors of the diverse domain of products liability. Although in many instances—as when one machine in a million contains a cracked or broken part—the meaning of the term "defect" will require little or no elaboration, in other instances, as when a product is claimed to be defective because of an unsafe design or an inadequate warning, the contours of the defect concept may not be self-evident. The formulation of a satisfactory definition of "design defect" has proven a formidable task. This court concludes that a product is defective in design either (1) if the product has failed to perform as safely as an ordinary consumer would expect when used in an intended or reasonably foreseeable manner or (2) if the benefits of the challenged design do not outweigh the risk of danger inherent in the design. This dual standard for design defects ensures an injured plaintiff protection from products that either fall below ordinary consumer expectations as to safety or that, on balance, are not as safely designed as they should be. At the same time, the standard permits a manufacturer who has marketed a product that satisfies ordinary consumer expectations to demonstrate the relative complexity of design decisions and the trade-offs that are frequently required in the adoption of alternative designs. Finally, this test reflects continued adherence to the principle that the focus of products liability actions is on the product, not on the manufacturer's conduct, and that in order to prevail, the plaintiff need not prove that the manufacturer acted unreasonably or negligently.

The drafters of the Restatement adopted the term "unreasonably dangerous" primarily as a means of continuing the application of strict tort liability to an article that is "dangerous to an extent beyond that which would be contemplated by the ordinary consumer who purchases it, with the ordinary knowledge common to the community as to its characteristics." However, in a previous case, this court flatly rejected the suggestion that recovery in a products liability action should be permitted only if a product is more dangerous than contemplated by the average consumer, refusing to permit the low esteem in which the public might hold a dangerous product to diminish the manufacturer's responsibility for injuries caused by that product. The flaw in the Restatement's analysis is that it treats consumer expectations as a ceiling on a manufacturer's responsibility rather than as a floor.

The defectiveness concept has embraced a great variety of injury-producing deficiencies ranging from products that cause injury because they deviate from the manufacturer's intended result (e.g., the 1 soda bottle in 10,000 that explodes without explanation) to products that, though perfectly manufactured, are unsafe because of the absence of a safety device (e.g., a paydozer without rearview mirrors) and including products that are dangerous because they lack adequate warnings or instructions (e.g., a telescope that contains inadequate instructions for assembling a sun filter attachment). The cases demonstrate that the concept of defect raises considerably more difficulties in the design defect context than it does in the manufacturing defect case.

In general, a manufacturing defect is readily identifiable because a defective product unit is one that differs from the manufacturer's intended result or from other ostensibly identical units. For example, when a product comes

continued . . .

continued . . .

off the assembly line in a substandard condition, it has incurred a manufacturing defect. A design defect, by contrast, cannot be identified simply by comparing the injury-producing product with the manufacturer's plans or with other units, because by definition, the plans and all such units will reflect the same design. Rather than employing any sort of deviation-from-the-norm test in determining if a design is defective, our cases have applied two alternative criteria in ascertaining whether there is something wrong—if not in the manner of production, at least in the product.

First, our cases establish that a product may be found defective in design if the product fails to perform as safely as an ordinary consumer would expect when the product is used in an intended or reasonably foreseeable manner. Note here that the instruction to the jury is erroneous because it suggested that only the intended use of a product is relevant in evaluating defectiveness rather than the product's reasonably foreseeable use. The design and manufacture of products should not be carried out in an industrial vacuum but with recognition of the realities of their everyday use. It may be that use of a loader by a relatively inexperienced worker is not an intended use, but it still is a reasonably foreseeable use.

The expectations of the ordinary consumer cannot be viewed as the exclusive yardstick for evaluating design defectiveness because in many situations the consumer would not know what to expect, having no idea how safe the product could be made. Thus, a product may be found defective in design— even if it satisfies ordinary consumer expectations—if through hindsight the jury determines that the product's design embodies excessive preventable danger or in other words, if the risk of danger inherent in the design outweighs the benefits of the design. In evaluating the adequacy of a product's design pursuant to this standard, a jury may consider, among other relevant factors, (a) the gravity of the danger posed by the design, (b) the likelihood that such danger would occur, (c) the mechanical feasibility of a safer alternative design, (d) the financial cost of an improved design, and (e) the adverse consequences to the product and to the consumer that would result from an alternative design. Because most of the evidence relevant to the risk-benefit standard involves technical matters particularly within the knowledge of the manufacturer, we conclude that the plaintiff must show only that the injury was proximately caused by the product's design. The burden then is on the manufacturer to prove that the product is not defective in light of the relevant factors.

The technological revolution has created a society that contains never-before-contemplated dangers to the individual. The individual must face the threat to life and limb not only from the car on the street but from a massive array of hazardous mechanisms and products as well. The radical change from a comparatively safe, largely agricultural society to this unsafe, industrial one has been reflected in decisions that formerly tied liability to fault but that now are more concerned with the safety of the individual who suffers the loss. The change has been from fault to defect. Plaintiffs are no longer required to impugn the maker; they are required to impugn the product.

The jury may have interpreted the erroneous instruction as requiring plaintiff to prove that the high-lift loader was more dangerous than the average consumer contemplated. Also, the instruction additionally misinformed the jury that the defectiveness of the product must be evaluated in light of the product's "intended use" rather than its "reasonably foreseeable use." Therefore, judgment in favor of defendants is reversed.

Barker represented an expansion in products liability law, by requiring that design defects be evaluated both in terms of consumer expectations and by balancing risks with benefits. Many other courts and state legislatures followed in the footsteps of *Barker*, and thus also came to rely on the separate tests in the appraisal of design defects. However, many states did not go this far, and continued to judge defectiveness on consumer expectations but not on risk/utility factors.

The consumer expectations test increasingly has come under attack, especially when it is the sole measure of a design defect. This is because it may serve to protect sellers of harmful products when safer alternative designs could have been utilized. This, in turn, may reduce the incentive for manufacturers to develop and utilize potentially safer designs. However, the consumer expectations test also has been criticized—this time by business interests—when it is used in addition to the risk/benefit test for appraising whether complex technical products are defective. This is because typical consumers, who might not fully understand all the technical constraints of a complex product, might expect the product to be safer than the manufacturer actually can achieve. Thus, when consumer expectations are evaluated separately from the risk/benefit balance, designs may be found to be defective even when there are no safer alternatives.

Failure to Warn   As alluded to in *Barker*, there is a third kind of product defect, which potentially can subject a manufacturer to strict products liability: the failure to provide adequate warnings about possible hazards. Attention focuses on the sufficiency of the warnings when the product is manufactured correctly and designed appropriately. Keep in mind that a product may be manufactured and designed in a defect-free condition—and still be dangerous. Strict products liability does not mandate absolute safety. Rather, it requires that an article be designed safely based on consumer expectations and within the parameters of the risk/benefit analysis.

AES An electrical appliance, such as the **AES**, invariably may cause severe injury in certain situations because of the high voltages used. A do-it-yourself home mechanic who dismantles the machine to fix it will be exposed to potential danger. One who plugs in the cord after it has been gnawed by the dog or exposed to moisture may be injured. One who uses the machine in the bathroom and tips it into the bathtub while soaking may be shocked. As a manufacturer, we may not have a duty to design around these potential hazards based on consumer expectations or a risk/benefit analysis. Maybe the cost of designing into the **AES** a manageable dogproof electric cord, for example, is simply too expensive to warrant its inclusion. However, since we are aware of the potential for harm in these situations, we may have a duty to warn the user about them so as to minimize the potential for injury. That is, we have a responsibility to ensure that the user may easily recognize the various risks inherent in the product. Otherwise, the product would have a defect making it unreasonably dangerous. This time the defect regards the ability of the consumer to appreciate the spectrum of product uses that may be hazardous.

As you likely guessed, there have been substantial debates about how much warning customers need to appreciate the potential risks of using products. Do the warnings have to apply to all the reasonably foreseeable ways that a product might be used or is it enough to limit them to normal uses of the product? Couldn't this lead to products having so many warnings that they may overwhelm consumers, thereby possibly causing users to simply ignore them all? What if the danger is obvious to an ordinary person? Does the manufacturer still have an obligation to warn, perhaps to make sure that individuals are thinking about the danger and considering possibly safer alternatives while they decide whether to use the product? In this regard, courts usually find no duty to warn of obvious dangers, but there have been notable exceptions. For instance, one court determined that a warning might be required on a meat grinder, stating that "one who grinds meat, like one who drives on a steep road, can benefit not only from being told that his activity is dangerous but from being told of a safer way."[7] Another issue is whether a manufacturer may always escape liability for a dangerous design by warning about those dangers. Although the analysis in *Barker* would imply that the answer is no, many courts have concluded otherwise. In fact, the second edition of the Restatement concluded in a comment: "Where warning is given, the seller may reasonably assume that it will be read and heeded; and a product bearing such a warning which is safe for use if it is followed, is not in defective condition nor is it unreasonably dangerous."

Disposable Lighters: An Example of Difficult Products Liability Issues In the early 1990s, Bic Corporation was sued on several occasions for damages sustained by children who played with disposable cigarette lighters that the company manufactured.[8] Bic's position in these cases was that is it should not be liable for the injuries, because the lighters were misused by individuals who were not even supposed to have them. The dangers of cigarette lighters were obvious to the adults who purchased them. In addition, the adults were warned to keep the lighters out of the reach of children. Nonetheless, children may have gained access to the lighters and may not have fully appreciated the hazards of playing with them.

Following the consumer expectation test, plaintiffs alleged that Bic should be liable because the company could reasonably foresee that children would misuse the product in a dangerous way. As stated in *Barker*, a manufacturer may be liable when it is reasonably foreseeable that its product will be used by one who is relatively inexperienced. Bic, on the other hand, argued that it had a duty to protect only purchasers—in this case, adults—from unreasonable risks of harm. Otherwise, it claimed, manufacturers of products such as knives and hammers also would be liable for injuries sustained by children who handle them inappropriately. In a key decision, the Seventh Circuit Court of Appeals agreed with Bic regarding the application of the consumer expectation test.[9] Although the law may be different in states such as California, the court held that in Illinois, consumer expectations must be measured with reference to ordinary consumers and not foreseeable users. The court seemed to be particularly concerned about including foreseeable users when children are at issue, because there then might be credible products liability suits every time a child injures itself with a potentially dangerous product.

Plaintiffs also argued that regardless of consumer expectations, the lighters should have been manufactured with child-resistant features because the benefits of such attributes outweighed their costs. According to this theory, if the risks of harm were sufficiently high and if enhanced child-resistant features could have been included at a reasonable cost without overly impinging on the utility of the lighter, then liability should result. The same appellate court, however, determined that application of the risk/utility test does not make sense when considering simple products with obvious dangers. Plaintiffs also complained that Bic had a responsibility to warn parents of the possible dangers to young children, even if the lighters otherwise were adequately designed. This claim, however, was not persuasive to the Seventh Circuit, which found that the company's statement to keep the lighters away from children was sufficient under the circumstances. Based on all these considerations, a very divided Seventh Circuit determined that Bic's disposable lighters were not unreasonably dangerous.

The New Restatement of Torts on Products Liability

In an effort to clear up some of the confusion regarding strict liability principles, the American Law Institute published a new chapter of the Restatement in 1998 that deals specifically with these issues. In Section 2(a), the new Restatement on products liability states that "a product contains a manufacturing defect when the product departs from its intended design even though all possible care was exercised in the preparation and marketing of the product." This, of course, merely restates generally accepted notions regarding manufacturing defects and thus has not been the source of any significant disagreement.

Section 2(b), which deals with design defects, is a different story, however. Essentially, the new Restatement exclusively adopts the risk/benefit test to determine the adequacy of product designs. No longer are consumer expectations to be the sole or even a separate determinant of whether a product is defective. Rather, consumer expectations are to be considered along with other factors when determining whether the benefits of the design outweigh its risks. The Restatement now provides that a product is defective in design "when the foreseeable risks of harm posed by the product could have been reduced or avoided by the adoption of a reasonable alternative design by the seller . . . and the omission of the alternative design renders the product not reasonably safe." According to the Restatement, the focus on reasonable alternative designs "is based on the common sense notion that liability attaches only when the harm is reasonably preventable." The factors courts may use to determine whether a reasonable alternative design renders the product not reasonably safe include:

1. The magnitude and probability of the foreseeable risks of harm;
2. The instructions and warnings accompanying the product;
3. The nature and strength of consumer expectations regarding the product, including expectations arising from product portrayal and marketing; and
4. The relative advantages and disadvantages of the product as designed and as it alternatively could have been designed. Evaluation of relative advantages may consider:
   a. The likely effects of the alternative design on production costs;
   b. The effects of the alternative design on product longevity, maintenance, repair and aesthetics; and
   c. The range of consumer choice.

Notice that these factors are very similar to those listed in *Barker*. However, consumer expectations are included among the risk/benefit factors, rather than standing alone as a separate criteria. As noted before, the Restatement is not law; it merely serves as an authoritative guide to what the law should be. Thus, there is no guarantee that this approach to design defects will be adopted by all the courts or legislatures.

The Restatement also provides new guidance regarding the duties that sellers have to warn users of dangerous conditions. The Restatement provides:

A product is defective because of inadequate instructions or warnings when the foreseeable risks of harm posed by the product could have been reduced or avoided by the provision of reasonable instructions or warnings by the seller . . . and the omission of the instructions or warnings renders the product not reasonably safe.

In appraising the reasonableness of a warning, the Restatement suggests that courts consider the following factors:

1. The gravity and risks posed by the product;
2. The content and comprehensibility of the warning;
3. The intensity of the expression; and
4. The characteristics of expected user groups.

The Restatement takes the position that there is no duty to warn about risks that are generally known by foreseeable product users. This is because warnings in these circumstances do not enhance product safety and indeed may diminish the significance of other warnings about less obvious risks. The Restatement also states that when "an alternative design to avoid risks cannot reasonably be implemented, adequate instructions and warnings will normally be sufficient to render the product reasonably safe." However, it notes that warnings are not a substitute for the provision of a reasonably safe design. In other words, warnings are a factor that may make a product reasonably safe, but sellers may not assume that the provision of a warning relieves them from any duty to make the product even safer. As you can see, the new Restatement takes a rather holistic approach to design and warning defects, folding considerations about consumer expectations and the effectiveness of warnings into a unified analysis of the risks and benefits of designs. Exhibit 8.2 presents the concepts to consider when analyzing a strict products liability situation.

Consumer Product Safety Committee Regulations

Liability for product defects is controlled mostly by state law. However, manufacturers of technology products also must be conscious of applicable federal policies. The most important federal regulatory body in this regard is the Consumer Product Safety Commission (CPSC). The CPSC's mission is to protect the public against unreasonable risks of injury from consumer products. To this end, the CPSC has established numerous rules mandating standards for various consumer products. For example, the CPSC has safety standards for lawn mowers that require, among other things, that they automatically shut off within three seconds after the operator's hands leave the normal operating position and that they carry specifically designed labels warning of the dangers of blade contact. In addition, the CPSC can require correction measures to protect consumers.

Firms also are required to disclose to the CPSC any information about possible product defects.[10] The primary rationale for such reports is to help the CPSC uncover substantial product hazards, so that the agency can work with companies to protect the public. If necessary, the agency may even demand that companies undertake certain preventative steps, which may include product recalls. The reports also help the CPSC to identify potential risks that the agency might prevent through education programs, labeling requirements, or new product safety standards.

According the CPSC regulations, a firm must notify the CPSC in four situations: (1) when information reasonably supports the conclusion that a product fails to

---

Exhibit 8.2
Strict Products Liability Analysis Issues

- **Manufacturing Defect**
  - The unit causing injury was not manufactured as safely as the manufacturer intended.

- **Design Defect**
  - **Consumer Expectation:** The product fails to perform as safely as an ordinary consumer would expect.
    - Intended uses
    - Reasonably foreseeable unintended uses
  - **Risk/Benefit Analysis:** The risk of danger in the design outweighs the benefits in the design. Important factors are:
    - Gravity of danger
    - Likelihood of danger
    - Feasibility of alternative designs
    - Cost of alternative designs
    - Comparative utility of alternative designs
  - **CASE:** *Barker v. Lull Engineering Co.*
  - **New Restatement of Torts on Products Liability**
    - Risk/benefit analysis is the sole test for design defect.
    - Consumer expectation is a factor in the risk/benefit analysis.

- **Failure to Warn:** Foreseeable risks of harm could have been reduced by the provision of reasonable instructions or warnings.
  - Important factors:
    - The gravity and risks posed by the product
    - The content and comprehensibility of the warning
    - The intensity of the expression
    - The characteristics of expected user groups.
  - No duty to warn about generally known dangers.
  - Warnings do not necessarily relieve a manufacturer of having to incorporate a safer design.

- **Manufacturers and Sellers Liable**
  - If regularly engaged in that business
  - To anyone injured by defective product
  - If product condition not substantially changed

---

comply with an applicable CPSC safety regulation or a voluntary industry standard upon which the CPSC relies in lieu of making its own rule, (2) when a product contains a defect that could create a substantial product hazard, (3) when a product creates an unreasonable risk of serious injury or death, or (4) when a product has been subject to three civil lawsuits within two calendar years that result in settlements or judgments in favor of the plaintiffs. A defect is defined by the CPSC as a fault, flaw, or irregularity that causes weakness, failure, or inadequacy in form or function. Much of this language, relying on terms such as "reasonably" and "inadequacy," makes some manufacturers uncomfortable because it is not absolutely clear when reporting is required.[11] This is particularly troublesome because a manufacturer who fails to report as required is subject to potentially costly civil and criminal penalties.[12] Notwithstanding these penalties, companies often are reluctant to report possible defects. Their worries include the belief that a report might constitute an admission that the product actually is hazardous; that the public will find out about the report, thereby leading to adverse publicity; and that the CPSC will respond with draconian measures.[13] However, the law is clear that such reports are confidential and do not have to constitute an admission. Nonetheless, many authorities believe that the annual number of reports received, which averages around 300, is substantially below what should be filed.[14]

Tort Reform Measures

Many business groups believe that negligence and strict products liability policies place an unfair burden on manufacturers and distributors in the United States. Liability without fault is a key point of contention, especially with design defects. Under the principles articulated in *Barker*, juries have wide latitude to make after-the-fact determinations that more precautions or warnings should have been provided. The new version of the Restatement may provide some relief, at least from the wide disparity of approaches to strict products liability, but it still relies on factors that allow for a great deal of discretion. Coupled with this is the belief that juries tend to be sympathetic with damage victims and will use the opportunity in court to reward them too generously for their injuries. In addition, firms believe that joint and several liability is unfairly burdensome when a business that was only slightly responsible for a victim's suffering is required to bear an unfair proportion of the financial burden. Other issues, such as the extent of attorneys' fees and the exposure to high punitive damage awards, are also on the agenda.

Business groups have been actively working to reform the tort system at the state and federal levels. So far, there has been some moderate success in various states. For instance, many states have eliminated joint and several liability or have limited it to those situations when the actions of a business were a substantial contributing factor to the victim's damages. In addition, damage limitations and restrictions on punitive damages and attorneys' fees have been enacted by several state legislatures. Even though there has been some relief in many states, business groups are still very dissatisfied with the overall national picture. The hodgepodge of state laws exposes business defendants to forum shopping, whereby injured victims seek out the state with the most generous tort policies to bring suit. Business groups, therefore, have attempted for several years to convince Congress to pass a federal products liability reform act, which would clarify tort standards and reduce potential burdens on a unified national basis. Due to opposition from consumer groups and the trial lawyers' association, many of the provisions initially sought by business interests have been watered down. As of 1999, the major types of provisions that remained include (1) a cap on punitive damages, at least for small businesses, (2) protection for retailers and distributors who unknowingly sell defective products, (3) relief from joint and several liability, (4) reduction in the allowable time limits to bring suits, and (5) deterrents for frivolous suits, such as a requirement that the loser pays for litigation costs. The prospects that a comprehensive bill will pass remain uncertain. Larger business organizations have lost some of their enthusiasm for the federal reform efforts, thinking that they no longer go far enough.[15] The opposition also derived strength in the 1990s from having a Democrat in the White House. The dynamic might change if the Republicans come to control both the Congress and the Oval Office. If not, however, reform at the federal level probably will be achieved only for very specific matters affecting narrow business interests.[16]

Examples of Strict Liability Policies in Other Countries

As we evaluate tort reform measures in the United States, it is instructive to consider the experiences of other countries employing different tort liability systems. Until recently, Japan may have provided the most extreme example.[17] The Japanese tort system traditionally did not give individuals who were injured by products the ability to sue based on strict liability principles. Rather, the sole means of recovery was through negligence. This reflected a longstanding philosophy in Japan that safety is best achieved when consumers are required to be more careful, rather than when manufacturers are forced to protect them. Due to international pressures, Japan passed its first strict products liability law in 1994. Although opposition in Japan called this move the first step toward America's "litigation hell," consumer advocates believe that the measure will not bring about much real progress.[18] For one thing, they claim that the definition of "defect" is much too narrow. Also, the reform did not address complications in the Japanese legal system that often prove to be burdensome on plaintiffs. For instance, in Japan, litigants have only limited rights to discovery, a process liberally allowed in the United States by which an injured party can learn information that is in the hands of the defendant. This means that it is difficult to prove what a company might have known about the safety of a product. In addition, regulatory oversight of unsafe products in Japan is weaker than in the United States. The result is that products sold in Japan may be less safe and carry fewer safety warnings than their counterparts in the United States. Indeed, Japanese companies that sell in both markets may design the goods destined for the United States with greater safety precautions than those they sell in Japan. Of course, this perturbs U.S. manufacturers, who believe the Japanese legal system gives its manufacturers a comparative advantage. This is not only because Japanese companies may need to spend less on research and legal costs but also because they have the freedom to test the safety of their products in the Japanese marketplace without incurring substantial risks of lawsuits. In the final analysis, one cannot say that one system is better than the other. The contrasting legal rules offer different incentives to manufacturers regarding the safety of their products. The proper formulation can be judged only with reference to one's social preference. However, as the international community becomes more interdependent, there will be continual pressures to find compromises that will permit greater unification of international tort policies.

Policies in the European Union (EU), in contrast, have moved more consistently in lockstep with those in the United States.[19] In 1985, the Council of the European Union passed a strict liability directive requiring the member states to pass legislation in conformity with its principles.[20] The philosophical underpinnings of the directive are similar to those found in the United States. For instance, the directive defines a defective product as one that "does not provide the safety which a person is entitled to expect, taking all circumstances into account." This language parallels the consumer expectation test followed in the United States. The directive places primary responsibility on the producers of the goods. However, if the goods are imported into the EU, then the importers also bear liability for defective products. In addition, when the producers and importers cannot be identified, other distributors and suppliers within the EU may be subject to liability. This ensures that those suffering injuries from defective products sold in the EU will have recourse against some identifiable source engaged in the distribution of the defective products within community borders. The directive also restricts producers from disclaiming or waiving their liabilities for injuries resulting from the use of defective consumer goods. As we shall see in Chapter 9, this policy conforms to that already prevalent in the United States.

Strict Products Liability and Computer Systems

Strict Liability for Computer Programs   As previously mentioned, designers of computer systems have to be increasingly concerned about their duties under negligence principles. However, attention to negligence would quickly be eclipsed by strict products liability if the latter were held applicable to computer systems. Until recently, computer software developers have believed that they were immune from strict liability doctrines. For one, there is a substantial issue whether software is even a product. Especially for custom-designed programs, a strong argument can be made that the programmer is providing the service of making a computer function as desired by the client. Services are not subject to principles of strict products liability.[21] This means that if problems develop, only the programmers should be judged regarding their duties of care; the software should not be evaluated in terms of defectiveness. This argument is eroding, however, as more and more software is sold off-the-shelf. The more standardized the program, the more it has the appearance of a product rather than a service.

Another aspect that might immunize software programmers from strict products liability is that the doctrine traditionally has been applied to tangible objects. In one sense, software merely instructs a user how to attain a desired result with a computer. In this way it may be considered little different from a guidebook, which instructs the reader about, for instance, how to select safe mushrooms. Courts have been unwilling to extend strict products liability to most books, even those that guide the reader through potentially dangerous activities. Besides the tangibility aspects, courts fear that enforcing strict liability on what could be considered defective instruction would have a chilling effect on freedom of expression. However, courts have been willing to view certain kinds of guidance materials in a different light. For instance, a company that converted government data into aeronautical charts was held responsible under strict products liability when certain charts were designed with improperly converted data.[22] In defending the distinction between these charts and other materials, one court stated:

> Aeronautical charts are highly technical tools. They are graphic depictions of technical, mechanical data. The best analogy to an aeronautical chart is a compass. Both may be used to guide an individual who is engaged in an activity requiring certain knowledge of natural features. Computer software that fails to yield the result for which it was designed may be another.[23]

The last sentence, although it was only conjecture by the court, unnerved computer programmers. Application of strict liability principles would mean that programmers could be liable even if they are extremely diligent in developing their software products.

Software presents some unique issues in the product liability context. For instance, when software causes unintended harms, there are substantial questions whether the problem should be characterized as a manufacturing or a design defect. Unlike the production of physical products, such as automobiles, all software usually comes off the shelf exactly the same. Even so, one might argue that there is a manufacturing defect when the coding does not implement the software design as planned. However, the more typical situation likely will involve defects in design. Thus, a risk/benefit analysis normally will be applied. The problem, though, is that it may be relatively easy to conceive of safe alternative software designs after the harmful consequences have surfaced. Therefore, application of strict products liability to computer software, no matter how a defect is characterized, may mean that programmers will be responsible any time their programs cause unexpected harms.

Expert Systems and Medical Treatment   An important development with computer technology involves what are called expert systems.[24] Expert systems represent an exciting frontier of computer technology that attempts to have the machines rise above simple data manipulation to the level of making reasoned judgments. In effect, the computer is programmed with judgment rules so that it can draw upon its enormous data banks of experience and then apply logic, inference, and intuition to reach a reasoned solution to a particular problem. The programming of expert systems is extremely complicated, relying on professionals in the field, on experts who synthesize decision rules, and on sophisticated computer programmers. Currently, the medical community is making the greatest inroads in using expert systems. For instance, some systems incorporate extensive medical databases containing information on thousands of diseases, symptoms, blood chemistries, and drug therapies. Based on this information, they recommend appropriate treatment protocols and warn doctors about potential problems.[25]

For obvious reasons, the medical community is excited about the prospects of better treatment with the aid of expert systems. However, there also is substantial concern about potential tort liabilities. Doctors who rely on information from expert systems or recommend medical devices utilizing them have to be concerned with their respective standards of care. How far can a doctor go in trusting the diagnosis or suggested treatment of an expert system? Conversely, one might pose the alternative question: If an expert system is available, would it be negligent for a doctor not to use the system in some advisory capacity?

Those involved in developing the system also must be concerned with tort liabilities. Under negligence principles, the various manufacturers, programmers, and experts must fulfill their appropriate standards of care. Whether the applicable standard is elevated to a professional level in this context is not yet settled, but as discussed before, one should expect it to be the trend. More threatening, of course, is the very clear potential that the system will be subject to strict products liability. The issue of whether the expert system is most like a textbook or an aeronautical chart comes alive in this context, and as at least one court has suggested, the resolution likely will be to apply strict liability. In that event, if the expert system provides an inaccurate diagnosis or treatment that leads to detrimental medical complications, then it should not be hard to prove that the system had a defect making it unreasonably dangerous.

Year 2000 (Y2K) Concerns   Toward the end of the 1990s, fears arose that computer systems might begin to fail or make mistakes as of January 1, 2000. The anxiety was due to a simple programming technique that was used to save valuable computer storage space: rather than designate a year with four digits, programmers designed computer systems so that they recognized the last two digits as representing the appropriate year in the twentieth century (the 1900s). Thus, the year 1981 was indicated simply with the number "81." As the year 2000 approached, the perceived problem was that in older computer systems, the year 2000 would be represented by only the last two digits, "00," which in turn would be understood as the year 1900 by the systems. Suddenly the elderly might not even be born. Shipping dates might never arrive. Air traffic control systems, utilities, and waste-water treatment plants might become disrupted. In fact, the predicted scenarios ranged from limited inconveniences to total catastrophic disaster.

With all of these potential problems looming on the horizon, companies began to worry about their legal exposure. What if our company does not make payments to employees or customers because of failures in our computer systems? What if we miss critical delivery dates? Could there be a domino effect? What happens if our suppliers do not deliver materials that we need to complete our obligations to other firms? What if our computers are used in the medical field, transportation, or heavy industry, and their failure results in bodily injury or death? As we shall see in Chapter 9, these issues sometimes may be resolved through contractual provisions, such as warranty terms and disclaimers. This is especially true for commercial transactions involving economic, as opposed to personal injury, losses. But even in these instances, it is clear that one of the parties to the transaction will be obligated to pay for any damage that results. The only real question, under the terms of the contract, is who? Thus, companies became involved in comprehensive Y2K audits, which required attorneys to evaluate the terms of existing contracts and to determine the extent of their firms' potential liabilities. Analyses then had to be conducted about how these problems should be rectified, if at all. Also, insurance carriers had to be contacted to review the extent that their policies might cover the losses.[26]

It was also evident that several potential Y2K problems might be characterized as torts and thus subject companies to potential lawsuits for negligence and strict liability. Again, contracts could take care of some of these concerns. But they generally offer little protection if consumers suffer personal injury. In addition, contracts do not prevent those who are not parties to the deal from suing when they have grievances. Thus the Y2K problem required companies to consider whether their computer systems might be "defective" because of the way they were designed. Under the risk/benefit analysis, the potential dangers and the extent of the efficiency savings are among the relevant considerations. But also consider how you would feel if you were on a jury evaluating the liability of a company for a Y2K failure that caused the death of several children? What if you learned that the company knew about the possibility for injuries when it devised its computer system and that it could have easily addressed them at that time? Corporate lawyers feared that sympathetic jurors might use these occasions to hit their companies with enormous punitive damage awards, such as those that were becoming more common in the automobile and cigarette industries. Also, lawyers worried how their companies might be stricken by joint and several liability, especially since several parties so often were involved in the design and use of computer systems.

Another products liability concern was whether there was any duty to warn those who might be economically or physically harmed by Y2K failures.[27] This is a little different from the duty to provide warnings when a product is initially sold. In this case, the products were sold long before the problems may have been recognized. Does a company have any duty to warn about dangers that it learns about from subsequent testing or new information? According to the Restatement, such a warning should be made when:

1. the seller knows or reasonably should know that a product poses a substantial risk of harm to persons or property;
2. those to whom a warning might be provided can be identified and may reasonably be assumed to be unaware of the risk of harm;
3. a warning can be effectively communicated to and acted on by those to whom a warning might be provided;
4. the risk of harm is sufficiently great to justify the burden of providing a warning.

There are several problems with warnings in these situations. Many of these are alluded to in the Restatement provisions, such as identification, communication, and cost. However, there are other issues. For instance, the warnings may serve to anger customers who, once alerted, expect more than a warning; rather, a solution to the problem. This could end up harming the reputation of the company and cause further litigation. Thus, the possible obligations to warn only added to the headaches faced by these companies.

Due to the magnitude of all these concerns, business groups approached Congress for legal protection from Y2K liability, which they received in July 1999. The powerful American Trial Lawyers Association opposed the law, leading to compromises on many issues. Some of the important protections ultimately adopted by Congress are:

1. For small companies and individuals, a cap on punitive damages to the lesser of three times compensatory damages or $250,000.
2. Proportionate liability rather than joint and several liability.[28]
3. Companies have 90 days to fix Y2K problems before lawsuits may be filed.

One important exception to the law, though, is that it does not cover suits for personal injuries. Nonetheless, the legislation is expected to substantially curb litigation resulting from Y2K problems.

Repetitive Motion Injuries   "Repetitive motion injuries" is an umbrella term that applies to any painful condition of the neck, shoulder, back, arm, or hand that occurs in a person engaged in repetitive physical duties.[29] Recently, there has been an explosion of complaints about repetitive motion injuries in the United States stemming particularly from uses of consoles, keyboards, and video display terminals associated with computers. Indeed, according to the U.S. Bureau of Labor Statistics, repetitive motion injuries are now the leading cause of occupational illness in the United States, accounting for 34% of all lost-workday injuries and illnesses.[30] For this reason, Robert Reich, secretary of the Department of Labor under President Clinton, called these ailments "the occupational diseases of the information age."[31] Of the variety of forms of repetitive motion injuries, the most prominent is carpal tunnel syndrome, a wrist disorder that many allege may be caused by the steady use of computer keyboards. Other forms of trauma may be caused by insufficient rest breaks and by inappropriate layouts of equipment, seating, and lighting.

Evidence is mounting that there is a correlation between certain workplace factors and the incidence of repetitive motion injuries, especially in manufacturing industries, such as those involved with meatpacking and automobile production. In addition, an increasing number of studies demonstrate that repetitive motion injuries may be reduced when employers implement prevention programs. Labor organizations and women's rights groups, among others, have lobbied vigorously at the federal, state, and local levels for workplace protection. Some states, such as California, have responded with legislation. However, most eyes have focused recently on efforts by OSHA to establish a comprehensive national ergonomic standard to address growing concerns over repetitive motion injuries.

Although OSHA has been studying repetitive motion injuries since the early 1980s, it did not formally begin the process for adopting an ergonomics standard until 1992.[32] OSHA spent the next several years working with interested groups to formulate appropriate requirements, but this effort was halted by Congress in 1995 when Congress prohibited the agency from using any of its annual appropriations allotment to further its work on the standard. This interruption proved to be temporary, since the restriction was lifted in 1996. Nonetheless, many members of Congress continue to be wary of OSHA's involvement. In 1999, OSHA provided a draft of its proposed ergonomics rule to small business, as it must do before formally proposing a standard for public comment. By the time this book is published, OSHA expects that it will have at least reached the more formal stages of adopting the standard. In fact, it is possible that the rule will have been implemented by this time. If so, it is likely that the rule at first will apply only to manufacturing industries and in certain situations where repetitive motion injuries have been reported. As for possible requirements, employers probably will have to set up ergonomics programs that may consist of the following elements:

1. Management leadership, which includes ways for employees to report problems, receive responses, and get involved in the program.
2. Hazard identification and information, which includes mechanisms to identify repetitive motion hazards and periodic reporting of information to employees.
3. Job hazard analysis and control, which requires analysis of problem jobs and implementation of measures to eliminate or control the hazards.
4. Training about the ergonomics program and repetitive motion hazards, which must occur periodically and at no cost to employees.
5. Medical management, including prompt access to health care professionals and possible work restrictions during recovery periods at no cost to the employee.

The other front where workers have raised the issue of repetitive motion injuries is in the courts. Employers, though, are not the only targets. Numerous lawsuits have been brought against computer manufacturers, alleging that the designs of their equipment, particularly keyboards, are defective and unreasonably dangerous. The lawsuits claim that the companies knew, or should have known, that the designs of their products were potentially dangerous and that the companies failed to adequately warn the workers who eventually used the products. Defendants include such companies as Northern Telecom, Apple Computer, Compaq, Digital Equipment, AT&T, IBM, and Wang. So far, users complaining of ailments, such as carpal tunnel, have found that there are many obstacles to winning these cases against the manufacturers. One major hurdle is proving that the injuries actually were caused by the design of the keyboard. Computer manufacturers often point to many other possible causes, such as personal physical deficiencies, preexisting injuries, or other factors in the work environment. Since these cases normally are based on a failure to warn, another problem for plaintiffs is proving that the manufacturers reasonably should have known about the problem. In this regard, users have had some success by demonstrating that manufacturers had established workplace procedures in their own operations to lessen the potential occurrence of repetitive stress injuries.[33] A final obstacle is proving that a warning might actually have affected a user's behavior. Until 1996, plaintiffs could claim no definitive successes against computer equipment manufacturers. Many cases were settled, and some simply were lost.[34] However, the industry was stunned in 1996 when a jury awarded two secretaries and a billing clerk close to $6 million for disabling wrist and arm injuries allegedly suffered from using keyboards manufactured by Digital Equipment.[35] Although all three of these awards were later overturned on appeal, computer companies now have substantial reasons to be worried.[36]

INTRUSIONS ON PRIVACY

Personal privacy is sacred within the culture of the United States. One only has to review the Bill of Rights to get a feel for U.S. reverence for individual privacy. The Fourth Amendment specifically protects individuals from government search and seizure. The Fifth Amendment states that government may not compel criminal suspects to testify against themselves. This serves to protect the privacy of information known by criminal defendants until they consent to testify. Even the Fourteenth Amendment, which protects liberty from government interference, has been interpreted by some to include elements of privacy. It is no wonder, therefore, that there has been a strong public reaction to the assault on privacy that new technologies have wrought.

The concept of privacy is elusive because one often does not think about it in concrete terms until the usual and expected patterns of conduct change. For example, experience with the common telephone has led the public to expect that a conversation is private between the acknowledged participants. New phone technologies have raised novel issues, however. Consider the case of new parents who monitor their infant from another room by using a baby monitor. Sometimes these monitors pick up the frequencies emitted by cordless phones, thus allowing the parents to overhear the phone conversations of their neighbors. Should the parents be expected to turn off the monitor when such a phone conversation is received? The whole point of using the monitor is to maintain constant contact with the infant, so this requirement does not seem fair or appropriate. Can we expect the parents to pay attention for baby noises but ignore all other sounds they hear? That seems impractical. At the same time, many people who use cordless phones think of them as no different from traditional phones. However, clearly the new technology must challenge accepted norms of privacy. Now, one has to consider whether the privacy of a conversation is dependent on the type of phone used. One also must reflect, in a more discriminating manner than before, about the kinds of behavior that might inappropriately interfere with privacy expectations. For example, whereas listening with the baby monitor might seem permissible under the circumstances, actively scanning the airwaves for the purpose of intercepting calls likely would appear less acceptable.

Privacy of Physical and Psychological Information

When the government or businesses take actions that allegedly impinge on privacy rights, they normally put forward certain reasons to justify the intrusion. The question, then, is whether these reasons are sufficiently important to outweigh the resulting degree of intrusion on legitimate expectations of privacy. A 1995 Supreme Court case, *Vernonia School District v. Acton*,[37] provides a useful illustration of the kinds of analysis that might be important in striking this balance. In *Vernonia*, the Supreme Court had to determine whether a drug testing policy for student athletes instituted by a public school violated either the Fourth or the Fourteenth Amendment of the U.S. Constitution. The school board adopted the policy because there was a sharp increase in drug use among students, and student athletes were the leaders of the drug culture. In addition, drugs increase the risks of sports-related injuries. According to the policy, students wishing to engage in sports had to sign a form consenting to drug testing. All athletes were required to submit to testing at the beginning of the season, and a pool consisting of 10% of the athletes was selected each week for random testing.

The Supreme Court determined that this policy was constitutional, since the interests of the school board in maintaining order and ensuring safety outweighed the intrusions on the athletes' reasonable expectations of privacy. In reaching this conclusion, the Court acknowledged that the disciplinary problems within the school district had reached epidemic proportions and that drug testing of student athletes was an effective way to address the problem. The Court also was impressed that the drug testing program was designed so that intrusions on privacy were minimized as much as possible. Urine was collected in ways that reduced the possibilities for personal embarrassment. Strict testing procedures were followed to assure accuracy. The tests only revealed the presence of certain illegal substances, such as marijuana, coke, and amphetamines, and did not provide other information, such as whether the student was epileptic, diabetic, or pregnant. If the testing resulted in a positive finding, then the student was given the option of suffering suspension or participating in a drug assistance program while continuing to play. Only the school superintendent, the principal, and the athletic director received notification of the results, and the information was not turned over to police.

The Court also concluded that student athletes do not have substantial expectations of privacy. First of all, parents authorize schools to exercise some degree of control over their children to assure civility and safety. To this end, schools often require physical examinations and vaccinations. Thus, with regard to medical examination and procedures, students within the school environment have a lesser expectation of privacy than do members of the public at large. The privacy expectations of athletes are reduced even further, since they often are undressed together in locker rooms. In addition, by trying out for the team, athletes agree to abide by additional rules of conduct and controls. In the final analysis, the Court concluded that the interests of the state were substantial while the intrusions on expectations of privacy were minimal. The testing program, therefore, was reasonable and constitutional.

Drug and alcohol testing programs have become increasingly common in the workplace. Government employers, like the Vernonia school board, must act in conformity with the Fourth and Fourteenth Amendments of the U.S. Constitution. Thus, any program must have sufficiently important rationales to justify the intrusions on privacy expectations. Although adults have greater privacy expectations than do student athletes, drug and alcohol testing programs can meet constitutional standards when there are substantial reasons to use them and procedures are carefully tailored to protect personal privacy interests. In this regard, an important factor involves the degree of harm that an employee might do to the government, the public, or other employees if a mistake occurs while under the influence. Thus, such programs often seem reasonable in the context of train engineers or when firearms may be carried.

The U.S. Constitution does not apply to the conduct of private businesses. However, a patchwork of federal and state laws have been passed to regulate drug and alcohol testing in various regions and industries. For the most part, they follow the balancing approach of *Vernonia*, allowing testing when the potential harms to the employer or the public are great, and the procedures intrude no more than necessary on the legitimate privacy expectations of the employees. Even more on the cutting edge are genetic testing techniques that allow employers and insurers to identify individuals especially prone to developing certain diseases and health risk conditions, such as Alzheimer's disease, cystic fibrosis, cancer, or heart disease. Such tests raise privacy concerns as well as accusations of unlawful discrimination.[38] However, there may be legitimate cost-saving and health rationales that justify their use in certain contexts. As of 1996, only a handful of states had laws specifically regulating how employers or insurance companies might use genetic tests. However, starting in 1997, there was a flurry of legislative activity, and now almost all states have statutes which regulate permissible uses of genetic information.[39]

Polygraph testing is another technological tool that employers have used to learn useful information, this time about personal beliefs and behaviors. By monitoring certain physiological parameters, such as pulse rates, respiration, and perspiration, a trained technician may use a polygraph to test the veracity of one's answers given in response to questions. Such testing, especially in the employment context, has come under fire for two reasons. First, there are questions about the reliability of polygraph testing. Second, there is substantial criticism about the types of information an employer or other interrogator strives to obtain through polygraph tests. Questions about previous drug and alcohol use, criminal fantasies, gambling activities, and prior personal relationships are just a few of the topics commonly probed. Before the advent of the polygraph, it was not necessary to consider whether employers or others had a right to learn this information, because it was not technologically possible to obtain it reliably. However, with the introduction of polygraph testing, the debate surfaced about the types of information an inquirer could access and the conditions under which such information could be obtained. Those concerns resulted in substantial regulation of polygraph testing, first at the state level and later by federal law. The federal policy prohibits polygraph testing by private employers in almost all industries and under most circumstances, including preemployment evaluations.[40]

Advances in technology will continue to raise new ways that the government and employers may learn information about individuals. What seems like science fiction for one generation often becomes reality for the next. For instance, the use of eye scanners to positively identify individuals once was only within the province of futuristic movies, such as Mission Impossible. However, in 1999, Bank United in Texas applied the technology to its ATM machines, allowing individuals to engage in transactions without the need of an ATM card or an identification number. Technologies are being developed that may allow individuals to be identified by other characteristics, such as voice prints or facial geometry. This science, called biometrics, has raised alarm bells among privacy advocates. Among other things, they worry about the accumulation of such information in databases that then might be used by inappropriate persons for unauthorized reasons. When new technological tools, such as these, threaten privacy concerns, one should follow the logic of *Vernonia* and balance the user's need to know the information with the degree of intrusion on the subject's reasonable expectation of privacy. Exhibit 8.3 depicts many of the issues that are important in this evaluation.

Monitoring of Communications and Personal Activities

Monitoring for Efficiency   Another area of concerns about privacy involves the monitoring of personal actions and conversations. Advancements in technology have allowed employers and others to monitor behavior that heretofore was free from close scrutiny. Electronic monitoring systems, as they are called, allow employers to measure employee efficiency in conducting routine duties. For instance, word processing and data entry tasks can be monitored for speed and errors through electronic systems that count keystrokes. The efficiency of phone operators can be checked by systems that clock the duration or count the number of calls in a given unit of time. Video monitoring allows employers to remotely view all actions taken by employees and/or customers. Such monitoring may be worrisome as a managerial tool because it may lead to such high performance standards that undue employee stress will result. Employees, too, may feel an undue intrusion on their personal privacy. Before electronic monitoring, supervision was likely to be periodic and with the knowledge of the employee. Electronic systems, on the other hand, may be operated remotely and constantly. In this way, there may be no way to engage in any private personal behavior—even rest—without employer awareness.

At this time, there are few laws that prohibit employers from using electronic monitoring systems. Following the balancing scheme used in *Vernonia*, employers often seem justified in ensuring that paid employees are using business assets only for legitimate purposes. In addition, when employees are being paid to perform duties at work, perhaps they should not expect to have personal moments to engage in private behavior. This latter claim, though, may not be entirely true in all contexts. Therefore, employers are advised to notify employees when monitoring will

Exhibit 8.3

The Privacy Balance: Relevant Considerations

IMPORTANCE OF BUSINESS OR GOVERNMENT PURPOSE	DEGREE OF INTRUSION ON REASONABLE EXPECTATIONS OF PRIVACY
• To protect individuals from physical harm • To protect corporate assets • To protect trade secrets • To ensure corporate assets used for business purposes • To reduce exposure to sexual harassment, defamation or other harmful consequences • To confirm reasonable suspicion of harmful activity	• The context of the intrusion • The extent of the intrusion • Existence of acceptable use policy • Notice of search or monitoring • Consent • Procedures to minimize privacy intrusions • Procedures to confirm results • Procedures regarding consequences if search uncovers problems • Procedures to guard secrecy of information

occur so that they do not expect to have privacy at those times. Also, there may be situations when employers have to be particularly careful. For instance, employers may want to engage in video surveillance of restrooms to monitor, let's say, drug use. Expectations of privacy in this environment are so great, however, that employers must take extra precautions, again within the spirit of *Vernonia*. In addition, they need to be especially cognizant of state laws, which may prohibit such surveillance altogether.[41] Those who are concerned about the effects of electronic monitoring on privacy periodically have approached Congress for federal relief. For instance, in 1993, Congress proposed the Privacy for Consumers and Workers Act that, among other things, would have substantially curtailed the ability of companies to engage in this form of monitoring. Although the proposal garnered substantial political support, it ultimately did not become law.

Monitoring Internet Activity   The more modern efficiency problem that employers have encountered regards employees who surf the Internet during work hours. A major concern is that employees may spend inordinate time using company computers to analyze their investment portfolios, make travel arrangements, locate friends, shop for merchandise, or follow their favorite sports teams. Possibly more disturbing may be the amount of time that employees use the Internet while at work to view indecent or pornographic material. For example, one study found that employees at IBM, Apple Computer, and AT&T together visited Penthouse's Web site 12,823 times in a single month in 1996.[42] In these cases, employers must be concerned not only with productivity losses, but with the possibilities that their work environments may be hostile to certain workers under federal antidiscrimination laws. In addition, Web sites often are able to trace customers back to the company system through which they hook up to the Internet.[43] You can imagine how disclosure of such information might embarrass the company, particularly if employees are visiting pornographic or other unwholesome sites. Another problem involves the sheer amount of a company's computer bandwidth capacity that employees sometimes utilize for personal reasons. This may be particularly true when company resources are used for downloading large music and video files, or for engaging in frequent securities day-trading.[44]

The tools are now available for businesses to follow every site that an employee visits, and some employers are choosing to use them.[45] Privacy advocates find this degree of scrutiny a little shocking. Employees often take time to rest and think about their personal lives while at work. Does an employer have a right to know what the employees are thinking about? So, what if a tired employee, rather than stopping simply to let the mind wander for a couple minutes, uses the Web to enhance the experience? An employee may sit back for a moment and wonder what the weather is like in a particular area, or check the Web to get better information. What difference does it make? Employees often take coffee breaks and chat with co-workers about their personal lives. Do employers have a right to know what topics interest their employees during these breaks? If not, why should they be able to review the Web sites visited by employees when they choose to use the Internet during rest breaks? Sometimes employees at the office pull out a magazine in their office and read it for a few minutes. Should an employer be able to come into a locked office at any time and see what the employee is reading? This could be particularly embarrassing if the magazine happens to be Playboy. Again, one needs to ask how this is different than monitoring the Web sites that interest the employee.

The extent to which Web monitoring should be used is as much a managerial decision as a legal one. Without question, if monitoring is to take place, employees should be notified. At least with notice, the employee is, in effect, told that the employer has the key to the office and may come in at any time to see what is going on. Thus, there is a reduced expectation of privacy. This, in turn, should influence what the employee chooses to view at the office. Also, the employer should establish an "acceptable use" policy for Internet resources, indicating if and when employees might use the Web for personal reasons.[46] Some businesses prohibit personal use of Internet resources under any circumstances. Others, though, have experienced employee resentment to full prohibitions. Thus, some businesses limit personal use only during certain peak periods when Internet resources may be strained or full employee attention is required. Others allow reasonable personal use within certain guidelines, but prohibit or even block access to pornographic sites.[47] The Internet is becoming an increasingly important force in the personal and professional lives of all workers. As this trend continues, employers will only have a more difficult time formulating the appropriate degree of scrutiny they should give to Internet usage.

Monitoring Telephone Conversations and E-mail   Possibly even greater attention has been given to the technical ability of employers to monitor conversations.

Concern about telephone wiretapping, for instance, led to significant regulation of wiretapping in the federal Omnibus Crime Control and Safe Streets Act. The next case discusses the federal wiretapping law and explains two important exceptions to the general prohibitions against the monitoring of phone conversations: (1) the consent of one party to the conversation and (2) monitoring in the ordinary course of business.

WATKINS V. L. M. BERRY & COMPANY
Eleventh Circuit Court of Appeals, 1983

FACTS: Carmie Watkins was employed as a sales representative by Berry & Company ("Berry"). Berry was under contract with South Central Bell to solicit Yellow Pages advertising from South Central Bell's present and prospective Yellow Pages advertisers. Much of this solicitation was done by telephone, and Watkins was hired and trained to make those calls.

All employees of Berry are informed of its established policy of monitoring calls as part of its regular training program. The monitored calls are reviewed with employees to improve sales techniques. Employees are permitted to make personal calls on company telephones, and they are told that personal calls will not be monitored except to the extent necessary to determine whether a particular call is of a personal or business nature.

In April or May 1980, during her lunch hour, Watkins received in her office a call from a friend. At or near the beginning of the call, the friend asked Watkins about an employment interview Watkins had had with another company (Lipton) the evening before. Watkins responded that the interview had gone well and expressed strong interest in taking the Lipton job. Unbeknownst to Watkins, Martha Little, her immediate supervisor, was monitoring the call from her office and heard the discussion about the interview. After hearing the conversation, Little told her supervisor, Diane Wright, about the call. Later that afternoon, Watkins was called into Wright's office and was told that the company did not want her to leave. Upon discovering that the supervisor's questions had been prompted by Little's interception of the call, Watkins became upset and tempers flared. Wright fired Watkins the next day, but after Watkins complained to Wright's supervisor, she was reinstated with apologies from Little and Wright. Nonetheless, within a week, Watkins left Berry to work for Lipton.

Watkins sued Berry, Little, and Wright for violating Title III of the Omnibus Crime Control and Safe Streets Act. The district court judge granted summary judgment against Watkins and dismissed her claim. Watkins appealed.

continued . . .

continued ...

DECISION AND REASONING: Title III forbids, among other things, the interception, without judicial authorization, of the contents of telephone calls. Section 2511(1)(b) provides:

> Except as otherwise specifically provided in this chapter, any person who ... willfully uses ... any electronic, mechanical, or other device to intercept any oral communication . . . shall be fined not more than $10,000 or imprisoned not more than five years, or both.

In addition to criminal remedies, Title III Section 2520 provides for civil remedies. The person whose communication is unlawfully intercepted may recover actual damages or statutory damages of $100 for each day of violation up to a maximum of $1,000. In addition, one is entitled to punitive damages, attorneys' fees, and litigation costs.

It is not disputed that Little's conduct violates Section 2511(1)(b) unless it comes within an exemption "specifically provided in" Title III. The defendants claim the applicability of two such exemptions. The first is the consent exemption set out in section 2511(2)(d):

> It shall not be unlawful under this chapter for a person not acting under color of law to intercept a wire or oral communication . . . where one of the parties to the communication has give prior consent to the interception. . . .

The defendants argue that, by using Berry's telephones and knowing that monitoring was possible, Watkins consented to the monitoring. The second exemption claimed is the business extension exemption in Section 2510(5)(a)(i), which defines the terms "electronic, mechanical, or other device," thereby establishing the kinds of monitoring subject to liability under Section 2511(1)(b). According to Section 2510(5)(a)(i), "electronic, mechanical, or other device" means:

> any device or apparatus which can be used to intercept a wire or oral communication other than any telephone or telegraph instrument, equipment, or facility . . . furnished to the subscriber or user by a communications common carrier in the ordinary course of its business and being used by the subscriber or user *in the ordinary course of its business* . . . [emphasis supplied].

Defendants argue that the monitoring of Watkins's call was in the ordinary course of Berry's business, that the interception therefore was not by an "electronic, mechanical, or other device" as defined in Section 2510, and that it therefore does not fall within Section 2511(1)(b).

The consent and business extension exemptions are analytically separate. Consent may be obtained for any interceptions, and the business or personal nature of the call is entirely irrelevant. Conversely, the business extension exemption operates without regard to consent. So long as the requisite business connection is demonstrated, the business extension exemption represents the circumstances under which nonconsensual interception is not violative of Section 2511(1)(b). Accordingly, we will first consider the scope of Watkins's consent to the monitoring of this call and then move to the question about whether the interception was justified as being in the ordinary course of Berry's business, notwithstanding the absence of consent.

Defendants argue that Watkins's acceptance of employment with Berry, with knowledge of the monitoring policy, constituted her consent to the interception of this call. This is erroneous with respect to Watkins's actual and implied consent.

It is clear that Watkins did not actually consent to interception of this particular call. Furthermore, she did not consent to a policy of general monitoring. She consented to a policy of monitoring sales calls but not personal calls. That consent included the inadvertent interception of a personal call, but only for as long as necessary to determine the nature of the call. So, if Little's interception went beyond the point necessary to determine the nature of the call, it went beyond the scope of Watkins's actual consent.

Consent under Title III is not to be cavalierly implied. Title III expresses a strong purpose to protect individual privacy by strictly limiting the occasions on which interception may lawfully take place. Stiff penalties are provided for its violation. It would thwart this policy if consent could routinely be implied from circumstances. Thus, knowledge of the capability of monitoring cannot alone be considered implied consent.

The cases that have implied consent from circumstances have involved far more compelling facts than those presented here. In one case, a police officer whose call was intercepted knew or should have known that the line he was using was constantly taped for police purposes; furthermore, an unmonitored line was provided expressly for personal use. (The police station had ten lines: eight were recorded continuously with an audible warning sound, one was recorded continuously without a sound, and one was not monitored.) In another case, the plaintiff made a personal call on telephones that were to be used exclusively for business calls and that he knew were regularly monitored. He had been warned on previous occasions to stop making personal calls from his business telephone; other telephones were specifically provided for personal use. In both cases, the employee was fully aware of the extent of the monitoring and deliberately ignored the strong probability or certainty of monitoring.

Such situations are worlds apart from Watkins's case, since Watkins had consented to a scheme of limited monitoring. We hold that consent within

continued . . .

continued ...

the meaning of Section 2511(2)(d) is not necessarily an all-or-nothing proposition; it can be limited. It is up to the judge or jury to determine the scope of the consent and to decide whether and to what extent the interception exceeded that consent.

If, as appears from the undisputed facts, there was no consent to the interception of the call beyond what was initially required to determine its nature, defendants must rely on the business extension exemption to shield them from liability for any listening beyond that point. It is not enough for Berry to claim that its general policy is justifiable as part of the ordinary course of business. The question, rather, is whether the interception of this call was in the ordinary course of business.

The general rule is that if the intercepted call was a business call, then monitoring is in the ordinary course of business. If it was a personal call, the monitoring was probably, but not certainly, not in the ordinary course of business. The undisputed evidence strongly suggests that the intercepted call here was not a business call, but rather was a personal call. Defendants argue, however, that the topic was Watkins's interview with another employer. Since this was obviously of interest and concern to Berry, defendants claim it was in the ordinary course of business to listen.

The phrase "in the ordinary course of business" cannot be expanded to mean "anything that interests the company." Berry might have been curious about Watkins's plans, but it had no legal interest in them. Watkins was at liberty to resign at will and so at liberty to interview with other companies. Her interview was thus a personal matter, neither in pursuit of nor to the legal detriment of Berry's business. To expand the business extension exemption as broadly as defendants suggest would permit monitoring of obviously personal calls on the grounds that the company was interested in, say, whether Watkins's friends were nice or not. We therefore conclude that the subject call was personal.

Whereas a business call is dispositive in one direction, a personal call is not dispositive in the other. In general, it is hard to see how intercepting a call involving nonbusiness matters could be "in the ordinary course of business," since such activity is unlikely to further any legitimate business interest. However, as an example, interception of calls reasonably suspected to involve nonbusiness matters might be justifiable by an employer who had had difficulty controlling personal use of business equipment through warnings. Thus, if interception of personal calls is permitted at all, it is permitted only for a very limited purpose. This might apply, for instance, to the situation in which monitoring occurs when personal calls are not allowed on business telephones.

Even in that limited situation, however, one is not entitled to monitor the contents of the entire call. We hold that a personal call may not be intercepted in the ordinary course of business under the exemption in Section 2510(5)(a)(i), except to the extent necessary to guard against unauthorized use of the telephone or to determine whether a call is personal or not. In other words, a personal call may be intercepted in the ordinary course of business to determine its nature but never its contents. The limit of this exemption for Berry's business was the policy that Berry in fact instituted. It thus appears that Little was justified in listening to that portion of the call that indicated it was not a business call; beyond that, she was not.

The violation of Section 2511(1)(b) is the interception itself, not the interception of particular material. It is not necessary to the recovery of damages that the violator hear anything in particular; she need do no more than listen. Thus, the reinstatement of Watkins and her subsequent departure, though they may affect the amount of actual damages, do not render her claim moot. Watkins's right to recover at least the minimum statutory damages flows from the interception, not from the actual damage caused.

We hold that this case should not have been disposed by summary judgment. Among the factual questions that should be considered are: What was the monitoring policy to which Watkins had consented? Did Little know that Watkins had received the call, and if so, did that necessarily indicate a personal call? How long was the call? When was the interview discussed? Were other subjects discussed? For how long did Little listen? How long does it take to discover that a call is personal? For example, is there an immediately recognizable pattern to a sales call? This list is not exhaustive, but it points out the directions in which further inquiries should be pursued.

The judgment of the district court is reversed.

PRIVACY OF E-MAIL COMMUNICATIONS The original wiretapping law was passed in 1968. Obviously, technology has changed substantially since that time, creating new ways not only to communicate but also to intercept discussions. Conversations no longer can be made solely over traditional phone lines, but now may be transmitted over the airwaves by cordless and cellular phones. When analog signals are beamed into space, however, individuals may intercept them easily with scanning devices. The emergence of e-mail is perhaps more important, though, since it has radically displaced much of the communication that traditionally occurred over phone systems. Stirred by these rapid changes in communications technologies, Congress passed the Electronic Communication and Privacy Act (ECPA) in 1986, which amended the 1968 wiretapping law to conform it to the new realities.[48]

A complete discussion of the ECPA is well beyond the scope of this book. Essentially, it carries over the privacy protection discussed in *Watkins* to electronic communications of various types, including cellular and cordless phones.[49] Thus, the act makes it illegal to intentionally use scanners to intercept conversations over these communication devices. The act also applies to e-mail services engaged in the business of transmitting interstate communications, such as AOL and CompuServe. Although there are many special exceptions, especially for the providers of the electronic communications services, one generally may not access e-mail sent through such interstate facilities unless there is consent or a business purpose.

Employers have special reasons to want to monitor e-mail messages beyond those that apply to phone conversations. Protection of trade secrets and important corporate information is one area of concern, since e-mail makes it so simple for employees to attach documents to correspondences. And it is not simply the nefarious corporate thieves that worry executives. The ease of e-mail results in a lot of inadvertent communications. Just consider how easy it might be to send a message by mistake to someone on a long "cc" list merely by replying to a note you received. There is also the problem of employees circulating offensive jokes and materials, especially if they may be construed as racist, harassing, or obscene to coworkers. For instance, an employer may be held responsible for establishing a hostile work environment if it does not take steps to prevent the widespread distribution of crude sexual jokes or pictures. Also, recipients of e-mail messages often treat them as if they have been written on corporate letterhead. Thus, personal messages may be misconstrued as official business communications, which can have various troubling consequences for the employer, such as harming its reputation.

Since the ECPA applies to e-mail services engaged in the business of transmitting interstate communications, employers have to be mindful of *Watkins* if they wish to access e-mail sent via these services. The applicability of the ECPA to internal corporate e-mail systems is not altogether clear, though. However, even when the federal act does not cover private internal e-mail systems, there are state statutes, constitutions, and common law that could be relevant. The following case provides a glimpse at how one court approached the subject of privacy in the context of corporate e-mail systems.

MICHAEL A. SMYTH V. THE PILLSBURY COMPANY
District Court for the Eastern District of Pennsylvania, 1996

FACTS: The Pillsbury Co. maintained an e-mail system in order to promote internal corporate communications between its employees. Pillsbury repeatedly assured its employees, including Michael Smyth, a regional operations manager, that all e-mail communications would remain confidential and privileged. Pillsbury further assured its employees that e-mail communications could not be intercepted and used by Pillsbury against its employees as grounds for termination or reprimand.

In October 1994, Smyth received certain e-mail communications from his supervisor over Pillsbury's e-mail system on his computer at home. In reliance

continued . . .

on Pillsbury's assurances regarding its e-mail system, Smyth responded and exchanged e-mails with his supervisor. At some later date, contrary to the assurances of confidentiality made by Pillsbury, company employees intercepted Smyth's private e-mail messages made in October 1994. According to Pillsbury, the e-mails concerned sales management and contained threats to "kill the backstabbing bastards" and referred to a planned holiday party as the "Jim Jones Koolaid affair." On January 17, 1995, Pillsbury notified Smyth that it was terminating his employment effective February 1, 1995 for transmitting what it deemed to be inappropriate and unprofessional comments over Pillsbury's e-mail system.

Smyth sued, alleging that he was wrongfully discharged because his termination was grounded on a violation of his right to privacy. Pillsbury asked the court to dismiss the case, arguing that Smyth would not be entitled to relief even if his recital of the facts were true.

DECISION AND REASONING: Pennsylvania is an employment-at-will jurisdiction and an employer may discharge an employee with or without cause, at pleasure, unless restrained by some contract. However, in the most limited of circumstances, exceptions have been recognized where discharge of an at-will employee threatens or violates a clear mandate of public policy. To date, the Pennsylvania Superior Court has only recognized three such exceptions. First, an employee may not be fired for serving on jury duty. Second, an employer may not deny employment to a person with a prior conviction. And finally, an employee may not be fired for reporting violations of federal regulations to the Nuclear Regulatory Commission. As this shows, a public policy exception must be clearly defined.

Smyth claims that his termination was in violation of public policy which precludes an employer from terminating an employee in violation of the employee's right to privacy as embodied in Pennsylvania common law. In support for this proposition, Smyth directs our attention to a decision by our Court of Appeals in *Borse v. Pierce Goods Shop, Inc.* In *Borse*, the plaintiff sued her employer alleging wrongful discharge as a result of her refusal to submit to a urinalysis screening and personal property searches at her work place pursuant to the employer's drug and alcohol policy. The Court of Appeals in *Borse* observed that one of the torts which Pennsylvania recognizes as encompassing an action for invasion of privacy is the tort of intrusion upon seclusion. As noted by the Court of Appeals, the Restatement (Second) of Torts defines the tort as follows:

> One who intentionally intrudes, physically or otherwise, upon the solitude or seclusion of another or his private affairs or concerns, is subject to liability to the other for invasion of his privacy, if the intrusion would be highly offensive to a reasonable person.

continued . . .

continued . . .

Applying the Restatement definition of the tort of intrusion upon seclusion to the facts and circumstances of this case, we find that Smyth has failed to state a claim upon which relief can be granted. In the first instance, unlike urinalysis and personal property searches, we do not find a reasonable expectation of privacy in e-mail communications voluntarily made by an employee to his supervisor over the company e-mail system, notwithstanding any assurances that such communications would not be intercepted by management. Once Smyth communicated the alleged unprofessional comments to a second person (his supervisor) over an e-mail system which was apparently utilized by the entire company, any reasonable expectation of privacy was lost. Significantly, Pillsbury did not require Smyth, as in the case of urinalysis or personal property search, to disclose any personal information about himself. Rather, Smyth voluntarily communicated the alleged unprofessional comments over the company e-mail system. We find no privacy interests in such communications.

In the second instance, even if we found that an employee had a reasonable expectation of privacy in the contents of his e-mail communications over the company e-mail system, we do not find that a reasonable person would consider Pillsbury's interception of these communications to be a substantial and highly offensive invasion of his privacy. Again, we note that by intercepting such communications, the company is not, as in the case of urinalysis or personal property searches, requiring the employee to disclose any personal information about himself or invading the employee's person or personal effects. Moreover, the company's interest in preventing inappropriate and unprofessional comments or even illegal activity over its e-mail system outweighs any privacy interest the employee may have in those comments.

In sum, we find that Pillsbury's actions did not tortiously invade Smyth's privacy and, therefore, did not violate public policy. As a result, Pillsbury's motion to dismiss is granted.

The result in *Pillsbury* seems harsh, and it might be a mistake for an employer to assume that courts in all states will take such a strict view about the privacy of e-mail communications. Many courts are likely to align their decisions more closely on the principles that underlie the ECPA.[50] Therefore, the best general advice that can be given to an employer who wants the ability to intercept or obtain employee e-mail messages is that the employer should follow the philosophical content of *Watkins*. For instance, the employer might consider instituting a policy that e-mail is to be used only for business purposes. This reduces an employee's claim to some expectation of personal privacy and strengthens the employer's allegation that there was a legitimate business purpose for its actions. The employer also should notify all employees that e-mail messages may be intercepted and read by the employer. Acceptance of work responsibilities by the employee with knowledge of this general review policy may be construed as implied consent. In addition, the employer should consider a requirement that all employees provide written consent for their e-mail messages to be monitored. Finally, employers must always carefully review their intentions to read e-mail messages in light of specific applicable state policies. For example, Maryland and Florida have laws that specifically prohibit employers from monitoring e-mail without an employee's consent.[51] Similarly, employers should conscientiously monitor pressures emerging at the federal level to more comprehensively protect personal privacy in the workplace. For instance, the Privacy for Consumers and Workers Act, which was proposed in 1993, would have required employers to notify employees about e-mail monitoring policies, along with providing other specific safeguards to protect the privacy of e-mail messages.

Measures to Protect Privacy in Communications

Anonymity

When individuals engage in conversation, they may protect their privacy by guarding their identities or the contents of their discussions. People often enjoy anonymity in their normal day-to-day routines. Have you ever met a total stranger and had an extremely relaxed and enjoyable conversation? Sometimes it can be cathartic to open yourself up to people who have no way of knowing who you are. Or think what you might do if you wanted to disclose information about someone who made you mad. Would you consider using a pay phone because you suspect that the call could not somehow be traced back to you? There are many reasons why individuals may want to protect their identities; most of these are harmless or even beneficial. For instance, anonymity allows people to discuss personal problems, test ideas, play jokes, file complaints, and ask dumb questions without fear of personal reprisals or embarrasement.[52]

When written messages are sent through the mail, anonymity can be maintained only by eliminating ways to trace the notes back to the sender. Thus, the author obviously should not put a return address on the envelope, and may want to use a common printer rather than write the note in long-hand. In addition, it may help to send the note from an arbitrary location, so that the postmark does not reveal any information. Those who want to preserve their anonymity on the Internet also must take appropriate precautions to remove leads that may be traced back to them. For starters, one might select an alias as an identifier for e-mail. In this case, the ISP likely knows personal information since it must bill the account, but it normally promises to keep this information confidential, unless forced to reveal it by a civil or criminal subpoena.[53] There are more extensive technical steps, though, that can be used to protect one's identity on the Internet. These include using a series of what are called "anonymous remailers" along with encryption techniques, which together make it very hard to trace a message back to the original sender.[54]

Although anonymity can encourage socially useful actions, it also clearly has its darker side, since it may allow individuals to engage in crimes or other deviant behavior without being detected. Anonymity facilitates deceit by allowing individuals to pretend to be who they are not. Thus, investment swindlers and pedophiles lurk behind the curtain of anonymity. The Internet certainly has not been immune to the potential evils that anonymity breeds. The incidence of fraud on the Internet is legion. But so too are other unlawful acts carried out on-line, such as defamation and copyright infringement. Anonymity also may help those who commit crimes off-line, by shielding their communications and transactions from law enforcement. A recurring question for regulatory policy is how much anonymity should be tolerated on the Net. What can be done to limit illicit behavior without overly stifling the good that might be derived from anonymity? Finding this balance will be one long-term challenge as the Internet continues to develop.

Encryption

Those who engage in conversation or commerce on the Internet often do not care to be anonymous, but they do find it important to protect the contents of their communications from prying eyes. Individuals sometimes want to make sure that employers or others will not be able to read their messages. Companies that want to send trade secret information over the Internet must ensure that their communications are secure. Consumers buying goods over the Web often are reluctant to release financial and credit card information without some guarantee that the information will not fall into the wrong hands. Governments, too, need protection since they so often deal with information that is vital to national security. The reasons for seeking security over the Web are virtually endless. In almost all cases, though, there are well-founded fears that unintended third parties may intercept the communications or find ways to access their contents by cracking the computer systems in which they are stored. In this event, the best protection is to ensure that the uninvited intruders are not able to read or decipher the information that has come into their hands.

Encryption encompasses techniques that translate communications into codes that are difficult for outsiders to read. You probably had your first experience with encryption as a child when you and your friends first cleverly devised schemes to keep you parents from reading your messages. A common first approach usually is to equate a number with each letter of the alphabet. All the parents can see, then, are sets of numbers. However, your friends can translate the number codes back to text simply by knowing the coding system or translation "key." Of course, parents are smart, and they can figure out the coding system if they really want to take the time to do so. Also, anytime you want to send a coded message to someone new, you have to find a way to get the key into their hands. Unfortunately, this transaction entails risk since it opens an opportunity for the parents or others to view the key. It also stretches the notions of trust, since the new recipient may lose the key or simply divulge the system.

With computers, messages now can be encoded with extremely sophisticated algorithms. At the same time, though, computers also make it easier for others to crack codes. And as computers get faster, they are more capable at deciphering encrypted text. Thus, there is a constant battle to use increasingly complex coding systems to keep the ever-speedier computers from being able to determine the keys. The strength of encryption products currently are measured in "bits"; the higher the number of bits used to encode the information, the harder it is for computers to determine the key. A rule of thumb is that each additional bit doubles the strength of the system. So, given the state of technology in 1998, a 40-bit system could be cracked in an hour while a 56-bit system might take a day. According to one estimate, though, a 128-bit system would take a "trillion trillion years" to decipher.[55] Thus, those wishing to maximize the security of their information certainly want to use systems using greater than 56-bit keys and obviously would prefer to use 128-bit systems, if allowed.

No matter how sophisticated the key, however, one still needs to find ways to minimize the risks when giving out that key to others. Fortunately, developers of encryption technologies have devised a very clever solution to this dilemma. The technique depends on the use of two keys, a "public" key that can be given to anybody, and a "private" key, which is kept securely in the hands of a particular individual. When the individual encrypts a message with the private key, all those who hold the public key may decrypt it. At the same time, messages that are encrypted using the public key may be decrypted only with the private key. This combination results in a number of powerful tools.

Suppose that two friends, Mike and Sarah, want to have a secure communication. To do this, Mike can give Sarah his public key, and Sarah may give Mike her public key. When Mike writes to Sarah, he can use Sarah's public key. This is secure, since only she can read it using her private key. Similarly, Sarah can write to Mike and encode the message using his public key. Mike, though, may be concerned because his public key is freely available. Perhaps someone with his public key is simply pretending to be Sarah. In fact, Sarah may not have written to Mike at all. The public-key, private-key system can be used to prevent impersonation also. To accomplish this, Sarah can encrypt her message with Mike's public key, and then encrypt that coded result with her own private key. To read this message, Mike must decrypt it with Sarah's public key and his own private key. The fact that the message could be decrypted with Sarah's public key means that she must have sent it, since her public key is only effective when her private key has been used to encrypt the original message. These principles are illustrated in Exhibit 8.4.

Note that the system can be used just as effectively in commercial settings as personal ones. Merchants can have public and private keys just as easily as individuals. But commercial transactions raise more complicated questions and problems, which now are in the process of being solved. For instance, Pete and Lucy may use their public and private keys to set up a business transaction. How does Lucy really know that Pete is who he says he is? After all, she may never have met him in person nor have any verification except his word. This problem can be dealt with using "certificate authorities," which vouch for certain levels of personal information about keyholders. If Lucy does not trust Pete, Pete may go to a certificate authority for verification. Pete can show the certificate authority whatever documentation the authority needs for it to certify specified personal information. The certificate authority then can create a statement verifying that the public key for a particular message belongs to Pete, and, if desired, providing other information about Pete, such as when he was born. This information is encrypted with the certificate

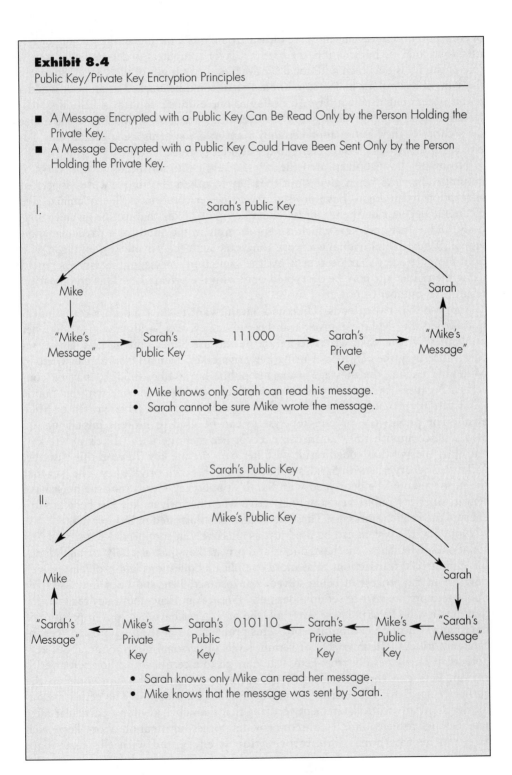

Exhibit 8.4
Public Key/Private Key Encryption Principles

- A Message Encrypted with a Public Key Can Be Read Only by the Person Holding the Private Key.
- A Message Decrypted with a Public Key Could Have Been Sent Only by the Person Holding the Private Key.

I.

Sarah's Public Key

Mike   Sarah

"Mike's ⟶ Sarah's ⟶ 111000 ⟶ Sarah's ⟶ "Mike's
Message"   Public Key   Private   Message"
                                             Key

- Mike knows only Sarah can read his message.
- Sarah cannot be sure Mike wrote the message.

II.

Sarah's Public Key

Mike's Public Key

Mike   Sarah

"Sarah's ⟵ Mike's ⟵ Sarah's 010110 ⟵ Sarah's ⟵ Mike's ⟵ "Sarah's
Message"   Private   Public   Private   Public   Message"
            Key   Key   Key   Key

- Sarah knows only Mike can read her message.
- Mike knows that the message was sent by Sarah.

Exhibit 8.5
Business Transactions and the Use of Certificate Authorities

■ Certificate Authority (CA) Validates the Identification of the Person Releasing the Public Key and Holding the Private Key.

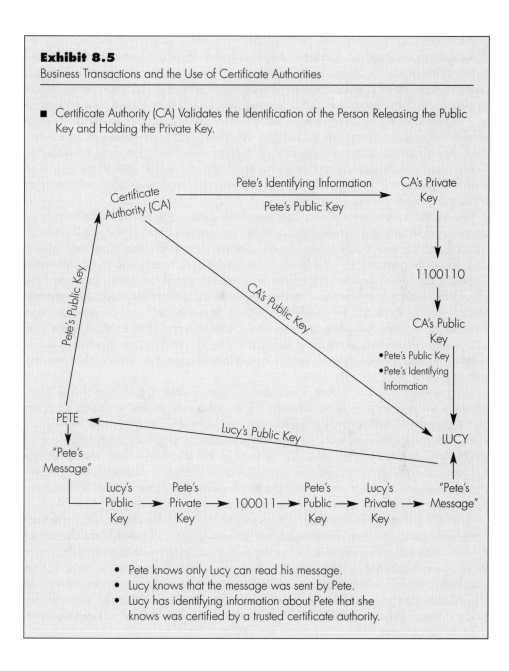

- Pete knows only Lucy can read his message.
- Lucy knows that the message was sent by Pete.
- Lucy has identifying information about Pete that she knows was certified by a trusted certificate authority.

authority's private key. When Lucy receives Pete's documents, she can verify who he is by relying on the statement of the certificate authority, which she knows is genuine, since she needed the authority's public key to decrypt the message. As long as Lucy trusts the certificate authority, she can proceed safely with the transaction.[56] Exhibit 8.5 shows how certificate authorities are used to validate identities.

Although encryption has many beneficial uses, the U.S. government is very concerned about the proliferation of strong encryption systems. Law enforcement and national intelligence officials have depended on wiretapping for years. However, if those engaged in criminal or threatening activities used 128-bit encryption devices to code their conversations and documents, they would then have a new and virtually impenetrable shield against detection. The government is particularly concerned that foreign sources may use powerful encryption technologies to hide activities that threaten national security or further international drug trafficking. Therefore, the U.S. government has supported initiatives that give it the legal and technical power to "break" strongly encrypted communications when necessary to further important national interests.

One of the earlier efforts dates back to 1993, when the Clinton administration announced that it was studying a policy, advocated by the National Security Agency, which effectively would have required those wishing to secure phone and data communications to rely on a particular data encryption chip, called the Clipper Chip. The purpose of the plan was to ensure that the government had the capability to decode messages, if necessary, by being able to gain access to the numerical encryption keys. To ensure the highest degree of personal privacy, the keys were to be divided into two pieces, which would have been held separately in escrow by different government agencies. Under the plan, a government official would have been able to obtain both pieces of any key only with a wiretap warrant.

Civil libertarians and industry executives, among others, objected to the plan. To them, there was something wrong with an arrangement under which a person was permitted to lock items up for security, but only if the government were given a copy of the key. Some worried that the government computers storing the keys might be violated, thereby allowing the keys to get into the wrong hands. Others did not trust the government to use the keys responsibly. Although the government's national security and criminal enforcement justifications did find sympathetic audiences, the Clipper Chip plan ultimately became shelved.

The U.S. government nonetheless took steps to control the sale of encryption devices in international markets through export regulations.[57] Indeed, until the end of 1998, it was very difficult to get a license to export encryption products that were more powerful than 40-bit technology. With the speed of modern computers, that essentially provided no protection at all. Those wishing to sell encryption products argued that foreign businesses already had the technical capabilities to manufacture much stronger products, and that the export controls therefore would merely allow them to take charge of lucrative foreign markets.

In December 1998, the Clinton administration issued new regulations that loosened export controls over encryption products.[58] Under this arrangement, weak encryption products using 56-bit technology or less still had to be reviewed for export licenses, but they normally received approval without much difficulty. However, encryption products employing stronger technology had to include some method by which law enforcement authorities in possession of a court order could gain access to the keys. This often involved an escrow plan, not unlike that proposed with the Clipper Chip. The regulations also provided for exemptions when the encryption products were designated for use in specified industries in approved regions. For instance, one was allowed to export strong encryption products to financial institutions, insurance companies, and certain types of health and medical organizations without incorporating methods for the government to recover the keys. The approved regions included Western Europe and Australia, among other important markets. The regulation included other exemptions as well, such as for exports designed to be used in wholly owned subsidiaries.

During the mid- and late-1990s, there were ongoing efforts in Congress to further loosen export controls on encryption products. For instance, for several years Congress debated the Security and Freedom Through Encryption Act, which would have allowed unrestricted export of nonmilitary encryption products without capabilities to access the keys. Other bills in Congress, though, more closely mirrored administration policy, reflecting concerns of security and law enforcement agencies. At the same time, there also were court challenges to the export regulations, usually on First Amendment grounds.[59] At least one of these initially was successful, when Dan Bernstein, a mathematics professor at the University of Illinois, sued the State Department after the agency denied his request that he be allowed to post the source code for an encryption formula on the Internet without a license. The appellate court panel determined that source code written for academic purposes by scientists was protected speech, and that the export regulations provided the government too much discretion to control the dissemination of ideas.[60]

In January 2000, the Commerce Department again substantially relaxed export controls over encryption products.[61] The revised policy removed licensing requirements for retail encryption products, regardless of their strength, exported to any country except certain terrorist nations. For some products, there still may be minor technical review requirements. In addition, post-export reports may have to be filed under some circumstances. The policy also withdrew licensing and technical review restrictions on source code that is available to the public. Civil libertarians hailed this new approach, as did purveyors of high-technology communications products that depend on encryption to protect privacy.

As this new policy was being formulated, the Clinton administration took steps designed clearly to appease law enforcement interests. For instance, it asked Congress to appropriate $500 million to help law enforcement officials deal with encrypted criminal communications. In addition, the administration asked Congress to consider legislation that it drafted called the Cyberspace Electronic Security Act.[62] The most controversial provision of this proposal would provide criminal investigators with increased powers to obtain warrants, allowing them to search covertly through personal computers for passwords and to install devices overriding encryption programs. Another section would allow the government to refuse to disclose how it recovered encrypted information used against a defendant in the course of a criminal proceeding. Clearly, public policy makers still are struggling to find the right balance between privacy concerns and the needs of national security. There is no reason to believe that the debate will end anytime soon.

Data Collection

An important attribute of personal privacy is that one can act as one wants without fearing that the behavior will be recorded in a form that is accessible to public scrutiny. If I go to a video store alone, for instance, I may take a peek at the covers of certain X-rated films, just for curiosity. Frankly, I am embarrassed to be near the section, but then, if anyone sees me there, it will only be the sales clerk, who does not know me. Imagine my reaction, then, if that sales clerk notes my name when I use my club card to rent *Titanic*, and then puts me on a list of those showing an interest in pornography.[63] That list may be sent to marketing firms that then send me catalogues for sex-related merchandise. All of a sudden, I am pegged as a sexual pervert in public eyes. Who else will get this list? Will I be branded a potential pedophile by the FBI? When information is recorded, all kinds of fears may be tapped. Who will have access to the information? What purposes will it be used for? What will happen to me if the information is not recorded correctly?

There have always been fears about data collection in the United States. But the computer revolution has greatly magnified the concerns and suspicions. Most people know that there are bits and pieces of information residing in public files if someone has the wherewithal to find them. For instance, real estate records and bankruptcy filings are public records at county courthouses. So too is information about lawsuits.[64] Until 1999, motor vehicle departments in many states allowed much of their information to be accessed easily by the public.[65] Thus, a lot of personal information, such as one's address, telephone number, age, height, and weight now reside in databases. Some departments even released medical limitations, Social Security numbers, and photographs. Did you ever obtain a fishing license? That information likely resides in a public database. Before computers, these data fragments were not of great concern because it was too hard for anyone to collect and organize it all into any form of useful profile. But this is no longer the case. Now there are private data warehousing firms that use vastly capable computer systems to access, store, and collate huge banks of information collected from these publicly available sources.[66] But this is only the beginning of the story. Think about what might happen when you use one of those supermarket discount cards to purchase groceries. When you applied for that card, you likely provided at least your name and address. Now all those items that were scanned into the supermarket's computers at checkout may be coupled specifically with you. How would you feel if that information also ended up in the computer files of a data warehouse corporation? And then there are your credit card purchases. And your magazine subscriptions. Suddenly, there are firms that may know more about you than you care to remember.

The ways that computers process the information have become more sophisticated also. It used to be that marketing firms would evaluate databases only to answer specific questions. For instance, they might crunch the numbers to see if there were any correlation between those buying diapers and purchasers of over-the-counter sleep aids. If so, then the information could be used to help target advertisements for these products. Modern mathematical and statistical techniques, however, now can sift through the data and find meaningful relationships without having to address specific hypotheses. And sometimes the results can be surprising. For example, the traditional wisdom in insurance circles was that drivers of performance sports cars were more likely to have accidents than were other motorists. However, one insurance company unexpectedly learned by using new computer analytical methods, that the accident rate with sports cars was not excessive when there were other cars in the household. This information allowed it to offer lower rates to some sports car owners.[67] Based on these new methods, firms now can build marketing profiles based on certain demographic and purchasing patterns to predict various kinds of potential interests and future behavior.[68]

Until recently, there has not been sufficient public interest to motivate Congress to pass many comprehensive laws governing the collection and dissemination of personal information. The federal Right to Financial Privacy Act restricts the federal government from reviewing bank account records but does not cover state agencies or private employers. There also is the Fair Credit Reporting Act, which limits access to credit reports, but it has notable exceptions for those having legitimate business needs to access such information. Federal regulation of personal information therefore has traditionally been somewhat spotty in the United States. Legislators, though, have begun to give this topic substantially more attention. Spurred by rapid advances in computer capabilities and in other technologies, the public has become alarmed about privacy intrusions on numerous fronts. Many of the concerns regard government initiatives that depend on the collection of data, such as health care proposals and efforts to track child support payments.[69] Others relate to the amount of information that private companies may access from governmental sources. For instance, in 1999, privacy concerns emerged after at least two states began to transfer files of driver's license photographs to Image Data, a private company involved with new methods to deter identity fraud.[70] Image Data's goal was to establish a computerized method for retailers to verify the identity of customers by enabling them to visually match the customers' appearances with their photographs. However, privacy advocates worried that the pictures might become available to others, such as telemarketers or detectives. In fact, there are a host of other emerging identity detection systems, such as retina scans and thumbprint readers, which raise similar privacy concerns since they depend on centralized databases of personal information. Private businesses have begun to take steps to qualm the fears of their customers before legislators feel compelled to act. Some supermarkets, for example, have dropped their discount card programs. However, these steps may not be enough to thwart new regulatory attention.

Data Collection on the Internet   Of all the modern technologies, the Internet is most responsible for the rising levels of concerns about the privacy of personal information. It is not simply that the Internet now gives individuals the opportunity to easily access enormous banks of information that once were available only to the most dedicated information sleuths. In addition, and perhaps more frightening, the Internet has become an extremely powerful tool that enables firms to actually create and disseminate new files of personal information. On one level, this may be viewed as an extension of methods already used off-line. For example, Internet businesses may record the items purchased by a customer and then use or sell that information for marketing purposes. However, Internet techniques enable merchants to monitor much more about what their customers do. For example, there likely have been occasions when you returned to an Internet page and you saw that previously explored items were highlighted in a distinctive color. Did you ever wonder how the Internet service knew what you had viewed on earlier visits? This is accomplished through a file, called a "cookie," that the service places on your computer to store various kinds of information.[71] For instance, a cookie may contain a special identification number assigned by the service to your computer. This does not, by itself, allow the service to know who you are, but it does permit it to determine if your computer has previously communicated with the Web site. The cookie also may store passwords that you selected so that you do not have to remember or retype them. In addition, a cookie may record your history of mouse clicks (sometimes called your "clickstream"), which then can be used by the Web service to refresh your memory—through the distinctive colors—about where you may have been before.

Cookies clearly have a number of functions that make life easier for Internet customers. However, they also raise privacy concerns, particularly with their ability to link clickstreams and search requests with particular computers.[72] Now, Internet services can act like the sales clerk at the video store, recording every item that draws your attention. Even without knowing who you are, this information can be enormously valuable to the site and to others. For instance, the Internet site might determine which of its services are most often accessed by purchasers, and then invest more resources into improving the information provided there. Marketers can use the information to improve their profiles about shopping behavior. Also, the information further enables Web sites to target advertisements to customers who are most likely to be interested in them. For example, all you have to do is read an article about golf on a general new service, and your computer may be noted as a good prospect for golf club or golfing vacation advertisements. This, in itself, may be somewhat disquieting. You may have thought that you were reading in the privacy of your own home, but in reality, you were engaging in a very public activity, where others may have been peering over your shoulder to determine what interests you. You might at least take some solace in the fact that the Web site does not know your name or who you are.[73] But, if you somehow volunteered that information, then your clickstreams all of a sudden may be pegged not just to your computer, but to you. And when you think about it, you may determine that you actually did provide this information, such as when you first registered to access the site or entered your name in a contest to win NCAA Final Four basketball tickets. Now consider how data warehousing firms might couple all this new information about you with their more traditional sources of personal data.[74] It is no wonder that a 1998 poll found that over 80% of Internet users were concerned about threats to their personal privacy.[75]

By 1998, Congress began to consider a number of bills dealing with the ways that Internet companies obtain and disseminate information.[76] However, the government put most of these in a holding pattern, based on some realistic expectations that industry members might be able to reduce anxieties about privacy without legislative interference. The problem for legislators is that companies often provide better services when they have more information. I may like the conveniences that cookies provide. Indeed, I already have the technical ability to erase or prohibit them on my browser if I choose, so banning them may seem like overkill. Similarly, I may appreciate the increased personal attention that sites can provide to me based on the information they obtain about my buying habits or needs. I may even value the specialized efforts that other firms direct toward me. Freedom of choice is a basic and powerful norm in U.S. society. Such freedom, however, is contingent on full disclosure of relevant information. For there to be real freedom, individuals must understand the terms under which their choices are made. Regarding the release of personal information, they should (1) be aware that personal information is being collected, (2) know how the information might be used, (3) be told how long the information might be stored, and (4) be informed of the conditions under which the information might be shared with others. If these concerns are addressed by the industry, pressures for regulation likely will ease. On the other hand, if the industry fails to meet these conditions, then government regulation surely will be forthcoming.[77]

Since freedom depends on the ability to make intelligent and informed choices, the government often directs special scrutiny when industry members appear to be taking advantage of the naivete of children. This has been no less the case with practices regarding the collection of personal information. By the late 1990s, many Web sites offered games, contests, and products to children who simply filled out application forms.[78] Spurred by the virtually blind desire to obtain attractive benefits, kids eagerly provided just about any information that the Web sites requested. Through these methods, operators were able to learn much more than the names and addresses of the children, however. For example, some Web sites also required children to submit personal information about other family members and their friends. In 1998, the government responded by passing the Children's Online Privacy Protection Act.[79] The act prohibits operators of Web sites or other online services directed to children from collecting personal information from children under the age of 13 unless the operators comply with FTC regulations authorized by the act. According to the act, the FTC regulations must require the operators to do the following:

1. Provide parents notice about their information collection and use practices;
2. Obtain verifiable parental consent for the collection, use and/or disclosure of personal information from children (with certain specified exceptions);
3. Provide parents with the ability to review the personal information collected from their children;
4. Provide parents with the opportunity to prevent further collection of information or use of information that already had been collected;
5. Limit collection of personal information for a child's participation in a game or prize offer to that which is reasonably necessary for the activity; and
6. Establish reasonable procedures to protect the confidentiality, security, and integrity of the personal information collected.

In October 1999, the FTC passed the regulations specified by the Child Online Privacy Protection Act.[80] The rules apply to operators of commercial Web sites and online services that are at least partly directed to children who are under 13 years old. As required by the federal legislation, the FTC regulations cover such topics as notice, parental consent and confidentiality, and provide for substantial civil penalties for violations of their terms.

INDUSTRY INITIATIVES TO PROTECT DATA PRIVACY ON THE INTERNET   Prompted by legislative proposals affecting interactions with adults, Internet ventures began to take meaningful steps in the late 1990s to notify customers about their data collection and privacy policies. In this regard, the Internet industry rallied behind three major initiatives. One was devised by TRUSTe, a labeling and certification organization sponsored by the Electronic Frontier Foundation and CommerceNet.[81] TRUSTe licenses logos, called "Trustmarks," that designate the strength of a participant's privacy practices. These range from "No Exchange," indicating that the site uses only personal information for billing and to carry out transactions, to "3rd Party Exchange," which warns that information may be collected and disclosed to third parties. Even in the latter case, though, the site is obligated to explain the kinds of personally identifiable information that might be gathered, what it will be used for, and with whom it might be shared. Participants are required to sign contracts in which they pledge to uphold their Trustmark obligations. They also are encouraged to have their data processing systems audited by an accounting firm. TRUSTe attempts to monitor compliance by seeding sites with false data, which is instructive if that information turns up somewhere else. TRUSTe also runs its own spot check audits.

A second set of ventures had similar objectives.[82] Industry organizations, such as the Alliance for Privacy, a group of over 50 key corporations and trade groups, issued guidelines instructing members what steps they must take to protect the privacy of Web customers. As with TRUSTe, the participants must inform customers about the kinds of information that will be gathered and how it might be shared. The guidelines also demand that customers be provided with "opt-out" privileges, meaning that they can request to be taken off marketing lists. In addition, the guidelines require stricter care when children are involved, such as by ensuring parental permission before asking kids for personal data.

The most ambitious plan is called the Platform for Privacy Preferences, or P3.[83] According to this standard, customers can fill out profile forms where they precisely indicate how much privacy they wish to be accorded to various kinds of information. For instance, a customer might specify that designated on-line merchants may relay promotional material on certain kinds of books, but that they may not share these preferences with others. The forms reside on the customers' PCs and can be accessed automatically by Web sites. A Web site also may use similar procedures to automate its side of the transaction. Thus, if its policies do not conform to the preferences established by a customer, then the customer will not be able to transact business at the site. In a sense, the site and the customer automatically negotiate the kinds of information that might be collected and the degree of privacy that will be accorded to it. This format appeals to many privacy advocates because it allows customers tremendous flexibility in fashioning their privacy preferences. In this way, it furthers freedom of choice. However, there still are concerns about whether industry participants truly will comply with their promises. Nonetheless, the combination of these efforts was enough to convince the FTC in 1999 to recommend to Congress that no new privacy laws were needed to police the privacy of personal information.[84]

EUROPEAN UNION DIRECTIVE ON INFORMATION PRIVACY PROTECTION On October 24, 1998, a sweeping European Union directive governing the collection and processing of personal information came into effect.[85] Since this is a directive and not a Regulation, the 15 member nations must enact laws that conform to the directive's principles. The basic purpose of the directive is to ensure that personal data is processed fairly and with informed consent. In this regard, the directive provides that companies involved with data processing have fundamental obligations to ensure that personal data are:

1. collected and processed for specified, explicit, and legitimate purposes;
2. adequate, relevant, and not excessive in relation to the purposes for which they are collected;
3. accurate and updated when necessary; and
4. kept in a form that permits identification of individuals for no longer than necessary, given the purposes of the processing.

Based on these principles, individuals have certain rights regarding the collection of personal information. For instance, as a general rule, individuals must unambiguously give consent to the processing of personal data.[86] They also are entitled to gain access to the data and to have the data rectified or erased if it is incomplete or inadequate. In addition, they have the right to object to data processing for the purposes of direct marketing.[87] Companies, on the other hand, have numerous disclosure obligations, including requirements to inform individuals when and why information may be collected and whether it might be disclosed or made accessible to others.

From the standpoint of the United States, possibly the most important feature of the Directive is that it prohibits the transfer of personal data to countries outside the EU that do not guarantee an "adequate level of protection." As we have just seen, there are very few laws in the United States that enforce privacy obligations. Instead, the United States has been moving in the direction of relying on industry guidelines and practices to ensure the privacy of personal information. The directive does not precisely define what measures are adequate, but rather indicates that the adequacy must be judged in light of all the circumstances. In this regard, the Directive states that particular consideration should be given to the following factors:

1. the nature of the data;
2. the purpose and duration of the processing;
3. the country of origin and the country of final destination;
4. the rules of law in the destination country; and
5. the professional rules and security measures that are complied with in the destination country.

The directive also provides for circumstances when data may be transferred to countries that do not provide adequate levels of protection, but these conditions are not well defined and often require the permission of administrative bodies.[88]

If it is determined that the United States does not provide an adequate level of protection, then many operations that depend on the transfer of personal data from Europe may be hampered.[89] For instance, those involved with maintaining centralized human resources records that contain benefits information or skills databases may have to be careful. Businesses that depend on processing personal data, such as investment banking, consulting, and auditing, also have reasons to study the directive closely. Obviously, direct marketing operations are affected. Some even speculate that the U.S. press, which is used to substantial freedoms in the United States, may need to think twice before reporting personal information on people in Europe.[90] Of most importance here, though, is the effect that the directive has on e-commerce operations on the Internet.[91] Many of the data collection methods described in this section will violate European laws unless U.S. levels of protection are deemed adequate. In 1998, the Clinton administration embarked on negotiations with the European Union to determine what must be done for U.S. levels of protection to meet European standards. The U.S. delegation argued that voluntary industry guidelines regarding privacy protection should suffice. However, EU officials at first were reluctant to accept them, due mostly to concerns about enforcement.

In March 2000, EU and U.S. negotiators agreed to a set of principles, based on self-regulation and government oversight, that would satisfy EU requirements that there be an adequate level of protection.[92] In a nutshell, U.S. companies receiving personal data from the EU must conform to conditions about notice, choice (such as the ability to opt-out or opt-in), onward transfer, security, data integrity, access, and enforcement. Companies may comply with these principles by joining a self-regulatory body that adheres to the principles or by instituting their own conforming practices. Government oversight is provided through reporting requirements to the Department of Commerce and through Federal Trade commission enforcement actions for unfair and deceptive practices. As this book goes to press, the agreement still must be formally approved with the EU and the United States. If it is adopted, as expected, then U.S. companies adhering to the principles will benefit, since they finally will know that they can transfer data from the EU without having to fear prosecution in the EU for violations of data protection policies.

Content Control and the Regulation of Indecent Speech

The Communications Decency Act of 1996   There can be little doubt that the Internet has brought enormous benefits to society. Just think of all the ways that it has made your life easier and more satisfying. You now can easily access information, engage in commerce, communicate with friends and within communities, and enjoy entertainment comfortably from your own home or place of business. That one can find much to commend with the Internet, however, does not mean that everything about it is necessarily "good." We have already discussed the ways that it facilitates copyright piracy. But for those who find fault with the Internet, the overriding concern almost always has to do with access to pornographic materials, especially by children. To some, the Internet is a sewer of smut that is constantly enticing children who are only fingertips away. Many parents are disgusted with what can be found on the Web and want their children to have no part of it. But kids can be hard to control, especially when prurient subject matter is so pervasive. And then there are the problems with lewd and licentious individuals who lurk the Net waiting to communicate with children via e-mail, chat rooms, and other discussion forums. The family unit is sanctified in the United States and many other countries. When social elements challenge the ability of families to determine their collective fates, strong reactions can be expected. In a sense, family decisions are private and should not be subjected to unwarranted intrusions from outside sources. By this notion, the availability of pornography on the Internet may be seen as a threat to the privacy interests of the family.

As we have seen, companies having operations that touch on privacy concerns have to tread very carefully. In these situations, special interest groups usually are more than ready to ask the legislatures to fashion remedies that appear to address their concerns. Legislative solutions, though, often cut a wide swath, reaching beyond the objectionable behavior and inhibiting activities that many people would prefer to enjoy freely. Offensive speech, therefore, may affect privacy interests in different ways. On the one hand, the speech may interfere with the privacy to determine what one sees or hears. On the other hand, regulation of that speech may affect rights to receive the kinds of information and materials that one wishes to enjoy. The companies may be in the best position to ward off both of these privacy issues if they can implement their own measures to address serious objections, since there then would be little coordinated motivation to seek legislative remedies. As we shall see, such technologies now are rapidly being developed, and the industry is beginning to adopt them. However, the technological solutions did not come in time to prevent hostility in the 1990s to the widespread availability of indecent materials.

The First Amendment prohibits the government from abridging the freedom of speech. Free discourse of ideas is considered essential to a democratic society. Therefore, any action that the government takes which might limit the ability to air views will be looked at with the closest scrutiny. Some limited types of speech, however, are not highly valued, and so they receive less protection from the First Amendment. Forms of communication that are "obscene," defamatory, or consist of "fighting words" are the most notable. For the government to regulate any other kinds of speech, though, it must have compelling justifications. In addition, the regulation must be narrowly tailored so that the government's purposes are satisfied in the least burdensome way. The courts have acknowledged that the government does have a legitimate interest in protecting children from harmful speech. This is why children can be prohibited from "R"-rated movies, for instance. When kids are involved, therefore, the inquiry usually focuses on how the regulation burdens the ability of adults to participate in legitimate communications, and whether there are other ways to protect the children while having less extensive effects on adults.

In 1996, the federal government adopted the Communications Decency Act to protect children from exposure to offensive messages and materials over the Internet. Immediately after the president signed the statute, the American Civil Liberties

Union along with several other groups brought suit, alleging that the act violated the First Amendment. The dispute marked a historic juncture for the Internet, since it emotionally involved so much that the public hopes and fears about the Net. It also provided the Supreme Court the opportunity to consider the role of the Internet in society, and how its growth might legally be curtailed.

RENO V. AMERICAN CIVIL LIBERTIES UNION
United States Supreme Court, 1997

FACTS: The American Civil Liberties Union, among other organizations, filed this lawsuit alleging that the Communications Decency Act of 1996 ("CDA") is unconstitutional. One provision of the Act prohibits the knowing transmission of obscene or indecent messages to any recipient under 18 years of age. Another prohibits the knowing sending or displaying of patently offensive messages (as measured by contemporary community standards) in a manner that is available to a person under 18. The Act provides two defenses. One covers those who take good faith, reasonable, effective and appropriate actions to restrict access by minors to the prohibited communications. The other covers those who restrict access to covered material by requiring certain designated forms of age proof, such as a verified credit card or an adult identification number or code.

The District Court ruled that the statute violates the First Amendment because it sweeps more broadly than necessary and thereby chills the expression of adults. The court also concluded that the terms "patently offensive" and "indecent" are too vague to meet constitutional standards of fairness. In addition, the court determined that the defenses are not technologically or economically feasible for most noncommercial providers to use. The District Court therefore enjoined the Government from enforcing the Act except as it relates to obscenity. The Government appealed to the U.S. Supreme Court.

DECISION AND REASONING: At issue is the constitutionality of two statutory provisions enacted to protect minors from "indecent" and "patently offensive" communications on the Internet. Notwithstanding the legitimacy and importance of the congressional goal of protecting children from harmful materials, we agree with the District Court that the statute abridges the freedom of speech protected by the First Amendment.

Anyone with access to the Internet may take advantage of a wide variety of communication and information retrieval methods. These methods are constantly evolving and difficult to categorize precisely. But, as presently constituted, those most relevant to this case are e-mail, automatic mailing list services ("mail exploders," sometimes referred to as "listservs"), newsgroups, chat rooms and the World Wide Web.

continued . . .

Sexually explicit material on the Internet includes text, pictures, and chat and extends from the modestly titillating to the hardest-core. Though such material is widely available, users seldom encounter such content accidentally. Unlike communications received by radio or television, the receipt of information on the Internet requires a series of affirmative steps more deliberate and directed than merely turning a dial.

Systems have been developed to help parents control the material that may be available on a home computer with Internet access. A system may either limit a computer's access to an approved list of sources that have been identified as containing no adult material, it may block designated inappropriate sites, or it may attempt to block messages containing identifiable objectionable features.

Technology exists by which an operator of a Web site may condition access on the verification of requested information such as a credit card number or an adult password. Credit card verification is only feasible, however, either in connection with a commercial transaction in which the card is used, or by payment to a verification agency. Using credit card possession as a surrogate for proof of age would impose costs on non-commercial Web sites that would require many of them to shut down. Moreover, the imposition of such a requirement would completely bar adults who do not have a credit card and lack the resources to obtain one from accessing blocked material.

The Government contends that the CDA is plainly constitutional under our prior decisions. In *Ginsburg v. New York*, we upheld the constitutionality of a New York statute that prohibited selling to minors under 17 years of age material that was considered obscene as to them even if not obscene as to adults. This decision was based in part on the State's interest in protecting the well-being of its youth. However, in important respects, the statute in *Ginsburg* was narrower than the CDA. First, we noted in *Ginsburg* that the prohibition against sales to minors did not bar parents who so desired from purchasing the magazines for their children. Under the CDA, by contrast, neither the parents' consent—nor even their participation—in the communication would avoid application of the statute. Second, the New York statute applied only to commercial transactions, whereas the CDA contains no such limitation. Third, the New York statute cabined its definition of material that is harmful to minors with the requirement that it be utterly without redeeming social importance for minors. The CDA fails to provide us with any definition of the term "indecent" and omits any requirement that "patently offensive" material lack serious literary, artistic, political or scientific value.

In *Renton v. Playtime Theatres, Inc.*, we upheld a zoning ordinance that kept adult movie theaters out of residential neighborhoods. The ordinance was aimed, not at the content of the films shown in the theaters, but rather at

continued . . .

continued . . .

the secondary effects—such as crime and deteriorating property values—that these theaters fostered. According to the Government, the CDA is constitutional because it constitutes a sort of "cyberzoning" on the Internet. But the CDA applies broadly to the entire universe of cyberspace. And the purpose of the CDA is to protect children from the primary effects of "indecent" and "patently offensive" speech, rather than any secondary effect of such speech. Thus, the CDA is a content-based blanket restriction on speech, and as such, cannot be properly analyzed as a form of time, place, and manner regulation.

We have observed that each medium of expression may present its own problems. Thus, some of our cases have recognized special justifications for regulation of the broadcast media that are not applicable to other speakers. In these cases, the Court relied on the history of extensive government regulation of the broadcast medium, the scarcity of available frequencies at its inception, and its invasive nature.

These factors are not present in cyberspace. Neither before or after the enactment of the CDA have the vast democratic fora of the Internet been subject to the type of government supervision and regulation that has attended the broadcast industry. Moreover, the Internet is not as invasive as radio or television. Finally, unlike the conditions that prevailed when Congress first authorized regulation of the broadcast spectrum, the Internet can hardly be considered a scarce expressive commodity. Through the use of chat rooms, any person with a phone line can become a town crier with a voice that resonates farther than it could from any soapbox. Through the use of Web pages, mail exploders, and newsgroups, the same individual can become a pamphleteer. The content on the Internet is as diverse as human thought. There is thus no basis for qualifying the level of First Amendment scrutiny that should be applied to this medium.

There are many ambiguities concerning the scope of the CDA that render it problematic for purposes of the First Amendment. Could a speaker confidently assume that a serious discussion about birth control practices, homosexuality, or the consequences of prison rape would not violate the CDA? This uncertainty undermines the likelihood that the CDA has been carefully tailored to the congressional goal of protecting minors from potentially harmful materials. The vagueness of the CDA is a matter of special concern for two reasons. First, the CDA is a content-based regulation of speech. Second, the CDA is a criminal statute. The severity of criminal sanctions may well cause speakers to remain silent rather than communicate even arguably unlawful words, ideas and images. In contrast to our previous cases, the CDA presents a greater threat of censoring speech that, in fact, falls outside the statute's scope

We are persuaded that the CDA lacks the precision that the First Amendment requires when a statute regulates the content of speech. In order to deny minors access to potentially harmful speech, the CDA effectively suppresses a large amount of speech that adults have a constitutional right to receive and to address to one another. That burden on adult speech is unacceptable if less restrictive alternatives would be at least as effective in achieving the legitimate purpose that the statute was enacted to serve. In evaluating the free speech rights of adults, we have made it perfectly clear that sexual expression which is indecent but not obscene is protected by the First Amendment.

In *Miller v. California*, we set forth the three-prong test for obscene expression which controls to this day: (a) whether the average person, applying contemporary community standards, would find that the work, taken as a whole, appeals to the prurient interest; (b) whether the work depicts or describes, in a patently offensive way, sexual conduct specifically defined by the applicable state law; and (c) whether the work, taken as a whole, lacks serious literary, artistic, political or scientific value.

It is true that we have repeatedly recognized the governmental interest in protecting children from harmful materials. But that interest does not justify an unnecessarily broad suppression of speech addressed to adults. The government may not reduce the adult population to only what is fit for children. Regardless of the strength of the government's interest in protecting children, the level of discourse reaching a mailbox simply cannot be limited to what would be suitable for a sandbox.

The District Court found that at the time of trial, existing technology did not include any effective method for a sender to prevent minors from obtaining access to its communications on the Internet without also denying access to adults. The Court found no effective way to determine the age of a user who is accessing material through e-mail, mail exploders, newsgroups, or chat rooms. As a practical matter, the Court also found that it would be prohibitively expensive for noncommercial—as well as some commercial—speakers who have Web sites to verify that their users are adults. These limitations must inevitably curtail a significant amount of adult communication on the Internet. By contrast, the District Court found that despite its limitations, currently available *user-based* software suggests that a reasonably effective method by which *parents* can prevent their children from accessing sexually explicit and other material which *parents* may believe is inappropriate for their children will soon be available.

The breadth of the CDA's coverage is wholly unprecedented. Unlike the regulations upheld in *Ginsburg*, the scope of the CDA is not limited to commercial speech or commercial entities. Its open-ended prohibitions embrace all nonprofit entities and individuals posting indecent messages or displaying them on their own computers in the presence of minors. The general, undefined terms "indecent" and "patently offensive" cover large amounts of nonpornographic material with serious educational or other value. Moreover, the

continued . . .

continued . . .

community standards criterion as applied to the Internet means that any communication available to a nationwide audience will be judged by the standards of the community most likely to be offended by the message.

The breadth of this content-based restriction of speech imposes an especially heavy burden on the Government to explain why a less restrictive provision would not be as effective as the CDA. It has not done so. The arguments in this Court have referred to possible alternatives such as requiring that indecent material be "tagged" in a way that facilitates parental control of material coming into their homes, making exceptions for messages with artistic or educational value, providing some tolerance for parental choice, and regulating some portions of the Internet—such as commercial Web sites—differently than others, such as chat rooms.

The Government argues that the CDA's defenses make the statute constitutional. First, the government suggests that "tagging" is a "good faith, reasonable, effective and appropriate" action to restrict access by minors. This suggestion assumes that transmitters may encode their indecent communications in a way that would indicate their contents, thus permitting recipients to block their reception with appropriate software. But the requirement that the good faith action be "effective" makes the defense illusory. The Government recognizes that its proposed screening software does not currently exist. Even if it did, there is no way to know whether a potential recipient will actually block the encoded material.

The government also points to the ability to restrict access by requiring use of a verified credit card or adult identification. Such verification is not only technologically available but actually is used by commercial providers of sexually explicit material. These providers, therefore, would be protected by the defense. However, it is not economically feasible for most noncommercial speakers to employ such verification. Thus, ironically, this defense may significantly protect commercial purveyors of obscene postings while providing little (or no) benefit for transmitters of indecent messages that have significant social or artistic value. We agree with the District Court's conclusion that the CDA places an unacceptably heavy burden on protected speech, and that the defenses do not constitute the sort of narrow tailoring that will save it.

The government asserts that—in addition to its interest in protecting children—its equally significant interest in fostering the growth of the Internet provides an independent basis for upholding the constitutionality of the CDA. The Government apparently assumes that the unregulated availability of indecent and patently offensive material on the Internet is driving countless citizens away from the medium because of the risk of exposing themselves or their children to harmful material. We find this argument singularly unpersuasive. The dramatic expansion of this new marketplace of ideas contradicts this contention. The growth of the Internet has been and continues to be phenomenal. In the absence of evidence to the contrary, we presume that governmental regulation of the content of speech is more likely to interfere with the free exchange of ideas than to encourage it. The interest in encouraging freedom of expression in a democratic society outweighs any theoretical but unproven benefit of censorship.

The judgment of the District Court is affirmed.

Private Control Through Labels and Software Filters   The problem with the CDA was not that it tried to protect children from indecent subjects, but that it achieved its objective in ways that overly burdened the rights of adults. The Supreme Court noted positively that user-based software would soon be available that would allow parents to control the types of communications received by their children. Much of the optimism in this regard comes from the Platform for Internet Content Selection (PICS), which was introduced in 1995. PICS essentially is a universal communications language designed so that Internet content and material can be labeled in a way that can be understood by software filters. PICS does not constitute a particular rating system. Rather, it is a protocol that enables ratings to be expressed, transmitted, and understood.[93] The language then opens the way for organizations to conceive of ways to actually rate the content of various Internet sites, and for developers to design software filters that take actions based on selected ratings.

Although the field is evolving quickly, there are two primary forms of rating systems. The first kind is a self-rating system. For this to work, some organization must establish certain labels that might be used to describe content. For instance, there might be labels for nudity, profanity, and violence. A Web site might then decide whether it has profanity and implement a PICS label so that a filter based on the rating scheme could take appropriate action, which likely would be to screen out the site so that an under-aged user would not be exposed to its contents. Although the site operator might be in the best position to know what kind of content resides on the site, one has to worry whether the operator will be honest, since attaching certain labels may reduce visitors and thus decrease potential revenue. Also, minds often differ on what constitutes violence or profanity, leading to inconsistent applications of labels. Self-rating organizations have taken steps to alleviate this latter problem by providing ways to better objectify the meanings of their labels. Nonetheless, the incentives for site owners to "fudge" on the labels they choose remain.

The other way for labels to be created is by independent rating services. Organizations can review the contents of Web sites and then construct databases that rate the sites based on their own criteria. Filtering software then can access these databases and take appropriate actions.[94] The sky is the limit when it comes to the goals of such rating bureaus. Obviously, many organizations rate material that their members consider to be indecent or immoral. Families sharing the same values then can employ filters that prevent access to sites that are given objectionable ratings. But not all ratings have to be negative. Family organizations can develop lists of sites deemed suitable for children. Filters then may grant access only to these sites. Medical organizations could do the same, indicating sites that provide useful information about diseases and treatments. In all of these cases, the trick is finding the organization that is likely to share one's values and that does a thorough job in rating sites on the Web.

Many consider PICS to be exciting because it supports competitive markets in rating systems and in the software that utilizes ratings. If the markets develop as some expect, then Internet participants should have the technological capabilities to substantially control what they or their families might find on the Web. Sure, much of what is going on here is censorship, but consumers have the choice of deciding what censors they want to employ. This is far different from the government deciding for everyone what is or is not acceptable. This is why the First Amendment applies to government actions regarding speech but has nothing to do with the actions of private organizations. Nonetheless, there may be reasons to worry about the development of these private ratings markets.[95] For instance, suppose you notice a rather sudden drop-off in visitors to your site. You may suspect that one of the heavily utilized ratings bureaus has for some reason given your site one of its unsatisfactory ratings. You may have trouble finding out which service is responsible, since the lists often are kept in confidence. After all, many ratings bureau are commercial enterprises that have proprietary interests in the lists that they develop. Even if you can establish that the members of a particular organization gave you a blemished rating, you then may have trouble changing their minds. If the ratings service is sufficiently important, you may suffer from substantial private censorship without any recourse.

Child Online Protection Act of 1998   Content control on the Internet is entering a turbulent period. The government may choose to act or let the private markets adapt on their own. If the government chooses to get involved, there are various ways that it may do so. The CDA was just one possible example, albeit one that was too vague and burdensome to pass constitutional muster. However, the federal government tried again in 1998 by passing the Child Online Protection Act (COPA), which, among other things, had provisions designed to address the accessibility of materials on the Internet that were considered harmful to children.[96] This time, the government attempted to stay within the contours of *Reno* by limiting the reach of COPA and more clearly defining the forms of speech that it covered.

COPA differed from the CDA in the following important respects:

1. It applied only to speech on the *World Wide Web*, and not to chatrooms, e-mail, and other means of communications on the Internet.
2. It applied only to communications made for *commercial* purposes.
3. Violation resulted in civil remedies but *not criminal* remedies.
4. COPA prohibited speech that is *obscene to minors* and defined obscenity in the

same terms that were approved by the Supreme Court in *Reno* and previous cases. This included a requirement that the material lacks serious literary, artistic, political, or scientific value for minors.

5. Minors were defined as persons under 17 years of age.

The government believed that COPA was constitutional because it so closely followed the parameters found lawful in *Ginsburg* and discussed with approval in *Reno*. Once again, though, the ACLU sued, claiming that COPA burdened speech that is constitutionally protected for adults. The district court agreed and granted a preliminary injunction in February 1999.[97] As with the CDA, COPA provided a defense for Web sites that required use of a credit card, adult access code, or adult personal identification numbers. It also allowed sites to rely on digital certificates that verify age or other reasonable and technologically feasible measures. However, the court was concerned that these verification systems might impose substantial economic costs on certain Web site operators. More important, though, the court thought it likely that these measures would deter users from accessing the sites because their use leads to a potential loss of anonymity. This, in turn, might create a disincentive for sites to provide the materials and cause the Web operators to self-censor the content from their pages. The court also believed that the statute likely could be tailored more narrowly to achieve its objectives. First, it was skeptical that COPA really could achieve its objectives, since material that is obscene to minors still could be obtained from foreign Web sites and noncommercial sites. Second, the court was impressed that filtering technologies may be at least as successful in achieving the statute's purposes without imposing the same degree of burden on adults. In April 1999, the government appealed this ruling to the Court of Appeals. Obviously one needs to pay close attention to developments regarding the future of COPA or any other subsequent legislative efforts.

Public Libraries and Filtering Software An interesting related issue regards the ability of public libraries to control the materials their patrons can view over the Internet. In 1997, the public library system in Loudoun County, Virginia, passed a Policy on Internet Sexual Harassment. This policy stated that the county libraries would provide Internet access subject to several restrictions. The most controversial provided that "all library computers would be equipped with site-blocking software to block all sites displaying: (a) child pornography and obscene material and (b) material deemed harmful to juveniles. The justifications for the policy were to minimize access to illegal pornography and the avoidance of a sexually hostile environment. The latter might occur if patrons roaming around the library were unwittingly exposed to degrading images displayed on computer screens. For implementation, the libraries put X-Stop site-blocking software on all their terminals. The method that X-Stop used to determine which sites would be blocked was proprietary. However, it did block sites such as The Safer Sex page, the Books for Gay and Lesbian Teens/Youth page, and the Renaissance Transgender Association page. Several organizations sued the county library system, claiming that the blocking software infringed their First Amendment rights.[98]

The library system argued that it has the right to select the books that it puts on its shelves. Thus, it also may determine what Web sites it "puts" on its computers. The court, though, did not believe that the situation was properly analogized with acquisition decisions. Rather, the court determined that use of blocking software was more like the censorship of content already available at the library. Thus, it would be as if a library used a black marker to line out objectionable passages from its books and magazines.

The court did not believe that the policy was necessary to further compelling interests. First, there was very little evidence that library patrons felt victimized by what they were forced to see on computer screens used by others. Anyway, there were less restrictive ways to police potential harassment problems, such as by installing privacy screens. Regarding the protection of minors, the court believed library staff might simply casually monitor what children were viewing. Or the library might put the filtering software on some machines for children but have other unlimited access machines for adults. The court also surmised that the library might use a filter system that adults easily could turn off. The court, relying on *Reno*, concluded that the filters unnecessarily burdened the rights of adults to access constitutionally protected materials. It thus enjoined use of the filtering software. Subsequent to this decision, the library installed filters that could be turned off by adults.[99] It also allowed parents to sign a statement indicating that their children could have unfiltered access. Clearly, filtering technologies hold much promise in settling the pornography hazards on the Web. But as noted before, they also may raise their own special brand of censorship issues.

DEFAMATION

The growth of electronic communications has brought new life to an old tort, defamation. In simple terms, one engages in defamation by making to the public a false statement about another person that harms that person's reputation. Before the age of computer bulletin boards and Web sites, it was relatively difficult for an individual to broadly disseminate defamatory statements. One might have stood on a soapbox in Central Park or published an independent newspaper. But neither of these likely would have had a large audience, and the latter would have been very expensive. A better option might have been to send a letter to the editor to a major national newspaper and hope that the newspaper published the letter in one of its editions. Or perhaps one might have written a book for an established book publisher, which then could have distributed the book through bookstores and libraries. The problem with these options, however, is that newspapers and book publishers have control over what they publish, and so review and edit the materials for such things as defamatory comments. Indeed, the law insists that they do so; by virtue of their ability to determine what they publish, newspapers, book publishers, and magazines are responsible for any defamatory comments that they release, even if they simply print information made by others. Thus, they will be liable to pay compensation for any personal damage that results from publishing the defamatory comments. Publishers do have one possible shield, though. Due to First Amendment considerations, publishers who make false statements about public officials and public figures (such as movie stars) are not liable for damages unless the statements were made with reckless disregard for the truth.

This system works very well to protect individuals from defamation in the traditional print media. Whenever a false statement is widely circulated, there almost always is a financially solvent publisher involved that can be easily identified and held accountable for the damages stemming from the defamation. Electronic communication systems substantially change the dynamics, however. Now it is easy and inexpensive for an individual to post a false statement on a bulletin board or on a Web site, thereby allowing the statement to be disseminated all over the world. For those who are the victims of such defamatory comments, numerous complex problems arise. For one thing, it may be difficult to identify who made the statements if that person hides behind aliases. Although the defamed individual might go to an Internet service provider and request that it reveal the identity of the speaker, the ISP may have contractual obligations to refuse to honor the request. Finding the person does not end the problems, however. Individuals engaged in making harmful statements often have no money. It does little good to sue someone for defamation when there is no chance for a meaningful monetary recovery. Also, those engaged in defamation might reside in other countries, thus raising all the issues regarding jurisdiction, the applicable laws, and foreign enforcement. The victims of defamation, therefore, need to find major business interests that can be held responsible for the harmful comments, akin to the role of newspapers and magazines in the traditional print world. In this regard, the most suitable targets have been Internet service providers.

Cubby, Inc. v. CompuServe Inc.[100] was one of the first important cases to address the responsibility of Internet service providers for transmitting defamatory comments of subscribers. CompuServe provided its subscribers access to special interest forums which were composed of electronic bulletin boards, interactive online conferences, and topical databases. One forum was the Journalism Forum, which focused on the journalism industry. CompuServe contracted with an independent company to manage the Journalism Forum. A publication that was made available via the Journalism Forum was Rumorville, a daily newsletter that provided reports about broadcast journalists. Rumorville published allegedly defamatory comments about a new competitor and its owner, having stated such things as that the owner was "bounced" from his previous job and that the new enterprise was a start-up scam. The owner sued CompuServe along with Rumorville and its operator. CompuServe claimed that it should not be held accountable, since it did not review the contents of the Journalism Forum and it had no knowledge that Rumorville was making defamatory comments. It argued that it should not be treated like a publisher, since it had no control over the statements made over its bulletin boards. Rather, its service should be analogized to a library or a distributor, which are not held liable under the law for defamation unless their owners know or have reason to know about the defamation. The court agreed with CompuServe, stating that its service was in essence a for-profit library that carried a vast number of publications. The court determined that it would be no more feasible for CompuServe to examine every publication it carried than it would be for a library, bookstore, or newsstand to do so. The court therefore held that CompuServe could not be held liable for any defamatory comments made by Rumorville.

The comfort that ISPs derived from *CompuServe* was quickly eroded in 1995 in *Stratton Oakmont v. Prodigy Services Co.*[101] Prodigy ran a bulletin board called "Money Talk" where members could post statements regarding stocks, investments, and other financial matters. An unidentified user posted on Money Talk that Stratton Oakmont, a securities investment banking firm, committed criminal fraud in connection with a stock offering. Stratton Oakmont sued Prodigy for these defamatory comments, claiming that Prodigy should be treated as a publisher and not as a mere distributor. The court agreed, basing its decision on several factors. First, Prodigy marketed itself as a family-oriented computer network and attempted to distinguish itself from competitors by trying to deter offensive language. In this regard it promulgated "content guidelines" instructing users to refrain from posting insulting notes and notifying them that such notes would be removed when Prodigy became aware of them. Prodigy also used a software screening program that automatically prescreened all bulletin board postings for offensive language. In addition, Prodigy contracted with "Board leaders" who were responsible for enforcing the guidelines. Prodigy argued that it was not feasible for it to manually review all statements posted by its users. Nonetheless, the court concluded that Prodigy was a publisher since it "uniquely arrogated to itself the role of determining what is proper for its members to post and read on its bulletin boards."

The ruling in *Prodigy* presented ISPs with a dilemma. If they exercised some editorial functions, for perhaps offensive language or pornography, then they opened the door to liability for defamation. On the other hand, if they did nothing, they were safe. This disturbed many groups, particularly parents, since the ISPs had a strong disincentive to do the good deeds that these groups wanted. Congress addressed the issue in the Communications Decency Act of 1996 by providing a safe harbor for ISPs. Although most of the CDA was found to be unconstitutional, the safe harbor survived. The law provides: "No provider or user of an interactive computer service shall be treated as a publisher or speaker of information provided by another information content provider."[102] This clearly protects ISPs in situations such as in *CompuServe* and *Prodigy*. But questions have arisen in more difficult contexts. For instance, in *Zeran v. America Online Inc.*,[103] the court had to address whether an ISP could be held liable for defamatory statements after it was notified of their nature. Although distributors traditionally may be found liable after notification, the court determined that the protection for ISPs under the new law was more absolute, insulating them even when they have notice. The next case follows in the footsteps of *Zeran*, although the court clearly was troubled by its decision. In addition, the court had to deal with the difficult topic of jurisdiction in cyberspace.

SIDNEY BLUMENTHAL V. MATT DRUDGE AND AMERICA ONLINE, INC.
District Court for the District of Columbia, 1998

FACTS: Matt Drudge is a resident of California who publishes from Los Angeles a gossip column called the Drudge Report that focuses on gossip from Hollywood and Washington, D.C. Drudge has a World Wide Web site that is available at no cost to anyone who has access to the Internet. The Web site has a hyperlink that causes the most recently published edition of the Drudge Report to be displayed. In addition, Drudge developed a list of regular readers to whom he e-mailed each new edition of the Drudge Report.

In late May or early June of 1997, Drudge entered into a license agreement with America Online ("AOL") that made the Drudge Report available to all members of AOL's service for one year. In exchange, Drudge received a flat monthly royalty payment of $3,000 from AOL. Upon signing the agreement, AOL posted a press release announcing the addition of the gossip column and urged potential subscribers to join AOL. Under the license agreement, Drudge was to create, edit and update and otherwise manage the content of the Drudge Report, but AOL could remove content that it reasonably determined to violate AOL's standard terms of service. Drudge e-mailed new editions of the Drudge Report to AOL and AOL posted them on the AOL service. During this time, Drudge continued to distribute each new edition of the Drudge Report via e-mail and his own web site.

On the Evening of August 10, 1997, Drudge transmitted from Los Angeles an edition of the Drudge Report that contained alleged defamatory statements about Sidney Blumenthal who was to begin work as Assistant to the President of the United States on August 11, 1997. The columns stated in part:

> The Drudge Report has learned that top GOP operatives who feel there is a double-standard of only reporting Republican shame believe they are holding an ace card: new White House recruit Sidney Blumenthal has a spousal abuse past that has been effectively covered up. . . . There are court records of Blumenthal's violence against his wife, one influential Republican, who demanded anonymity, tells the Drudge Report.

The edition was transmitted by e-mail to direct subscribers and posted on Drudge's web site. It also was transmitted to AOL which in turn made it available to AOL subscribers. After receiving a letter from Blumenthal's attorney on August 11 alleging defamation, Drudge retracted the story through a special edition of the Drudge Report that was transmitted though the same channels.

continued . . .

continued . . .

Blumenthal and his wife sued AOL and Drudge for defamation. In this action, AOL asked the court to dismiss the case against it by summary judgment, claiming that under the law it cannot be held liable even if Drudge's statements were defamatory. Drudge asked the court to dismiss or transfer the case because it could not exercise jurisdiction over Drudge (or in other words, because it did not have the power to make Drudge come to D.C. and defend the case).

DECISION AND REASONING:

A. *AOL's Motion to Dismiss the Case*

The Internet is a unique and wholly new medium of worldwide human communication. It enables people to communicate with one another with unprecedented speed and efficiency and is rapidly revolutionizing how people share and receive information. The near instantaneous possibilities for the dissemination of information by millions of different information providers around the world to those with access to computers and thus to the Internet have created ever-increasing opportunities for exchange of information and ideas in cyberspace. This information revolution has also presented unprecedented challenges relating to rights of privacy and reputational rights of individuals, to the control of obscene and pornographic materials, and to competition among journalists and news organizations for instant news, rumors and other information that is communicated so quickly that it is too often unchecked and unverified. Needless to say, the legal rules that will govern this new medium are just beginning to take shape.

In February 1996, Congress made an effort to deal with some of these challenges in enacting the Communications Decency Act of 1996. Whether wisely or not, it made the legislative judgment to effectively immunize providers of interactive computer services from civil liability in tort with respect to material disseminated by them but created by others. In recognition of the speed with which information may be disseminated and the near impossibility of regulating information content, Congress decided not to treat providers of interactive computer services like other information providers such as newspapers, magazines or television and radio stations, all of which may be held liable for publishing or distributing obscene or defamatory materials written or prepared by others. While Congress could have made a different policy choice, it opted not to hold interactive computer services liable for their failure to edit, withhold or restrict access to offensive material disseminated through their medium.

Section 230(c) of the Communications Decency Act of 1996 provides, "No provider or user of an interactive computer service shall be treated as the publisher or speaker of any information provided by another information content provider." The statute goes on to define the term "information content provider" as "any person or entity that is responsible, in whole or in part, for the creation or development of information provided through the Internet or any other interactive computer service." In view of this statutory language, the Blumenthals' argument that the *Washington Post* would be liable if it had done what AOL did here—publish Drudge's story without doing anything whatsoever to edit, verify, or even read it (despite knowing what Drudge did for a living and how he did it)—has been rendered irrelevant by Congress.

The Blumenthals concede that AOL is a provider of an interactive computer service and that if AOL acted exclusively as a provider of an interactive computer service it may not be held liable for making the Drudge Report available to AOL subscribers. They also concede that Drudge is an information content provider because he wrote the alleged defamatory material about the Blumenthals contained in the Drudge Report.

AOL acknowledges both that Section 230(c) would not immunize AOL with respect to any information that AOL developed or created entirely by itself and that there are situations where there may be two or more information content providers responsible for material disseminated on the Internet—joint authors, a lyricist and a composer, for example. While Section 230 does not preclude joint liability for joint development of content, AOL maintains that there simply is no evidence here that AOL had any role in creating or developing any of the information in the Drudge Report. The court agrees. It is undisputed that the Blumenthal story was written by Drudge without any substantive or editorial involvement by AOL. AOL was nothing more than a provider of an interactive computer service on which the Drudge Report was carried, and Congress has said quite clearly that such a provider shall not be treated as a publisher or speaker and therefore may not be held liable in tort.

The Blumenthals make the additional argument, however, that Section 230 does not provide immunity to AOL in this case because Drudge was not just an anonymous person who sent a message over the Internet through AOL. He is a person with whom AOL contracted, whom AOL paid $3,000 a month—$36,000 a year, Drudge' sole consistent source of income—and whom AOL promoted to its subscribers and potential subscribers as a reason to subscribe to AOL. Furthermore, the license agreement between AOL and Drudge by its terms contemplates more than a passive role for AOL; in it, AOL reserves the right to remove or direct Drudge to remove any content which, as reasonably determined by AOL violates AOL's then-standard Terms of Service. In addition, shortly after it entered the agreement, AOL issued a press release captioned: "AOL Hires Runaway Gossip Success Matt Drudge." The release noted that "maverick

continued . . .

continued . . .

gossip columnist Matt Drudge has teamed up with America Online," and stated "Giving the Drudge Report a home on America Online opens up the floodgates to an audience ripe for Drudge's brand of reporting . . . AOL had made Matt Drudge instantly accessible to members who crave instant gossip and news breaks." Why is this different, the Blumenthals suggest, from AOL advertising and promoting a new purveyor of child pornography or other offensive material? Why should AOL be permitted to tout someone as a gossip columnist or rumor monger who will make such rumors and gossip instantly accessible to AOL subscribers, and then claim immunity when that person, as might be anticipated, defames another?

If it were writing on a clean slate, this court would agree with the Blumenthals. AOL has certain editorial rights with respect to content provided by Drudge and disseminated by AOL, including the right to require changes in content and to remove it; and it has affirmatively promoted Drudge as a new source of unverified instant gossip on AOL. Yet it takes no responsibility for any damage he may cause. AOL is not a passive conduit like the telephone company, a common carrier with no control and therefore no responsibility for what is said over the telephone wires. Because it has the right to exercise editorial control over those with whom it contracts and whose words it disseminates, it would seem only fair to hold AOL to the liability standards applied to a publisher or, at least, like a book store owner or a library, to the liability standards applied to a distributor. But Congress has made a different policy choice by providing immunity even where the interactive service provider has an active, even aggressive role in making available content prepared by others. In some sort of tacit *quid pro quo* arrangement with the service provider community, Congress has conferred immunity from tort liability as an incentive to Internet service providers to self-police the Internet for obscenity and other offensive material, even where the self-policing is unsuccessful or not even attempted.

Any attempt to distinguish between "publisher" liability and notice-based "distributor" liability and to argue that Section 230 was only intended to immunize the former would be unavailing. Congress made no distinction between publishers and distributors in providing immunity from liability. If computer service providers were subject to distributor liability, they would face potential liability each time they receive notice of a potentially defamatory statement—from any party, concerning any message, and such notice-based liability would deter service providers from regulating the dissemination of offensive material over their own services by confronting them with ceaseless choices of suppressing controversial speech or sustaining prohibitive liability—exactly what Congress intended to insulate them from in Section 230. While it appears to this court that AOL in this case has taken advantage of all the benefits conferred by Congress in the Communications Decency Act, and then some, without accepting any of the burdens that Congress intended, the statutory language is clear: AOL is immune from suit, and the court therefore must grant its motion for summary judgment.

B. *Drudge's Motion to Dismiss for Lack of Personal Jurisdiction*
The legal questions surrounding the exercise of personal jurisdiction in cyberspace are relatively new, and different courts have reached different conclusions as to how far their jurisdiction extends in cases involving the Internet. Generally, the debate over jurisdiction in cyberspace has revolved around two issues: passive web sites versus interactive web sites, and whether a defendant's Internet-related contacts with the forum combined with other non-Internet related contacts are sufficient to establish a persistent course of conduct.

Despite the attempts of Drudge to label the Drudge Report as a "passive" web site, the court finds this characterization inapt. The Drudge Report's web site allows browsers, including D.C. residents, to directly e-mail defendant Drudge, thus allowing an exchange of information between the browser's computer and Drudge's host computer. In addition, browsers who access the web site may request subscriptions to the Drudge Report, again by directly e-mailing their requests to Drudge's host computer. In turn, as each new edition of the Drudge Report is created, it is then sent by Drudge to every e-mail address on his subscription mailing list, which includes the e-mail addresses of all browsers who have requested subscriptions by directly e-mailing Drudge through his web site. The constant exchange of information and direct communication that D.C. Internet users are able to have with Drudge's host computer via his web site is the epitome of web site interactivity.

Not only is Drudge's web site interactive, the subject matter of the Drudge Report primarily concerns political gossip and rumor in Washington, D.C. Even though Drudge may not advertise in physical locations or local newspapers in D.C., the subject matter of the Drudge Report is directly related to the political world of the nation's capital and is quintessentially inside the beltway gossip and rumor. Drudge specifically targets readers in D.C. by virtue of the subjects he covers and even solicits gossip from D.C. residents and government officials who work here. Drudge also has a number of non-Internet related contacts with Washington, D.C. He sat for an interview with C-SPAN in Washington, and visited D.C. on at least one other occasion. He also contacts D.C. residents via telephone and the U.S. mail in order to collect gossip for the Drudge Report. These non-Internet related contacts with the District of Columbia, coupled with the

---

continued . . .

interactive nature of Drudge's web site, which particularly focuses on Washington gossip, are contacts that together are sufficient to establish that Drudge engaged in a persistent course of conduct in the District of Columbia. Thus, the court concludes that the circumstances presented by this case warrant the exercise of personal jurisdiction. Drudge's motion to dismiss or transfer for want of personal jurisdiction therefore will be denied.

Exhibit 8.6 summarizes the key aspects of defamation law in the United States. It also outlines the disparate ways that courts addressed the potential liability of ISPs, and how section 230(c) of the Communications Decency Act came to the ISPs' aid.

OTHER HIGH-TECHNOLOGY TORT ISSUES

Intrusions on Computer Systems

Computer systems are vulnerable to various forms of intrusive behavior. Some of these we have already discussed, such as e-mail monitoring. Many of the intrusions are akin to theft. Sophisticated computer "hackers" find ways to infiltrate computer systems to steal data, transfer funds, or change records. They also devise schemes to impersonate computer users so that they can steal services or engage in other forms of mischief. Most of these activities are unlawful under criminal and civil statutes. Many of them may be prosecuted under traditional laws, such as those applying to embezzlement, larceny, forgery, malicious mischief, and receiving stolen property. In some cases, there are special federal or state laws applying specifically to misuses of computers.

Computer Viruses and Worms   One threat that most people fear is the possible introduction of viruses into their computer systems. A virus is really just a computer program that carries out instructions. What is special and so dangerous about viruses, however, is that they can create copies of themselves whenever they come into contact with computer systems. Thus, viruses may replicate and be transmitted to computers over telephone lines or cable, or from disk to disk, usually without users even knowing that their systems have been infected. The fear, of course, is about what the virus may cause the computer to do. Most viruses are developed only to engage in clever fun, such as to relay comic messages. Some, though, have the potential to cause widespread catastrophic effects if preventative steps are not

---

Exhibit 8.6

Defamation and the Internet

■ **Requirements**
  - False statement
  - About another person
  - In the presence of others (public)
  - That harms the person's reputation

■ **Defense**
  - False statement about public figure must be made with reckless disregard for truth

■ **Publisher Liability**
  - Magazines, newspapers
  - Strictly liable for defamatory statements made by others in publications
  - Liable even without notice about the defamatory statements

■ **Distributor Liability**
  - Bookstores, libraries
  - Generally not liable for defamatory statements made by others in distributed publications
  - Liable only with notice about the defamatory statements

■ **Internet Service Provider Liability for Defamatory Statements**
  - *Cubby, Inc. v. CompuServe, Inc.*
    — CompuServe treated as a distributor
    — ISP not liable for defamatory statements of user unless it had notice of defamation
  - *Stratton Oakmont v. Prodigy Services Co.*
    — Prodigy treated as publisher
    — ISP may be strictly liable for defamatory statements of user even without notice of defamation
    — Based on existence of content guidelines and some enforcement
  - Communications Decency Act, Section 230(c)
    — ISP not liable for defamatory statements made by others
      - Even if it exercises editorial control
      - Even if it has notice of defamation
    — **CASE:** *Sidney Blumenthal v. Matt Drudge and America Online, Inc.*

---

taken. One notable example was the Michelangelo virus, which was programmed to destroy computer files on the anniversary of Michelangelo's birthday in 1992. Other feared names have included the Melissa and Chernobyl viruses, which spread rapidly in 1999.

There are other forms of programs related to viruses that may be equally as destructive. For instance, a "worm" may enter a computer system and do damage there, but cannot replicate itself. Nonetheless, the effects may be widespread because worms may easily be transmitted to millions of users through attachments to e-mail messages. For instance, the "ExploreZip" worm was sent in 1999 with an e-mail message that read, "I received your e-mail, and I shall reply ASAP. Till then, take a look at the zipped docs."[104] Those users who clicked on the attached file launched the worm into their computers; it then destroyed Microsoft Outlook, Express, and other e-mail related documents. Viruses and worms cause tremendous economic damage through lost productivity and repair costs. As an example, one study indicated that businesses lost $7.6 billion in just the first half of 1999 due to viruses and worms.[105]

The introduction of a computer virus may be a crime under federal and/or state laws. For instance, the Federal Computer Fraud and Abuse Act makes it a crime to intentionally access or cause damage to any computer used substantially for U.S. government purposes or by financial institutions. The first conviction under this statute was against a Cornell University graduate student who crippled the Internet computer network with a virus in 1988. The virus affected systems at universities and military installations and cost as much as $15 million for systems operators to eradicate.

Manipulative and Coercive Devices   Sometimes individuals plant potentially harmful programs into computer systems and use them to pressure their operators to take certain actions. In one case, a law firm hired a computer consultant to install a new computer system and to modify its insurance claims processing software. The programmer installed a bug in the program so that the system would stop working once claim number 56789 was processed. The consultant planted the bug so that the law firm would be forced to retain him once again to correct the problem. In litigation by the law firm against the consultant, the court awarded the $7,000 the firm had to pay to correct the problem and an additional $18,000 in punitive damages.[106]

In another series of cases, purveyors of computer systems have been held liable for damages caused by "drop-dead" or "time-bomb" devices installed in the software. A drop-dead device causes the program to shut down at the instruction of the programmer, and a time bomb automatically locks up the program at a particular time unless the programmer deactivates it beforehand. Some computer specialists who have installed these devices have allowed them to shut down systems when clients have failed to pay appropriately, at least in the programmers' minds, according to contracts made for their services. Courts have not looked favorably on these devices, holding the installers liable for damages and punitive damages. However, one should note that in these situations, the clients were unaware that their system had disabling devices installed. If a client has agreed in the contract to the installation of a disabling device that could be activated against defined operations with reasonable notice, then it is likely that use of the device would not give rise to liability.

Spamming   Internet users usually pay a flat fee for Internet access but do not have to pay per-message charges for the e-mail they send to recipients. This financial arrangement provides an opportunity for marketing firms to send unsolicited commercial advertisements to hundreds of thousands of Internet users at virtually no cost. Junk-mail operators responded quickly. By 1998, AOL reported that it handled between 700,000 and 4.2 million pieces of unsolicited advertisements each day.[107] Recipients found the volume and repetitive nature of the advertisements so annoying that the mail soon became known as "spam," a term derived from a skit performed on Monty Python's Flying Circus in which a restaurant offered only repeated varieties of Spam (such as Spam on Spam with Spam).

In one sense, spam is an intrusion on the recipients' privacy rights to receive the information they want to receive. However, spam also negatively affects ISP's since they must bear the complaints of their customers. In addition, the volume of spam may put such a burden on the finite processing and storage capacities of ISP computers that it clogs the ability of the ISP to deliver its customers' messages. In the 1990's, ISPs took steps to block the transmission of spam by using filters to search for certain words, such as "sex" or "get rich" in the subject line, but spammers learned to evade these measures. ISPs also tried to block messages from sources that they previously identified with spam, but the spammers learned how to disguise the origins of their messages.

In the 1990s, Cyber Promotions, Inc. may have been the most notable company involved with the business of sending spam, and ISPs sued it on several occasions. In one important case, CompuServe requested a preliminary injunction on the theory that Cyber Promotions was engaged in a form of trespass on CompuServe's computer system.[108] Trespass, though, may not occur when there is consent, and Cyber Promotions argued that CompuServe, by linking to the Internet, tacitly invited anyone in the public to send e-mail messages to its subscribers. However, the court was not persuaded, since CompuServe specifically asked Cyber Promotions to stop using CompuServe's equipment for sending junk e-mail messages. Cyber Promotions also believed that it had a First Amendment right to send unobstructed e-mail to CompuServe customers. However, the First Amendment applies only to government action and does not normally cover the actions of private companies. Thus, this argument was not persuasive either. The court, therefore, issued a preliminary injunction preventing Cyber Promotions from sending unsolicited advertisements to any CompuServe customers.

In the late 1990s, a few states enacted legislation specifically dealing with the problems of spam.[109] A California law passed in 1998, for example, regulates commercial messages that promote the sale or distribution of goods or services.[110] The law requires such messages to contain "ADV:" in the subject line, which thereby enables customers to use filters that search for that term. Spammers also must provide valid return e-mail addresses, along with instructions informing recipients how they can ask that they be removed from mailing lists. There are also rules requiring the spammers to keep good records of these requests. Spammers who violate these requirements may face criminal misdemeanor charges, punishable by fines and/or imprisonment for each offense. In addition, the law authorizes civil actions by the recipients of the spam. Several similar proposals also were introduced at the federal level during this time, and it seems likely that increased federal involvement may soon be at hand.

Intrusions on Publicity Rights

Few things can be considered so personal as one's individual identity. In a very real sense, the special attributes that make you who you are belong only to you. This includes your appearance, your personality, your voice, the way you walk, and your individual style. How would you feel if others somehow took or mimicked these special attributes and put them on public display without your permission? What if those others went so far as to make money from their appropriation? The law recognizes that individuals have rights to their personal identity, and it protects them from intentional invasions by others. This is especially true when commercial advantage is to be gained from such appropriation. In many states, these rights in identity are often collected together under an umbrella phrase called the "right of publicity."

Disputes about publicity rights often arise in the context of advertising, although they have been alleged in a variety of other commercial settings. The following is just a short list of disputes involving possible misappropriation of publicity rights:

1. The vocal imitation of Bette Midler's voice in an advertisement for Ford's Mercury Sable automobiles developed by the agency Young & Rubicam.
2. The use of a guitar riff almost identical to one played by Chris Isaak in his hit song "Wicked Game," for a Nissan commercial for its Infiniti automobile.
3. Imitation of the stage persona of the rap group the Fat Boys, by Joe Piscopo in a Miller beer commercial.
4. Imitation of Bobby Darin's rendition of "Mack the Knife," including the singer's inflections, phrasings, and arrangement, in a McDonald's "Mac Tonight" advertising campaign.
5. A robot recognizable as Vanna White used in a portrayal of the future in an advertisement for Samsung VCRs.

Disputes involving publicity rights sometimes are associated with copyright disputes. This happens when an actual recording or picture is used in creating the allegedly offending work. Digital sampling and digital imaging are two frequent contexts for this occurrence. As discussed in Chapter 6, when one uses digital means to alter portions of songs or pictures, copyright infringement may take place. However, invasions of publicity rights also may result, as when McKenzie River Corporation used a sampled version of Chuck D's voice for a commercial, or when *Los Angeles Magazine* integrated Dustin Hoffman's head (from the movie *Tootsie*) with the body of a model.[111] Publicity rights clearly take on added importance when one simply imitates a voice, likeness, or style, as opposed to copying a song or a picture. This is because there may be no copyright privileges upon which one can rely for damages. Based on all this, the best advice is to get permission before copying or imitating the distinctive style, voice, or appearance of a well-known individual.

CONCLUSION

This chapter should have made you more sensitive to the wide range of personal and social obligations that one incurs when offering a new product or service. Not only must one be careful, but one also must ensure that the technology does not cause harm when used in foreseeable ways. In addition, consider that uses of advanced technologies may arouse public action leading to new forms of protection of personal rights. In this regard, one needs to look no further than to the Internet and how it has raised concerns about personal privacy.

In the next chapter, we will explore some important contracting issues for those managing technology. As we shall see, some of the concerns over torts may be handled through contract provisions. However, one usually cannot negotiate absolute protection from tort liabilities when dealing with knowledgeable parties. Also, the more the context involves consumers rather than sophisticated commercial businesses, the less protection contracts can provide. In addition, although contracts may resolve liability issues between the parties to agreements, they do not offer relief when others suffer damage from use of the technology. Torts, therefore, will always be a critically important concern for those doing business in the technological world.

NOTES

1. Employees who are negligent may be held personally liable for damages to those injured. Employers also may be held responsible to pay for the damages that result from an employee's negligence under a doctrine called respondeat superior. In addition, employers may be directly liable if they do not exercise due care in supervising the employees who caused the harm.

2. United States v. Carroll Towing Co., 159 F.2d 169 (2d Cir. 1947).

3. Calabresi and Hirschoff, "Toward a Test for Strict Liability in Torts," 81 Yale L.J. 1055 (1972).

4. W. Buckley, "Databases Are Plagued by Reign of Error," Wall St. J. (May 26, 1992) at B6.

5. In July 1999, a jury awarded $107 million in compensatory damages and $4.8 billion in punitive damages to six people who were burned when their General Motors car exploded after being hit from behind by a drunk driver. The jury determined that GM's fuel tank was defectively designed, and that it could have been safer with relatively inexpensive measures.

6. The judge reduced the $4.8 billion dollar punitive damage award to $1.09 billion, stating that the original award was excessive.

7. Liriano v. Hobart Corp., 170 F.3d 264, 271 (2d Cir. 1999).

8. See e.g., Todd v. Societe Bic, 21 F.3d 1402 (7th Cir. 1994); Carlson v. Bic Corp, 840 F.Supp. 457 (E.D. Mich. 1993); Bondie v. Bic Corp., 739 F.Supp. 346 (E.D. Mich. 1990).

9. Todd v. Societe Bic, 21 F.3d 1402 (7th Cir. 1994).

10. Consumer Product Safety Act, 15 U.S.C. § 2064(b). For an informative discussion about the duties of sellers under CPSC laws and regulations, see CPSC Document #8001, "A Guide for Manufacturers, Importers, Distributors, and Retailers on Procedures Relating to the Enforcement of Standards and Regulations Issued Under the Consumer Product Safety Act, The Federal Hazardous Substances Act, the Flammable Fabrics Act, and the Poison Prevention Packaging Act," 2d Ed. (February 1994) available at www.cpsc.gov.

11. See M. Lemov, "The Current Federal Product-Safety Requirements for Reporting Potentially Dangerous Products Have Caused Confusion Among the Nation's Manufacturers," Nat'l L. J. (August 10, 1998) at B4.

12. Civil penalties may be as high as $1.25 million. 15 U.S.C. § 2069. Willful disregard of the reporting requirements can give rise to a one-year prison term. 15 U.S.C. § 2070.

13. M. Lemov and M. Woolf, "Underreporting Defects Is Risky," Nat'l L. J. (December 14, 1992) at S6.

14. M. Lemov, "The Current Federal Product-Safety Requirements for Reporting Potentially Dangerous Products have Caused Confusion Among the Nation's Manufacturers," Nat'l L. J. (August 10, 1998) at B4.

15. R. Schmitt, "Some Big Firms Are Trying to Kill Legislation on Product Liability," Wall St. J. (July 7, 1998) at B15.

16. For instance, in 1994, Congress passed legislation banning suits against manufacturers of small planes that are more than 18 years old.

17. The information provided on the traditional tort system in Japan was reported in L. Helm, "It's Buyer Beware in Japan," L.A. Times (February 6, 1993) at A1.

18. See J. Sapsford, "Japanese Firms Brace for First Laws on Consumer Rights, and Insurers Gain," Wall St. J. (March 8, 1994) at A12.

19. See S. Hurd and F. Zollers, "Product Liability in the European Community: Implications for United States Business," 31 Am. Bus. L.J. 245 (September 1993).

20. Council Directive 85/374/EEC of July 25, 1985, on the approximation of the laws, regulations, and administrative provisions of the member states concerning liability for defective products, 28 O.J. Eur. Comm. (No. L 210) 29 (1985).

21. Some services, however, are treated under strict liability principles if they are deemed ultrahazardous activities.

22. Aetna Casualty & Surety Co. v. Jeppsen & Co., 642 F.2d 339 (9th Cir. 1981).

23. Winter v. G. P. Putnam's Sons, 938 F.2d 1033, 1035 (9th Cir. 1991).

24. This discussion on expert systems is based on B. Knowles, "Artificial Intelligence and Legal Liability: Some Observations," Am. Bus. L. Assoc. Nat'l Proceedings, 1989 at 545.

25. W. Marbach, J. Conant, and M. Hager, "Doctor Digital, We Presume," Newsweek (May 20, 1985) at 83.

26. For a good article on insurance issues, see J. Pabarue and R. Maniloff, "Insurers Can Expect a Swarm of Millenium Bugs," Nat'l L. J. (June 29, 1998) at B8.

27. For a nice discussion, see R. Werder, Jr., "Year-2000 Bug May Affect Companies' Products," Nat'l L. J. (April 13, 1998) at B10.

28. There are exceptions in cases of fraud, or where individuals suffer harm that exceeds 10% of a net worth that does not exceed $200,000.

29. Other terms, such as "repetitive stress injuries" and "work-related musculoskeletal disorders," often are used to describe the same conditions.

30. Occupational Safety & Health Administration, "Background on the Working Draft of OSHA's Proposed Ergonomics Program Standard," (February 19, 1999), available at www.osha.gov.

31. B. Fellner and E. Scalia, "Ergonomic Rules May Jump the Gun," Nat'l L. J. (October 25, 1993) at 17.

32. OSHA uses the term "work-related musculoskeletal disorders (WMSD's)" which it describes as injuries and disorders of the muscles, nerves, tendons, ligaments, joints, cartilage, and spinal disks. According to

OSHA, WMSD's are caused when workers must repeat the same motion throughout their workday, must do their work in awkward positions, or use a great deal of force to perform their jobs.

33. *See* J. Auerbach and L. Johannes, "Companies Split on Warnings for Keyboards," Wall St. J. (February 11, 1996) at B1; J. Engen, "IBM, Apple Defendants in Major Wrist-Injury Trial," Nat'l L. J. (February 20, 1995) at B1.

34. J. Engen, "IBM, Apple Defendants in Major Wrist-Injury Trial," Nat'l L. J. (February 20, 1995) at B1; G. Taylor, "Loss in First RSI Trial Viewed as First Step," Nat'l L. J. (March 21, 1994) at A9; J. Moses, "Carpal-Tunnel Lawsuits Are Consolidated," Wall St. J. (June 3, 1992) at B8.

35. *See* E. Milstone, "Keyed Up, Repetitive Stressed Out," A.B.A.J. (February 1997) at 22.

36. Geressy v. Digital Equipment Corp., 980 F.Supp. 640 (E.D. NY 1997); Rotolo v. Digital Equipment Corp., 150 F.3d 223 (2d Cir. 1998).

37. 515 U.S. 646 (1995).

38. For an excellent discussion of social and policy issues regarding genetic testing, see L. Andrews, Body Science, A.B.A.J. (April 1997) at 44.

39. *See* W. Mulholland, II and A. Jaeger, "Genetic Privacy and Discrimination: A Survey of State Legislation," 39 Jurimetrics (Spring 1999) at 317. At the federal level, the Americans with Disabilities Act prohibits discrimination against qualified persons with disabilities. This law may constrain employers from taking actions based on genetic information.

40. Employee Polygraph Protection Act of 1988, 29 U.S.C. §§ 2001 et seq.

41. A New York law bars hidden cameras from changing rooms, restrooms, or hotel rooms. In California, employers may not use cameras in employee restrooms or changing rooms without a court order. *See* M. Higgins, "High Tech, Low Privacy," A.B.A.J. 52 (May 1999) at 57.

42. J. Rigdon, "Curbing Digital Dillydallying on the Job," Wall St. J. (November 25, 1996) at B1.

43. Web sites can use reverse directories to translate the Internet Protocol numbers of their customers, and determine the companies that operate the computer systems used to access the Web. *See* M. Moss, "A Secret Cat-and-Mouse Game Online," Wall St. J. (October 13, 1999) at B1.

44. M. McCarthy, "Now the Boss Knows Where You're Clicking," Wall St. J. (October 21, 1999) at B1.

45. Examples in 1998 included SurfWatch Professional Edition, WebSense, LittleBrother, and Elron Internet Manager. *See* D. Branscum, "bigbrother@the.office.com," Newsweek (April 27, 1998) at 78. Another product, called Telemate.net, reportedly can generate a wide variety of Web usage statistics according to numerous company-wide, department-wide, and individual usage parameters. M. McCarthy, "Now the Boss Knows Where You're Clicking," Wall St. J. (October 21, 1999) at B1. For a good article about other Internet monitoring tools and company use policies, see R. Yasin, "Web Slackers Put on Notice," Internet Week (October 18, 1999) at 1.

46. A study by SurfWatch indicated that over 50% of companies had Internet acceptable use policies in place as of May 1998. D. Plotnikoff, "Bosses Lean on Internet Abusers," San Luis Obispo Telegram-Tribune (November 25, 1998) at D-1. *See* D. Branscum, "bigbrother@the.office.com," Newsweek (April 27, 1998) at 78.

47. This was the policy at Intel in 1998. See D. Branscum, "bigbrother@theoffice.com," Newsweek (April 27, 1998) at 78.

48. Pub. L. No. 99-508 (1986) codified at 18 U.S.C. §§ 2510 et seq.

49. Cordless phone conversations were not covered by the ECPA until 1994. Now, the radio portion of a cordless call is protected from intentional interception.

50. A good example is Bourke v. Nissan Motor Corp., California Court of Appeal, 2d App. Dist. (July 6, 1993). In this case, the court determined that an e-mail search did not violate California's state constitution, which expansively protects privacy. The court's decision rested heavily on the existence of an e-mail policy in which the employee agreed that the company's e-mail system was to be used only for company purposes. In addition the policy stated that people other than the intended recipient might review the e-mail.

51. *See* M. Higgins, "High Tech, Low Privacy," A.B.A.J. 52 (May 1999) at 54. In October 1999, the governor of California vetoed legislation that, among other things, would have (1) prohibited employers from

secretly monitoring employee e-mail and computer files, (2) required employers to distribute copies of e-mail policies to all employees and verify that they were read and understood, and (3) allowed employees the right to access personal electronic data collected through monitoriing.

52. E. Dyson, *Release 2.0* (Broadway Books, 1997) at 231–32.

53. In one case, AOL revealed the name and address, as well as credit card and checking account information, of a subscriber using the alias Jenny TRR after receiving a petition for discovery in a civil suit. In that suit, the individual using the name Jenny TRR was accused of defaming a Caribbean resort and one of its diving instructors in a critical message posted on an AOL bulletin board. *See* C. Johnson, "Anonymity On-Line? It Depends Who's Asking." Wall St. J. (November 24, 1995) at B1.

54. For a thorough discussion of protecting anonymity on the Internet, see E. Dyson, *Release 2.0* (Broadway Books, 1997) at 232–239. For a good article on anonymous remailers, see S. Lohr, "Privacy on the Internet Poses Legal Puzzle," N.Y. Times (April 19, 1999) at C4.

55. *See* R. Mainland, "Congress Holds the Key to Encryption Regulation," Nat'l L. J. (April 20, 1998) at B9, n.1.

56. A mathematical technique also can be used to verify that the contents of messages have not been altered. A number, called a "hash" value, is calculated that uniquely corresponds to the contents of a digital document. The hash and the document are encrypted with the sender's private key. The recipient decrypts the hash and the document with the sender's public key. The recipient then recalculates the hash for the document. If the two hash values are the same, then the recipient knows that the document has not been altered, and that it was sent by the person who holds the private key.

57. For an excellent discussion about the application of export regulations to encryption products, see B. Dayanim, "New Encryption Rules Relax Some Restrictions," Nat'l L. J. (February 1, 1999) at C11.

58. For a full discussion of the 1998 export licensing regulations, *see* B. Dayanim, "New Encryption Rules Relax Some Restrictions," Nat'l L. J. (February 1, 1999) at C11.

59. Bernstein v. Department of Justice, 1999 U.S. App. LEXIS 8595 (May 6, 1999); Karn v. Department of State, 925 F.Supp 1 (D.D.C. 1996), *remanded* 1997 U.S. App. LEXIS 3123 (January 21, 1997).

60. Bernstein v. Department of Justice, 176 F.3d 1132 (9th Cir. 1999).

61. Department of Commerce, Bureau of Export Administration, "Revisions to Encryption Items," Interim Final Rule, Fed. Reg. Vol. 65, No. 10 (January 14, 2000).

62. *See* R. O'Harrow Jr., "Encryption Battle Enters Home, Office," Wash. Post (August 20, 1999) at A1; M. Godwin, "The New Cryptographic Landscape: What Is the U.S. Encryption Policy Now?" E-Commerce Law Weekly (October 19, 1999) at 24.

63. Due to a very specialized law, video rental stores must keep information about their customers' rental histories in confidence.

64. Information about medical malpractice or workers' compensation claims may be of interest to insurance companies or prospective employers. *See* A. Miller, J. Schwartz, and M. Rogers, "How Did They Get My Name?" Newsweek (June 3, 1991) at 41.

65. The 1994 Drivers' Privacy Protection Act barred the release of this information if an individual notified the motor vehicle department that it wanted the information to be kept private. However, most people did not take the step to "opt-out" of public disclosure. In October 1999, the law was strengthened, making the information private unless the individual consented to its release. Drivers' Privacy Protection Act, 18 U.S.C. §§ 2721–2725, amended by Pub. L. 106-69, Stat. 986 (October 9, 1999).

66. For an excellent article on data warehousing companies, see R. O'Harrow, Jr., "Say Goodbye to Privacy," Wash. Post Nat'l Weekly Ed. (March 23, 1998) at 6.

67. L. Bransten, "Looking for Patterns," Wall St. J. (June 21, 1999) at R16.

68. D. Bank, "Know Your Customer," Wall St. J. (June 21, 1999) at R18.

69. *See* W. Leibowitz, "Medical Database Spotlights Tech Privacy Issues," Nat'l L. J. (August 3, 1998) at A8; R. O'Harrow, Jr., "Is Uncle Sam Enforcing the Law or Snooping?" Wash. Post Nat'l Weekly Ed. (July 5, 1999) at 30. Another brewing controversy regards the collection of DNA data from convicted felons, and how that data may be used. *See* G. Gugliotta, "The Rush to DNA Judgment," Wash. Post Nat'l Weekly Ed. (July 12, 1999) at 31.

70. *See* R. O'Harrow Jr., "They Know Who You Are," Wash. Post Nat'l Weekly Ed. (February 1, 1999) at 29.

71. For more complete discussions of cookies and related information gathering tools, see T. Weber, "Browsers Beware: The Web Is Watching," Wall St. J. (June 21, 1996) at B10; S. Haar, "Beyond Cookies, the Web Gets Personal," Inter@ctive Week (July 22, 1996) at 67; P. McGrath, "Knowing You All Too Well," Newsweek (March 29, 1999) at 48; S. Hansell, "Big Web Sites to Track Steps of Their Users for Advertisers," N.Y. Times (August 16, 1998) at 1.

72. Privacy advocates have been outraged by other methods that they fear might be used for impermissible identification purposes. For example, Intel designed its Pentium III chips with unique serial numbers so that Web sites could access them for user verification. Although the feature was intended to help promote e-commerce security methods, the clamor was so vociferous that Intel developed a method for users to turn the feature off.

73. The Web site may be able to determine the entry point of your computer to the Web, thereby allowing it to determine the company or government agency for which you work. In 1999, Amazon.com used this information to publish "best seller" lists by various categories, such as by specified businesses, universities, or government agencies. *See* "Amazon's 'Fun' New Feature Stirs a Privacy Controversy," San Luis Obispo Telegram-Tribune (August 29, 1999) at A11. Web sites also can learn when employees from competitor companies are making visits, allowing them to post screens especially designed for their eyes, or to block them from access altogether. In a similar way, Web operators trying to evade criminal investigations may be able to detect when law enforcement personnel are trying to access their sites and screen them out. *See* M. Moss, "A Secret Cat-and-Mouse Game Online," Wall St. J. (October 13, 1999) at B1.

74. In 1999, it was reported that DoubleClick, Inc., a leading on-line advertising company, had embarked on a strategy to combine data from on-line activity with information about purchases in the real world to generate personal profiles for marketing purposes. *See* A. Petersen and J. Auerbach, "Online Ad Titans Bet Big in Race to Trace Consumers' Web Tracks," Wall St. J. (November 8, 1999) at B1. Other companies are involved in research to determine linkages between on-line behavior and off-line consumer purchases. *See* K. Kranhold, "Tracking the Clicks of Online Shoppers," Wall St. J. (October 13, 1999) at B16.

75. R. Morin, "A Matter of Privacy," Wash. Post Nat'l Weekly Ed. (June 29, 1998) at 34.

76. *See* W. Leibowitz, "Medical Database Spotlights Tech Privacy Issues," Nat'l L. J. (August 3, 1998) at A8.

77. Toward the end of 1999, the FTC began to hold public workshops to address privacy concerns about Internet data gathering techniques. *See* A. Petersen and J. Auerbach, "Online Ad Titans Bet Big in Race to Trace Consumers' Web Tracks," Wall St. J. (November 8, 1999) at B1.

78. *See* J. Sandberg, "Ply and Pry: How Business Pumps Kids on Web," Wall St. J. (June 9, 1997) at B1.

79. Pub. L. No. 105-277, 112 Stat. 2681 (October 21, 1998).

80. 16 C.F.R. 312 (1999).

81. For a thorough discussion of TRUSTe, see E. Dyson, *Release 2.0* (Broadway Books, 1997) at 202–205.

82. *See* R. Quick, "On-Line Groups Are Offering Up Privacy Plans," Wall St. J. (June 22, 1998) at B1.

83. A similar approach is called the Open Profiling Standard. *See* E. Dyson, *Release 2.0* (Broadway Books, 1997) at 206–210; D. Clark, "Rivals Microsoft and Netscape Team Up to Protect Consumer Privacy on the Web," Wall St. J. (June 12, 1997) at B8.

84. The FTC was impressed with a study indicating that the number of popular Web sites posting privacy policies rose from 14% in 1998 to almost two-thirds in 1999. *See* AP, "Report: No Need for New Internet Privacy Laws," San Luis Obispo Telegram-Tribune (July 13, 1999) at D2; G. Miller, "As Net Sites Give Privacy a Priority, Offline Concerns Grow," San Luis Obispo Telegram-Tribune (May 13, 1999) at A6.

85. Directive 95/46 of the European parliament and of the Council of October 24, 1995, on the protection of individuals with regard to the processing of personal data and on the free movement of such data (OJ 1995 L 281/31).

86. There are limited exceptions to this rule, such as when the data processing is necessary for the performance of a contract to which the individual is a party.

87. *See* A. Gidari and M. Agliion, "E.U. Directive on Privacy May Hinder E-Commerce," Nat'l L. J.

(June 29, 1998) at B7, noting an opinion of the Working Party on the Protection of Individuals with Regard to the Processing of Personal Data.

88. Article 26. For instance, the directive provides for exceptions if the individual unambiguously consents to the transfer, or if the transfer is necessary for the performance of a contract involving the data subject. *See* F. Carlin, "EU to Install Data Privacy Standards," Nat'l L. J. (October 27, 1997) at B7, B14.

89. A Swedish court prohibited American Airlines' Sabre Group from transferring to the United States personal information regarding Europeans, such as whether a passenger is Jewish and prefers kosher meals, or requires wheelchair assistance on arrival from transatlantic flights. *See* "Privacy Law Worries U.S. Businesses," Informationweek (October 26, 1998) at 26; "Privacy Here and Abroad," Wash. Post Nat'l Weekly Ed. (November 9, 1998) at 25.

90. P. Swire, "The Great Wall of Europe," CIO Enterprise (February 15, 1998) at 26.

91. It has been reported that U.S. Robotics was fined for failing to register under the United Kingdom's Data Protection Act and for obtaining information about visitors to its Web site for marketing purposes. A. Gidari and M. Aglion, "E.U. Directive on Privacy May Hinder E-Commerce," Nat'l L. J. (June 29, 1998) at B7, B19.

92. Draft International Safe Harbor Privacy Principles Issued by the U.S. Department of Commerce (March 17, 2000). Substantial information about the agreement and draft principles is available at www.ita.doc.gov/td/ecom/menul.html.

93. For an excellent discussion of PICS, see E. Dyson, *Release 2.0* (Broadway Books, 1997) at 169–191.

94. Organizations also might sponsor an Internet Service Provider that screens content for its members according to their preferences. FamilyClick.com, a 1999 proposed joint venture between AT&T and Tim Robertson (son of evangelist Pat Robertson), is designed to give families control over content in this way. L. Cauley, "AT&T Plans Internet Venture with Son of Evangelist to Block Data for Children," Wall St. J. (July 19, 1999) at B6.

95. *See* L. Lessig, "What Things Regulate Speech: CDA 2.0 vs. Filtering," 38 Jurimetrics 629 (Summer 1998) at 652–665.

96. Child Online Protection Act, Pub. L. No. 105-207 (October 21, 1998) *codified* at 47 U.S.C. § 231.

97. American Civil Liberties Union v. Reno, 31 F.Supp. 2d 473 (E.D. Pa. 1999).

98. Mainstream Loudoun v. Board of Trustees of the Loudoun County Library, Civil Action No. 97-2049-A, (E.D. Va. 1998).

99. W. Leibowitz, "Future of Web Filtering," Nat'l L. J. (December 14, 1998) at A18.

100. 776 F.Supp 135 (S.D. NY 1991).

101. 1995 N.Y. Misc. LEXIS 229 (NY Sup. Ct. 1995).

102. 47 U.S.C. § 230(c)(1).

103. 129 F.3d 327 (4th Cir. 1997).

104. D. Satran, "ExploreZip Virus Hits Computers Around the World," Yahoo! News, Reuters, (June 11, 1999).

105. "Computer Virus Costs to Business Surging—Study," Yahoo! News, Reuters (June 18, 1999).

106. Werner, Zaroff, Slotnick, Stern and Askenazy v. Lewis, N.Y. Superior Ct. (August 3, 1992).

107. D. Branscum, "The Big Spam Debate," Newsweek (June 22, 1998) at 84.

108. CompuServe, Inc. v. Cyber Promotions, Inc., 962 F.Supp. 1015 (S.D. Ohio 1997).

109. By the end of 1998, California, Nevada, and Washington had enacted laws to combat unsolicited commercial e-mail.

110. California Business and Professional Code §§ 17538.4, 17538.45; California Penal Code § 502.

111. *See* A. Kuczynski, "Dustin Hoffman Wins Suit on Photo Alteration," N.Y. Times (January 23, 1999) at A30.

Important Contract and Antitrust Issues for Technology Companies

9

INTRODUCTION

This final chapter presents important issues which high-technology companies must consider when entering into contracts. The intent of the chapter is not to provide an exhaustive treatment of the subject. An entire book dedicated to the topic of contracts would barely suffice to cover even the most fundamental aspects of contract principles. The attempt, here, therefore is simply to familiarize the reader with a carefully selected set of the most pressing contract-related issues typically encountered by high-technology enterprises.

In this chapter, we first will take a look at product warranties, a topic of critical importance for all sellers of high-technology goods. What are the standards of performance that the goods should be expected to meet? How can the seller precisely define the limits of those expectations in the contract? This section will address these important concerns. In addition, we will evaluate contract techniques that may be used to reduce the seller's monetary risks when the goods do not live up to standards promised under the warranty.

After the discussion of warranties, the chapter considers two relatively modern contract issues that have substantial importance to technology companies. One involves the use of shrink-wrap or click-wrap licenses—techniques that firms use to facilitate the process of obtaining approval of contractual conditions by their customers. The other regards recent efforts to develop new model laws specifically governing software contracts and licenses of information.

Next, we will review some representative contract issues raised when firms work together in what is often called a strategic alliance to develop, manufacture, and/or distribute high-technology products. Among other things, we will have an opportunity here to pull together certain of the intellectual property concepts that have been raised throughout this book. In addition, we will briefly examine alternative dispute resolution techniques. These methods, which strive to avoid litigation, have now proven their effectiveness, especially in situations when long-term business relationships are essential.

Following this discussion, we will take a look at how various contractual relationships typically entered by high-technology concerns may raise substantial antitrust concerns. Clearly, the antitrust scrutiny recently received by such firms as Microsoft and Intel highlights the potential implications that antitrust may have for high-technology business strategies. Also, we will consider some of the special antitrust problems that may be raised when a company enjoys exclusive intellectual property rights in the marketplace.

For reference, a very simplified sample software development agreement is provided at the end of this chapter. This sample is intended merely to demonstrate how some of the issues discussed in the chapter might be resolved in contractual form. Please keep in mind that a comprehensive agreement would address many more topics, treating all of the relevant considerations with substantially more specificity than does this sample. Thus, you never should rely on the sample as a checklist of all the important aspects of a software development contract. In addition, the language used in the sample has been greatly simplified so as to enhance its role as an educational tool. Therefore, neither its format nor any of its provisions should be used to draft legal documents.

WARRANTIES, LIMITATIONS, AND REMEDIES

(AES) Purchasers of the **AES** will be very excited about the new addition to their home entertainment system. They likely will have a host of expectations about the product including the capabilities of the product, conditions for performance, and durability. Some of these presumptions just come with the territory. One who buys an **Audio Enhancement System** naturally will expect it to improve the sound of a record collection to some reasonable degree. In addition, the purchaser will rightfully assume such things as that the product will not be damaged and that it will hold up under normal operating conditions. Other expectations may be derived from our statements and actions. Perhaps we made specific oral or written promises about how the **AES** would perform. Or maybe the sales staff gave certain assurances after learning what the customer wanted. It is even possible that salespeople demonstrated the performance of various features of the **AES** in a listening room environment, leading the customer to assume that the **AES** would perform the same at home. All of these scenarios involve implicit or explicit promises made to customers about the performance, qualities, and characteristics of the **AES**. Such promises are called warranties.

Throughout the following discussions about warranties, disclaimers, and remedies, the text uses the **AES** as an example to demonstrate how the law may be applied and how contract provisions might solve certain problems. The entire section, therefore, should be viewed as a continuation of the **AES** thread-case scenario.

As mentioned in Chapter 1, contractual relationships are governed primarily by state law. Fortunately, all 50 states have adopted the Uniform Commercial Code (UCC), which was developed by legal experts to simplify, clarify, and modernize policies governing commercial transactions.[1] For this discussion regarding warranties, the important provisions are within Article 2, which deals with sales and licenses of goods.[2] In addition to Article 2, many states also have adopted more particularized legal codes dealing with warranties for consumer goods. For instance, when we sell the **AES** in California, not only must we be cognizant of the UCC, but also we must consider the Song-Beverly Consumer Warranty Act. Finally, sellers of consumer products, such as **AES**, are subject to federal law under the Magnuson-Moss Warranty Act, which imposes additional requirements when written warranties are made. Magnuson-Moss is enforced by the Federal Trade Commission.

Article 2 of the UCC was designed over 40 years ago, before the introduction of modern information technologies such as computers and the Internet. This explains why the article applies only to transactions in goods. Article 2, however, is beginning to show its age, as modern economies enter the information age. Although its provisions clearly apply to certain tangible items such as computer diskettes, there are substantial questions whether and to what degree they cover the intangible information contained on such disks. The issues become even more vexing as the tangible items are removed altogether, such as when information is transferred over the Internet. For this reason, a massive effort was undertaken in the 1990s to develop a new article of the UCC, titled Article 2B, intended to apply specifically to software and information contracts. These efforts stalled in 1999, due to disputes over certain key issues, such as the legality of click-wrap licenses. Nonetheless, the effort to develop a model law undoubtedly will continue, and one should expect the adoption of Article 2B or some similar package relatively soon.[3]

With respect to international transactions, the United States is a party to the Convention on Contracts for the International Sale of Goods (CISG), which has over 40 participants. The CISG applies to commercial contracts for the sale of goods when made between companies having their places of business in different nations that have ratified the convention.[4] The provisions of the CISG often are somewhat similar to those in the UCC. However, there are many technical differences that may be important, such as with risk of loss and the acceptance of offers. In addition, application of the CISG is limited to commercial transactions, whereas the UCC applies also to consumer sales. Warranties under the CISG are governed by Article 35. For the most part, warranties are treated the same under the CISG as with the UCC. Once again, though, there are some variations that could prove to be important. For example, the CISG provides merchants more flexibility in disclaiming implied warranties than does the UCC. The forthcoming treatment of warranties does not include consideration of the CISG.[5] However, it should be clear that those engaging in international transactions must consult the CISG whenever it is applicable to their international dealings.

Express Warranties

Express warranties consist of the actual promises made by the seller, whether communicated orally, in writing, by description, or through a demonstration. Article 2, Section 313, of the UCC explains that express warranties may arise in three ways. It provides:

1. Any affirmation of fact or promise made by the seller to the buyer which relates to the goods and becomes part of the basis of the bargain creates an express warranty that the goods shall conform to the affirmation or promise;
2. Any description of the goods which is made a part of the basis of the bargain creates an express warranty that the goods shall conform to the description;
3. Any sample or model which is made part of the basis of the bargain creates an express warranty that the whole of the goods shall conform to the sample or model.

Express warranties typically are incorporated in the written sales agreement or provided in writing with the goods. For instance, we may include with the **AES** written assurances that the product will exceed certain defined technical specifications, that it will be free of material defects for a specified length of time, or that it will improve the audio quality of certain types of recordings. However, this may not be the total extent of our express promises. The UCC provides that we do not have to formally declare that a promise is a warranty for it to serve as one. Thus, oral allegations made by salespersons that are more definitive than mere opinions come within the definition of express warranties. In addition, the language makes it clear that descriptions in promotional literature and demonstrations of units at trade shows or in showrooms may lead to express warranties.

How to Control and Limit Express Warranties   Providers of high-technology products and services prize a dedicated and hard-working sales staff. Often, remuneration schemes, such as those based on commissions, are established to ensure that marketing personnel have sufficient incentives to push the merchandise aggressively. Those involved in sales and marketing must be carefully trained about the statements and promises they make, for such allegations ultimately may bind the company as express warranties. However, even with careful training programs, there will be the occasional incident—such as an oral assurance that a desired objective can be obtained or a promotional booklet that highlights an unproven feature—resulting from an overwhelming desire to close a sale. Thus, most sophisticated sellers take steps to reduce their legal exposure from statements or demonstrations made by sales staff. High-technology sellers must understand how these steps might serve to protect the company. Purchasers in turn must be aware of them to ensure that promises made in the negotiation process actually survive the sale.

When we manufacture and market the **AES**, we have a strong desire to satisfy the expectations of our customers. We hope that our salespeople and distributors do not promise more than we can deliver, but we can never be sure, and in all likelihood some substantial mistakes or misunderstandings will arise. Our goal, therefore, is to maintain as much control as possible over our potential legal liabilities to customers who allege that we have not fulfilled our promises. Our best means for accomplishing this is to clearly express in a written agreement precisely what the customer should expect from the AES and what our obligations are to fulfill these commitments.

One of the most important lessons about contract negotiations is to document in writing all the important aspects of a deal. In almost all negotiations, various issues are raised and discussed but not always clearly answered prior to closure of the transaction. Invariably, some of these issues will arise later on, leading to honest disputes about what the contracting parties actually promised each other. Although it may take more time to finalize the deal, it is far better for the parties to definitively address every conceivable issue that might affect their business relationship and clearly write down how they intend to handle those issues should they eventually materialize. Although this exercise may not reduce the physical problems that might occur, the clarity that it lends to expectations should result in more congenial solutions.

Beyond this practical reason for memorializing a deal in writing, there are legal reasons as well. The legal system has a strong preference for written contracts. Because proof about the existence and terms of oral agreements may come only from the memories and allegations of the individuals involved in the deal, oral arrangements raise the specter of dishonesty and fraud. For this reason, all states have passed laws that require certain types of contracts to be in writing if the parties wish to bring lawsuits regarding them.

ENTIRE AGREEMENT CLAUSES   Far more important for this discussion, however, is how written contracts affect oral and even written statements made prior to finalization of a deal. In general terms, the policy is that once the parties finalize their agreement in writing, the writing takes substantial precedence over all previous promises. All prior (or contemporaneous) contradictory statements will be thrown out by a court if a dispute arises. A court might consider a supplementary promise, such as when a salesperson orally makes an additional warranty pledge, if the promise is otherwise consistent with the written terms in the final contract. However, if the parties indicate that the written contract is to be treated as the exclusive statement of the terms of the agreement, then even consistent statements made prior to the contract will be ignored by the courts. Such contracts, called integrated contracts, are the key for the company to help control its warranty obligations. If the parties agree that their written contract is integrated, then the buyer cannot later allege that the seller made warranty promises that are not somehow contained within the four corners of the contract. This effectively means that statements and demonstrations made by salespersons may not be considered part of the express warranty terms of the deal if a dispute arises.

The following type of language in written contracts makes it clear that the agreement is to be treated as an integrated expression:

This contract constitutes the complete and exclusive statement of the agreement between the parties and it supersedes all proposals, oral or written, and all other communications between the parties relating to the subject matter of this contract.

Companies intending to rely on integrated written contracts to control express warranties must always remember that the law ultimately will strive to protect the reasonable expectations of the parties. If one's goal is to take advantage of unsophisticated buyers by luring them with promises that are ultimately taken away in the final written agreement, then the purchasers likely will have legal recourse. Fraud provides one theory of liability, notwithstanding the integration clause in the written contract. In addition, some courts might decide in egregious situations that it is unconscionable to enforce the integration clause, thereby giving them the freedom to evaluate whether other promises were made that might not have been included in the final written expression.

The message from all this for the buyer should be very clear. When there is a written contract specifying the terms of an agreement—and there always should be—then the buyer should take care to ensure that the contract includes all important promises made by the seller during the sales negotiation process. Since the seller often uses a standard form contract, the buyer should require that an appendix be attached that clearly specifies any promises the seller made that the buyer considers to be a key aspect of the deal. Such allegations may have been made orally by salespeople, claimed in sales brochures, or indicated through sales demonstrations. Whatever the source, failure to include them in the written agreement may raise substantial obstacles if a dispute ever arises.

Implied Warranties

In addition to any express warranties made by the seller, the UCC provides that the seller makes certain implied warranties simply because the transaction occurred. According to UCC Section 2-314, merchants who enter into a contract for the sale (or license) of goods imply in the contract that the goods will be *merchantable*. Here, a merchant is a person who regularly deals in the goods under consideration, a definition that clearly covers our company when we sell the **AES**.[6] In order for **AES** units to be considered merchantable, they should meet at least the following standards:

1. Be fit for the ordinary purposes for which such audio equipment is used.
2. Be adequately contained and packaged.
3. Conform to any promises made on the packaging.
4. Meet other standards expected from the way we deal with the **AES** or that ordinarily arise in the audio trade.

Besides the implied warranty pertaining to merchantability, we also may make an *implied warranty that the goods are fit for a particular need or purpose* expressed to us by the customer. UCC Section 2-315 states:

> Where the seller at the time of contracting has reason to know any particular purpose for which the goods are required and that the buyer is relying on the seller's skill or judgment to select or furnish suitable goods, there is . . . an implied warranty that the goods shall be fit for such purpose.

This situation could easily arise with the **AES**, as with all audio equipment. For instance, customers may explain to our salesperson that they are searching for a way to improve the sound quality of special records or that they will need to store the audio equipment in a very hot or moist environment or that the unit must be compatible with certain types of components. In all likelihood, the salesperson will know that customers are relying on the salesperson's superior knowledge and judgment about audio equipment to guide their decision. If the salesperson ultimately recommends and sells the **AES** knowing about these special needs, then by implication we have promised that the **AES** will satisfy them.

One final kind of implied warranty that may be important to sellers of high-technology goods is the *warranty of title and against infringement*. When a company sells products incorporating intellectual property, then, by implication, it promises that the product does not infringe the intellectual property rights of another. A purchaser of the **AES**, for instance, could be liable for patent infringement when using the machine if the machine contains patented technology owned by someone other than our company. If this ultimately damages certain customers, they could sue us for compensation.

Exclusion of Implied Warranties Implied warranties are unattractive to manufacturers and sellers who wish to maximize control of potential liabilities stemming from alleged deficiencies in their products. Anytime a court has the flexibility to infer a promise from actions or a course of dealing, sellers are susceptible to unfavorable interpretations. This is particularly true with the implied warranty of fitness for a particular purpose, wherein liability can depend on the believability of testimony regarding the knowledge of the seller about the needs of the purchaser. Thus, manufacturers often strive to exclude the implied warranties so that they may be committed only to their express promises.

Under the UCC, all three kinds of implied warranties may be excluded. However, one must be careful to communicate the exclusion clearly to the purchaser by using appropriate language. In addition, one also must be mindful of state and federal consumer warranty laws that may affect one's ability to limit or exclude implied warranties.

One method to disclaim all implied warranties is to clearly state in the contract that the goods are sold "as is" or "with all faults." Generally, such language is used when the seller makes no warranties, either express or implied, regarding the products. However, this is not the method of choice, especially for sellers of new merchandise, for purchasers usually expect some level of warranty protection. You can imagine the response if we tried to sell new **AES** units "as is." The more common method is to clearly state express warranties and then particularly exclude the implied warranties. The most important requirement when using this method is that the exclusion be conspicuous. This means that a reasonable person in the buyer's position would not be surprised if later shown that the exclusion is in the contract. Typically, it is a good idea to print the exclusion close to the signature line, using a larger-size typeface than the rest of the contract and bold print. The UCC also requires that the disclaimer of the implied warranty of merchantability must actually mention the word "merchantability." The following clause provides an example of how the implied warranties of merchantability and fitness can be effectively excluded in the contract:

> **to the extent allowed by law, seller hereby disclaims all implied warranties, including, but not limited to, the implied warranties of merchantability and fitness for a particular purpose.**

WARRANTY LIMITATIONS AND THE MAGNUSON-MOSS ACT Since the **AES** is a consumer product, we will have to comply with the federal Magnuson-Moss Act and possibly state consumer warranty laws if we wish to reduce our exposure to implied warranties. The Magnuson-Moss Act states that if we make a written express warranty, then that warranty must be either a Full Warranty or a Limited Warranty, as those terms are defined by the act. For our purposes, the major difference is that implied warranties may not be limited or excluded if a Full Warranty is provided. Thus, assuming we wish to control this aspect, we will have to provide a Limited Warranty. Even with this, however, we are not able to fully exclude the implied warranties. Rather, we may only limit their duration to either the length of our express warranty or a reasonable amount of time, whichever is longer. In addition, we must indicate in a conspicuous way that the laws of certain states may give different rights with respect to limitations on implied warranties. In California, for instance, the Song-Beverly Consumer Warranty Act allows implied warranties to be coextensive in duration with the express warranties, but in no event less than 60 days. Other states may be even more restrictive, possibly not allowing any limitation at all. According to the Magnuson-Moss Act, our disclaimer of implied warranties must conspicuously inform purchasers of their potential rights under state laws with the following language:

> **some states do not allow limitations on how long an implied warranty lasts, so the above limitation may not apply to you.**

In sum, the best course is to provide written express warranties and to disclaim implied warranties as much as possible. With consumer products, however, one will have to conform this strategy both to the federal Magnuson-Moss Act and to appropriate state consumer warranty laws. These considerations are summarized in Exhibit 9.1.

Remedies for Breach of Warranties and Limitations of Remedies

Compensatory Damages When an **AES** unit does not work as warranted, the buyer likely will suffer damage. For instance, one important warranted feature of the **AES** is that it improves sound quality to a defined degree according to some technical measure. If that improvement is not achieved with a

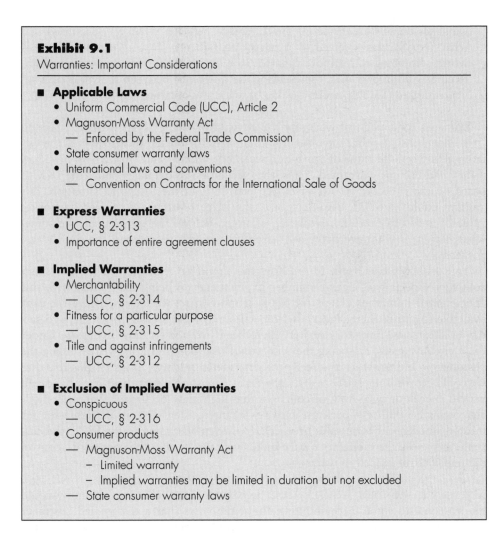

Exhibit 9.1
Warranties: Important Considerations

- **Applicable Laws**
  - Uniform Commercial Code (UCC), Article 2
  - Magnuson-Moss Warranty Act
    - — Enforced by the Federal Trade Commission
  - State consumer warranty laws
  - International laws and conventions
    - — Convention on Contracts for the International Sale of Goods

- **Express Warranties**
  - UCC, § 2-313
  - Importance of entire agreement clauses

- **Implied Warranties**
  - Merchantability
    - — UCC, § 2-314
  - Fitness for a particular purpose
    - — UCC, § 2-315
  - Title and against infringements
    - — UCC, § 2-312

- **Exclusion of Implied Warranties**
  - Conspicuous
    - — UCC, § 2-316
  - Consumer products
    - — Magnuson-Moss Warranty Act
      - – Limited warranty
      - – Implied warranties may be limited in duration but not excluded
    - — State consumer warranty laws

purchased machine, then the buyer has not received the product for which that buyer bargained and paid. In this case, our company should have to compensate for this damage. For instance, assume a consumer could have purchased a competing brand for $500. However, the customer opted for our StatFree brand, even with its $1,300 price tag, because we warranted that it could achieve a 14-ptu quality boost while the competitor's model could yield an improvement of only 10 ptus. If it turns out that our customer's StatFree delivers only a 10-ptu increase, then the buyer clearly has suffered damage. The extent of the damage depends on how one looks at the situation. On one hand, the buyer paid $800 more for the machine than it is worth. On the other, the buyer paid $1,300 with the expectation of receiving a 14-ptu quality improvement.

Damages could be considered the difference between what was promised and what actually was received. If it turns out that in reality, a 14-ptu machine is worth something much more than $1,300, say $5,000, then the buyer has suffered $4,500 in damages, representing the difference between the value of what was expected ($5,000) and the value of what was obtained ($500).

Damages for breach of warranty are covered by the UCC in Article 2, Section 714, which provides that the measure of damages for breach of warranty is the difference between the value of the goods accepted and the value they would have had if they had been as warranted. Thus, the calculation of damages under the UCC is based on the expectations raised by the warranty. In the foregoing situation, this amount could be $800, assuming our sales price represented the actual market value of a 14-ptu machine. However, as noted before, the figure could be somewhat higher, if what we promised actually is worth more than the $1,300 we charged.

You probably can begin to see how this could be troublesome for our small company, especially if a large number of units end up being distributed with this deficiency. If numerous claims for $800 or more arise, we may not have the cash available to satisfy them. Proceeds from sales may have already been spent to satisfy creditors and investors or may have been invested in new inventory. Under these circumstances, replacing the unit would be a better alternative, assuming the customer would allow us to remedy the situation in this way. It also is possible that we could fix the units fairly easily if the customers simply sent them back to us and waited a week or two. And, of course, if that nightmare occurs wherein only models costing $5,000 will perform as we warranted, then we will be liable for far more than even our total sales proceeds. However, according to the UCC, the customer may seek the monetary award unless we take steps in the contract to control the remedies for breach of warranty.

METHODS TO CONTROL COMPENSATORY DAMAGES   As a seller, we certainly would like to come to some understanding about the ways that a dissatisfied customer may remedy the situation. For instance, we would want the customer to agree that we should have the opportunity to repair or replace the model rather than our having to pay monetary compensation. Presumably, if those efforts cannot achieve the performance warranted, then we would have to satisfy the customer with money. Our fear then is what the value of the warranted product ultimately may be determined to be—potentially $5,000 as described earlier. To alleviate this concern, we also want the customer to agree that our maximum responsibility is to return the purchase price should we fail in our efforts to repair or replace the unit satisfactorily.

Fortunately, the UCC, in Section 719, allows us to reach such agreements with our customers. Section 719 provides that the agreement may provide for other types of remedies such as (1) return of the goods and repayment of the purchase price or (2) repair and replacement of nonconforming goods. This section also allows us to limit the available remedies solely to those provided for in the agreement as long as we expressly provide that they are exclusive. Thus, we are given a lot of room to fashion the purchaser's remedies to meet our needs. However, this right is not unlimited. Section 719 provides that when circumstances cause an exclusive or limited remedy *to fail of its essential purpose*, then the buyer may resort to the remedies normally available under the code. In other words, we ultimately must be able to satisfy the buyer in a reasonable fashion. For instance, our contract might provide that we will repair or replace the unit so that the customer receives the performance warranted. If after a reasonable number of attempts we are unable to provide a unit conforming to the warranty, then our remedy has failed of its essential purpose. In this case, the buyer is entitled to the compensation needed to fulfill expectations under the bargain.

One way to soften the sting of this result is to provide a fallback remedy in the agreement that becomes effective if our efforts to repair or replace fail. Again, though, one must keep in mind that the fallback must be reasonable. Therefore, to be somewhat extreme, one might consider a clause stating that if repairs are not effective, the buyer is entitled to $1. Clearly, this would be unreasonable and would make the entire remedy fail of the essential purpose. Obviously, by doing this, we are trying to make the buyer bear the total responsibility for the deficiency in our product. This is the type of solution we must avoid. Rather, our fallback remedy should provide for the return of the entire purchase price or of some amount of compensation that is reasonable under the circumstances. The following is an example of an effective remedy limitation with a reasonable fallback provision:

> If the product does not conform to the warranty, Seller shall at its sole and absolute option repair the product at no charge or replace the product with the same model or its equivalent at no charge. If, after repeated efforts, Seller is unable to provide correction for the nonconformity, then Buyer's exclusive remedy and Seller's entire liability is to refund the amounts paid by Buyer to Seller upon return of the product to Seller.

Consequential Damages   The foregoing discussion focused on damage to the buyer because the **AES** we delivered was not worth as much as we promised. However, there are other ways that a purchaser could be damaged that potentially could be far more costly. For example, suppose some of the **AES** machines somehow erased or damaged records even though we promised that the machine would have no effect on prerecorded material. Unfortunately, one of the purchasers just happened to have a particularly treasured collection of old classical and jazz LPs and did not discover the problem until most of them had been played. Clearly, this buyer not only will demand that the defect be repaired but also will want to be compensated for the other dire consequences of our breach of warranty—and under the circumstances, this could total thousands of dollars, even though we received only $1,300 in payment for the machine. As another example, consider a buyer who made it clear to the salesperson that the StatFree was going to be the central feature of a new kind of '50s nightclub premised on the premier sound quality of music performed by the original artists. Since much of this music is available only on LP format, the concept depends on the StatFree's working as warranted. If the StatFree does not perform adequately and the nightclub fails, the owner may blame us for the demise and expect compensation for all the losses on the project. One final illustration involves a buyer who is severely electrocuted by a damaged power cord, even though we warranted that the product would be free of material safety defects. Obviously, damages of these kinds, which are called consequential damages, may be staggering.

Section 714 provides that a buyer not only is entitled to compensation for loss of the benefit of the bargain but also may receive incidental and consequential damages. Of these, consequential damages are by far the most important and threatening. According to Section 715 of the UCC, consequential damages include:

1. losses resulting from general or particular requirements and needs of the buyer about which the seller had reason to know and which could not be reasonably prevented by the buyer; and
2. injuries to persons or property which the seller knew or reasonably should have known would have resulted from any breach of warranty.

This definition of consequential damages covers all of the scenarios presented earlier. Therefore, we could be liable by our breach of warranty for potentially enormous consequential damage awards unless we are able to limit or exclude our exposure to them through the contract.[7]

CAN CONSEQUENTIAL DAMAGES BE LIMITED?   The UCC provides us some flexibility if we desire to reduce our exposure to potential consequential damages. Section 719 provides:

> Consequential damages may be limited or excluded unless the limitation or exclusion is unconscionable. Limitation of consequential damages for injury to the person in the case of consumer goods is prima facie unconscionable but limitation of damages where the loss is commercial is not.

According to this provision, a company may limit its exposure to consequential damages as long as the limitation is not *unconscionable*. Unconscionable is not defined, but clearly it refers to situations or behaviors that are socially reprehensible. For instance, the methods that one uses to "convince" another to enter an agreement may be so distasteful as to be considered unconscionable. As an example, a company may bury particularly oppressive terms in a sea of legalese using consistently small print with the intent that the other party will overlook them. Or the firm may place the terms in unexpected places, such as within standard provisions about minor conditions that normal people usually ignore. Other scenarios may involve high-pressure salespersons who prey on particularly needy individuals, especially those who do not understand the language very well. Or imagine the power a hospital might have if it included burdensome terms within contracts that it forced patients to sign before having emergency surgery. All of these raise instances where a contract may be deemed unconscionable for procedural reasons. As you might expect, when firms get unsuspecting individuals to enter contracts in such ways, the courts typically will not enforce their agreements, claiming that they violate public policy.

One special type of agreement that is deemed procedurally unconscionable is called a *contract of adhesion*. A contract of adhesion arises when a consumer has no choice but to enter a standardized contract because there are only a few other firms offering the product or service, and they all require adherence to the same burdensome conditions. Many people object to shrink-wrap and click-wrap licenses, calling them unconscionable for procedural reasons. We shall see that at least one court has agreed, ruling that they are contracts of adhesion.

Along with procedures, courts also may analyze the substantive content of the contract provisions to determine if they are unconscionable. Thus if the terms "shock the conscience" because they are unusually unfair or oppressive, courts will refrain from enforcing them on the grounds of public policy. Putting the procedural and substantive notions of unconscionability together, one now can begin to piece together the extent to which companies may limit consequential damages. Perhaps it is best to envision a spectrum running from "certainly unconscionable" to "clearly not unconscionable." Section 719 defines one scenario that is certainly unconscionable: that involving a consumer good that causes personal injury. Therefore, we will not be able to limit our exposure for the power cord mishap with the AES. At the other extreme are situations involving straightforward agreements between commercial parties having equal bargaining power. These clearly are not unconscionable because the parties are able to fend for themselves and thus can make purposeful decisions about how they wish to allocate the risks of their transaction. For those other situations that lie in the middle ground, the types of characteristics that often are relevant include (1) the business sophistication of the buyer, (2) whether the buyer had an opportunity to read the limitation and could understand its ramifications; and (3) how much power the buyer was able to exercise in bargaining for changes in the contract. Exhibit 9.2 reviews the basics of unconscionability.

Regarding consequential damages, some states have adopted laws that are more restrictive than the UCC, especially when dealing with consumer goods. A seller has to pay attention to particular state laws, such as the Song-Beverly Act in California, before attempting to limit the ability of buyers to recover consequential (or incidental) damages. Indeed, the federal Magnuson-Moss Act requires the following statement to conspicuously appear on the face of a warranty for consumer products:

some states do not allow the exclusion or limitation of incidental or consequential damages, so the above limitation or exclusion may not apply to you.

CAN CONSEQUENTIAL DAMAGES BE LIMITED WHEN EXCLUSIVE REMEDIES FAIL?   Sellers who wish to limit their exposure to consequential damages must deal with one other area of uncertainty. Section 719 of the UCC is somewhat ambiguous about

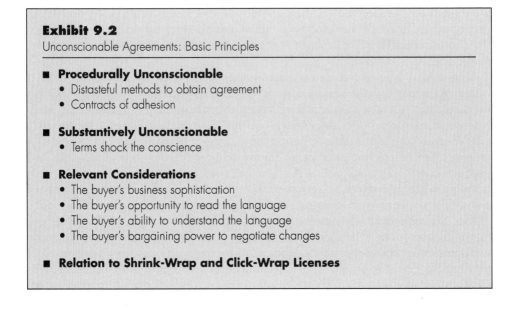

Exhibit 9.2
Unconscionable Agreements: Basic Principles

■ **Procedurally Unconscionable**
  • Distasteful methods to obtain agreement
  • Contracts of adhesion

■ **Substantively Unconscionable**
  • Terms shock the conscience

■ **Relevant Considerations**
  • The buyer's business sophistication
  • The buyer's opportunity to read the language
  • The buyer's ability to understand the language
  • The buyer's bargaining power to negotiate changes

■ **Relation to Shrink-Wrap and Click-Wrap Licenses**

what happens to a consequential damage limitation if an exclusive remedy fails of its essential purpose. For instance, it is typical for a seller to have an exclusive remedy of repair or replacement along with a limitation of consequential damages. If the seller ultimately is unable to repair or replace the product satisfactorily, then that remedy has failed of its essential purpose. Does that mean that the limitation of consequential damages has also failed? After all, the buyer may have agreed to the restriction on consequential damages on the assumption that the unit ultimately would work as warranted. Under these circumstances, one might argue that it is unconscionable to enforce the limitation on consequential damages.

The courts vary widely on this issue. Some are inclined to package the exclusive remedy with the limitation on consequential damages, so that when the exclusive remedy fails, the consequential damage limitation is thrown out with it. Others treat the subjects more discretely. In these courts, there are circumstances in which an exclusive remedy could fail of its essential purpose while a limitation on consequential damages remains conscionable. In this regard, judges tend to scrutinize the relative sophistication of the contracting parties and the expression of their intent very closely.[8] If the business subject to the limitation has substantial bargaining power and often is involved in complex contract negotiations, then it normally is harder for this firm to argue that it was unaware of what was going on, thereby allowing the other party to take advantage of it. On the other hand, if the complaining party is a consumer, then the courts may be much more skeptical. In addition, when the breach of contract leads to consequential losses that were within the normal expectations of the parties at the time they entered the contract, then courts are most likely to enforce provisions that allocate the expected risks. Finally, it often is important that the breaching party acted reasonably and tried in good faith to uphold its end of the bargain. As you can imagine, judges are not inclined to enforce provisions that were cleverly designed to facilitate unconscionable conduct.

Companies that provide exclusive remedies along with consequential damage limitations certainly want a court to enforce the consequential damage restriction when the exclusive remedy fails. Certain steps can make it more likely that a court will do this. The best means is to ensure that the exclusive remedy does not fail. Having an effective backup remedy may be helpful in this regard. Also, the seller should make it very clear in the contract that the two issues are considered to be separate and discrete aspects of the deal. To this end, the contract should provide the consequential damage limitation in a clause that is separate from the one providing the exclusive remedy. Packaging them in the same paragraph may lead a court to believe that the two should be treated together. Also, the consequential damage limitation should expressly state that the parties intend the limitation to remain effective even if the exclusive remedy fails. Such language clearly demonstrates how the parties intended to allocate the risks of the venture, especially if they are both sophisticated in commercial matters.

Exhibit 9.3 summarizes the major considerations regarding remedies for breach of warranties. In addition, it indicates how one might control exposure to compensatory and consequential damages.

Y2K Issues

As noted in Chapter 8, companies began to focus enormous attention on potential Y2K computer problems as the year 2000 approached. There was no question that the "defect" existed, and that it could cause significant economic disruptions and personal harms in a wide variety of contexts. The fundamental issue, therefore, was determining who would be responsible to pay for the damages that would result if the problems were not rectified in time.

Consider the questions that might confront a typical business that operates within a supply chain of distribution. For instance, a manufacturer of irrigation parts requires parts and raw materials to make its final products. This means that the manufacturer depends heavily on its suppliers to meet its predicted needs. Likewise, many of the suppliers depend on others to carry out their businesses. On the other side of the supply chain, the manufacturer has obligations to buyers who need the irrigation parts to incorporate into their irrigation systems. They, too, likely have obligations to their buyers, who may need the systems to, let's say, water golf courses or football fields.

So, let's assume that a Y2K problem in the manufacturer's computer systems cause disruptions in its operations, resulting in production delays or faulty parts. These, in turn, create hardships for its purchasers. Indeed, one of the buyers encounters a catastrophe on its contract to irrigate Texas Stadium before the Dallas Cowboys home opener. Undoubtedly, the manufacturer will have some responsibility to compensate its customers for their losses. The extent of that responsibility

Exhibit 9.3
Remedies for Breach of Warranties and Limitations of Remedies

- **Remedies for Breach of Warranties**
  - Compensatory damages
    - Benefit of the bargain
    - UCC, § 2-714
  - Consequential Damages
    - Other losses resulting from breach about which the seller reasonably should have known
    - UCC, § 2-715

- **Methods to Control Compensatory Damages**
  - Agreement provides for alternative remedies
  - Alternative remedies may not fail of their essential purpose
    - Repair or replacement
    - Fallback remedy
      - Return of payments made

- **Limitations on Consequential Damages**
  - May not be unconscionable
    - UCC, § 719
    - Consumer goods and personal injury damage limitations
  - State consumer protection laws

- **Enforcement of Consequential Damage Limitations when Alternative Remedies Fail**
  - May depend on relative sophistication of parties
  - Contract should demonstrate intent to treat damage limitation separately

will depend on the warranties and the forms of exclusive remedies and limitations it may have negotiated in its contracts. The manufacturer might then look to its software vendors and consultants to indemnify it for the payments it must make to its aggrieved customers. However, to obtain the software and services, it may have signed standard contracts which warranted the systems for, perhaps, only one year and limited remedies to repair or replace. Thus, the manufacturer may become stuck with shouldering some potentially large losses suffered by its customers.

This type of scenario explains why companies such as this manufacturer adopted measures to ensure that their own systems were Y2K compliant. In this regard, firms closely scrutinized their software systems to determine if they might encounter significant Y2K problems. If so, then it usually made economic sense to try to fix the problems before they actually disrupted operations. Since software vendors often had some financial exposure, depending on the circumstances and their contract warranty provisions, they also may have been brought into the compliance effort. Optimally, the companies could complete their system overhauls and verify Y2K compliance before encountering any significant negative repercussions. In addition, firms were advised to enter new contracts only with software vendors and consultants that warranted their products and services for Y2K compliance.

Although the expenses to meet such Y2K compliance may have been large, at least the manufacturer ultimately had the ability to control whether its own systems would work. However, this does not mean that ensuring its own compliance definitely solved all of the manufacturer's potential Y2K problems. If one of its suppliers had Y2K issues that caused its parts to be delayed or defective, then the manufacturer might not be able to satisfy its customers as promised. This time, however, the solutions would not be totally within the manufacturer's control. If the manufacturer suffered losses due to its supplier's Y2K difficulties, then it might be able to sue the supplier for compensation, but again, contract provisions could limit the amount of recovery. Also, the supplier might be small and not have the funds to cover its liabilities. Similar kinds of issues could arise from the other direction in the supply chain as well. For instance, customers faced with Y2K problems might miss payments or cancel orders, which might then affect the manufacturer's ability to meet its obligations to suppliers. Thus, Y2K problems had the potential to send tremendous ripples both up and down the supply chain.

At this time, it is unclear how long the Y2K problems may affect commercial transactions. Companies entering deals now normally expect their suppliers and customers to warrant that Y2K problems will not interfere with their performance under contracts. However, there are questions about how far these responsibilities should go. As a buyer, for instance, the irrigation manufacturer may want its suppliers to take responsibility for any Y2K problems that arise anywhere down the supply chain. However, this may be overreaching. In fact, most companies should think long and hard before signing contracts that require them to cover Y2K failures to such an extent. A more appropriate solution might have the following features:

1. Each party promises that its own computer systems are Y2K compliant.
2. Each party promises to request Y2K compliance in contracts with other parties.
3. The parties promise to share information about Y2K problems so that they might minimize the potential impacts from those problems.
4. If a party complies with these conditions, then it is not liable should it not be able to perform under the contract due to Y2K failures beyond the party's reasonable control (such as due to problems with suppliers or from the government).[9]

Since Y2K issues really come down to allocations of risk, you can see why warranties and limitations on remedies have such an enormous impact on how the problems are solved. This clearly is an area where contracts have to be scrutinized very carefully. In addition, one needs to pay close attention to applicable laws. For instance, Section 719 clearly is relevant if a Y2K failure related to a consumer good could result in personal injuries. Also, as we have seen, new federal statutes may offer some degree of relief in certain situations.

SHRINK-WRAP AND CLICK-WRAP LICENSES

General Principles Regarding Standardized Forms

A fundamental objective of contract law is to allow people to depend on the promises that others make to them. When parties complete a deal, they come away with reasonable expectations about what each is supposed to do. The goal of the law is to protect these reasonable expectations. At the same time, contract law is designed to allow the parties the freedom to determine the terms of their arrangement using the methods that they desire. Therefore, contract law does not usually specify what steps must be used to enter a deal. Rather, it generally only provides solutions when the evidence does not make it clear what the parties expected from the arrangement. Also, the law generally will enforce the promises that each party makes in a contract, unless there is some strong indication that they do not reflect the reasonable expectations of the parties. This is where the doctrine of unconscionability comes in. When judges strike down contract clauses due to unconscionability, it is usually because they do not believe that the complaining parties would have agreed to the allegedly objectionable terms if they had known about them, understood them, and had some choice to walk away from them.

Shrink-wrap and click-wrap licenses are merely extensions of a trend toward using form contracts in business dealings. When commercial firms do business with each other, their executives normally do not haggle over every component of their arrangement before beginning to perform. Through experience, each firm has a formula which it likes its deals to follow, and for efficiency puts that formula in a standard contract. When it comes time to formally strike a deal, one firm typically makes an offer on its form contract, which includes key features such as the price, quantity, and shipment dates along with a lot of standard provisions about such things as insurance, risk of loss, and warranties. The arrangement is concluded when the other party accepts by agreeing to the key terms on its own form contract. Sure, there sometimes are problems with this approach, especially when some of the standard provisions in the two forms are not the same. After all, contracts are supposed to involve a "meeting of the minds," which has not happened when the acceptance differs in any respect from the offer. However, the law has evolved to enforce commercial deals based on form contracts because they are an efficient method of conducting business. In addition, commercial parties reasonably expect that they have a deal even when certain terms have not been ironed out or individually negotiated. As always, the law works to protect those fundamental expectations, while providing rules for deciding which secondary terms control when there are differences.

Standardized Forms in the Consumer Context

Businesses no longer confine the use of form contracts to commercial parties, however. It is now common practice for firms to use standard forms for dealing with individual customers in the mass markets. This raises a number of concerns. These are not situations where customers reply with their own standard forms. Usually, the business simply provides the form with the understanding that these are the conditions, take them or leave them. Often, this is not a problem, since the terms would not surprise or offend a reasonable person. However, there is always a fear that businesses will try to take advantage of consumers, knowing that they will not read the forms or have any choice about them. That is, businesses might try to slip into the legal verbiage something particularly nasty that some consumers might not agree to if they were aware of it. This problem becomes especially acute when the consumers do not even have an opportunity to read the forms until after they have initiated the transaction, for instance by paying money for a product and taking it home. Just think about the last time you purchased electronic equipment. Did you even see the warranty disclaimers before you opened the box? Did you ever even read the document that included them? Is it fair that you might be bound to conditions that were not specifically brought to your attention before you handed over your money? Thus, there are dual concerns in the consumer context. One has to do with *unconscionable* behavior. The other has to do with *timing*—when the deal was struck, and what terms were included at that time.

Shrink-wrap licenses came to prominence in the software industry with over-the-counter sales to customers. Software often includes numerous trade secrets. When a copy of a computer program is sold to a customer, copyright laws prevent the customer from doing certain things, such as making additional copies for the office or for friends. Notably, though, copyright protects only expressions and not ideas. In addition, the trade secret laws permit individuals to reverse engineer the program and learn its ideas unless they have otherwise agreed not to do so. Thus, without more, individual purchasers might be able to study the programs they buy and determine valuable programming strategies and techniques. As we learned in Chapter 4, one way to prevent reverse engineering is to have customers agree that they will not take specified steps to learn or disclose the trade secrets. A shrink-wrap license is a method to do this in a mass-market environment. Essentially, the computer program is wrapped in cellophane, with a statement on the front stating that if the wrap is broken, then the customer agrees to certain terms and conditions. These terms make it clear that the program is being licensed—rather than sold—with numerous restrictions. One example that was subject to litigation in the case, *Vault v. Quaid*, stated:

> Important! Vault is providing the enclosed materials to you on the express condition that you assent to this software license. By using any of the enclosed diskette(s), you agree to the following provisions. If you do not agree with these license provisions, return these materials to your dealer, in original packaging within 3 days of receipt, for a refund.
>
> This software is licensed to you, the end-user, for your own internal use. Title to the licensed software and all proprietary rights in it shall remain with Vault. You may not transfer, sublicense, rent, lease, convey, copy, modify, translate, convert to another language, decompile or disassemble the licensed software for any purpose without Vault's prior written consent.

The theory behind the shrink-wrap license is that by breaking the seal, customers implicitly acknowledge their acceptance of the terms through their actions. In addition, at least in the case above, the seller has pretty good evidence that the buyer specifically saw the key terms in the license, since they were visible through the cellophane.

Click-wrap licenses are designed to reach the same result, but in the environment of the Internet rather than over-the-counter. With a click-wrap license, an online merchant indicates that by clicking in a particular place or manner, the customer agrees to certain specified conditions. Thus, with a click-wrap, the act of breaking a seal is merely replaced with the act of clicking the mouse.

Shrink-wrap and click-wrap licenses raise all the concerns of mass-market licenses. Perhaps the antipathy is greater because they prevent conduct that many people expect they should be allowed to do. It is not hard to imagine the complaints: "What do you mean I can't sell my copy to a friend?—Everybody does it and anyway it's legal for me to sell my copy under the copyright laws." Customers sometimes argue that they never would have purchased the software if they had really known about or understood the restrictions before handing over the money. Also, they may point to the futility of the situation, since any company that has functionally equivalent software uses the same shrink-wrapped restrictions.

The Trend in the Courts

Vault Corporation v. Quaid Software Ltd.[10] was one of the first important appellate court decisions dealing with the legality of shrink-wrap licenses. Vault sold a specialized computer diskette that provided protection against unauthorized duplication of its contents. The protection device consisted of a proprietary program which instructed a computer not to run unless it detected a special mark that was physically placed on the magnetic surface of the diskette. When a program was sold on Vault's diskette, a person could copy that program to another diskette, but it would not run because the new diskette would not have the appropriate physical mark. Vault's diskettes were sold with the shrink-wrap license provided above, which among other things, provided that the purchaser would not copy or disassemble the contents. Quaid purchased a disk and then copied and disassembled it so that he could develop a commercial diskette that was able to defeat the protection device.

Vault sued Quaid, alleging that the company breached the shrink-wrap license.[11] The court assumed that the shrink-wrap license was a contract of adhesion. Although the court did not discuss this conclusion, it apparently rested on the theory that the license was drafted by a dominant party and presented on a take-it-or-leave-it basis to a weaker party who had no real opportunity to bargain about the terms. Since the shrink-wrap license was a contract of adhesion, it normally would be viewed as unconscionable under state public policies and thus unenforceable by the court. Louisiana, though, had passed a special statute specifically stating that software providers could impose license terms prohibiting reverse engineering, among other actions. Therefore, the Louisiana legislature had specifically determined that shrink-wrap licenses did not violate the public policy of Louisiana. The court, however, essentially threw the state statute out, declaring that it conflicted with the Copyright Act. Section 117 of the Copyright Act allows an owner of a computer program to make a copy or adaptation of the program (1) if the copy or adaptation is necessary to use the program or (2) if it is made for archival purposes. According to the court, the license provision went so far as to prevent owners from doing some of these actions even though they are specifically authorized under the copyright laws. Based on this inconsistency, the court determined that the statute was preempted by federal law and thus could not serve as a valid policy in Louisiana. This meant that the contract of adhesion had to be viewed as unconscionable under general policy notions, thereby making its terms invalid.

Those who opposed the use of shrink-wrap licenses hailed the decision in *Vault v. Quaid*. The case effectively stated that shrink-wrap licenses violate public policy and that state governments might have a hard time implementing a contrary view. Nonetheless, many analysts criticized the court's conclusions. According to them, the copyright laws provide rules indicating what the general public can or cannot do with copyrighted materials. These laws, however, should not constrain what copyright owners might want to achieve through contracts. People who enter contracts, after all, are not strangers, but rather are individuals who are dealing directly with the copyright owner. Another argument noted that Section 117 applies to owners of computer programs, and thus has nothing to say about what licensees are able to do. The result was confusion over the legality of shrink-wrap licenses. Through the mid-1990s there were only a few court decisions dealing with the topic, and they often were decided on alternative grounds.[12] Then in 1996, the Seventh Circuit Court of Appeals released the following decision, which tackled the issue head on and persuasively argued that shrink-wrap licenses are enforceable.

ProCD Inc. v. Zeidenberg
Seventh Circuit Court of Appeals, 1996

FACTS: ProCD compiled information from more than 3,000 telephone directories into a computer database and software package. The database cost more than $10 million to compile and is expensive to keep current. Likely, the database could not be copyrighted even though it is more complex than the directory at issue in *Feist*.

The database and associated software package are more valuable to business customers than the general public. Therefore, ProCD decided to engage in price discrimination by selling the database to the general public for personal use at a much lower price (approximately $150) than that charged to

continued . . .

continued . . .

business customers. Price discrimination likely benefits members of the general public since it allows ProCD to charge them a lower price than it otherwise could if it were required to charge all customers the same price for the product. To make price discrimination work, ProCD had to devise a way to keep low price purchasers from reselling to commercial users. One way this could have been done would have been to make the general consumer database inferior to the commercial database, such as by having less current data. Instead, though, ProCD relied on contracts to prevent the unwanted sales. Every box sold to general consumers declared that the software package came with restrictions stated in an enclosed license. This license, which was printed in the manual, encoded on the CD-ROM disks, and which appeared on a user's screen every time the software ran, limited use of the program to noncommercial purposes.

Mathew Zeidenberg bought a consumer package in 1994 from a retail outlet. He formed a company that sold the database over the Internet at a price that was substantially below the price ProCD charged to commercial users. ProCD sued, requesting an injunction against further dissemination of the package beyond that allowed in the license. The district court determined that the license terms were not binding as contracts because they did not appear on the outside of the packages. The court also concluded that federal law would forbid enforcement of the terms even if the licenses were contracts. ProCD appealed.

DECISION AND REASONING: Must buyers of computer software obey the terms of shrink-wrap licenses? Zeidenberg argues, and the district court held, that placing the package of software on the shelf is an "offer" which the customer "accepts" by paying the asking price and leaving the store with the goods. A contract includes only the terms on which the parties have agreed and one cannot agree to hidden terms. So far so good—but one of the terms to which Zeidenberg agreed by purchasing the software is that the transaction was subject to a license. Zeidenberg's position therefore must be that the printed terms on the outside of the box are the parties' contract—except for printed terms that refer to or incorporate other terms. But why would state law fetter the parties' choice in this way? Vendors can put the entire terms of a contract on the outside of a box only by using microscopic type, removing other information that buyers might find more useful (such as what the software does, and on which computers it works), or both. Notice on the outside, terms on the inside, and a right to return the software for a refund if the terms are unacceptable (a right the license expressly extends), may be a means of doing business valuable to buyers and sellers alike.

Transactions in which the exchange of money precedes the communication of detailed terms are common. Consider the purchase of an airline ticket. The traveler calls the carrier or an agent, is quoted a price, reserves a seat, pays and gets a ticket, in that order. The ticket contains elaborate terms, which the traveler can reject by canceling the reservation. To use the ticket is to accept the terms, even terms that in retrospect are disadvantageous. Consumer goods work the same way. Someone who wants to buy a radio set visits a store, pays, and walks out with a box. Inside the box is a leaflet containing some terms, the most important of which usually is the warranty, read for the first time in the comfort of home. By Zeidenberg's lights, the warranty in the box is irrelevant; every consumer gets the standard warranty implied by the UCC in the event the contract is silent; yet so far as we are aware, no state disregards warranties furnished with consumer products.

Next consider the software industry itself. Only a minority of sales take place over the counter, where there are boxes to peruse. A customer may place an order by phone in response to a line item in a catalog or a review in a magazine. Much software is ordered over the Internet by purchasers who have never seen a box. Increasingly software arrives by wire. There is no box; there is only a stream of electrons, a collection of information that includes data, an application program, instructions, many limitations, and the terms of sale. The user purchases a serial number, which activates the software's features. On Zeidenberg's arguments, these unboxed sales are unfettered by terms—so the seller has made a broad warranty and must pay consequential damages for any shortfalls in performance, two "promises" that if taken seriously would drive prices through the ceiling or return transactions to the horse-and-buggy age.

According to the district court, the UCC does not countenance the sequence of money now, terms later. To judge by the flux of law review articles discussing shrink-wrap licenses, uncertainty is much in need of reduction—although businesses seem to feel less uncertainty than do scholars, for only three previous cases touch on the subject, and none directly addresses it. One concerned a situation in which the parties exchanged forms with incompatible terms. Another did not reach the question because the court found that the buyer knew the terms of the license before purchasing the software. The third, *Vault Corp. v. Quaid Software Ltd.*, held that Louisiana's special shrink-wrap statute was preempted by federal law, a question to which we return.

What does the UCC say? Section 204(1) states, "A contract for sale of goods may be made in any manner sufficient to show agreement, including conduct by both parties which recognizes the existence of such a contract." A vendor, as master of the offer, may invite acceptance by conduct, and may propose limitations on the kind of conduct that constitutes acceptance. A buyer may accept by performing the acts the vendor proposes to treat as acceptance. And that is what happened. ProCD proposed a contract that a

continued . . .

continued . . .

buyer would accept by *using* the software after having an opportunity to read the license at leisure. This Zeidenberg did. He had no choice, because the software splashed the license on the screen and would not let him proceed without indicating acceptance. So although the district court was right to say that a contract can be, and often is, formed simply by paying the price and walking out of the store, the UCC permits contracts to be formed in other ways. ProCD proposed such a different way, and without protest Zeidenberg agreed. Ours is not a case in which a consumer opens a package to find an insert saying "you owe us an extra $10,000" and the seller files suit to collect. Any buyer finding such a demand can prevent formation of the contract by returning the package, as can any consumer who concludes that the terms of the license make the software worth less than the purchase price. The UCC consistently permits the parties to structure their relations so that the buyer has a chance to make a final decision after a detailed review.

Some portions of the UCC impose additional requirements on the way parties agree to terms. For instance, a disclaimer of the implied warranty of merchantability must be "conspicuous." The special provisos reinforce the impression that, so far as the UCC is concerned, other terms may be inconspicuous.

The district court held that, even if state law treats shrink-wrap licenses as contracts, section 301(a) of the Copyright Act prevents their enforcement. The relevant part of section 301(a) preempts any "legal or equitable rights [under state law] that are equivalent to any of the exclusive rights within the general scope of copyright." One function of section 301(a) is to prevent states from giving special protection to works of authorship that Congress has decided should be in the public domain. But are rights created by contract "equivalent to any of the exclusive rights within the general scope of copyright"? Rights "equivalent to those within the general scope of copyright" are rights established *by law*—rights that restrict the option of persons who are strangers to the author. A copyright is a right against the world. Contracts, by contrast, generally affect only their parties; strangers may do as they please, so contracts do not create exclusive rights. Someone who found ProCD's software package on the street would not be affected by the shrink-wrap license—though the federal copyright laws of their own force would limit the finder's ability to copy or transmit the application program.

Think for a moment about trade secrets. After *Feist*, a simple alphabetical list of a firm's customers, with addresses and telephone numbers, could not be protected by copyright. Yet *Kewanee Oil* holds that contracts about trade secrets may be enforced—precisely because they do not affect strangers' ability to discover and use the information independently. Think, too, about everyday transactions in intellectual property. A customer visits a video store and rents a copy of *Night of the Lepus*. The customer's contract with the store limits use of the tape to home viewing and requires its return in two days. May the customer keep the tape on the ground that section 301(a) makes the promise unenforceable? A law student uses the LEXIS database, containing public domain documents, under a contract limiting the results to educational endeavors; may the student resell his access to this database to a law firm from which LEXIS seeks to collect a much higher hourly rate?

Although Congress possesses power to preempt the enforcement of contracts about intellectual property, courts usually read preemption clauses to leave private contracts unaffected. Terms and conditions offered by contract reflect private ordering, essential to the efficient functioning of markets. Section 301(a) prevents states from substituting their own regulatory systems for those of the national government. Just as section 301(a) does not itself interfere with private transactions in intellectual property, so it does not prevent states from respecting those transactions.

The contract between ProCD and Zeidenberg does not withdraw any information from the public domain. Everyone remains free to copy and disseminate all 3,000 telephone books that have been incorporated into ProCD's database. Anyone can add SIC codes and zip codes. ProCD's rivals have done so. Enforcement of the shrink-wrap license may even make information more readily available, by reducing the price ProCD charges to consumer buyers. Licenses may have other benefits to consumers: many licenses permit users to make extra copies, to use the software on multiple computers, even to incorporate the software into the user's products. But whether a particular license is generous or restrictive, a simple two-party contract is not "equivalent to any of the exclusive rights within the general scope of copyright" and therefore may be enforced.

Shrink-wrap licenses are enforceable unless their terms are objectionable on grounds applicable to contracts in general (for example, if they violate a rule of positive law, or if they are unconscionable). Because no one argues that the terms of the license at issue here are troublesome, we enter judgment for ProCD.

Reversed.

The Conscionability of Shrink-Wrap Licenses

ProCD effectively sanctions the use of shrink-wrap and click-wrap licenses. According to the case, the terms of the license do not even have to appear on the outside of the package. Rather, it is enough if the customer is aware that the purchase is subject to a license and is given a reasonable right to return the merchandise after having the opportunity to review the terms of the license later on. As the last paragraph states, the parties did not argue that the terms of the license were unconscionable. Instead, the arguments were more about the contracting process. But the court makes it clear that unconscionable shrink-wrap licenses still are not going to be enforced. In this regard, the following factors are likely to be relevant:

1. How bizarre is it to use particular terms in the industry?
2. How conspicuous is the notice given to the customer about the existence of a license and the terms that the license contains?
3. How sophisticated is the customer with business affairs in general and with practices in the industry?
4. Are the terms contrary to other agreements made with the customer about the transaction?
5. Does the customer have the ability to obtain the goods, services or information without having to agree to the objectionable terms, either from the same merchant or from other vendors?

These elements are interrelated, and all should be considered when addressing conscionability. For instance, the more that the terms deviate from what is normally experienced in the industry, the greater are the demands on the merchant to make those terms conspicuous. Printing the restrictions in bold letters at the front of the license clearly is a step in this direction. A better practice is to make sure that the customer has an opportunity to review and approve the specific clause. As an example, an Internet purveyor might prevent customers from continuing with the purchase process unless they click a button indicating that they specifically "approve" of that condition. Also, the merchant needs to consider the sophistication of its buyers. There may be a greater need to use plain language instead of legalese when dealing with consumers (as opposed to commercially experienced businesses) to make sure that they actually understand the conditions.[13]

At this time, it seems that the battle is being won by merchants who wish to use shrink-wrap and click-wrap licenses. The benefits that these contracts bring to the commercial process in terms of efficiency outweigh the fears that their terms will be routinely abusive. However, merchants are advised to take steps to ensure that they do not appear to be taking advantage of unsuspecting consumers. The law will give them the flexibility to use these devices to carry on their transactions, but they must use them in ways that satisfy the reasonable expectations of their customers. Saying this another way, if businesses overstep the bounds of appropriate behavior through their licensing techniques and provisions, then they should not expect the courts to come to their assistance. The legality of these licensing practices continues to be the source of tremendous conflict. Many of the frustrations with finalizing Article 2B of the UCC were related to this very issue. Thus, one should not expect the controversies regarding shrink-wrap and click-wrap licenses to end anytime soon. Exhibit 9.4 summarizes the issues related to these licenses.

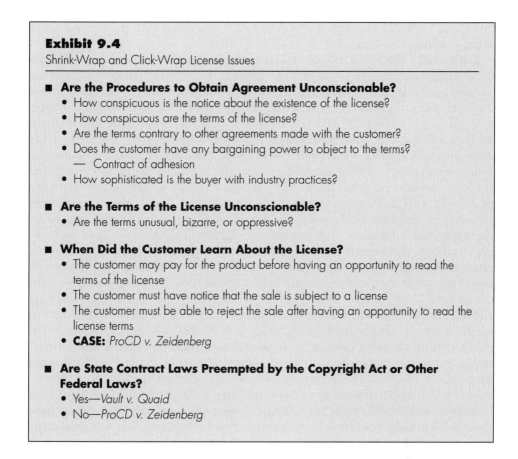

Exhibit 9.4
Shrink-Wrap and Click-Wrap License Issues

- **Are the Procedures to Obtain Agreement Unconscionable?**
  - How conspicuous is the notice about the existence of the license?
  - How conspicuous are the terms of the license?
  - Are the terms contrary to other agreements made with the customer?
  - Does the customer have any bargaining power to object to the terms?
    — Contract of adhesion
  - How sophisticated is the buyer with industry practices?

- **Are the Terms of the License Unconscionable?**
  - Are the terms unusual, bizarre, or oppressive?

- **When Did the Customer Learn About the License?**
  - The customer may pay for the product before having an opportunity to read the terms of the license
  - The customer must have notice that the sale is subject to a license
  - The customer must be able to reject the sale after having an opportunity to read the license terms
  - **CASE:** ProCD v. Zeidenberg

- **Are State Contract Laws Preempted by the Copyright Act or Other Federal Laws?**
  - Yes—Vault v. Quaid
  - No—ProCD v. Zeidenberg

PROPOSALS FOR NEW MODEL LAWS

Article 2B, UCITA, and UETA

During the past decade, we have witnessed unprecedented growth in new industries involving transactions in information. The revolution arose on the heels of the computer, which fueled demand for products such as computer software, data, text, and images. The movement exploded in the 1990s due to the Internet, which greatly facilitated access to information and spawned a new electronic dimension to commerce. The interesting thing is how the role of "goods" has diminished in this developing environment. The basic computer is a good, just like a stereo or a car. So are some of the other items one might use with a computer, such as a printer, a diskette, or speakers. For obvious reasons, these goods are important to have. In a sense, they are like the entrance ticket to a favorite event. But what people really are after is the world that the computer opens up to them. And most of this world is devoid of tangible property; rather it is filled with the creative juices of the intellect.

Beginning in the 1990s, policy makers formally began to deliberate whether the UCC Article 2 needed to be updated to address the needs of the new commercial paradigms. Article 2 was developed in a commercial environment having two fundamentally distinct offerings: goods and services. Given the overwhelming importance of tangible products, Article 2 addressed most major concerns with its focus on transactions in goods. However, in today's business regime, the market has something new to offer—information—and its commercial significance is growing explosively. The markets for intangible properties sometimes depend on very different business constructs than do those for goods. For instance, owners of intangible property usually do not make sales in the classic sense. Rather, they license rights to access or make use of the property. Just think of the various rights enjoyed by copyright owners—such as copying, altering, distributing, displaying, and performing—and how these rights might be allocated. Perhaps a computer diskette or the physical pages of a book may actually be sold, but the intellectual property is not, and that is what the consumer really values. Thus, there is an increasing need for the UCC to structure rules that specifically address licensing practices in software and information industries. Also, electronic commerce raises a host of contract issues that are not cleanly resolved by Article 2 of the UCC. Many provisions in Article 2 depend on proof in writing. Does this mean that one cannot rely on electronic contracts, since they are not written on paper? How does one sign a document in cyberspace? Electronic commerce also changes the nature of transactions. Can a computer serve as an agent and sign a contract? Should mass-market licenses be treated differently? Numerous issues and questions such as these have already led to some confusion in the new information markets. The solution, many believed, was a new UCC article that specifically addresses them.

In 1994, the American Law Institute and the National Conference of Commissioners on Uniform State Laws (NCCUSL) started a joint effort to design a new model code to govern information licenses and on-line commerce. The process was extremely deliberative, allowing the public substantial opportunities to comment on proposed drafts and to participate in committee meetings. Many different approaches were considered, but ultimately the drafting committee decided to formulate a new article to the UCC, titled Article 2B. By 1998, the framework of Article 2B was substantially developed, and included more than 100 sections dealing with such topics as transfers, standard and mass-market forms, warranties, disclaimers, acceptance and rejection, and electronic commerce. However, the effort was continually plagued with dissent—from consumers who thought that the drafts did not provide sufficient specific protections to industry participants who worried that some provisions were too inflexible. Members of the entertainment and communications fields also objected. They argued that Article 2B's rules might be appropriate for the software and Internet industries but that they might have unintended consequences in their fields. In 1999, the NCCUSL abandoned Article 2B based on seemingly irreconcilable differences. In its place, the organization offered the Uniform Computer Information Transactions Act (UCITA) and the Uniform

Electronics Transactions Act (UETA) as separate pieces of legislation that would be adopted separate from the UCC.[14] UCITA mirrors Article 2B in most respects, however, and quickly raised many of the same objections. Thus, it is hard to predict at this juncture exactly what new laws, if any, states will soon adopt. It is clear, though, that uniform laws are needed, and that efforts to adopt them will continue. In this light, it is instructive to look at some of the approaches that were considered within Article 2B. Given the time and thought that went into designing the sections of Article 2B, one certainly can gain insights into what many of the final solutions might be.[15] In addition, if states start to pass laws based on UCITA, then Article 2B, for the most part, will be resurrected in that form. For this reason, the following discussion provides references to parallel UCITA and UETA provisions in the footnotes.[16] The text also addresses a few instances where UCITA differs from Article 2B. Exhibit 9.5 outlines several important issues raised by information licenses, and indicates the solutions that generally have been recommended in the model laws.

Electronic Commerce Issues

Proof by Records   Any new model code will have to account for the movement toward a paperless society. Many provisions of the UCC rely on written words or signatures to verify who entered contracts and on what terms. Article 2B proposed to modernize the notion of a "writing" by employing the concept of a "record" in its place. A record was defined as "information that is inscribed on a tangible medium or that is stored in an electronic or other medium and is retrievable in perceivable form."[17] So, for instance, the UCC's version of the statute of frauds dictates that a writing is required to prove the existence and terms of certain contracts. Article 2B would have changed this requirement so that a record would suffice.[18]

Digital Signatures   Under the UCC, a valid signature on a written document serves as proof (1) that the document is in its original unaltered form and (2) that it has been approved by the person who signed it. In electronic commerce, however, there are no written documents and no hand signatures. Thus there have to be new procedures to verify that a particular person approved of the terms contained in a record.

In Chapter 8, we discussed how encryption techniques can be used to verify who sent a document and that its contents have not been changed. These methods are sometimes called *digital signatures*, since they satisfy the roles of written signatures in the electronic marketplace.[19] The steps of one process works as follows:

1. A person drafts the document to be signed.
2. The one-way hash value of the document is calculated. This is a unique digital representation that the recipient can use to check that the document has not been altered. It is a one-way function because a person can calculate the value from the document but cannot produce the document from the hash value.

Exhibit 9.5

Model Laws for Information Licenses and Software Contracts: Selected Important Issues

---

■ **E-Commerce Issues**
  • Proof by records: To substitute for proof by written documents
  • Digital signatures: To enable secure ways to prove the identities of the parties and that the documents have not been altered
  • Electronic agents: To allow formation of contracts without human intervention

■ **Mass-Market Licenses**
  • Model laws generally adopt the reasoning of *ProCD v. Zeidenberg*
  • License provisions are enforceable unless they are unconscionable
  • Possible extra security for license terms that may interfere with other public policy objectives

■ **Warranties**
  • Model laws generally retain Article 2 provisions, but "update" them to conform better to information and computer technologies
  • Possible warranty for the accuracy of information content for customized advice

■ **Disclaimers and Limitations of Warranties**
  • Model laws generally retain Article 2 provisions
  • Consequential damage limitations are enforceable even if exclusive remedies fail

■ **Choice of Law and Forum**
  • License may provide for court forum unless the forum is unreasonable and unjust
  • License may select governing laws, but may not use license to bypass a state's consumer protection laws

■ **Self-Help Remedies**
  • Model laws generally allow self-help
  • Notice requirements, limitations on their use, and remedies for wrongful use

---

3. The hash value is encrypted with the person's private key and is attached to the document.
4. The encrypted hash value and document are transmitted to the recipient.
5. The recipient decrypts the hash value with the public key.
6. The recipient computes a new hash value for the document and checks that it is identical to the value that was decrypted.

If the hash value can be decrypted and is identical, then the recipient knows that the person who holds the corresponding private key sent the document and that the document was not altered. As discussed in Chapter 8, the recipient still may need to verify the identity of the person who claims to hold the private key. After all, the person who distributed the public key may have lied about his or her identity. To solve this problem, the maker can go to a trusted certificate authority (CA) for validation. The validation process works according to these principles:

1. The CA validates certain identifying information about the holder of the private key, such as the holder's name and address.
2. The CA uses its own private key to encrypt the holder's public key and the identifying information, thereby making what is called a digital certificate.
3. The person signing the document attaches the digital certificate to the document along with the encrypted hash value.
4. The recipient uses the CA's public key to decrypt the holder's public key and the identifying information. If the recipient is successful, then the recipient knows that the trusted CA must have validated the identity of the person who claims to hold the private key.
5. The recipient uses the holder's public key to decrypt the hash value as described above.

Although these steps sound complicated, the process can be almost entirely automated. It also is more reliable than traditional measures that rely on written documents and signatures. The major concern comes when a private key has been stolen or compromised, for then a person might successfully serve as an imposter. However, there is substantial protection even for that occurrence, since the release can be reported to the CA, which then can add the certificate to its certification revocation list. Thus, as an additional step, the recipient should check the CA's "certification revocation list" to verify that the digital certificate is still valid. Of course, the owner of the private key might not report that it has been compromised. In this event, one might fairly conclude that the owner should take responsibility for any problems that an imposter might cause.

Article 2B accounted for digital signatures by broadening the ways that parties might manifest assent to contracts.[20] Rather than rely merely on terms such as "signature," the proposed new provisions introduced the concept of "authenticating records" and provided that encryption techniques could be used for such purposes. In this regard, Article 2B relied heavily on the ways that digital techniques might be used to assure that a record could be "attributable" to another.[21] As discussed above, digital techniques are available to validate the identity of a party and to assure that the contents of a record have not been changed. Article 2B effectively endorsed the use of these techniques to authenticate records as long as the procedures were "commercially reasonable." It also answered questions about who should bear the loss when things go awry, such as when a private key is stolen.

Electronic Agents   In the digital world, individuals increasingly will rely on computerized processes to relieve them of tasks they otherwise might have had to do themselves. For instance, as discussed in Chapter 8, individuals soon will regularly automate their privacy relationships with Web sites, such as through the Platform for Privacy Preferences. Computers may play a large role in contractual relationships as well. Since most people do not have the time to personally negotiate and finalize all their required business arrangements, they often authorize other individuals to act as their agents. Such agents have the power to enter deals according to the instructions they receive.

In digital environments, one easily can imagine situations where it may be more efficient to have computers act as agents rather than humans. And why shouldn't they? Computers are no less capable of receiving and following instructions than are humans. For instance, consider a consumer who is interested in collecting renditions of the song "Blue Suede Shoes." This consumer might formulate a Web search program with instructions to download all renditions that it locates according to various maximum acceptable royalty rates. Web sites likely will use computer programs to automate their replies to search requests, relying on them to indicate the terms under which they will release audio files. Indeed, the programs may do all the work without human intervention—from finding each other, to negotiating the terms of the transaction, all the way to providing access to the music that is desired.

Almost all the case law dealing with the power of agents was formulated with reference to human actors. There are substantial questions, therefore, about the legal consequences of using electronic agents. Can computer programs bind individuals to business arrangements? How can one prove that a contract was formed? Is it enough that the Web site computer program transmitted a digital audio file to the consumer's computer?

Article 2B proposed that digital agents could enter binding agreements. It made this abundantly clear in one section which provided that "operations of one or more electronic agents which confirm the existence of a contract or indicate agreement form a contract even if no individual was aware of or reviewed the actions or results."[22] Another section acknowledged the ways that electronic agents might manifest assent to contract proposals. It stated:

a. A person or electronic agent manifests assent to a record or term thereof if, acting with knowledge of, or after having an opportunity to review the record or term, it:
   (1) Authenticates the record or term, or
   (2) Engages in affirmative conduct or operations that the record conspicuously provides or the circumstances, including the terms of the record, clearly indicate will constitute acceptance, and the person or electronic agent had an opportunity to decline to engage in the conduct or operations. . . .
d. A manifestation of assent may be proved in any manner, including by a showing that a procedure existed by which a person or an electronic agent must have engaged in conduct or operations that manifests assent to the record or term in order to proceed further in the use it made of the information.[23]

This section made it clear that under the appropriate circumstances, operations initiated by an electronic agent—such as the release of digital audio files—would be sufficient to prove that a contract was formed. Article 2B, in other sections, also provided legal frameworks for resolving disputes regarding the terms of contacts negotiated by electronic agents.[24]

Mass-Market Licenses

Article 2B addressed an enormous number of different issues that specifically affect information licenses and software contracts. Of all of these issues, the most contentious likely concerned the legality of mass-market licenses—the umbrella term used by Article 2B to refer to shrink-wrap and click-wrap licenses. Much of the debate focused on fears that consumers unknowingly would be forced to swallow oppressive terms. Thus, early proposals considered establishing official lists of potentially surprising terms and conditions that could become binding only if consumers specifically and independently approved of them. However, these ideas were dropped because the industry feared that they would unduly lengthen the contracting process. In the end, Article 2B returned to the catch-all requirement of unconscionability, stating that "a term does not become part of the contract if it is unconscionable."[25] Thus, Article 2B would not have changed the general principles regarding the legality of mass-market licenses, as discussed earlier in this chapter. The article did add one protection to benefit consumers, however. It provided that a term in a mass-market license would not be effective if it conflicted with a previous express agreement between the parties.[26] This provision amounted to a deviation from the parol evidence rule and was designed to ensure that merchants did not slip conditions into mass-market licenses that unexpectedly altered previously negotiated conditions.

Except in situations involving unconscionablity, Article 2B approved of the use of mass-market licenses. This was made clear in the section on manifest assent, documented above with reference to electronic agents. According to this provision, license terms are effective if the consumer has an opportunity to review them and engages in some affirmative conduct that the consumer understands will indicate acceptance. This might include opening a cellophane wrapper or clicking in a box after having the opportunity to read the license terms.

Article 2B also addressed the situation considered in *ProCD* where consumers do not have an opportunity to review the terms in the mass-market license until after payment is made.[27] Article 2B essentially adopted the reasoning of *ProCD*, stating that consumers are entitled to a refund if they object to the terms once they are made aware of them. However, Article 2B provided some additional consumer protections. It provided that the merchant must reimburse the consumer for any reasonable expenses in returning or destroying the information. More importantly, it also required merchants to compensate consumers for any foreseeable losses caused by the installation of the information, including reasonable expenses in restoring the system to its prior condition. Thus, if a merchant set up a situation where a consumer could not read a license until after installation of a program or information on a computer, then it would have to be prepared to fully compensate the consumer if the consumer ultimately objected to the license conditions. This was considered to be a major concession by business interests and would have required them to carefully consider the ways that they might present postpayment license conditions.

UCITA's approach to mass-market licenses is very similar to that proposed for Article 2B. It, too, strongly supports private contracts and makes them enforceable unless they are unconscionable. If there is any difference at all, UCITA may offer a slightly broader concept of the kinds of mass-market contracts that may be perceived as unconscionable. UCITA provides that if a term of a contract violates a fundamental public policy, a court may refuse to enforce it to the extent that the interest in enforcement is clearly outweighed by a public policy against enforcement of the term.[28] This clearly was meant to pacify those who fear that mass-market licenses will go too far in restricting rights normally enjoyed under fair use and free speech principles. Thus, distributors of information may not be able to restrict consumers from using small portions of their works in accordance with the fair-use doctrine, even if the mass-market license is absolute in its terms. This provision also may negate attempts by licensors to make users agree to extraneous conditions, such as that they will not make public statements criticizing the company. The language of UCITA essentially leaves this debate open and allows the courts to address the issues on a case-by-case basis.

Warranties

Article 2B essentially maintained the same warranties that are provided under Article 2, but with some modifications that make the language more consistent with information and computer licenses.[29] Thus, Article 2B had sections dealing with express warranties and many of the same implied warranties we found in Article 2, such as merchantabililty, fitness for a particular purpose, and noninfringement. The language of some of these warranties provided details that are not found in Article 2. For instance, the implied warranty of fitness included a warranty that information would not fail to achieve the licensee's articulated purpose due to a lack of reasonable care or effort by the information provider.[30] The fitness warranty also provided a guarantee that a system would be successfully integrated, assuming the licensor were reasonably aware that the licensee was relying on its skill in combining systems.[31]

Article 2B would have codified a new warranty dealing with the accuracy of information content.[32] Does a Web site that publishes medical information, for instance, warrant that the information is accurate? What if an investor sells a stock because an Internet site reported, in error, that the stock price had risen 20% when in fact it had fallen by that amount? The traditional rule is that information purveyors do not warrant the accuracy of their information unless they have some fiduciary relationship with the recipient. This is based on the same First Amendment rationales that limited strict tort liability for publicly disseminated information. Article 2B for the most part adopted this approach. It provided that a merchant in a special relationship of reliance warrants that there are no inaccuracies in informational content due to a failure to exercise reasonable care. However, the warranty would not have extended to "published informational content," which was defined as information prepared for or made available to all recipients (or a class or recipients) in substantially the same form and not provided as customized advice tailored for a particular licensee.[33] Thus, Article 2B's new implied warranty on the accuracy of informational content would have been limited to entities providing customized advice or those having some other form of special relationship with the licensee. In addition, the warranty would not have assured accuracy in an absolute sense but would have required only that licensors use reasonable care in preparing information.

Other Issues

Disclaimers and Limitations   Article 2B's provisions regarding warranty disclaimers essentially were no different than those that currently exist under Article 2.[34] The new forms of implied warranties could be disclaimed as you would expect. For instance, the implied warranty of fitness could be disclaimed with language such as, "There is no warranty that this information or my efforts will fulfill any of your particular purposes or needs." The only requirement for a disclaimer of the information accuracy warranty was that it mention the word "accuracy." Also, Article 2B required that disclaimers of implied warranties had to be conspicuous when used in mass-market licenses.

Article 2B also made no material changes to Article 2's rules regarding damage limitations.[35] The only notable nuance was that Article 2B was more explicit about what happens to a consequential damage limitation when the exclusive remedy fails. It provided, "Failure or unconscionability of an agreed remedy does not affect the enforceability of terms disclaiming or limiting consequential or incidental damages if the contract expressly makes those terms independent of the agreed remedy."[36] Thus, as recommended earlier, you should make sure the consequential damage limitation is in a clause separate from the exclusive remedy and clearly states that it survives even if the exclusive remedy fails.

Choice of Law and Forum   Article 2B contained provisions that generally allowed the parties to determine where disputes would be litigated and under what laws. In Chapter 1, we reviewed some of the considerations that go into determining where an aggrieved person might be able to bring a case. As we saw, the choice merely cannot offend traditional notions of fair play and substantial justice. Depending on the circumstances, this may open the door to suits being brought in a host of potential court sites, especially when Internet commerce is involved.

When parties enter contracts, they have the ability to agree to where their potential disputes will be resolved. Usually these agreements do not present problems, since both parties have an interest in controlling uncertainties about where they might have to litigate. The fear, of course, is that a dominant party in a contractual relationship will select a court jurisdiction that is so remote that the weaker party could not afford to bring suit there. For instance, a contract for services provided in Maine might state that any dispute must be resolved in the courts of California, or perhaps Belize. Article 2B's approach to this problem was to allow the contracting parties to choose an exclusive judicial forum for litigation unless the choice was "unreasonable and unjust."[37]

Article 2B also provided parties substantial flexibility to choose the laws that govern their contracts.[38] It stated, "The parties in their agreement may choose the applicable law." However, it also provided that a contract may not override a consumer protection statute. Thus, General Motors could not avoid California's state consumer warranty act, the Song-Beverly Act, simply by having purchasers agree that the laws of Michigan will apply to their disputes. Article 2B also provided rules for determining the applicable law when a contract does not have an enforceable clause specifying it. As one example, it stated that "a contract providing for electronic delivery of a copy is governed by the law of the jurisdiction in which the licensor is located when the agreement is made."

Self-Help Remedies In Chapter 8, there was some discussion about potential tort liability for certain self-help measures, such as drop-dead and time bomb functions in computer programs. There were substantial debates during drafting sessions of Article 2B about the propriety of using such measures and the notice that might be required before using them. The final Article 2B draft indicated that when a license is cancelled, the licensor has the right to possess all copies of licensed materials in the hands of the licensee and to prevent continued access to the licensed information.[39] It also provided that the licensor could exercise these rights without judicial process if it could be done *without a breach of the peace* and *without foreseeable risk of personal injury or significant damage* to information or property.[40] It is worth noting that UCITA deals more specifically with self-help remedies and puts several additional constraints on their use.[41] For instance, UCITA requires that the contract include provisions indicating that self-help remedies might be used. It also mandates that notice be given at least 15 days before the self-help measures are implemented. In addition, UCITA provides that the licensee is entitled to damages for wrongful uses of self-help remedies.

STRATEGIC ALLIANCES: INTELLECTUAL PROPERTY AND OTHER CONCERNS

There are numerous business concepts that currently have aroused the interest of the press. "Competitiveness" and "total quality management" provide two notable illustrations. Another favorite is the growing importance of "strategic alliances" or "strategic partnering." As with the other terms, the notion of a strategic alliance is somewhat vague. On one level, people often are simply referring to a spirit of working together. However, on a more important plane, strategic alliances constitute a growing trend by companies to join forces in relatively long-term formal ventures to pursue common goals.

The move toward forming strategic alliances appears to be especially important in high-technology industries. A 1992 survey of CEOs in the electronics industry stated that "[a]lliance building now is fundamental to the way U.S. electronics companies conduct business."[42] The computer field has been a source of alliances for years, including (1) the notable link between Apple Computer, IBM, and Motorola to develop the Power PC family of microprocessors, and (2) SEMATECH, a consortium consisting of 14 U.S. computer chip makers. One of the most consistent headline business topics of the 1990s was the formation of strategic alliances between telecommunications, computer, and media corporate giants with the goal of developing interactive multimedia capabilities. Business partnering surged with the advent of the Internet, especially since it offers such huge opportunities in the face of enormous risks. New alliances now are announced on an almost daily basis between companies involved with the development of content, delivery techniques, software, search engines, browsers, servers, hardware components, and computers. Clearly, strategic alliances are becoming the rule rather than the exception for technology ventures.

High-technology concerns may enter strategic alliances for a variety of reasons. The following list indicates just some of the possible benefits that a company might seek from a strategic alliance.[43] It should be clear from the list that a partner likely is attempting to benefit from a few, but not all, of the items on the list. In addition, each partner may be entering a particular strategic relationship to achieve different long-term goals.

- *Acquisition of Technology:* An alliance may be formed to gain access to technologies or to combine technologies.
- *Tapping of Manufacturing Capacity:* One may prefer to use the existing plant and equipment of another firm rather than make the investment independently.
- *Access to Distribution:* The importance of distribution channels for high-technology products may lead one to seek out a partner with established networks.
- *Risk and Cost Sharing:* With a particularly risky venture, it might make sense to join forces with other firms to share the costs of the enterprise.
- *Access to Capital:* The need for money often is a motivation for strategic alliances.
- *Geographic Expansion:* A strategic alliance with firms doing business in other regions may be a way to more quickly and easily enter these areas. In the international environment, this may be especially helpful in countries that have concerns about ventures run by foreigners.
- *Marketing:* Strategic alliances may further marketing objectives in various ways. Joining forces with a company having a solid reputation may improve the chances of raising public awareness and acceptance of the technology. Or one might expand the product line with complementary products or services to better meet the needs of consumers.
- *Reduction of Infringement Risks:* Uncertainties about the extent of intellectual property rights owned by another company, for example in software, may make an alliance with that company attractive. This may prevent that company from

bringing a costly litigation action when one plans to develop or sell similar technology.

- *Prevention of Competitors' Access to Technology:* One might consider an alliance as a defensive measure in order to keep competitors from being able to use important technologies.

When one enters a strategic alliance, a whole spectrum of legal issues must be considered. What business structure will the alliance take? The partners may choose to stay separate, forming the team solely through contract. Or they may opt to unify the relationship under the umbrella of a more formal structure, such as a partnership, joint venture, or corporation. The decision will rest on such variables as tax considerations, liability concerns, the expected length of the relationship, the manner in which resources may be pooled, and the extent to which risks will be shared. For some of these forms, securities laws will have to be consulted. In addition, as we shall see later in this chapter, the parties should review how the antitrust laws might bear on the arrangement. As you surmised, the allocation of risks and liabilities between the parties, including such things as warranties and limits on liabilities, will be crucial decisions in forming a successful alliance. Also, since intellectual property rights undoubtedly will be involved, substantial decisions will have to be made regarding their ownership and protection. In addition, since partners often have the expectation of entering the alliance for the long haul, they should give serious thought about the ways disputes will be resolved should they arise. And, of course, if the alliance plans to move into international circles, an overlay of additional complex issues arises, such as customs regulations, export and technology transfer controls, foreign ownership restrictions, and foreign political practices.

When considering these legal issues, those involved in the alliance must never lose sight of the strategic business concerns and objectives that led the parties to contemplate the union in the first place. For example, if the goal of the alliance is to create a new technological standard upon which other companies will build their products, then it might make sense to make the technology freely available rather than tightly control it through intellectual property protection licenses. Also, the partners must be very wary of the distinct corporate cultures of each of the participants in the alliance. One only has to look at the computer industry to understand how these differences can affect the relationship between partners in an alliance. Some companies in the computer field have a culture that supports trade secret protection and the substantial security measures required to implement it. Employees in these firms generally accept the importance of various security measures and are willing to put up with certain physical impediments and intrusions on privacy. Other companies take more of a maverick approach, encouraging employees to freely share and use their ideas with little corporate scrutiny. Such differences must be recognized before these companies form a strategic alliance, especially if they will need to share trade secrets in the arrangement. As you can imagine, employees in the maverick company are likely to reject and ignore the demands for security that the more protective company naturally will want implemented. Clearly, the participants in a successful strategic alliance must not only grasp the business and economic issues supporting the effort but also fully consider the human and cultural implications of the partnership as well.

Suppose we decide that our company cannot develop, manufacture, market, and distribute audio components using the **AES** technology successfully on its own. In particular, we need help in developing the software, and we require partners for product design, manufacturing, and sales. After extensive negotiations, we determine that SoftWave Corporation is best suited to develop the software that will control certain basic functions of the **AES** and that Scherer Audio Company has the skill and capacity to design, manufacture, and market **AES** products using our technology and SoftWave's software. We decide that we will keep our business entities separate and will handle the partnering through contracts.

A multitude of contract issues must be evaluated by all three parties to this arrangement. Indeed, the contracts should spell out with great detail how the parties expect to handle every aspect of the deal. What specific tasks is each supposed to perform for the others? When are the tasks supposed to be completed? When is payment required? Is there a period for testing the products, and how will it be determined if the tests have been passed? Is one party responsible for training the others to use or install software or components? How, from where, and by whom will ultimate products be distributed to consumers? When does the relationship end? The parties should have answered these and a litany of other questions in their contracts before engaging in operations. Although all of these considerations are vitally important, they are not the subjects of this discussion. Rather, the attempt here will be to resurrect some of the intellectual property and liability issues already raised in previous chapters of this book. To do this, the book relies heavily on examples pertaining to the **AES**. These analyses, therefore, should be treated in their entirety as continuations of the **AES** thread-case. The book then turns its focus to alternative methods to resolve disputes other than through the use of formal litigation in the traditional court systems. Such possibilities, called alternative dispute resolution (ADR) techniques, have become an increasingly important aspect of strategic partnering arrangements in high-technology fields.

Patent Issues

We learned in Chapters 2 and 3 that we can receive patents for computer software and machines that use software. In developing the **AES**, many patent issues may arise, particularly between SoftWave and ourselves. If SoftWave develops patentable software, that company likely will be considered the inventor. Thus, SoftWave will have to file the patent applications. However, we still must deal with the very important issue of ownership. If we wish to control the patent on the software, then SoftWave will have to agree to assign the patent to us. This will be very important if we integrate the software into a patentable **AES** machine or process. If SoftWave owns the patent on the software, then we will have to negotiate a license to use the invention in the **AES**. Otherwise, our product or process, although patentable, would infringe SoftWave's patent. Similarly, we need to address with SoftWave which company will own any software improvements that might be created in the future.

Since we are dealing with potentially patentable inventions, all the parties should agree to take the requisite steps to verify dates of invention and diligent reduction to practice. In addition, we need to work out who will undertake the responsibility to file for and obtain the patents in the United States and abroad. Obviously, as part of this, we must address how the parties expect to pay for the expenses that will be incurred in these efforts. In addition, we have to take care in the contracts to ensure that the participants do not carelessly destroy the chances for international patent protection. For instance, we might want to put certain constraints on Scherer not to market the product until an international application is filed with the PTO.

In our arrangement, the technology essentially is developed by SoftWave and our company, while Scherer is in charge of product design and marketing. A typical transaction might have our company (along with SoftWave, if necessary) license the technology to Scherer with the understanding that Scherer is to pay a sizable royalty based on a percentage of its ultimate sales revenues. Disputes often arise from this form of agreement when the marketing firm ends up shelving the technology, thereby yielding no return to the inventors. This is especially true when the technology license is given exclusively, because then the inventors are dependent solely on the success of the marketer. The inventors may feel aggrieved, believing that the marketer failed to try hard enough to push the technology. In their view, the marketer had an obligation to use its "best efforts" to commercialize the technology, and its failure to give the requisite attention amounted to a breach of contract. Although the contract may not have expressly mentioned the marketer's obligations to use best efforts, they can be implied from the nature of the contract.

The courts are reluctant to read into a contract an implied condition to use "best efforts."[44] However, they may do so if the arrangement makes the licensing firm totally dependent on royalty payments for compensation. Think of it this way. If we grant Scherer an exclusive deal, and give up our rights to make arrangements with other companies, surely we would expect something in return. It might be an up-front fee or an advance royalty payment. Such a payment, of course, would provide Scherer some incentive to make sales to recoup its investment. In addition, though, it will satisfy a court that we received at least the minimum compensation for which we bargained. On the other hand, if Scherer gives nothing but its promise to pay future royalties, then surely we must expect it to use its best efforts to generate those royalties. Why else would we enter such a deal? Thus, a court may determine from the context that Scherer was obligated to use its best efforts to commercialize the technology, even though the contract did not expressly say so.

As with all contract matters, the best way to avoid such disputes is to fully address all potential outcomes at the beginning of the relationship. Thus, from our point of view, we would like the contract to specifically state that Scherer will use best efforts to market the technology. In the alternative, we would probably be satisfied with a substantial up-front payment for an exclusive license to market. Scherer likely will not want to leave it up to a court to determine if it used best efforts, especially if sales turned out to be somewhat dismal. On the other hand, it likely will desire an exclusive license. Its best option, therefore, is to have the contract explicitly say that it does not have to use best efforts. However, we likely will not buy into that. If sufficient advance compensation is not possible, then Scherer might consider discussing the possibility of terms that allow it to terminate the relationship on short notice. In this way, Scherer could end our dependency on its efforts should those efforts not be resulting in satisfactory sales.

Trade Secret Issues

As part of this development and distribution partnership, the participants probably will be exchanging numerous trade secrets. In our dealings with SoftWave, we will have to disclose information about our technology and the ultimate product concept so that SoftWave can develop the appropriate software. After creating the software, SoftWave will have to provide us with sufficient information about the functional parameters of the program so that we can utilize it in the product. Also, since we are relying on Scherer to manufacture and distribute the ultimate **AES** products, we will have to disclose an enormous amount of information to that company about the attributes and constraints of the technologies we created along with SoftWave. Much of this information will be valuable as long as it is not in the hands of competitors. Also, we likely will not rely on patent protection for some, if not all of it, either because of perceived negative strategic implications with the patent system or because the information does not meet the standards for patentability. Therefore, the partners will all have to be very conscious of how the trade secrets will be protected as they are passed among themselves.

The two most important considerations for dealing with trade secrets are (1) ownership of the secrets and (2) ensuring that the secrets are the subject of reasonable measures to preserve their secrecy. The ownership issue is little different from the one that applies with patents. Since much of the valuable information and ideas will be jointly developed, it is important for the parties to determine at the beginning of the relationship how the fruits of the innovations should be shared. For instance, if we expect that all secrets ultimately should belong to us, then we must take care in the contracts to provide for this outcome. The final determination about ownership will depend on a number of factors, such as the relative importance of each company's technological contributions, each party's relative bargaining strengths, the most efficient ways to control and improve the technologies, and compensation schemes.

As we know, once the ownership issues are ironed out, then the trade secret owners, as determined under the agreements, must take measures that are reasonable under the circumstances to protect the secrecy of their information. We have already seen in Chapter 4 how difficult this can be simply within the confines even of one's own firm. Confidentiality agreements in conjunction with a host of physical measures are always required. Such steps are just as important when other companies are entrusted with the information. However, the problems are multiplied. When we furnish trade secrets to SoftWave, for instance, we have to watch over that company to ensure that it handles the information as we do within our own enterprise. To this end, our agreements should very specifically enumerate (1) whom the information can be shared with, both within and outside SoftWave; (2) that confidentiality agreements must be signed by all who have access to the information; (3) any physical security measures that must be undertaken by SoftWave; (4) that SoftWave must ensure that reasonable security measures be taken by those who are allowed access to the information outside SoftWave; (5) whether other protections such as enforcing covenants not to compete with particular individuals are necessary; and (6) what measures we will take to monitor SoftWave's compliance with these terms. The last item is important not to overlook. Part of our responsibility in preserving the secrecy of the valuable information is engaging in periodic audits, not only within our company but also within the confines of all businesses entrusted with the secrets. Thus, our agreement with SoftWave should ensure that we have permission to inspect its operations under mutually agreed-to terms so that we are satisfied SoftWave is adequately preserving the secrecy of our technologies.

Clearly, this all becomes more and more complicated as the number of parties and trade secret owners increases. If SoftWave owns trade secrets in its software, then it will want similar assurances from us and rights to ensure our compliance. Likewise, we both will have to extend these protections to Scherer's operations. And, of course, both companies will have to work very closely with Scherer, once distribution begins, in order to make sure that the distributors and retailers take whatever steps we think are necessary to preserve the secrecy of information given to them to help explain, sell, and maintain the products.

Copyright Issues

It is likely that the copyright laws will be used to protect portions of the computer program utilized in the AES.[45] Also, various written documents, such as manuals, instructions, and sales brochures are susceptible to copyright protection. As previously discussed, however, protection for just about any other facet of the AES will not be possible via the copyright laws in the United States.

A particularly important issue will again be ownership. In this regard, we must follow the principles laid down in *CCNV v. Reid*. Unless we come to some other understanding in the contract, it is likely that SoftWave will be the owner of the copyright to the AES program. This is despite the fact that we came to SoftWave with the idea to create the program. We would not even be a joint owner in this situation, since we did not contribute to the expressive portions of the ultimate program. Thus, if we expect to be the owner of the copyright in the program used by the **AES**, then in the contract, SoftWave will have to assign its copyright in the program to us. As for all the other copyrightable materials, we will have to be similarly conscious of copyright ownership principles, especially those applying to works made for hire.

The owners of the copyrights in these various items will have to license to developers and marketers the rights to copy and/or distribute the works. For instance, if we design an instruction booklet to explain the **AES** to users, then Scherer will need permission to duplicate it for inclusion with each **AES** it produces. In addition, some participants in the sales channels, including Scherer, may need permission to distribute the copies along with the product. In this regard, the first-sale doctrine of Section 109 should be consulted to determine if permissions are necessary.

Similar principles will apply to the computer program. Scherer will need to receive from the copyright owner, whether it is us or SoftWave, the authority to duplicate the program if it must make copies in order to manufacture the product. Of course, if we provide Scherer with components that already integrate the program, then Scherer will not require a license to copy. Also, if Scherer wishes to improve the **AES**, necessitating changes in the program, then permission from the copyright owner will be required to make derivative works. In this regard, another possibility is that the copyright owner may commit itself to make these updates so that they can be integrated into Scherer's new products. Beyond these issues, Scherer and possibly others involved in distribution may need licenses to carry out their marketing duties, just as was necessary with the instruction booklet. As you can see, the copyright owner has tremendous flexibility in determining how to allocate its rights, requiring the parties to give tremendous thought to their allocation, preferably at the beginning of the deal. Failure to clearly come to grips with all the potential ways that the relationship might develop may inevitably lead to tensions between the parties. Part of the dispute between Apple and Microsoft, for instance, questioned whether Apple's license allowing Microsoft to sell Windows 1.0 extended to Microsoft's improved version, Windows 2.03.[46]

Trademark Issues

Trademark issues are usually somewhat easier to resolve. Assuming that the alliance has chosen the word "StatFree" to serve as a trademark, the first question again centers on ownership. Likely, our company or Scherer will own the trademark and will be responsible for federal and international registrations. If we are the owner of the trademark, we will need to consider what persons involved in manufacturing, marketing, and distributing the product might need permission to use the trademark to carry out their responsibilities. This obviously will include Scherer but likely will encompass others as well. In a similar fashion, we must consider who has rights to register and use relevant Internet domain names.

Another issue involves the steps the parties will take in policing use of the trademark to ensure that it does not lose trademark significance, such as by becoming generic. For instance, we may require those involved in marketing the product to follow certain guidelines specifying linguistic dos and don'ts when promoting the product. In addition, we may want those involved in distribution and sales to police improper customer usage, by perhaps correcting customers when they use the word "statfree" in a product sense rather than with brand significance. Finally, the parties need to resolve whether they should have rights to use the name on other products they may develop. Scherer, for instance, may want to ensure that it has the right to use the StatFree name on a line of **AES** accessory products that it later may choose to manufacture and distribute.

Liability Issues

When parties undertake a strategic alliance, it is crucial that they fully comprehend the potential risks of the relationship and appropriately divide responsibility for negative outcomes should those consequences materialize. Clear definitions of what each party should expect from the others in the alliance lead to unambiguous solutions to the problems and disappointments that inevitably occur. This is not to say that such understandings will reduce the financial pain when a party is obligated to bear the costs. However, such clarity does tend to narrow the extent of disagreements among the parties, leading to less contentious outcomes to problems. This, in turn, can help ensure the harmony that is necessary for a successful long-term strategic relationship.

To this end, it is common for commercial parties to articulate very specifically in the contract exactly what types and levels of performance should be expected from their products and services. In other words, sophisticated businesspersons will make somewhat elaborate express warranties and usually will disclaim the implied warranties of merchantability and fitness. Keep in mind that the restrictions on disclaiming implied warranties discussed earlier in this chapter applied only to the sale of consumer goods. This conforms to the philosophy that commercial parties (who in theory do not need such extensive protections of the law to look after their interests) should have the flexibility to structure a deal according to their particular needs.

Similarly, commercial contracts can be quite specific about the types and extent of remedies that one party can enforce against another. For instance, SoftWave must be very concerned about its financial exposure if a defect in its software causes distributed **AES** units to fail. In its contract negotiations with us, SoftWave may try to come to some mutually agreeable outcome that allows it to limit its exposure to potentially enormous consequential damages. Of course, any reduction of SoftWave's ultimate responsibility to pay for these consequential damages means that we must absorb the losses, even though the error was committed by SoftWave. However, we can reduce the risk of such an outcome by requiring the computer software to pass certain specific tests before we accept it. In addition, we may find that we simply have no choice but to assume responsibility for consequential damages just so the alliance can come together in the first place.

Likewise, commercial parties may allocate the risks from potential tort liabilities through contracts. For instance, there may be some concern that the components we supply to Scherer may cause severe electrical shocks when being installed and tested by Scherer employees. If these shocks were to materialize and employees were thereby injured, we could be liable through negligence or strict liability principles. Given that we are a small company, such potential tort liabilities should give us pause. Indeed, the risks may be so high that we might not be willing to enter the deal at all. The members of the strategic alliance may reallocate these risks through the contract so as to reduce our uncertainty, thereby allowing the deal to go forward. For instance, we may agree that Scherer should bear the total responsibility for injuries caused by the shocks should they occur.

Indemnification An important element of risk allocation among strategic partners is the ability to seek indemnification against other participants. *Indemnification* is the right to be reimbursed for payments made to third parties to satisfy their legal claims. For instance, assume a third party alleges that Scherer violates the third party's copyright in a computer program when Scherer copies and distributes the program designed by SoftWave. Not only will Scherer have to pay for its defense in court, but should the court find that the program does unlawfully infringe, then Scherer would be liable for damages as well. Clearly, Scherer was depending on SoftWave to create a program that would not cause legal problems. Indeed, among the participants in the alliance, SoftWave is in the best position to control whether the software violates the rights of any third party. Under circumstances such as this, the partners will want the contract to clearly specify that SoftWave will indemnify them should legal problems arising from the software require payments to third parties.

Since SoftWave ultimately is responsible to pay these third-party claims, it naturally will want to have the opportunity to control the litigation. Thus, indemnification clauses normally allow the responsible party, here SoftWave, to have a say in the selection of legal counsel, the choice of litigation strategies, and the course of settlement negotiations. Such input usually is not absolute, however, for the party being sued has a stake in the outcome if the indemnifier does not have the financial means to satisfy the ultimate judgment. For example, Scherer may want to accept a settlement offer while SoftWave would prefer to fight in court. Suppose the offer is turned down according to SoftWave's wishes. If the defense fails in court and the losses are much larger than the settlement offer, then Scherer is on the hook should SoftWave not be able to pay the damages fully. Thus, indemnification clauses should be given tremendous forethought and must be carefully tailored according to the needs and financial means of the parties involved.

Indemnification clauses are essential to high-technology alliances. The previous example illustrates that when companies are making and distributing products dependent on intellectual property, there are enormous risks of infringement. Thus, indemnification clauses often deal with potential copyright, patent, trade secret, and trademark issues. However, indemnification clauses may be broader, depending on the context. For instance, they may extend to potential tort and contract liabilities, as well as to more specialized issues, such as the possible violation of particular rules, regulations, and statutes applicable to the situation at hand.

Alternative Dispute Resolution

From the simple overview of contractual matters presented in this chapter, you can recognize the varied scope of issues that arise in any strategic venture. You also should be aware that it is simply impossible to address every potential problem up front in a contract. One certainty when entering any long-term strategic alliance is that disputes invariably will arise. Many of these disagreements may be settled through discussions and negotiations. However, when these measures fail, the parties will require more formal channels to resolve their differences.

The traditional avenue for resolving disputes is by litigation in the state or federal court systems. However, litigation presents a number of problems, particularly for high-technology strategic ventures. Possibly the biggest drawback to litigation hinges on its very nature, based on confrontation, hostility, and distrust. One fairly certain outcome of litigation is that the parties will not be friendly once it concludes. Such a state of affairs, of course, is hardly consistent with a strategic venture, which depends on long-term working relationships among the participants. A second pitfall with litigation is the time frame for handling disputes. Depending on the jurisdiction, it may take years before a civil case comes to trial. In the fast-paced world of high technology, in which firms must move quickly and decisively, delays of this magnitude to the smooth operation of the partnership may doom the venture. Another drawback with litigation is that the decision makers often are inexperienced with the subject matter underlying the dispute. We have already seen what happens to computer copyright disputes when they are resolved by judges and juries who do not fully appreciate the technology. High-technology litigants often invest substantial resources into teaching the decision maker about the technology, with little assurance that the intricacies can be assimilated in a relatively short amount of time. This often leads to poor decisions that only increase the frustration surrounding the dispute. An additional deficiency with litigation is the public nature of the proceedings. This can lead to substantial hardships when the dispute involves modern technologies, especially those consisting of trade secrets. Although there are ways for the litigants to preserve the confidentiality of their trade secrets during litigation, the course may be perilous. Finally, litigation can be extremely expensive, mostly because of high attorneys' fees and extensive discovery requirements.

Alternative dispute resolution (ADR) techniques are designed to help the parties reach a satisfactory decision while minimizing the deficiencies inherent in the traditional litigation system. The key to ADR is that it can be tailored to the special needs of the parties involved. Many firms now specialize in advising firms on the proper forms and implementation of ADR. The techniques being used are extremely varied, ranging from highly informal to very formal. However, some attributes are fairly consistent. For instance, the process is private, thereby alleviating

---

Exhibit 9.6

Selected Alternative Dispute Resolution Techniques

■ **Mediation**
- A process that facilitates negotiations between the parties
- Effective mediators have excellent "people" skills and have expertise in the field of the dispute
- Informal, consensual, nonbinding process

■ **Minitrial**
- A mock run to illustrate how arguments and evidence might appear at trial
- A "jury" of executives from both sides deliberates with the assistance of a mediator
- Nonbinding, consensual process

■ **Binding Arbitration**
- Parties agree to be bound by the decision of the arbitrator(s)
- Only limited rights to appeal decisions
- Often relatively fast decisions
- Often cheaper than trial
- Flexible procedures
- Flexibility regarding the number of arbitrators and methods of selection
- Flexibility with rules governing how arbitrators fashion relief

---

fears of trade secret disclosure. Also, selection of the decision maker(s) is up to the parties. This means that the parties are free to find people who have expertise in the matters under dispute. Other key aspects, such as time and expense, vary considerably, depending on the technique being used. We will now take a brief look at three types of ADR that have received substantial attention in high-technology contexts. They are mediation, the minitrial, and arbitration (see Exhibit 9.6).

Mediation   In mediation, the parties engage a neutral person to help them resolve their differences. The mediator is not a decision maker. Rather, the role of the mediator is to facilitate settlement of the dispute by removing obstacles and helping the parties explore avenues of potential agreement. More than anything else, the effectiveness of the mediator depends on trust. The mediator is like a shuttle diplomat, working between the parties to resolve their differences. The mediator's goal is to buffer the animosity between the disputants and to find ways to have them overcome their differences so that an effective working relationship can be restored. The mediator often is able to identify the key issues, allowing the parties to see through their hostility to the real points of disagreement. An effective mediator may render impartial assessments of positions, highlight the consequences of not reaching a settlement, and explore mutually acceptable bases for agreement. From the foregoing, one can tell that mediators must have skills in diplomacy more than anything else. Mediators must be good listeners and have excellent "people" skills so that they can effectively facilitate negotiations between the parties. However, to be most effective, the mediator also must have expertise in the particular field of the dispute. This expertise should cover both the relevant business and legal issues that are at the heart of the disagreement. Organizations such as the Center for Public Resources and the American Arbitration Association maintain panels of highly qualified mediators and should be consulted if mediation is pursued.

The entire mediation process is consensual and informal and can be terminated by any party at any time. Because there is no binding commitment and, thus, little downside to its use, mediation often is selected as a first crack at finding a solution to the problem. If it fails, then the parties can resort to more formal methods of dispute resolution. With this in mind, commercial parties entering a long-term relationship should consider including the following form of provision in their agreement:

> In the event that there is a dispute or claim relating to this contract, and the parties are not able to resolve it through direct negotiations, then the parties hereby agree that they will attempt to settle the dispute or claim first by means of mediation according to the Commercial Mediation Rules of the American Arbitration Association. The parties further agree that they will proceed to litigation, arbitration or any other resolution procedure only if they fail to resolve their differences through mediation.

This provision is just one example of a very simple type of mediation agreement. Often the strategic partners will want to be much more specific in the agreement about the mediation process if it becomes necessary to use it. For instance, they may specify the number, qualifications, and possibly the identity of the mediators. They also may be more concrete about what resolution process might follow mediation should it fail, such as by requiring arbitration in lieu of litigation.

Minitrial   A minitrial is not really a trial; rather it is a test run so that the disputing parties may explore what might happen if they pursued litigation all the way through the trial process. The procedure is relatively informal, and like mediation, it is confidential and has no binding effect on the parties. Often minitrials are pursued when mediation is unable to bring the sides to agreement—usually because the parties have widely divergent views about the probabilities of success at trial or the amounts of money that might be recovered.

A minitrial neither takes place in a courtroom nor uses a judge to render a decision. However, it has attributes that mirror a trial setting. The parties make presentations of their views about the situation to "juries" consisting of business executives with settlement powers from both of the contesting corporations. Often the case is facilitated by a neutral third party, who has expertise in mediation. The goal of the minitrial is to have the executives get a realistic feel for what might happen at trial should that avenue be followed. The presentations are informal without the constraints of rules of evidence. However, in complex cases, such as those involving patents, realism is ensured by allowing experts to "testify" and by allowing the parties flexibility to learn various facts from each other (called "discovery") prior to the proceeding. The neutral participant facilitates the proceeding and may ask questions during the presentations. After the presentations, the neutral party may be asked to give the executives an advisory opinion about the risks each side would face at trial and a prediction of the outcome. The jury of executives then "deliberates," sometimes with the neutral individual mediating the discussions. If the minitrial is successful, the sides will see the merits of each other's arguments, substantiated by the independent thoughts of the neutral participant. These insights may lead the parties to reach a settlement in a relatively swift, inexpensive, and consensual manner.

Arbitration   Arbitration essentially is a private, trial-type proceeding that is conducted according to the wishes of the disputing parties. Although the parties may choose a nonbinding form of arbitration, it is far more common that they opt for *binding arbitration.* Binding arbitration means that the parties agree to be bound by the decision of the arbitrator, an aspect that marks an important difference from the preceding styles of ADR, in which voluntary resolution was the goal. With binding arbitration, the parties have determined that the neutral will decide the outcome of their dispute and fashion the appropriate relief. And there is little recourse if a party is dissatisfied with the decision. Although one might appeal the determination to the appellate courts, the grounds for any appeal are extremely limited, to, say, fraud or illegality. More typical reasons for dissatisfaction, such as that the arbitrator did not understand the facts or did not apply the law correctly to those facts, normally will not be reviewed by the courts. Thus, the choice to use arbitration must be made with the understanding that binding really does mean binding.

Arbitration is increasingly preferred by high-technology firms over litigation because it is private, relatively fast, and decisive. Also, the participants may fashion the ground rules for the arbitration in their contractual relationship so that it is tailored to their specific needs. Typical issues that must be resolved involve who will serve as the arbitrator or arbitrators, how much discovery will be allowed, what rules of evidence will control the arbitration, and what types of relief may be granted.

Normally, an arbitration agreement will specify how many arbitrators will be used and how they will be selected. Obviously, it is less expensive to use only one arbitrator to make the decision. But many times, companies prefer panels of arbitrators, most often consisting of three individuals. There are several explanations for this preference. Probably of most importance, the parties may disagree about what types of expertise an arbitrator should have. For instance, in a software dispute, one party may want a software engineer while the other prefers an intellectual-property attorney. A panel containing both kinds of experts solves the impasse. Another important virtue of panels is that they may be perceived as more able to impart a fair decision than a single arbitrator could.

The arbitration agreement should establish not only the number of arbitrators but also the methods whereby each will be selected. The American Arbitration Association maintains lists of arbitrators who have expertise in a variety of areas, such as the National Panel of Patent Arbitrators and the National Panel of Commercial Arbitrators. These can be very useful in filling the slots. The selection techniques range anywhere from methods of chance to specification of the particular arbitrators in the agreement. One typical arrangement is for each party to select an arbitrator of its choice and leave it to those two individuals to select a third.

One of the principal advantages of arbitration is that the parties may specify simplified rules about discovering information prior to trial and about trial procedures. Discovery of information in traditional litigation can be very expensive and time consuming. The parties may control discovery in arbitration by limiting or even prohibiting it in their arbitration agreement. Indeed, in some states, discovery is restricted by law unless the agreement provides that increased discovery will be used.[47] Similarly, the rules of evidence used to conduct the hearing may be tailored by the parties. Usually these are more relaxed than civil trial procedures. Often the parties will agree to use the American Arbitration Association's Commercial Arbitration rules or will follow the Center for Public Resource's Model ADR Procedures for technology disputes.

One other key issue is the type of relief the arbitrator is empowered to grant. Typically, the arbitrators are given the authority to decide the appropriate relief based on their own discretion. This flexibility is no different from what exists in normal civil litigation. Sometimes, the arbitrators are more constrained in fashioning relief. One example is called "final offer arbitration" or "baseball arbitration." When this approach is used, each party submits to the arbitrator a single proposed award. After hearing the evidence at the hearing, the arbitrator is required to pick one of the two submitted alternatives without modification. This procedure tends to discourage the sides from taking extreme positions, since the arbitrator is not likely to accept an unreasonable recommendation. In addition, the narrowing of the differences in this manner may help lead to an early settlement.

ADR certainly presents a lot of potential advantages to high-technology firms.[48] This explains the explosive growth in the use of ADR procedures by businesses in the past few years. One survey, for instance, found that 88% of Fortune 1000 corporations had used mediation over a three-year period, while 79% had used arbitration.[49] However, ADR is not a universal panacea. Sometimes arbitration can turn out to be more expensive and time consuming than litigation. Also, ADR techniques may disclose certain weaknesses if the dispute ultimately gets to trial. In addition, some observers contend that arbitrators have a tendency to pursue the middle ground, a possible negative if your rights are the ones being sacrificed. Other factors, such as the publicity surrounding civil trials and the desire to have juries consider sympathetic cases also may trigger a preference for traditional channels of litigation.[50] In sum, firms conducting business in the technology field should seriously consider the potential benefits of ADR techniques when devising strategic partnerships, but they should not perfunctorily assume that ADR is the way to go. The decision is a crucial one that demands substantial consideration.

Antitrust and Anticompetitive Conduct

When high-technology firms enter contractual or other business arrangements, they need to assess what effect those deals might have on competition and whether those consequences will be acceptable to the public and to key policy makers. The barrage of media attention recently given to Microsoft and Intel, among many others, for engaging in practices that some say may be unduly anticompetitive, points out the importance of this policy area. Usually competition policy comes within the broad umbrella of what is called antitrust. However, there is another doctrine, called "misuse," that also is relevant to firms dealing with intellectual property. This chapter closes by providing a sense of how high-technology firms might be affected by these important competition policies.

Overview of Antitrust

Antitrust policy in the United States has its roots in the Industrial Revolution. The time was marked by a substantial shift in economic and political power from the once-dominant farming community to the emerging industrialists. There also was a notable change in the way economic power was controlled. Whereas before the Industrial Revolution, economic wealth was diffused over a multitude of owners of small businesses and entrepreneurs, the era brought with it new breeds of empires that sometimes controlled substantial economic assets and power. The result was a populist reaction around the turn of the 20th century. It was during this tumultuous period that antitrust policies were born.

The fundamental antitrust statutes are the Sherman Act, the Clayton Act, and the FTC Act. The Sherman Act, which serves as the cornerstone of antitrust policy, prohibits contracts, combinations, and conspiracies in restraint of trade. In addition, it states that monopolizing is unlawful. The Clayton Act deals with a number of practices such as price discrimination. However, its major thrust is its merger clause prohibiting mergers that may substantially lessen competition. The FTC Act empowers the Federal Trade Commission to prohibit unfair methods of competition.

A notable similarity between these statutes is how vague they are in describing unlawful conduct. What does it mean to restrain trade? What kind of conduct constitutes monopolizing? Under what circumstances will a merger have the possible effect of lessening competition? What kinds of business methods are unfair? One frightening aspect of antitrust is that there is no clear guidance about the meanings of these terms, leaving businesses constantly exposed to the vagaries of the policy makers in charge of interpreting them.

Philosophical Justifications for Antitrust   Those responsible for giving meaning to the vague terms of antitrust generally search the historical origins of the policy to determine the philosophical constructs from which it evolved. Unfortunately, such historical analyses have led to two substantially different notions of what antitrust is designed to achieve. One school of thought attaches a *populist* philosophy to antitrust. According to this approach, antitrust arose to protect small farms and businesses from the powerful industrial enterprises. Antitrust was conceived to ensure a vital system of small producers and sellers, thereby ensuring that American entrepreneurial ingenuity thrives through the incentives of universal opportunity. Following this line of reasoning, antitrust is based on a generalized distrust of big business. Although one legitimately might make arguments that big business can be more efficient in the production and distribution of goods and services, that notion is viewed with skepticism, especially when taking a long-term perspective. Those advocating the importance of small business to society believe that any economic benefits that might conceivably be achieved through size ultimately will be enjoyed by the large-business powerhouses to the detriment of consumers and society. The small-business supporters therefore are inclined to use antitrust to attack the formation and growth of big business, even when faced with convincing arguments that greater size might yield lower costs. From all of this, one should not be surprised that those entertaining a small-business philosophy on antitrust usually support an active program of antitrust enforcement.

One can review the history of antitrust and reach an entirely different construct about the purposes of antitrust. One of the concerns of the Industrial Revolution was the rise of true economic monopolies that faced little if any competition in their industries and that had the means to deter any firm that might consider entering the field. Economists consider monopolies to be inefficient not only because they transfer wealth from consumers but also because they impose an unrecoverable cost on society through the income redistribution process. Thus, it makes sense for the government to interfere with the free market when the unfettered market otherwise would result in monopoly power. Here, monopoly power does not mean that the business is big. Rather, it is related to the capability of the business to dominate firms that try to compete with it.

Following this line of reasoning, the other philosophical approach to antitrust is founded on the principle of maintaining *economic efficiency*. Those supporting this view of antitrust policy believe that enforcement is proper only when the free market, left to its own devices, would not render an efficient outcome. However, this scenario is considered the exception rather than the rule. Decisions and arrangements normally made by business firms through the natural forces of the competitive process are viewed as serving the public interest by increasing economic efficiency. The strategies adopted by firms are to do better than their rivals, ultimately leading to lower prices or better products for consumers. If the process leads to more powerful firms, then it likely is because their added scope enhances certain economic efficiencies that allow those businesses to be more formidable competitors. Big business, therefore, is not seen as something that is necessarily bad. In fact, it may be viewed positively, as long as there are market forces in place to ensure competitive practices, such as with pricing. Therefore, those advocating the efficiency objectives to antitrust, based on these observations, normally call for a hands-off or passive approach to antitrust enforcement, under the assumption that the free market normally will result in the most efficient outcome.

Antitrust Policy Makers   Antitrust policy initially derives from Congress through statutes. However, as already noted, Congress has been somewhat vague in articulating antitrust standards. On occasion Congress has been more forceful, providing greater clarity for certain specific areas of antitrust concern. For example, in 1984, Congress reduced the antitrust exposure for companies engaging in joint research and development projects when it passed the National Cooperative Research Act. This move stimulated a number of joint research efforts that otherwise may not have occurred for fear of antitrust enforcement. For example, thanks somewhat to this amendment to the antitrust laws, the big three auto makers jointly developed a manufacturing process for a lightweight material that could someday substitute for steel. In addition, they received a joint patent for the process in 1993. Nonetheless, for most arrangements, congressional statutes remain vague about the potential applicability of antitrust. Under circumstances such as these, policy making shifts from Congress to administrative agencies, the president, and the courts.

The Federal Trade Commission and the Antitrust Division of the Justice Department are charged with enforcing the antitrust laws for the public. As you can imagine, the degree of scrutiny these agencies give to various business practices is a function of the philosophies held by their top administrators. In the 1960s, for instance, these agencies were ruled by the small-business philosophy, thereby leading to somewhat aggressive enforcement practices. However, in the 1980s, both agencies were much more passive, due in large part to philosophical shifts that at that time supported the efficiency approach. Since the top administrators are appointed by the president, one can quickly see one way the president can influence antitrust policy. The marked change in enforcement activity, for instance, can be ascribed somewhat to the different philosophical approaches held by the Democratic administrations in the 1960s compared to President Reagan's in the 1980s.

In the 1990s, the antitrust agencies became slightly more aggressive. This may be explained somewhat by changes in the economic environment. As a result of the numerous mergers and acquisitions in the previous decade, many industries had become highly consolidated, raising the likelihood that firms might be able to exercise market power. Coupled with this were rapid changes in the international and technological environments, which also created new challenges for antitrust enforcement. President Clinton, too, played an important role through his appointments, who were less likely than their Republican predecessors to rely on unfettered markets to address antitrust concerns.

When the administrative agencies bring enforcement actions, the cases either are initially heard in the federal courts or may ultimately be reviewed by them. In addition, private parties may bring antitrust actions in the federal courts when they believe they have been damaged by violations of the antitrust laws. When such cases are brought, the federal courts must interpret the vague language of the statutes to answer the question at hand. For example, if a case is brought against a company and it is shown that the company fixed prices with a competitor, then the court must determine if this practice is the type of restraint that Congress intended to be unlawful under the Sherman Act. As with administrative agencies, the decision of the court likely will be influenced by the antitrust philosophies held by the presiding judges. Looking at the 1960s and the 1980s, we see a marked difference in the approaches taken by courts. Whereas in the 1960s there was concern for the protection of small business, in the 1980s the focus was on maintaining economic efficiency. This change again can be ascribed somewhat to the influence of the president, who is responsible for nominating federal judges when vacancies occur.

Violation of the antitrust laws may carry severe penalties. When private parties are successful in antitrust litigation, they are entitled to three times their proven damages (treble damages), plus attorneys' fees and court costs. Also, the Justice Department may bring criminal proceedings against alleged violators of the Sherman Act. In addition, the FTC and the Justice Department may initiate civil cases, asking the tribunal to impose injunctions and possibly to order the payment of damages. The potential degree of liability, coupled with uncertainty about how the law will be enforced and interpreted, can make antitrust litigation a very frightening prospect indeed.

Application of the Antitrust Laws

The Rule of Reason   Section 1 of the Sherman Act prohibits contracts, combinations, and conspiracies that unreasonably restrain trade. The ambit of this provision is so broad that firms must evaluate any contemplated business transaction with other companies in terms of its reasonableness. What makes an arrangement reasonable, therefore, is the key question for the Sherman Act, Section 1. When cases are brought to the federal courts, judges use what is termed the "rule of reason" to make this analysis. The rule of reason can be likened to a scale, illustrated in Exhibit 9.7, balancing how the arrangement might harm competition against the possible ways it could benefit competition. If the likely harms to competition outweigh the benefits, then the transaction is unreasonable and unlawful; if the benefits outweigh the harms, then it is reasonable and lawful.

For example, a common distribution practice is for manufacturers to provide

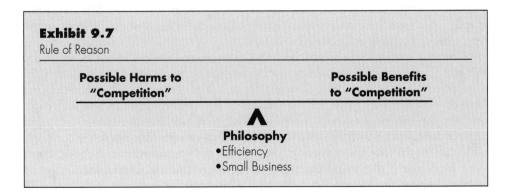

Exhibit 9.7
Rule of Reason

| **Possible Harms to "Competition"** | **Possible Benefits to "Competition"** |

Philosophy
• Efficiency
• Small Business

retailers the exclusive rights to sell in particular regions. Such an arrangement may harm consumers because they will not be able to comparison shop for the manufacturer's goods at different retail outlets in the area. On the other hand, the exclusive privilege might encourage the retailer to more aggressively push the manufacturer's brand, since the retailer knows that customers, once persuaded, have no choice but to buy the brand from it. Other manufacturers may be forced to match the increased promotion with vigorous competitive responses, such as lower prices or enhanced services, thereby benefiting consumers. Whether the arrangement is reasonable depends on the particular facts and the relative weights given to each possibility by the courts. *Eastman Kodak v. Image Technical Services*, presented later in the chapter, also illustrates how arrangements conceivably may have both positive and negative effects on competition.

The rule of reason raises significant ambiguity for businesses. One never knows which arguments, information, or expert testimony ultimately will persuade the court. In addition, as mentioned earlier, "competition" may be defined in different ways by different judges. Some may evaluate the transaction by considering the effects on economic efficiency. Other judges may be more concerned with how the transaction might impact the ability of small businesses to survive.

Per Se Illegality   The courts have developed one shortcut that adds more certainty to their judgment about certain kinds of transactions. Those sitting on the courts have concluded that some arrangements are potentially so harmful that no alleged benefits could ever outweigh their dangers in a rule-of-reason analysis. Rather than waste everyone's time by reviewing evidence regarding the reasonableness of such deals, the courts skip the weighing analysis and jump directly to the conclusion that they are unlawful. In other words, to be successful, all the plaintiff must do is prove that the defendant engaged in one of these arrangements. This is substantially easier and more predictable than in the typical rule-of-reason scenario wherein the plaintiff must prove not only the existence of the transaction but also that it is unreasonable on balance. Since unreasonableness is assumed, these transactions are called *illegal per se* (literally, illegal in and of itself).

As you might imagine, those advocating the small-business approach to antitrust are more inclined to support illegal per se determinations than are those who favor efficiency. This is because they are more suspicious of business arrangements that might increase the competitive power of firms in the marketplace. For this reason, numerous arrangements were judged illegal per se in the 1960s when small-business proponents dominated the courts. However, by the 1980s, the efficiency-minded judges then in place were more inclined to fully review the economic effects of particular transactions rather than perfunctorily deem them illegal. Thus, the list of illegal per se offenses began to shrink. The most important change was in vertical nonprice restrictions, which were illegal per se prior to 1977. However, the Supreme Court changed its mind in that year, ruling that these important arrangements should be fully evaluated under the rule of reason.[51] Similarly, in 1997, the Supreme Court ruled that vertical maximum price agreements, which previously were illegal per se, should be appraised under the rule of reason.[52]

Currently, certain practices are still illegal per se, but the courts often are very particular about the circumstances that make a practice unlawful out of hand. For instance, tying arrangements, which are the primary subject of *Eastman Kodak v. Image Technical Services*, are illegal per se, but only if (1) there are two products and (2) the company has appreciable market power in the tying product. If these aspects are not found, then the arrangement is judged under the rule of reason. Vertical minimum price fixing, in which parties at different levels of the distribution chain agree to resale price floors, is illegal per se, but again, the courts have substantially narrowed the kinds of conduct that come within the definition of the offense.[53] A few practices, such as price agreements between competitors, have steadfastly remained illegal per se. However, one should not be surprised if the courts continue the trend toward using the rule of reason for antitrust analysis as the twenty-first century begins to unfold.

Monopolizing and Other Antitrust Offenses   The Sherman Act, Section 2, prohibits monopolizing. In the 1940s and 1950s, a company seemingly could run afoul of this provision simply by obtaining a market share that was too large.[54] However, as antitrust policy makers focused more on efficiency considerations, they rejected the notion that the attainment of high market share alone should be condemned. After all, one could achieve market dominance due to the implementation of the most cost-effective business practices. Such conduct should be rewarded, not outlawed. Also, it would not make sense to prevent large companies from implementing new and more efficient business practices, even if they ended up hurting competitors. On the other hand, big firms have the ability to harm competition because market participants are so dependent on them. Thus, modern antitrust analysis evaluates the conduct of big firms to appraise whether they have engaged in monopolizing. If a company's actions are designed to improve economic efficiency, then they are lawful; if they make sense only in terms of destroying competitors, however, then they violate the antitrust laws. *Eastman Kodak v. Image Technical Services*, which follows, explains how the courts evaluate monopolization charges.

Eastman Kodak v. Image Technical Services deals with a critical subject for high-technology firms: the contractual provision, imposed by some manufacturers of high-technology equipment, requiring purchasers to have their products serviced by the manufacturers. In antitrust terms, this may be likened to a tying arrangement, a situation wherein the manufacturer limits the right of customers to purchase a product they desire (the tying product) without also buying some item they do not necessarily want (the tied product). For this arrangement to be illegal per se, one must show that repair services are distinct from the equipment and that the manufacturer has appreciable market power in the desired equipment. Keep in mind that if the arrangement is not illegal per se for want of one of these elements, then it still might be unlawful under the more extensive rule-of-reason analysis.

The tying of service to hardware has become somewhat common in the computer industry. One can point to a number of reasons why such tying arrangements might be reasonable under certain circumstances.[55] For instance, some customers prefer a turnkey solution to computer problems, which includes hardware, software, software updates, and maintenance. For some manufacturers, it may not be feasible to offer all these features unless the features are packaged in some attractive way. Another important consideration is that vendors of computer software often have substantial trade secrets that they wish to protect in their products. Maintenance agreements ensure that the software developer does not have to relinquish source code to the customer or third-party maintenance firms so that problems can be corrected. Also, customers who experience substantial problems in the servicing of their computer products may attribute the problems to the products, when poor service may actually be the problem. Thus, service maintenance agreements can preserve a company's goodwill and make it a more respected competitor with other firms. On the other hand, tying arrangements requiring service may have certain pernicious effects. For instance, the requirement may simply be a way for the manufacturer to force third-party service providers out of business so that the manufacturer can raise service prices and sustain a high-level stream of future income. Those adhering to the small-business philosophy to antitrust naturally would be especially sensitive to this possibility.

Kodak is a 1992 Supreme Court decision that evaluates some of the important antitrust issues respecting service maintenance agreements. This case discusses service contracts both as tying arrangements under Section 1 of the Sherman Act and as a means for monopolizing under the Sherman Act, Section 2. Given the propensity of the Supreme Court in the early 1990s to favor the efficiency role of antitrust, there was some expectation that the court would side with the defendant, Kodak, in the proceeding. As you will see, however, there always are surprises lurking in the world of antitrust.

EASTMAN KODAK COMPANY v. IMAGE TECHNICAL SERVICES, INC.
United States Supreme Court, 1992

FACTS: Kodak manufactures and sells technologically complex, high-volume photocopiers and micrographics equipment. This equipment is serviced by Kodak and by independent service organizations (ISOs), such as Image Technical Services (ITS). ITS and other ISOs sued Kodak after Kodak adopted policies limiting the availability of parts to ISOs, thus making it harder for the ISOs to compete with Kodak in servicing Kodak equipment. The ISOs alleged that Kodak's policies amounted to illegal-per-se tying and monopolization, as prohibited by Sections 1 and 2 of the Sherman Act. The district court granted summary judgment for Kodak. This means that even if all the facts alleged by the ISOs were true, the ISOs would not prevail after a trial. According to the District Court, since Kodak did not have market power in the

continued . . .

continued . . .

equipment market, it could not have market power for service or parts. Consequently, it could not have engaged in *illegal per se* tying or unlawful monopolization. The Court of Appeals reversed, and Kodak appealed to the Supreme Court.

Summary judgment is improper, and the case should go to trial if the ISOs could potentially win at trial based on their version of the facts. To determine the propriety of summary judgment, the Supreme Court assumes that the facts alleged by the ISOs are true. If the ISOs persuade the Supreme Court that summary judgment is improper, then the case proceeds to trial both for determination of the actual facts and for proper resolution of the dispute based on those facts. Thus, the "facts" presented in this case are only the allegations of the ISOs.

Kodak provides to its customers service and parts for its equipment. It produces some of the parts itself; the rest are made to order for Kodak by independent original equipment manufacturers (OEMs). Kodak provides service after an initial warranty period either through annual service contracts, which include all necessary parts, or on a per-call basis.

Beginning in the early 1980s, ISOs began repairing and servicing Kodak equipment at substantially lower prices than Kodak. Some of the ISO customers purchased their own parts and hired ISOs only for service. Others chose ISOs to supply both service and parts. ISOs kept an inventory of parts, which were purchased either from Kodak or from other sources, primarily OEMs.

In 1985, Kodak implemented a policy of selling replacement parts for equipment only to buyers of Kodak equipment who use Kodak service or who repair their own machines. Kodak also sought to limit ISO access to other sources of Kodak parts. Kodak and the OEMs agreed that the OEMs would not sell to anyone other than Kodak those parts fitting Kodak equipment. Kodak also pressured Kodak equipment owners and independent parts distributors not to sell Kodak parts to ISOs. In addition, Kodak took steps to restrict the availability of used machines. Due to these actions, ISOs were unable to obtain parts from reliable sources, and many were forced out of business.

DECISION AND REASONING:
Tying Arrangements. The ISOs allege that Kodak unlawfully tied the sale of service of Kodak machines to the sale of parts. A tying arrangement is an agreement by a party to sell one product but only on the condition that the buyer also purchase a different (or tied) product or at least agree not to purchase that different product from any other supplier. Such an arrangement violates Section 1 of the Sherman Act if the seller has tied the sale of two products and has appreciable economic power in the tying product.

For service and parts to be considered two distinct products, there must be sufficient consumer demand so that it is efficient for a firm to provide service separately from parts. Evidence in the record indicates that service and parts have been sold separately in the past and still are sold separately to self-service equipment owners. Indeed, the development of the entire high-technology service industry is evidence of the efficiency of a separate market for service.

Kodak insists that because there is no demand for parts separate from service, there cannot be separate markets for service and parts. By that logic, we would be forced to conclude that there can never be separate markets, for example, for cameras and film, computers and software, or automobiles and tires. We have often found arrangements involving functionally linked products at least one of which is useless without the other to be prohibited tying devices.

Also, the ISOs have presented evidence that service was tied to parts. The record indicates that Kodak would sell parts to third parties only if they agreed not to buy service from ISOs.

Having found sufficient evidence of a tying arrangement, we now consider whether there was appreciable economic power in the tying market. Market power is the power to force purchasers to do something they would not do in a competitive market. It has been defined as the ability of a single seller to raise price and restrict output. The existence of such power ordinarily is inferred from the seller's possession of a predominant share of the market.

The ISOs allege that Kodak's control over the parts market has excluded service competition, boosted service prices, and forced unwilling consumption of Kodak service. The ISOs have offered evidence that consumers have switched to Kodak service even though they preferred ISO service, that Kodak service was of higher price and lower quality than the preferred ISO service, and that ISOs were driven out of business by Kodak's policies.

Kodak counters that even if it concedes monopoly share of the relevant parts market, it cannot actually exercise the necessary market *power* because competition exists in the equipment market. Kodak argues that it could not have the ability to raise prices of service and parts above the level that would be charged in a competitive market because any increase in profits from a higher price in the aftermarkets at least would be offset by a corresponding loss in profits from lower equipment sales as consumers began purchasing equipment with more attractive service costs.

The extent to which one market prevents exploitation of another market depends on the extent to which consumers will change their consumption of one product in response to a price change in another. Although competition in the equipment market may impose a restraint on prices in the aftermarkets, this by no means disproves the existence of power in those markets.

continued . . .

continued . . .

There is no immutable law—no basic economic reality—that competition in the equipment market cannot coexist with market power in the aftermarkets.

Significant information and switching costs constitute one possible explanation of this potential coexistence. For the service market price to affect equipment demand, consumers must inform themselves of the total cost of the package—being equipment, service, and parts—at the time of purchase; that is, consumers must engage in accurate life-cycle pricing. Life-cycle pricing of complex, durable equipment is difficult and costly. In order to arrive at an accurate price, a consumer must acquire a substantial amount of raw data and undertake sophisticated analysis. The necessary information would include data on price, quality, and availability of products needed to operate, upgrade, or enhance the initial equipment, as well as service and repair costs, including estimates of breakdown frequency, nature of repairs, price of service and parts, length of downtime, and losses incurred from downtime.

Much of this kind of information is difficult—some of it impossible—to acquire at the time of purchase. Moreover, even if consumers were capable of acquiring and processing the complex body of information, they may choose not to do so. Acquiring the information is expensive. If the costs of service are small relative to the equipment price, or if consumers are more concerned about equipment capabilities than service costs, they may not find it cost-efficient to compile the information.

As Kodak notes, there likely will be some large-volume, sophisticated purchasers who will undertake the comparative studies and insist that Kodak charge them competitive prices. Kodak contends that these knowledgeable customers will hold down the package price for all other customers. There are reasons, however, to doubt that sophisticated purchasers will ensure that competitive prices are charged to unsophisticated purchasers too. As an initial matter, if the number of sophisticated customers are relatively small, the amount of profits to be gained by supracompetitive pricing in the service market could make it profitable to let the knowledgeable consumers take their business elsewhere. More important, if a company is able to price-discriminate between sophisticated and unsophisticated consumers, the sophisticated will be unable to prevent the exploitation of the uninformed. Therefore, it makes little sense to assume, in the absence of any evidentiary support, that equipment-purchasing decisions are based on an accurate assessment of the total cost of the equipment, service, and parts over the lifetime of a machine.

A second factor undermining Kodak's claim that supracompetitive prices in the service market lead to ruinous losses in equipment sales is the cost to current owners of switching to a different product. If the cost of switching is high, consumers who already have purchased the equipment, and are thus locked-in, will tolerate some level of service-price increases before changing equipment brands. The ISOs have offered evidence that the heavy initial outlay for Kodak equipment, combined with the required support material that works only with Kodak equipment, makes switching costs very high for existing Kodak customers.

In sum, there is a question of fact whether information costs and switching costs foil the simple assumption that the equipment and service markets act as pure complements to one another. We conclude, then, that Kodak has failed to demonstrate that the ISOs' inference of market power in the service and parts market is unreasonable. Kodak thus is not entitled to summary judgment on the tying claim.

Kodak contends that despite the appearance of anticompetitiveness, its behavior actually favors competition because its ability to pursue innovative marketing plans will allow it to compete more effectively in the equipment market. A pricing strategy based on lower equipment prices and higher aftermarket prices could enhance equipment sales by making it easier for the buyer to finance the initial purchase. It is undisputed that competition is enhanced when a firm is able to offer various marketing options, including bundling of support and maintenance service with the sale of equipment. Nor do such actions run afoul of the antitrust laws. But the procompetitive effect of the specific conduct here—elimination of all consumer parts and service options—is far less clear.

Monopolization. The offense of monopolization under Section 2 of the Sherman Act has two elements: (1) the possession of monopoly power in the relevant market and (2) the willful acquisition or maintenance of that power as distinguished from growth or development as a consequence of a superior product, business acumen, or historical accident.

The existence of the first element—possession of monopoly power—is easily resolved. As has been noted, the ISOs have presented the plausible claims that service and parts are separate markets and that Kodak has the power to control prices or exclude competition in service and parts. Monopoly power under Section 2 requires something greater than market power under Section 1. The ISOs' evidence that Kodak controls nearly 100% of the parts market and 80% to 95% of the service market, with no readily available substitutes, is sufficient, however, to survive summary judgment under the more stringent monopoly standard of Section 2.

Kodak contends that a single brand of a product or service can never be a relevant market under the Sherman Act. We disagree. The relevant market, for antitrust purposes, is determined by the choices available to Kodak equipment owners. Prior cases support the proposition that, in some instances, one brand of a product can constitute a separate market.

continued . . .

continued . . .

The second element of a Section 2 claim is the use of monopoly power to foreclose competition, to gain a competitive advantage, or to destroy a competitor. Liability turns, then, on whether valid business reasons can explain Kodak's actions. Kodak claims that it has three valid business justifications for its actions: (1) to promote interbrand equipment competition by allowing Kodak to stress the quality of its service; (2) to improve asset management by reducing Kodak's inventory costs; and (3) to prevent ISOs from free riding on Kodak's capital investment in equipment, parts, and service. Factual questions exist, however, about the validity and sufficiency of each claimed justification, making summary judgment inappropriate.

As to the quality of service, there is evidence that ISOs provide quality service that is preferred by some Kodak equipment owners. With respect to asset management, Kodak's actions appear inconsistent with a need to control inventory costs. The justification fails to explain, for example, the ISOs' evidence that Kodak forced OEMs, equipment owners, and parts brokers not to sell parts to ISOs—actions that have no effect on Kodak's inventory costs. Finally, Kodak's argument that the ISOs are free-riding by not entering the equipment and parts markets is not persuasive. One of the evils proscribed by the antitrust laws is the creation of entry barriers to potential competitors by requiring them to enter two markets simultaneously.

The judgment of the Court of Appeals denying summary judgment is affirmed.[56]

The foregoing discussion dealt only with fundamental principles regarding the Sherman Act. Always keep in mind that there are other federal antitrust laws and policies that also must be considered before embarking on any new venture. All 50 states have their own antitrust laws as well. As just one example, companies contemplating mergers must make evaluations in terms of the Clayton Act, Section 7, as well as relevant state statutes. Federal merger and joint venture policy has undergone substantial changes during the past 25 years. In the 1960s, mergers creating firms of just 5% market shares were attacked by the federal administrative agencies and found to be unlawful by the courts.[57] More recently, however, following the efficiency approach to antitrust, one finds that the federal enforcement agencies are much more permissive and that the courts are considerably more tolerant of mergers and joint ventures.[58] This is especially true of mergers involving companies that handle different product lines. A relatively permissive antitrust attitude could prove to be important to certain emerging high-technology industries, such as those using multimedia technologies, for those industries likely will depend on strategic relationships and mergers between existing corporate powerhouses. As stated before, only time will tell whether the efficiency attitude will continue to prevail or whether there will be a resurgence of efforts to have antitrust policy protect the viability of small-business enterprises. The only thing that is clear is that the course of antitrust will always be an important variable for firms doing business in high-technology fields in the United States.

The Antitrust Debate About Microsoft

Microsoft Corporation fundamentally is a computer software development company, specializing in operating systems and applications software. During the 1980s and 1990s, Microsoft experienced phenomenal growth, becoming one of the largest and most profitable corporations in the world. Its owners and managers became multimillionaires, while the CEO, Bill Gates, became the richest person in the world. The public reaction to Microsoft's "success" typifies the struggle inherent in antitrust. On the one hand, Microsoft is perhaps the premier example of the virtues of marketplace capitalism. The company has enjoyed prosperity because it is highly efficient and continually develops innovative and profitable products. Microsoft, however, also has attained such enormous size and economic power that it has become worrisome to an American population that culturally distrusts those who have the capability to wield excessive control. The very nature of the U.S. governmental structure is based on checks and balances to preserve individual liberties from unbounded governmental interference. The distrust is only greater when such power is held by private hands. As mentioned, antitrust arose during the Industrial Revolution, a time when the owners of large corporate empires were termed "robber barons." The challenge for antitrust policy is to distinguish businesses that act in ways worthy of praise from those that deserve to be vilified. Obviously, this is not simply an economic exercise but a political one as well.

The Issue of Monopoly Power   Although numerous private lawsuits have been brought against Microsoft alleging unlawful behavior under the antitrust laws, the actions brought by the Justice Department in the 1990s clearly are the most important and have garnered the most attention. The focal point of the government's allegations is Microsoft's dominance in the market for computer operating systems. As mentioned, monopolies are feared in part due to cultural and political concerns. However, economists also worry about monopolies because they have the power to exclude competition and control prices in the market. From an economist's point of view, a company is not necessarily a monopoly just because its market share is high. For instance, a firm may have a very high market share but know that if it raises prices, it will face potential entry of numerous competitors into its industry. Monopoly, therefore, requires not only a large market share but also the ability to keep other businesses from effectively competing. One way that this might result is when it would be very expensive for new firms to enter the business to compete—a situation that is characterized by what are called 'barriers to entry."

Through the 1990s Microsoft consistently held an exceedingly high market share of the personal computer operating system market. By most accounts, over 90% of personal computers ran on Microsoft operating systems by the end of the decade. According to the Justice Department and others, this size translated into monopoly power due to the special nature of the market for operating systems, which raised enormous barriers to entry. For one thing, operating systems are subject to *network effects*. Network effects are present when a product's value to one user is related to how many other people are using the product. A telephone provides a simple example. A person who owns the first phone really has nothing of value since no one else has a means to converse with him. However, that phone becomes much more valuable as others begin to buy and use phones. In fact, every phone user on the phone network benefits when new users enter the system. The benefits from the network make it hard for a company having an alternative means of communication to enter the market. Think how reluctant you would be to give up your telephone so that you could use a new system that reaches only a few people. Likely, the new company would have to convince you that its system could reach almost as many people as your old system before you would switch, even if the new system had certain advantages, such as greater clarity or ease of use. You can imagine, though, how hard this would be for the new company to do. Thus, network effects tend to protect old technologies from competition by superior new technologies.

The market for operating systems is subject to network effects. For one thing, one who uses Microsoft Windows as an operating system benefits when others adopt the same system. Just consider how much easier it is to use your computer at work if it has the same operating system that you use at home. Also, when you want to exchange files with friends or others, it is much easier if they also use the same system. Thus, users are reluctant to buy new computers having less pervasive operating systems for fear of how that might affect their relationships at work and with friends. Software is also a big player in the operating system network. One major reason that consumers select a particular operating system is because it can run the largest selection of applications software products. Applications programmers almost always develop their products for Windows, since it has such a large share of the market. However, they often shun alternative operating system platforms because the potential sales markets are too small to justify investments in alternative versions of the software. Thus, a vicious circle is created. Applications programmers develop software for Windows because there are so many potential computer users that may buy their titles, and computer users select Windows because there are so many applications program titles that are developed for the Windows operating system. Any new operating system that wants to compete with Windows, therefore, has to ensure that numerous software titles are available for use on the system. This is true even if the new system offers certain technical or other kinds of operating advantages over Windows.

Windows benefits from other barriers that make competition difficult in the operating system market. Due to network effects and the availability of software applications, a customer is reluctant to switch to another operating system. This hesitation may be compounded by other factors. For instance, a customer who has used Windows for a relatively long period likely will have accumulated a large number of software applications programs. If the customer were to switch to a new platform, all that software would have to be replaced. Also, there is a time factor involved with making a change. A Windows user not only would have to take the time to decide if it's worth changing to a new system, but also would have to adapt to the new requirements of that system once the change was made. All of these effects tend to "lock in" customers to the operating system that they already use, which almost invariably is Windows. On top of all this, the research and development costs that are needed to design a new operating system are considerable. Based on all of these factors, the Justice Department was convinced that Microsoft not only had a large share of the market but had the ability to exercise monopoly power within it.

The Potential Threat from Internet Browsers   As noted before, one does not violate the Sherman Act simply by being a monopoly. The offense requires that one "monopolize," which, according to *Kodak*, means that a company must use its monopoly power to foreclose competition, gain a competitive advantage, or destroy a competitor. Government antitrust enforcers argued that Microsoft in the early 1990s perceived a potential threat to their operating system monopoly from Internet browsers—a threat that was sufficiently significant that it seemed likely to overcome the barriers to entry that had deterred so many other firms and technologies. Internet browsers can run in conjunction with any operating system. Their primary role is to act as an interface to the Internet, making it easy for Internet users to access information over the Web. Browsers, however, also can serve as a platform for computers to run applications programs over the Internet. This means that a Windows machine with an Internet browser can run an application program designed for the browser and not for Windows. Software developers no longer had to write programs strictly for Windows for them to run on Windows machines. Now they could be written for the browser instead. Since the browser also can be used with any other operating system, other systems, all of a sudden, might have a large stock of available software titles that could be used on them via the browser. In addition, browsers easily can overcome network effects that traditionally plagued operating systems, since they are universally purchased to access the Internet. Thus, Microsoft feared that Internet browsers would effectively commoditize traditional operating systems and would become the key interface to run applications programs instead.

In addition, browsers threatened Microsoft because they could be used to distribute a new universal programming system, called Java, which is designed to interface with several different operating systems. The beauty of Java is that applications programmers can make products that are compatible with Java and have them operate on multiple operating systems. This, again, diminishes the network effects traditionally enjoyed by Microsoft. In fact, with Java, one does not even need a traditional full-function computer to run applications programs. Thus, a person could use a browser in conjunction with a simplified network device to access the Web and operate an applications program written in the Java programming language. In this way, computers someday may not even be necessary to do the tasks that computers traditionally have done. Obviously, these developments startled Microsoft, since it depended so heavily on computers using its operating systems.

The early market leader in the development of browsers was Netscape. In 1995, Netscape could claim over 70% of the market with its Navigator browser. Microsoft responded to the threat by developing its own browser, called Internet Explorer. However, the Justice Department claimed that Microsoft was not content to have its Internet Explorer compete on the merits. Rather, Microsoft used its monopoly power in operating systems as leverage to take control of the browser market. According to the Justice Department, it did this through a series of anticompetitive practices that had no rational business justification besides the intent to destroy Netscape. For this reason, the Justice Department, along with the state attorneys general from 20 states, sued Microsoft in 1998 for violating the antitrust laws.[59] The thrust of the complaint was that through its anticompetitive actions, Microsoft monopolized the market for operating systems and browsers. As evidence of this, the Justice Department noted that Internet Explorer's share of the browser market rose from less than 5% in 1996 to over 50% in 1998. The complaint also alleged that Microsoft engaged in illegal tying arrangements, in violation of Section 1 of the Sherman Act.

Preliminary Justice Department Antitrust Proceedings   Although the Justice Department filed suit in 1998 to address Microsoft's actions regarding Netscape and other competitive browsers, the antitrust saga actually began earlier. In 1994, the Justice Department sued Microsoft, alleging that the company had engaged in anticompetitive practices with original equipment manufacturers (OEMs) so that it could maintain its monopoly in its operating system. For instance, the department alleged that Microsoft offered deep discounts to OEMs that agreed to pay royalties to Microsoft for every computer they shipped, regardless of whether the computers were installed with Microsoft's operating system or not (this was called a "per-processor" agreement). At the time, Microsoft's operating system was MS-DOS, and the interface was Windows 3.11. The department claimed that the agreement prevented other operating system developers such as Novell, which had created DR-DOS, from selling their systems to OEMs because the OEMs would have to pay royalties to two companies—the operating system developer and Microsoft under the agreement—if the OEMs chose the alternative system. Microsoft and the Justice Department settled the suit in 1995. Microsoft agreed to discontinue certain allegedly anticompetitive practices, such as the "per-processor" discount arrangement. The agreement also contained a clause stating essentially that Microsoft would not force other companies to enter tie-in arrangements (where obtaining a desired item is conditioned on buying another product). However, this was qualified by language stating that the provision "shall not be construed to prohibit Microsoft from developing *integrated products*" (emphasis added).

Microsoft began distributing Internet Explorer to OEMs in 1995 along with its operating system, which at that time was Windows 95. Microsoft required the OEMs that wanted to install Windows 95 on their machines to also install Internet

Explorer. In 1997, the Justice Department filed a complaint asking the court to hold Microsoft in contempt for violating the 1995 agreement, which prohibited tie-in arrangements. The district judge concluded that Microsoft had not violated the 1995 agreement because Internet Explorer was "integrated" with Windows 95 under the terms of that agreement. However, the judge also determined that even though Internet Explorer might be "integrated" with Windows 95, it still might be a separate product under the antitrust laws. Thus, by bundling the two products together, Microsoft likely had violated the antitrust laws. For this reason, the district judge, on December 11, 1997, entered a preliminary injunction prohibiting Microsoft from licensing Windows 95 or any other operating system on the condition that the licensee also preinstall any Microsoft Internet browser, including Internet Explorer. Microsoft then filed an appeal of the district court's December 11 preliminary injunction order with the Court of Appeals for the District of Columbia.[60]

On April 21, 1998, the Court of Appeals vacated the preliminary injunction.[61] The major factor for this decision was procedural. The Justice Department asked the court to find Microsoft in contempt. The district court determined that Microsoft was not in contempt, but nonetheless issued the preliminary injunction. The Court of Appeals determined that Microsoft did not receive sufficient notice about the potential extent of the remedies that the court might consider. In this regard, the appellate court ruled that the district court was wrong to appraise Microsoft's actions under the antitrust laws when no request had been made for it to do so. Possibly the most controversial aspect of the court's opinion was its discussion of what it means for Internet Explorer to be *integrated* with the Windows operating system. The Justice Department argued that Internet Explorer was a product separate from the Windows operating system, and that Microsoft had simply licensed the desired operating system on the condition that the OEMs also include the browser. The court, however, stated that the products were integrated, since Microsoft had provided plausible evidence that the bundled version of Windows with Internet Explorer was superior to the combination of a separate operating system with a stand-alone browser. It thereby concluded that the version of Internet Explorer that was included with Windows 95 was different from the version that could be obtained alone. Although this discussion was really only about the meaning of the term "integrated" in the 1995 agreement, many observers believed that it sent a strong signal about what the court might rule if an antirust case were brought based on a claim of unlawful tying. Since tying under the antitrust laws requires that there be two separate products, the Justice Department would have to prove that a bundled version of the browser and operating system is merely a packaged version of what is offered separately in the marketplace. If nothing else, the Court of Appeals showed some skepticism on this score.[62]

The 1998 Antitrust Complaint and Trial   On May 18, 1998, the Justice Department, commenced the antitrust suit against Microsoft by filing its complaint.[63] Although one of the charges brought by the Justice Department was that Microsoft unlawfully tied the browser to the Windows operating system, the complaint was more far-reaching, charging that Microsoft engaged in monopolizing by engaging in numerous anticompetitive practices, including tying. The complaint alleged that Microsoft leveraged its power in operating systems to maintain its dominance in operating systems and to monopolize the market for browsers. In this regard, the complaint listed six different examples of Microsoft's anticompeititve conduct that demonstrated the company's intent to destroy Netscape and take command of the market for browsers:

A. *Microsoft Attempted to Divide the Browser Market with Netscape.* The government charged that in 1995, Microsoft met with Netscape executives and proposed that the two companies not compete in the sale of browsers. Microsoft allegedly proposed that Microsoft would offer Internet Explorer only to users of Windows, and that Netscape would sell browsers designed only for other operating systems. Although Netscape declined the deal, the proposal indicates that Microsoft was willing to engage in unlawful anticompetitive activities to protect its operating system monopoly and to take control of the browser market. This charge clearly is the Justice Department's weakest claim in the case.

B. *Exclusionary Agreements with ISPs.* Since more than 90% of new computers have the Windows operating system installed by OEMs, ISPs can gain an enormous marketing boost if they are permitted to advertise and distribute their services through an icon or folder on the Windows desktop. According to the Justice Department, Microsoft agreed with ISPs to give them attractive placements on the desktop. In return, the ISPs agreed (1) to promote and distribute Internet Explorer nearly exclusively to their subscribers; (2) to eliminate links on their Web sites from which subscribers could download competing browsers; (3) to ship their access software with only Internet Explorer as the browser; and (4) to use Microsoft-specific programming extensions in their Web sites so that the sites would look better when viewed with Internet Explorer. The gist of this allegation is that ISPs would do just about anything to get a prime spot on the ubiquitous Windows desktop. This would include giving up the power to promote or distribute Netscape Navigator, even if they felt that it was a better product or offered them or their subscribers certain advantages.

C. *Exclusionary Agreements with Internet Content Providers.* Newer versions of Internet Explorer had "channel" buttons appearing on the right side of the Windows desktop screen. Channel buttons provided advertising for and direct access to Web sites that occupied the channel. Microsoft gave Internet content providers, such as Disney and CBS Sportsline, the opportunity to license channel buttons having different levels of desirability. Those that wanted the most prominent placement had to agree to various conditions inhibiting their promotion or distribution of competing browsers. They also had to agree to use Microsoft programming extensions so that their sites would look best when viewed using Internet Explorer. The Justice Department claimed that content providers had substantial marketing-based motivations to enter these agreements, even if they otherwise may have preferred to work with Netscape. Before the Justice Department filed suit, Microsoft announced that it planned to discontinue these agreements. Nonetheless, the Justice Department felt that they already had caused substantial harm, requiring an antitrust remedy.

D. *Contracts with OEMs about Boot-Up and Desktop Screens.* Microsoft required OEMs, as a condition of obtaining a license for Windows, to agree that they would not modify the appearance, sequence, sounds, or content of the boot-up screens. They also agreed that they would not modify the appearance of the Windows desktop screen (beyond certain narrowly circumscribed permitted changes). The Justice Department charged that these restrictions ensured that if an OEM installed a competing browser, the OEM could not give that browser more prominence or visibility than it gave to Internet Explorer. They also ensured that Microsoft could honor its agreements with ISPs and content providers, under which Microsoft promised to give preferential placements on the desktop. The government charged that these agreements reduced the ability of OEMs to customize and differentiate their products in ways that might enhance competition between Microsoft products and other vendors. They also furthered Microsoft's attempts to leverage its monopoly power in operating systems to the browser market.

E. *Tying of Internet Explorer to Windows 95.* The Justice Department argued that Internet Explorer was a separate product from the Windows 95 operating system. It claimed that many accepted indices of how product markets should be defined, such as sales, distribution practices, promotion policies, and industry customs demonstrated that the browser must be treated as a product separate from Windows 95. Similarly, the department argued that browsers are in a competitive product market that is separate from the market for operating systems. According to the Justice Department, since Internet Explorer is a separate product from Windows 95, Microsoft engaged in unlawful tying by requiring OEMs to license and install Internet Explorer in order to put the Windows 95 operating system on their machines. Based on this allegation, Microsoft may not only have furthered its campaign to monopolize, but it also may have engaged in a per se violation of the Sherman Act, Section 1.

F. *Tying of Internet Explorer to Windows 98.* The Justice Department claimed that Microsoft had no legitimate business reason to more tightly bundle Internet Explorer with the operating system as it did with Windows 98. Rather, its sole intent was to defeat Navigator. If this were not the case, the department posed, why wouldn't Microsoft offer bundled and unbundled versions of its operating system, and let customers and OEMs choose which solution was superior? In the Justice Department's eyes, Windows 98 offended the antitrust laws in the same ways as did Windows 95 by tying Internet Explorer to the separate operating system.

On October 19, 1998, the Justice Department and Microsoft delivered their opening arguments, thus marking the beginning of this historic trial. Ironically, the case was argued before the same judge who issued the December 11, 1997, preliminary injunction. The parties offered testimony for five months. During this time, there was substantial speculation that Justice Department lawyers were being very persuasive in making their case. Thus, there was a lot of discussion about what the remedy might be should the judge determine that Microsoft did, indeed, violate the antitrust laws.

The least intrusive form of remedies would be *conduct* relief. With these, the court would prohibit Microsoft from continuing to employ the types of actions and agreements that the judge determined were anticompetitive. Thus, the judge might forbid Microsoft to limit how OEMs present information on the desktop or during the boot-up sequence. Or he might require Microsoft to offer OEMs a current and working version of Windows that does not include Internet Explorer. The problem with these remedies is that they do not make up for any competitive advantage that Microsoft may have gained while it used the offensive practices. Justice Department data, for example, indicates that Internet Explorer's new users rose from 28% in the second quarter of 1997 to 60% in the third quarter of 1998, while Netscape's share decreased from around 70% to 30% in the same period.[64] Thus, the competitors might need a "kick-start" to get back to where they should have been.[65] It is not clear what kinds of remedies the court could use to allow competitors to overcome the unwarranted advantages enjoyed by Microsoft as a result of its unlawful conduct. Perhaps the court could forbid Microsoft to distribute Internet Explorer for a certain period of time. However, courts often are not willing to meddle in the markets in this fashion. Nor, some experts believe, should they.[66] For this reason, there was talk during the trial that the judge should consider *structural* relief. Structural remedies would require Microsoft to divest certain assets or business units so that the market could attain the level of competitiveness that would have existed had Microsoft not engaged in unlawful practices. For instance, Microsoft could be broken up along functional lines, or at least be ordered to divest its browser business. Or perhaps the judge might break Microsoft up into several integrated companies.

The two sides presented their closing arguments in September 1999. Even though the case was heard at breathtaking speed in antitrust terms, there was speculation that the pace of change in the technology world still had outstripped it. For instance, during the proceedings, America Online bought Netscape, putting it into the hands of the world's most dominant ISP. In addition, a new operating system called Linux had risen dramatically in popularity. Thus, to some, the case had become moot, and indeed, Microsoft argued that it could not be characterized as a monopoly in light of these and other developments.

After closing arguments, the parties had to await Judge Jackson's decision. The judge broke up this phase of the trial so that it extended over a period of time, perhaps to encourage the sides to settle before he had to render a judgment and determine the appropriate remedy. The judge issued his *findings of fact* on November 5, 1999.[67] The findings strongly supported the government's allegations, and there was tremendous speculation that Microsoft would lose the case should it not settle.

The next step was scheduled for February 22, 2000, when the parties had to make oral arguments to the judge regarding whether the conduct amounted to antitrust violations. In the meantime, Judge Jackson ordered the parties to attempt to mediate a solution. To help the parties narrow their differences, Judge Richard Posner, the very respected and somewhat conservative chief justice of the Seventh Circuit Court of Appeals, agreed to serve as mediator. During this period, there was some speculation that Microsoft would find a way to settle the case. Besides worrying that Judge Jackson was likely to decide in the government's favor, Microsoft had to consider that under the antitrust laws, private parties could introduce a final judgment against the company as prima facie evidence in their legal actions. This might result in numerous successful treble damage lawsuits against the company. Nevertheless, the parties did not reach a settlement before February 22, and so the next step in the decision phase commenced.

During the following two months, settlement negotiations again intensified, especially after Judge Jackson announced that he was about to release his *conclusions of law*, which would provide his final judgment specifying whether Microsoft's actions violated the antitrust laws. Indeed, the judge gave Richard Posner more time to mediate an agreement, as the sides appeared to be narrowing their differences. Nonetheless, the negotiations broke down on March 31, 2000, perhaps because the numerous plaintiffs had different notions about the appropriate remedy. Therefore, on April 3, 2000, Judge Jackson issued his conclusions of law.[67]

Judge Jackson determined that Microsoft violated Section 2 of the Sherman Act since it had unlawfully used the power it enjoyed with Windows to maintain its dominance in the market for Intel-based PC operating systems. Further, Microsoft violated Section 2 by leveraging its power in operating systems in an attempt to take control of the browser market. Judge Jackson also ruled that Microsoft violated the Sherman Act, Section 1 by unlawfully tying its browser to the operating system. On this point, the judge was careful to address the previous concerns of the Court of Appeals, and indicated his confidence that the determination was consistent with Supreme Court precedents. Finally, the judge found that Microsoft had violated state antitrust laws in all of the states involved in the lawsuit.

Exhibit 9.8 provides a chronology of the key developments through April 2000 in the Justice Department's lawsuit against Microsoft. Since Judge Jackson concluded that Microsoft violated the antitrust laws, the proceeding at this juncture entered its next stage—determining the all-important remedies. As this book heads to publication, there is speculation that the Justice Department will request that Microsoft be required to divest certain businesses, such as, perhaps, its Office applications software division. Still, many experts believe that the judge will rely on conduct relief rather than more extensive structural remedies. In either case, Microsoft pledged to appeal the decision, believing that the higher courts will understand that the company did not stifle competition, but rather acted as an innovator in fiercely competitive markets. Thus, it may be years before the proceeding ultimately is concluded. No matter what that final outcome may turn out to be, the Microsoft case clearly has raised enormous philosophical questions about the legitimacy of antitrust in the rapidly changing technology landscape. The resolution of this particular case will not answer these questions. Rather, it likely will serve to

---

Exhibit 9.8

Justice Department Actions Against Microsoft: Timeline

July 1994 Justice Department sues Microsoft, alleging that Microsoft engaged in several anticompetitive practices with equipment manufacturers (OEMs) to preserve its monopoly in operating systems.

August 1995 Justice Department and Microsoft settle the dispute; Microsoft consents to a judgment and order entered by the court.

Court order prohibits Microsoft from entering tying arrangements with OEMs but allows Microsoft to develop integrated products.

October 1997 Justice Department charges Microsoft in contempt of 1995 court order for requiring OEMs to install Internet Explorer with the Windows operating system.

December 1997 District court concludes that Microsoft was not in contempt of the 1995 court order because Internet Explorer was "integrated" under the terms of the order.

District court determines that Microsoft likely violated the antitrust laws and enters a preliminary injunction forbidding Microsoft from requiring OEMs to license Internet Explorer as a condition to obtaining a license for Windows.

April 1998 Court of appeals vacates the district court's December 1997 preliminary injunction on procedural grounds.

May 1998 Justice Department sues Microsoft, alleging unlawful tying of Internet Explorer to the Windows operating system, and for monopolizing the operating system and Internet browser markets.

October 1998 The trial begins.

September 1999 The trial judge hears closing arguments.

November 1999 The trial judge issues his findings of fact.

April 2000 The trial judge issues his conclusions of law stating that Microsoft violated sections 1 and 2 of the Sherman Antitrust Act.

---

frame new issues regarding the role that regulation must play to preserve competition in the twenty-first century.

International Dimensions of Antitrust

Most high-technology enterprises now take on global dimensions and thus must be concerned not only with the antitrust policies of the United States but with those of other nations as well. Strategic alliances in high-technology fields increasingly involve an international host of partners. For example, IBM, which has formed over 20,000 business relationships worldwide, clearly is carrying out a strategy of creating global networks of alliances for technology, marketing, and manufacturing.[68] Such an international posture is not simply for the corporate giants, however. For instance, Xilinx depends substantially on Japanese partners for much of its manufacturing and overseas distribution.[69]

As with all international matters, there is not a uniform standard for competition policy. Thus, a company must consider the competition policy of any nation that might be affected by its operations. This does not mean simply consulting the laws of the country where manufacturing takes place or where the corporate headquarters is housed. For instance, even foreign companies that have no assets in the United States may be subject to U.S. antitrust laws if their operations have a substantial and reasonably foreseeable effect on either the import trade or the domestic commerce of the United States. Other nations, too, may have policies with similar extraterritorial effect.

The competition policies of different nations vary widely, depending on their respective philosophies toward economic relationships. The WTO has begun to consider ways to develop a multilateral framework for antitrust enforcement by organizing the Working Group on the Interaction between Trade and Competition Policy.[70] However, the prospects for achieving uniformity through this route likely will be remote for many years to come. Thus, one always must scrutinize local competition laws when entering new international markets. As just one example, we will take a brief look at the antitrust policies of the European Union (EU), which mirror those of the United States to some degree.

Antitrust in the European Union   The Treaty of Rome governs competition policy in the European Union. Article 85, Section 1 of the treaty prohibits agreements that prevent, distort, or restrict competition in such a way that trade among the member states is affected. This wording somewhat parallels the Sherman Act, Section 1, especially in terms of its vague language and potential breadth. However, Article 85(1) goes further and specifically lists sets of practices that come within the general definition. These include concerted actions which (1) fix prices or trading conditions, (2) limit or control production, markets, or technical developments, (3) share markets, (4) discriminate against competitors, and (5) require supplementary and illogical tie-in obligations. At first blush, this seems to condemn many types of transactions that might pass muster under U.S. antitrust laws through application of the rule of reason. Indeed, Article 85(2) provides that all agreements that fall within Article 85(1) are automatically void. Thus, one might get the notion that many more types of business arrangements fall within an *illegal per se* status in the EU than in the United States. However, Article 85(3) reduces the sting of these provisions by allowing for potential exceptions to the blanket prohibitions. It states that an agreement or transaction may be declared lawful if it:

1. contributes to improving the production or distribution of goods or to promoting technical or economic progress in the EU;

2. allows consumers a fair share of the resulting benefit;
3. imposes only restrictions that are indispensable to the attainment of those objectives; and
4. does not eliminate competition in a substantial part of the market for the products involved.

Based on this provision, businesses that are planning to engage in potentially restrictive transactions in the EU may notify the EU Commission and request that the body clear their deals for antitrust purposes. In effect, the commission then may exempt the deal based on its judgment that the benefits outweigh the harms according to the criteria of Article 85(3). This process raises enormous difficulties for business entities, however. For one thing, it may take years for the commission to examine a transaction and render its answer. Also, the commission sometimes may grant an exemption only on the condition that the parties make certain changes to their planned activities.[71] There is another option, which is to request a "comfort letter" from the commission, assuring the parties that the commission will not undertake an enforcement action. Although a comfort letter is easier to get than an exemption, it does not carry as much legal weight in the courts if others should file complaints.[72]

As you might suspect, the EU Commission would be buried with requests for exemptions if it had to rely solely on these methods to assure businesses about the antitrust consequences of their transactions. For this reason, the commission has devised a system to give preliminary approval to sets of activities by means of "block exemptions." Block exemptions have been issued for various practices such as certain patent licensing agreements, exclusive dealing situations, research and development agreements, know-how licenses (which protect trade secrets), and franchising arrangements, among others. The block exemptions are somewhat detailed and provide substantial guidance not only about agreements which are permissible but also about those that almost assuredly are not. For instance, the block exemptions on patent and know-how licensing contain three categories: (1) the White List, which indicates agreements that are compatible with the spirit of Article 85(1); (2) the Gray List, which designates transactions that normally do not violate the law, but under special circumstances might run afoul of it; and (3) the Black List, which identifies agreements that are not protected by the block exemption nor likely by any other means, such as through an individual exemption. In 1999, the commission proposed a new block exemption that is designed to provide greater coherency and coverage for those businesses involved with distribution agreements.[73] Viewing all of these procedures together suggests that antitrust in the EU ultimately is governed by principles akin to the rule of reason analysis used in the United States. However, the specific methods of applying the standards differ markedly and must be recognized before pursuing transactions within the EU.

Article 86 of the treaty prohibits the abuse of a dominant position—language that is reminiscent of Section 2 of the Sherman Act. As with the Sherman Act, it is not enough that one holds a dominant position. To be unlawful under Article 86, there also must be abusive exploitation of market power. Again, though, one should not be tempted by this similarity with U.S. policy to assume that EU antitrust principles always mirror those in the United States. For instance, private parties cannot bring causes of action for damages. In addition, the broad extraterritorial application of U.S. antitrust law is offensive to many European countries. Thus, the EU Commission usually does not take jurisdiction over activities that are conducted outside the European Union.[74]

EU MERGER POLICY   A more recent addition to EU competition policy came with the adoption of the EU Merger Regulation, which became effective in September 1990. The regulation provides that a "concentration" is incompatible with EU antitrust policies when it "creates or strengthens a dominant position as a result of which effective competition would be significantly impeded in the common market or a substantial part of it." The regulation essentially requires that all *concentrations* having a *community dimension* must be reported to the EU Commission's Merger Task Force in a preclearance procedure to make a determination about their *dominance*. Although this may seem burdensome, businesses actually want to be subject to the terms of the regulation. Under the regulation, the Merger Task Force has exclusive jurisdiction over concentrations that come within the regulation's terms. Thus, when a concentration has a community dimension, the participants need to deal only with the Merger Task Force to gain approval, rather than having to negotiate with the antitrust authorities in all the individual EU countries that may be affected by the transaction.

According to the 1990 Merger Regulation, a *concentration* occurs when there is a change in control. This may happen in various ways, such as through mergers, spin-offs, acquisitions, stock swaps, management buyouts, and privatization. A key determinant is whether a firm has obtained a decisive influence over the strategic decisions of another entity, such as with its business or budgetary plans, financial investments, or board memberships.[75] Difficult issues sometimes have arisen in situations involving joint ventures. In 1997, amendments to the Merger Regulation added some clarifications and expanded the types of joint ventures that were included within the definition of a concentration.

The *community dimension* requirements are by far the most important aspect of the EU Merger Regulation. According to the 1990 regulation, a concentration has a community dimension if:

1. the aggregate worldwide turnover (sales) of all the parties involved is more than 5 billion European Currency Units (ECU); and
2. aggregate turnover in the EU of at least two of the parties involved is more than 250 million ECU.

As noted before, if the merger does not meet the community dimension criteria, then it is subject to the varying standards and procedures of the member states. This can be quite onerous, especially since most of the 15 member countries have their own premerger clearance procedures. Thus, businesses have a continual interest in expanding the scope of the community dimension standards. In 1997, they received some relief when the Merger Regulation was amended. According to the new regulation, a community dimension can be established by the old criteria, or by complying with new thresholds. The new alternative way provides that there is a community dimension when:

1. the aggregate worldwide turnover of all the parties involved exceeds 2.5 billion ECU;
2. at least two of the parties involved independently have turnover in the EU exceeding 100 million ECU;
3. the combined turnover of all the parties involved exceeds 100 million ECU in each of three EU member states;
4. in each of these three member states, at least two of the parties involved must individually have turnover exceeding 250 million ECU.

This alternative standard includes more complicated criteria than the traditional measure. It also is not as sweeping as many desired. Nonetheless, the EU commissioner in charge of competition policy estimated that the 1997 amendments might raise the number of annual filings with the EU Merger Task Force by as much as 50%.[76]

Once the EU Merger Task Force takes jurisdiction over a concentration, the analyses for *dominance* and its effect on competition follow principles similar to those used in the United States. The Merger Regulation states that there is an indication of compatibility if the combined market share of the concentration does not exceed 25% in the EU or a substantial part of it. This provides some security about the minimum market share that a combination must attain before it may be subject to further scrutiny. Above this level, the size of the resultant market share will be an important determinant of dominance, along with other factors, such as market structure, barriers to entry, and efficiencies.[77]

U.S. firms would be foolish to ignore the antitrust ramifications of their actions in Europe and in other foreign nations. Some people were shocked in 1997 when the EU Commission raised objections to the proposed merger between Boeing and McDonnell Douglas, especially since U.S regulators had already approved the deal. The EU Commission and the U.S. regulatory agencies have begun to work together to coordinate some of their activities. Up until recently these efforts mostly involved procedural matters, such as notifications and the sharing of information.[78] However, a joint agreement signed in 1998 provides hope that there soon will be greater coordination of enforcement activities.[79] This would be a welcome development for technology businesses, and perhaps might serve as an important springboard for expanded global antitrust coordination through the WTO.

Antitrust, Intellectual Property, and the Doctrine of Misuse

Those high-technology firms dealing with intellectual property must come to grips with an inherent tension between intellectual property and antitrust policies. Intellectual property laws grant exclusivity to intangible assets so that creators have sufficient economic incentives to develop and disclose their works. In effect, the laws provide a form of limited monopoly, preventing others from accessing the intellectual property in ways proscribed by statute. For instance, the patent laws prevent others from making, using, or selling an invention, while the copyright laws keep the public from copying expressions. Since the purpose of the limited monopoly is to allow creators to earn economic benefits from exclusivity, one should expect those having such legal protection to try to maximize the economic returns from the rights bestowed.

Interesting questions arise, however, since these goals must interface with antitrust policies. That a company is granted a monopoly by the law does not mean it is immune from antitrust. In fact, just the opposite may be true. Those applying the antitrust laws are most worried about firms that enjoy a position of economic strength in the marketplace. This rings true for those holding either of the philosophical foundations of antitrust. For example, in *Kodak*, we saw that tying arrangements are automatically condemned if applied by firms having market power. Otherwise, the more relaxed rule of reason is applied. Thus, firms enjoying intellectual property rights, together with the monopoly-like status that attends them, must be particularly wary. This does not necessarily mean that anything these firms do is unlawful. Most transactions are not illegal per se, even for the most powerful firms, and thus may be lawful as long as they are reasonable under the circumstances. Also, just because a company has a legal monopoly, such as from a patent, copyright, or trademark, does not mean that the business has market power in an antitrust sense. For instance, an inventor who receives a patent on an autofocusing device for cameras does not necessarily have market power, because cameras using that invention arguably must compete with cameras utilizing different autofocus technologies. In addition, they may have to contend with other types of cameras, such as those having manual focus and even static focus capabilities. Therefore, one should not jump unduly to the conclusion that intellectual property rights become a straitjacket under the antitrust laws. Rather, a firm with intellectual property rights simply must refrain from engaging in anticompetitive conduct, just as all firms must do. The only proviso is that special attention must be given to how the intellectual property rights affect one's particular economic position in the market.

Firms owning intellectual property violate the antitrust laws when they use their legally bestowed rights as leverage to achieve anticompetitive ends. For example, the following practices are just a few typical intellectual property transactions that may unreasonably restrain trade under certain factual conditions: (1) tying arrangements, wherein customers are forced to purchase products they do not want in order to get the legally protected technology they do want; (2) covenants not to deal in competing goods, in which licensees promise not to deal with products using competitive technologies; (3) resale restraints, wherein certain controls are placed on how purchasers of products utilizing intellectual property may sell those products; (4) price-fixing agreements, in which prices for products with protected technologies are specified; and (5) grant-back provisions, requiring licensees to assign to the licensor ownership to inventions developed by the licensees during the license term. When situations such as these arise, courts do not alter their antitrust analysis simply because intellectual property is involved. The rule of reason, or per se illegality, if relevant, will be applied, just as if intellectual property were not the subject of the litigation. Again, though, one must always keep in mind that the courts may find that intellectual property rights bestow market power, a conclusion that may seriously tip the scales in an antitrust suit.

Intellectual Property Antitrust Guidelines   Periodically, the federal antitrust enforcement agencies issue *Antitrust Guidelines*. The guidelines are not the law; rather they represent the agency's interpretation of what the law is and the forms of conduct that may violate it. Antitrust Guidelines are useful to businesses because they indicate the circumstances under which the agencies might be inclined to bring enforcement actions. Before the 1990s, the Department of Justice and the FTC would issue their guidelines independently. However, the agencies now often work together and jointly release guidelines that reflect a common approach to enforcement. Perhaps the most well-known Antitrust Guidelines are the Merger Guidelines, which were issued by the Justice Department in 1984 and later were updated in a joint effort with the FTC in 1992. The agencies recently have issued other important guidelines dealing with such matters as antitrust enforcement of international operations and the health care industry.

On April 6, 1995, the Department of Justice and the FTC jointly released Antitrust Guidelines for the Licensing of Intellectual Property. For the most part, these guidelines provide substantial comfort to those dealing with intellectual property. One needs to look no further than the general principles to recognize that the guidelines embody a flexible and somewhat tolerant philosophy regarding intellectual property licensing. The general principles are:

a. for the purpose of antitrust analysis, the agencies regard intellectual property as being essentially comparable to any other form of property;
b. the agencies do not presume that intellectual property creates market power in the antitrust context; and
c. the agencies recognize that intellectual property licensing allows firms to combine complementary factors of production and is generally procompetitive.

Thus, the guidelines essentially confirm that the federal enforcement agencies will treat intellectual property just like any other factor of production. The fact that intellectual property may be defined as a limited monopoly in legal terms does not presumptively mean that it provides monopoly power in economic terms. Indeed, if anything, the guidelines offer reasons that intellectual property licensing might be looked at more favorably than more typical property arrangements. For instance, they discuss how integration of intellectual assets can benefit consumers through the reduction of costs and the introduction of new products. They also indicate how cross-licensing may be an efficient way to overcome certain problems encountered with intellectual property ownership, such as we noted in Chapter 2 with patent blocking.

The guidelines make it clear that the general approach to intellectual property licensing is through the rule of reason. Thus, in general, the agencies first will consider whether an arrangement in conjunction with market structure is likely to produce anticompetitive effects. If so, then the agency will look further and determine whether the licensing arrangement is necessary to achieve desirable procompetitive efficiencies. The guidelines discuss a variety of typical licensing techniques and provide insights about the types of conditions that might make them seem more or less reasonable in the eyes of the agencies. For instance, the guidelines specifically address tying arrangements, exclusive dealing, cross-licensing and pooling arrangements, grant-backs, and resale price agreements.

THE GUIDELINES SAFETY ZONE   The guidelines provide numerous assurances to business interests through its applications of the rule of reason. Nonetheless, the very nature of the rule of reason means that businesses never can be sure that their conduct will not be challenged. The guidelines make a stunning contribution in this regard by providing for a "safety zone." The guidelines state that absent extraordinary circumstances, the agencies will not challenge licensing arrangements in which the contracting companies collectively account for no more than 20% of each relevant market significantly affected by the license.[80] This provision obviously is critical to small companies involved with intellectual property licensing, since it almost completely relieves them from antitrust concerns. The guidelines also make it clear that arrangements outside the safety zone are not presumed to be unlawful. Rather they simply may be subject to scrutiny. In this regard, the guidelines provide that the great majority of licenses falling outside the safety zone still will be viewed as procompetitive and lawful, in conformity with the general principles noted above.

THE GUIDELINES AND INNOVATION MARKETS   Although the Intellectual Property Guidelines for the most part serve to comfort businesses involved with licensing, they do formalize a relatively new concept—called *innovation markets*—that might raise some concerns. Usually, antitrust analysis considers the potential competitive effects that arrangements may have on products and technology markets that already exist. However, the Justice Department and the FTC recently have been concerned with how combinations of intellectual property assets might affect competition in research and development efforts directed to new or improved goods or processes. Their apprehension is that if one or a few firms tie up all the specialized assets needed to engage in the development of new products, then competition will be stifled to the detriment of the markets and consumers. As an example, the guidelines hypothesize that two companies specializing in advanced metallurgy agree to cross-license future patents relating to the development of a new component for aircraft jet turbines. If innovation in the development of the component requires the capability to work with very high tensile strength materials, then there may be reason to determine the effect that the cross-license agreement will have on the ability of other firms to engage in high-tensile research for jet engines.

Commentators and scholars have argued heatedly about the propriety of considering innovation markets.[81] The Justice Department and the FTC clearly have embraced the idea, though, since they each have brought several enforcement actions based on potential anticompetitive effects on innovation markets.[82] The FTC, for instance, brought a highly publicized complaint against Intel in the late 1990s. The FTC charged that Intel withheld vital information about its chips from computer manufacturers, such as Digital Equipment and Compaq, which had sued Intel for violating their intellectual property rights. The thrust of the allegation was that Intel used its dominance in microprocessor chips to prevent technology companies from asserting intellectual property claims against it. The FTC alleged that this, in turn, might reduce the incentive for technology companies to develop innovations and compete in new markets. On March 8, 1999, the FTC reached an agreement with Intel.[83] Thus, the courts did not address the concept of innovation markets in this dispute. Nonetheless, the theory of innovation markets definitely has gained a solid toehold in antitrust analysis. Therefore, technology firms now must consider how their licenses or other actions might retard the ability of other firms to engage in the research of promising new products or processes.

Misuse of Intellectual Property

PATENT MISUSE   Intellectual property owners, in general, must pay attention to the antitrust laws with the same respect as do other business operators. However, there is another, possibly more pernicious, doctrine that intellectual property owners must consider when transacting business involving their legally protected rights. The doctrine, called misuse, has its roots in the patent realm. According to a long line of patent cases, patentholders who misuse their legal privileges may not enforce their patent rights until the misuse terminates. What makes this doctrine so extreme is that it applies even when others knowingly and purposively infringe the patent. Making this more extreme is the fact that others may lawfully infringe the patent even if they are not personally subject to the misuse. This means that even if the conduct amounting to misuse is restricted to only a few business dealings, all patent rights nonetheless are essentially shelved until those incidents of misuse are completely purged.

Patent misuse arises in two contexts. From an academic sense, perhaps the least troubling is when a firm is using a patent in a way that violates the antitrust laws. At least one can take solace that the firm has done something tangibly wrong with the patent by using it to achieve anticompetitive ends. However, patent misuse has a life independent of the antitrust laws. In 1942, the Supreme Court made it clear in *Morton Salt v. Suppiger*[84] that one may engage in misuse, even without violating the antitrust laws, by unlawfully extending the patent monopoly. Some situations of this type are easy to understand. For instance, if a licencer attempts to extend the life of a patent by requiring licensees to pay royalties beyond the patent term, then there clearly is a disruption of the patent system's careful balance between incentives and disclosure. Note that this practice might pass muster under the antitrust laws. However, reference to antitrust is unnecessary because competitive effect is not the real issue. Rather, the concern is focused on the period of public and individual rights of access.

The difficulty with the independent line of misuse arises because most patent practices raise concerns only in a context of restraining competition. In these situations, it is more difficult to argue that a practice judged reasonable under the antitrust laws should nevertheless be considered too anticompetitive under the patent laws. One notable judge probably stated it best when he asked, "If misuse claims are not tested by conventional antitrust principles, by what principles shall they be tested?"[85] However, misuse based on anticompetitive conduct without reference to antitrust remains alive in the courts.

Congess has questioned whether there can be patent misuse without an antitrust violation. In 1988, the Senate supported new legislation that, had it become law, would have prohibited a finding of patent misuse unless the patentholder had violated the antitrust laws as well.[86] However, the House of Representatives did not go along with such a broad policy change. What resulted was the Patent Misuse Reform Act of 1988, which effectively removed refusals to deal from allegations of patent misuse and which instructed that misuse claims based on tying arrangements must conform more to antitrust principles.

COPYRIGHT MISUSE   Soon thereafter, in 1990, a new twist was added to the misuse saga by the case, *Lasercomb America, Inc. v. Reynolds*.[87] Lasercomb developed a CAD/CAM program that it licensed to several businesses, including a competitor, Holiday Steel. Many of the licenses had durations of 99 years and provided, among other things, that during the license term and for one year thereafter, the licenses could not sell CAD/CAM programs. These terms were negotiable, and Holiday was not subject to the restriction on competition. Holiday circumvented protective devices on Lasercomb's CAD/CAM program, and then made several copies of it for its own use and developed a commercial equivalent for sales to others. Lasercomb sued for copyright infringement.

Given these facts, you probably expect that Lasercomb won this case in slam-dunk fashion and, indeed, it did convince the lower court to find in its favor. Nontheless, the appellate court agreed with Holiday that Lasercomb's licenses amounted to copyright misuse. The lower court judge determined that the license restrictions on competition were reasonable to protect Lasercomb's trade secrets in the program. The appellate court, though, ruled that this did not matter, on the assumption that reasonableness was related to antitrust concerns. The court stated, "The question is not whether the copyright is being used in a manner violative of antitrust law (such as whether the licensing agreement is reasonable), but whether the copyright is being used in a manner violative of the public policy embodied in the grant of a copyright." And the court did find that the clause violated copyright policy, due to its breadth and length. The court believed that Lasercomb went too far with its licenses, since it prevented the licenses from exercising their creative abilities to make and sell CAD/CAM programs for an extremely long time—in fact, longer than the duration of Lasercomb's copyright itself.[88] Relying on the patent misuse doctrine, the court also ruled that it did not matter that Holiday was not subject to the misuse in its licenses. The court therefore ruled that Lasercomb could not enforce its copyrights until it purged its licenses of the copyright misuse.

For two reasons, Lasercomb shocked many legal analysts in the field. First, it confirmed the continuing viability of patent misuse based on anticompetitive conduct even when the actions are reasonable under antitrust policies. Second, it extended the misuse doctrine, which heretofore had been traditionally confirmed to the patent arena, to copyrights. This latter aspect has drawn the most attention because it raises the very real possibility that owners of copyrights in computer programs, among others, must now contend not only with antitrust but with misuse as well.

The appellate court was very critical of the methods used by Lasercomb to prevent licensees from accessing the ideas in its programs. This, in turn, has heightened concerns that trade secret protection methods may be incompatible with software licenses. One should not take these fears too far, though. Lasercomb's strategy for protecting its trade secrets was to employ covenants not to compete, a technique which, as we have seen, is viewed skeptically by many courts. They are, after all, somewhat of a hammer approach for ensuring that licenses do not use trade secrets in developing competitive products. Perhaps, then, one lesson from *Lasercomb* is that noncompete provisions may not be the safest course to take to protect trade secrets. An effective alternative would be to have a contract provision stating that any competing product made or sold by the licensee will be presumed to contain trade secrets obtained from the licensed product. This provision, which shifts the burden to the licensee to prove independent development, should be effective in deterring trade secret abuses without having the appearance of overreaching.

The length of the agreements also disturbed the court, especially since the noncompete restrictions potentially lasted longer than the copyright in the program. As with patents, attempts to extend protection beyond the statutory term should be criticized under copyright policy without reference to antitrust or competition. This aspect, too, certainly contributed to the finding of copyright misuse. Therefore, although copyright misuse apparently has viability, one should not overreact, as some have, from its appearance in this case. Maintaining prudent trade secret protection procedures, along with keeping a watchful eye on how courts treat future cases, seems to be the best approach.

CONCLUSION

The message throughout this book should now be very clear. A high-technology company must fully understand what might be done before deciding what should be done. Business strategy cannot be formulated in a vacuum. Rather it must be made with reference to the possible techniques that exist to achieve various ends. Obviously, an understanding of contracts and how they are treated within the legal system is a critical component of this strategy formulation process.

You now have a sophisticated understanding of the most important legal policies that affect firms managing advanced technologies. You know what currently can be done within the policy constraints of the law. You understand the pros and cons of various approaches, including the likelihood and extent of protection, their costs, and the liabilities if things do not go as planned. The decisions about what should be done are now up to you. Part of the fun of learning about the legal frameworks is the power such learning gives you to make meaningful business strategy decisions. But always remember that with the ever-increasing pace of change in the world of high technologies, legal constructs are increasingly under pressure to adapt. Thus, what you have finished learning today may be out of date tomorrow. I hope this book has alerted you to that very prospect. It is incumbent on you, therefore, as a manager in a high-technology enterprise, to keep constantly abreast of changes to legal policies not only in the United States but in the international environment as well. It is only with that kind of perseverance that you can be confident your business strategies are based on the most recent array of legal policies governing your decisions.

NOTES

1. Louisiana has not adopted all the articles of the Uniform Commercial Code.

2. Although certain provisions of Article 2 specifically are directed to the sale of goods, courts in major jurisdictions, such as California and New York, have applied those provisions to licenses as well. In addition, Article 2A, which specifically applies to leases, treats warranties in a fashion similar to that under Article 2.

3. For instance, rather than add a new article to the UCC, states may choose to conform their laws to other proposals, such as the Uniform Computer Information Transactions Act (UCITA).

4. For a multinational corporation, its place of business is the country that has the closest relationship to the contract and is closest to where it will be performed. CISG Article 10.

5. For a very good discussion of the CISG, see R. Schaffer, B. Earle, and F. Agusti, International Business Law and Its Environment, 3d ed. (West Publishing Co., 1996), Chapter 5.

6. UCC § 2-104 provides additional situations in which a person may be defined as a merchant.

7. For an interesting example of the potential scope of consequential damages, consider the financial exposure that PanAm-Sat Corporation may have faced when a failure in its communications satellite caused millions of pagers across the country to be temporarily silenced. According to one report, PanAm-Sat and its retailers were protected by clauses in their contracts which (1) limited liability for consequential damages and (2) provided that the exclusive remedy was for "a refund of fees paid for lost services." *See* D. Van Duch, "Few Beeper Suits Foreseen," Nat'l L. J. (June 1, 1998) at A11.

8. For an excellent case that thoughtfully explores the interrelationships between exclusive remedies and consequential damage limitations, see Chatlos Systems, Inc. v. National Cash Register Corporation, 635 F.2d 1081 (3d Cir. 1980).

9. D. Cohn, and P. Wittman, "How Y2K Could Affect the Supply Chain," Bus. L. Today (September/October 1998) at 39.

10. 847 F. 2d 255 (5th Cir. 1988).

11. Vault also raised copyright infringement claims, but the court denied them. One particularly fascinating argument was that Quaid contributed to the unlawful infringements of its customers—who mostly used Quaid's diskettes to make unlawful reproductions of computer programs stored on Vault's diskettes—based on the argument that there were few noninfringing uses of Quaid's diskettes. The court determined that Quaid's diskettes could be used to make operational back-up copies of programs stored on Vault's diskettes, a practice that is specifically authorized by Section 117(2) of the Copyright Act.

12. *See* Step-Saver v. Wyse Technology, 939 F.2d 91 (3d Cir. 1991).

13. For some good advice about using click-wrap licenses, see E. Hansen and C. Covello, "Click-Wrap Licenses: The Pros and Cons," Nat'l L. J. (September 20, 1999) at B8.

14. The NCCUSL approved UCITA by a 43-6 vote on July 29, 1999. UCITA applies to commercial agreements to create, modify, transfer, or distribute computer software, multimedia interactive products, computer data and databases, and Internet and on-line information. UCITA does not cover the broadcast or distribution of digital motion pictures or sound recordings. In July 1999, the NCCUSL also approved the Uniform Electronics Transactions Act (UETA), which expressly validates the use of electronic records, signatures, and contracts.

15. The following discussion refers to the August 1, 1998, draft of the "Uniform Commercial Code Article 2B: Software Contracts and Licenses of Information," [hereinafter called "1998 Article 2B Draft"].

16. References to UCITA refer to the draft that was approved by the NCCUSL at its July 29, 1999, meeting.

17. 1998 Article 2B Draft, § 102. UCITA's definition is provided in UCITA, § 102. UETA's definition is in § 2.

18. Similarly, UETA provides, "A contract may not be denied legal effect or enforceability solely because an electronic record was used in its formation." UETA, § 7(b).

19. For an excellent discussion of digital signatures, see Information Security Committee, Section of Science and Technology, American Bar Association, "Tutorial," 38 Jurimetrics J. 243–260 (1998).

20. 1998 Article 2B Draft, §§ 111, 113–120. UCITA's approach is very similar and can be found in §§ 107, 108, 112, and 214–218. UETA also authorizes the use of digital signatures in §§ 7 and 9.

21. UETA's approach to digital signatures and attribution is provided in § 9. For instance, it provides, "An electronic record or electronic signature is attributable to a person if it was the act of the person. The act of the person may be shown in any manner, including a showing of the efficacy of any security procedure to determine the person to which the electronic record or electronic signature was attributable." UETA, § 9(a).

22. 1998 Article 2B Draft, § 204(a). The language in UCITA is very similar. UCITA, § 107. UETA follows the same approach in § 14.

23. 1998 Article 2B Draft, § 111. Similar language can be found in UCITA, § 112. UETA deals with electronic agents in § 14.

24. 1998 Article 2B Draft, § 209(b).

25. 1998 Article 2B Draft, § 208(a)(1). The same solution can be found in UCITA, § 211(a)(1).

26. 1998 Article 2B Draft, § 208(b)(2). UCITA provides the same protection in § 211(a)(2).

27. 1998 Article 2B Draft, § 208(b). UCITA deals with the topic in the same way. UCITA, § 211(b).

28. UCITA, § 105(b).

29. 1998 Article 2B Draft, §§ 401-409. UCITA's warranty provisions also are in §§ 401–409.

30. 1998 Article 2B Draft, § 405(b). UCITA has a similar provision in § 405(a)(2).

31. 1998 Article 2B Draft, § 405(d). UCITA offers the same warranty in § 405(c).

32. 1998 Article 2B Draft, § 404. UCITA provides for the same warranty, also in § 404.

33. 1998 Article 2B Draft, § 102. UCITA's definition also can be found in § 102, and is virtually the same.

34. 1998 Article 2B Draft, § 406. UCITA deals with disclaimers in § 406 as well.

35. 1998 Article 2B Draft, § 703. UCITA approaches damage limitations in the same way. UCITA, § 803.

36. 1998 Article 2B Draft, § 703(c). UCITA has the same provision in § 803(c).

37. 1998 Article 2B Draft, § 108(a). UCITA follows the same approach in § 110.

38. 1998 Article 2B Draft, § 107. The same language can be found in UCITA, § 109.

39. 1998 Article 2B Draft, § 715(a).

40. 1998 Article 2B Draft, § 715(b).

41. UCITA, § 816.

42. Survey conducted by Ernst & Young and *Electronic Business*, reported in S. Almassy, "A New Mind-Set for Electronics Executives," Electronic Bus. (March 30, 1992) at 83.

43. This list is derived from a superb article that comprehensively explains the reasons for and forms of

strategic alliances. D. Scrivner, "Strategic Alliances in the 1990s," Comp. Law. (December 1992) at 24–32.

44. *See* Permanence Corp. v. Kennametal, Inc., 908 F.2d 98 (6th Cir. 1990).

45. If the program ultimately is embodied in a semiconductor chip, then protection may be sought not only under copyright but also under the Semiconductor Chip Protection Act. This will protect not only the program but the mask, which is used to manufacture the chip. The mask, in essence, is like the blueprint of a house in that it contains the pattern of the circuitry to be implanted on the chip. The Semiconductor Chip Protection Act thereby extends protection to the creative efforts of the engineer who designed the chip to implement the program. *See* Lipner and Kalman, Computer Law (Merrill Publishing Co., 1989) at 36-40.

46. Apple Computer, Inc. v. Microsoft Corp. and Hewlett-Packard Co., 799 F. Supp. 1006 (N.D. Cal. 1992).

47. *See, e.g.,* Cal. Civ. Proc. Code § 1283.

48. For a good discussion of the advantages and disadvantages of ADR, see S. Weiss, "ADR: A Litigator's Perspective," 8 Bus. L. Today 30 (March/April 1999).

49. D. Lipsky and R. Seeber, "Top General Counsels Support ADR," 8 Bus. L. Today 24 (March/April, 1999).

50. For a thorough discussion of the possible drawbacks to ADR, see D. Friedman and M. Broaddus, "Computer Contract Disputes in the 1990s: Choosing ADR or Litigation," 5 J. of Proprietary Rights 2, 5–8 (April 1993).

51. Continental T.V., Inc. v. GTE Sylvania Inc., 433 U.S. 36 (1977).

52. State Oil Co. v. Khan, 522 U.S. 3 (1997).

53. Business Electronics Corp. v. Sharp Electronics Corp., 485 U.S. 717 (1988).

54. *See* United States v. Aluminum Company of America, 148 F.2d 416 (2d Cir. 1945).

55. *See* J. Yates and A. DiResta, "Software Support and Hardware Maintenance Practices: Tying Considerations," 8 Comp. Law. 17 (June 1991).

56. After this ruling, the parties finally went to trial. The jury determined that Kodak had violated the antitrust laws and rendered a verdict totaling close to $72 million after damages were trebled. The district court also imposed a 10-year injunction, requiring Kodak to sell parts to ISOs and end users on nondiscriminatory terms. The damage award and the injunction were modified on appeal. Image Technical Services, Inc. v. Eastman Kodak Co., 125 F.3d 1195 (1997). For a thorough discussion, see H. Applebaum and T. Barnett, "Ninth Circuit Upholds Kodak's Liability for Monopolizing the 'Aftermarket' for Servicing of Its Equipment but Vacates Some Damages and Modifies Injunction," Nat'l L. J. (September 29, 1997) at B4.

57. *See* Brown Shoe Co. v. United States, 370 U.S. 294 (1962).

58. U.S. Department of Justice and Federal Trade Commission Horizontal Merger Guidelines (April 2, 1992), reprinted in 4 Trade Reg. Rep. (CCH) 13,104.

59. The Justice Department, 20 state governments, and the District of Columbia filed suit. One of the states, South Carolina, later dropped out.

60. Other "events" took place before Microsoft filed its appeal. For instance, on December 15, 1997, Microsoft publicly announced that any OEM that did not agree to license and distribute Internet Explorer could not obtain a license to a current working version of the Windows 95 operating system. Microsoft stated that any OEM that declined to distribute Internet Explorer could obtain only a 2-year-old version of Windows 95, or a current version (excluding Internet Explorer) that Microsoft admitted would not work. On December 15, 1997, the Justice Department asked the court to hold Microsoft in contempt of its December 11, 1997, order.

61. United States v. Microsoft Corp., 147 F.3d 935 (D.C. Cir. 1998).

62. Microsoft also requested a ruling that the December 11 preliminary injunction would not bar the sale of Windows 98, which more completely bundled Internet Explorer with the operating system. On May 12, 1998, the Court of Appeals granted this request, stating that it was very unlikely that the government could prove that Windows 98 was not an integrated product under the terms of the 1995 agreement. United States v. Microsoft Corp., 1998 U.S. App. LEXIS 9492 (D.C. Cir. 1998).

63. The Justice Department complaint can be found at www.usdoj.gov/atr/cases/f1700/1763.htm.

64. K. Donovan, "Microsoft Judge Gets Decision 'Roadmaps'," Nat'l L. J. (August 23, 1999) at A7.

65. The Supreme Court has ruled that once a Section 2 violation has been proven, "it is the duty of the court to prescribe relief which will terminate the illegal monopoly, deny to defendant the fruits of its statutory violation, and ensure that there remains no practices likely to result in monopolization in the future." United States v. United Shoe Machinery Corp., 391 U.S. 244, 250 (1968).

66. See J. Lopatka and W. Page, "A (Cautionary) Note on Remedies in the Microsoft Case," Antitrust (Summer 1999) at 25.

67. The conclusions of law can be found at www.usdoj.gov/atr/cases/f4400/4469.htm.

68. J. Markhoff, "Unable to Beat Them, IBM Now Joins Them," N.Y. Times (July 6, 1992) at C1.

69. C. Compton, at 862. See D. Hamilton, "U.S., Japan Focusing on Electronic Gear," Wall St. J. (July 12, 1993) at 1.

70. See P. Marsden, "'Antitrust' at the WTO," 13 Antitrust 28 (Fall 1998).

71. R. Tritell, "The Application of Block Exemptions to Intellectual Property Licensing in the European Community," 5 J. of Proprietary Rights (July 1993) at 12.

72. A business may also request that the commission grant what is called a "negative clearance." This is a determination that the transaction is not restrictive under the general terms of Section 85(1). As with exemptions, this process may take a long time.

73. See F. Carlin, "Commission Seeks to Change Competition Rules," Nat'l L. J. (March 1, 1999) at B7.

74. R. Schaeffer, B. Earle, and F. Agusti, International Business Law and Its Environment, 3d ed. (West Publishing Co., 1996) at 716–720. However, mergers may be subject to scrutiny, even when most of the assets are outside the EU, if there are substantial sales in the EU.

75. See F. Fine, "A Practical Guide to EU Merger Control Jurisdiction and Procedure," 13 Antitrust 34 (Fall 1998) at 35.

76. F. Fine, "A Practical Guide to EU Merger Control Jurisdiction and Procedure," 13 Antitrust (Fall 1998) at 34. The average number of filings between 1994 and 1997 was 127. The commissioner predicted that the amended regulation would result in an additional 60 filings per year. Many of these may come from changes regarding the application to joint ventures, however.

77. For an excellent discussion of how dominance is analyzed in the EU, see F. Fine, "The Substantive Test of the EEC Merger Control Regulation: The First Two Years," 61 Antitrust L. J. (Spring 1993) at 699.

78. Agreement Between the government of the United States of America and the European Communities Regarding the Application of Their Competition Laws (September 21, 1991) available at www.usdoj.gov/atr/public/international/docs/ec.htm.

79. Agreement Between the government of the United States of America and the European Communities on the Application of Positive Comity Principles in the Enforcement of Their Competition Laws (June 4, 1998) available at www.usdoj.gov/atr/public/international/docs/1781.htm.

80. Licensing arrangements that involve facially anticompetitive per se violations of the antitrust laws are excluded from the safety zone.

81. See "Symposium: A Critical Appraisal of the 'Innovation Market' Approach," 64 Antitrust L. J. (Fall 1995).

82. See R. Hoerner, "Innovation Markets: New Wine in Old Bottles?" 64 Antitrust L. J. 49 (Fall 1995), which lists in the Appendix numerous enforcement actions by the Justice Department and the FTC involving innovation theories.

83. In the settlement, Intel agreed that it would not withhold technical information necessary for computer makers to go to market. The agreement provided certain exceptions, such as for when the other companies do not pay their bills or try to misappropriate Intel's technologies. See K. Donovan, "Smart Lawyering Inks Intel Deal," Nat'l L. J. (March 22, 1999) at B1.

84. 314 U.S. 488 (1942).

85. USM Corp. v. SPS Technologies, Inc., 694 F.2d 505, 512 (7th Cir. 1982) (opinion written by Justice R. Posner).

86. The Intellectual Property Antitrust Protection Act of 1988, § 438.

87. 911 F.2d 970 (4th Cir. 1990).

88. At the time of this decision, the duration of copyright protection for works made for hire was 75 years from the date of publication or 100 years from the date of creation, whichever expires first. In 1998, these terms were extended for an additional 20 years, to 95 and 120 years respectively.

SIMPLIFIED SAMPLE SOFTWARE DEVELOPMENT CONTRACT

[NOTE: This sample agreement is intended solely to demonstrate how a few important issues might be addressed in a written contract. Although it presents several topics that typically are covered in development agreements, this highly simplified exposition should not be used as a checklist of pertinent considerations. In addition, its form and language should not be used in any way to draft legal agreements.]

THIS AGREEMENT is made this _____ day of _____ 20 ___ between Optico Imaging Company (hereinafter referred to as "Client") and the Neptune Corporation (hereinafter referred to as "Developer").

WITNESSETH:

WHEREAS, Client requires computer software to control Client's specialized machinery used to grind mirrors for optical telescopes; and

WHEREAS, the operations and characteristics of Client's machinery are carefully guarded as trade secrets; and

WHEREAS, Client requires the software to achieve a detailed set of defined tasks; and

WHEREAS, Developer has the expertise to develop said software to meet the defined tasks;

IT IS, THEREFORE, AGREED as follows:

1. DEFINITIONS
    (a) *Software.* "Software" means all computer programs, subroutines, translations, and any other specialized software produced or provided by Developer to satisfy its obligations under this Agreement.
    (b) *Functional Specifications.* "Functional Specifications" means (1) the set of tasks and functions that must be performed by the Software to fulfill the needs of Client, and (2) the design specifications which indicate the way the Software must be organized to accomplish those tasks and functions.
    (c) *Documentation.* "Documentation" means the instructions necessary for Client to operate the Software and its features.
    (d) *Services.* "Services" means all tasks provided by Developer under this Agreement, including, but not limited to analysis, design, programming, testing, consulting, and installation.
    (e) *Modifications.* "Modifications" means (a) changes to Software allowing it to be used on hardware other than that for which the Software was initially designed, and (b) any changes to source code resulting from the addition of a substantial feature or capability not present in the original Software.
    (f) *Proprietary Information.* "Proprietary Information" means all information relating to the Software, including, but not limited to, source code, object code, listings, printouts, flow charts, research materials, programming notes, operational and performance specifications, test results, and Documentation.

2. SCOPE OF SERVICES
    (a) PART I. In consultation with Client, Developer will analyze Client's business and machinery, and create the Functional Specifications for Software intended to meet the set of Client needs specified in Exhibit A.

(b) PART II. Upon acceptance of the Functional Specifications by Client, Developer will code, test and debug Software that meets the Functional Specifications, prepare the Documentation, and install the Software on the equipment specified in Exhibit A. Delivery of the Software and Documentation under PART II must be made within 180 days of the day that this Agreement is signed.

(c) Modifications. Client shall provide Developer the opportunity to develop any modifications to the Software and Documentation created under this Agreement.

3.   PAYMENT

(a) PART I. Developer shall be paid for the Functional Specifications developed under Part I on a fixed fee basis, in the amounts and according to the timetable specified in Exhibit B.

(b) PART II. Developer shall be paid for the Software and Documentation developed under Part II according to the fixed fee and royalty schedules provided in Exhibit B.

(c) Modifications. Developer will be paid to develop modifications according to the schedule provided in Exhibit B.

4.   ACCEPTANCE

(a) PART I. Upon delivery of the Functional Specifications due under Part I of this Agreement, Client shall have 15 business days to examine the Functional Specifications to determine if they conform to this Agreement. If the Functional Specifications conform, Client shall notify Developer of acceptance in writing within the acceptance period. If they do not conform to this agreement, Client shall notify Developer within 15 days of delivery and specify the deficiency. Client shall have the opportunity to correct the deficiency within a reasonable time and to deliver the Functional Specifications for acceptance as specified herein.

(b) PART II. Upon delivery of the Software and Documentation due under PART II, Client shall have 30 business days to conduct the acceptance tests, listed in Exhibit C, on the Software on Client's hardware and machinery in its facilities to determine if the Software meet the terms of this Agreement.

(b.1) If the Software passes all acceptance tests, based on reasonable judgment when necessary, Client shall notify Developer in writing within 5 business days from the date that the last test is fulfilled.

(b.2) If the Software does not pass all acceptance tests listed in Exhibit C, then Client shall notify Developer in writing within 5 business days of failure, and Developer shall have a reasonable time to correct the Software so that it can meet the acceptance tests. Thereafter, Client shall have 20 business days to conduct the acceptance tests. This process may be repeated as many times as required until the Software meets the acceptance tests; provided, however, that if the Software does not successfully pass all acceptance tests within 180 days after initial delivery of the Software under PART II, Client shall be entitled to consider Developer to be in default of this Agreement.

5.   WARRANTIES

(a) *Limited Software Warranty.* Developer warrants that the Software delivered under this Agreement, excluding Modifications, will conform to the Functional Specifications and any other requirements described in this Agreement, and will be free of defects that materially affect the performance of such features. The warranty is effective for 180 days following the acceptance date of PART II. This warranty shall not apply to nonconformities or defects due to any of the following:

(i)   misuse or modification of the Software by the Client or a third party;

(ii)   failure of the Client or third party to maintain proper operating conditions;

(iii) hardware equipment defects or operating system software error; or

(iv) interaction with software not provided by Developer.

(a.1) *Exclusive Remedies for Breach of Limited Software Warranty.* If at any time during this 180 day Limited Software Warranty period Client notifies Developer in writing of any nonconformity or defect, Developer shall at its sole and exclusive option either (1) provide all reasonable programming services to repair such nonconformity or defect, or (2) replace the nonconforming Software with conforming Software. If Developer reasonably is unable to repair or replace the nonconforming or defective Software, Developer shall refund to Client all sums paid by Client to Developer under this Agreement for the Software.

these remedies are the sole and exclusive remedies for breach of the limited software warranty provided herein.

(b) *Noninfringement Warranty.* Developer warrants that the Software will not infringe any United States copyright, trademark, or patent or misappropriate any trade secret of any third persons.

(b.1) *Exclusive Remedies for Breach of Noninfringement Warranty and Indemnification*

(b.1.A) In the event that a lawsuit is brought against Client claiming that the Software infringes a United States patent, copyright or trademark, or misappropriates trade secrets:

(i) Client must give prompt notice to Developer of the lawsuit;

(ii) Developer shall have the option to defend the lawsuit at its expense. Under this circumstance, Client agrees to (a) give Developer the right to control and direct the investigation, preparation, defense and settlement of the claims, and (b) fully cooperate with Developer in the investigation, preparation, defense and settlement of the claims; and

(iii) Developer will indemnify Client for all damages and costs awarded against Client, except that Developer will not be responsible for any cost or expense paid, or settlement made, by Client without Developer's written consent.

Client agrees that Developer will not be liable if the claims of infringement or misappropriation result from modifications to the Software made by the Client or any third party, or are based on the use of the Software in combination with software not developed by the Developer.

(b.1.B) If Client receives notice regarding the Software of any alleged infringement of any United States copyright, trademark, or patent, or any alleged misappropriation of trade secrets, Developer may at its option and expense:

(i) obtain for Client the right to continued use of the Software for the purposes intended under this Agreement,

(ii) replace the Software with functionally equivalent and noninfringing Software, or

(iii) modify the Software so that it no longer infringes or misappropriates said rights.

THESE REMEDIES ARE THE SOLE AND EXCLUSIVE REMEDIES FOR BREACH OF THE NON-INFRINGEMENT WARRANTY PROVIDED HEREIN.

(c) Client expressly acknowledges that no representations or warranties other than those contained in this Agreement have been made respecting the Software, Modifications, Documentation or Services to be provided, and that Client has not relied on any representation not expressly set out in this Agreement.

6. WARRANTY DISCLAIMER

TO THE EXTENT ALLOWED BY LAW, DEVELOPER EXPRESSLY DISCLAIMS ALL IMPLIED WARRANTIES, IN-

CLUDING WARRANTIES OF MERCHANTABILITY AND FITNESS FOR A PARTICULAR PURPOSE. SHOULD A
COURT DETERMINE THAT THE PRODUCTS ARE "CONSUMER PRODUCTS" UNDER THE MAGNUSON-MOSS
WARRANTY ACT, THEN IMPLIED WARRANTIES ARE LIMITED IN DURATION TO A PERIOD OF 180 DAYS AF-
TER ACCEPTANCE. AFTER SUCH 180 DAY PERIOD, ALL IMPLIED WARRANTIES ARE EXPRESSLY DISCLAIMED.

SOME STATES DO NOT ALLOW LIMITATIONS ON HOW LONG AN IMPLIED WARRANTY LASTS, SO THE
ABOVE LIMITATION MAY NOT APPLY TO CLIENT.

7.   LIMITATION OF LIABILITY

IN NO EVENT SHALL DEVELOPER BE LIABLE FOR ANY SPECIAL OR CONSEQUENTIAL DAMAGES, IN-
CLUDING, BUT NOT LIMITED TO LOST PROFITS, LOSS OF GOODWILL, OR LOSS OF BUSINESS OPPORTUNI-
TIES, EVEN IF DEVELOPER HAS BEEN ADVISED OF THE POSSIBILITY OF SUCH DAMAGES. IN NO EVENT
SHALL DEVELOPER BE LIABLE FOR ANY SPECIAL OR CONSEQUENTIAL DAMAGES BASED UPON NEGLIGENCE
OR STRICT PRODUCTS LIABILITY. CLIENT UNDERSTANDS THAT THESE LIMITATIONS APPLY EVEN IF IT IS DE-
TERMINED THAT THE REMEDIES PROVIDED UNDER THIS AGREEMENT FAIL OF THEIR ESSENTIAL PURPOSE.

SOME STATES DO NOT ALLOW THE EXCLUSION OR LIMITATION OF SPECIAL OR CONSEQUENTIAL
DAMAGES SO THE ABOVE LIMITATION OR EXCLUSION MAY NOT APPLY TO CLIENT.

8.   MAINTENANCE

Following expiration of the warranty, Developer agrees to provide all maintenance services
necessary to correct and resolve any errors or defects which appear in the Software as a result
of its use by Client. Developer's obligation to provide such maintenance services is contingent
upon payment of the maintenance fees, as specified in Exhibit B, and the accurate and timely reporting of any problems with the Software. Maintenance services shall not apply to any problems resulting from modifications to the Software by Client or any third party.

9.   OWNERSHIP

All Software developed pursuant to this Agreement, and all corresponding copyrights, Proprietary Information, and patents, shall be owned by Client. Developer agrees to take all actions
and execute all documents and assignments reasonably necessary to carry out this intent.

10. CONFIDENTIALITY

(a) Each party acknowledges that, during the course of this Agreement, it will be entrusted
with trade secrets relating to the business and products of the other party. Each party agrees that
it will not use such trade secrets for any purpose except for the performance of this Agreement,
and that it will not disclose any such trade secrets to any person unless such disclosure is authorized by the other party in writing.

(b) Developer agrees to comply with the trade secret protection measures provided in Exhibit D. Developer hereby grants to Client the right to visit Developer's site during normal business hours upon reasonable notice for the purpose of verifying that the trade secrets and Proprietary Information are being protected in accordance with this Agreement.

11. TERMINATION

Client may, for any reason, terminate this Agreement at any time effective upon Developer's
receipt of written notice. In the event of termination, Client will pay all sums due to Developer, including pro-rata fees and expenses for items partially complete at the time of termination, as well
as any expenses associated with termination. After receipt of the payment of such sums, Developer will deliver to client copies of its work product completed to that date.

12. MEDIATION AND ARBITRATION

(a) In the event that there is a dispute or claim relating to this Agreement, and the parties are not able to resolve it through direct negotiations, then the parties hereby agree that they will attempt to settle the dispute or claim first by means of mediation according to the Commercial Mediation Rules of the American Arbitration Association.

(b) If mediation fails to resolve any dispute or claim arising under this Agreement, then it shall be submitted to binding arbitration. The procedures for conducting binding arbitration are detailed in Exhibit E.

(c) Except where clearly prevented by the area in dispute, both parties agree to continue performing their respective obligations under this Agreement while the dispute is being resolved.

13. CHOICE OF LAW

This Agreement shall be governed by and construed in accordance with the laws of the State of California.

14. ENTIRE AGREEMENT

This Agreement constitutes the complete and exclusive statement of the agreement between the parties with respect to the subject matter herein, and supersedes all prior proposals, agreements, negotiations, representations and communications, whether oral or written, between Developer and Client.

15. ATTORNEYS' FEES

In the event that any action or proceeding is brought by either party in connection with this Agreement, the prevailing party shall be entitled to recover its costs and reasonable attorneys' fees.

16. AMENDMENTS

This Agreement may not be changed except by a written agreement, executed on behalf of Developer and Client.

17. EXHIBITS

Exhibits A, B, C, D, E and F, which are attached, are included in this Agreement. No other exhibits or appendices form a part of this Agreement.

IN WITNESS WHEREOF, the parties hereto, intending to be bound hereby, have caused this Agreement to be executed by their duly authorized representatives as of the day and year hereinabove set forth.

Attest: Optico Imaging Company

_____   By _____

Attest: Neptune Corporation

_____   By _____

Index